MAYNOOTH COLLEGE
1795–1995

MAYNOOTH COLLEGE 1795–1995

Patrick J. Corish

GILL & MACMILLAN

Gill & Macmillan Ltd
Goldenbridge
Dublin 8
with associated companies throughout the world
© Patrick J. Corish 1995

0 7171 2241 7

Design and print origination by
O'K Graphic Design, Dublin

Printed by
ColourBooks Ltd, Dublin

A catalogue record is available for this book from the British Library.

1 3 5 4 2

CONTENTS

CHAPTER V: A NEW ORDERING

CHAPTER VI: INTO THE NEW ORDER

CHAPTER VII: THE BISHOPS' COLLEGE, 1870–95: STRUCTURES, FINANCES, BUILDINGS

CHAPTER VIII: THE BISHOPS' COLLEGE, 1870–95: STAFF, STUDIES, COLLEGE LIFE

CHAPTER IX: UNIVERSITY STATUS ACHIEVED

CHAPTER X: THE NEW CENTURY: THE FABRIC OF LIFE

CHAPTER XI: THE NEW CENTURY: TENSIONS AND ENTHUSIASMS

LIST OF
ILLUSTRATIONS

BETWEEN PAGES 176 AND 177

Plate

BETWEEN PAGES 240 AND 241

Plate

PREFACE

St Patrick's College, Maynooth celebrates its second centenary in 1995. By Irish standards at any rate this makes it a venerable institution. Founded in 1795 as a seminary to replace those so suddenly swept away in the French Revolution, it has sent out over ten thousand priests in its two hundred years of existence, the great majority of them to minister in the dioceses of Ireland. It did this work unobtrusively, so unobtrusively indeed in times past that it tended to figure in popular consciousness either as the place Ireland was really ruled from or as having something to do with a mission to China, possibly indeed in China itself.

The approach of the bicentenary naturally suggested the writing of a history, and with a certain inevitability the task moved in my direction, having taught history in Maynooth all my life and having retired a reasonably suitable time before the commemorative history would be due to appear. I can only say that I regard it as an honour to have come my way, to trace the story from the time when by chance rather than planning the college settled in Maynooth in the shadow of the old Geraldine castle. The ancient yew-tree under which tradition has it Silken Thomas played his lute is just inside its gate, and it would seem churlish to note that historical revision suggests that the young Fitzgeralds matured too fast to have much time for that kind of thing. Two hundred years later an institution has developed that the founding fathers could hardly have envisaged, stretching now both north and south of what will no longer be the Galway road when the new bypass opens in the bicentenary year (Plates 14, 36).

As I tried to bring things into focus one possibility that presented itself was to write the history of the second hundred years, to continue John Healy's *Maynooth College: its Centenary History*, published in 1895. It soon became apparent, however, that this would not be the best way of doing things. Healy's study has many merits. It has preserved in accessible form a great deal of information about the first hundred years. Indeed if one considers the conditions under which it was written it is a remarkable piece of work, for the decision to include a history in the centenary celebrations of 1895 was taken at a comparatively late stage, and when he agreed to write it Healy was no longer living in the college, having been appointed coadjutor to the Bishop of Clonfert in 1884. But for a number of reasons a history of the first hundred years written for 1895 and of the second hundred written for 1995 would not have run easily in tandem. Every human generation brings a new perspective to the past; it asks new questions of the same evidence. It is hardly necessary to stress that the perspective at the end of the twentieth century must differ quite a bit from the perspective at the end of the nineteenth. In short, it appears beyond question that a history written for 1995 would have to go back to 1795, not indeed to supersede Healy's work but to supplement it.

In writing the present volume I have had much more time than Healy had, and the consciousness of needing it can only increase appreciation of his achievement. Over the years I have come to owe much to many people. There is no question where the greatest debt is due. It is to Monsignor Ledwith, President for ten years until April 1994. When I accepted his invitation he followed it up by extending to me every facility, with a characteristic largeness of mind and sense of style. Towards the end of this book, feeling it was time to bring things to a close, I wrote: 'Here the story is beginning to enter the areas of current affairs and unfinished business.' I am not sure exactly when that sentence took shape, but I am sure that when it was written there must have been few indeed who were not assuming that he would be President for the bicentenary in 1995. But his ten-year term was coming to an end, and he judged wisely that ten years was enough for any individual in this particular office given the pressures of time. When retiring he expressed the wish to continue in the service of the college in an academic role and hopefully this is what will happen.

He must certainly be remembered as one of Maynooth's outstanding presidents. When he took office ten years ago the burden of debt seemed uncontrollable. Not merely has the debt been paid off, but money has been raised for very extensive repair and refurbishment of the heritage buildings of the seminary, the latest being a commitment of a million dollars for the restoration of the College Chapel. This work on the seminary buildings only reflected his solicitude for the seminarian student. As total numbers more than doubled, from under 2,000 ten years ago to 4,000 today, it was necessary to support seminarian confidence. That this did not hinder care for the whole student body is clear from the new student restaurant, sports complex and recreation centre, and the 'University Village Apartments'. The Callan Building represents the first half of the needs of the Faculty of Science. And as the college grew the academic and support staff grew. It is a measure of the developments during his term of office that when he retired it had to be accepted that it needed two to replace him. On 22 June 1994 Canon Matthew O'Donnell was appointed President and Rector of the Pontifical University and Dr W. J. Smyth to the new post of 'Master' of the National University College (Plate 94).

I am deeply indebted to him for assistants to get the source material under control. In the year 1989/90 I had Joe Leydon as research assistant. In that year material was traced and copied in many repositories: in Rome the Congregation for the Evangelisation of Peoples and the Irish College; and in

Ireland in many places, including the archives of the Irish dioceses, the National Library, the National Archives, and the Public Record Office of Northern Ireland. I am grateful to the authorities in all these places for their courtesy and help. In that same year notable progress was made in putting the college archives in order, and this continued in 1990/91 with Fionnuala O'Driscoll as archival assistant.

Names indeed multiply. I owe a continuing debt to Dr Dermot Farrell, executive assistant to the President and himself vice-president since October 1993. I owe the same continuing debt to Mary Moriarty and Marie Murphy in the President's Office, who cheerfully coped with the longhand of someone whose relationship with computers might literally be described as a state of idiocy. I am grateful too to the library staff, in particular Penny Woods and Suzanne Redmond, who helped me in selecting illustrative material and having it photographed; and to Jim Keenan, cartographer in the Department of Geography, for professional assistance. I acknowledge permission to reproduce copyright material from the Ordnance Survey (Government permit no. 5906); the National Library of Ireland; the Royal Irish Academy; Mr Lee Mallaghan of Carton House; and Father Joe Dunn of Dublin.

There are things this history does not attempt to probe, for it is not really the historian's business to probe them. Forty years ago in the student magazine, the *Silhouette*, a seminarian marked out the boundaries:

> Not all that we experience in Maynooth can be made articulate. Not all that we articulate can be printed. Over seminary life, so much of which is lived inside ourselves, in prayer and study, all of which is lived within a rigid daily order within four walls, hangs a heavy curtain of privacy and reticence.

Neil Kevin, in *I Remember Maynooth*, written in 1937 within the same framework, noted the inward-looking life of the 'roll-call of six hundred young men between the dream-swept years of eighteen and twenty-five.' Times have changed. The seminarian's life is more outgoing, and he is a minority in a student body of four thousand young men and women. But they all inhabit 'the dream-swept years', where the historian, like everybody else, has to tread softly on dreams.

Some time in the eleventh or twelfth century someone whose name is lost to us wrote a short poem which, like many poets of the time, he ascribed to that great figure of the heroic age of Irish Christianity, Colm Cille. The opening line surely echoes the thought of many a scriptorium: 'Is scíth mo chrob ón scríbainn', 'my hand is weary with writing'. In truth, even Colm Cille's hand grew weary. In that chapter of austere beauty that records his passing Adomnán wrote: 'And when he came to that verse of the thirty-third psalm where it is written, "But they that seek the Lord shall not want for anything that is good", he said: "Here, at the end of the page, I must stop. Let Baithene write the rest".'

CHAPTER I

A SEMINARY
IN IRELAND

The Irish Seminary Tradition

For by far the greatest part of its two hundred years' history St Patrick's College, Maynooth, has been exclusively a seminary preparing young men for ordination to the Catholic priesthood. The institutionalisation of such training began at an early date. In Christian antiquity an important step was taken by St Augustine, who insisted that the candidate for ordination should spend some time in the community of clerics gathered round the bishop. When Augustine died in 430 the civil organisation of the Roman Empire was disintegrating in the West. There were to be centuries ahead in which almost the only literate people were the clergy, and the schools of the bishops and the monasteries the only institutes of learning. But even in these times there were outstanding organisers: Isidore of Seville and the Council of Toledo (633) and the *Regula Canonicorum* (c. 755) of Chrodegang of Metz. The structures these drew up for the cathedral schools had been established all over his empire by Charlemagne before his death in 814.

By the twelfth century learning was shifting to the towns, where it became institutionalised in the universities. It was to these that the scholars were attracted, and the cathedral and monastic schools decayed, despite attempts at the very highest level to revive them, for example at the Lateran Councils in 1179 and 1215. Inexorably, theological teaching came to be concentrated in the universities, and it got new life under this stimulus. It was to the universities that the brightest of the aspirants to the priesthood came. What proportion of the total they were cannot be quantified exactly, but they were a minority. The lot of those who could not get university education was worse than it had been before: many of them got little more than some kind of apprenticeship with a priest who gave them little learning because he had little to give. As for those who went to university, in the beginning provision was made for their moral and spiritual formation by having them lodge in special houses, but in time this broke down. By about the year 1400 theology and other ecclesiastical studies were concentrated almost exclusively in the universities; the life-style of candidates for the priesthood could differ little from that

1

of their companions; and their studies were career-directed, concentrating on canon law. As an Irish reformer complained about 1515,

> The church of this land use not to learn any other science but the law of canon, for covetyce of lucre transitory; all other science, whereof grow none such lucre, the parsons of the church doth despise . . .

The challenge to the whole system initiated by Luther in 1517 was essentially directed against what were widely seen as the pretensions of a clerical order riddled by scandals. Inevitably, much of the efforts of many Catholic reformers centred on reform of the priesthood. Claude Le Jay, Jesuit and missionary in Germany, saw clerical formation as central. The foundation of the German College in Rome in 1552 was a direct result. There had been two striking efforts in England, another country very much divided in religious matters. Here the reformers were Henry VIII's archbishop of Canterbury, Thomas Cranmer (1489–1556), and the Catholic archbishop of his daughter Mary, Reginald Cardinal Pole (1500–58). Pole's extensive legislation on the training of priests at his legatine synod in 1556 got no chance to be put into practice in England, but in 1563 it was substantially incorporated into the decrees of the Council of Trent (sess. xxiii, c. 18, *de reformatione*).

Trent faced so many problems that it had to concentrate on reform of the episcopate, in the hope that good bishops would produce good priests. When it began, it seems to have thought that a reform in the abuses in the appointment of clergy would solve the problems of the priesthood, but it came to see that more positive action by way of formation was also required. With its attention concentrated so heavily on the bishop, it is not surprising that what Trent finally decided was essentially a renewal of the cathedral school. Pole had envisaged the possibility of such a school educating lay and cleric together, but what emerged from the debates at Trent was an exclusively clerical institution: students were to be tonsured and to wear clerical garb from the day they entered. Every cathedral church was to have a school for the education of the clergy of the diocese. By way of exception, smaller and poorer dioceses within the same ecclesiastical province might pool their resources, and very large dioceses might have two or even three seminaries if the bishop so decided. The Council was not in favour of appointing regular clergy to teach in seminaries, though it realised there were few qualified diocesan clergy, and inevitably the regulars, especially the Jesuits, came to play a large part. But the Council's emphasis is always on the bishop and the diocese. It is the bishop who is to prescribe the courses of study and lay down the rule of discipline.

However, the real shapers of the modern seminary came from seventeenth-century France, Vincent de Paul (c. 1580–1660), John Eudes (1601–80) and Jean-Jacques Olier (1608–57), whose foundation at Saint-Sulpice in Paris became the model for many others, some of them staffed by his own priests, the 'Sulpicians', though his seminaries always remained under the ultimate authority of the bishop. The principal development was the division of the seminary. Trent had envisaged the students as ranging in age from about twelve to the age of ordination, about twenty-four, but from now on the seminary proper was to be confined to those engaged in strictly professional or vocational studies, while the minor seminary, the *petit séminaire*, gave a preparatory training in the humanities to boys between twelve and eighteen. The universities still maintained themselves as teachers of theology, so some seminarians attended courses in the university, while courses for the others were provided within the seminary. In places, even in Sulpician seminaries, a situation developed where those who attended university were those who could pay the fees. In eighteenth-century Angers, for example, the choice was between three years of university theology and a 'poor man's seminarist crash-course' of fourteen months. But for all, as in all Sulpician seminaries, the chapel rather than the library was at the heart of the house, as was the regulation that staff and students live a totally common life.

Perhaps it might be more accurate to say 'in all Sulpician seminaries except one'. Already in the early eighteenth century the mother-house in Paris held many graceless young aristocrats, going through the minimum preparation necessary to qualify for a benefice, living in elegantly furnished rooms with their own servants, preparing to be great gentlemen rather than pastors, what reading they did being in the *philosophes* rather than in the theologians. It would appear that the effect of this element on general seminary formation was minimal. Certainly provincial France was essentially a conformist Catholic country, apart from some among the upper classes in the towns. The parish priests were men of character and leaders in local life. Almost everyone had a relative who was a priest. There were complaints against the system, against the great and widening gap between the privileged and the unprivileged in what was theoretically the privileged First Estate of French society, and against the narrow 'clericalist' education in the seminaries, a novitiate for monks, some would call it, or even a penal establishment for galley-slaves. But when the rural *curé*, the *vicaire savoyard* of real life, read his Rousseau, it was not because he rejected his theology (in which his interest was limited and probably declining) but rather because he was dissatisfied with his social and economic status. What he was learning was democracy rather than irreligion, but in the event this proved explosive enough.

Eighteenth-century France had particular relevance for Ireland because the training of the Irish Catholic clergy had come to be heavily concentrated there. In the later Middle Ages Ireland had suffered from the same ills as western Christendom generally. It may have been no great additional handicap that the country failed to develop a university. In any case, numbers of young Irishmen, many of them candidates for the priesthood, made their way abroad, principally to Oxford and Cambridge. What is coming to be seen as a significant element in the rejection of the Anglican settlement by the bulk of the Irish people occurred when these young men began to go, not to the English

3

universities, but to Catholic centres on the Continent. This change is of its nature badly documented, even by Irish standards, but it appears more and more certain that some were going from early in the reign of Elizabeth I, and that they were going in significant numbers once the issues came to be seen clearly in the 1570s. Not all went to become priests, but some did; others took the decision while abroad; and almost all came back firmly committed to the Catholic Reformation.

Inevitably, these young scholars lived precariously, certainly until some stroke of fortune allowed them to gather in a house bought, or more often rented, which became, usually a little grandiloquently, 'the Irish College'. These institutions often led an uncertain existence, if only because there was often the possibility of being unable to pay the rent. An organised group appears in Paris in 1578, but nothing further about them surfaces for about forty years. The first institution to begin a continuous history was the 'Royal College of the Irish Nobles', St Patrick's, Salamanca, founded with the approval and promise of financial help from Philip II of Spain on 23 July 1592, a few months after the grant of a royal charter to the College of the Holy and Undivided Trinity of the University of Dublin on 3 March, the long-delayed university which it was hoped would provide the legally established Church in Ireland with an adequate ministry. Catholic colleges multiplied rapidly on the Continent, their number reflecting the political disunity at home: too many of them, too many of them too poor, and some of them in consequence imper-manent. The Penal Code of the eighteenth century had a blanket prohibition of Catholic education, but here as in other areas a level of education that would not disturb the social order came to be tolerated, elementary education, but not higher education, and, needless to say, not the education of the clergy. Aspirants to the priesthood and the sons of any Catholics of rank or wealth had to look to Europe. By the close of the eighteenth century nearly five hun-dred seminary places had been provided, with some, but far from sufficient, endowments to support the students who filled them. It was common practice not to send young men abroad to study theology until they had already been ordained priests at about the age of twenty-four, so that they might help to support themselves by the exercise of their ministry, with the regrettable if inevitable result that some found a congenial niche in the richly endowed *ancien régime* church of France and did not return to Ireland. Detailed figures were supplied to Parliament by the secretary of the Trustees of Maynooth College in 1808:[1]

College	Staff	Students	Priests	Burses	Pensioners
Paris: Collège des Lombards	4	100	100		
Paris: Irish College	3	80		60	20
Nantes	3	80	80		
Bordeaux	3	40	20	20	
Douai	2	30	30		
Toulouse	1	12		12	
Lille	1	8			8
Louvain	2	40		20	20
Antwerp	2	30	30		
Salamanca	2	32		32	
Rome	2	16		16	
Lisbon	2	12		12	
Total	27	480	260	172	48

It was a modest but real patrimony. The students who supported themselves by their ministry as priests came to 55 per cent of the total, while almost 35 per cent enjoyed burses established by Irish or foreign benefactors. Of the 480 places, 418, or 87 per cent, were in France and the Austrian Netherlands. After some hesitation the colleges in France had been exempted from the law of 2 November 1789 confiscating church property, and their inmates were exempted from the oath imposed on the clergy on 12 July 1790. This however did not save them from initiatives taken by local officials or the mob as the Revolution became more radical, and they were all seized after war broke out between France and Britain on 1 February 1793. The Austrian Netherlands had been overrun by the French armies, and the two colleges there were included in the closure. In Rome the little Irish College had had problems since the suppression of the Jesuits in 1773, and was in any case to be closed when the French occupied Rome in 1798. In 1794 the Congregation of Propaganda agreed to admit four additional Irish students to its own college, but nothing appears to have been done, and nothing that could possibly be done could compensate for the losses in northern Europe.

These losses were a catastrophe. Some possibility of better things began to appear with the fall of Robespierre in 1794, but the Concordat of 1801, while it closed the rift between Church and State, did not restore the previous situation but created a new one. As well, the war between France and what became the United Kingdom of Great Britain and Ireland dragged on with only minor interruptions until 1815. When it was over the only Continental colleges to be restored were Rome, Paris and Salamanca.

A Seminary in Ireland: Political Problems

At least the possibility of filling the gap had begun to open up in Ireland, where the Penal Code was being slowly dismantled, through a combination of the spread of Enlightenment ideas, fears that the common resentments of Catholics and Presbyterians might develop into common interests, and pressure from Britain through the Irish administration on an Irish ascendancy unwilling to move and yet afraid to stand still. A Relief Act of 1782 allowed Catholics to open schools, on certain conditions: the schoolmaster must take the Oath of Allegiance drawn up in 1774; a licence had to be granted by the Protestant bishop, who could withdraw it without giving any reason; and these schools might not be endowed. The grudging relief measures of April 1792 did abolish the obligation to seek a licence from the Protestant bishop, and the broader measures of April 1793 allowed Catholics to hold professorships or masterships or take degrees in any college that might be founded, provided this college was a member of the University of Dublin, and was not founded exclusively for the education of Catholics (a royal proclamation the following year allowed them to take degrees in Trinity College). The prohibition on the endowment of Catholic schools was not repealed.

After 1782 advertisements for Catholic 'academies' began to appear in the newspapers. Colleges set up in Carlow and Kilkenny for the education of boys broadened their aims to admit seminarians after 1793, because of the rapidly worsening situation in France. Other bishops in poorer parts of the country were resorting to more desperate expedients, some trying to provide some theological education from resources scantier than those in Carlow and Kilkenny, others, it appears, ordaining priests with no theological education at all—'hedge priests', as a young theological student at Maynooth was to priggishly call them.[2] No doubt they hoped that in time something would turn up to supply the education for which they would hitherto have been sent to a Continental college immediately after ordination. Even Carlow and Kilkenny were struggling, both of them from poverty, and Carlow in addition facing the hostility of the Protestant bishop.[3]

Attempts to provide a wider remedy for what had been a national calamity were hampered by the reluctance of the Irish bishops to come together (episcopal meetings, even at provincial level, were developed very circumspectly). However, on 5 December 1793 the four archbishops and five bishops, two from the southern province and one from each of the other three, wrote from

Dublin to the Congregation of Propaganda in Rome about the problems involved in establishing a seminary or seminaries in Ireland.[4] They considered it a real possibility that if one were to be set up it might have to be affiliated to Trinity College under the terms of the Act of 1793. This they declared they could never accept, but even if it could be avoided there was a real problem in financing a seminary, given the poverty of the country and the legal ban on endowments. To the difficulties that might be feared from the government were added others coming from the radical element which had taken over the Catholic Committee and won the Relief Act of 1793 from an unwilling Parliament. This group was prepared to work for the education of both clergy and laity, but in return expected some measure of control. The Catholic Committee had dissolved itself after the passing of the Relief Act, but not before it set up a committee of seven to work towards 'procuring an improved system of education for the Catholic youth of the Kingdom of Ireland'. Three of the seven were United Irishmen. In this committee a plan took shape which would have pleased the thinkers of the Enlightenment or the framers of the Civil Constitution of the Clergy but would be very unacceptable to the Irish bishops. Their plan was for the education of both clergy and laity. It was designed for Catholics, but would not exclude students from other denominations. It was to draw its financial support from the public and not from the government, and clergy and laity were to share control.

The bishops were also moving, for their need left them no option. They sought the patronage of Edmund Burke and support from the government. Burke, a member of the Established Church, had a broadly Catholic background. Such people were often no great friends to things Catholic, but Burke was exceptional in that he had an unusual largeness of mind which had made him a good friend to the Catholics since the relaxation of the Penal Code was first mooted. As he himself claimed in 1780,

> I have been a steady friend, since I came to the use of reason, to the cause of religious toleration; not only as a Christian and Protestant, but as one concerned for the civil welfare of the country in which I live, and in which I have for some time discharged a public trust. I never thought it right . . . to force men into enmity to the state by ill-treatment, upon any pretence of either civil or religious party.[5]

His help was now all the more valuable because he was so implacably and eloquently opposed to the French Revolution. His advice was that in their approach to the Government the bishops should insist on exclusive control of the college, and that in addition to nominating agents in London to manage their affairs—he suggested his son Richard and the Irish chaplain to the Spanish embassy, Thomas Hussey—an Irish bishop should also go to London. The bishops felt this might not yet be necessary, but they agreed to the agents

Burke had suggested. On 17 December 1793 they presented an address of loyalty to the King, and followed this up with a memorial to the Lord Lieutenant dated 14 January 1794. In this they asked to be allowed to set up a seminary for the training of their clergy, under Catholic superiors and with no link to Trinity College. They further asked that it be licensed to seek endowments. The Lord Lieutenant, the Earl of Westmorland, was no friend to further concessions to Catholics. A reply did not come until almost a year later. It was dated 2 January 1795 and was signed by the under-secretary, Sackville Hamilton, and it merely said that the request had been submitted to the law officers of the crown, who had declared it illegal to grant it.

Much water had flowed under many bridges during that year. The Irish bishops sent to Rome a copy of the memorial they had addressed to the Lord Lieutenant on 14 January. This was discussed at a meeting of the Congregation of Propaganda on 8 July. The reaction was favourable, but it emphasised that the bishops must insist on control of all staff appointments. In London, under the pressures of war with France the moderate Whigs led by the Duke of Portland had formed a coalition government with Pitt's Tories. Portland himself became Home Secretary, and as such ultimately responsible for Ireland. Ireland was the issue on which there was the greatest divergence of opinion among the coalition partners. The Whigs inclined to the view that potential Irish disaffection could best be dealt with by bearing down on the forces resisting further concessions in Dublin and granting what was already being referred to as 'Catholic emancipation', the right of Catholics to sit in Parliament. Against this background the question of a 'Catholic college' might not be expected to cause serious trouble. It was agreed that there should be a new Whig Lord Lieutenant, the Earl of Fitzwilliam.

Richard Burke had died on 2 August 1794, and though his father struggled to deal with business despite his shock and grief, much of the negotiation concerning the 'Catholic college' now devolved on Thomas Hussey.[6] Hussey, senior chaplain at the Spanish embassy in London and a seasoned diplomat, had been born in Co. Meath, probably in 1741. He had been educated for the priesthood at Seville and Salamanca, and was ordained in 1769. A later story, that he had been a Cistercian for a time, has no documentary foundation, and he appears to have become a chaplain at the Spanish embassy soon after his ordination. Here he won the trust of the British as well as the Spaniards. He had earlier worked with Richard Burke as agent of the Catholic Committee. The Irish bishops were fortunate to have the services of this seasoned and trusted diplomat, for although the political situation looked very favourable there were still obstacles to be negotiated. Was provision to be made for the education of the laity as well as the clergy? The bishops would have preferred a college for the clergy alone, both because of the urgency of their need and because they felt there was better hope that the management of such a college would be left exclusively in their hands. But many leading political figures, including Portland, Fitzwilliam and Burke, urged on Hussey that the laity should be included. Burke was insistent that while state funding was necessary there should be no state 'intermeddling'. Henry Grattan, who might be expected to be an influential figure under the new administration, was approached by Burke and he agreed. At the end of the year Hussey crossed to Dublin, where Fitzwilliam took office on 4 January 1795.

The Whigs would have liked to grant 'Catholic emancipation', but Fitzwilliam left England with instructions agreed by both coalition partners to move very circumspectly on the Catholic question and to refer back for further instructions before committing the government to anything. He arrived in Dublin as a very vigorous new broom. Powerful officials were dismissed, led by John Beresford, the most powerful of all. It easily came to be assumed that 'Catholic emancipation' would be passed in Parliament, which opened on 22 January. Fitzwilliam let it be known that he felt the demand could not be resisted, and Grattan introduced an emancipation bill on 12 February.

By now the bishops were anticipating, not unreasonably, that the bill for their college would go through without much controversy. On 2 February they addressed a letter to Grattan, signed by eighteen bishops, who seem to have been all present in Dublin in an unprecedented gathering.[7] In this letter they asked, with some confidence, for four colleges, one for each ecclesiastical province, exclusively for the education of the clergy, under the exclusive control of the bishops, and supported by a grant from Parliament. On 6 February the Lord Lieutenant received a delegation consisting of Bishop Plunkett of Meath and Bishop Teaghan of Kerry. It began to appear that the Government might insist on some voice in appointing staff. It further appeared that they might have in mind to propose a package involving not merely some control over education in the proposed college or colleges but some control over the nomination of bishops. These issues had been lurking since the debates on the bill of 1782 which had repealed much of the penal laws against religious practice. John Hely Hutchinson, provost of Trinity College, wanted the Catholic clergy to have a 'liberal' education in Ireland, paid for by the government. He was reported as wanting this to be imparted in Trinity, with, he accepted, a separate professor of divinity. A number of people claimed credit for raising the issue of what came to be known as the 'Veto'. In 1778 it took the form of a proposal that the crown should nominate Catholic bishops from a panel of three chosen by the clergy of the diocese.[8] While it would be easy to find parallels for these proposals in Catholic Europe of the late 1770s, the historical interaction between Irish Catholicism and the Anglican settlement made anything approaching them difficult to the point of impossibility in Ireland, and first religious and then political emancipation were in fact granted in Ireland without any such strings attached.

Shortly after the middle of February 1795 it began to appear as if the proposed final stage of 'Catholic emancipation' was forcing bigger issues on an episcopate whose attention had been focused on their college. But by now Fitzwilliam was in serious trouble, and he was dismissed from office on 23

February. He was dismissed not so much for the concessions he had proposed for the Catholics, though here he had blatantly gone against his instructions, but because of the power of the people he himself had dismissed. When he fell these returned to favour, and the future for concessions to Catholics did not look bright. 'Catholic emancipation' came only in 1829, after a long struggle which did much to set Irish politics in a sectarian mould. By contrast, the proposal for the 'Catholic college' drew some benefits from the imbroglio, because it represented a useful sop to Catholics. At first it was naturally assumed that everything was lost with the fall of Fitzwilliam, and Hussey thought in terms of leaving Dublin, believing there was nothing now to keep him there, but he first wrote to Portland, on 27 February 1795, a few days after the fall of Fitzwilliam. In reply, Portland assured him there would be a college, and told him to stay.

About the only thing certain was that there was to be one college, not four; indeed four colleges never seem to have been seriously considered. But all the other questions were open. Was it to be a college for the clergy only, or for the laity as well? Was there to be government financial support, and would the government demand some measure of control in return? On 17 March Burke wrote to Hussey urging that control should not be conceded as the price of an endowment. When the new Lord Lieutenant, Camden, was sworn in on 31 March, Hussey put the bishops' proposals to him: that there should be one college, founded by royal charter, and under Catholic episcopal control. Camden referred the matter to the Lord Chancellor, Fitzgibbon, and the Chief Baron of the Exchequer, Barry Yelverton. Between these on the one side and Hussey and Archbishop Troy on the other a bill was hammered out which with a measure of careful ambiguity was acceptable to both government and bishops. The new college would not have a charter of incorporation, but Troy and Hussey seem to have been assured it would be built from public funds and get an annual grant of £5,000. A site near Dublin was acceptable to the government, but not one in the city itself. The Catholic side had to accept the four chief judges on the board of trustees, all of them Protestants, of course, but other proposals—that the Protestant Archbishop be a visitor and that the professors be appointed by the King or Lord Lieutenant—were, Troy wrote to Archbishop Bray of Cashel on 25 April 1795, 'at length given up'.[9]

The bill, when leave was given to introduce it on 23 April, continued the ambiguities, which may indeed have helped it through all its stages without serious opposition, down to the royal assent on 5 June 1795 (35 Geo. I, c. 21). What debate there may have been was not judged worthy of notice in the *Parliamentary Register*. As presented to Parliament, the financial provision was less generous than Troy and Hussey had been led to believe. Permission was sought to apply 'the sum of £10,000, or part thereof, for establishing a college for the better education of persons professing the popish or Roman Catholic religion, and intended for the clerical ministry thereof.' However, the bill actually introduced the next day did not have this last clause, no doubt indicating continuous complex tensions behind the scenes. The change was a paper victory for the government, but, as will be seen, the bishops won in fact. Indeed, according to a newspaper report the Chief Secretary, Thomas Pelham, stated explicitly that originally provision had been made for the education of the laity, but this had been dropped at the request of the clergy.[10] On 29 April there was a petition from a group calling itself 'his Majesty's Catholic subjects of Ireland'. The core of this group must certainly have been the education committee set up by the Catholic Committee in 1793. They asked that the proposed college should be governed by its principal and professors, not by nominated trustees; that students be admitted by examination, not by nomination; and that it be open to Protestants as well as Catholics. In the circumstances of April 1795 it is hardly surprising they got no hearing. The only modification introduced in committee was the reduction of the figure of £10,000 to £8,000, obviously another compromise between opposing views.

As enacted in June 1795, the bill named twenty-one trustees, for the purpose of 'establishing . . . maintaining and endowing an academy . . . for the education exclusively of persons professing the Roman Catholic religion' (it was explicitly stated that no Protestant was to be admitted). The Trustees, who were also to act as Visitors, fell into three distinct groups. The first consisted of the four 'high judges', John Fitzgibbon, the Lord Chancellor, John Scott, Viscount Clonmel, Chief Justice of the King's Bench, Lord Carlton, Chief Justice of the Common Pleas, and Barry Yelverton, Chief Baron of the Exchequer. The Act implied, but did not state, that the post of trustee was attached to the judicial office. In an act passed in 1800 (40 Geo. III, c. 85) the judges ceased to be trustees but remained as visitors. From the beginning, in fact, they had performed their functions as trustees in a very limited way. They—or more accurately three of them on each occasion—attended only two Trustees' meetings. Both of these were held in the Lord Chancellor's chambers in the House of Lords. The very first meeting, held on 24 June, had as its sole business to advertise for a site for the college. It was attended by Clonmel, Carlton, and Yelverton. The list of those present is headed by an erasure, but the letters 'Cl' are clearly decipherable. This must mean that the Lord Chancellor had been expected but did not turn up (he had been created Earl of Clare just twelve days before, on 12 June). Five meetings followed in rapid succession, much occupied with detail. No judge attended any of them. Then there was a meeting on 28 July, again in the Lord Chancellor's chambers. Its sole purpose was to accept the offer of 'Mr Stoyte's house' in Maynooth as a site. Clare, Clonmel and Yelverton attended. No judge came to any other meeting.

Of the seventeen Catholic trustees, six were laymen, drawn from the Catholic nobility and gentry. They were all politically conservative. Four of them had seceded from the Catholic Committee in 1791: Lords Fingall, Gormanston and Kenmare, and Richard Strange. So had the father of a fifth, Sir Edward Bellew. The sixth was Sir Thomas French, from an old Connacht gentry family; he was to be raised to the peerage in 1798 for his loyal services during the rebellion. It would be wrong to see these men as in any way subservient to the bishops. If anything, indeed, the bishops were deferential to the nobility. In any case their common fear of any hint of radicalism gave them a great measure of common interest. The situation became even more comfortable because it became the practice that when one of the lay trustees died his son and successor was invariably co-opted in his place. This was quite legal according to the terms of the Act, but it effectively excluded from the Trustees any element that might be either innovative or disturbing, depending on the point of view. Like the laymen, the eleven Catholic ecclesiastics were appointed by name and not by office. All were bishops except Thomas Hussey. He could hardly have been excluded, but he was the only Catholic ecclesiastic to be a trustee who was not a bishop. The ten bishops named were the four archbishops and six bishops who had been prominent in the negotiations with the government. Again, vacancies were to be filled by co-option, and only bishops were co-opted.

In their task of establishing the academy, the Trustees were empowered to set up endowments by receiving subscriptions and donations, and to purchase lands in value not exceeding £1,000 a year. They were also effectively constituted the governing body, being empowered to appoint a president and all necessary staff. All—staff, students and servants—were to take the Oath of Allegiance of 1774.[11] They were further empowered to make rules, regulations and statutes; of these, those 'not affecting the exercise of the popish or Roman Catholic religion' had to be laid before the Lord Lieutenant, who might disapprove of them within a month. Finally, a sum not exceeding £8,000 was to be paid out of the money voted by Parliament to the treasury 'towards establishing the said academy'.

A few points remain to be noted. According to the text of the statute, the proposed institution was not to be exclusively for the education of the clergy. Again according to the text of the statute, government control was minimal, and in practice it decreased. What exactly was brought into existence was uncertain, beyond a group of trustees empowered to found and manage a college. Strictly speaking, the statute did not bring the college into existence. It will be recalled that at the beginning of April 1795 Hussey had asked for a college under episcopal control to be founded by royal charter. This did not happen. The college did not receive a charter, and the Trustees did not become a legal body corporate (as has been noted, all the trustees, Protestant and Catholic, were appointed as individuals, not in virtue of their office). As Professor O'Connell has commented, 'The plan of Fitzwilliam's government to give the clergy some form of partial establishment and recognition was one thing: very different was the plan implemented by Camden's administration of granting money to a group of individuals for the ostensible purpose of merely improving the education of Catholics.'[12] Yet, as will be seen, there was a kind of impetus built into the Act of 1795 which set the college firmly towards becoming an ecclesiastical seminary under a corporate body of Trustees and under episcopal control.

Settling In at Maynooth

The Trustees now had to bring together students, staff and buildings. At their first meeting, on 24 June 1795, they decided to acquire lands and buildings in the vicinity of Dublin, and to advertise for a suitable site. The next day they appointed Thomas Hussey President and on 27 June Francis Power vice-president and bursar. The same day they appointed the first professors. There were plenty of suitable people, *émigrés* from the Revolution, Irish as well as French. Francis Power in particular, sometime canon of Avignon, was to be a permanent focus of stability in a troubled institution until he retired in 1810. Nor was there any shortage of prospective students, as soon as arrangements could be made for them.

At least three sites in what was then 'the vicinity of Dublin' were seriously considered: Glasnevin House, Barry House in Donnybrook, and Stillorgan House. Indeed negotiations for this third site had advanced so far that the proprietor believed that agreement had been reached on 8 July, and expressed his sense of grievance when he learned that the Trustees had decided on another location when they met on 28 July. This was the house that John Stoyte, a steward of the Duke of Leinster, had just built at the western end of the main street recently laid out in Maynooth (Plate 33). With it they invested in about sixty acres of land, on a lease for lives renewable for ever granted to them by the Duke of Leinster. Part of this was Stoyte's property, part of it that of his neighbour, Mr Chamberlain. The overall cost was just over £4,000 (Plate 1).

Maynooth in those days could hardly be described as being 'in the vicinity of Dublin'. What induced the Trustees to move so far out was undoubtedly the active good will of Ireland's premier nobleman, the Duke of Leinster, his wife, the Duchess Emily, and her sister, Lady Louisa Connolly.[13] The 'Catholic college' does not appear to have been very welcome in other places, so the patronage of the Duke, a liberal according to his friends, a radical according to his enemies, was an important factor.

Though knocked about a bit by renovations in the 1950s, Stoyte House — it still bears the name — is still recognisable as the nucleus of the college. It was a small gentleman's house, not particularly distinguished, two storeys and attic over basement. It had been built shortly before on the site of the old Geraldine 'Council House', whose remains were removed at the time, the 'council table' being removed to Carton House, while the doorway was re-erected as the entrance to the Church of Ireland school. Contemporary maps show an entrance gate in the centre of a curved wall which follows the same line today, though today's gate and wall are replacements of the 1950s (Plates 3, 4, 10). A description written in 1818[14] notes the ornaments on the piers: two sphinxes on the gate-piers, flanked by lions couchant and urns. These, regretfully, went in the 1950s, though indeed they were then close to disinte-gration. It must be assumed they were put there by Mr Stoyte rather than by the Trustees, though the latter must be responsible for the ornate sundial that still stands at the front of the building, for it is dated 1796 (Plate 14). Two parallel lines are drawn on the 1795 maps between the Stoyte and Chamberlain properties. In later maps, the Carton map of 1821[15] and the Ordnance Survey of 1838 (Plates 5, 34), they resolve themselves into lines of trees, not quite aligned with Stoyte House, which in turn is not quite aligned with the street of Maynooth and its prolongation, the avenue leading to the west gate of Carton. These lines of trees still stand, obviously antedating the building of Stoyte House and therefore the oldest object on the grounds of Maynooth College, known to generations of students as 'the glade'. It shows its age now, becoming quite gapped as the old trees fall, gaps the replacements will take long years to fill.

On 28 July it was decided to begin by admitting fifty students. As agreed, the Trustees took possession of their property on 1 September. On 16 September, as noted in the first entry in the first account-book of the college, the sum of £1 14s 1½d was paid 'to a carriage to and from Maynooth, for Messrs Aherne [professor of Dogma] Flood [professor of Moral] and Dunne [secretary to the Trustees], by direction of Most Rev. Dr Troy, to inspect and report on the extent of the accommodation for professors, students etc.' By the end of 1795 only forty students had been admitted, and not all the profes-sors had yet turned up, but even so Stoyte House could not cope. A memoran-dum from the Trustees in April 1799, preserved in Castlereagh's papers, states that while all students were maintained from the day of their admission some were lodged in houses in Maynooth.[16] Additional buildings were clearly need-ed, and on a fairly large scale.

What buildings were to go up depended on what resources were available and what students were to be catered for. A long advertisement inserted in the *Dublin Evening Post* of 26 November 1795 shows the Trustees still trying to focus their problems. From what they say it appears clear that they envisaged lay students attending lectures with the clerics, and hoped that people might come forward to build boarding-houses for them as a commercial venture. Of the £8,000 voted by Parliament, half had already been spent in the purchase of property, and what was left was being steadily diminished by recurring daily charges. Yet while Parliament had granted only £8,000 'towards establishing the said academy', there was an understanding cloaked in ambiguities that more money might be available. Shortly after the Trustees had advertised in the *Post* their fortunes improved considerably when Thomas Pelham, the Chief Secretary, advised Hussey and Troy that the government planned to make more money available, seemingly considerably more money.[17] Pelham must have been further encouraged by a letter dated 31 December from John Foster, Speaker of the Commons and implacable defender of the Protestant ascendancy, proposing 'an Irish solution to an Irish problem', saying he considered that Pelham 'very properly' intended 'to continue a yearly allowance', 'but there is no reason to give it a fixed place in the speech'[18] or in more modern terminology, there is no objection to making the grant provided it does not appear in the Book of Estimates. In consequence, when the Trustees petitioned from their meeting of 23 February 1796 for support for the establishment for one year to 25 March 1797 and for erecting buildings, Parliament responded with a grant of £7,000. A similar petition on 20 January 1797, detailing the cost of the building at £12,420, the expense of fitting it out at £4,181 16s 11d and annual expenses at £2,679 15s, resulted in a grant of £10,000. In all this Pelham had proved a very good friend to the college, but even he drew back from any grant of a charter,[19] and the grant for 1796/97 was made in the name of the individual trustees who had signed the petition, while those for 1797/98 were made to their secretary, Andrew Dunne. Yet in January 1798 what was now becoming an annual petition to Parliament asked confidently for a grant for the completion of the building works, for the maintenance until 25 September of the 'present establishment'—sixty-nine students, as events would shortly show—and the maintenance until the end of the financial year, 25 March 1799, of the 'full establishment', set at two hundred students. For all this the Trustees asked a sum of £10,622.

The petition came before Parliament on 1 February. It is clear even from the laconic *Commons' Journal* that questions were raised. Sectarian tension was rising in the country, and there were understandable misgivings at the way in which an annual grant to the 'Catholic college' was being introduced. Parliament asked for and received details of all sums already paid to the college, and a list of all who held office in it. On 28 February 1798 the *Hibernian Journal* singled out two members who spoke critically against the institution. One was John Foster, who urged that the sums granted were too great and asked that they be reduced. He did not, however, ask that the petition be rejected. Total rejection was proposed by the second speaker, Patrick Duigenan. Duigenan was an example of the vehement anti-Catholicism sometimes found in converts to the Established Church. He was born in Leitrim in 1735, the child of a farmer who would have liked to see his promising son a priest. However, he was patronised by the local Protestant rector, who helped him to enter Trinity College in 1756. He proved himself a brilliant student, and was made a fellow. In 1767 he was called to the bar, where he concentrated his attention after taking a prominent part on the losing side in the quarrels over the appointment of Hely Hutchinson as Provost in 1774. He became MP for Old Leighlin in 1791. Rough and quarrelsome, but a conservative churchman to the point of caricature, he now called for the termination of any government assistance to the 'Catholic college', and declared himself opposed to it in principle. There may have been an element of reaction to his intemperance in the decision taken by Parliament to vote the full sum requested.

In their petition for funds in January 1798 the Trustees had made it clear they expected to have their new building ready to receive students by the beginning of the academic year in September. The events of that disturbed spring and summer forced them to postpone the opening, but it is now time to see what they were doing with their money. In a letter of 20 February 1796 to Archbishop Bray of Cashel, Archbishop Troy of Dublin set out hopes and plans:

> Our present savings and parliamentary aid will enable us to expend £12,500 in building the front side of a square to accommodate 200 students, besides halls, a temporary chapel, refectory etc. to be covered on the 25th March of next year. Stapleton's improved plan was preferred and presented to Parliament and government with the accounts and estimates. We have also in hands £500 to be expended in building, or renting if possible, a large lodging house for the immediate accommodation of additional students, particularly lay pensioners, to render the institution more generally useful and palatable to the public.[20]

Plans for two buildings took shape, because the Trustees envisaged two colleges, lay and ecclesiastical. At their meeting on 10 August 1796 they approved 'Dr Hussey's contract with Samuel Parker for the erection of a building intended to lodge the scholars until the large buildings are completed, and afterwards to serve for the reception of pupils not designed for the ecclesiastical state'. The building cost £1,000 and was unpretentious indeed. Its location, between the present College Chapel and the senior infirmary, then discreetly removed from the ecclesiastical college, appears clearly on the Carton maps (1821) and the Ordnance Survey (1838), where it is marked 'Infirmary'. It was occupied by clerical students when it was completed in the summer of 1798. Eugene Conwell, a student of Armagh who entered Maynooth as a priest in September 1798, wrote several letters that autumn to his uncle Henry, parish priest of Dungannon, describing his room in a building about forty perches from the college, a cold room, because the building had been finished only that summer. It housed about thirty students. They hoped to move to 'the new building' in the spring, when the one they now occupied would be given over to the 'externs' now lodging in the town.

In fact it was the spring of 1800 before the clerics vacated this building, which then briefly became a lay college until the neighbouring property of Riverstown Lodge was bought for this purpose in 1802.[21] The clerics returned, and in due course it became their infirmary, when precisely it is not easy to say, but probably in 1804, when at their meeting on 11 October the Trustees set aside £2,000 to be spent on an infirmary. It is doubtful if all this money was spent, for the inadequacies and, increasingly, the decrepitude of the old building are continuously complained of. It was demolished in the early 1860s and replaced by the present infirmary; and in truth it does not appear to have required much demolition.

Work on the major building was approved by the Trustees and was begun when Parliament had approved their request for funds. The architect was

Michael Stapleton, a Catholic and a master builder and stuccodore of some repute, whose work has survived in several places, and—unfortunately in modern reproduction only—in St Joseph's Chapel in Maynooth (Plate 72). Work must have begun as soon as Parliament had given approval towards the end of February. The contract stipulated that the shell of the building was to be finished by 25 March 1798 and to be fitted out for use by 25 September—dates, it might be suspected, more related to the government's accounting year than to anything else. In fact the building was occupied piecemeal over the year 1799.

Practically no detail of the building process has survived. All that remains are the accounts of the laying of the foundation-stone by Lord Lieutenant Camden on 20 April.[22] He arrived accompanied by the four judge-trustees and many Castle officials. The clerical trustees present were the Archbishops of Armagh and Dublin, Bishop Plunkett of Meath, and the President, Dr Hussey, with the staff and students of the college, together with 'the Duke of Leinster and the principal nobility and gentry in the neighbourhood'. When the Lord Lieutenant alighted at the gate the band of the Londonderry Militia played 'God Save the King'. As soon as he was seated he was greeted with Greek and Latin odes composed by James Bernard Clinch, professor of *belles-lettres*, the Greek ode being delivered by Patrick Coleman, a Dublin clerical student, and the Latin ode by William Ahern of Cloyne. There was also an English ode composed by Rev. John Eustace, Professor of Rhetoric, and delivered by a young man called Cooney, seemingly a lay student. The Lord Lieutenant then laid the foundation stone, the band once again playing 'God Save the King', 'to which the students and an immense concourse of people joined in the chorus.' Then there were presentations—an inscribed silver trowel for Camden, saluting him as 'fautor' and 'patronus', and an inscribed gold snuff-box for Pelham, saluted as 'patronus' and 'Macaenas'. 'His excellency partook of some refreshments, and returned to the Castle, where the Trustees of the seminary had the honour of dining with him,' in the plain wording of the newspaper report.[22] In his diary Lord Clonmel, Chief Justice of the King's Bench and no great respecter of bishops of any persuasion, put it more acidly:

> Lord Camden laid the foundation stone of the popish seminary at Maynooth. I attended him with the Chancellor and the other two chief judges, and we dined at the castle with several popish bishops, and other Trustees. N.B. A very new scene in this kingdom, and important in its consequence.[23]

One of the 'popish bishops', Patrick Plunkett of Meath, recorded the same conviction, but more hopefully, in a long letter to his Roman agent, John Connolly OP, written from Navan on 12 October:

> We received at Maynooth cards of invitation to dine that day with the

Lord Lieutenant at the Castle of Dublin, and his Excellency had the goodness to order his carriages to convey the ecclesiastical Trustees from Maynooth to Dublin, a distance of eleven miles. Doctors O'Reilly, Troy, Abbé Hussey and I came to the capital in the Viceroy's splendid coach and six attended by his servants. We had the honour of dining that day along with the other Trustees at the Castle with the Lord Lieutenant. The dinner, you may be sure, was suitable to the place and the occasion: the politeness, attention and affability of the Lord Lieutenant was such as to leave us nothing to wish for.

It was not the least remarkable circumstance of that extraordinary day, that the Lord Lieutenant called on Doctor O'Reilly of Armagh to bless the table. 'Doctor O'Reilly, be so good as to give us grace'. After the King and royal family, the first toast given by the Viceroy was 'success and prosperity to the Seminary of St Patrick'. The Duke of Leinster, on whose estate the college is situated, assisted with delight at the ceremony of the laying of the first stone and was one of the guests at the Castle dinner that day. His Grace behaved towards us with marked civility and kindness. The scene exhibited on the 20th of April was in every respect so new, I thought this detail would not be unacceptable.[24]

'Foundation Day' is still marked in Maynooth on 20 April. Unfortunately there is no trace of the foundation stone, all the more remarkably because a drastic reconstruction in the early 1950s laid bare every stone that was to be left in the original building. Yet there was an inscription on a 'a plate fixed in the foundation-stone', according to J. B. Clinch, and as he gives the inscription in his pamphlet it deserves reproduction if only because there is no other trace of it:

COMES DE CAMDEN, Hiberniae Pro-Rex
ad Religionis et Litterarum incrementum, hujus
R. Collegii Catholici Deo, sub nuncupatione S.
Patricii dicati patriaque Munificentia dotati,
primum lapidem collocavit; praesentibus, praeter
Aulicum Comitatum, plurimis ex Collegii Curatoribus,
et frequentissimo populo: XII Kal. Maii
Anni Salutis M.DCCXCVI Regni Georgii III. Regis
Augusti XXXVI.[25]

It does indeed contain two pieces of information: that the college was to be dedicated to St Patrick, though this was perhaps inevitable; and that its other and legal title was ambiguous, in that people would expand 'R. collegium Catholicum' either as 'Royal Catholic college' or 'Roman Catholic college'.

There is a fine contemporary print of Stapleton's building,[26] and a large watercolour by an unknown but amateur artist has recently been discovered and now hangs in the President's office (Plates 11, 35). It was a great block of a building (unfortunately made 'blockier' by the extensive reconstruction of the early 1950s). When at that time its condition gave cause for concern, close examination indicated that it was remarkable it had lasted so long. It was clearly designed to enclose as much space as possible as cheaply as possible, and yet it was a building with some character, one might venture to say not without elegance. The line of building was attached to the back of Stoyte House, running out about 200 feet on either side of it and in some of its features replicating it. At each end and in the centre it was an attic over two storeys, and the three blocks were linked by wings of two storeys, each of these pierced by an archway large enough to take carriages. On the ground floor of the block to the south was the students' refectory, while the chapel took up two floors of the northern block. In between, the ground floor was divided into five large lecture halls. The first floor and attics were to accommodate 200 students, Stoyte being reserved for the staff.

There was still much to be done to make the building habitable. Accommodation was very tight, and in the cavernous attics it was very bad. The surroundings were no more than a green field ploughed up by builders. The general layout introduced that lasting problem of Maynooth life: how to get from anywhere to anywhere without going out in the rain. Before these problems were tackled, however, even before the building was completed, the very existence of the college was threatened.

'Dark and Evil Days'

On 30 March 1798 martial law had been declared throughout Ireland. Lord Chancellor Clare held a visitation of Trinity College between 19 and 21 April, as a result of which nineteen students were expelled on suspicion of being United Irishmen. When he declared his intention of holding a similar visitation at Maynooth the Trustees decided to forestall him by holding a special meeting on 11 May.[27] In consequence of reports in circulation charging some with disaffection, they ordered the President 'to interrogate in the most solemn manner each individual relative to said reports'. The following day the President interviewed the sixty-nine seminarians. Fifty-nine swore an oath that they had never been United Irishmen. Eight admitted they had taken the United Irishman oath but had repented and taken the Oath of Allegiance. Two refused to answer. All ten were immediately expelled, for the Trustees had left the President no discretion. The lay students lodging in the town and attending lectures in the college were then interrogated. Six said they had taken the United Irishman oath but had since taken the Oath of Allegiance. One would only say that he was loyal. The seven were informed that they would no longer be allowed to attend the schools of Maynooth College.[28]

Some indication of student mentality may be gleaned from evidence given to the Commission of Inquiry in 1826 by John Cousins. Cousins had been admitted as a student for the diocese of Ferns in 1799. Ordained priest in 1805, he had later defected and officiated as a clergyman in the Established Church. The evidence he gave to the Commissioners is factual in tone and seems devoid of anything like rancour. For himself he said he entered Maynooth a rebel and left it a rebel, and that he would have been fighting with the Wexford rebels in 1798 had his mother not locked him up. Most Maynooth students, 'coming from retired parts of the country', had little in the way of political views when they entered the college but quickly developed them as they talked to one another. There was, Cousins said, much sympathy for the rebels. In particular, the students used to 'dwell with pleasure on the bravery with which the rebels fought' and regret their failure. This, however, was sympathy, not active support, and some students, but not many, particularly from the north of the country, were described by Cousins as very loyal.[29] But even this represented an alarming gap between the student body and the Trustees, a conservative group indeed, and the staff, all of them refugees from the Revolution in France.

Active revolt began on 23 May, most successful in Wexford but widespread all over Leinster. The Trustees, who had forwarded an address of loyalty to the Lord Lieutenant after their meeting on 11 May, took comfort in the fact that the college staff gave some help in suppressing the rebellion in the vicinity of Maynooth, but they took the unprecedented step of sending all the students home for the summer months, because, they said, there were well-grounded fears the rebels planned to force those not in holy orders to join them.[30] In this there may have been an element of understatement.

On 24 June, three days after the defeat at Vinegar Hill had effectively ended the rebellion, Peter Flood, the President, wrote to his friend Bishop Plunkett of Meath. He had received government assurance, he said, that Maynooth would not lose its grant. Vacation was beginning that day, and he hoped to resume studies on 24 or 25 August. It would be impossible, however, to receive additional students, for all work on the new building was suspended since the insurgents had forced the workmen away (a careful sentence, possibly with elements of both overstatement and understatement). He added that some of the insurgents even threatened to make the students march in their ranks. He wrote again on 21 August. The academic year would begin, but not without problems. Very little building work had been done for three months, and the 450 soldiers quartered in Maynooth occupied every available house, including those used as lodging-houses for students. He hoped to be able to accommodate 50 in the new building, rising to 75 by mid-September, 125 by Christmas, and the full 200 by March 1799, an estimate he had to revise downwards in a letter of 5 March: he now planned to have 150 by the end of April and the full 200 by the end of June. Unless this number was reached there was danger that a substantial part of the grant would be lost.[31]

As will be seen, what was by this date happening in Parliament gave good grounds for such fears. Outside Parliament, Maynooth was prominent in the wild rumours that swept the country. In his pamphlet *A Fair Representation of the Present Political State of Ireland* Patrick Duigenan said it was stated and generally believed that about thirty-six Maynooth students had joined the rebels and fought at Kilcock and elsewhere, and that it was certain sixteen or seventeen had been expelled. As has been seen, ten clerical students were expelled and seven lay students excluded from lectures. It may be taken as certain that no Maynooth student fought with the rebels at Kilcock or elsewhere in the locality, and as equally certain that some men from the locality working on the college buildings did, probably not all of them under compulsion.

Attention ultimately focused on two students, Francis Hearn and John Power. Hearn was one of the two students who had refused to answer in May 1798. Like most of those expelled, he had tried to continue his studies for the priesthood, and had been admitted to Carlow College, where he spent three months. But he also managed to get himself so deeply involved in the insurrection that he had no defence when captured at Carlow in the opening days of October 1799. He was sent for trial to his native Waterford, where he was executed on 28 October. On 1 October the military had turned up at Maynooth College, seeking Hearn and John Power. They were told that there were no people of that name in the college, that Francis Hearn had been expelled, that there never had been a John Power and that a Maurice Power had left in October 1797, 'not wishing to take orders'. There was a Thomas Power, described as 'an inoffensive, harmless young man', which however did not stop him being arrested. The next day the vice-president, Francis Power, called agitatedly on Archbishop Troy, who immediately sent him to the Castle with his information. Presumably Thomas Power was released; a few days later a John Power was arrested with Hearn in Carlow and sent with him to Waterford. It is quite possible he was as innocent as his namesake Thomas; at any rate, no more is heard of him.[32] The connection between Maynooth students and the 1798 insurgents was, then, very indirect, but that did not stop the Dublin papers. On 9 November 1799 *Faulkner's Dublin Journal* reported: 'Great exertions were made by the Roman Catholic clergy of Dublin to obtain pardon for Hearn, a student of Maynooth College, who was lately tried by court martial and pleaded guilty.' An indignant protest from Archbishop Troy to the Lord Lieutenant the following day resulted only in a backhanded disclaimer published on 12 November: 'No such application was made on behalf of Hearn—his guilt was of a nature so atrocious as to preclude the most distant hope of pardon.' In any case the story had been sent on the rounds and could not be overtaken; on 20 November Troy was writing again to the Castle complaining that the London papers were taking up the story and asking that they also publish the correction.[33]

1799 had been a difficult year indeed. In the aftermath of the insurrection the government was determined on a union of the two kingdoms. It was hoped to win Catholic support by a promise of 'emancipation', that is, final admission to the political nation. In return, the Catholics should grant the government some measure of control over clerical appointments. The episcopal members of the Maynooth Trustees, after their meeting in January 1799, took upon themselves to accept, subject to the approval of the Holy See, proposals allowing the government to reject the name of a candidate put forward for an Irish diocese should they raise 'a proper objection' against his loyalty to the crown. This was a contentious concession, even in the circumstances of January 1799.

The Trustees' meeting had forwarded to Lord Lieutenant Cornwallis their petition for a grant of £8,000 for the maintenance of 200 scholars over the year 1799/1800. Relations between the administration and Parliament were edgy, but the question of the day was the Union, not the Catholic college. The Commons did deduct £1,383 15s 10d, alleged to be unexpended from the previous year's allocation, but it granted the residue without any demur, agreeing that 'the petitioners deserve the aid of Parliament'. Trouble erupted, however, when the bill came to the Lords. The laconic *Lords' Journals* record only that on the second reading a proposal to consider the request in committee on 1 August (a day Parliament would not be in session) was carried by twenty-five votes to one. Other sources allow a little fleshing out. Anti-Catholic sentiment surfaced in an abusive debate. The motion was moved by Lord Farnham, but the real damage was done by Clare, the Lord Chancellor. He later claimed that the Lords had rejected the request because it had emerged that an arrangement had been made privately with 'Dr Troy and other popish bishops, though by whom I could never find out', to agree to a permanent annual grant of £8,000 'for maintaining a mere monastick institution, for the education exclusively of papist priests'. It was intolerable that the clergy be educated apart from the laity, and intolerable also that they be educated without any payment whatsoever, for this meant they would in future be taken from an unacceptably low class in society, educated in 'an asylum for paupers'.

The Lord Lieutenant was appalled, for the Chancellor had given him no advance notice of what he proposed to do. He knew that what had happened in the Lords would be interpreted, in the heated atmosphere of the times, as a proposal to put an end to Maynooth. While this might comfort extreme Protestants, it could politically alienate even moderate Catholics. The Chancellor's reply was in a measured tone, but was hardly calculated to mollify. He declared that he and the Lords sought the regulation of Maynooth, not its abolition. The Lords had taken the course they did because it was the only way open to them: they could not insert the regulations they wished for into a money vote. But if money was really needed, there was no problem. A new bill for a lesser amount could be introduced in the same session.[34] Clare followed up this letter by declaring from the woolsack in the Lords that he did not wish to see Maynooth abolished but rather run on 'more liberal principles', these to include the admission of lay students. From a meeting the Maynooth Trustees issued on 22 April a firm but eirenic statement, pointing out their desperate need for 200 seminary places—less than half of what had been lost—and appealing for an end to the bitter attacks in the newspapers. It appeared that the situation might be cooling.[35]

Unfortunately, it soon appeared that Clare had given the Lord Lieutenant bad advice when he said that it was possible to introduce another money vote. This proposal was put before Parliament, a precedent for it being cited. But John Foster, the Speaker of the Commons, declared the precedent to be a bad one. A confrontation seemed inevitable when the Chief Secretary, Castlereagh, declared that, since the Commons had voted the money and the Lords had said they wanted Maynooth supported, he trusted the executive would be justified in making the necessary payments before the next session of Parliament. The Commons agreed unanimously, thus avoiding confrontation by consenting to questionable practice.[36] On 30 April Troy could inform the Archbishop of Cashel that for this year the government would give a grant to support 100 students 'on its own responsibility', and a week later this was known among the student body.[37]

In his letter to Clare on 18 April, the Lord Lieutenant had said that he awaited his suggestions for reform of the college. Other people were forwarding suggestions, the chief among them being Bishop O'Beirne of Meath. Thomas Lewis O'Beirne (c. 1748–1823) had been sent with his brother to Saint-Omer. The brother became a Catholic priest, but Thomas conformed to the Established Church, and according to tradition for a time ministered in the same parish as his brother in his native Co. Longford. A Longford parish did not hold him long, however. He attached himself to the Whig political interest, and in due course became a bishop. He was beyond question a gifted man, and by all accounts a good bishop. On both headings he had grave suspicions of popery. The advice he and others tendered went to support the views of Clare. 'We have giddily made this establishment', he said, 'with strange precipitance and want of forethought', where students 'from the lowest ranks of community' were 'educated in a monastery' for the Catholic priesthood. The answer was not to suppress Maynooth but to give it money, if necessary even more liberally, but at the same time turn it into an instrument of government where all diocesan priests had to be educated. It would be controlled by having more Protestant trustees, perhaps even a majority. Certainly a majority of the visitors should be Protestants, and dignitaries such as the Church of Ireland Archbishop of Dublin and Bishop of Kildare, and the Provost of Trinity College, should be either trustees or visitors. The institution should not be exclusively clerical. All were agreed on this and Clare was especially strong on it, though they all seem to have had a subconscious reservation that while it was good for the clergy to be educated with the laity it was not quite so good for the laity to be educated with the clergy. Yet the mix was necessary if there was to be any hope of substituting 'a rational system of classical, scientific, religious and moral education for the perverted and mischievous scholastic jargon'. The text of the divinity lectures was to be approved by the Lord Lieutenant, who would nominate the President and have a veto on other appointments.[38]

This is further proof that the Protestant establishment would have given the Irish Catholics a seminary under its close control, rather like what Joseph II had done in Austria or Febronius counselled in Germany, except that in Ireland the situation would be much worse, because the establishment was hostile rather than reformist. It was even suggested that just as the college was not to be exclusively clerical neither was it to be exclusively Catholic. Catholics and Protestants were educated together in the Netherlands and in parts of Germany, it was pointed out, and Trinity College now admitted Catholics. But a practical statesman like Cornwallis knew that most of these suggestions would be totally unacceptable to Irish Catholics, and he asked Clare to discuss things with 'leading Catholics', who seem to have been Archbishop Troy and Lord Fingall. Clare 'submitted very reluctantly at Lord Cornwallis's request' and soon had to submit himself to what was practical. What were ostensibly the two principal issues—that lay pupils be admitted and that the clerics be asked to pay something—seem to have caused no contention. Troy accepted the latter and agreed to have a certain number of lay students as soon as accommodation could be provided.

It is clear there was hard bargaining on the issue of control, and it is equally clear that Clare lost. The issue narrowed down to the question of visitation. It was agreed that the judges should no longer be Trustees—as has been seen, they did not in fact attend Trustees' meetings. Instead it was proposed that the four chief judges—designated now by office, not by name—should hold frequent visitation. The Catholic side won two vital modifications. There were to be three Catholic visitors, 'Arthur, earl of Fingall, the Reverend Richard O'Reilly and the Reverend John Thomas Troy'—designated by name only, but in the event of a vacancy a new visitor was to be elected by the Trustees, now all Catholics—and anything relating to 'the exercise of the Roman Catholic religion or the religious doctrine or discipline thereof' was to be exclusively the concern of the Catholic visitors. The President was to be appointed by the Trustees as hitherto; the appointment had to be approved by the Lord Lieutenant, and the new President had to take a special oath in the Court of Chancery, a quite innocuous formula being prescibed. All 'bye-laws, rules, regulations and statutes' were to be submitted to the Lord Lieutenant for approval, and did not bind if he disapproved of them within a month, but 'nothing contained herein shall extend, or be construed to extend, to any bye-laws, rules and regulations affecting the exercise of the Roman Catholic religion, or the doctrine or discipline or worship thereof.' Finally, a small and tentative step was taken towards giving corporate recognition to the Trustees in that they were allowed to sue and be sued 'by and in the name of their secretary.'

All this was incorporated in an Act of Parliament (40 Geo III, c. 85), which received the royal assent on the last working day of the Irish Parliament, 1 August 1801. In a letter to Bray of Cashel on 19 April Troy had commented that the legislation was not really necessary, but to preserve an appearance of consistency the Chancellor felt he had to make some change to justify what he had said the previous year.[39] In hindsight it is clear that he got little of what he had hoped for. If anything, the college was now more clearly established as a Catholic institution governed by Catholics. This being so, the power of the Protestant Visitors was almost altogether an empty one, for little was left after the exercise, doctrine, discipline and worship of the Catholic religion was removed from them. The grant was still dependent on an annual vote of Parliament, but it had acquired some additional stability, at least in fact. The Trustees could confidently build up the student numbers to the two hundred they had planned for, and they had a building that could shelter them, even if with some crowding and some discomfort.

CHAPTER II

'INTERESTING TIMES'

Building Up a Staff

Once the college had come into being, the Trustees were fairly quickly transformed by pressure of events into the real governing body of the institution, even though they were legally empowered only to collect funds and make rules. Only scanty records of the triennial visitation survive, all of them from the same college source, but even when allowance is made for a natural bias tending to play down its significance, it appears clear that visitation was not in fact an important influence in the government of the college. From the beginning the Trustees held their principal annual meeting at the beginning of the year, in January or February. This was done to prepare their accounts for presentation to Parliament and to petition a renewal of the grant for the following financial year. The college could not in fact have continued without this annual grant, for only small resources came from other quarters, normally in the form of a burse in favour of a diocese, allowing additional student places for that diocese to be established (a comprehensive list of 'Private Foundations for Burses' was printed annually in the *Calendar* up to the early 1970s).

At their first business meeting, on 26 June 1795, the Trustees approved constitutions for the clerical government of the college, and ordered their insertion in a 'Book of Statutes'. No such book is extant, but these domestic regulations survive as the 'Regula Pietatis et Disciplinae' in the first printed statutes. These were finally approved at meetings on 17 and 18 November 1800. The 'statutes' as distinct from the 'Regula Pietatis' were submitted to the Lord Lieutenant for his approval and were published in 1801 by Hugh Fitzpatrick of Dublin, now established as 'publisher and bookseller' to the college. Here it will suffice to call attention to one fact, namely that in these statutes the Trustees appear as lawgivers only, not as part of the institution. A more detailed examination must come after a description of the collegiate body which had by now been rather untidily built up.

It was both fitting and to a degree inevitable that Thomas Hussey should become first President. It was not an easy assignment, and indeed was to turn out more difficult than might have been anticipated, as is clear from the fact that the seventh president was appointed just eighteen years after the foundation of the college, giving each of his predecessors an average of just three years' tenure of office. In the matter of public relations Hussey was a real asset, no doubt, but he was not so useful in the affairs of the struggling institution itself, principally because he was often away, for he did not regard the appointment as full-time. He did not resign his chaplaincy at the Spanish Embassy in London, and London and Dublin seem to have seen more of him than Maynooth did. As early as January 1796 Archbishop Troy was writing to Bray of Cashel saying, wishfully it appears, that it was probable Hussey would resign the presidency. He did not resign, not even after he had been appointed Bishop of Waterford in December 1796. In December 1797 Troy was writing rather more testily to Bray that if he did not resign he would be got rid of, and this is what was done, at least implicitly, when his successor was appointed on 17 January 1798, 'in place of Rt Rev. Dr Hussey now RC bp of Waterford.' Hussey's great services had been in securing the foundation of the college, not in his short and intermittent spell as President.

Maynooth, indeed, was never his primary commitment, nor indeed was his diocese of Waterford, though he did end his days there. He had returned to Spanish diplomatic circles in 1798, first in London and then in Paris. Here he was reputed to have played an important role behind the scenes in the negotiations leading to the Concordat of 1801. He was certainly instrumental in securing the return of the Irish College that same year. A letter to its rector, John Baptist Walsh, dated 6 September 1801, may be revealing. 'The institution of the Roman Catholic College of Maynooth', he wrote, 'is undoubtedly a munificent foundation, and very beneficial to the Catholic clergy of Ireland'; but, he went on, it could not share 'advantages which Colleges situated only on the Continent, having full and free communication with the Head of the Church and with the rest of the learned Catholic world, can attain, and which an insular situation and local laws and customs may eventually deny—a sister house in Paris fully answers the purpose of communication.'[1] It would seem that Thomas Hussey found it harder to settle in the Maynooth backwater than even Louis Delahogue or François Anglade.

His successor was Peter Flood, a priest of the diocese of Ardagh, now perhaps fifty years of age. He had had a distinguished career in Paris, being among other things superior of the Lombard College, but he appears to have been prematurely aged by the hardships he had experienced in the Revolution. He had been appointed professor of Moral Theology at Maynooth on 27 June 1795, but he had declined the appointment and had become parish priest of Edgeworthstown. Now however he was persuaded to come to Maynooth as President. It was the beginning of a time of external troubles, and though the college moved towards stability in expanding its numbers to two hundred students and moving into its new buildings, it was not without serious internal tensions, which flared up as Peter Flood was dying. He died on 26 January 1803 and was buried in the north aisle of the College Chapel (now St Joseph's

Oratory). His unmarked grave was discovered during the reconstruction of the 1950s, and is now marked by a plain cross in the tiled floor.

The man who acted as a kind of 'sheet anchor' through several presidencies was Francis Power. He was also an *émigré*, but his background was not academic. His official appointment was as vice-president, but from time to time he acted as bursar as well, and he must also have been dean until the dean appointed at the beginning of 1798 finally arrived in June 1799. Indeed, the statutory provisions for the offices of vice-president and bursar as laid down in 1800 seem to have been primarily a description of what Francis Power was in fact doing. To the historian he left a legacy of the first internal records of the college, the first account books (Plate 12) and a record of annual ordinations and prize-lists, in which he inserted records of such things as staff appointments and visitations, terse indeed, but often the only record in these first years. Born in 1735, he was not a young man when he came to Maynooth. He died on 5 June 1817 and was the first to be buried in the college cemetery, blessed by Archbishop Troy on 30 May, no doubt in anticipation of his death.

The first dean, Edward Ferris, was appointed on 17 January 1798. As described in the statutes, the office of dean was clearly very important: under the direction of the President, he was responsible for all formation of students outside the class-room. Ferris, now nearly sixty years old, seemed well qualified for his work. He too had been forced into exile after a distinguished career in France, where he had gone as a young man and joined the Vincentian Congregation. When appointed he was in Italy, and he did not arrive until the middle of June 1799. He had a reputation for learning marked by rigidity, and holiness marked by extreme austerity, but he and Peter Flood seem to have had good relations with the students for the short time he was dean. He was appointed professor of Moral Theology on 4 November 1800, and his successor was a young man, Thomas Coen, the first student accepted into the college, on 30 June 1795. He was then twenty-four years of age and probably already ordained, but he spent five years at studies, which would have been recently completed when he was appointed, provisionally on 24 February 1801 and 'fully' on 28 July 1802. Quite certainly he was too young and inexperienced to be given this responsible relationship with young men who had recently been his fellow-students. There is also more than a suspicion that Ferris kept up some measure of his previous relationship with the students, and that this made things much harder for Coen. At any rate he had a stormy passage until a more or less forced resignation in 1810, though five years later he became coadjutor bishop of his native diocese of Clonfert, and succeeded as bishop in 1831.

It will be clear from the appointments listed above that there was no shortage of suitably qualified staff, both French and Irish, who had fled from the French Revolution to both Britain and Ireland. There was some inevitable untidiness at the very beginning, as staff were sought out to teach a student body as yet only being assembled. A notice in the *Dublin Evening Post* of 26 November 1795 stated:

From the want of a more ample accommodation at present, it has been found necessary to confine the studies of the current academical year to a course of Moral Theology, of the first part of Mathematics and Philosophy, of Rhetoric and Belles Lettres, and of the first class of Humanity: professors in each of these departments are now resident at Maynooth. Lectures in the first two branches have already commenced: and the professors of Rhetoric and Humanity will proceed to lecture, as soon as the scholars qualified for each class will be given to the establishment.

However, by the time an 'establishment' could be said to exist, in 1800, a full corps of teachers had assembled.

The Council of Trent had envisaged a wide range of studies for the seminary, but it was thinking in terms of students ranging from boys of about twelve to young men of about twenty-four on the eve of ordination. As the 'major seminary' developed, the emphasis on studies there concentrated on the 'professional' theological subjects, with courses in Philosophy regarded both as studies in their own right and as a preparation for Theology. Because the basic language of teaching was Latin, and indeed because the Classics were still considered the foundation of all education, a preparatory year of classical studies, 'Rhetoric', was usually desirable. Indeed Maynooth at its beginning left open the possibility of three years of classical studies, partly because very ill-prepared candidates for the priesthood might be expected and partly because the idea of a lay college was present, but not sorted out. So, the preparatory course might extend from one to three years, a preparatory year, then Humanity, then Rhetoric. The preparatory year was soon dropped as unnecessary, but it was nearly a century before the secondary education system was sufficiently developed to allow the Humanity class to be dropped. *Belles-lettres* earned a separate year only if the term was used to describe the preparatory drilling in the Classics. Insofar as it might be used to denote English literature, it was an adjunct to be filled in in evening classes, as were French and Irish, both these being studied in a severely practical way.

Two years were to be devoted to Philosophy, one year to mental or rational philosophy, one year to natural philosophy, Mathematics and Physics. Natural philosophy had made its way into Catholic education centres by the middle of the eighteenth century, despite some resistance to any idea that Aristotle had left things yet to be discovered, and suspicions of inductive reasoning. Maynooth's equal division of time between mental and natural philosophy lasted for nearly a hundred years, the idea that a grounding in the latter was a necessary part of a general education being only grudgingly abandoned in the face of the growing complexities of both philosophy and science.

In Mental Philosophy, as in Theology, the language of instruction was Latin. Teaching was by question and answer, the professor interrogating the student on work which he had prepared. A drawback of this method was that it focused the students' reading on one book, and while it is surely undesirable that students at university undergraduate stage should be regularly operating at the limits of knowledge, it is correspondingly desirable that their reading should be wider than a single textbook. The problem was even worse in the early days of Maynooth, in that textbooks in the philosophy and theology of clerical instruction were simply not to be had, so that the professor had to spend much time dictating to students matter on which he might examine them the next day. In the report laid before Parliament in 1808 it was noted that while there was no problem in getting classical texts, and in natural philosophy 'several English authors' were used, in mental philosophy 'the professor is obliged through paucity of books to compile the treatise, and dictate the same to his scholars', and in Dogmatic Theology 'the professor [is] obliged to compile these treatises chiefly from books cited in the margin: he dictates his courses.' Things may have been slightly better in Moral Theology: the professor explains, the scholars study Paul Antoine and Peter Colet, though the indications are that while there may have been enough books to go round there was far from being one per student.

Within the seminary, Theology was still 'the queen of sciences'. What was regarded as a good course lasted three years, and it was this which had been introduced at Maynooth, though it was soon evident that not all bishops could always allow their students to complete it. Theology in the world of 1800 was already a vast, sprawling subject, even though it was slow to react to the new challenges being constantly thrown up. As taught in the seminaries it was practical rather than speculative, designed, reasonably indeed, to produce the good pastor rather than the abstract theologian, and closely tied to the two great tasks given by the Council of Trent to the parish clergy: that they should preach every Sunday and holyday, and that they should be good and exact confessors, trained to judge the state of the penitent as part of the administration of the sacrament of penance.

Dogmatic Theology, then, was basically a preparation for preaching, a preaching structured by the *Catechism of the Council of Trent*, which had been prepared on the order of the Council and finished in 1566. While the *Catechism* did have an appendix attempting to relate the gospels appointed for each Sunday to its schematic theology, the attempt was as unsuccessful as attempts in modern times to do the reverse, and Sunday preaching developed as a programmed instruction. In so far as seminary theology went beyond this, it emphasised the Reformation divisions, 'controversies', and was much less alive to the fact that the controversies of the eighteenth century had developed into being between any form of Christianity on the one hand and unbelief on the other.

This programme lent itself to producing a series of 'tracts' designed for student instruction, claiming to distil into a single book all they needed to know. This was even more marked in Moral Theology, which had aimed at producing a 'manual' to equip the good confessor. The Jesuit *Ratio studiorum*, which

30

appeared in 1599, required a course on 'cases of conscience' in addition to an explanation of the *Summa Theologica* of Aquinas. A member of the committee which drew it up, the Spanish Jesuit Juan Azor, produced his *Institutiones Morales* in three volumes in Rome between 1600 and 1611. While older manuals for the guidance of confessors had, necessarily, discussed 'cases of conscience', Azor's work is a new type of textbook of Moral Theology. Its basic divisions follow the commandments, not the virtues as hitherto, and in consequence there is a greater preoccupation with sin. A preoccupation with penance as a 'tribunal' gives rise to a forensic imagery that is in danger of reducing morals to law; and as this line of exposition grew more and more refined, there was a temptation to believe that all possible cases had been anticipated, that there was no room for surprises.

Dogmatic and moral theology, then, formed the solid core of the priest's intellectual formation for his mission. By comparison, everything else was subsidiary, even the formal study of Scripture, though the reason Maynooth did not have a full-time professor of Scripture for some years was the severely practical one that no-one suitable could be found. In any case, especially since the Reformation, Scripture studies had concentrated on 'proof texts' for doctrines, and these were set out in the dogmatic treatises. In the same way, all the Canon Law a priest needed to know formed part of his course in Moral Theology. As for Ecclesiastical History, it was little more than a kind of *belles-lettres* of Theology, and again the essentials were to be found in the dogmatic treatises.

Maurice Ahern was appointed professor of Dogma. He had had a distinguished academic career in the Sorbonne. He was sixty years of age when appointed to Maynooth and he died in 1801. He was succeeded by another distinguished professor of the Sorbonne, the Frenchman Louis-Gilles Delahogue, who had been appointed professor of Moral in 1798. Now into his sixties, he was one of the two Frenchmen who lived out their lives in Maynooth. He became a kind of father-figure of its theological school, and died in 1827 at the age of eighty-eight. Edward Ferris succeeded him in Moral Theology, and taught until his death in 1809. Thomas Clancy, an Irish Franciscan from Prague, was appointed to teach Scripture in 1796, but after a short time he returned to Bohemia. The Trustees then approached John Lanigan, an *émigré* Irishman from Italy, where he had taught at the University of Pavia. However, Bishop Moylan of Cork demanded that he sign an anti-Jansenist declaration in terms at which Lanigan took umbrage. He became secretary to the Royal Dublin Society, and Maynooth remained without satisfactory arrangements for teaching Scripture for some time.

Natural Philosophy was entrusted to Justin Delort, and Mental Philosophy to André Darré. In 1801 Delort sought leave of absence to go to France, and he did not come back to Ireland. Darré took over Natural Philosophy, while yet another Frenchman, François Anglade, replaced Darré. Darré was to return to France in 1813, but Anglade was to remain on, becoming professor of Moral Theology in 1810 on the death of Ferris. He died in 1834.

Appointments in the junior, preparatory, classes present a tangle which cannot be fully sorted out from the surviving records (the annual *Calendar* carried informative notes in this matter down to the early 1970s). What happened in the class of Rhetoric is clear: John Eustace was appointed in 1795, James Bernard Clinch on his resignation in 1798, and Charles Lovelock when Clinch in turn resigned in 1802. These two appointments were in fact promotions, for in 1795 Clinch had been appointed to a post confusingly referred to as 'the first class of Greek and Latin', *'belles-lettres'* and 'humanity' and Lovelock had been appointed to the 'second class of Greek and Latin', being promoted to the first when Clinch was promoted to Rhetoric. Further, the earlier accounts indicate payments to temporary lecturers in this area whose appointments were not formally recorded, and it is clear that some of these at least taught lay boys, and for a time lay boys and clerics together. After the lay college got a clearly separate existence, the ecclesiastical establishment settled down with chairs of 'Rhetoric' and 'Humanity'.

Mark Usher, a layman, was appointed professor of English Elocution. The fact that this was among the first batch of appointments would suggest that the Trustees regarded the subject as very important, but only very inadequate provision was made after his resignation in 1816. Provision had been made for the teaching of Irish, but it was not easy to find a teacher. There was a student passing through the college, Paul O'Brien, a native of Meath but of the diocese of Armagh. He had developed a personal interest in the language, and he was appointed to teach it in July 1804. A few years later a man from Dublin named Keenan left in his will £1,000 to endow a chair of Irish, but this was contested by his nephews, and judgement in favour of the college was given only in 1820. And lastly there is the shadowy figure of Augustine Clotworthy McCormick, appointed sacristan at a pittance in 1799. An Augustinian Canon Regular, described as 'abbot general of Bangor', he had spent his life in France, principally, it would seem, as an army chaplain. It was a kindly thought to give the old man what was in fact a refuge, and when he died in 1807, leaving the college '£25 7s 9d cash', no successor was appointed.

Putting Roofs over Heads

It is only in a relative sense that large buildings can be said to be finished, and their defects show up only when they begin to be lived in. On 1 August 1799 Louis Delahogue wrote to a patron in England, Lord Clifford of Chudleigh, giving his reactions to his first year's work at Maynooth.[2] The climate he described as even more unpredictable than that of England, and he found the damp trying. Access to the beautiful demesne of the Duke of Leinster was welcome, and the canal brought Dublin closer, though it was sometimes frozen in winter and dry in summer. The new buildings were on a huge scale, but he judged the interior totally unsuited for a community. This consideration must have been the motive of the Trustees when at the end of 1800 they ordered drastic changes in the building. The two large arches were to be closed up, leaving only a window on the west side and a door on the east. A corridor was to run the entire length of the west side of the building, from the refectory in the south block to the chapel in the north. This fairly extensive work was finished only at the end of 1803, so that the students crowded into the building that must soon have picked up the name that it has since retained, 'Long Corridor', had to put up with the discomfort of building activities as well as overcrowding.[3] Though Eugene Conwell wrote to his uncle on 7 January 1800 that the chapel, refectory and kitchen were completely finished, the Trustees authorised the spending of £200 in fitting out the chapel in May 1800, and a further £100 the following November (the first ordinations took place on Friday of Pentecost quarter-tense, 6 June 1800). At the beginning of the year the Trustees allotted £40 'to enclose the grounds', and 'for cleansing paving and gravelling the grounds immediately surrounding the new buildings', while in November they ordered the purchase of 'the cabins contiguous to the college', a row just at the front gate, indicated very clearly in the drawing accompanying the Grand Jury map of 1783 (Plate 9). They do not appear on the Carton maps (1821) and presumably were demolished.

Even though the clerical students regained a building from the laity in September 1802 they were still living in crowded conditions, which certainly contributed to the troubles of January 1803.[4] In May 1804 the Trustees set aside £2,000 for additional buildings to meet the 'urgent necessity' of providing accommodation for the sick. These, however, do not seem to have been built, and it may well be that it was at this time that the old lay building, or part of it, was set aside for this purpose, which it discharged until the 1860s. In any case, space was so badly needed that in 1806 a beginning was made on the north side of the projected square. The college records show that about this time a few small legacies, amounting to about £2,000, were quickly sold for building purposes, but because of the high prices of wartime the building had to stop when only partly finished because there was no more money. It was in this state when the Lord Lieutenant, the Duke of Bedford, visited the college. When showing him round, the President, Andrew Dunne, pointed to what he called 'our *pierres d'attente*'. Bedford suggested that he deal with his expectations by applying to Parliament for a special grant, which he did at once, apparently without waiting to consult the Trustees.[5]

The application came before Parliament on 2 February 1807, where everything favoured it. Grenville's ministry was well disposed towards Catholics, and prepared to grant even more to Maynooth than the £5,000 asked for to finish the building. It was made all the more favourable because of attempts now coming to a head to entice Irish seminarians back to Paris. Here, as the fury drained out of the Revolution, the Abbé Walsh was working successfully to restore the Irish College, already legally re-established; he planned to reopen it in September 1805. His problem was to find students, and it was an attempt to entice some from the Irish College in Lisbon that drew on him an extremely strong condemnation from the Irish bishops on 24 January 1807.

The bishops stigmatised Walsh's efforts to attract seminarians as 'calculated to inspire them with veneration for and attachment to the present French government . . . at the same time actuated by a desire to alienate them from that allegiance which they owe to the government of their own country'; and they went on to say that 'bound as we are by every tie of gratitude to the government for the very liberal support of our ecclesiastical establishment at Maynooth, and which under the auspices of the present administration we hope will very shortly be considerably enlarged', they 'utterly reprobated' Walsh and declared they would deal severely with any students foolish enough to accept his 'insidious offer'.[6]

Parliament was disposed to give Maynooth what it wanted, realising that as yet it could not accept all the students that were needed and believing that it was better to have Irish Catholic priests not only educated at home but educated well, and so what seemed a modest request for £5,000 went through with little discussion. Then Grenville over-reached himself, proposing Catholic concessions that caused George III to develop scruples about his coronation oath. This in turn led to a general election, fought on the 'no popery' issue, and, fairly predictably, Grenville lost. The new Prime Minister had to take account of the mood displayed in the election, and even the extra £5,000 was in danger, because while it had been voted it had not yet been formally allocated. It was finally granted because the Trustees had incurred extra expenditure relying on the good faith of Parliament, but a pledge had to be given that there would be no repetition of such an extra grant.

On 21 April 1808 the Trustees decided that the new building would allow them to receive fifty extra students, 250 in all. They had applied for a repetition of the previous year's grant, and this led to what was described as a 'pretty warm debate' in Parliament. On 29 April John Foster, Chancellor of the Irish Exchequer, proposed the sum of £9,250. This could be defended both as some kind of compromise between £8,000 and £13,000 and as taking account of the fact that there were now fifty more students to be supported. His proposal was accepted, and the annual grant remained at about this level for the years ahead (reckoned as £8,928 sterling after the currencies were merged in 1825). There were people who felt Maynooth had been shabbily enough treated. Bedford, who retired from politics after the 'no popery' election, wrote on 11 July 1808 to the Trustees a letter they judged worthy to be inserted in their Journal, saying apologetically that it was the best that could be done.

The New House, as it has been called then and since to distinguish it from the 'old buildings' of Long Corridor, must have been occupied in two parts, as each was completed, over the academic years 1807/08 and 1808/09. A monochrome wash, now in the Russell Library, depicts the two buildings from the north-east (Plate 13). Warburton writing in 1818 gave a good impression of the new addition: 'It was originally intended that the front range should form one side of a square, but from lack of sufficient funds the front and north-west wing only have been as yet completed. This wing is principally laid out in dormitories, opening off galleries about 300 feet in length, which serve as ambula-tories to the students in wet weather, and on a plan not only judicious in the arrangement but in the execution neat, simple and inexpensive.' He added: 'In the rere of the building is an extensive tract of level ground, part of which is appropriated to a garden and part laid out in spacious gravelled walks for the convenience of the students; this is decorated with plantations, and particular-ly with a fine avenue of stately elms.'[7] This landscaping can be seen in the Carton maps of 1821 and in detail in the Ordnance Survey of 1838 (Plates 5, 34). Buildings and grounds were taking shape, and so too were the people who lived there, with perhaps a little more difficulty.

Students, Clerical and Lay

When the bishops began sending students to Maynooth they naturally fol-lowed to some extent the previous practice of sending young men whom they had just ordained in order to study their theology. Government officials did not like this, and neither did the college authorities, fearing, as the experience of some Continental colleges had shown in the past, that it was hard to main-tain seminary discipline in a community where budding seminarians of eigh-teen mixed with ordained priests of twenty-four or more. From the beginning, then, the Trustees attempted to exclude ordained priests.

They met opposition from a number of bishops, but in 1799 it was finally introduced as a rule that hereafter no priest would be admitted as a student, and that after twelve months no student over twenty years old could be admit-ted unless he was qualified to enter at least the class of Logic. In 1804 the Bishop of Limerick was lamenting that he could not find enough candidates under twenty with enough Latin to pass the entrance examination to fill up the places allotted to him in Maynooth, and in this predicament he was hardly alone.[8]

Much of the human routine of life at this early date can be recovered from the 'Regula Pietatis' and the document presented to Parliament in 1808. As the President, Bartholomew Crotty, informed the Commissioners in 1826, the 'Regula Pietatis' or 'jus vetus' as it was already coming to be called, was in 'great measure' taken from the rules of the Irish College, Rome, and Archbishop Troy was its 'principal author'.[9] These documents show the prospective student presenting himself in the college, for the first few years in mid-September, a date soon changed to the end of August. With him be brought certificates of his age, parentage and baptism, a letter of nomination from his bishop, and a duly attested declaration that he had taken the Oath of Allegiance. He was examined in the Classics and if admitted paid the entrance fee imposed in 1799 and signed an undertaking to keep the college rule. He was now entitled to commons, tuition, and coals and candles during the hours of study in the halls. He had to pay for his washing and mending and for can-dles in his own room, which he shared with at least one other and, at the bot-tom of the social scale up in the attics, with as many as six. He had to provide himself with more or less the usual paraphernalia of tableware and linen, and with a cassock and the college gown and cap. According to the 'Regula Pietatis' his attire was to be black on Sundays and holydays and grey or some dark colour at other times. This left room for some measure of personal predilection, as appears from a letter from a student to a priest, probably his parish priest, in 1803.[10] The student was very short of money, and would like his mother to send material for a soutane and riding-coat. He would prefer 'blue rug' for the soutane and 'blue rug' or perhaps 'dark mixed bearskins' for the riding coat—two coarse friezes that would certainly be warm enough if not very elegant.

Having entered the college, more likely than not he would stay there until the end of his course, committed to an unrelenting round, apart from a week at Christmas and Easter and the long vacation in summer, originally August and the first half of September, but soon (probably as early a 1804, for reasons that will be seen) extended to almost all of July and August. But permission was required to go away even in the summer vacation, and most spent it in the college, enjoying a regime that was a little more relaxed and gave time for some general education. This continuous residence was not felt as any great hardship, for people were not accustomed to much moving about. Indeed a number of students, as well as some of their bishops, felt quite aggrieved when they were sent home in the summer of 1800 because the war had made provisions so dear, and in 1801 when those who wanted to stay on were asked to pay an extra five guineas. And, term or vacation, residence was taken literally. The gate porter was ordered to keep the gate locked and to have a book in which the names of all who went in or out were to be entered. (A reference to 'the right-hand gate which is near the old buildings' being left open for wheeled traffic must indicate the wide gate near the Protestant church which disappeared only in the rebuilding of the 1950s and which would probably be very useful today because of developments since then.)

From letters of Eugene Conwell in 1798 it is clear that what might be called the standard seminary regime had been introduced while everything was still crowded into Stoyte House and most students still in lodgings in the village: a round of prayer, class and study from rising at six to night prayer at nine. Conwell thought it 'very severe', but worse was to come. The first dean, Edward Ferris, arrived in June 1799. An austere man, he himself got up at four o'clock (to the discomfort of staff members living near him), so he must have judged it no great hardship to ask students to rise at five. A new horarium, which must have owed a great deal to Ferris, was sanctioned in November 1800. Though students had to rise at five, night prayer was still at nine and all were in bed at ten. The space between rising and breakfast was stretched from three to three-and-a-half hours; the main meal ('dinner') was changed from three to one o'clock and a recreation period lost. For divinity students there was a merciless unbroken grind from rising at five to dinner at one. It proved just too much for Irish conditions, and must have been a factor in the tensions that came to a head at the beginning of 1803. In 1804 the Trustees approved a new horarium, which proved sustainable, though it was more rigorous than the original one.

The details were as follows:

Summer (March–October)	Winter (November–February)
5.00 Rising	6.00 Rising
5.30 Prayer	6.30 Prayer
6.00 Study	7.00 Study
7.30 Mass	8.30 Mass
8.00 Breakfast, recreation	9.00 Breakfast, recreation
9.00 Study	

10–11.30 Class
11.30 Recreation
12.00 Study
1.30–3.00 Class
3.00 Dinner, recreation
5.00 Class, 'for modern languages'
6.00 Study
7.00 Conference [perhaps not every day]
8.00 Supper, recreation
9.00 Night prayer
9.30 All retire

The practice of having a lighter class load and an organised walk outside the college on Wednesdays seems to have been a feature almost from the beginning, while on Sundays there was High Mass at ten and Vespers at three, with evening study only, at six o'clock.

In class the student met his professor, an imposing figure in soutane, with a gown edged with ermine and a white tassel in his cap if he were a professor of Theology, and if of another subject with a cloak edged with green silk and a green-tasselled cap. (The traditional Maynooth gown is the gown of the eighteenth-century Sorbonne, and it would appear that this is the Theology gown described above: in any case it must have come in at an early date.) The general teaching methods have already been described. In addition to the routine interrogation in class there was a more elaborate literary exercise, an *exercitatio*, once a month. As well as the professors there were 'lecturers', who get a whole chapter in the statutes of 1800. These were students who had finished their course and were kept on to act as tutors or substitutes when a professor was not available. The office did not prove lasting, partly because of a couple of unfortunate appointments, but also because the growth of a post-graduate department, the Dunboyne Establishment, provided a more useful source for tutors and substitutes.

Originally there were four examinations in the year, in December, March, May and August, but they were soon reduced to two, in January and June (this probably happened after the troubles of 1803). The examinations were oral and exhausting. A supplementary written test for the better students was introduced later, but it took the simple fact of cheap and abundant paper to make it possible for the written examination to displace the traditional oral one. This oral was ideally to be conducted before the whole faculty, but to shorten the examinations the President was empowered to divide the board, but not in the examinations at the end of the year. In keeping with tradition, the examinations were competitive as well as being oral and public. Prize-lists were drawn up, based on assessment throughout the year as well as on performance in examination. The first recorded prize-list is dated 1799, and a printed list for 1802 has survived in the diocesan archives of Down and Connor.

Outside the class hall the student was very much in the hands of the dean, another imposing figure, gowned like a professor of Theology. One aspect of his duty was to act as watchdog. Either in person or through students chosen by him, his monitors, he supervised morning and evening prayer and communal study in the halls. He was to visit students' rooms twice in the fortnight, not merely inspecting them for cleanliness but keeping an eye on what students were reading. He was empowered to inflict punishments, including a small fine, which, however, soon fell into disuse. Frequent offenders were to be admonished by the President in his presence, and if this brought no improvement they were liable to expulsion, as they were for a number of named serious transgressions of rule. But a dean was expected to be more than a watchdog: it was enjoined on him 'to constantly imbue the students with precepts of piety and modesty'. In forming the students heavy emphasis was placed on the observance of rule, the routine of prayer, study and silence, which would tame the natural heedlessness of youth and allow virtue and good habits to flourish—too much emphasis, Bishop Plunkett of Meath thought, calling for more 'spiritual direction' to balance book-learning.[11] The theme was to recur. However, in the 1804 horarium the hour of seven in the evening is set aside for a 'conference', and, as will be seen, it soon becomes explicit that the dean does give regular conferences to the students as an important element in their formation. Confession once a fortnight, the staff acting as confessors, communion once a fortnight and on the greater feasts, retreats 'at stated times', an hour's catechism for first-year students on Sunday evenings from, of course, Francis Power—that about sums up the 'spiritual direction' as the institution tried to settle down.

Already the 'Maynooth cleric' was being categorised, mostly from hostile sources. From the ascendancy came sneers, resting on fears, about the pauper priests educated at government expense that the institution was sure to produce. In a pamphlet published in 1810 Cornelius Keogh, a son of John Keogh, advanced the speculation that the pauper products of the 'anti-Irish servile seminary' would not be revolutionaries but lickspittles, in contrast with the clergy who in the past had come back accomplished scholars from the Continental seminaries, not brooking degradation at home because they had been educated in Catholic countries.[12] The reality, in so far as it can be recovered, is more ordinary but more human. In his letters Eugene Conwell reveals himself as a high-spirited young man with no mean opinion of himself, cock-a-hoop because he has been selected to preach in the chapel in Maynooth after only one trial run in the college, and remarking after a walk to Castletown House, where the students were shown around by Mr and Mrs Connolly, 'I must endeavour to cultivate an acquaintance there if I can.'

The college authorities argued that Maynooth education was by no means free. There was the entrance fee and various expenses calculated to come to about £20 a year—almost certainly an exaggeration. The information laid before Parliament in 1808 gave the father's occupation in the case of the 229 students then in residence. It gives useful information, even though three-quarters described their father simply as 'farmer'. The figures are:

In his evidence to the Commission in 1826 the President, Bartholomew

Occupation	Number	Percentage
Farmer	172	75.1
Grazier	11	4.8
Trade	21	9.2
Manufacture	17	7.4
Other*	8	3.5

innkeeper 2, carpenter 2, apothecary, clerk of coal mines, land surveyor, architect.

Crotty, confirmed this pattern. Most students came from farming families that were at least 'comfortable', with quite a few rich farmers and graziers; some too were the sons of tradesmen and shopkeepers, again with 'quite a few opulent merchants', while from the Catholic gentry there had been 'a good many from time to time'. He pointed out that in Ireland a Catholic priest had a hard and dangerous life, with the consequence that no-one would look down on a zealous priest because his parents were poor. He showed the growing confidence of Irish Catholics when he added that may persons of such poor families were recommended by clergymen for the University of Dublin and received there, where they were often induced to conform, and there seemed no hesitation in advancing them to orders. Some of these had been the first to upbraid Maynooth students with the lowliness of their origin. It was painful to see this charge levelled against 'the children of Roman Catholics who perhaps at no very remote period were in competent circumstances, but are now reduced to the inability of supporting them in college', or that they 'should be excluded, in consequence of the misfortunes of their parents'. He finally gave as his opinion that the Maynooth students probably came from a rather better-off class than their predecessors in the eighteenth century, and William Crolly, student in 1801, professor in 1810, and in 1825 bishop of Down and Connor, was inclined to agree.[13] This is a not unreasonable position, especially if it is recalled how many of the earlier students were priests with some capacity to support themselves, whereas priest-students were not accepted in Maynooth after 1799.

Some tensions arose from the fact that the students of the lay college, who for nearly twenty years were educated beside the clerics, regarded themselves as coming from a higher social class. As has been seen, the Act of 1795 did not envisage an educational establishment for clerics exclusively, and the Trustees acted as if provision for the laity was also expected of them. At first their hope was that hostels for lay students would be built as a business venture, but in August 1796 they contracted for a building to house the lay college.[14] This was planned as little more than a dormitory, as the lay students were to go to the clerical college for chapel, classes, and their main meal of the day. Even before their building was ready they were attending classes from lodgings in the town, as indeed were most of the clerics. The clerics moved into the new main building over the academic year 1799/1800, and the lay college opened in its own building in the autumn of 1800, the Trustees having set aside £1,000 for unspecified 'improvements' to it. The first President was Patrick Coleman, a young Dublin priest who had entered Maynooth in 1795 at the age of twenty-three; it was he who had read the Greek ode at the laying of the foundation-stone. For two years he presided over what must have been a fairly ramshackle establishment, for in November 1801 the Trustees voted a further £1,000 for more improvements or to buy a new building. By this time, however, the lay college had got caught up in politics.

The first visitation prescribed by the Act of 1800 took place in July 1801. Lord Chancellor Clare did not attend, but the other three judges did. No formal report was made, but in October the Chief Justice of the King's Bench, Arthur Wolfe, Lord Kilwarden, queried the Lord Lieutenant if the lay college—which, he said, the Visitors had been quite surprised to see—were not 'a departure from the original intention'. Wolfe was only one of many who felt that Catholic youth should not be diverted from Trinity College, and Trinity itself was keeping a wary eye on any developments at Maynooth that might seem to parallel its own programmes.[15] The Maynooth lay college had powerful defenders, however. The Duke of Leinster said that formal government approval should be sought for it, and Lord Fingall spoke of the possibility of opening a separate lay college in Maynooth, which was of course perfectly legal. The government decided the best line was to insist that any lay college should be quite separate from the clerical establishment and receive no public support, directly or indirectly. This was conveyed to the Trustees through their 'agent', Alexander Knox, one of the only two tasks he discharged during his lifetime, while he drew £300 a year from the scarce college funds for an office which he had 'always considered . . . as a sinecure'.[16] At this stage Clare objected. In the wranglings of the few years just passed he had publicly committed himself to the principle that the Catholic clergy and laity should be educated together. However, the Lord Lieutenant told him that if he wished to challenge the decision it would have to go to the Cabinet in England, and Clare did not press the matter.[17]

On 5 May 1802 a number of Catholic laity met at Fitzpatrick's bookshop in Capel Street. Lord Fingall took the chair. It was agreed there was need for a lay college close to the clerical college in Maynooth, and that subscriptions should be invited. Five trustees, all laymen, were set up to oversee the project. On 27 September Riverstown Lodge and its lands were bought for £1,000. These immediately adjoined Maynooth College, and indeed were shortly to become part of it. Riverstown Lodge is still there. It is an older house than Stoyte, though probably not much older, an elegant small Georgian house that has managed to retain its quality despite the decidedly inelegant clutter that now surrounds it. There is a good map of the lands, dated 1809 (Plate 2). As well as the lands north of the canal, which became the Junior House grounds, there were a number of fields on the other bank, at first let to tenants and later expanded to become the 'Newtown farm'.[18] The main entrance gate, beside the church, was later closed, and the gate itself is probably the ornate 'White Gate' inserted further up the wall to communicate between what became the Junior House and the rest of the college. This wall ran just a little beyond the enclosed garden which is still there. It ensured the separation of the lay college from the clerical one immediately beside it.

The trustees met again on 1 April 1803 and reported progress. Thirty-two subscribers, including five bishops, had contributed £1,513 15s. A total of £1,376 14s 9d had been spent, including £290 on 'alterations etc.' Nearly fifty students were in the college, and it was estimated that an additional £2,000 would be needed to provide for the hundred it was hoped to attract.[19] It seems certain that nothing like this was ever subscribed, and it seems highly likely that the only addition made to the lay college was the shoddy wing built on to the back of Riverstown Lodge at its western end. This single wing appears on one of the Carton maps of 1821, and also would appear to be on the 1809 map, though this indicates the buildings only very roughly (Plates 2,3).

No formal records of the lay college have survived, so information on how it functioned must be collected from bits and pieces.[20] In Autumn 1802 it opened its doors to the 'sons of the nobility and gentry of the Catholic persuasion, of which there are several at present who are not designed to graduate for the church, or enter into holy orders'[21]—though a few graduates of the lay college did cross the boundary later into the clerical one. A prospectus of 1806 stated that the age of admission was ten to fifteen years, and amid a tangle of information on fees, tableware and bed-linen states that 'the holyday dress is uniform, and consists of a coat of superfine blue cloth, with yellow buttons; waistcoat, buff—great finery indeed as the lay students joined the more soberly dressed clerics in their common chapel. Apart from the chapel, however, the only intermingling seems to have been informal meetings after some classes in one of the colleges which were attended by a few students from the other.

In his study of the lay college, John Brady suggests that it is reasonable to estimate that a student body of between 75 and 90 was consistently maintained. The courses may be presumed to have been standard: there was an annual prizegiving, at which students, no doubt carefully chosen and carefully coached, delivered formal orations in Latin and English in praise of the benefits of a liberal education before their teachers, the trustees of the lay college, and sometimes the trustees of the ecclesiastical college. Three neatly printed orations from the prizegiving of 1805, two in Latin and one in English, have survived among Archbishop Troy's papers in Dublin, and in Maynooth chance has preserved manuscript orations in Latin and English for the years 1810, 1812, 1813 and 1814, some in fair copy, others showing second thoughts, additions and cancellations.[22] It is not possible to draw up anything like a full list of staff, and here there appears to have been some overlapping with the clerical establishment. Brady has collected all the scanty information on the four presidents, William Russell (1802–05), Morgan D'Arcy (1805–07), Paul Long (1807–14), the three of them priests of Dublin, and Patrick M'Nicholas (1814–17), from Achonry. He was appointed when Long left to take charge of the Irish College in Paris after the downfall of Napoleon. He had entered Maynooth as a student in 1795 and had been appointed to its staff in 1806, a post to which he returned when the lay college closed in 1817.

On 26 June of that year the trustees of Maynooth paid the trustees of the lay college £1,000 for their property. No particular pressure dictated this step: it is to be explained by the fact that few ever regarded the lay college as more than a stopgap. That it had four presidents in fifteen years may be indicative, and the fragmentary surviving evidence indicates that its trustees were constantly changing. Even more important, however, was the steady growth in the numbers of Catholic boarding schools in the first two decades of the century. In particular, Clongowes Wood College, opened in 1814 a few miles away, proved a greater attraction for 'the sons of the nobility and gentry of the Catholic persuasion'.

Embattled Presidents

The clerical students were living in crowded conditions, two hundred packed into Long Corridor, later two hundred and fifty into Long Corridor and New House—some improvement, but not much. The seminary regime was hard, and under Edward Ferris hardness became harshness. Resentments boiled over into confrontation in January 1803. There are two detailed accounts of the incident, one a memorial drawn up by the students on the day it occurred, to present to the Trustees, and the other a long letter, written eleven days later, from a student to a young priest who had just left the college to return to his diocese. Both are in substantial agreement, down to quite small detail.[23]

Trouble erupted at breakfast on the morning of 3 January, Monday of the second week of term, at the fire in the kitchen. It is not known where this kitchen was. It cannot have been the building put up in 1823, but it is unlikely that it was still in the basement of Stoyte House, for at the beginning of 1800 Eugene Conwell refers in a letter to 'the kitchen now finished', together with the chapel and the refectory. Wherever it was, it was overcrowded. That morning a servant wanted to toast bread for a professor's breakfast, but a student was boiling a kettle at the fire. The servant asked him to take it off, but he refused. The servant reacted with language which led to the student saying that if he spoke to him again like that he would kick him. Students and servants crowded into the kitchen, and the angry gathering was joined by a professor, Louis Delahogue, who in turn lost his temper, though he was not the professor whose toast was delayed. He must still have been an exotic figure to the average student. It probably did not help that he was small in stature (two passports he got when leaving France have survived among his papers, showing him as slightly less than five feet six inches tall).[24] What really stung the students in his abuse was that he called them 'peasants', then an opprobrious word in both France and Ireland. Someone rang the bell, and the students gathered in one of the halls and began to talk about sending a joint remonstrance to Delahogue. The dean, Thomas Coen, appeared and ordered them out, but they refused. He took the names of four he maintained were 'ringleaders', but they continued to draw up their remonstrance and agreed all would sign it. After dinner, when the document was ready, twenty senior students tried to find Delahogue to present it to him. According to the student accounts, he and other staff members were ignominiously barricaded into a room upstairs. The thwarted students decided to draw up a petition to the Trustees, which they all signed and despatched. When Coen tried to address the students after supper he was shouted down. Over the next few days individual staff members began to work on individual students, and solidarity began to crumble at the edges. On Friday the President, Peter Flood, returned to the college. He was a very ill man, and was to die before the month was out, but he was in unyielding mood when he met a student delegation on Saturday morning. That evening the students were addressed by Ferris, who got a hearing and seems to have made some impression, for the next delegation to Flood was talking in terms of 'no victimisation'. Flood remained unyielding, however, and said he would expel all who did not return to their duties, even if he had to call in the civil authorities. The students yielded, declaring they would await justice from the Trustees.

When the Trustees met on 24 February they first elected their secretary,

Andrew Dunne, as President (Peter Flood had died on 26 January). They spent over two days reaching a careful decision, if only because they did not want intervention from the Visitors. However, their options were very limited, and they decided to expel the four ringleaders as noted by Coen on the morning of 3 January, and a fifth who had been prominent in drawing up the petition of the Trustees. He was Michael Collins, who was later ordained priest and indeed became bishop of his native diocese of Cloyne and Ross in 1827. His fellow-diocesan, John Roche, a brilliant student, did not continue his studies for the priesthood. He was the only one of the five not to express regret to the Trustees. Of the two Limerick students, it was reported that Ferris had got Edward Byrne accepted by the Jesuits in Stonyhurst, and Thomas Hogan— 'the Goose Hogan' to his fellows—was ordained for his own diocese. Finally there was William McMullan of Down and Connor, nephew of the bishop. His uncle treated him coolly at first, but soon ordained him. All five give the impression of being natural leaders, and Hogan is the only one who appears as a possible mob-leader. The other four seem to have been serious young men of ability above the average. There were many pieces to be picked up after the five were publicly expelled in the College Chapel on 3 March.

It was a serious incident, denoting serious tensions. To begin with, there were the physical discomforts of being overcrowded in a building still being remodelled. The pressures of the horarium are not explicitly mentioned by the students, but they must have been seen as contributing, for relaxations were introduced. What must have been an important factor was the mix of students, ranging in 1803 from eighteen-year-olds to ordained priests up to ten years older (the question of discipline with such a community had earlier raised problems in the Continental colleges, and in Paris had led to the setting up of a second college, for priests only). There were students beginning to make the transition from student to staff as monitors and lecturers, set in authority over priests older than themselves while not yet themselves priests. The first two full appointments from the student body to the staff were contentious. Michael Montague was appointed bursar on 30 July 1802. He was temperamentally a saver, and when he died as president in 1845 he had completed the front square and built the Junior House out of money saved from the annual grant. His parsimony first appeared at the students' table, for it was wartime and food was dear. Thomas Coen's appointment as dean in February 1802 was even more contentious. The President was failing, the vice-president, Francis Power, was a gentle person, and Edward Ferris, Coen's predecessor as dean, kept interfering. Of this there can be no doubt. In a letter to William McMullan of 8 October 1803 Ferris said that two staff members, Lovelock and Montague, were accusing him of having supported the students, while Delahogue and the President, Andrew Dunne, charged him with 'invading all the jurisdiction in the college'.[25] To the *émigré* staff it must have seemed, even more than in 1798, that the tocsin of revolution might be sounding in Maynooth when it showed signs of quietening in France, and they must have held their breath when extensive disturbances broke out in the Maynooth area in conjunction with Emmet's rising on 23 July that year. There was possibly some sympathy among the students, but no active support (the fact that the rising took place on the Saturday the summer examinations ended may have been a factor). When the rising collapsed quickly André Darré was approached by the local rebels to mediate with the Duke of Leinster, which he did successfully. Nevertheless, an investigation into the college's alleged role in the rising was ordered. It was carried out by the Solicitor-General, James McClelland. His report, made in August, was very hostile, though he had to admit he could find no direct involvement. But, he said, the very foundation of the college had been a provocation that must have nurtured the rebellious spirit, and the staff and the students had advance warning of the rising. No evidence for this was proffered, but in the atmosphere of religious confrontation of those days it came to be widely believed.[26] And the temper of the student body must have been still brooding. As they had reminded the Trustees, it was hard to have been dismissed as 'paupers' by Patrick Duigenan, or to have to endure 'the protection given to similar language from the scholars of the lay house', who seem clearly to have regarded themselves as coming from a higher social class, but to have been called 'peasants' in front of the servants by a professor was harder still.

Andrew Dunne, appointed President on 20 February 1803, had been secretary to the Board of Trustees since 1795. He inherited a tense situation that was not healed after the five expulsions had taken place on 5 March. There is little detailed information on his presidency. Most of what there is comes from a number of letters written by Edward Ferris to William McMullan, one of the five students expelled in 1803, and now a priest working in his native diocese of Down and Connor. Predictably, Ferris laid most of the blame for the tensions on the dean, Thomas Coen. To the extent that Coen was not making a success of the job Ferris was right, but as the job came to him it was very hard to handle. And the problems were not all centred on an individual. Dunne got the easy start any newcomer might expect, and something was done in regard to some of the grievances. The rigours of the horarium were relaxed a bit; food in the refectory improved, and for a while the staff ate at a high table in the students' refectory, though this seems to have given satisfaction to nobody and was discontinued. There were still problems of student discipline, and a number of expulsions. Inevitably the dean was at the centre of these tensions, but the President got drawn in too. In January 1807 he tendered his resignation to the Trustees. They persuaded him to stay on until the next meeting at the end of June, and expressed the hope that he might be persuaded to stay on a little longer, at least until a suitable successor could be found.[27] Unfortunately for himself, this is what he did.

Disaster struck him at the visitation held on 20 June. Because no formal report was made from these early visitations, the only continuous record is the series of brief notices written into the college records by the vice-president.

These laconic accounts would indicate that the visitation was normally a formality, as indeed it must have been because the powers of the Visitors were so limited. The normal procedure was for the visitation to take place regularly every third year, at the end of the academic year. Formal notice was given by the President, and on the appointed day staff, students and servants assembled at 11 a.m. 'in the large hall adjoining the chapel'. The Lord Chancellor asked if there were any grievances, and when no-one spoke up he expressed his satisfaction at the happy state of the college. No doubt it would have been a healthier situation if there had been a more open visitation, where students might feel freer to speak, but this was almost impossible because the visitors included the four Protestant judges. Almost, but not quite impossible: the visitation of 1819 records an appeal against expulsion made to the Visitors by a student called Shannon, on the grounds that unfitness for the priesthood was not a reason for expulsion. His appeal was rejected, Lord Norbury, Chief Justice of the Common Pleas, who presided, giving as the reason that the college was 'practically an ecclesiastical establishment' and that candidates unsuitable for the ministry had no right to remain. He added that he knew from personal experience that in 1795 the government's intention in establishing the college was 'to supply the place of foreign ecclesiastical colleges'.

What Francis Power did not record in 1807 was that a similar case had come before the Visitors in that year, and the outcome had not been so favourable to the college. Two students from the diocese of Ossory had been expelled, picked as scapegoats, according to Ferris, when there was 'a great noise and general murmuring at the opening of lectures.' One of them, named Kennedy, appealed to the Visitors.[28] It seems certain the Visitors inclined to support him. An anonymous contributor to the *Irish Magazine* for January 1813 said they gave as their reason that the law did not compel the college to confer Holy Orders on those disobedient to the seminary rule, so such disobedience was not in itself a justification for expulsion. The *Irish Magazine* is not the most reliable of sources, especially where Maynooth is concerned. Its proprietor and editor, Watty Cox, was to fix a disapproving eye on the college for a number of years after he began the paper in 1808. An eccentric United Irishman, with a truly vitriolic pen, he detested the college Trustees, lay and episcopal, for their conservative outlook, most of all Lord Fingall. For five years the paper was to chronicle the problems of Maynooth, always diverting even if always partisan, and increasingly inaccurate. It is certain that his information came from inside the college, and fairly certain that not all of it came from students. More immediate even if rather ambiguous evidence comes from Bishop Plunkett of Meath, one of the Trustees, who noted in his diary four days after the visitation that 'an appeal to the judges, in their quality of Visitors, made by an expelled student, was prevented by accepting his submission.' The situation would appear to have been untidy, but the Visitors in 1807 were not prepared to give the ruling they were to give in 1819, that whatever the strict legal situation the college was in practice an ecclesiastical institution.

A few days later Dunne resigned the presidency. His successor, Patrick Byrne, was appointed the same day. A priest of Armagh, he had been rector of the Irish College, Nantes, and when appointed was parish priest of Donaghmore. He got the customary welcome given a newcomer, especially when it became known that he did not approve of more Frenchmen being appointed to the staff. Friction between French staff and Irish students had been surfacing from the beginning, but it now begins to appear as one of the principal tensions. The second was provincialism. This was nothing new among Irish seminarians: it had regularly become serious in the Continental colleges, where it might have been more destructive were it not for the fact that in some of these colleges students from one province or another predominated. Now students from all over Ireland were being gathered into Maynooth, where the unpopular dean was from Connacht, so that it was not surprising that 'Connachtman' became a term of abuse.

Patrick Byrne certainly began well. According to Ferris (who may just have been influenced by the thought that Coen was being put in his place) the new President captivated everyone by his openness, his sense of fair play, and his willingness to listen to grievances. He attended morning and evening prayer and, in a word, looked after everything. There had been no such thing as the observance of silence, but he had only to express a wish that silence be always observed except at recreation and it was immediately complied with.[29] In May 1808 he and Francis Power, the vice-president, invited Daniel Murray to Maynooth to help to investigate the students' grievances. Next year Murray was named coadjutor to the ageing Dr Troy: he was to remain until his death in 1852 a good friend to the college. The students had genuine grievances, he wrote to Bishop Plunkett of Meath on 10 May, the most serious being the fact that the medical attendant, Dr Egan, came from Dublin only on 'a cursory visit once a month, and the sick left to the mercy of a young apothecary'.[30] Egan was a distinguished Dublin physician, who owed his appointment to the patronage of Lord Fingall. An anonymous letter addressed to Fingall, dated Maynooth 17 December 1809, published in the *Irish Magazine* of January 1810, reproached him among other things with 'the tragedy of the boys who died'.

The situation was slipping out of Byrne's control. At their meeting on 3 July 1809 the Trustees set up a committee to investigate the insubordination and general relaxation of discipline, which, they bluntly said, was 'caused principally by the want of cordial co-operation between the President, dean, professors and masters.' In the concrete, as already suggested, the tensions were twofold: between French staff and Irish students, and among the staff and students between those from Connacht who were alleged to support the dean and those who opposed him. Unfortunately Coen's opponents soon came to include the President. The Trustees' committee consisted of the Archbishops of Armagh and Dublin, the Bishop of Meath, and Lord Fingall. It might be noted that Armagh, Dublin and Fingall were the Catholic visitors, and as the situation in the college went from bad to worse they decided to call a special meeting of the Trustees at the beginning of December, in order to ward off a special visitation which by law the Lord Lieutenant was empowered to call at any time. The situation was by now alarming. In a letter to Archbishop Bray of Cashel dated 17 November explaining why it had been decided to call a special meeting, Troy spoke of 'the late scandalous riots' in the college.[31] They had been sparked off by a letter in the *Evening Herald* of 4 October, signed 'Hibernicus' and clearly written by a student, which the Trustees when they met considered to contain 'a libel on the government and legislature'. The dean decided to search the students' rooms for newspapers or other incriminating material. He found a door locked against him and, it was alleged, kicked it in.

The Trustees' meeting was called for Maynooth on 1 December. It then appeared that the Trustees themselves might be added to those who were not co-operating, for the meeting had to disband for lack of a quorum.[32] They had got into the habit of meeting more conveniently in Dublin, and it was here they finally assembled on 7 December. They considered their problems for the best part of a week, and on 13 December issued a long list of resolutions. These reveal a background verging on anarchy, manifesting itself in 'disorderly noises' everywhere, in the corridors, refectory, class halls, and prayer hall, culminating in the room search which had left the student body seething. However, the Trustees had no remedy except to expel the ringleaders, and the ringleaders were hard to find. Although one student named another as the writer of the letter to the *Evening Herald*, the Trustees could not pin it on him when they examined him, and a grateful Watty Cox soon had a flow of copy in the form of anonymous letters from Maynooth. Coen was described as 'a vulgar poor man', fit only 'to quest oatmeal for a Connacht friary'; it was remarked that the Trustees' decision that students' doors must never be locked against authority would lead to a great saving, for 'such is the mild temper of the dean, that whenever any opposition is ever made, a broken door will immediately be the consequence'; while resentment against the French surfaced in allusions like 'a fellow here we call Abbé Baboon, a French sycophant and a mean creature'. A letter dated 19 January 1810 spoke of 'the memorable investigation' conducted by the students to effect 'an active change' in the administration and the present superiors. The writer implies they would be satisfied to see Coen gone, but they got nowhere.[33] In a letter dated 13 January to the Bishop of Ossory, which has survived in the diocesan archives, Archbishop Kelly of Tuam, himself a trustee, remarked with what seems unwarrantable detachment that he understood the Trustees had not been able to take any decisive action in restoring discipline at Maynooth, and that unless there was a speedy remedy the outcome could be fatal to the college. Time was certainly running out for the President and dean. It ran out at the statutory meeting of the Trustees on 27 June 1810, held, again, in Dublin. Bishop Plunkett's entry in his diary seems to indicate that the Trustees themselves were to some extent bemused: 'Dr Byrne, President of the College, signified

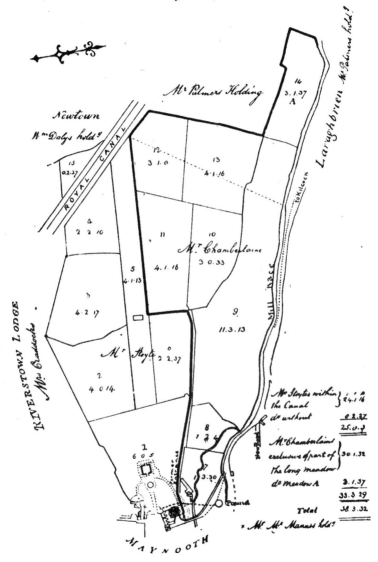

A Survey of Part of the LANDS of MAYNOOTH, Intended for the Roman Catholic College ~ by Thos Sherrard 1795.

The College holding 1795 (*MCA*)

Plate 1

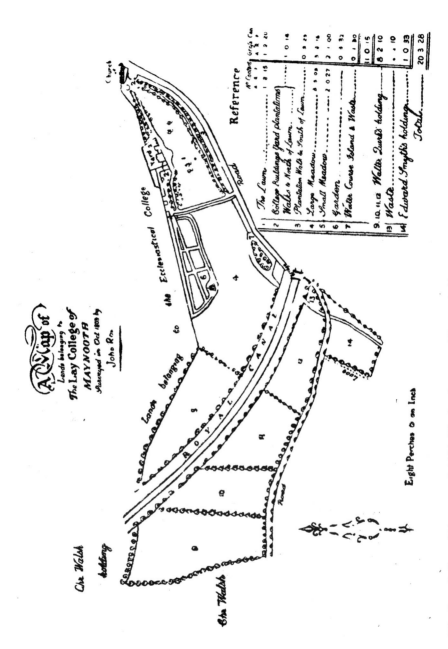

The Lay College (Riverstown) 1809 (Healy, *Centenary History*, 317)

Plate 2

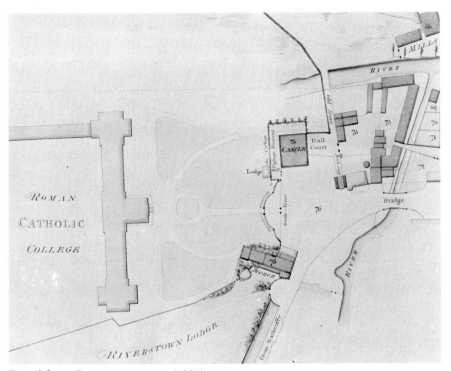

Detail from Carton estate map (1821)

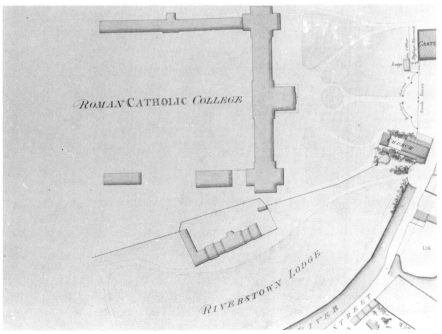

Detail from Carton estate map (1821)

Plate 3

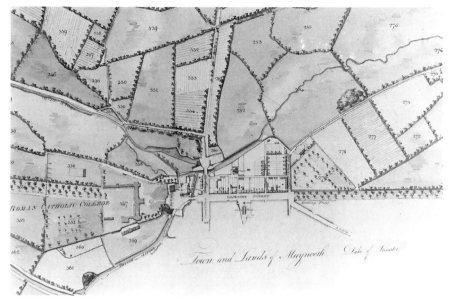

Detail from Carton estate map (1821)

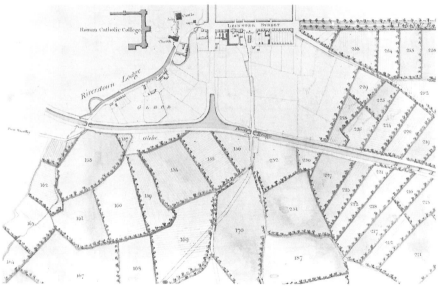

Detail from Carton estate map (1821)

Plate 4

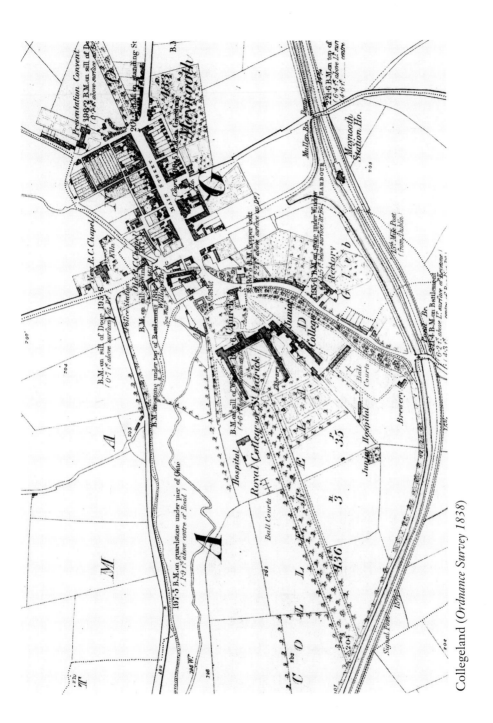

Collegeland (*Ordnance Survey 1838*)

Plate 5

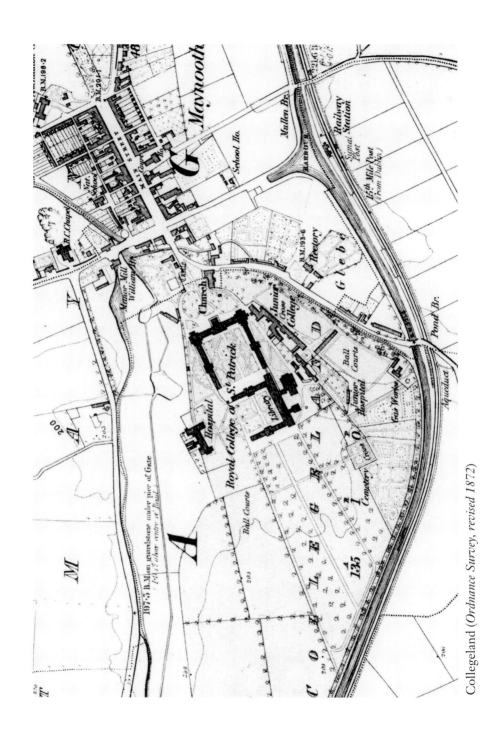

Collegeland (*Ordnance Survey, revised 1872*)

Plate 6

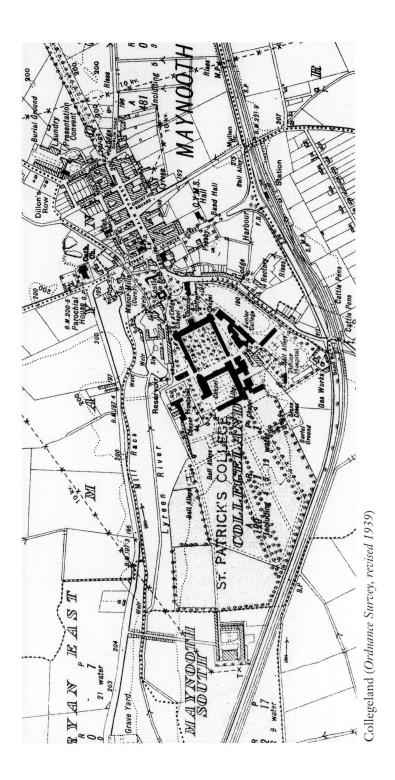

Collegeland (*Ordnance Survey, revised 1939*)

Plate 7

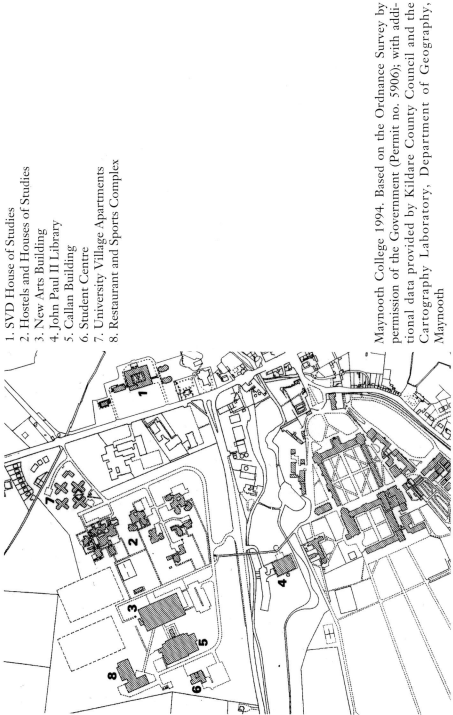

1. SVD House of Studies
2. Hostels and Houses of Studies
3. New Arts Building
4. John Paul II Library
5. Callan Building
6. Student Centre
7. University Village Apartments
8. Restaurant and Sports Complex

Maynooth College 1994. Based on the Ordnance Survey by permission of the Government (Permit no. 5906); with additional data provided by Kildare County Council and the Cartography Laboratory, Department of Geography, Maynooth

Plate 8

From Alexander Taylor's map of County Kildare, 1783 (*Courtesy of the Royal Irish Academy*)

Plate 9

Stoyte House and entrance gate, photographed 1895, but apart from the cross on the pediment little changed from 1795

Plate 10

Engraving of the College from J. Warburton, J. Whitelaw, R. Walsh, *History of the City of Dublin* (1818), at p. 1316

Plate 11

Books and Stationary

Paid Hugh Fitzpatrick, for Books and Stationary to 26 Nov 1800		31 18 8
John Boyce .... Stationary & Binding Books to 20th		20 9 10
Cornt McLoghlin ..... Freight & other Charges of Books Imported }		20 17 2
Jas Vallance, for Books purchased by Auction		10 11 10
	Books & Stationary .... (20)	101 9 7

Rent, Tythe, Insurance &c —

Paid His Grace the Duke of Leinster, One Years Rent of the College Lands, to 1st Nov 1800 }		74 .. ..
Revd Nichs Ashe, Tythe of Meadow Ground for the Year 1800		4 15 10
Robt Clayton, Parish Cess		. 6 4
Sundry Persons, County do		2 . 10
Sun Fire Insurance Company Premium of Insurance Duty &c on £3,000, on the Buildings of the College }		14 8 9
	Rent, Tythe, Insurance &c	95 11 9

Labourers in the Garden, Manure & Horsehire

Paid Sundry Persons for Labour, Horsehire & Manure to 29 Dec 1800		53 16 6
	Labourers Manure &c	53 16 6

Furniture & Utensils

Paid Jas Kelly, for Sundry Earthen Ware, Linen		10 5 11
Laughlin Daly, for Wooden Ware		3 12 .
Richd Bodkin ... Diaper		3 5 .
Jas Keane .... a Kitchen Jack, & fixing up do		12 10 5
Wilde & Co, for Ironmongery .... to 29 July 1800		9 16 11
J. J. O Brien & Co for Linen & Diaper ..... 20 Sep		53 10 11
John Raper .... Window Glass		3 9 2
John Proudfoot ...... a Mahogany Clothes Press & Cupboard		11 12 7
Luke Foley .... Sundry Tin Ware ... to 18 Octr 1800		10 5 4
Wm Anderson ..... 2 Surplices, Washing &c		4 2 .
The Steward's Returns of Expenditures for Sundry Articles of Furniture &c to 31 Dec 1800 }		10 10 10
	Furniture and Utensils	151 4 3

A page (1808) from the first account book (*MCL*)

Plate 12

Monochrome wash by G. P. Coddan *c.* 1810 (*MCL*)

Plate 13

George Butler a Student in the
College of Maynooth ——————

came into open Court, at a Sessions of the Peace held at *Maynooth*
the *11th* day of *January* 183 *3* and did then and there take and
subscribe the Oath and Declaration, pursuant to an Act of Parliament passed
in the 13th and 14th Years of the Reign of George the Third, and another Act
passed in the 33rd Year of the same Reign.

Which I certify.

George Medlicot } Clerk of the Peace for the
County of Kildare.

Certificate of Oath of Allegiance taken 1833 by George Butler, later Bishop of
Limerick 1861–86 (*MCA*)

'Silken Thomas yew tree' and sundial (1796)

Plate 14

Old kitchen with remains of passage refectory, as it stood until the early 1960s

Rhetoric House, Riverstown, St Mary's Church (*Church of Ireland*)

Plate 15

R. P. JOAN. STEPHANI
MENOCHII,

DOCTORIS THEOLOGI,

È SOCIETATE JESU,

COMMENTARII

TOTIUS

SACRÆ SCRIPTURÆ,

EX OPTIMIS QUIBUSQUE AUCTORIBUS COLLECTI.

JUXTA EDITIONEM A P. TOURNEMINIO RECOGNITAM.

TOMUS II.

Dublinii :

EX TYP. HUGONIS FITZPATRICK, IN VIA VULGO DICTA, CAPEL-STREET,

TYPOG. & BIBLIOP. ROM. CATH. COLL. MAYNOOTH.

⟶ ⊕ ⟵

M,DCCCXIV.

Title-page of 'Menochius' with Fitzpatrick imprint and woodcut (*MCL*)

Plate 16

his resignation. Mr Coen promised the same in September. Dr Everard appeared to be chosen President.'[34]

Patrick Everard, to whom this uninviting offer was now extended, was of old Catholic gentry stock from Fethard, Co. Tipperary. He had been educated for the priesthood in Salamanca, where he was ordained in 1783. He had been rector of the Irish College at Bordeaux from 1786 to 1793, and barely escaped with his life during the Terror. He arrived in England and opened a boys' school at Ulverston. He had been invited by the Maynooth Trustees to become first President of the lay college, but he did not come. Not surprisingly, he approached this new offer with circumspection. His school at Ulverston was successful, but he accepted that the Maynooth post was important; and so he decided to go to Ireland to see the situation for himself. He arrived in July and agreed to accept, but only for a limited time, which he envisaged as a short time, though he may not have made this as clear to the representatives of the Trustees as he did to his friends.[35] Needless to say, he began the academic year in the autumn with their full support, which they formally assured him of at a special meeting held on 15 October, at which they also expressed their appreciation of the improvement in discipline since his arrival and approved all the measures he had taken. By this date Thomas Coen had left the college, and William Fitzpatrick was appointed dean in his place. This did not solve the problem of the dean, for he lasted only a year, and was succeeded in 1811 by Andrew Hart, who lasted no longer, but the students seem to have been prepared to work with the dean now that Coen was gone. At the same meeting of the Trustees Francis Power, now seventy-five years old, resigned the vice-presidency. It has been seen that he had been in many ways a centre of stability through troubled years, but he was temperamentally too mild to give decisive leadership. In his place the Trustees appointed Peter Magennis, a Dominican.

There was good will for the new administration, which seems to have lasted to the end of Everard's presidency. A series of articles entitled 'The Tears of Maynooth', published in the *Irish Magazine* for August, September, November and December 1813, is a diatribe against Everard, but by this stage the bias has turned to inaccuracy; it is a reasonable suspicion that some of the alleged incidents never happened at all or, if they happened, must have happened while Coen was dean and therefore before Everard became President. By the time they were published Everard had long left Maynooth: indeed a permanent successor had been appointed on 13 November 1813, before the last of them was published. One can only conclude that they were written to prevent him returning (which he had no intention of doing) and that Watty Cox would not relinquish juicy copy once it came into his hands. What evidence there is indicates that Everard's initial success with the students was sustained. In one or two things he did show poor judgement, notably in the appointments he gave to Matthias Crowley, and there are suggestions that the manly and energetic qualities everyone praised went with a strain of haughtiness which might contain the seeds of trouble. Yet Andrew Hart, the dean, writing to Archbishop Daniel Murray on 14 November 1811 could refer to 'the present happy situation of the house . . . a hint of the President's wishes is sufficient to lead the students to do anything', though he admitted that 'the fact of it being the President's plan is sufficient to call down the unqualified condemnation of another portion of our community', by which he must mean the staff, or at least a part of them.[36] Everything, he said, depended on Everard staying on to finish his work. But Everard's commitment was less permanent than others hoped for. He was absent in England, presumably at his school in Ulverston, during the winter of 1810/11 and again in 1811/12. He tendered his resignation on 29 January 1812, pleading ill-health. The Trustees felt he might be persuaded to change his mind, for they decided to make a provisional arrangement for a situation where the worst storms were dying down but a strong hand was still needed. Archbishop Daniel Murray, coadjutor to Troy, agreed to take the presidency for a year to allow for the possibility that Everard might be persuaded to change his mind. He demanded that he be allowed to nominate his own vice-president, and he named Peter Kenney SJ.[37] It must have been Kenney more than Murray who attended to detail in Maynooth over this year, for though he was preoccupied with his plans for a college which came to fruition with the opening of Clongowes Wood in 1814, Murray, in addition to his duties as coadjutor-archbishop, was parish priest of St Andrew's, Westland Row. In 1826 Charles McNally, then a professor in the college, told the Commission of Inquiry of his memories of Kenney in the academic year 1812/13, when he was a student in his final year. He recalled his learning, zeal and piety, and his anxiety to give the students spiritual instruction. He conducted the retreats, and composed meditations for the students, which were read to them at morning and evening prayer.[38] No doubt the situation was further stabilised when after the year's administration by Murray and Kenney it was decided to seek a new President, since it was now clear that Everard would not return. The Trustees appointed Bartholomew Crotty, who remained for nineteen years. It took a little longer to find a dean with similar staying power, but he turned up in the person of Philip Dowley in 1816.

A Student Community

The academic side of the college might be expected to have troubles because of this unsettled situation, and indeed it had academic troubles of its own as well. It was necessary to give some assistance to the single professor in both Moral and Dogmatic Theology, as the class numbers crept up to about 170 students. The only possibility was to appoint a bright student who had just finished his course, with the title of lecturer. In some respects it was a risky step to take: part of Montague's troubles as bursar arose from his parsimonious nature, but they were heightened by the fact that when appointed he had been so recently a student. To describe the first two appointments to academic lectureships as 'unfortunate' is an understatement. David Sinnott was appointed lecturer in Moral Theology in 1804, the year in which he completed his own studies. He seems to have discharged his duties without comment until 1809, by which time he was showing many signs of eccentricity. He had lost faith in transubstantiation, so he had to leave the Catholic Church, but he would agree to join the Church of Ireland only if he was not required to subscribe to the thirty-nine articles. He withdrew to his native Co. Wexford, where he lived miserably.[39]

Matthias Crowley of Cork, appointed lecturer in Dogmatic Divinity in 1802, ran a more colourful course. He had entered the college before the clerics were housed in Long Corridor, and was expelled after about six months because, on his own admission, he led 'an idle and refractory life'. He then spent two years in the college in Carlow and got himself readmitted to Maynooth, where he was ordained after two more, when he was appointed lecturer. His intellectual gifts may not have quite matched his ability to advance himself: he was known to the students as 'the French wagtail', because, they alleged, he owed his appointment to his servility towards the French professors. On 30 June 1808 a Frenchman, Francis Eloi, was appointed to the chair of Scripture, which it was proving so difficult to fill (Ecclesiastical History was thrown in). Eloi's patron was Francis Moylan, Bishop of Cork, and Crowley's political sense seems to have deserted him when he applied for the chair, demanding that a concursus or public competition be held, in accordance with the college statutes. On this point the statutes did not altogether back him, and instead of getting a concursus he found himself withdrawn to his native Cork. Unfortunately, Eloi, like other Frenchmen, did not stay. He left at the beginning of July 1809, and the post was still vacant when Everard accepted the presidency a year later. He proposed that Crowley be asked to teach Scripture, and he was appointed professor on 15 October 1810. While he may have been satisfactory enough as lecturer in Theology, where all he had to do was explain Delahogue's dictates, he was completely out of his depth as professor of Scripture, so much so that when William Fitzpatrick announced in May 1811 that he was resigning as dean Everard appointed Crowley in his place, intending to have the appointment ratified by the Trustees at the end of the academic year. Before this, however, Everard had refused to back Crowley's demand that a student be expelled. Crowley marched out in high dudgeon and joined the Established Church, where he made a respectable career for himself. He gave evidence before the Commission of 1826, factually and without rancour.[40]

The 'core-curriculum' of philosophy and theology found professors who served it well. Theology was taught over a three-year cycle, to a class that built up to about 170. After Maurice Ahern's death in 1801 Louis-Gilles Delahogue took over Dogmatic Theology and Edward Ferris moved to Moral. When Ferris died in November 1809 he was succeeded by François Anglade, who had taught philosophy since he had arrived in 1802. This left a gap in Philosophy, and it took a few years before it was filled successfully. Scripture too took a while to settle down, for a variety of reasons, but the situation was reasonably stabilised with the appointment of James Browne in 1817.

Textbooks had next to be provided. There were plenty to choose from, but unfortunately no supply for seminarians in Ireland. In Moral Theology, in 1796, the Roman Congregation of Propaganda had recommended the work of Gabriel Antoine SJ, and sent a few copies to Maynooth. Antoine's *Theologia Moralis Universalis*, first published in 1726, had been very widely used: it was rigoristic in its approach despite its Jesuit authorship. After Anglade became professor in 1810 it was decided it was time to have a textbook printed in Dublin. The choice fell on the moral section of Louis Bailly's *Theologia Dogmatica et Moralis*, published in eight volumes in Paris in 1789. Its general approach was in the rigorist strain of Antoine, and it would appear that the main reason Bailly was preferred was that it was shorter. This continued to be the textbook in Maynooth until the early 1850s, and over the same period it was widely used in France. The Irish edition was produced by the college publisher, Fitzpatrick. In one way the Irish printings developed into a bibliographical curiosity, in that they continued to refer to royal edicts of pre-revolutionary times, whereas successive French editions took account first of the Concordat and then of the Civil Code. A textbook link between Catholic moral theology and British and Irish civil law was first provided by George Crolly, professor from 1844 to 1878.[41] When Anglade became professor he had been teaching philosophy for eight years and had been compiling his own course of philosophy. In dogma Bailly had been the principal textbook, though available only in a few copies, until Delahogue composed his own treatises. Publication began in 1808 and continued at regular intervals. Though there had been problems in getting someone to teach Scripture, the students were provided with a textbook when in 1814 Fitzpatrick published a Dublin edition of Stefano Menochio SJ, *Brevis Explicatio Sensus Litteralis S. Scripturae*, first published in three volumes in 1630 (Plate 16). Fitzpatrick's successor, Coyne, published a cheaply priced Douai Bible in 1825. 'Menochius', Delahogue, Bailly and Anglade served as basic textbooks until the middle of the century.

Hugh Fitzpatrick and Richard Coyne, publishers, clearly had an important role in the history of the college. As the Penal Code was relaxed, the Catholic printers and booksellers began to move out of the warren of alleys around Cook Street. In 1793 a group of them were admitted to full guild membership, a great advance indeed. One of these was Hugh Fitzpatrick, official printer to the Catholic Committee and publisher and bookseller to Maynooth College from its beginnings. When he died in 1819 the business went down, and it was taken over at the same address, no. 4 Capel Street, by Richard Coyne in 1822. Both Fitzpatrick and Coyne were talented men, who moved on terms of equality with the Catholic leaders, lay and clerical.

Of necessity, the library had humble beginnings. In May 1800 the Trustees ordered one of the large halls to be fitted out for this purpose. They appointed their secretary, Andrew Dunne, librarian, with authority to name a deputy at

£20 a year. The statutes of 1800 required the library to be open four hours each class day, and the 'prefect' was to be present during opening hours. Who was actually there is nowhere stated: it might be suspected that it was the vice-president, Francis Power. The library grew slowly. Edmund Burke had already made 'a handsome present of classical books', which had belonged to his dead son, Richard. In 1812 the Trustees set up a committee of four of their bishop-members to oversee the spending of £1,000 'for the purchase of books for the use of the college'. In 1818 Warburton reported that there were 5,000 books, mostly theology but including commentaries on Scripture written by Christians 'of every persuasion'.[42] For some years it must have caused little hardship that only the staff and students of four years' standing had the right of admission. And of course there was little time or opportunity for individual research: specifically, students were forbidden to publish anything without the permission of the President. So, almost unbelievably, were the professors, a prohibition that lasted, with growing insecurity, until 1848. More unbelievably still, this prohibition was reintroduced in the 1872 statutes, and though it was a dead letter from the beginning it proved to have a remarkable power of survival.

In the preparatory courses the college was left to find its own way. There was one interesting intervention by a well-disposed Prime Minster, but it came to nothing. In April 1806 Grenville wrote to the Chief Secretary, William Elliot, suggesting that 'an allowance of a small salary' might be made 'for a chemical . . . and a medical knowledge' and 'a little mathematical, or at least arithmetical instruction' to supplement what was believed to be the 'purely and exclusively theological' education at Maynooth. Elliot was not enthusiastic and seems to have killed the proposal by pointing out that Trinity College would object to anything in any way suggesting the development of a lay university at Maynooth, and saying that he doubted if it would be 'agreeable to several of the superior Catholic clergy'.[43] The details as furnished to Parliament in 1808 indicated respectable courses in Classics and in 'Natural or Experimental Philosophy', including Mathematics—'algebra, geometry, conic sections' and 'Chymistry'. The course in Irish was briefly described: 'McCartin's Grammar, Irish Testament explained, fragments translated into English'. In 1809 Fitzpatrick published *A Practical Grammar of the Irish Language* by the professor, Paul O'Brien.

A student community was being slowly put together. On 16 January 1812, just after term began after the Christmas examinations, Delahogue congratulated the body of students he had angrily dismissed as 'peasants' nine years before, in English that still halted a little:

> If you certainly foreknew what I had to tell you upon the last examination, I cannot find too expressive words, to testify to you my satisfaction on every respect, for your numerous attendances during all the days, your constant attention, and your answers to the different questions

proposed to you. I exhort you, gentlemen, to continue—you have great motives of emulation. I consider the three courses of divinity as three divisions of the same army which are to be competitious, one with another for honour. Gentlemen, this day, which is my birthday, permits me to address you some words on that account. I begin in the 73rd year of my age. 30 years ago I enjoyed commodity of life, very sufficient income, honourable situation, and general estime of the bishops of France . . . I have many thanks to return to Almighty God who procured for me such an honourable situation as to have been called to the young clergymen of Ireland. I neglected nothing to fulfil my duty for the greatest advantage of them. I have the satisfaction to have finished the fourth tract on the Trinity and the Incarnation.[44]

Studies were further developed by the beginnings of a postgraduate school, to be known as the Dunboyne Establishment from the circumstances of its origin. John Butler was appointed Bishop of Cork in 1763. His family was an aristocratic one, and in December 1785 he succeeded to the title of Lord Dunboyne. He became convinced it was his duty to carry on the line, and applied for a dispensation to marry. When this was refused he conformed to the Established Church on 19 August 1787 and married a distant cousin, Maria Butler. When he felt the end approaching, he wrote to Archbishop Troy asking to be reconciled. Troy forwarded his request to Rome, but when he heard he was dying he sent him William Gahan OSA as his confessor. Butler indicated to both Troy and Gahan that in order to make amends he proposed to leave lands to Maynooth College, and both claimed they dissuaded him. When he died on 7 May 1800 it was discovered that in a will dated 1 May he had left to the Trustees his lands in Meath, worth £1,000 a year, subject to a life interest to his sister, and a charge of £200 a year to his wife during her lifetime. His sister petitioned Chancery to set the will aside as not only inequitable but also in contravention of the unrepealed statute invalidating bequests of land made by persons who had conformed to the Established Church and later returned to Catholicism. This was awkward, for even Lord Chancellor Clare was of the opinion that the failure to repeal this particular statute in 1793 was an oversight, it having been the intention to repeal all such laws. Clare died on 28 January 1802, when the petition had dragged through many inconclusive hearings in Chancery. Finally the Master of the Rolls decided it should be put before a jury at Trim assizes, where it came up on 24 August, the judge being Lord Kilwarden, Chief Justice of the King's Bench.

Both parties agreed that the testator was of sound mind, and both Troy and Gahan repeated the evidence they had already given in Chancery, that they had dissuaded him and implored him to leave his property to his family. The crucial question was whether he died a Catholic, and William Gahan was the crucial witness. He declared that as Dunboyne's spiritual counsellor he could disclose only what he had been authorised to disclose; that as a priest he knew nothing and that as a citizen he was not bound to incriminate himself and incur the penalties for reconciling a Catholic who had converted to the Established Church. The judge committed him to Trim gaol for contempt, then released him immediately on the grounds that the fact of his committal had sufficiently discharged his contempt. On the question of fact the jury found that Dunboyne had indeed died a Catholic, and the question of law was referred to the court of King's Bench next term for a ruling.

Talk of a compromise began. On 26 June 1805 the Trustees, on counsel's advice, accepted compromise in principle. Before they could accept it in fact an Act of Parliament was necessary, for they had no legal power to compromise suits. This was given by Parliament on 25 June 1808 (48 Geo. III, c. 143). By then progress had been made in working out the details, and the deed of compromise was signed on 14 November 1809. The Meath lands were divided equally between the Trustees and the Butler claimants. The Trustees got lands yielding £400 a year, and further lands yielding £100 in return for a rather complex settlement by which they finally paid the Butlers just under £1,000.[45] At the meeting at which they accepted the compromise, in June 1805, the Trustees had decided to organise a scheme whereby outstanding students, with the permission of their bishop and the President, might remain in the college for further studies. It was a brave decision, at a time when they were trying to scrape money together to put up desperately needed additional buildings. On 29 January 1812 they decided to set aside the entire income from the Dunboyne estate to endow these scholars. It was another brave decision, for this was the meeting at which Patrick Everard tendered his resignation.

CHAPTER III

THE CATHOLIC ENLIGHTENMENT: AFTERNOON

The Greening of the Staff

It has already been suggested that one of the major problems facing the college of Maynooth was to find a president who might be willing and able to stay the course. But the problems of a president did not arise exclusively from the turbulence of the students: there was also the problem of communication, or rather lack of communication, with the Trustees. Two draft memoranda which have survived in the papers of Louis Delahogue, one dated late 1813, the other 1814, indicate that when the Trustees consulted him on the problems of the college his reply was blunt. The last time they had met in the college, he claimed, was in June 1810, when they had forced the resignations of Byrne and Coen. Since then they had met in Dublin: there was no communication between the Trustees and the college officials, and neither party knew what the other was doing.[1] The Trustees seem to have taken the point, for, beginning with 1815, the June meeting was henceforth held in the college, with another meeting in the opening months of the year held in Dublin. This was reasonably satisfactory, for the main business of this latter meeting was to prepare the petition to Parliament for the annual grant, while most college business was done in June. There were still problems with some of the Trustees, especially some of the lay Trustees, who were not over-zealous in attending meetings, and problems too in communicating decisions to the college administration (the vice-president's record book begun by Francis Power notes, sometimes in the form of a letter from the secretary, the decisions which it was felt the college should know about). It was only in 1826 that the Trustees decided that resolutions affecting members of the college should be recorded by the secretary in a book to be deposited in the library.

By now the Trustees had developed an unrestricted authority. The powers of the Visitors had always been tenuous, and after their rejection of student appeals in 1819 visitation became little more than a formality. No report was made to public authority, and no official record of the visitation was made. Nevertheless, the Trustees' authority could not be effectively exercised without a competent administration in the college. Here there were four key figures. Pride of place must certainly go to Daniel Murray, coadjutor Archbishop of Dublin from 1809 and Archbishop after the death of Troy in 1823. After his term as emergency President in 1812–13, as Trustee he attended every meeting and sat on every committee (the practice of setting up joint committees of Trustees and staff to discuss important matters in detail, which now makes its appearance in the Trustees' minutes, may almost certainly be attributed to him). Next there was Bartholomew Crotty, appointed President on 13 November 1813, at the age of forty-four. He had been a student in the Irish College in Lisbon, where he had been appointed to teach philosophy immediately after his ordination in 1791. Ten years later he became rector, and over the years 1806 and 1807, though the French were occupying Lisbon, he successfully resisted Napoleon's attempts to bring himself and his students to the reconstituted Irish College in Paris. In 1811 he returned to Ireland and was appointed parish priest of Clonakilty. No record seems to have survived to show who or what induced him to take up the presidency of Maynooth, but Daniel Murray must have had an important role in it: the two men were contemporaries, Murray having been ordained in Salamanca in 1790. Having accepted the post, Crotty proved robust enough to hold it until he was appointed Bishop of Cloyne and Ross in 1833.

Michael Montague, the third key figure, once expressed the opinion that Crotty was not stern enough: 'the President', he wrote to a priest friend, 'is very indulgent and of course masters and students ready to complain if there is the least cause and often without cause.'[2] This may tell us more about Montague than about Crotty. He came from the heart of Gaelic Ulster, the parish of Errigal Kieran in Co. Tyrone. Here at the time of his ordination in 1798, and for years afterwards, it was from his family home that the table and vestments were brought to the Mass-rock on Sundays.[3] He entered Maynooth in 1795, never left it for another appointment, and died as President in 1845. He had been a leading prizeman in his student years, but it was not here that his interests lay. After ordination he substituted for Darré during one of his absences, but he found his niche, first as assistant bursar to Francis Power and as college bursar in 1802. It has earlier been suggested that his parsimony in the students' refectory contributed to the disturbances at the beginning of 1803, and while he did not repeat this mistake he never wasted money. He was appointed vice-president in 1814, and over the following years the college buildings were very greatly extended, out of money saved from the annual parliamentary grant when the price of provisions collapsed after the Napoleonic wars. Dr Patrick Murray, who had entered as a student in 1821 and been appointed to the staff in 1838, saluted him as 'the father of the college' in an obituary in the *Dublin Evening Post* of 30 October 1845, the day after his death. The tribute was deserved.

The fourth figure is the dean who made the office, Philip Dowley of Waterford, appointed 'sub-dean' immediately after his ordination in 1816 and dean four years later. In 1834 he was appointed vice-president, but declined the office because he had made up his mind to leave to join a number of newly ordained priests who under his guidance had already taken the first steps in a venture that was to develop into the Irish Vincentian congregation.

As well as contending with distant Trustees and restive students, the college administration had to deal with hostile Protestant opinion. For a number of reasons relations between Protestant and Catholic deteriorated in the first decades of the nineteenth century. Both sides had wounds to lick after 1798. Politically, the Catholic demand for 'emancipation', or full admittance to the political nation, was resisted, all the more doggedly as it became more inevitable, or at best considered in the context of a veto on episcopal appointments, which Catholics were not willing to accept. Religiously, the strengthening of evangelical Protestantism, coupled with an active mission to Catholics, roused real bitterness. Maynooth became a focal point in these tensions for fairly obvious reasons. By the 1820s it was ordaining most of the Catholic priests of Ireland, teaching them, so extreme Protestants believed, the well-known Catholic principles on how to deal with heretics, individually and collectively, and all this at the public expense. Even moderate Protestants might have legitimate fears as they tried to grapple with the idea of the British crown having full Catholic subjects, not far away in Canada but in the home islands. And the opportunity to air these questions came up every year, when the Maynooth vote came before Parliament. Indeed anxieties about Catholicism in general tended to focus on the college. On 7 July 1817, for example, anxious Protestants in the House of Commons were seeking reassurances about what was being taught in Maynooth College, and being referred to the information on this matter that Parliament had sought and got in 1808, and again in 1813. These fears, however, were not fanned by what might be in Delahogue or Bailly. They sprang from the fact that that same day an aggregate meeting was being held in Dublin to protest against the treatment of Richard Hayes, the Franciscan who had gone to Rome with a protest against the Veto, who had been ordered to leave the Papal States on 23 May, and was to be forcibly deported on 16 July.

A few years later Maynooth became even more the focus of controversy with the publication of the 'Letters of Hierophilos'. Thirty-two letters in all appeared under this signature, between January 1820 and May 1823. All were dated from Maynooth College, where no attempt was made to conceal the fact that the author was John MacHale, appointed assistant to Delahogue in 1814 and his successor on 22 June 1820. MacHale set out to defend Catholics against the attacks made upon them. These were often couched in offensive language and MacHale gave as good as he got. The slanging match continued. In 1826 Crotty explained the problems of a President. What was he to do when the *Dublin Journal*, 'supposed to be the organ of a large part of the Protestant population of Ireland, including many of the clergy', asserted that 'the Roman Catholic clergy of Ireland was composed of men taken from the plough, and trained up in the college of Maynooth in principles of treason and sedition'? He had in fact done nothing, only to see both charge and language repeated in London papers. He then appealed to the Lord Lieutenant asking for a special inquiry or, failing this, an investigation by the Commission to inquire into education in Ireland, set up on 14 June 1824. The Lord Lieutenant told him to raise the matter with the statutory Visitors who were to meet in June 1825, only a few months away. This Crotty did, and they declared the calumnies to be utterly without foundation.[4] But by this stage the Visitors were not a body who might be expected to do very much, so in 1826 the Education Commission added Maynooth to the educational problems to be investigated in Ireland.

There were five commissioners. The one Catholic, Anthony Richard Blake, the first Catholic ever appointed to a government commission of inquiry, was supposed to give some assurance to Catholics, but he was automatically suspect for having taken office under the Crown and was publicly denounced by O'Connell. This judgement does seem unfair, for he worked hard in the limited time he could spare from his official duties. The one Irish Protestant, John Leslie Foster, son of the bishop of Clogher, was opposed to Catholic claims. There were two Scots, William Grant and James Glassford, scarcely heard of in Ireland before their appointment. Grant was opposed to the proselytising campaign in Ireland, but simply could not comprehend the Catholic position on scripture-reading. Lastly there was Thomas Frankland Lewis, of English and Welsh background, old Etonian, 'a careful and accomplished man, but formal, verbose and dull . . . employed in political and administrative posts of the second rank'.[5]

The Commissioners collected evidence from the staff, selected students, and others between 19 October and 7 November 1826. Their Report, with this evidence and supporting documentation, was laid before the House of Commons on 2 June 1827 and ordered to be printed on 27 June.[6] The evidence and documentation is much more interesting than the Report itself, which, as might be expected from such a mixed body, is dull, uninformative and inconclusive. In 1844 Anthony Blake told the Lord Lieutenant that three of the Commissioners wanted a more liberal endowment under new conditions, while two wanted the college suppressed.[7] Though the Report states that the primary purpose of the inquiry was to investigate the political implications of Catholic teaching on oaths and the temporal power and infallibility of the Pope, the Commissioners in fact confine themselves to a brief history of the college and a bald summary of the principal points of the evidence given, from which they draw no conclusions.

Indeed, the Report did little more than provide ammunition for renewed attacks on Maynooth, one of them by one of the Commissioners, Leslie Foster, in the *Quarterly Review*, and a particularly worrying one, because of the status of its author, Lord Bexley, entitled, seemingly innocuously, *Address to the Freeholders of the County of Kent*. Nicholas Vansittart, first Lord Bexley, had had a short and undistinguished appointment as Chief Secretary for Ireland, but a long and to some unexpectedly successful tenure of office as Chancellor of the Exchequer from 1812 to 1823, difficult years, in which the great war had to be first pursued and then paid for. He had the general reputation of being a moderate man, but not where Catholicism was concerned, for he was a strong evangelical Protestant. His attack on Maynooth was set in the wider context of Catholic Emancipation, and soon drew a reply from the Catholic education commissioner, Anthony Richard Blake.[8] Blake however was more concerned with the wider political issues, and when no reply came from Maynooth he was among those who kept urging the President that something must be done. Pressure also came from the formidable Bishop of Kildare and Leighlin, James Doyle,[9] and Crotty penned a reluctant reply, carefully phrased for the most part but here and there displaying flashes of a robust patriotism he had earlier shown in his replies to the Commissioners.[10] His overall judgement that replying was futile was borne out by the fact that the attacks continued to come from a Protestant society reluctantly coming to terms with Catholic Emancipation; and when this receded as a political issue the growing strength of Evangelicalism resulted only in a slight modification of the thrust of the attacks. They became so virulent that in 1830 a group of Irish MPs gave serious consideration to a proposal that the annual parliamentary grant should be renounced. This set alarm bells ringing in Maynooth, where an ambitious building programme had so strained resources that in 1831 the Trustees applied for an additional £5,000 for building purposes, similar to what had been given in 1808. This time, however, they did not get it.[11]

Between various hammers and anvils Maynooth was beginning to develop a distinctive personality. In the beginning the French influence had been pervasive, producing a kind of afternoon of the Catholic Enlightenment, a rustic Sorbonne in north Kildare. The Trustees—lay and episcopal—were naturally opposed to everything the French Revolution stood for; Lord Fingall was probably the most active in trying to ensure that the tone of the institution would be that of France before the Revolution, and this is precisely what the original staff represented, Irish as well as French. Not all the Frenchmen stayed: Eloi lasted only one year (1808–9), Delort six (1795–1801), and Darré finally returned to France in 1813, after eighteen years. But Anglade and Delahogue lived out their lives in Maynooth, holding the two most influential professorships, those of Theology. Montague, the man from the Ulster Massrock, may have merited the title of administrative 'father of the college', but these men from the Sorbonne were its intellectual fathers. Little bits of remembered lore recalled a whole life-style.[12] It was remembered that French had been the language of the professors' table, though the story had it that Paul O'Brien, professor of Irish, a man about whom stories seemed to gather, organised a corner where the language was Irish. Delahogue, it was recalled, wept at the very mention of the name of Voltaire. The formal garden, which appears in its full development in the Ordnance Survey map of 1838, seems to have been known as 'the French plot', and the stringed harp in trimmed boxwood, though said by some to be the work of Paul O'Brien, was more credibly attributed by others to 'the French professors, who were believed to have a great taste for such things'. Anglade, it will be recalled, had spent six years as gardener with a Protestant family in Wales before coming to Maynooth.

As the years passed, however, a more native imprint began to appear; indeed from the beginning there were deep tensions between Irish youth and middle-aged to elderly refugees from the French Revolution. Young Irishmen began to be appointed to the staff. One of the the first was John MacHale, appointed initially as assistant to Delahogue and then as his successor on 22 June 1820. Before this date he had published the first of the 'Letters of Hierophilos', dated 29 January. In these letters the Maynooth cleric appears in an unmistakably Irish context, reacting angrily to attacks on his Church and his college, and demanding religious equality, to include disestablishment and disendowment of the state Church of Ireland, as a political right. Despite attempts to play down their influence in evidence given to the Commissioners in 1826, it appears clear that these letters, appearing first in the newspapers, then as pamphlets, and in collected form from 1821, circulated widely among the students.

The last letter signed 'Hierophilos' is dated May 1823 and the next, signed 'John, bishop of Maronia' is dated October 1826. There is no doubt that the Frenchmen mounted a counter-attack, and indeed seem to have brought 'Hierophilos' to heel. In May 1824 Bishop James Doyle issued a long public letter entitled 'Conciliation of Ireland'. Today it is best remembered for its proposals for the union of the churches, quite startling for the time, but it was his remarks on the Irish Catholic clergy that raised hackles in Maynooth. He warned that, in ruling Ireland,

> the ministers of England cannot look to the exertions of the Catholic priesthood: they have been ill-treated, and they may yield for a moment to the influence of nature, though it be opposed to grace. This clergy, with few exceptions, are from the ranks of the people; they inherit their feelings; they are not, as formerly, brought up under despotic governments; they have imbibed the doctrines of Locke and Paley more deeply than those of Bellarmine, or even Bossuet, on the Divine Right of Kings; and they know more of the principles of the constitution than they do of passive obedience.

One evening at the very end of May or beginning of June, 'while the professors were at dessert', one of them read out this passage. Delahogue and Anglade blenched: '*Mon Dieu*', Delahogue exclaimed, '*est-ce possible qu'il prêche la Révolution?*' '*La Révolution*', Anglade echoed, '*c'est horrible.*' The upshot was the 'Maynooth Manifesto', published on 4 June 1824, signed by Delahogue, Anglade, John MacHale, professor of Dogmatic Theology, James Browne, professor of Sacred Scripture, and Charles McNally, professor of Logic and Moral Philosophy. They declared that their statement was occasioned by 'recent published allusions to the domestic education of the Catholic clergy', and, having recapitulated Catholic tradition on the obedience due to constitutional authority, concluded that 'if any change has been wrought in the minds of the clergy of Ireland, it is that religious obligation is here strengthened by motives of gratitude, and confirmed by sworn allegiance, from which no power on earth can absolve.'

The three Irishmen went on to become bishops, and it was from them in later years that W. J. Fitzpatrick, Doyle's biographer, derived his information. There is no doubt that, theology apart, an institution so dependent on public money and so regularly assailed as unworthy of it must have felt the bishop's remarks unnecessarily provocative, but there can be little doubt that in later years the three Irishmen recalled the incident with embarrassment. But Hierophilos did not break his silence until MacHale became a bishop, and Bishop Browne's account of the incident is revealing in that he attributes what happened to Paul O'Brien's ability to read any passage so as to produce the effect on his hearers that he wanted to produce. It would be quite in character that Paul O'Brien should have had this histrionic ability, but he cannot have been the reader on that early summer evening in 1824, for he had died four years earlier.[13]

In 1814 Delahogue had urged on the Trustees the desirability of the college providing its future staff as far as possible from its own graduates. As this situation developed, there developed with it the institution of 'concursus', or public competition between candidates for a chair. The statutes of 1800 envisaged a concursus only for student-candidates for lectureships, but the revised statutes of 1820 extended it to all appointments. When a vacancy occurred, a notice was to be posted in several places in the college that a concursus would be held in sixty days. There was no advertisement in the papers, but the students could be relied on to spread the news. Candidates, who must have a testimonial from their bishop and the permission of the Trustees, were to announce themselves to the President. The assessment board consisted of the President, the vice-president, the deans and the professors of theology, with a professor from the department to which the appointment was being made, should it have a second professor. Each candidate was examined for two hours a day for four days. Candidates for theology or philosophy were to be examined in both disciplines, including natural philosophy, and candidates for the humanities, though examined mainly in the Classics, were expected to prove their theological and philosophical abilities as well. At the end, each member of the board wrote out his recommendation, giving the reasons for it (an example of such a recommendation, dated 1 May 1829, given by William Higgins, appointed Bishop of Ardagh on 20 September of that year, has survived in the diocesan archives).[14]

The concursus was a reasonable test as long as education was supposed to produce universal scholarship, and with modifications from time to time it served Maynooth for long years. It took a little time to become established because the Trustees, having very judiciously set it up, went on to ignore their own decision. However, in 1825 they found themselves having to appoint Thomas Kelly, the junior dean, to succeed MacHale as professor of Dogmatic Theology, because he was the only candidate, and they decided that in future, even when there was only one candidate, they would require 'a satisfactory performance in the form of a concursus'. Ironically, Kelly became Bishop of Dromore the following year, coadjutor in Armagh in 1828, and Archbishop of Armagh and therefore a Trustee on the death of Archbishop Curtis in July 1832. Perhaps even more ironically, his appointment to Dromore was questioned in Rome, because he was teaching theology in Maynooth, for by 1826 some Roman authorities had become convinced that Maynooth was a theological hotbed of something called 'Gallicanism'.[15]

The appointment of Thomas Kelly was far from being the only case in which there was only one applicant. It also illustrates the fact that candidates often had their eyes set on a chair of theology, because it was regarded as being at the top of a hierarchy of subjects rather than because of the fact that the administrative staff and the theology professors were paid slightly more. Not that the highest-paid was highly paid, because money was always tight; even when prices fell after the war there was an ambitious building programme to be financed out of the annual grant. In 1820 the Trustees announced a new scale of salaries, ranging from £100 a year for the senior administration and professors of theology through £90 for philosophy and £80 for the humanities to £70 for the junior dean and 'others'. These salaries were increased in 1827, the President doing quite well, the professors of theology rising to £122 a year, other professors to £112, and the junior dean being put on the same level as the professors of philosophy and the humanities.[16] This may have stabilised the office of junior dean. Certainly it had hitherto been regarded as a post in which nobody lingered, and the tradition did not altogether die. In view of the importance and difficulty of the office this was regrettable.

Buildings and Grounds

The office was indeed increasing in importance and difficulty as the college and its student numbers grew. The annual grant supported 250, but in 1820 there were 350, and in 1830 numbers were approaching 450. This committed the college to an extensive building programme, which had to be financed out of the annual budget. Payments for building were made piecemeal, and the Trustees' minutes do not record them all. However, the college accounts do, at least to the extent of making it clear that building costs bulked larger at certain times, and this fact can be related to specific building projects, so that while establishing when certain buildings were erected is not a straightforward inquiry it is nevertheless possible to reach certainty.

Despite the pressure of numbers, priority was given to a building to house the 'Dunboyne Scholars'. This was begun even before the wartime difficulties were over, and though it was cheaply built progress seems to have been slow. In August 1814 the Trustees noted that the building was unlikely to be ready before the academic year 1815/16. The college accounts show Peter Magennis OP beginning to be described as 'Prefect of the Senior Scholars' in that year, and it is a reasonable assumption that this appointment coincided with the opening of the new building. The architect was John Taylor, the contractor John Curran. It was a plain building, separated from the others, facing the western end of New House (though, as will appear, not quite the western half of it). It was clearly designed and sited with the completion of a square in mind. What distinguished it externally from the corresponding part of New House was a row of bulky chimneys, only half of which survived the reconstruction of the 1950s. Each of the twenty students provided for was to have a fire in his room, these being on the ground and middle floors. The top floor was undivided, and the college library transferred there, conveniently close for the students but alarmingly situated over as many as twenty open fires.

The Trustees acquired the lay college when it closed in 1817, and it became a separate establishment for the freshmen, irrespective of what class they matriculated into. This gave some relief to the accommodation problem, but far from enough. There was a pressing need for further building, and the obvious development was to close the gap between the Dunboyne building and Long Corridor. To find out how this happened it is necessary to consider the evidence of the 'Carton maps'. These have been referred to more than once already, but in the present context it is necessary to describe them in a little detail. They were commissioned by the Duke of Leinster from the Dublin firm of Sherrard Bassington and Greene. They are beautifully coloured ornate maps, showing the Leinster estate house by house and field by field. When finished they were bound in a volume, bearing the date 1821, and now in Carton House. Clearly the preparation of these maps extended over a fairly long period. A copy of one of them is attached to a deed concerning the Stoyte property, dated 8 August 1820. The college buildings appear in four of the sheets, and none of the four agree. Two of them show the detached Dunboyne building and Riverstown Lodge, but only one of these indicates the wing built on to the back of this latter in the early 1800s. What is most puzzling is that three of the four show a building between Dunboyne and Long Corridor, a large building but not completely filling the gap. Two show the same curiously irregular outline, but the third is different (Plates 3, 4).

It can be said with certainty that there never was such a building there. This can be shown conclusively by two lines of argument. Firstly, the college accounts show only token sums spent on buildings between the payment for Dunboyne in 1816 and 1825, when there is a very substantial payment, followed by small but significant ones for a few years following, and this tallies with what may be gleaned from the Trustees' minutes concerning a building programme over these years. Even more significantly, and quite exceptionally, there has survived, in two copies, one in Dublin and one in Maynooth, a very detailed 'Specification for Addition to the South Wing', dated 26 April 1822.[17] It is a specification for a building to connect Dunboyne with Long Corridor to match New House precisely and so complete another wing of the square. What is involved is the eastern half, the centre block, and something to the west of it. How much exactly was made clear when the buildings were stripped of their plaster in the early 1950s: the original Dunboyne House, badly built, stopped two windows short of the centre block, and the later work was much better building, as would indeed appear from the detail of the 1822 specification.

The essential factor in the great programme now begun was a buildings committee, first set up by the Trustees in 1821. There can be no doubt that the central figure within the college was the vice-president, Michael Montague. Though he had been relieved of the duties of bursar in 1816, his successor, John Cummins, was an invalid, and when he retired at the beginning of 1828 Montague was appointed bursar again. The first building contract was approved in February 1822, for an extension of the south wing of the college, the architect being again John Taylor but the builder the firm of Henry, Mullins and McMahon. The contract, for part of the building only, was for £2,300, but a year later, in February 1823, the Trustees approved a contract for £4,200 'for the completion of the extension of the buildings from the Dunboyne Establishment and also for the building of a new kitchen and its appurtenances.' The kitchen is the square building at the east end of Riverstown Lodge, and it is probable that the wing running back from this end of Riverstown was constructed at the same time. The kitchen was connected to the neighbouring refectory by a covered passage, clearly shown on the Ordnance Survey map (Plate 5): the kitchen end of this passage survived until the most recent adaptation of the building (Plate 15). It is still possible to see where the wall between the Riverstown and Stoyte properties was deflected to fit in with the new arrangements.

Numbers still pressed on space, and a contract for another building was signed in August 1828. There may have been some delay in beginning it, for money was very scarce. In 1831 Parliament refused a petition for a building grant of £5,000, but in that year the Trustees paid about £6,000 for building, and about £6,500 again in 1833. These payments represent the two buildings, to be called Rhetoric and Logic from the classes they were designed to accommodate, who with the small Humanity class that came to settle in the wing between Dunboyne and Long Corridor formed a separate 'Junior House' (Plates 15, 32), with its own class halls, chapel and refectory (Science departments have now taken over the class halls and Geography the refectory, while the computer lives in what had been the chapel). Finally, over the years 1835 and 1836 the sum of £2,750 was paid to put up the small separate infirmary building beyond the walled garden. For reasons to be discussed later, the idea of 'completing the square' had been abandoned.

A contributor to the *Dublin Review* in 1836 summed up the development. The buildings had been put up out of pressing need, with money painfully saved from a meagre annual grant. The result was that 'the general appearance of the house, although free, perhaps, from any substantial defect, is tasteless and inelegant.'[18] To an extent this is true, yet if one stands in the front square on a sunny morning when the shrubs are in bloom it is hard to resist the thought that when building within a tradition it is hard to go badly wrong, more especially perhaps if there is not much money to spend.

Anyway, these buildings represented a serious drain on meagre resources. In the forty years between 1795 and 1835 the college had spent 10 per cent of its annual grant on buildings, and about 15 per cent in the twenty years after 1815. In June 1822 the buildings committee was instructed to treat with a Dr Meyler to build 'hypocausts' to 'ventilate the four great halls with cold and warm air and the refectory and prayer hall with cold air'; a year later the library was added to the places to be heated. However, the system kept breaking down, and Meyler was regularly called in for repairs. The last reference to repairs is in 1833, and it seems likely that the 'hypocausts' were then abandoned and the students regained a right to a fire in the halls where they studied during the winter. Any remains of the system would of course have been demolished in the reconstruction of the 1950s.

Turning from buildings to grounds, the map of 1809 shows that Riverstown had a wall from the entrance gate at the Protestant church to the canal bank, which still stands, and on the north side from the church to slightly beyond the garden, most of it still there (Plate 2). There is no indication that the Stoyte property was walled. In the summer of 1824 a wall to enclose the whole college property was begun, from where the Riverstown wall ended at the canal. Doubts were raised whether the project might not be over-ambitious, but in June 1825 it was decided that 'the wall be continued round the college grounds exclusive of long meadow'. It was finished 'last week', Crotty informed the visiting Commissioners on 19 October 1826.[19] The wall appears very clearly on the 1838 Ordnance Survey map (Plate 5): nearly all of it still stands, except where part had to be demolished in the building of the new infirmary in the early 1860s. A little later the wall along the Galway road was built to enclose the long meadow.

Brewer, visiting the college in 1824, reported that 'behind the buildings a large proportion of the attached land is laid out in retired walks and admirably adapted to the uninterrupted exercise of the students.'[20] In reality things were a little rougher. The Carton and Ordnance Survey maps show the field boundaries still undisturbed, apart from the land occupied by buildings, the formal garden, admittedly a large one, and a walk on either side of the glade, a gravelled walk, Crotty told the Commissioners in 1826. But even the cemetery, blessed in 1817 to receive the remains of Francis Power, was still unenclosed (Maurice Ahern, who died in 1801, was buried in neighbouring Laraghbryan, where there is still an inscription to his memory; so presumably was Clotworthy Augustine McCormick, though he has no memorial; while the remains of Edward Ferris, buried there in 1809, were removed to the Vincentians in Castleknock in 1875).

Student bodies quickly give local names to their surroundings, and a few from the early days were preserved by John Gunn, who entered as a student in 1829 and became a dean in 1838. Some were gone even when he wrote in 1884: 'on the terrace near the senior infirmary there was a hawthorn called the third year's divines' bush, because the budding of its leaves in spring gave notice to that class, then the highest, to prepare for flitting'; while others that survived at least into living memory can lead his reader to much poring over maps and speculation on how placenames may migrate, when, for example, displaced by buildings: 'the wall that extends from the cemetery by the ball-courts formed in early days the college boundary on that side, before the enclosing wall was built. About the central part of it, between the two rows of trees, it was interrupted by a pond . . . long since closed up, its site being trace-able only by a slight depression in the ground.'[21]

Rules, Deans and Students

As student numbers climbed under the inexorable pressure of necessity, questions began to be posed not just about how to put a roof over their heads but about how to accommodate such numbers within the traditional idea of a seminary, for nothing like this had happened before. The Council of Trent had thought of a seminary in terms of an extension of each bishop's household, and the systematisers of the seventeenth century were agreed that between eighty and a hundred seminarians was the ideal number, large enough to make possible an adequate teaching staff, small enough to ensure that relationships between staff and students were kept on a personal level. Some tensions were only to be expected in so large a group of young men living under a strict discipline. When Crotty became President a number of students asked him to sanction a Literary and Historical Society. He agreed, but after a short time he began to have doubts and approached the Trustees, who suppressed it—quite rightly, said Delahogue, no doubt recalling the revolutionary clubs; these things cause nothing but trouble. But a year later the Trustees were considering what they called 'deliberate meetings' the students had recently held, and asking the President to deal with them. Three years later, in 1819, Dr Daniel Murray and Everard, now coadjutor in Cashel, were asked to go to the college 'to inquire into the grounds of various matters mentioned in the memorials,' which seems to have brought this particular problem to an end. But because of its size Maynooth was in danger of becoming impersonal: in 1822 the Trustees were grumbling about students being absent from common exercises on the pretext of being with a superior or professor, and in 1824 they absolutely forbade staff members to entertain students in their rooms. At the 1826 visitation the dean, Philip Dowley, said the college was simply too large; it was very hard 'to ascertain the dispositions of individual candidates', while Archbishop Murray said he was inclined to agree with those who thought that rather than enlarge Maynooth further a second college should be built to supply the extra priests all agreed were necessary. As has been seen, what happened was the Junior House.

When Murray visited the college in 1819 he seems to have taken the initiative in having a committee set up to revise the college statutes. In consisted of himself, the President, and an ex-president, Andrew Dunne, now again secretary to the Trustees. Their deliberations led to the publication of new statutes in 1820. By 1826, however, it appeared that in some respects the written statutes were being modified in practice. As well as requiring the President to consult with the deans and vice-president on the admission of students to Holy Orders, these statutes had also envisaged a kind of *ad hoc* council, consisting of the President, vice-president, deans and professors of theology, apparently to act as judge should a staff member be guilty of breach of statute. What happened in practice was that this second council met only to select Dunboyne students, for a concursus for a chair, and in some cases when it was proposed to expel a student, while the President, vice-president and deans became a real if non-statutory council which effectively ran the college.[22] As will be seen, this gave the deans a considerable voice in academic affairs, the theology staff a very small voice in administrative affairs, and other staff no voice at all. This imbalance was compounded by the fact that it was hard to find a dean other than a recently ordained student, and hard too to get even such a dean to stay long in the office. His responsibilities were quite heavy: as described by Crotty in 1826, they involved enforcing the discipline of the house, giving the students moral and religious instruction (once a fortnight, it would seem), normally conducting the retreat, accompanying the students on walks outside the college on Wednesday afternoon, attending morning and evening prayer and visiting students in their rooms.[23]

As has been seen, Coen's two successors as deans each lasted only a year. With the second of them, Andrew Hart, the Trustees had appointed a recently ordained student, Daniel Malone, with the title of 'sub-dean', soon changed to the perhaps less invidious title of 'junior dean'. Malone took over when Hart departed in July 1812, but he in turn accepted a lectureship in Moral Theology in August 1814. The Trustees immediately appointed Thomas Murphy, a priest of Waterford, with James Browne of Ferns, recently ordained, as 'sub-dean'. But Murphy ceased to be dean in April 1816, so Browne became dean, with John Cantwell of Meath, recently ordained, as 'sub-dean'. Browne accepted the chair of Scripture on 7 February 1816, and Cantwell became dean and Philip Dowley, a Dunboyne student not yet ordained, became 'sub-dean'. He became dean when Cantwell returned to his diocese in 1820, and though for quite a while to come deans tended to migrate to teaching posts Dowley remained and with him there was a hand on the helm.

This instability in the office of dean, coupled with the fact that the dean was too often in a position of authority over young men who had recently been his fellow-students, must have contributed to the instability that can be sensed in the early years of Crotty's presidency. The fact that the office of vice-president was ill-defined may have been a further complication. Perhaps significantly, Montague told the 1826 commission that he saw himself as discharging nearly the same duties as the deans. At this time, and indeed for a long time to come, the vice-president did not have teaching duties, but Montague continued to discharge much of the duties of his former office of bursar. As well, the sheer size of the student body must have emphasised the disciplinary aspect of the dean's office. He simply had to do things which nature resented: he had to visit students' rooms not merely when they were there but when they were not; outgoing mail passed through his hands, the Commissioners were told in 1826, though he did not open it, while incoming mail did not even pass through his hands, for this would have been illegal. In imposing penalties for breach of rule he had the protection of the informal council which had developed. The ultimate penalty was expulsion; in some cases the larger council was convened to enforce this penalty. Below this was the solemn warning or 'caveat' ('cat' in student slang) administered by the President in council: three of these automatically led to expulsion. The statutes had always provided for punishment by fine, but this soon ceased to be the practice, if indeed it ever was. Some regrets were expressed to the Commission in 1826 at the lack of any penalty less weighty than a presidential caveat, though it was admitted that the fear of exclusion from Orders was in practice sufficient.

The deans were assisted by monitors, selected by the dean from among the divinity students and approved by the President. They are mentioned in the first statutes of 1800. Their duties were to report absences from morning and night prayer, should the dean not be there, and to preside over study in the halls during the winter months. In earlier and less settled times they tried to exercise a wider authority, with unhappy results. Significantly, Dowley assured the visiting Commissioners in 1826 that there had been no complaints against monitors for the previous twelve or thirteen years, though one can accept that there were complaints in the past without agreeing with the verdict of that very suspect document, 'The Tears of Maynooth',[24] that when Everard was away the college was left 'to the guidance of a snarling dean and a merciless junto of monitors', the monitors being all from Connacht because the dean was Coen, the rhetoric ignoring the awkward fact that Coen had left before Everard arrived.

In 1826 Crotty was able to report to the Commission that there were now no more than three students in any room apart from fourteen in 'the long dormitory of the lay college, where the freshmen are'. Henry Inglis, who visited the college in 1834, spoke of a table 'plentifully and wholesomely supplied', though he must have been thinking primarily of the dinner, at which there was meat every day, except on Fridays and fast days, when there was 'eggs, bread and butter, pie or pudding'; breakfast and supper were simply bread and cocoa. Many details of student life were recorded by Charles W. Russell, the future distinguished professor and President, in letters to his sister Margaret during his student days between 1826 and 1835. He must have recovered them when she died in December 1877, for they have survived among his papers.[25] Among his culinary memories are going to the infirmary on Wednesday to avoid the salt ling and pea soup, and the eggs and butter at breakfast on Easter Sunday morning, a great treat after the long fast of Lent. Inglis describes the student accommodation as spartan: 'The dormitories of the students are precisely the same as those in the convents abroad. Each has a small window, a table, a chair, a little bedstead, a mattress and a crucifix'; but Russell recalls the flowers in his room—half a dozen geraniums, a 'monthly rose', and 'another very handsome thing', whose name he could not remember. Inglis went on to say: 'There is a large area for play ground at Maynooth; but I did not see many taking advantage of it. The students did not, in general, look like individuals fond of play.'[26] Yet the young Russell wrote to his sister in his second year describing 'a great bowling match', adding 'I spend a good deal of time at it'; the next year he told her 'we play a good deal of cricket'. In 1826 Crotty and Dowley had explained that the main recreation was walking along the two walks on either side of the glade; that the students also had access to 'one or two fields along the avenue' but that football, though formerly allowed, was now prohibited as 'dangerous and not very decorous' (probably a fairly apt description of the game as then played). There were, however, plenty of ball-courts, and the juniors played 'prisoner's bar'. Indoors students were allowed backgammon and chess in the corridors, but cards were strictly forbidden. Walks outside the college every Wednesday were accompanied by a dean, occasionally by a Dunboyne student. Students were free to choose and change their friends, but 'the students of the same diocese do often associate and walk together after breakfast and dinner, in parties of three or four', either because they had known one another before coming to the college or because they wished to cultivate an acquaintance knowing they would share the same mission afterwards. Students were allowed to go to the gate at fixed hours to meet tailors and shoemakers, and visitors were freely allowed during recreation, and at other times with the permission of a dean.[27]

During term, departures from the daily round were rare. Russell recalls St Patrick's Day in his second year, with an evening session in the refectory that began with 'a long spiritual exhortation' from a senior student and ended with a sing-song, the songs including, interestingly, 'Royal Charlie'. He recalled similar refectory festivities on Easter Sunday, 19 April 1829, to celebrate 'Catholic Emancipation', passed in Parliament six days before. He told Margaret 'Dr Crotty was in high spirits. Made a strong speech and sang an old song for us'. Things were a little freer during vacation. The seminary tradition had not encouraged vacations outside the college, but by the 1820s 'a considerable number' went away for the summer vacation, some for health reasons, others encouraged to go because it meant a little more money spared for the building programme. The permission of the student's bishop was required in each case, and while some bishops gave permission freely others did not. The students who remained enjoyed a more relaxed regime but were far from idle. However, there were fewer hours of study, few lectures (these mostly in things like elocution), no High Mass, Vespers, or weekly student sermon. There was more time than during term to use the library, and it was in fact much used.[28]

It is sometimes said that in an all-male society there is a danger of slipping into roughness, and there is some evidence of this. In 1820 and again in 1823 the Trustees called the President's attention to the need to keep the college clean inside and out and to see that the students dressed 'conformably to the regulations'. In 1828 they ordered the bursar to buy in bulk cloth better than what the students usually got for their college cloaks, and ordered that they be obliged to use it. In June 1830 they laid down that all students wear the clerical collar from the beginning of the next academic year. That September Russell complained to his sister that instead of a cravat they now had to wear a 'rabbat', as worn by Dublin priests. It consisted of a black silk covering for the shirt-front, with a piece of white muslin coming half way down. It was supplied by the Presentation Convent at an 'outrageous' price. More expense arose from the fact that the muslin had to be changed every day; and besides, the whole thing looked 'ridiculous'.

The great cholera epidemic of 1832 raised real fears in the college as elsewhere. A month before the first outbreaks in Belfast and Dublin in mid-March the Trustees ordered the setting up of a 'Board of Health', made up of the medical officers, the President, vice-president and deans, with the prefect of the Dunboyne, Charles McNally, and the professor of Sacred Scripture, Laurence Renehan. Renehan proved the guiding spirit of the committee, showing for the first time that gift of organisation which led him to the presidency of the college in 1845. This too must be the reason why the draft minutes of a meeting of this body are among the limited records that have survived from before 1845[29] (Renehan was the first President to leave records other than account-books or lists of ordinations and prizemen). These minutes reveal what by present-day standards would have to be called squalor, though contemporaries might not have seen it quite that way, except under the immediate threat of a cholera outbreak. The committee ordered the whole college to be whitewashed immediately and the corridors kept clean. It noted the practice of getting rid of waste by simply throwing it out the window, and ordered that 'a donkey-cart and butt' be employed to cart things away from the buildings. It then adjourned, but only until the following Thursday. The measures taken contributed to lessening the risk in overcrowded buildings—about 440 students packed into the front square, Riverstown, and either Rhetoric or Logic (one of these houses was built, the second was building). At any rate the college escaped the cholera, and it proved unnecessary even to send the students home.

The seminary tradition had centred on spiritual and intellectual formation, and on both of these the evidence given to the Commission in 1826 provides detail to an extent not available before. Spiritual formation centred on the chapel, but was not confined to it. The chapel at the north end of Long Corridor had from the beginning been regarded as temporary, but it had to serve for nearly a hundred years. As numbers grew it got more and more crowded, even when Junior House got its own chapel. This latter remained a plain box of a room, but Inglis in 1834 noted that an attempt had been made to decorate the main chapel: 'Everything within the college is plain, excepting the chapel, which is ornamented, as Catholic chapels are everywhere.'[30] The reconstruction of the early 1950s, while it faithfully copied Stapleton's stucco work, of necessity destroyed the wall paintings around the altar, and the chapel is now very plain indeed. There is no evidence as to when the paintings were made; the Trustees' minutes record only such things as the purchase of 'vestments, altar-linen and a carpet for the altar'. At the 1826 inquiry there is a slightly defensive note about the teaching of church music, from which it seems a fair inference that while it was taught it did not get a very high priority. It was normally a part-time task of a professor, but in 1826 it had to be entrusted temporarily to a student, who taught a group of fourteen or fifteen, who in turn taught the others.[31]

The traditional seminary rule called for silence at all times except at recreation. It is interesting to see two explanations being given for this, reflecting two different traditions. The President, Bartholomew Crotty, told the Commission that the purpose of this silence, even the night silence, was not religious but was for the maintenance of good external order in a large community; only the silence at retreats had religious significance. On the other hand the dean, Philip Dowley, a younger man, maintained that all seminary silence had a religious as well as disciplinary significance. There was, naturally, silence at meals, with a reader. At dinner there was read first a chapter of Scripture, then a religious book, and lastly the entry for the day in the Roman Martyrology (this proved to be a very enduring programme). There is not so much evidence on what students read for themselves. Charles McNally listed as among the books he had when he entered as a student in 1808 the Douai Bible, Hay's *Sincere Christian* and St Augustine's *Confessions*. Coyne's inexpensive Douai Bible in 1825 made it available to all, though it was noted that even before this nearly every student had his Bible. In 1827 Coyne had produced a cheap Breviary, primarily for students of the college. In 1824 the Trustees ordered him to print 500 copies of *A Memorial of the Christian Life* by Luis of Granada, the sixteenth-century Spanish Dominican who had developed a method of prayer he felt every Christian could practise. In continuation of the work begun by Francis Power, the vice-president, Michael Montague, twice a week took the Humanity and Rhetoric classes combined through *Butler's*

Catechism. He had begun by introducing them to the Scriptures through *Reeves's Bible History*, but moved on to get them to read the historical books of the Old Testament and as much of the Pentateuch as there was time for.[32]

Students were expected to go to confession once a fortnight, and to communicate as often as advised by their director. With the exception of the President, all priests in the college acted as confessors. Students chose their confessor at the beginning of the year, and while they might change him if they felt they had good reason frequent change was naturally discouraged. There were two retreats, in September at the beginning of the year and before ordinations at the end. The dean normally conducted the retreat, but someone from outside the college was sometimes asked: in his evidence to the Commission Father Kenney from Clongowes said he had been invited three or four times since he had left thirteen years before. The retreat-master conducted the morning meditation, and gave one religious conference each day. The rest was spent in private devotion. It was the duty of the dean to give the regular spiritual talks. It may be that they were not given altogether regularly. A student in evidence went so far as to say that they were given only occasionally, that there had been none in the year 1825/26, and none so far in the current year.[33] In 1818 the Trustees had asked the President to invite superiors and professors and 'such Dunboyne scholars as he may think proper' to give religious instruction to the students occasionally.

There was long suspicious quizzing by the Commissioners on the Sodality of the Sacred Heart, introduced in 1822 by the authority of the Archbishop on the recommendations of the Trustees, and it might be sensed that they were not altogether mollified when told that it was a voluntary society and that the sole obligation of its members was to say some prayers, for they still sensed a kind of secret Jesuitry. Lastly, perhaps small but perhaps significant, in that same year 1822 the Trustees ordered the Angelus bell to be rung three times a day, reflecting developments in the country which gave all the churches the right to ring a bell to call people publicly to prayer.

Studies

In France, the best point of comparison with Ireland, the standard seminary course in the early nineteenth century was four years, two years studying Philosophy and two years of Theology. The aim was to produce a man of pastoral piety who had learned his trade well. It was not so important that his textbooks might have devoted more space to problems of the past as compared with those of the present: that is the way of textbooks, and in any case these problems did not greatly concern the priest in the parish. From the beginning, however, Maynooth had three years of theology; indeed in 1817 a proposal emanated from the Trustees to extend the course to four years. Delahogue, now coming to the end of his teaching career but a respected elder statesman, pointed out the problems. The fact was that because of the needs of the dioceses bishops were ordaining students before they had completed a three-year course of theology, and if the course were extended to four years it had to be presumed that even more would be ordained before they had finished it.[34] Although the Trustees in 1820 set up a committee to arrange a four-year course, the practical difficulties must have seemed too great, and no change was made at the time.

The college offered courses extending over four years before students began theology. About half the entrants were assigned to the class of Humanity, a year spent studying Classics for those whose previous schooling was considered deficient (quite a number of entrants in the early years had studied at Protestant classical schools, because there were no Catholic schools convenient for them). Nearly all the remainder entered the class of Rhetoric, another year of the Classics, though a handful were judged sufficiently prepared to begin Philosophy. The entrance examination programme for 1821[35] listed the classical texts required for admission to Humanity. For Rhetoric there were still more texts, for Philosophy more again, and nothing else. The concern of the Trustees about entrance standards is shown in a minute of June 1820 requiring that every student admitted spend his first year in Humanity before joining a higher class, while the pressing need for priests is reflected in a minute just twelve months later saying that if a bishop who was very short of priests made a written request his students might pass directly from Humanity into Philosophy. In 1829 additional requirements for entrance were laid down—English grammar, geography and arithmetic for Humanity, ancient history and algebra for Rhetoric, and English and Irish history and six books of Euclid for Philosophy—but the successive minutes postponing these requirements show how hard it was to insist on them.

Professors of Humanity were normally promoted to the chair of Rhetoric, where they were more inclined to stay, though some moved into Theology. In both courses there were nine lectures a week. Humanity was a grind over texts and composition, making up for deficiencies in previous education. Jeremiah Donovan, the professor of Rhetoric, gave an interesting account to the Commissioners of the course he had specially devised for ecclesiastical students. He began the year with texts such as Quintilian, Aristotle and Longinus, and then in February or March he gave lessons in English elocution, taught them how to compose in English and Latin, and how to write the exordium of a sermon.[36] English and French were amalgamated in 1820 in the person of Christopher Boylan. In the words of Bartholomew Crotty in 1826, the classes in English, French and Irish 'constitute no addition to time but are merely incidental to certain periods of the other classes'.[37] There were four classes a week in English, held in the evening between five and six. Up to 1824 they had been attended by all students of the first three years, but after that by the freshmen only irrespective of the class they had matriculated into. The name 'English Elocution' tended to cling to the course, and describes it fairly aptly: students were taught to compose and declaim. At this period, no further formal instruction was given in these matters, apart from someone who might be engaged on a temporary basis, sometimes during the summer vacation, and what practical experience might be gained by students of Theology when they delivered their sermons. But the formal instruction does seem to have been given far too early in the course, and this would appear to mark a decline from earlier days. French was even more peripheral than English, two classes a week, on Tuesdays an hour before breakfast and on Saturdays at one o'clock. It was claimed that nearly all got a reading knowledge and some got a speaking knowledge, but inevitably French influence was fading.

Irish had the same auxiliary role. The classes were attended by students of the second-year theology class, or rather those of them from parts of the country where it would be useful to them as priests. It was fortunate in its first professor, Paul O'Brien, a distinguished scholar and a man of many other gifts as well. What he could inspire in his students was shown in two publications that appeared shortly after his early death in 1820. The first was an edition of Donlevy's *Irish Catechism*, published in 1822, a fairly thorough reworking of the original, published in Paris in 1742. The editor was John McEncroe, slightly disguised in the college records as 'McIncroe'. He had been ordained for the diocese of Cashel in 1819. Shortly after publishing the *Catechism* he spent seven years with Bishop England in Charleston in the United States, and though he returned in poor health he left for Australia in 1834, where he had a long and distinguished career. The second publication was a translation of *The Imitation of Christ* by Daniel O'Sullivan, ordained for the diocese of Cork in 1822. The Trustees took 200 copies of the *Catechism* and 300 of the *Imitation* for use in the Irish class in the college. Unfortunately, Paul O'Brien found no successor. When William Crolly, past student and professor and now Bishop of Down and Connor, told the Commission in 1826 that there were not many parts of Ireland where instruction in Irish was required, and in Ulster only 'in those rough districts, where the people are confined to mountains and places of that kind,'[38] he gives the impression of merely stating a melancholy fact, and indeed the Irish language was facing what was nearly a terminal decline. O'Brien's successor, Martin Loftus (1820–27) is a shadowy figure, but that he had a real interest in instruction through Irish appears from the fact that he published a bilingual catechism in 1839. When he left it was indeed hard to find anyone. James Tully, ordained for Tuam in 1825, was reluctantly appointed in 1828, the Trustees reluctant because they did not consider him a good candidate, the candidate reluctant because he was far more interested in going to a parish than in teaching Irish. Until his death on 2 October 1876 he presided over the decline of the language, a little sadly, one gets the impression.

The next step after Rhetoric was Rational Philosophy, Logic, Metaphysics and Ethics, usually abbreviated to 'Logic'. It was a long course to cover in a single year, even with nine lectures a week, but there was only a short treatment of Ethics on the ground that this course would be covered in Moral Theology.

The first professors had been French, Andrew Darré (1795–1801) and François Anglade (1802–10). When Anglade moved to Moral Theology there were a few years of instability. William Crolly, appointed professor in 1810, left to become parish priest of Belfast in 1812. His successor, Patrick McNicholas, became president of the lay college in 1815. Charles McNally (1815–29) stabilised the situation. In 1810 Anglade was far advanced in writing a textbook which was to have a long run of life. Volume I (Logic) was published by Fitzpatrick in 1813 and volumes II (Metaphysics) and III (Ethics) in 1815. It derived substantially from a noted course prepared for the seminary in Lyons ('Philosophia Lugdunensis'), which in turn drew heavily on the *Ars Cogitandi* of the seventeenth-century author Pierre Nicole. The course was taught in Latin—rightly so, Delahogue maintained: the University of Paris had never allowed a French text, and there was all the more reason for excluding English texts, full of the principles of scepticism and invectives against popery.[39] Nevertheless—or so the Commissioners were told—the students had access to Locke, especially his *Essay on the Human Understanding*, though their attention was called to a few points in which he was considered unorthodox.[40]

Then followed a full year of 'Natural Philosophy', mathematics up to and including conic sections and quadratic equations being taught until January or February, followed by experimental science. The quality of its professors, especially Nicholas Callan, was important among the reasons why this legacy of the Catholic Enlightenment established itself so firmly at Maynooth. The first professor, Pierre-Justin Delort (1795–1801), was very distinguished indeed, but he did not stay. He began his classes in 1795, with three pupils and no 'philosophical apparatus'. It was not a situation to content a person of Delort's calibre, and when things began to look better in France in 1801 he obtained leave to go there 'on family business' and did not return. He was succeeded by André Darré (1801–13). He too had to lecture on experimental science without having anything to experiment with, but he did write a *Treatise on Plane and Solid Geometry* which, as revised by his successors, remained in use in the college until the end of the century. It was unusual among textbooks used in Great Britain or Ireland in that it was not based on Euclid. But Darré too was not a contented exile and his health was poor. He sought leave of absence in 1806, from which he returned, and again in 1813, and this time he did not. His successor, Cornelius Denvir (1813–26), was the first of the Irishmen. He was fortunate when in 1815 'a person called Barclay, who went through the country as a lecturer in experimental philosophy' offered his apparatus to the college for £250. It was a big sum, given the overall resources, but the Trustees provided it. Denvir, 'who had a turn for mechanics', improved this apparatus and added to it. He resigned to return to his diocese in 1826 and was succeeded by Nicholas Callan, professor from 1826 until his death in 1864. Over these years he played a distinguished part indeed in the development of applied electricity. By 1833 he had given his students a textbook, *Electricity and Galvanism*, and they no longer had to buy the expensive *Cambridge Course*.

In Theology too the Irish replaced the Frenchmen. Delahogue retired in 1820 and died on 9 March 1827, aged eighty-eight. Anglade retired in 1828 and died on 12 April 1834, aged seventy-six. Each found 'a grave in green Kildare' in the college cemetery. Delahogue had taught the whole course in Dogmatic Theology, and Anglade the whole course in Moral, to a single class of all the divinity students. In 1818 Delahogue provided details of the courses, as taught, he said, since he had come twenty years before:

Cycle I:
Dogma: De religione naturali et revelata, cum confutatione Dr Gibbon.
Moral: De iure et iustitia: de contractibus et restitutione; de legibus et similia.

Cycle II:
Dogma: De ecclesia.
Moral: De matrimonio, quoad dogma et moralem praxim; de decalogo et ecclesiae praeceptis, de variis statibus vitae.

Cycle III:
Dogma: De sacramentis in genere, de Eucharistia, de Trinitate et Incarnatione.
Moral: De Poenitentia, quoad dogma et moralem praxim, de censuris, irregularitatibus, purgatorio et indulgentiis, de actibus humanis, conscientia et peccatis.[41]

Though some parts of what would be regarded as a complete theology course were omitted, it was a hard grind, nine lectures a week to a class that grew unmanageably large. Students in their first year got tuition from the junior lecturers, if such were available, but, Delahogue claimed, never before, either in France or elsewhere, had he seen so much demanded of students in so little time; but despite this he found them excellent. The Trustees introduced a fundamental change in 1828 when they appointed an extra professor of Theology and put one professor in charge of each class. The classes now were much more manageable though still large, but the professors had twice as many lectures, each having to cover the complete year's course in Dogma and Moral.

The teaching of Scripture had great problems. The first three appointments were short-lived, for different reasons: Thomas Clancy, Francis Eloi and Matthias Crowley. In 1810 Peter Magennis, a Dominican, had been appointed vice-president, possibly at Everard's instigation, when Francis Power retired. Magennis had been successively student, professor and rector at the Dominican college of Corpo Santo in Lisbon from 1782 to 1799. It is not clear when he returned to Ireland, nor what he did on his return, nor indeed what led to his appointment in Maynooth. Then Archbishop Murray insisted on having Peter Kenney as his vice-president, and Magennis took up the chair of Scripture. He left the college in 1813, and when he returned in 1815 he was reappointed to Scripture but shortly afterwards was named 'Prefect of the Senior Scholars', in which capacity, according to the college account-books, he was paid until the beginning of 1817, when he left for good, having, according to a Dominican source, clashed with Delahogue and Anglade, whose teaching he had criticised.[42] Meantime, Christopher Boylan, ordained in 1815, had been selected to study Hebrew, and received private tuition for eight months from John Barrett, professor of Greek and Oriental Languages and vice-provost of Trinity College. Boylan was appointed professor of Oriental Languages in Maynooth in June 1816. It seems clear that this was an over-ambitious appointment, given the slenderness of the college resources: what is quite unclear is why James Browne, ordained in 1812 and appointed junior dean in 1814, ended up as professor of Scripture in 1817, while Christopher Boylan had to be content with the post of professor of English Rhetoric.

With James Browne the teaching of Scripture was stabilised. Both he and the President, Bartholomew Crotty, gave details of the course to the Commission in 1826.[43] It extended over a three-year cycle, with all the theology students forming one class, meeting twice a week on Wednesday and Saturday. The professor lectured in English, on the Vulgate text, because this was the basis of the commentary of the textbook, Menochius. While it was claimed that the Greek text was 'constantly referred to', it does appear that much of the drilling in Greek in the early years was not fully utilised in Scripture study. The texts studied in detail were almost all from the New Testament: Matthew, John, Romans, Corinthians, Hebrews, Timothy and Titus. Crotty adds the Pentateuch and Psalms, the latter important because they formed a great part of the priest's daily office, the Pentateuch, it is reasonable to suspect, treated more selectively. Perhaps significantly, he added that the Messianic prophecies were treated of in the class of Dogmatic Theology. Browne explained that it was part of his duty after the Wednesday class to hear the students who were to give exhortations on the Gospel the following Sunday. Every student in the three theology classes took his turn in Sunday preaching, in the presence of members of the staff, one of whom was invited to comment at the end, but because of the great numbers of students the first-year theology class usually escaped.

It would be a mistake to suggest that the delay in setting up a Scripture class was based on a conviction that Scripture was of secondary importance, for the problems were very real. Nevertheless there was some kind of conviction that all the good pastor needed to know, even if not quite all truth in heaven and on earth, was contained in the textbooks of Dogmatic and Moral Theology. This was certainly true of Canon Law: the practical questions were treated in Moral Theology, and any deeper study could await the postgraduate stage for the select few. The same was true of Ecclesiastical History, which was taken seriously in only a handful of Catholic seminaries. In 1818

Delahogue had strongly opposed any separate lectures in history, saying that the course was already overloaded and that the students would meet the important issues, all they would in fact remember, in their general theology studies. His own course on natural and revealed religion included a 'confutation of Dr Gibbon'; and in the same way the messianic prophecies were treated in the theology class. But in the near future both Scripture and History were to develop independent existences, and the response of he seminary course was dilatory. For the moment, Ecclesiastical History was relegated to the postgraduate years, and even when it was later introduced as a full undergraduate subject it was not easy to convince students of its practical utility, in its more esoteric parts at any rate. In his reminiscences, Dean Gunn recalled a student being asked about the Three Chapter controversy, admittedly at all times a distant land to the Irish seminarian. 'The answer not seeming sufficient, the professor asked the question a second and third time, with the same result, when the student said: "I believe, sir, in the three answers I have given I have replied indirectly that I don't know anything of the matter".'[44] Yet there was an interest among many of the staff in the ecclesiastical history of Ireland. William Kelly, a young staff member, writing to a Franciscan in his native Wexford on 14 April 1834, said: 'The writing of an ecclesiatical History of Ireland is a matter that has been talked of in the college these last eight years. Mr Boylan [a member of the staff from 1816 to 1828] commenced a continuation of Lanigan. He was unable to proceed for lack of materials.' The next year Patrick J. Carew, a professor of Theology, published *An Ecclesiastical History of Ireland from the Introduction of Christianity . . . to the Commencement of the Thirteenth Century*. It was heavily dependent on John Lanigan's *Ecclesiastical History of Ireland*, published in 1822, and did not wear as well as it.[45]

The evidence given to the Commission provided more detail on the teaching method.[46] The professor appointed what was to be studied, and explained any points which he felt might be obscure. The students listened, but now that they had textbooks normally did not take notes. The next day the professor called on individuals to explain the issues. The language was Latin, though it was admitted that English was allowed 'more freely' in Philosophy than in Theology, which does seem to imply that even in Theology communication could so break down in Latin that it was necessary to fall back on English. The rule laid down that students were not admitted to the library until they had spent four years in college, but in practice all students of Theology were admitted, and students in Natural Philosophy had a small library of their own. However, the students had little time for reading beyond the textbooks, which were bought in bulk by the bursar and sold to individuals through the library. Nevertheless, when students went to the gate to meet tailors and shoemakers there were also booksellers there, and, according to one of the professors, 'it often happens that clergymen, especially in distant parts of the country, send their books to the college to be sold, and they are brought into the public hall and a sort of auction gone through.'[47] It is possible that the young men buying the books may sometimes have wondered why their elders were selling them, particularly those from 'distant parts of the country'.

Dunboyne and Degrees

It has been seen that the first income from the Dunboyne bequest appears in the college accounts in 1811, that the first two scholars were admitted in January 1813, that a special building for them was given priority, and that it was probably ready in the autumn of 1815. The endowment provided twenty scholars with a stipend of £25 a year in addition to their free commons. These were nominated by the President and approved by his council for a three-year course of study. They might be ordained priests at the end of the second year. In its early years, however, the Dunboyne Establishment was usually about half full. The principal reason for this was that bishops needed priests as soon as their normal course was finished: they were indeed sometimes compelled to ordain them even earlier. There was the further reason that organising a course of studies was difficult. There were only two professors of Theology, both of them old men who had no more assistance than two young lecturers appointed in 1814. It is not surprising, then, that the committee appointed in June 1813, consisting of the President, these two professors, and the secretary to the Trustees, and ordered to draw up a programme of studies, was dissolved in June 1816 with nothing done. At the same meeting the Trustees provisionally adopted a report by Peter Magennis. As has been seen, he was 'Prefect of the Senior Scholars' from 1815, probably September, when they moved into their own quarters. But Magennis left the college early in 1817, and the Dunboyne scholars reverted to the unsatisfactory condition of being left very much to themselves to revise the whole course of theology they had already studied as undergraduates.

It was in these circumstances that an application to the Roman Congregation of Propaganda for authority to confer degrees came to be mooted. The initiative seems to have come from the four archbishops rather than from the Trustees as a body. Though no copy of the application has come to light, the Roman reply, dated 30 August 1817, was businesslike.[48] It asked for details of all courses, an assurance of the orthodoxy of the professors, because there had been complaints on this head, and an assurance that the civil power would approve. The Trustees at their meeting in June 1818 were sufficiently encouraged to commission Troy to apply for authority to confer the baccalaureate at the end of the first year of Dunboyne studies, the licentiate after the second year and the doctorate after the third. The initial response to this gave no hint of a problem. Propaganda wrote on 4 July to say that it now appeared that the reports of unsound doctrine were false, and that the petition would be granted as soon as a list of the books used in the college was supplied. Another letter followed on 12 September saying that the Pope had granted the privilege, and that an account of the foundation, studies, and privileges of the college should now be sent.[49] In the event, Troy sent to Rome a complete set of the text-books in Theology and Philosophy. They arrived at the end of August 1819 and were given to a theological consultor of the Congregation, Pietro Ostini of the Collegio Urbano. When he saw the bulk of the unfamiliar tomes Ostini asked for a lot of time, and he took it. Long before he reported, Maynooth's application was in deep trouble.

It began on the morning of 12 October, when the Dominican Master-General sent to Propaganda a copy of a letter he had just received from Dublin.[50] Much of it concerned Dominican affairs, and Maynooth may have come in because of the unhappy experiences there of the Dominican Peter Magennis, but the college was attacked as a hotbed of Gallicanism, inculcated by its French professors. The letter that did most damage, however, came from Bishop Walsh of Waterford at the end of 1819 or the very beginning of 1820.[51] Walsh was in deep trouble himself. He had got involved with factions in his diocese, and had been summoned to Rome to explain himself. He was not allowed to return, and died in Rome on 1 October 1821. He was no friend of Maynooth, and some of what he said is either ill-informed or malicious, but he did have some points of substance to make. He listed the priests ordained in Maynooth who had apostatised (they seem to come disproportionately from his own diocese). He gave what he claimed were instances of successive appeals to the 'Protestant' Visitors—confusing, either maliciously or in igno-rance, the Visitors and the Trustees—and asserted that the college had been plagued by disputes since its foundation. He pointed to its links with the gov-ernment, in particular its heavy dependence on an annual grant, and said that if it were given power to confer degrees without the formal approval of the government, Parliament and Trinity College, the least that might be expected was the loss of the grant, followed inevitably by the collapse of the college. Finally, he demanded that nothing be done without the consent of all the bish-ops, not merely the eleven who were Trustees. He followed this up by for-warding to Propaganda a letter he received from John Hogan OFM, dated Dublin 22 May 1820, containing the standard attacks on the teaching in Maynooth.[52] Meantime, in a letter of 24 April 1820 Troy had repeated his request that Maynooth be given authority to confer degrees, as part of his rou-tine dealings with Propaganda, and without appearing to sense any danger,[53] even though news of danger had reached Maynooth, from where Christopher Boylan wrote to a friend in Rome at the end of January 1820 regretting the bad opinion held of Maynooth there and pointing out that Delahogue could only be expected to adopt the Gallican position on matters open to discussion and that it was publicly known that his 'coadjutor and presumptive successor, Mr McHeal', was in perfect conformity with Bellarmine, as were Browne and the other young Irishmen.[54]

The Trustees considered the situation at their summer meeting, and the

Archbishops of Armagh and Dublin were deputed to reply to the charges. Archbishop Curtis of Armagh wrote to Propaganda on 28 July.[55] He said he had recently been present in Maynooth as Visitor and Trustee. He found everything there in impressive good order, with no reason for complaint. The Trustees were amazed to hear that fellow-Irishmen had spread reports in Rome that the teaching of the college was hostile to the Holy See. The power to grant degrees had been requested because Maynooth was now the only seminary the Irish Church had, and he felt that he and the other bishops might have been trusted to be vigilant custodians. The textbooks used there had been sent to Rome by Archbishop Troy, and there had been no word of complaint. Of course, Delahogue followed the 'view of the Paris schools' in the matter of papal infallibility, but in practice the Irish Catholics were ultramontanes, and even the French were heading in that direction.

There was sound common sense in this. The current political scene indicated that if the Irish were to develop doubts on the Pope it would be because it was feared he might not be sound on the Veto question, and not because of theological opinion in the Sorbonne before 1789. In this matter the evidence given to the 1826 Commission is particularly revealing, especially that of Anglade and MacHale.[56] Both agreed that the first Gallican article, denying the Pope power in civil and temporal matters, had always been taught at Maynooth. In regard to the second, on the superiority of a general council to the Pope, Anglade said it was discussed as an open question, the arguments for and against being given, but MacHale said that on this point the Gallican teaching went too far in that it set up as a general rule a position adopted at the Councils of Basel and Constance to meet a specific problem, and he concluded that in Maynooth 'we have neither taught the ultramontane doctrine, nor the liberties of the Gallican church.' The two were agreed in accepting the third article, that the exercise of papal authority should be moderated by accepted Canon Law, MacHale however rather grudgingly: 'I suppose it is held at Maynooth', while as to the fourth, the personal infallibility of the Pope, he merely said that on this there were different opinions and it was not an article of faith, which is in fact the position he had learned from Delahogue in his treatise on the Church.

Yet even Gallicanism of this moderate hue was no longer acceptable in Rome, especially now that the French themselves seemed to be abandoning it. In replying to Curtis on 9 September Propaganda confined itself to saying that it was pleased to hear that things were going so well at Maynooth, but that Delahogue's Gallicanism was not acceptable at a time when Félicité de Lamennais was more representative of the French church. The Maynooth textbooks were still being examined, and an answer would be given when a verdict on them was reached. The matter was raised at a full meeting of the Congregation on 12 February 1821, but there was still no word from Ostini, and the only decision taken was to await his report.[57] At least that was the answer given to Archbishops Curtis and Troy, though a sense of growing suspicion and perhaps even hostility might be detected in the fact that letters were sent to a number of other Irish bishops on the same day detailing the charges made against Maynooth and suggesting that they might offer an independent opinion. A week later the same request was sent to Curtis and Troy.[58] No reply from Troy has come to light, and it is possible he did not send one. Curtis, however, replied on 30 July, having clearly taken time to think things out and consult the other Trustees. He said that everyone he consulted was agreed that it was necessary to give Maynooth authority to grant degrees, in view of the loss of the foreign colleges. There had been troubles there in the past, but they had been firmly dealt with. The Lord Lieutenant had assured Archbishop Troy that there would be no opposition from the government or from Trinity College, after Troy had explained to him that the Maynooth degrees would have no civil effects. Nevertheless, he added, it would probably be safer if Maynooth were not yet constituted a university but merely got authority from the Pope to confer degrees: university status might come later, if things went well.[59]

A month before this letter was written, on 24 June, Ostini's long-delayed report arrived in Propaganda, nearly two years after it had been commissioned. It is a lengthy document, most of it taken up with Delahogue's writings. He goes into much detailed criticism of his admittedly moderate Gallicanism, which he inevitably found unacceptable. On all matters he found him orthodox, and indeed conceded that there was much to praise. His only criticism of Anglade was that in his treatise on Ethics he followed a system of probabiliorism verging on rigorism. He admitted he had not read Bailly, and contented himself with quoting a eulogy of a new French edition from a newspaper entitled *L'ami de la religion et du foi*.[60] The officials of Propaganda considered this report satisfactory, and the Cardinal Prefect wrote to Curtis on 8 September 1821 saying that the Pope would be approached for the authority to confer degrees. However, an oral assurance from the Lord Lieutenant was not sufficient: it must be given formally and in writing.[61] No corresponding letter was sent to Troy, though Curtis assumed, not unnaturally, that he had got one. When he found he had not, he sent him his own letter from Propaganda, with a covering note dated 8 November, in which he gave as his opinion that the prospects in Rome looked good. He had discussed the situation with Lord Fingall, but had found him apprehensive and cool, but, he said, the Trustees could consider the whole matter at the next meeting.[62] The minutes of this meeting, however, contain no mention of the proposed degrees, and it must be assumed that the matter was shelved. It is worth noting, however, that this was not because of Roman fears of Maynooth's orthodoxy but because of Irish fears of political repercussions if the government were asked for formal approval.

The attacks on the teaching in Maynooth did not stop, and found a listening ear in Rome in the new secretary of Propaganda, Pietro Caprano, appointed 11 March 1823. It was not just that Maynooth was too rigorous: curiously, it was also too lax. On 10 May 1825 John Furlong, an Augustinian friar in Callan, Co. Kilkenny, wrote complaining of the spread in Ireland of the detestable doctrine, first taught by Delahogue in Maynooth, that Protestants who were in good faith could be saved.[63] At the meeting of the Trustees in June 1825, Daniel Murray, now Archbishop of Dublin, read a letter from one of his priests, Michael Blake, who had gone to Rome the previous September to try to reopen the Irish College there. It would be advisable, Blake suggested, for the Irish bishops to write immediately to Rome to efface the fatal impression created there concerning the doctrine, discipline and morals in the Irish seminaries, especially in Maynooth. Archbishop Curtis replied on behalf of the Trustees in two very strong letters to Blake, dated 27 June and 3 July 1825, knowing they would be passed on to Caprano, as indeed they were.[64] He recalled that some years ago he had several times written to Propaganda on Maynooth, and the Cardinal Prefect had replied expressing satisfaction. The Trustees were most indignant that these charges had been revived by Caprano. They would have refuted the calumnies long ago had they received them officially, instead of having to suffer the 'degrading indignity' of becoming aware of them 'by the contemptible medium of popular rumour'. The second letter, a week later, shows his anger still hot, and must have been written only because he felt there was something he had forgotten or not made sufficiently clear in the first. Caprano's 'heavy charges', he wrote, were based merely on the fact that 'worthy old Mons. de la Hogue dictated to his disciples at Maynooth the Parisian propositions, the only ones, perhaps, he knew, or could explain. The thing is absurd. That Gallican opinion is not more taught or adopted at Maynooth or on the mission of Ireland that at Rome. It is a mere abstract scholastic question.' He did not convince Caprano. It has already been noted that when it was proposed to make Thomas Kelly Bishop of Dromore objections were raised on the grounds that his orthodoxy was suspect because he was teaching theology at Maynooth, and when on 29 May 1826 it was finally decided to appoint him a rider was added 'that Monsignor Secretary insist by all convenient means that the teaching in Maynooth be changed.'[65] However, Caprano moved from Propagnada in 1828, and the matter does not seem to have been pursued further; but a suspicion of Maynooth orthodoxy lingered in Rome.

Meanwhile Maynooth had to organise its postgraduate school without having the authority to give degrees. In June 1822 the Trustees set up a committee of Archbishops Curtis and Murray, with the President, Bartholomew Crotty, to make proposals. Murray was the driving force, as is clear from two letters, dated 4 July 1822 and 30 May 1823, which have survived in the diocesan archives of Kildare and Leighlin, and show that he sought and got the active help of the influential bishop, James Doyle. The committee reported a year later, in June 1823, and the Trustees accepted their proposals with a few minor modifications and the major one of explicitly adding courses in Canon Law and Ecclesiastical History. The 'senior scholars' were to be proposed by the President and approved by his council. They were to have an allowance of £25 a year in addition to commons. The course was to last for three years, but those who did not give satisfaction might be culled after the first year, and again after the second. The proposal that outstanding students might stay on after the third year, as ordained priests, with an increased allowance and acting as tutors, was not formally adopted, but there do seem to have been a few of them, though not many. There was detailed provision for the spiritual life of the students, more detail in fact than for their academic courses, though it was specifically laid down that they were to be specially trained in writing in English at a popular level.[66]

At the same meeting the Trustees appointed Nicholas Slevin prefect and librarian, two offices which were to be conjoined for a long time. Slevin was a wandering scholar, ordained in the Irish College, Salamanca, in 1804 as a priest of the diocese of Clogher. He taught there for a number of years, then returned to Ireland, but after a brief stay went to Rome in 1815 and back again to Salamanca in 1821, where he taught for a year until ill-health forced him to return to Ireland. His appointment to Maynooth must have been on the re-commendation of Archbishop Curtis, who had been rector of Salamanca dur-ing his student years. He put up an impressive theological performance at the Commission of 1826. It was he, then, who put together the first 'Dunboyne' course, though he remains a curiously elusive figure. His students were allowed much time for the reading they had not had time for in their earlier years.[67] He met them four times a week, twice for Theology, once for Canon Law and once for Ecclesiastical History, while the professor of Scripture took them once a week for Hebrew, a class open to all theology students but in practice attended by few except the senior scholars.[68] A schedule for the January examinations of 1825 has survived. It lists thirty-two questions on the canon law of benefices, seven question on Ecclesiastical History, and fifteen 'theses' in Theology, which indicate that what they were principally expected to do was to get a more mature grasp of what they had earlier studied.[69] Slevin's health was always poor, and when he died he was succeeded on 13 February 1829 by Charles McNally. McNally was a Maynooth alumnus, ordained for the diocese of Clogher in 1813 and appointed professor of Logic in 1815. With him the highest theological post in the college was occupied by a home product.

The library had grown slowly, for in truth there was not much money to spend. Small as it was, it does not seem to have been successfully catalogued until it was transferred to the top floor of the Dunboyne building, or indeed until Nicholas Slevin was appointed librarian in 1823. He gave a detailed account to the Commission in 1826.[70] He said he had two assistants, Dunboyne students. They actually looked after the library, under Slevin's superintendence. It was open for four hours on Monday, Tuesday, Thursday and Friday and until one o'clock on Saturday: it was closed on Wednesdays and Sundays. It was also open during vacation. Students could not borrow books, but there was free access to the shelves. While there was no list of pro-hibited books, they were not allowed to read 'books of bad tendency'. He esti-mated that it contained about 10,000 volumes. As Brewer described it in 1824, it was 'in a retired part of the original building . . . a neat and eligible, but not extensive apartment, containing numerous theological works, but at present lamentably defective in other branches of literature.'[71] In 1823 Dr Meyler had been paid £80 to 'ventilate [it] with hot air', but, as has been seen, he was not always successful in such operations.

The Maynooth Priest, c. 1835

In 1834 the English traveller Henry Inglis gave as a very considered opinion:

> I found the old foreign-educated priest, a gentleman; a man of frank, easy deportment, and good general information; but by no means, in general, so good a Catholic, as his brother of Maynooth: he, I found, either a coarse, vulgar-minded man, or a stiff, close, and very conceited man; but in every instance, Popish to the backbone: learned, I dare say, in theology; but profoundly ignorant of all that liberalises the mind: a hot zealot in religion; and fully impressed with, or professing to be impressed with a sense of his consequence and influence. I need not surely say, that I found exceptions; that I found some, whom the monk-ish austerities, and narrow education of Maynooth, had left unscathed; and that I found very many—I might say, the greater proportion—who, notwithstanding the defects of education which clove to them, were charitable and heedful of the poor; and who grudged no privations in the exercise of their religious duties.[72]

It is certainly condescending, but it is not uncomplimentary, and the contrast between the Maynooth priest and his foreign-educated predecessor (the youngest of these now nearly forty years ordained) may be attributed too much to the college and too little to a changing society and the gap that always exists between the older and the younger. It is noteworthy that he does not mention the political role of the priest, and from the evidence given to the 1826 Commission—where, of course, it was necessary to speak guardedly—the student body does not appear as greatly interested in politics. Newspapers had been forbidden since some students had got into the habit of writing anonymously in them earlier in the century, but it was accepted that some might come in in the post, which was delivered directly to students, and this did not seem to cause great concern. One witness said the students were natu-rally in favour of 'Emancipation', that they occasionally spoke in support of 'Repeal' or against the Established Church, but that their conversation between themselves was normally either about their class work or banter.[73]

Not merely the students but the superiors and servants had to take the 1774 Oath of Allegiance before being admitted to the college, and the first statutes in 1800 list a duly attested certificate of having taken the oath among the documents each freshman must present on arrival.[74] Inevitably, students turned up without the certificate, and these were taken to a magistrate to take the oath. In 1826 Bishop William Crolly testified that this was already the practice when he entered in 1801: he said the oath was explained to them beforehand and no-one had any scruple in taking it. Others testified in 1826 that 'for many years' it had been the practice that students entering in September took the oath collectively in the courthouse in Maynooth at the quarter sessions the following January in 'something like a loft where the students all stood up . . . on both sides of the courthouse'. The dean handed a list of students to the clerk of the peace, and when he returned to Dublin he transmitted individual certificates to the dean or bursar (a bundle of such certificates for 1833 has chanced to survive) (Plate 14).[75] By 1826 it was being suggested that some of the more scrupulous individuals were getting unhappy about the oath. There were clauses in it that Catholics had found offensive even in 1774, and they grew more offensive as the years passed. The Commissioners who visited the college in the 1850s expressed their view that the oath was not so administered as 'to give proper solemnity to the occasion'. It was in truth becoming an anachronism, and when in 1868 an Act of Parliament (31 & 32 Vict., c. 72) did not mention Maynooth in its list of those required to take oaths on various occasions the Maynooth oath was quietly dropped.

There still exists in the college a bust of King George III, sometimes referred to with mild irreverence as 'our holy founder' by those who still think about such things. Where it came from is not known, but it arrived shortly after his death in January 1820. In June 1821 the Trustees ordered it placed in the niche in the front hall. In June 1822 they ordered it to be placed in the south window of the front parlour before 25 August and decided that henceforth the King's birthday was to be a free day. It might be that they felt the front parlour was a more protected spot, for it must be significant that it was necessary in January 1823 to decree that it be placed on a bracket in the President's room, where it must have been moved. Still, when Lord Mulgrave, the Lord Lieutenant, paid an extended visit to the college on 19 December 1825 the walks were lined by cheering students. Again it would be a mistake to judge his reception in political terms. They asked him to get them dispensed from the Christmas examination, and he did.[76] Impending examinations could loom larger than political issues. And when Sir Francis Head visited the college in August 1852 he found in the library—at that time still on the top floor of Dunboyne House—'a statue of King George III, the founder of the institution', described as being on 'the fireplace at the end of the room'.[77] Head is usually meticulously accurate, but he must surely be referring to the bust, not to a 'statue'. It would appear that now it was considered safe to have it in a public room again, possibly in the belief that very few would now know who it was.

CHAPTER IV

THE CATHOLIC ENLIGHTENMENT: EVENING

Staff: Developments and Tensions

When Bartholomew Crotty departed as bishop of Cloyne he left behind him in Maynooth a reasonably stable institution. That institution retained the stamp he had put on it for another twenty years, from 1833, the year he left, to 1853, give or take a year. In 1853 Maynooth faced another public inquiry, this time by a Royal Commission.[1] Like the previous inquiry in 1826 it had in the first place the effect of getting down on paper many things about the college that might otherwise never have been recorded, though in this matter it may not be quite so valuable as the earlier visitation, for many things had not changed in the meantime, or had not changed very much. It remains, however, a comprehensive record of a system that was soon to be changed considerably.

The only limitation on the power of the Trustees was that imposed by the nature of the body. The lay trustees had quickly become in fact hereditary, and the episcopal trustees held office for life. The 1853 Commission did not think that this led to good government, and they suggested changes,[2] which, however, were not implemented. In one respect things had improved since the early years of the century, when Delahogue had complained that the college's governing body had not seen the place in four years. But there was still no organic link between the governors and the governed. It is true that any member of the college could address the Trustees, and, as their secretary put it to the Commission a little complacently, this was in every case 'kindly received and considered with the most patient attention', and always received a reply. But, as one of the staff put it, while a professor might address the Trustees, 'he did not know what is going on'.[3] Even the President attended the Trustees' meetings only by invitation, and he was not always invited. The President, nevertheless, was the key figure. When Crotty departed the Trustees appointed Michael Slattery, parish priest of Cashel, on 19 June 1832. He was now nearly sixty years of age. He had read for a degree in Trinity, and had then gone on to Carlow College, where he was ordained in 1809. After a few years teaching philosophy in Carlow he had returned to his native diocese, becoming parish priest first of Borrisoleigh and then of Cashel. No doubt an important factor in bringing him to the attention of the Trustees was a strong recommendation from James Warren Doyle, the influential Bishop of Kildare and Leighlin. But Slattery was himself appointed Archbishop of Cashel in December 1833, and the Trustees were once again looking for a President.

So far, presidents had always been brought from outside, not unreasonable in a young institution. But the institution was now close on forty years old, and the indications are that there was a feeling among the staff that it was now mature enough to provide its own president. The obvious candidate was Michael Montague, who as vice-president and bursar could claim to have built most of the college. But though he had had a distinguished scholastic career he had lost interest in such things, which may be assumed to be one of the reasons Archbishop Murray did not wish to see him president. Another possible candidate was the long-serving dean, Philip Dowley, but his mind was definitely turning towards joining the young men he had encouraged to take on a life that developed into the Irish Vincentian congregation.

When the Trustees met in February 1834 they offered the presidency to Nicholas Foran, parish priest of Dungarvan, who was to become Bishop of Waterford in 1837. It was embarrassing for them when he refused the invitation, all the more so as the Maynooth staff were annoyed the post had been offered to an outsider. Yet the Trustees, and Murray in particular, were reluctant to consider Montague. It is quite possible Murray might have put forward Paul Cullen, the young rector of the Irish College in Rome. He wrote to him on 14 May as Cullen was setting out for Ireland: 'If you had started sooner you might be here before the meeting of the Maynooth Trustees in the latter end of June. If so, I should certainly make a push to lay hold of you for the vacant presidency of our national college.'[4] But the June meeting came with Michael Montague the only candidate, and he was appointed. The next day, 25 June, Philip Dowley was elected vice-president, but he resigned the following day and the day after, 27 June, left to join his embryonic Vincentians. The same day Laurence Renehan was elected vice-president.

The appointment of Philip Dowley as dean in 1816 had given the office a measure of stability, but instability persisted because his assistants were regularly tempted to migrate to teaching posts (they were normally Dunboyne students when appointed). Thomas Kelly, appointed dean in 1820, became a professor of Theology in 1825. His successor, Laurence Renehan, lasted only two years, securing the chair of Scripture in 1827. Thomas Furlong, the new dean, lasted no longer, moving to the comparatively junior chair of Humanity in 1829. He was succeeded by Joseph Dixon. When the Junior House had been formally set up in 1833 the Trustees decided to appoint a third dean and John Derry was given the post on 20 June. A year later, in June 1834, Dowley left to join his future Vincentians, and in September Dixon was appointed professor of Scripture in succession to Renehan. That left only one dean, John Derry, priest of the diocese of Clonfert, three years ordained and one year a dean.

Not surprisingly, the Trustees decided to look outside for their senior dean, and in September they appointed Miles Gaffney, a priest of Dublin, curate in Townsend Street. He had not been a student of the college, and there can be little doubt that his name was put forward by Archbishop Murray. That still left only two deans instead of three, and to make matters worse they did not agree, for, perhaps understandably, Derry resented Gaffney's appointment, as he saw it, over his head. On 14 February 1835, in reply to a request from Gaffney, the Trustees gave a ruling that the junior dean was subordinate to him 'in every department of the college', and in June they set up a subcommittee to clarify the respective competences of vice-president and deans and make any further regulations they might deem advisable.

The position of the vice-president was a further complication. He did not have teaching duties, and as well as standing in for the President when necessary he exercised a general but poorly defined authority throughout the college. Both Montague and Renehan had played a role in the office of bursar, but the chief activity of the vice-president was considered to be in the area of student discipline, leaving an unresolved question as to how his authority related to that of the deans, of the senior dean in particular. The Trustees gave their decisions in June 1836. They said that while the vice-president and deans had an overall right of supervision, the size of the establishment dictated a division of authority. The division they made was not altogether clear-cut. The senior dean was to have charge of the junior students, and in addition he gave an instruction to the senior division once a fortnight. The vice-president and junior dean were to have special charge of the senior students, with the obligation, again between them, of a fortnightly instruction to the juniors 'as the junior dean appears to labour at present under a delicacy of health'. The reference to ill-health was probably tongue-in-cheek; at any rate Derry resigned on 19 September 1836. Ironically enough, he was appointed Bishop of Clonfert in 1847 in succession to Thomas Coen, the dean of the previous generation who had also left Maynooth in some dudgeon.

Gaffney was therefore left alone at the beginning of the academic year in September 1836. There had to be a special meeting of the Trustees on 22 November to appoint as dean Robert Cussen, clearly a man of some maturity of years, for he is described in the records as curate of St Michan's, Limerick, and formerly honorary canon and professor of theology at Meaux.[5] At their statutory meeting in January the Trustees appointed as third dean Walter Lee, ordained for the Dublin diocese in Maynooth a few years before and now pursuing his studies in Rome. Cussen resigned in September 1838 when he was appointed parish priest of Bruff, and John Gunn of Elphin diocese, a Dunboyne student, was appointed to succeed him. That same month Gunn had been an unsuccessful candidate for two chairs, one of Theology, the other of English and French. By this time, however, the Trustees had just made a ruling that would prevent him applying for an academic post. In January 1837 they had requested the 'college council', that is, the President, vice-president, deans and professors of theology, to give an interpretation of the statutes as to whether deans were eligible to apply for professorships (this, incidentally, seems the only recorded instance of the Trustees consulting this council). It was requested to report to the June meeting of the Trustees. The report interpreted the relevant statute literally, and declared that it meant that candidates from within the college had to be teaching staff or Dunboyne students, so that deans could not be candidates for an academic chair while holding the office of dean. This ruling was accepted.

The senior dean, then, resided in the Junior House, and the other two on either side of the square. At the end of 1845, when student numbers had increased still further, the President, Laurence Renehan, began to speak of the appointment of an additional dean.[6] There was opposition, and real problems. It could be argued, even if not with total conviction, that no money to pay an additional dean could be taken from the parliamentary grant under the terms of the Act of 1845. This argument was taken up by members of the teaching staff who resented the way they were excluded by the deans from any share in the formation of students. Weight was added to their argument by the consideration that the existing three deans may not have been deployed to the best advantage: even as the day approached in the early 1850s when the students would finally move into the new buildings, it did look as if the situation could be met by one of the two Senior House deans going with them. On 30 March 1852 the senior dean, Miles Gaffney, wrote a very frank letter to Archbishop Paul Cullen. He was arguing in support of a fourth dean, though what he had to say would equally indicate that three might be enough if they worked at it. One of his colleagues, Walter Lee, was, he said, absent on sabbatical (he implied that Lee had developed a taste for travel to Italy). The other, John Gunn, was in effect doing nothing, he claimed, showing a positively disedifying lack of zeal, impervious to appeals from the senior dean and the President and even to a threat to appeal to Archbishop Cullen of Armagh.[7] Gaffney's arguments for a fourth dean were accepted, and James O'Kane, appointed on 24 June 1852, proved to be one of the outstanding deans in the history of the college. There were still only three deans, for Gunn resigned the same day, on the grounds of ill-health. The parting seems to have been reasonably amicable, and he was awarded a small pension.

The evidence given to the Commission in 1853 showed indeed a number of areas where things did not work out in practice quite the way they were supposed to do in theory. In November 1846 the Trustees set up a committee to revise the college statutes, originally drawn up in 1800 and revised in 1820.[8] The committee was drawn from the episcopal members of the Board of Trustees, and they were instructed to work 'in consultation with the President and such of the staff as they may wish to consult.' There is no clear evidence how far this consultation extended, but there are indications that it did not extend very far. In his evidence to the Commission, Professor Patrick Murray testified that when it was reported that the statutes were to be revised he and some of his colleagues approached the Trustees' committee seeking abrogation of the statutory ban on the professors publishing anything at all without the previous permission of the President. Though it was their right to make such an approach, he said that some members of the committee resented their initiative.[9] Nevertheless, the revised statutes, as published in 1848, granted the staff the right to publish, without any previous permission, 'compositions in theological, philosophical or literary subjects'. One thing the limitation seems clearly designed to exclude is politics. Just now, the staff was being drawn into the political excitement generated round the names of Peel and O'Connell in the 1840s; and as Murray himself was shortly to discover, the line between theology and politics can be thin when the theologian addresses himself to problems of Church and State.

The main problem found with the statutes in general was that so much of them was in practice a dead letter. Part of the reason for this was the fact that at every meeting the Trustees passed resolutions which would effectively modify the statutes, some of them, it was claimed, even directly opposed to the statutes; but only about half of these were put into practice, the basic reason being that an institution as large as Maynooth College had developed a kind of momentum of its own, 'routine usages and customs' that could override formal statutes and Trustees' resolutions.

This was particularly evident in the matter of the college councils. In fact, no matter how carefully one reads the 1848 statutes, it is hard to find in them any statutory body that could be properly described as a council. The Commissioners of 1853 claimed to have discovered two statutory councils in them, one consisting of the President and the professors of theology to supervise studies in theology and the other of the President and all the professors to supervise studies generally. In fact, the statutes only envisage the President as consulting with these groups for these purposes whenever he chooses to do so; they also envisage him consulting with the vice-president and the deans in the matter of calling students to Orders, which would seem to give this group the same right as the others to be regarded as a council—a greater right, indeed, for unlike them it actually functioned regularly. As a further complication, in his evidence Professor George Crolly claimed—with what basis in the statutes it is not easy to see—that there was in fact only one council, 'the President's council'. Its functions were to conduct the concursus, to choose Dunboyne students, to draw up the programme of examinations, and to interpret the statutes. This 'meeting of masters' had three statutory meetings a year, but it had not met since Crolly's appointment nearly ten years before, and to the best of his knowledge it had never met.

There were in fact two bodies in the college that in practice functioned as councils. One was the President, vice-president and deans, who met to discuss promotion to Orders and general disciplinary matters. The second, known as the 'concursus board', seems to have been what Crolly had in mind when he spoke of the 'meeting of masters'. As its name indicates, its principal function concerned the concursus for the appointment of new staff. Crolly was able to deny this body the title of council because, in addition to the President and professors of Theology and Scripture (a non-theology professor might be added for a concursus for a non-theology chair, but he need not), the vice-president and deans were also members and all members had an equal vote. The Commissioners were sharply critical of these arrangements, especially the voting power of the deans in the appointment of academic staff. They recommended two working councils, a council of discipline, with some marginal influence from the professors, and a council of studies, with some marginal influence from the deans. There was no immediate response to this recommendation.

The tensions between deans and professors explain why Patrick Murray, in his evidence to the Commission, said that to give more power to an internal council was not the answer to the problems posed by the remoteness of the Trustees, and George Crolly would seem to be speaking for more than himself when he referred to resentment at the the total exclusion of the teaching staff from a voice in the formation of the students, which led to the professor existing on the margin of seminary life, meeting the students in class but otherwise living apart. There was sharp resentment at the fact that the administrative staff, if they acted together, held an unassailable control over all appointments. A further dean had been appointed in 1852, and he sat and voted on the 'concursus board'. Numbers of staff had opposed this appointment, ostensibly because it was not needed, in reality because they disapproved of the power of the deans in academic appointments, and not, as Archbishop Cullen cattily wrote to John Miley, rector of the Irish College in Paris, because they did not want their salaries reduced by a few pounds.[10] In fact, it did not prove legally possible to pay the additional dean from the parliamentary grant, and a salary for him had to be put together out of college resources. This must be what lies at the back of the charge that the fourth dean had not a statutory position, but the text of the statutes would not support this complaint. When a third dean had been appointed in 1834 the text of the 1820 statutes, which spoke of two deans only, had been duly emended by a resolution of the Trustees approved by the Lord Lieutenant, which was incorporated into the 1848 revision, and did not specify the number of deans.

Tensions between the administration and teaching staff continued, leading to suspicions and allegations. The fact that the allegations were sometimes unsustainable only showed the depth of the suspicions. It was particularly resented that the deans, who had been appointed without concursus, should have such a dominant voice in the concursus for the election of professors. By now such a concursus was routine. For all its faults it was essential to retain it, Crolly told the Commissioners in 1853, otherwise chairs would go to the best canvassers. The programme for a Theology concursus in 1838[11] lays down a scrutiny extending over three days. On the first day each candidate was to deliver a 'premeditated dissertation' for twenty-five minutes on a proposition chosen by lot and defend it against objections raised by the other candidates for a further twenty-five minutes. On the second day ten questions from Moral Theology were to be proposed to each candidate and on the third each was to interrogate each of his competitors for half an hour in Logic, Metaphysics and Ethics and to demonstrate four propositions from algebra, geometry, mechanics and astronomy, thereby proving his competence in both Rational and Natural Philosophy. The same source gives the programme for a concursus in the same year in the humbler department of French and English. This too lasted for three days, and it began with at least a nod towards Theology. On the first day each candidate first answered two questions from Moral and one from Dogmatic Theology, then two questions from Rational and two from Natural Philosophy, and each had to answer the objections of his competitors for ten minutes. On the second day the topics were grammar and rhetoric, where the candidates examined and interrogated one another. They also had to read passages from English and French classics. On the third and final day they were given a theme for English composition and a passage of English to be translated into French. The votes of the assessors have not survived in these two instances, but they have in two others, held in September 1845.[12] These show the usual grapplings with the attempt to translate assessment into firm recommendation. For the chair of Rational Philosophy Joseph Behan of Meath got five votes, but two went to John McEvilly of Tuam, on the grounds that this was his third concursus and that he was a candidate who should get a chair. Behan was recommended and appointed. Denis Gargan of Meath was recommended and appointed to the chair of Humanity, by a margin of four votes to three, against a candidate described as 'exceedingly bashful and timorous', but it would appear the better of the two academically; Laurence Renehan, the President, submitted a very critical judgement of Gargan's academic attainments. Finally, the problem of appointment boards, as distinct from assessment boards, emerges in a letter from Archbishop Cullen to John Miley of 17 November 1852. The vacancy was in Scripture, consequent on the appointment of Joseph Dixon to the archbishopric of Armagh. There were three candidates. One was Dr McGettigan, nephew to the bishop of Raphoe. He would not do, Cullen had decided. In his view the best candidate was Daniel McCarthy of Kerry, but if the vote split between him and the third candidate, Laurence Gillic of Meath, McGettigan might well slip in.[13] Gillic was appointed on 18 January 1853, but he died after a year and McCarthy succeeded on 22 June 1854.

Once appointed, the staff member was entitled to his commons and a small salary, £112 a year, non-incremental. All were agreed it was too small, but there was no means of increasing it until Peel's improved provision in 1845. Up to this most of the staff still lived in Stoyte House, which must indeed have been crowded. The exceptions were noted by a visitor in 1840. The Prefect of the Dunboyne students lived 'in the midst of those more immediately under his care', as did the three deans, of whom the senior dean, Miles Gaffney, lived with the Junior House students, and the other two on either side of the square. Other staff members may have lived dispersed among the students, as they did later, but there is no evidence one way or the other. It was at first envisaged that all the staff would move to the new buildings, but as things worked out only some did.[14]

When Sir Francis Head visited the college in 1852, notebook in eager hand, he left a detailed description of the staff common room and dining-room—the two rooms on the south side of Stoyte House—worth reproducing at length as a record of the first age now at an end. The common room was

> a comfortable small room of three windows, handsomely furnished with scarlet and black carpet; scarlet curtains edged with yellow lace, with white muslin curtains underneath; a round table, covered with scarlet and black cloth; ten dining-room chairs, with black hair bottoms; a dumb waiter; a brass fender; common grate; a painting of a man, with both hands uplifted, on his knees before two friars, one standing, the other sitting on the ground close to a cross surmounted by Alpine scenery.

Through an open door he saw 'in a spacious adjoining room . . . a large dining table (standing on a scarlet and black carpet), four silver decanter stands, a large full-length picture of St Francis on a pedestal, and about a dozen and half of plain hair black-bottomed chairs.' Here he later met the staff, and was entertained to dinner. Both pleased him: of 'the Principals of the College . . . I need hardly say that in appearance and in reality they were exceedingly clever-looking men', while

> our dinner was exactly what it had been described to me, plain, simple and homely. It consisted of a large joint of mutton, a great dish full of fowls, ham and vegetables of various sorts. We then had one immense fruit pie, with cheese, butter and a slight dessert. The wine consisted of super-excellent port and sherry; and as soon as the cloth was removed, a large jug of hot water, a couple of small decanters of whiskey, a bowl of white sugar and a tray of tumblers, each containing a little ladle, were successively placed on the table.[15]

What is sometimes referred to as 'the Maynooth Mission to India' may be introduced as a final vignette of the Maynooth staff of the first age. In the early nineteenth century English-speaking power was expanding all over the world. That power, British or American, was culturally Protestant but ruled over many Catholics. The Catholic Church in all these territories was under the jurisdiction of the Roman Congregation of Propaganda. In a search for English-speaking priests the Congregation turned naturally to Ireland. Activity was speeded up when in 1831 the Prefect of Propaganda, Cardinal

Cappelloni, became Pope as Gregory XVI. In India he set out to break the Portuguese *padroado*, a privilege granted in 1514 whereby no bishop could be appointed without the approval of the King of Portugal. It was now an anachronism in India, where the British had replaced the Portuguese as the imperial power. Gregory XVI set up four vicariates-apostolic, Madras in 1832, Bengal in 1834, Ceylon and Pondicherry in 1836. This was resented and resisted by the clergy of the *padroado*. The Pope had appointed an Irishman vicar-apostolic of Madras in 1832, but he was soon looking for a coadjutor on the grounds of ill-health. His coadjutor was named in 1838. He was Patrick J. Carew, professor of Theology in Maynooth, from the diocese of Waterford.

That year, 1838, saw the first recorded movement of Maynooth students and priests in numbers out into this English and Protestant world. In February seven students had gone out to Bishop Polding in New South Wales, no doubt a response to the fact that Polding had preached the summer retreat in 1837, and in May three Limerick priests had gone to Scotland. On 24 June Carew was consecrated bishop in the College Chapel in Maynooth, and in September he sailed for India, bringing with him five priests and one student. One of the priests was a young colleague from the Maynooth staff, William Kelly of the diocese of Ferns, appointed professor of English and French in 1830. In 1840 Carew was transferred to the vicariate of Bengal, and John Fennelly of the diocese of Cashel and college bursar was consecrated bishop to succeed him in the College Chapel on 27 June 1841. He brought with him to India three priests, three students, three teaching Presentation Brothers and three teaching nuns with a lay sister.[16]

Writing to Paul Cullen in Rome on 2 February 1840, the senior dean in Maynooth, Miles Gaffney, expressed his regret that the college could do no more for the India mission. He said that over the past two years it had sent nearly forty priests to dioceses and missions outside Ireland, but it simply could not sustain this effort. The institution was very overcrowded, and all the places it could offer were needed for priests for Irish dioceses, where the ratio of priests to people was now only being stabilised after a continuous disimprovement since the 1790s, but the level of stabilisation was in many dioceses quite unacceptably poor, and in the worst cases it still verged on the disastrous. On the other hand, Gaffney went on, there were some dioceses—he named Cloyne, Cashel, Ossory and Meath—which already had far more candidates than they could accept. Many, he said, were talking of the need for a missionary college, and he believed that if money could be found for this it would soon have a hundred students.[17] In fact All Hallows College, Dublin, opened in 1842 specifically to supply foreign needs. When the great Famine changed the demographic situation in Ireland it also created an Irish emigrant community whose needs had first call on Irish priests. These came from All Hallows and the regional seminaries, while the percentage of priests for Irish dioceses educated at Maynooth increased. When later a growing number of Irish dioceses had so many priests that the newly ordained had to seek a mission abroad until there was a vacancy at home this was regarded as a temporary exile, though in the nature of things some did not come back; and it was to be nearly eighty years before Maynooth priests turned again to the even wider world of people not yet Christian.

Rags to Riches

A new bursar was needed when Montague became President, and John Fennelly, ordained twelve months previously for the diocese of Cashel, was appointed on 18 September 1834. Almost immediately the college ran into serious financial trouble. It is true that prices rose markedly in the 1830s, and it may be that the new bursar was less parsimonious than his predecessor, but it is clear beyond doubt what the main reason for the crisis was. The building programme had come to an end, and the Trustees, beginning in 1834, greatly increased the number of free places to be provided from the annual grant. It was soon evident that they had increased them to an extent it could not bear. In 1838 £1,000 had to be borrowed to balance the books, and there was talk of a memorial to the Lord Lieutenant seeking an increased grant. Though forty-one of the additional free places were suppressed in 1839, the next year there was a deficit of £2,500 and twenty-seven more were suppressed. On 15 April 1841 Fennelly resigned, on being appointed vicar-apostolic of Madras in India, in succession to his colleague, Patrick J. Carew. Three days before, Renehan was asked to take on the duties of bursar as well as vice-president, as Montague had in 1827. The debt by now had reached the disturbing figure of £4,600, and though Renehan was twice congratulated over the next two years for his success in reducing it, it was clear that the enlarged institution faced commitments beyond its means. In November 1841 the Trustees sent a deputation to the Lord Lieutenant with a petition for an increase in the annual grant. He immediately forwarded the petition to London, but the reply which came back was only an assurance that a grant not less than the previous one would be laid before the next session of Parliament and a note that an increase could not be recommended without previous deliberation and inquiry. Though Archbishop Murray replied on behalf of the Trustees to say that such an inquiry was reasonable and would be welcomed, no further steps were taken.[18]

There was good reason for this, for the political problems were formidable. In the 1830s 'Popery' was seen as a growing threat, not just in Ireland, where Catholic Emancipation had led to papists in Parliament, but also in England itself, where the Tractarians were preaching a 'Puseyism' scarcely distinguishable from 'Popery'. This led to a strong evangelical reaction, centring on Exeter Hall in the Strand in London, built in 1830, and the Protestant Association, inaugurated there in 1835. The annual vote on the Maynooth grant provided an obvious target for the evangelicals in Parliament, their members strengthened by the Reform Act of 1832. It led to monotonous and repetitious attacks on the anomaly of a government grant to what was at best a tolerated sect and at worst an institution producing ministers of a religion which was both treasonous and idolatrous. Various suggestions had been put forward to try to avoid the tirade, such as having the grant removed from the annual estimates, or instituting a formal parliamentary inquiry into Maynooth, but the problem was one ministers preferred to leave alone if at all possible.

As is the way of politics, what many saw as a measure of justice was brought forward as a measure of expediency.[19] Sir Robert Peel had climbed to power on the general conservative reaction to such events as Catholic Emancipation and the Reform Act. Nevertheless his 'Tamworth Manifesto' of 1834, while emphasising such themes as law and order and the Church, also included a moderate, rational and indeed liberal programme of progressive improvement and the broadening of the base of society. It was of course pragmatic in aim, designed to win to the Conservative Party the many Dissenters who had been enfranchised in 1832, while not losing the Anglican Evangelicals; but there was built into it a drive towards turning a confessional society into a liberal one.

When Peel became Prime Minister in August 1841 there was general agreement in his cabinet on one element in this delicate programme: if at all possible Ireland should be left alone, for Ireland raised the demon of Popery. Above all, Maynooth must be left alone, for it was in the guise of Maynooth that Irish Popery surfaced annually in the House of Commons, leading to debates that grew in acrimony over the 1830s. This explains the reaction to the petition of the Trustees in November 1841. It is true that Eliot, the Chief Secretary, inclined to the view that an increased grant would afford an opportunity to get more control of the college by a more effective system of visitation, and that this was well worth paying money for; but Peel and his Home Secretary, Sir James Graham, were more cautious, and, as has been seen, nothing was done except to confirm the existing grant and hold out the possibility that there might be an improvement subject to visitation and report. What changed Peel's mind was the 'Repeal Year' of 1843. Ireland was calling for 'justice', and some measure of justice it had to have. This, inevitably, meant a turn towards the liberal state and inevitably roused conservative opposition. And if there was to be Irish legislation, it was unthinkable that Maynooth should not figure in it, and it was inevitable that the conservative opposition should find its focus in the Maynooth proposals, for these raised very deep constitutional issues indeed.

Over the winter of 1843–4 the Cabinet discussed five possible measures for Ireland. Of these, three were brought forward and enacted, all of them dealing with religious issues. They were the Charitable Bequests Act (1844) and the Maynooth College Act and the Queen's Colleges Act (1845). Legislation concerning Maynooth bristled with difficulties, but it nevertheless seemed the safest way of showing generosity to the Catholic clergy, far safer than, for example, any proposal to pay them a salary from public funds. In further subsidising Maynooth the government would be meeting a concrete and admitted need, on which it had been petitioned a few years before. Chief Secretary Eliot convinced Peel that it was a safe project, and continued to press that more control be built into the legislation. In the event, he did not get much in the way of control, and the project turned out to be not as safe as he had represented it.

In February 1844 the Cabinet approached its Irish problems gingerly. There was broad acceptance of some kind of indirect endowment of the clergy, but any proposal to increase the Maynooth grant was opposed by two influential figures, Henry Goulbourn, the Chancellor of the Exchequer, and W. E. Gladstone, the President of the Board of Trade. At the end of the month the only proposal put before the Commons was what was to end as the Charitable Bequests Act, regarded as a form of indirect endowment. Peel went on to propose in Cabinet that there be far-reaching changes in Irish higher education, involving the joint education of the laity and the Catholic clergy, and an extension of the role of Trinity College. This proved so unacceptable in so many quarters that what came out of it in the end was two separate pieces of legislation, the Maynooth College Act and the Queen's Colleges Act. But before Parliament rose at the end of July Peel would commit himself no further in response to a questioner than to say that the government was considering the Irish universities question, and to add that it was considering Maynooth too. By November it was clear that an important but discreet role was being played by Anthony Blake. Blake, one of the first Catholics to have won the trust of the government, was well informed on Maynooth, having been one of the Commissioners who carried out the visitation of 1826. Early in November he submitted a memorandum to the Cabinet which was the foundation for the legislation subsequently enacted. He strongly opposed the common education of the laity and the Catholic clergy, appealing in this to the authority of Edmund Burke. Instead, he argued, Maynooth College should be given a status and income that would allow it to discharge properly its function of educating the Catholic clergy. The Trustees, he said, should be legally incorporated to enable them to acquire land, and they should be empowered to grant degrees. The annual grant should be considerably increased—he suggested £25,000. There should be a separate seminary nearby for the junior classes, and a hundred and fifty free places should be provided here.

Enough information was reaching the Trustees to induce them to submit a further petition to the Lord Lieutenant in November 1844. When it was presented by the four archbishops he raised with them the matter of visitation, for the petition had made it clear the Trustees would not welcome any change and the government still hankered after increased control through more effective visitation. The archbishops opposed the change: MacHale opposed it vehemently. By now trouble was mounting over the Charitable Bequests Act, and the government was content to incorporate in the Maynooth Bill a suggestion from Anthony Blake that gave the college a system of visitation about as innocuous as the previous one.

The needs of the college had been set out by Laurence Renehan, vice-president but effective head of the institution, for Michael Montague, the President, was bedridden with what proved to be his last illness. All who had spoken in favour of the college in the parliamentary debates, he said, were agreed that the needs were great. The staff were poorly paid at £112 a year. It was accepted that this established a real temptation 'to exchange the exhausting study and discipline of college life, at the very time when that person would be best qualified to serve the college, for the greater liberty and richer emoluments of a parish priest'; but the money simply had not been there to give any increase. A modest increase in the allowance for commons was also needed—five pounds a year was suggested—to relieve staff and students of the need to buy for themselves their own 'groceries', tea, sugar and the like. The students even had to pay for their own candles. This increase in commons, Renehan mused, would allow 'lighting the whole house better with candles or gas'.

Much was needed by way of buildings. The existing buildings needed extensive repairs and were overcrowded and badly furnished. There was general agreement that they had had to be built in a very plain style, 'inferior to the ordinary style of a workhouse or a barrack', and it was 'desirable and would not cost very much' that both embellishments to these buildings and new buildings to be erected might 'give something more of an academical character to the general appearance of the college.' As well as general accommodation 'we want a church', for the College Chapel, regarded even in 1795 as temporary, and now with the Gothic revival beginning to appear positively unecclesiastical, was in any case much too small to accommodate the student body, while the recently designated oratory of the Junior House was no more than an overcrowded room. As well, 'we want a library—the place devoted to that purpose at present is situated on a third storey, and exposed to considerable peril from the fourteen fires burning night and day directly under it in the rooms of so many Dunboyne students', and there was need of 'a more commodious infirmary for the senior house', for the old lay college that served as the infirmary was threatening to fall down.[20]

The bill was drafted by the Irish attorney-general in January 1845. The Trustees got nearly all of what they wanted, without really having to accept increased control by way of visitation. On the government initiative, it was proposed that the grant be no longer paid directly to the Trustees *en bloc*, but only against detailed claims duly certified by the bursar. This introduced a measure of inflexibility, counterbalanced however by handing over responsibility for repairs to the buildings to the Board of Works. This had been requested by the Trustees, but unfortunately for them it ran into problems and the Board ceased to carry out repairs after 1852. The bill was approved by the Cabinet without substantial change at the end of January. This led to the resignation of Gladstone, which he had for some time intimated. He tried to explain to Peel that he had no basic objection on either political or religious grounds, but he had attacked the annual grant to Maynooth in a book published a few years previously in 1838, and as he had never publicly repudiated this view he felt he could not in conscience remain in a Cabinet which approved the new bill. Pragmatic politicians like Peel and Graham found it hard to grasp what he meant, but he seems to have reached the stage in his development when he believed that the state had a duty to support religion but that the old system, whereby it supported only its established Church, was no longer tenable and he did not know what should take its place. When it came to a decision in the Commons he actually voted for the bill, and it was in fact his wrestling with his conscience on the Maynooth issue that convinced him beyond doubt that he could no longer defend the position he had taken up in 1838.

Peel made a preliminary announcement of what he proposed in the Commons shortly after the bill was approved in Cabinet. Even before the details were known it was clear there would be serious opposition from the Evangelicals, though churchmen at the time were principally preoccupied by the Tractarian problem. It was more ominous that the Dissenters showed signs of wavering. Hitherto they had made common ground with Catholics on the platform of political and civil rights, but it began to appear that numbers of them would not give their support to state subvention of religion. What prevented the development of a really wrecking opposition was the inability of Dissenters and Evangelicals to shape a common attack.

On 19 March Peel told the Commons that he proposed to make the Maynooth grant a permanent endowment. The next day a Central Anti-Maynooth Committee was set up, and it was to meet daily while the debate lasted. When the bill was introduced on 3 April a decision was challenged on the first reading. This was most unusual, but the government had a majority of 216 to 114, though most of those who voted against were Tories. The next day *The Times* came out in opposition, which it was to lead and organise to the bitter end. An unprecedented number of petitions descended on the House of Commons, ten thousand in all, it was estimated. The debate on the second reading began on 11 April and followed a predictable course. The arguments in favour of the proposal were in the main pragmatic. It was argued that the Irish Catholic clergy had developed into a potent political force, and that if the sense of injustice they felt could be alleviated they could be relied on to bring the laity with them in support of the Union, a laity who could be convinced that they were being put in a position of equality with Protestants in Ireland and even in England. Ireland needed more priests and better-educated priests, and it was in the common political interest to make means available to provide them, to try to deal with the 'Irish Catholic question', which had weakened and divided every government since the beginning of the century.

There were some MPs—Gladstone among them—who were prepared to support this reasoning but were galled to see what they regarded as a matter of justice being introduced by Peel for reasons of expediency. The tone of the opposition, however, did not hold out any temptation to waver. For the most part it was unashamed bigotry, but beneath there were currents of real unease, not just about Maynooth, nor even the Irish Catholics, but about the Church of Ireland, and even the Church of England itself. The debate revealed growing anxieties about the tenability of the position of the Church of Ireland, and about the nature of the Church of England. It is quite remarkable to see the assumption surfacing that the Catholic Church was the 'old church'. It might have been expected from O'Connell, who referred to it as 'the ancient religion of this land—the religion of Alfred and Edward, and of Sir Thomas More', but it is striking to see Macaulay saying, in a passage that has often been quoted:

> When I consider with what magnificence religion and science are endowed in our universities; when I call to mind their long streets of palaces, their venerable cloisters, their trim gardens, their chapels with organs, altar-pieces and stained windows; when I remember their schools, libraries, museums and galleries of art; when I remember, too, all the solid comforts provided in those places for instructors and pupils, the stately dwellings of the principals, the commodious apartments of the fellows and scholars; when I remember that the very sizars and servitors are lodged far better than you propose to lodge those priests who are to teach the whole people of Ireland and when I remember from whom all this splendour and plenty are derived; when I remember the faith of Edward III and Henry VI, of Margaret of Anjou and Margaret of Richmond, of William of Wykeham, or Archbishop Chichele and Cardinal Wolsey; when I remember what we have taken from the Roman Catholic religion—King's College, New College, my own Trinity College and Christ Church—and when I look at the miserable *Do-the-Boys-Hall* we have given them in return—I ask myself if we and the Protestant religion are not disgraced by the comparison.

The vote on the second reading on 19 April was 325 to 178, 161 Tories for, 148 against (the Tory vote in the Lords held firm, the second reading being carried by 226 to 69). In the vote on the third reading, on 19 May, 148 Tories voted for the bill, 149 against, but it was carried by the same large cross-bench majority as had the Emancipation Act of 1829. The Maynooth vote made permanent the split in the Tory party, and the evidence is that Peel knew it. Royal assent was given on 30 June (8 & 9 Vict., c. 25).

One consequence of the fierce debate that raged about principle during the passage of the bill was that its details got very little parliamentary scrutiny, and the bias towards the interests of the Trustees which had emerged from the parliamentary draftsman and had survived Cabinet discussion survived also the debates in Parliament. The Act began by forming the Trustees into 'a body politic and corporate', ostensibly to enable them to acquire additional lands. The Act of 1808 (48 Geo. III, c. 145) had authorised them to purchase or acquire lands up to £1,000 annual value, but in practice what this had authorised them to do was to accept Lord Dunboyne's bequest. Now as a body corporate they were given power to acquire land up to an additional £3,000 annual value, the statutes of mortmain notwithstanding. More fundamentally, though it is not mentioned in the Act, as a body corporate they now became unambiguously the legal owners of the college.

The Act went on to provide up to £6,000 annually for the salaries and commons of the college staff, envisaging increased numbers and improved salaries. Unlike the other sections of the bill, however, there was no breakdown of the total to cover individual cases, perhaps understandably, and again perhaps understandably the staff showed some anxiety over the possible outcome, so much so as to send a delegation of two of their colleagues, Robert ffrench Whitehead and Charles W. Russell, to wait on Peel in London. This move seems to have had the approval of the President, and at least of Archbishop Murray among the Trustees, who indeed requested them to remain in London until the bill was safely through. On 10 April 1845 they presented a petition to Peel asking that no charge should be introduced for commons, and that the Act should fix individual salaries and specify new professorships. There is no record of what happened if and when they met Peel, but the law as enacted did no more than include a general provision for commons within the £6,000 allotted for the staff, but without specifying any sum for this purpose.[21] The legislation then turned to the students, first the 'senior' or 'Dunboyne' students, twenty in number. It noted that up to this they had been maintained by the rents of the Dunboyne estate and £700 a year from the government grant, and went on to enact that as long as the Dunboyne rent was applied to them exclusively (it had been diverted to general college purposes in the lean times of the previous decade) each was to receive an annual stipend of £40 a year from government funds. These funds had hitherto maintained 250 free places for other students; as noted above, the attempts to charge the annual grant with additional free places had been the principal cause of the financial crisis. The Act now doubled the number of free places, allotting 250 between the students of the four junior classes and 250 between the students of the three senior classes of Theology. These latter were to receive in addition a yearly stipend of £20. A sum of up to £28 a year was allowed for the commons of every student, Dunboyne, theology and junior. Overall this came to an annual provision of £26,360: £6,000 for the staff, £14,560 for student commons, £800 for Dunboyne stipends, and £5,000 for the stipends of the Theology students.

Next the Act turned to buildings, the provision and furnishing of new buildings, and the badly needed repair and furnishing of the old ones. All this was entrusted to the Commissioners of Public Works. At the request of the Trustees and with the written approval of the Treasury they were to contract for new buildings which when completed were to be demised to the Trustees. For the erection and furnishing of the new buildings and the repair and furnishing of the old ones a sum not exceeding £30,000 was granted. As events were to show, this was not enough to put up the new buildings required, much less to carry out the extensive repairs needed by the old ones. But there was a great clear gain in that it was enacted that all the money voted was to be a charge on the consolidated fund, both the £30,000 for buildings and the annual grant of £26,360. This latter was an important gain, for grants under the consolidated fund were not debated in Parliament, and it now seemed as if the annual abuse of Maynooth might be over. But from the point of view of accounting the college had new obligations. The previous grant was paid and no questions were asked about how it was spent: as has been seen, very substantial buildings had been erected out of money it had been possible to put aside from it. But the new increased grant was directed to specific objects: so much for staff salaries, so much for student stipends, so much for student commons. The problems arising from this generated quite a correspondence between the college bursar, the Chief Secretary, and the Treasury. The problem was that payment would be made only against specified claims, and these had to be designated in advance. It was finally agreed that before the end of each quarter the bursar would transmit to the Lord Lieutenant a statement showing the amount he estimated would remain at the end; and if it appeared excessive he would be directed to repay part of it to the consolidated fund. With this he would transmit the names of all entitled to sustenance, support or stipend, on the basis of which the payment of a 'sum which may appear to be required' would be authorised. The bursar was told that the quarterly statements need not be detailed, but detail was expected in the annual accounts, which would be inspected by Treasury auditors, and it was recommended that the best time to present these was in connection with the annual visitation. In practice, the full sum of £26,360 was paid each year; there was only one relatively minor matter, the Dunboyne stipends, where the college did not always have its full complement of twenty. There was also correspondence on a sum, finally agreed at £2,232, remaining unexpended on 30 June 1845, when the new arrangements began. The Treasury was at first inclined to require that this be repaid, but after a lengthy correspondence, stiffened with a memorial from the Trustees, it finally waived its claim on 6 March 1849.[22]

Finally the Act dealt with visitation. Many people wanted to make a tighter system of visitation the price of an increased grant, but the Trustees were not anxious to concede this. Essentially, the Trustees got their way, even in so far as the provisions of the Act were concerned, and even more as things worked out in practice. The Act of 1800 had entrusted a triennial visitation to the four chief judges, all Protestants, and to three Catholic Trustees, 'Arthur James, Earl of Fingall', 'the Reverend Richard O'Reilly of Drogheda, doctor in divinity' (and Archbishop of Armagh), and 'the Reverend John Thomas Troy, of the city of Dublin, doctor in divinity' (and Archbishop of Dublin), and had in practice denied an effective role to the judges by laying down that only Catholic Visitors might inquire into matters involving the Catholic religion. Because of the way the Board of Trustees had perpetuated itself, the Catholic visitors in 1845 were the Earl of Fingall and the Archbishops of Armagh and Dublin. These were to remain as visitors under the new Act. To them were to be joined 'such other five persons as her Majesty shall . . . from time to time nominate'. They were to carry out a visitation every year and in addition whenever the Lord Lieutenant might require them. The text of the Act envisaged a searching inquiry, but once again it was laid down that only the Catholic Visitors might examine anything concerning 'the exercise of the Roman Catholic religion or the religious doctrine or discipline thereof' (it was hardly to be expected that a right asserted in 1800 could be withdrawn in 1845). The secretary to the Trustees or some other official of the college was to take minutes of the meetings and keep a minute book, and each meeting was to present a report to her Majesty, a copy of which would be communicated to Parliament. Even this innocuous procedure did not quite work out.[23]

Student Life

The sheer size of the student body posed problems that could not be solved simply by multiplying the number of deans. The fact was that it was hard to devise a discipline that was not largely external. There was wide agreement that the duties of each dean should be further demarcated, and that the students of the Senior House should be physically divided into two groups. Some indeed felt that not even this was enough, and in this context there had been some debate on what was called 'the Sulpician system', which got aired before the Royal Commission in 1853. It took its name from the leading French seminary, Saint-Sulpice in Paris, or rather the two linked seminaries, one for theologians, with two hundred students and up to thirty staff, the other for philosophers, with the same number of staff but only one hundred students. It was not just in staff-student ratios that Maynooth and Saint-Sulpice differed. Maynooth, increasingly, took the bulk of students for Irish dioceses, but Saint-Sulpice could afford to select the best, with bishops all over France begging for places. Some students had already completed a seminary course elsewhere, and some of them were taking degree courses at the Sorbonne. Within the seminary, staff and students mingled on equal terms without distinction. This contrasted sharply with Maynooth, where teaching staff were excluded from student formation and the numbers involved forced on the deans a very external system of discipline, more so than in the other, smaller, seminaries in Ireland.

The need for Maynooth to come round to the Sulpician system was forcefully put to the Commissioners in 1853 by David Moriarty, a priest of the diocese of Kerry and rector of All Hallows College, Dublin. Here he claimed to have introduced the Sulpician system, the only model, he asserted, for a properly functioning seminary. All Hallows by now had a student body of about eighty, with a staff (or, to use the word he preferred, a community) of eight. This was not quite up to the levels of Saint-Sulpice, but it was far better than the position in Maynooth. In any case, there were problems going beyond staff-student ratios. The Maynooth staff was divided on the merits of the Sulpician system. The fact that it in effect abolished the distinction between deans and professors touched a raw point. Laurence Renehan, the President, did not like Saint-Sulpice; it was paternal, he said, but absolute, and in this respect inferior to what he and others described as the 'constitutional' system of Maynooth, better suited to adult young men, where the clear definition of duties involved a clear definition of rights. Opponents of the Sulpician system claimed that it could degenerate into a community where each spied on the others, and no doubt some potential for this was built into it. Renehan indeed claimed that the Trustees had earlier introduced the system in Maynooth, but had abolished it.[24] No documentary evidence to support this statement is extant, but Renehan's memory would have gone back to at least 1818, when he entered as a student. It may be that the simple fact of increasing numbers imposed its own kind of discipline. In any case, by 1853 the 'Sulpician option' was scarcely open, if only because of the completed new buildings, which the college was just beginning to colonise. In a revealing statement, Dean Gaffney said it had been his hope that these would have been erected at the far end of the grounds,[25] but they now stood beside the old buildings, forming with them so close a unity as to impinge on all attempts at division.

The old buildings had begun to take on an air of almost slatternly comfort, despite the intolerable pressures of increased numbers in the years immediately after 1845. The 'mean, roughcast and whitewashed range of buildings', as they impressed themselves on Baptist Wriothesley Noel in 1836,[26] had, for all their modest appearance, stretched the means of their builders and quickly showed signs of dilapidation and disrepair. Thackeray, visiting in 1842, raged about what he saw as slatternliness everywhere in Ireland, but was apoplectic about 'the supreme dirt and filth of Maynooth—that can but belong to one place, even in Ireland . . . An Irish union-house is a palace to it. Ruin so needless, filth so digusting, such a look of lazy squalor, no Englishman who has not seen can conceive.'[27] Thackeray's constant references to himself as a 'Cockney' would seem to show a desire to give the impression of great bravery in venturing so far from civilisation, and other visitors, while they stress the poverty, do not support Thackeray's charge of dirt and slatternliness outstanding even by Irish standards—Johnson in 1844,[28] for example, or Head in 1852,[29] when pressures were at their worst. Nevertheless, the poverty was real. Despite a cautious resolution of the Trustees in June 1823 'to inquire into the probable expense of a gasometer' the college remained lit by oil lamps and flickering candles; while a resolution of 1834 regarding ways of heating 'the halls, corridors and apartments' indicates that Dr Meyler's hypocausts were beyond repair. The lecture halls doubled as study halls during the winter, and were heated by fires, as was the library. There was no heat in the students' rooms. Of these the newly arrived Lord Lieutenant, the Earl of Clarendon, wrote to Lord John Russell, the Prime Minister, on 31 July 1847: 'I saw the rooms of which we heard so much in England. They have three or four beds in them and are wretched comfortless and ill-ventilated, such as no one in England would ask a servant to sleep in for a night . . . The single-bedded rooms are not much larger or better than those at Pentonville Prison.'[30] The Commissioners of Public Works summarised the situation dispassionately in their report to Parliament for 1848: 'Many parts of the buildings were found in a dilapidated state when placed under our charge. A considerable expenditure will be required for some time.'

Between 1845 and 1853 these buildings had to accommodate a hundred extra students. Before the increased grant there had been an average of about 425 students a year, of whom 250 had been grant-supported since 1809. The legislation of 1845 provided support for 500, and the enrolment increased at once to about 525 and stayed there. Of these, Renehan reported to Archbishop Murray in November 1845, about 250 were accommodated in single rooms, the rest in rooms with up to seven beds.[31] The Commissioners of Public Works in August 1845 set out the furnishings it was proposed to supply, furnishings so modest that one might surmise the quality of what they were designed to replace: an iron bedstead, 'a palleass matress,' that is, one stuffed with straw, three blankets and counterpane, a chest of drawers, a table, a 'washhandbasin etc.', two chairs and a small bookshelf.[32] The Board of Visitors noted on 22 June 1847 that this 'better furniture' had now been supplied to seventy rooms, and that it was intended to continue the process. The visitations between 1847 and 1850 show the progressive substitution of boards for flagstones in the floors of the lecture and study halls in Long Corridor. They also leave a definite impression that this, the earliest building and now fifty years old, was in general in a bad state of repair.

The daily round of student life had changed little if anything from what had been established almost from the foundation of the college and revealed in detail in the 1826 visitation. From six o'clock in the morning (five o'clock after Easter) to ten at night the day was spent in a round of duties, interspersed with brief periods of recreation, everything regulated by the bell, which, Battersby noted when he visited the college in 1840,[33] was situated underneath the clock over the central door in the west façade of Long Corridor. Interestingly, a number of the teaching staff told the Commission in 1853 that they thought the system 'too laborious and monotonous', and perhaps even more interestingly there was the feeling that rather less time might be devoted to study and rather more to relaxation and religious exercises.[34] However, with the resilience of youth most students coped with the system. How they fared in general emerges from statistics supplied by Laurence Renehan to cover the decade 1844–53,[35] which may be tabulated as follows:

	Number	Percentage
Entered College	920	
Expelled	34	3.7
Left	124	13.5
Died	37	4
Left because of ill-health	24	2.6
Ordained priests	701	76.2

As usual, only the extremes get noted as individuals. There was the young man who coped so badly that he threw himself to his death from a top-storey window of his room in the newly built Rhetoric House on 26 February 1841. No details are known: the tragedy is only referred to by Daniel McCarthy in his diary in April 1860 when recording details of a similar tragedy from the same room—the notorious 'ghost room' of Rhetoric House. A spectacular rejection of the system that was less tragic, comic even, was also recorded. It concerned a student who had a pint of whiskey smuggled in to him in the infirmary. After imbibing he left the college and spent the night in the village, where he was accosted the next morning by a justifiably anxious President and vice-president. The young man clearly had not slept it off: he used rough language and even struck the vice-president. The last document in a little dossier on his case[36] is a letter from him, dated 15 July 1847, explaining his conduct by saying he had decided to leave in any case. It might be asked if he figured in the President's statistics as 'left' or 'expelled': it is clear that some of those listed as having 'left' had been strongly encouraged to go.

Recreation and vacation in 1853 were very much as they had been in 1826, though it is possible to detect differences which may have some significance. One was that more students went away for the summer vacation. The first visitation under the Act of 1845 was told that 'usually all are allowed, and many prefer, to remain during the whole or part of a vacation', and that it was considered a grievance when all were sent home in the summer of 1841 because of the financial position of the college. Yet the Commissioners in 1853 were told that the numbers remaining for the summer vacation had steadily decreased, from 115 in 1849 to 33 in 1853. One reason for this, of course, was that after 1845 the students were financially better off. Another was the improvement in transport, notably the spectacular development of the railway system after 1845. There appears, however, to have been a further reason, namely that through the 1840s discipline was becoming tighter during both term and vacation. There were no striking changes, and indeed no indication of a wish to impose a stricter regime. Student petitions for additional recreational space in the early 1850s consequent on the erection of the new buildings were favourably received by the Trustees. There do, however, appear to have been restrictions on what must have been a useful safety-valve, the weekly walk outside the college. For one thing, the old practice was discontinued of postponing the walk until the next fine day should Wednesday afternoon be wet, and indeed this practice could be disruptive of academic timetabling. As well, there appear to have been difficulties about students walking through neighbouring fields: an exchange of letters has survived between Renehan and a peppery landowner in November and December 1848, in which Renehan bluntly told him the students had been warned not to enter his lands and had been told precisely where they were.[37] It would seem that incidents like this may have contributed to the privilege being restricted: in June 1851 the Trustees granted a student request to walk the neighbours' fields during vacation, provided no damage was done and the President and deans were satisfied the owners had given express consent. And the evidence given to the Commission in 1853 does indicate a certain tightening of discipline as compared with 1826. It is clear that the custom of students of the same diocese taking recreation together after dinner was now regarded, at least by students, as having the force of law; 'singularity' was a matter of concern to the authorities, said Thomas Furlong, who began as a dean and was now a professor of Theology; games like chess and backgammon, simply described as 'permitted' in 1826, were still permitted, but 'discountenanced'. In 1826 it had been noted that football, though once allowed, had been forbidden; in 1853 hurling was included in the prohibition, which must indicate that some hardy spirits had tried to introduce it.

As has been seen, spiritual formation was exclusively in the hands of the deans, and some at least of the teaching staff resented their exclusion. Some of them too might even have agreed with David Moriarty when he implicitly compared Maynooth unfavourably with Saint-Sulpice, where, he said, spiritual training preponderated over intellectual. In the Junior House, the senior dean regularly addressed the students on Wednesday and Saturday mornings and on the greater festivals. His topics were how to make mental prayer and how to observe the rule. Instruction in the Senior House was more intermittent: once a week, sometimes twice, and, if a student who gave evidence to the Commission is to be believed, sometimes omitted. Apart from the morning and night prayer prescribed by rule, the Rosary was recited publicly during Lent, and at other times almost all said it privately. Students went to confession once a fortnight, choosing their confessor at the beginning of the year and being free to change him. Saturday evenings from six to eight were set aside for confessions. The general practice was to communicate weekly, but many did so twice a week, on the advice of their confessor. The Blessed Sacrament was reserved in both chapels and in both also there was Benediction on the greater feasts, the octave of Corpus Christi, and the first Sunday of each month.

It was a bitter disappointment when the money granted in 1845 was not sufficient to provide a new College Chapel. The Junior House chapel was no more than a plain room in Rhetoric, and the Senior House or 'College'

Chapel, regarded as temporary even in 1795, looked very inadequate fifty years later as new Catholic churches went up all over the country. Stapleton's stucco work was still its principal decoration. It even lacked an organ. It was crowded when occupied, as it normally was, by the students of Senior House, and it is hard to find a word to describe it when these were joined by the Junior students for the retreats at the beginning and end of the year. An attempt was made, led it seems by the senior dean, Miles Gaffney, to enlarge it by extending it thirty feet to the front,[38] but the President would not agree and it had to serve as it was for another generation.

When he visited the college in 1836 Baptist Wriothesley Noel said of the students:

> They were generally athletic youths, with good countenances, and with all the appearance of robust health . . . their caps and gowns are very much like those of the smaller colleges at Cambridge . . . many of the gowns were indescribably ragged, and occasionally I observed a yawning rent at the knee;

and as he left he reflected gloomily

> with melancholy interest on the prodigious moral power lodged within the walls of that mean, roughcast, and whitewashed range of buildings, standing without one architectural recommendation, on that dull and gloomy flat. What a vomitory of fiery zeal for worthless ceremonies and fatal errors! Thence how the priestly deluge, issuing like an infant sea, or rather like a fiery flood from its roaring crater, pours over the parishes of Ireland, to repress all spiritual improvement by their anti-Protestant enmities and their cumbrous rites! For those poor youths themselves, many of them with ingenuous countenances, I felt a deeper pity still.[39]

Thackeray in 1842 was, predictably, equally gloomy. Speaking of some students going to Maynooth whom he met on a coach he praised them as 'simple, kind-hearted young men, sons of farmers or tradesmen seemingly, and, as is always the case here, except among some of the gentry, very gentlemanlike and pleasing in manners'; but he added:

> With the happy system planned within the walls of their college, those smiling good-humoured faces will come out with a scowl, and downcast eyes that seem afraid to look the world in the face . . . men no longer, but bound over to the Church body and soul: their free thoughts chained down and kept in darkness, and their honest affections mutilated.[40]

From judgements like these it is easy to see how Peel's proposals in 1845 raised such a storm of abuse, in which it was hard to make the point that whatever Maynooth College was doing it was at least something rather more complicated than was suspected either by those who feared its politics or those who feared its popery.

Writing to Renehan on 9 May 1845 Archbishop Slattery of Cashel, noting that Peel's Bill was virtually passed, expressed the hope that it might produce all the good expected of it, but also the fear that unless there was an increased spirit of piety and humility the college would be more difficult to control, 'and certainly still more difficult for the bishops to govern them after leaving the college, with the notions of rights and of independence that this measure is naturally calculated to engender.'[41] An unusual number of student petitions, preserved among Renehan's papers, and no doubt inspired by hopes of better times to come, might seem to indicate that there was substance to his fears, but when examined they turn out to concern for the most part small improvements in diet, and the reason there were so many of them was because the Trustees were so slow to move. There were potential flashpoints, however. A petition to the Trustees in June 1845 had been met with procrastination. At the beginning of December Archbishop Murray was writing to Renehan in some perturbation saying the Lord Lieutenant had shown him a number of petitions he had received from Maynooth students and asking what he should do about them. Renehan expressed astonishment that students should write to the Lord Lieutenant, said there was never less discontent in the college and never less reason for discontent, but pointed out that the slow pace of the Trustees had left him in the position of having had to grant what he regarded as reasonable improvements on his own authority.[42] The pace of the Trustees quickened only slightly, but the fact that the Lord Lieutenant did not intervene allowed them to keep the situation under control. Their repeated deferring of a request for tea for breakfast every day in place of what seems to have been really execrable cocoa was the kind of thing that led to the setting up of a student committee of grievances, another potential flashpoint that seems to have existed for some years before the Trustees finally put an end to it at their meeting of 18 October 1853. Regulations they made on student dress give a kind of visual foretaste of the new clerical discipline. On 27 June 1848 they decreed that the standard dress was to be 'black pantaloons, short black gaiters, and the standing clerical collar to the coat'. They went a step further in June 1854, laying down that ecclesiastical dress as prescribed for seminarians by the synod of Thurles was to be introduced from the coming September, from which time the soutane and 'round hat' were to be worn always, even on walks outside the college. At least, so the Trustees' minute says. If they meant this literally they were going beyond the regulations laid down at Thurles, namely that the soutane and biretta were to be worn inside the college walls; and thankfully this is what happened, and, it appears, only after some resistance.

MAYNOOTH COLLEGE, 1795–1995

Studies

The new affluence after 1845 did not bring great changes in the teaching programme. There were two new professors, one in Theology and one in
Ecclesiastical History, but otherwise change came slowly. In point of age the
student body was becoming more homogeneous. Men already ordained priests
were not accepted from the beginning of the century, but for a time there
tended to be some spread in age over those beginning their course because of
variation in schooling opportunity. As time went on, however, the student
body tended to be made up almost exclusively of young men who entered at
eighteen or nineteen and were ordained at twenty-four or twenty-five. One
reason that made this streamlining possible was the growth of secondary colleges, most of them diocesan, but this growth was slow and there were gaps in
the system where the situation probably deteriorated about mid-century,
because of the effects of the Great Famine in the poorer districts. As David
Moriarty explained to the Commission in 1853:

> The means and opportunities of procuring preparatory education are
> less than they were some years ago. The famine nearly eliminated classi-
> cal education; and the better class of farmers, who used to procure such
> education for their children, has been broken down or has emigrated.
> The smaller classical schools are nearly all gone, the masters were in
> many instances obliged to take refuge in the poorhouse or on the public
> works, and very few can now support their children in the diocesan or
> provincial seminaries; but the few schools that now are found in the
> country are pursuing a better method of preparatory instruction than
> was pursued in the classical schools formerly. They are combining with
> classical education a more extensive study of English and mathematics.[43]

It will be noticed that Moriarty used the word 'seminary' to describe these colleges, and, admirer of all things French as he was, he hankered after the
French *petit seminaire*, though even he had to admit that Ireland could not
afford it. Others, Patrick Murray, for example, gave a robust defence of the
practice of educating together boys destined for the priesthood and for lay life,
and this is how the diocesan secondary schools developed, though the name of
'seminary' attached itself to them. Despite Moriarty's praise for the broadening of the curriculum in these schools, the aptitudes of the young man presenting himself for the entrance examination in Maynooth at mid-century
tended to be still narrowly classical. A whole series of resolutions of the
Trustees show continued concern with deficiencies in mathematics. And over
a broader front, the Trustees had tried, in 1829 and again in 1841, to demand
something over and above classical texts for aspiring students. The 1829 programme was still in place in 1853, but the Commissioners summed up the
state of the requirements for matriculation: 'This resolution, though retained
on the entrance-card, has remained a dead letter, and there is, in fact, no

A pre-photography 'Class-Piece' (1861)

Plate 17

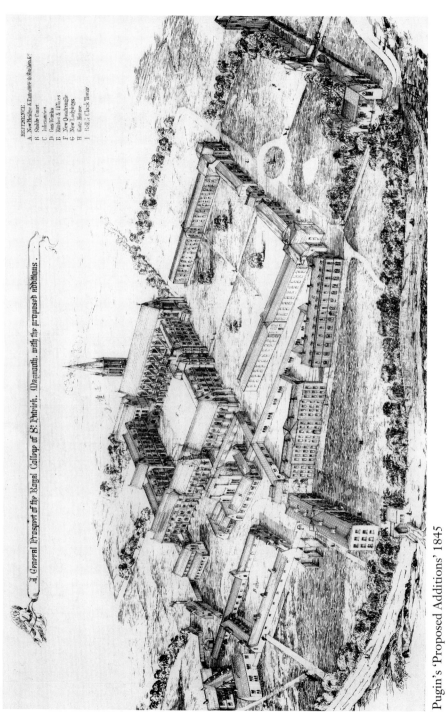

A General Prospect of the Royal College of St. Patrick, Maynooth, with the proposed additions.

Pugin's 'Proposed Additions' 1845

Plate 18

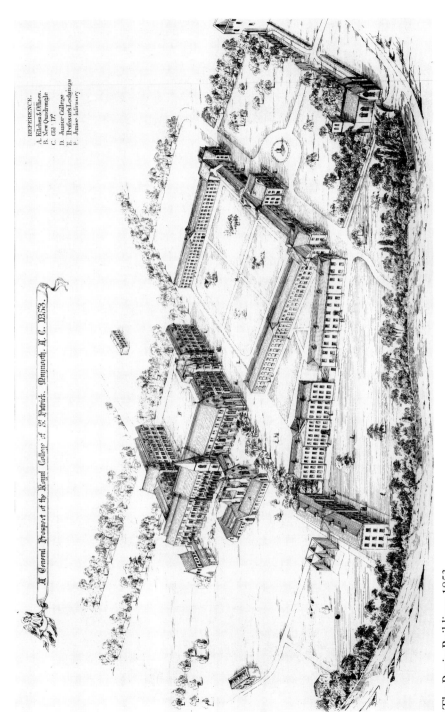

A General Prospect of the Royal College of S.t Patrick. Maynooth. A.C. 1853.

The Pugin Buildings 1853

Plate 19

A Pugin cloister

Plate 20

Pugin Buildings: community dining-room

Plate 21

The original High Altar

Plate 30

A COLD MORNING WITH BEWERUNGE

THE UPLIFTED FINGER INDICATES THAT WE ARE "LOSING THE BITCH".

Henry Bewerunge, professor of Church Chant 1888–1923, as seen by James Cassin (Ossory 1921)

Plate 31

The Junior House

The dividing walls go up, 1880s

Plate 32

examination at entrance in English grammar or composition; nor is the examination in history a substantial or effectual one, no student being ever rejected for deficiency, however great, in that respect.'[44]

The courses for the first four years remained in 1853 very much as they had been in 1826, but the evidence from the annual visitations prescribed in the 1845 Act and the searching inquiry of 1853 provide useful additional information and comment. About half the freshmen still matriculated into Rhetoric and half had to begin in Humanity. The two courses were very parallel, the respective professors having seven lectures a week in Classics, the professor of Humanity taking in addition two lectures in algebra (which he did not like) and the professor of Rhetoric having two lectures in geometry. As well, both classes had four lectures in English and two in Catechism and Bible History, given by the vice-president. Bishops under pressure sometimes allowed their students to skip the Rhetoric year, and occasionally the year of Natural Philosophy. Missing Rhetoric was possibly the more serious, as it was here and in the English class that students got their only formal training in elocution. The drilling in Latin may have served them well later in the schools of Philosophy and Theology, but Greek was not similarly subsumed into Scripture studies, and in most cases it may be presumed that much of it was forgotten. And when Matthew Kelly, professor of English and French, listed for the Commission his essay subjects for the previous year, most of them in his own preferred area, ecclesiastical history, it is legitimate to wonder how they came to be written, for at this time there was no library at all in Junior House. There had been one (the Trustees had started it with a very modest grant of £40 in 1834), but pressure on space with the increased numbers immediately after 1845 meant it was needed for a dormitory, and the books were removed to the College Library in Dunboyne House.

'Logic' or Rational Philosophy still occupied the third year, a short space for a wide-ranging subject. There were two lectures a week in French, which further cut in on the time available. And when the year was over, instead of passing on to the cognate subject of Theology, the students had to spend an intervening year at 'Natural Philosophy', which to some of them remained a mystery. The traditional course consisted of algebra, geometry and what today would be called experimental physics, but the natural sciences were beginning their great expansion, and subjects like chemistry and geology were pressing for admission into what was already a very crowded course. The professor, Nicholas Callan, was something of an experimental genius: he had produced what is accepted to be the first induction coil in 1837. Natural Philosophy was always reasonably generously funded at Maynooth: in 1835 the Trustees made £200 available for 'physical apparatus', and when the Board of Works moved in in 1845 Callan was not slow to get them to do work 'in connection with his construction of experiments' or to build a shed (which turned out to be 'very large') outside his lecture hall to house his 'new nitric acid battery', brushing aside civil service misgivings about whether such things could legally come under the heading of 'repairs'.[45] He exercised the prerogative of the genius to be a bit crotchety and unpredictable. He had resented an intrusion of two hours of Ecclesiastical History on his students after 1845; resented too that he had to teach much more elementary mathematics than he would have wished if his students were to keep up with him at all, despite the labours of the professors of Humanity and Rhetoric; and resented finally that he could not reach some of them despite all attempts to come down to their level. The question whether Natural Philosophy was a part of everyone's general education was beginning to present itself, and it became more pressing as science rapidly became more complex.

The evidence given to the Commission indicated that no-one was really satisfied with the courses over these four years. There were too many diverse things, badly taught because there was not enough staff and there was not enough time. The criticisms were summed up most incisively by George Crolly, professor of Theology. The system, he said, was 'radically and essentially vicious'. Theology should form no part of the concursus for a chair in these departments. It automatically excluded lay applicants, and priests appointed were tempted not to study their own subjects but keep an eye on the next vacant chair in Theology. A large number of tutors was needed, and he felt that laymen would certainly be better here.[46] The Commission accepted all these points and their recommendations tried to remedy the defects. They recommended that separate professors of French and Mathematics should be appointed, together with a body of tutors to supplement the work of the professors; that Logic and Natural Philosophy should be taught together over two years, with some Natural Philosophy in all years; and that Ancient History should be taught in the first and second years, with Modern History in the third and fourth. None of these recommendations was implemented. It may have been just as well, because the real problem was not so much the shortage of teaching staff as the fact that they were trying to teach too much in too little time, with too little pattern to it. Not surprisingly, much of it was forgotten fairly quickly.

Dogma and Moral continued as the core-curriculum of Theology. A teaching system had developed that seemed designed to waste scarce resources. It has been seen that up to 1828 there were two professors, one of Dogma, one of Moral, each teaching a course which was necessarily cyclical to the three theology classes combined. When a third professor was appointed in 1828 each was given charge of a single class, to which he taught both Dogma and Moral. This was an improvement from one point of view, in that the professor had to deal with smaller numbers to whom he could give more individual attention, even if this was limited to more frequent class-calls. The disadvantage to the professor was that it doubled his work load, but worse was to come. In June 1836 the Trustees called for new arrangements, which would allow each professor 'to teach in succession the whole course of Theology'. This was truly the worst of all worlds; the professor had twice as many lectures as before

1828, and he had to cover twice as much ground, being responsible for both Dogma and Moral; and because he taught his way over this vast course in a three-year cycle, the student still met his theology cyclically, beginning at whatever part the professor of first-year theology lectured on in that particular year.

No matter how it was packed, a three-year course necessarily omitted some of 'universal theology'. Up to about 1840 most bishops could not afford to leave their students in college any longer, and indeed some had to ordain them before the three years were completed. In 1834, however, there is reference to students staying on for a fourth year in addition to those nominated for the Dunboyne course. The Trustees decided these should be taught Dogma and Moral by the professor of Scripture, whom they probably considered seriously underemployed at less than four hours' teaching a week. That the number of such students was small appears from a further resolution of 1839, to the effect that when their numbers did not exceed six they were to be allotted to one of the ordinary theology classes or to the Dunboyne. With the increased grant in 1845 a further chair of theology was established, and as bishops became less hard-pressed for priests a four-year theology course became the norm. But the pattern remained unchanged: the student still met his course over a cycle, now of four years. By the early 1850s the professors were trying very hard to get rid of this strange system and the Trustees were regarding any change with a suspicious reluctance. In June 1853 the professors petitioned the Trustees to group the classes two and two, each group having two professors, one teaching Dogma and one teaching Moral over a two-year cycle. When the Commissioners came to the college in October the theology professors made strong representations to them on the need to change what they called among other things an extraordinary system which seemed to have every possible defect. Although the Commissioners were naturally reluctant to venture into the teaching of theology, they did support the professors' pleas for a change in structures, a change which the Trustees were very slow to implement.

Scripture studies continued to occupy the same relatively humble niche: two lectures a week to the three theology classes combined, with detailed exegesis of much of the New Testament and the opening chapters of Genesis, with a more generalised approach to the rest of the Old Testament. The language of instruction was English, the textbook was in Latin, and the Vulgate text was used. Inevitably, even the best students forgot much of their hardly-acquired Greek; and if and when they graduated to the Dunboyne they had lectures in the biblical languages, thus exchanging exegesis without languages for languages without exegesis. While resources were undoubtedly scarce, this may not have been the best way of using them.

It will be recalled that Francis Eloi had been appointed to teach Ecclesiastical History in 1808, but that nothing had come of it. A professor was appointed in 1845, in consequence of the increased grant. He found it hard to establish a niche for himself in what everyone regarded as an overcrowded curriculum. He secured two lectures a week with the first-year theology class because the Scripture class was transferred to the second, third and fourth years. It was decided that these lectures be also attended by the students of Natural Philosophy, much to the indignation of their professor. An attempt had to be made to give some kind of survey over the two-year course thus established. A further hour's lecture for the second, third and fourth years combined, in which selected questions might be treated in rather more detail, was found by reducing the overall lectures in Dogma and Moral from nine to eight a week.

The real Cinderella of the theology years was the Irish language class. As has been seen, attendance was compulsory for students from dioceses with Irish-speaking areas, on average rather more than half the class. There is evidence, however—it once reached up to a resolution of the Trustees—that not all who were expected to attend actually did so. The professor was uninspiring and the language regarded as doomed. Bishop Murphy of Cloyne summed up the feelings of many in a letter to Laurence Renehan dated 22 May 1852. He expressed his gratification that one of his students was so highly regarded in the college, and he added: 'I know of only one deduction to his future brilliancy and usefulness (to be sure it be deemed a vulgar one) that is, a want of Irish.'[47]

Two striking gaps in the training of priests emerged in the evidence given to the Commission in 1853. One has been adverted to already: the sketchy nature of the instruction given on how to compose and deliver a sermon. Formal instruction was indeed confined to the junior classes of Rhetoric and *Belles-Lettres*. In the first years of the college there had been a full professor of English Elocution, but he was succeeded by a visiting lecturer, who was in turn demoted to lecturing during the summer vacation, for which, as has been seen, progressively fewer students remained in the college. A student from each of the theology classes preached a sermon every Sunday in the presence of a designated group of students and staff, but the exercise seems to have been lackadaisical. Student witnesses told the Commission that sermons were frequently written for preachers by fellow-students or even copied from books, all this with impunity, and they said they would like more instruction and supervision. However, the theology professors opposed the appointment of a professor of 'Pastoral Theology' or 'Sacred Rhetoric'. The furthest they would go was to express a willingness that the professor of *Belles-Lettres* should give some lectures to the theology students, which they claimed he was willing to do.

If preparation for preaching was defective, training in catechetics did not exist. The question was raised by David Moriarty. He stated that in Saint-Sulpice the seminarians went out on Sundays to teach catechism to children, and said this system had been introduced in All Hallows. There was widespread objection from the Maynooth staff to the introduction of such a system. It crystallised around two points: that it would interfere with the seminarians' own studies, and that it would involve 'a number of students outside the college, and not subject to the inspection of a superior at the time.' Curiously, no-one seems to have adverted to a more fundamental, and possibly insuperable, problem: given the number of students in the college and its rural location, the number of potential catechists would be hard put to it to find sufficient groups to catechise.

So it would appear that the preferred formation centred on hard pounding at Dogmatic and Moral theology—too hard indeed, some of the professors told the Commission; Patrick Murray, himself a devoted student, was particularly eloquent in recommending rather less time at books for his students than the nine hours daily laid down in the timetable for most days of the week. The textbooks remained the same: Delahogue for most of Dogma, Bailly for Moral and the dogmatic treatises Delahogue had not got round to writing. Both Delahogue and Bailly were, each in his own way, essentially pre-French Revolution, and becoming increasingly dated and in need of supplementing and even correction by the professor—Delahogue with his *ancien régime* pattern of Church structures, and Bailly (as printed and reprinted in Dublin) with his illustrations of knotty points in contracts, family law, wills and other such things by reference to edicts of dead kings of France. As has been seen, the professor lectured for about half an hour and then interrogated the students, in turn but not in order, on the lecture of the previous day. The language of instruction was Latin, but it is clear from repeated remarks made to the Commission that neither professors nor students felt inhibited about breaking into English if contact could not be otherwise established. It was admitted that under this system the weaker students suffered from a lack of individual tuition, but the staff were reluctant to allow the Dunboyne students to act as tutors, even though this was envisaged in the statutes—again, for fear this might interfere with their own studies. At the end of his first year of teaching theology Edmund O'Reilly, himself a graduate of the Roman schools, gave his view to Tobias Kirby, the vice-rector of the Irish College, Rome. Overall, he was impressed by the solidity of even the weaker students; but, he complained, their study habits were bad, and their practice of returning the professor's notes almost verbatim was much to be deplored. He might have adverted to the fact that the teaching method seemed designed to encourage this age-old, and indeed regrettable, form of student insurance policy.[48]

There were examinations twice a year, at the beginning of January and at the end of June, each consisting of an oral test lasting ten minutes. In 1833 the Trustees ordered the President to report to each student's bishop on his performance in the January examination. These examinations tended to drag out, and with the increased numbers after 1845 the Trustees decided that the four theology classes be examined simultaneously, and set up four examining boards to assist the professor. The staff's objections to this change may have been increased by the fact that they were not consulted in the making of it, and the picture given of a lone professor examining before an audience of five or six may possibly be exaggerated, but there was some substance to the view that for the ordinary student the end-of-year examination was a small ordeal compared with his 'class-call' during the year. For the student who aimed higher than a pass the oral examination was, of course, only the beginning of his ordeal. This was described in detail by Edmund O'Reilly at the end of his first year's teaching, this time in a letter to his old rector, Paul Cullen:

> The answering and examinations were extremely satisfactory—very few *weak men*, as we call them. Then came the work of *first class*, which as you are perhaps aware consists of a selection of the best in the school (not exceeding the fourth part, by a recent rule of the Board) out of whom alone are to be chosen the persons for premiums and distinctions. To these *chosen few* a subject or rather subjects are given on which to write, and from the inspection of the dissertations jointly with the year's answering and examinations, the *grades* of honor are determined. They are not in the habit of writing so long a time as in Rome. The determination of this rests with the professor. I gave mine two sittings, the one in Dogma, the other in Moral, the first over two hours, the second about an hour and a half. In Dogma I gave them the proof of the divinity of the Word from the *ratio filii* . . . In Moral a case of a physician who having caused a patient's death, by administering unsafe medicine excused himself from restitution, because the remedy was *probabiliter profuturum* and he was a probabilist . . . The pieces were all passable and generally very good. It cost me a great deal of calculation to determine the premiums and distinctions, which as well as the first class rested entirely with me.[49]

This general framework of examination was to remain unchanged for a long time, as indeed was the general nature of the questions. That the answers too had a long life ahead of them appears from the chance preservation of forty-six students' essays in Dogma. Each student signs with his name and diocese, which means they can be placed at the very end of the 1830s or the beginning of the 1840s. One student adds '2nd year's divinity class', and this indicates a batch of essays of students of Edmund O'Reilly. The essays are in English. Some of the writers were to have distinguished careers, a few as bishops. The pieces, in O'Reilly's words, are 'all passable and generally very good,' written by intelligent young men genuinely trying to grapple with ideas. But there is also the timeless quality of the manual tradition, and over a hundred years of life lay ahead of it.[50]

To crown all, there was prizegiving in June, in the presence of the student body, the staff and the Trustees. As the Visitors noted in 1847, 'the prize essay in the Dunboyne class, which is composed in English, and the best compositions in Greek, in Latin and in French, English and Irish, are read by the composers in the presence of the Trustees and the whole college community.' The general shape of the prize-list, unchanged almost from the beginning, was to remain unchanged for a long time to come. In each subject there were one or more prizes: under each prize there was a group of names, most commonly three. These drew lots or 'cut' to see who should get the prize, a collection of books half-bound in leather with the college seal, still referred to in book-sellers' catalogues as 'the Maynooth binding' (Plate 39). Those unlucky in the 'cut' received a book as a consolation prize, so to be top of the list or 'first of first' did not necessarily mean ending up with a large pile of books—an element of luck or chance which may have added interest especially for those whose names were not called at all.

Charles McNally (1829–43) was succeeded as Prefect of the Dunboyne by John O'Hanlon, who was to enjoy a long term of office indeed, ending only with his death in 1879. But a Dunboyne course of studies was slow to take shape. In 1826 the Prefect had met his students four times a week in a lecture-seminar, two in Theology, one in Canon Law, and one in Ecclesiastical History.[51] They also had a class in Hebrew once a week, given by the professor of Scripture. McNally reduced the weekly classes to three, but the fourth was restored by the Trustees when they appointed O'Hanlon, rejecting a student petition that they be left at three. It is not clear how the class in Ecclesiastical History fared through these changes. Presumably it was dropped by McNally. In their evidence to the 1853 Commission neither John O'Hanlon nor Charles Russell, appointed professor of Ecclesiastical History in 1845, refers to a course in history for Dunboyne students. It may well have been concluded that the courses now followed by the students through their theology years were sufficient.

The students selected for the Dunboyne course were not ordained priests with their class-fellows, and were subject to the full college discipline. They necessarily spent much time re-reading courses they had already done, but this could now be genuinely enlarging because they had time to read in the library, conveniently located on the top floor. Yet the surviving documentation—and it is very patchy—would seem to indicate that the Dunboyne was not a very stimulating place. Normally, not all the allotted places were filled. There were, of course, non-academic reasons for this: many dioceses continued to be so short of priests that releasing a young man for further studies was an unaffordable luxury; and because the places were allotted between the four ecclesiastical provinces, if a province could not take up its full allotment it was reluctant to see its places go even temporarily to another. There can be no doubt that the lack of an academic degree was a grave handicap. Within the college the desirability of degrees was fully appreciated, and the possibility of doing something about it surfaced again at the end of 1844. The only surviving documentation is a long detailed letter from Laurence Renehan to Archbishop Murray, which has survived in Dublin and in final draft in Maynooth.[52] It is clear that Renehan's letter is a reply to a request from Murray that he consult with his colleagues on the expediency of having a papal brief authorising Maynooth to confer degrees. Renehan in reply said he had consulted them all, but more particularly those who had experience of foreign colleges. All were agreed it would be beneficial to have degree courses, and all were agreed too on the need to preserve high standards: 'the home-made doctor, in order to secure the same respect as a foreign graduate, must possess over and above the same merit, a superplusage sufficient to counterbalance the value which prejudice sets upon distant things.'

It would appear that there was no doubt among the staff of Maynooth's ability to hold its own. They certainly aimed higher than the Roman practice, where in Philosophy a baccalaureate was given after one year, a licentiate after two, and a doctorate after three: in Theology these degrees were given after the second, third and fourth years respectively, and a candidate for the doctorate did not need to have taken the lower degrees first. There was a much higher standard in Paris, Salamanca, and Louvain. The courses were longer, and for the higher degrees more specialised, the examinations more testing, and the securing of a lower degree was necessary before attempting a higher one. In regard to the British universities Renehan felt that, at least after the four years' baccalaureate, what was required was 'much standing rather than much talent or learning', in that an MA could be secured only after three more years, a BD after seven, and a DD after four more at Oxford and seven at Cambridge.

He then put forward proposals for Maynooth. The junior classes would take the BA and MA degrees, the BA after at least one year in the college, completion of at least the Rhetoric course, possibly the first year of Philosophy. For this degree what he described as 'average talent' should be required. Rather more should be demanded for the MA, taken at the end of the second year of Philosophy. The BD would be taken at the end of the third year of Theology, with a 'long and solemn' examination on the year's course in Theology and Scripture and 'a written piece on some question in each of these departments'. The licentiate would come after two further years (as a Dunboyne student) demanding superior talent, more testing examinations, with two written theses, one on Theology, one on Ecclesiastical History or Canon Law; and the doctorate after one further year (making six in all), demanding uncommon talent, with two 'full theses', one on the year's study, the other on questions selected from the entire course of Theology, Scripture and History. Of every twelve students entering, he would expect six to secure the BA, four the MA, three the BD, two the STL, and one the DD.

A good deal of thought had clearly gone into these proposals, which, Renehan claimed, 'attempted to combine the encouragement of moderate abilities with a necessity of continuously applying talents, however extraordinary'. But absolutely nothing further is heard of the scheme. What can only be conjectured, but it is a very reasonable conjecture, is that it was overtaken by the prospect of an increased grant which appeared shortly afterwards. Not merely had administrative resources to be concentrated in this area, but the proposal aroused such public hostility among Protestants as to urge great caution in the matter of seeking authority to grant degrees.

So, even the Dunboyne students had to continue their reading without the stimulus of a degree. The library remained on the top floor of their building right through the 1850s, for money could not be put together to furnish the great library which was part of Pugin's new buildings. Sir Francis Head made his way to the library in 1852, and, as usual, jotted down details in his note-book. He recorded that it was 115 feet long, with thirteen bays on each side, lettered A to K, with a passage in the middle. In each bay there was a reader's table, and there was 'a fireplace at the end of the room . . . on it a statue of King George III'—for Head, as already suggested, an unusual lapse from total accuracy.

The Commissioners in 1853 were told that it was overcrowded, with the books overflowing into two store-rooms. There was a general complaint that those who used it talked too much there, and several professors said they never used it (except, presumably, to exercise their right to borrow books). The opening hours were much as they had been in 1826, 'in the morning' on Monday, Tuesday, Thursday, Friday and Saturday, and now in addition on Wednesday, 'occasionally'. Head expressed satisfaction at the number of books, and special satisfaction at the number of Bibles and commentaries, but he did note that there was no Bible in Irish.[53] A small, and apparently inter-mittent, book-purchase fund allowed acquisitions of newly printed books, but the principal source of accessions continued to be from libraries of deceased clergy, either by legacy or purchase. In 1833, for example, the Trustees bought Christopher Boylan's library after his early death. There were substan-tial legacies from Bishop Murphy of Cork, who died in 1846, and from Bishop Crotty of Cloyne, a past President, who died in 1847. In 1848 Bishop Murphy's brothers decided on a very handsome gift to the college, the Irish manuscripts of their deceased brother.[54] Passing references show purchases of large items, such as the *Acta Sanctorum* in the 1830s, and about the same time the acquisition, presumably by donation, of the Ordnance Survey maps. The state of the library in 1840 was described in some detail by the librarian, Charles McNally, in a letter to Paul Cullen in Rome, asking his help in secur-ing theological works, for which he had £150 to spend, the residue of a legacy of François Anglade, who had died in 1834. What he wanted, he said, were

works strictly theological, in which I regret to say our library has been hitherto lamentably defective. In the other departments of ecclesiastical literature, the H. Fathers of various editions, commentaries on the S. Scriptures, Ecclesiastical History, Canon Law etc. the library is compar-atively well furnished. We have to be sure a pretty good supply of the French compilers, but of the works of St Thomas, Bellarmin, Suarez etc. only parts or odd volumes, and of many of the standard divines no part at all. Of all of these I wish to have the works complete and of the best editions, and indeed of all the theologians of repute or merit, as far as our means will go.[55]

French Heritage, Irish Heritage

In many ways Maynooth was developing its distinctive character. The French influence of the early days persisted in the theology textbooks, though it was recognised that these needed amplification and even correction by the professor. It will be recalled that one result of the application to Rome for the power to confer degrees in 1817 had been that the college had got the reputation there of being 'French', 'Jansenistic', 'Gallican'. The charge of 'Jansenism' or 'rigorism' persisted. In 1836 Aidan Devereux, a priest in Wexford, ordained in Maynooth ten years earlier, wrote to Paul Cullen in Rome to say he was sending him two students. There was, he said, a need for Roman-trained priests to oppose a spirit of disregard for papal authority which had been growing over the past twenty years among the younger and more ignorant of the clergy, and also to combat the excessive rigorism 'introduced into the national seminaries by French professors and their disciples'.[56] Some fourteen years later, Cullen, now just returned to Ireland as Archbishop of Armagh, received another letter on the same topic. It was written from Kingston-on-Thames by William Young, describing himself as a 'missionary apostolic' (he had been ordained in Maynooth in 1822 for the diocese of Dublin). He claimed that Father Dominic Barberi had always held that religion in Ireland suffered from excessive rigorism, and that this was the consequence of the training in Maynooth. He deplored the lack of 'tender, religious training' in the five or six years he himself had spent there and the use of rigorous French textbooks, all leading to grinding penances, intolerable exactions, and 'poor and insufficient opportunities' offered to working people to discharge their religious duties.[57] It can be said with some certainty that these charges were less true in 1850 than they were in 1820. The appointment of Edmund O'Reilly to teach theology in 1838 would have been an important factor, for he brought with him from the Roman schools a Moral Theology kinder than that of the French rigorists, associated in particular with the name of St Alphonsus Liguori. O'Reilly, however, would have been only one factor in the complex changes of the times. Nicholas Callan had studied for a doctorate in theology in Rome in the mid-1820s, and had returned committed to the teaching of St Alphonsus, on which, indeed, he published as extensively as he did on 'Natural Philosophy'. After a year teaching in Maynooth O'Reilly wrote to Tobias Kirby in Rome giving his impressions. He had left Maynooth in 1830 to continue his studies in Rome, and he admitted that when he returned there as professor in 1838 it was with prejudices, but that after a year's teaching these were 'considerably abated, altho' not totally removed'. He still saw defects, but there was much to admire: spirituality, order and regularity were greatly improved. He had a high opinion of the superiors and professors. He had previously disapproved of how little they mixed with the students, but he now saw how hard it would be to change the system, and noted that some who set out to change it later regretted what they had done. Gallicanism, he said, was almost dead, and 'the papal infallibility is not looked on in any odious light, and is certainly inclined to by several of the professors'. 'Of course', he concluded, 'the temporal power is not dreamt of, and why should it?'[58]

The 1853 Commission of inquiry showed that 'Gallicanism', by now a very ill-defined idea, was almost dead indeed, and yet not quite dead. The staff had to be careful in their replies to the Commissioners' questions, for one of the questions on which the Protestant public inevitably sought assurance was that of the authority of the Pope. Thomas Furlong, appointed professor of Theology in 1845, had been interviewed as a student in 1826. He summarised the position in very measured terms: he said the college held the first Gallican article, namely that God had conferred on the Pope as successor of St Peter power over spiritual things but not over temporal; indeed, he said, 'we affirm it on oath'. He added that in these matters there had been no change since 1826, 'save that a more decided bias prevails in favour of the infallibility of the Pope and his authority in spiritual matters'.[59] One might doubt this on reading the evidence of his senior colleague, George Crolly, which sounds decidedly Gallican,[60] but it must be borne in mind, first, that he resented very much how the reputation of his uncle, the late Archbishop Crolly, had been blackened because of his support for the Queen's Colleges, and second, that in his evidence he displayed a kind of donnish determination to explain the matter fully, even if it was a theological issue in which the Commissioners were not greatly interested. As will be seen, this was an indiscretion which was to cause him much pain.

A feeling that what might be represented as anti-papalism still lingered in Maynooth was strengthened, at least in the minds of those who believed it, by an unfortunate incident in the summer of 1849. On 3 July Archdeacon John Hamilton wrote to Laurence Renehan on behalf of Archbishop Murray. The Pope had written, he said, inquiring about devotion to the Immaculate Conception among priests and people, and asking also if it was considered it should be made a defined doctrine. He asked for a reply addressed to the Archbishop by 24 July. Renehan's answer in fact bears that date. He pointed out that many of the staff and students were on holiday, but that he had managed to assemble nine of the staff. They were agreed that devotion to the Immaculate Conception was very widespread, they would even say universal, but they showed much reluctance to see it defined, only one being openly in favour, on the grounds that it had never been the practice to define doctrine except out of necessity, and there was no heresy or movement urging definition; that the time was not propitious because of the political disturbances (the Pope was in fact still exiled from Rome); and that a definition would stir up controversy among Catholics.[61] It was unfortunate that none of those Renehan had managed to consult was a professor of Theology, and when these returned they declared that their collective opinion was quite the opposite. By now, of course, the 'Maynooth view' had been sent to Rome, and all they could do was to depute Edmund O'Reilly, as senior professor, to approach Archbishop Paul Cullen of Armagh at the Trustees' meeting in June 1850 to tell him that the collective opinion of the professors of Theology was quite the opposite of this. They had drawn up a document to send to Rome, Murray informed his friend Charles Gavan Duffy, but on reflection they did not send it because they feared Archbishop Cullen of Armagh would use it as another weapon to attack Archbishop Murray of Dublin.[62] By the time this letter was written in February 1855 much further embittered controversy had taken place, but it is clear that by the end of the 1840s theology and politics, secular and ecclesiatical, were already intertwining at Maynooth.

The staff got drawn into the political debates of the late 1840s, and like the rest of the country they divided into those who supported O'Connell and those who opposed him on the proposed legislation concerning Charitable Bequests and the Queen's Colleges. These divisions among the staff communicated themselves to the students. Patrick Murray said he spoke explicitly to students in their final year on the 'delicate topic' of priests in politics. He and his friend George Crolly were well known as opponents of O'Connell and supporters of Archbishops Crolly of Armagh and Murray of Dublin, the former being George Crolly's uncle. According to Charles Macauley, a Dunboyne student, Murray spoke very strongly on dictatorial priests, and insisted on the distinction between a priest's rights as a priest and his rights as a citizen. George Crolly and Henry Neville agreed with this, but John O'Hanlon, senior theology professor and prefect of the Dunboyne students, declared that a priest might instruct voters from the altar to vote for a particular candidate, especially 'simple and ignorant people'.[63]

O'Hanlon, a priest of Ossory, appointed professor of Theology in 1828 and advanced rapidly to the post of Prefect of the Dunboyne in 1843, was an outspoken man who generated strong friendships and strong enmities. He was an enthusiastic supporter of O'Connell, and of his leading advocate among the hierarchy, Archbishop John MacHale. In this O'Hanlon was rather exceptional among what might be called 'the older generation', but a clear division of the staff on political lines was now superimposed on the divisions between the administration, especially the deans, and the professors, especially the professors of Theology. In 1852 three of the latter gave as a central point of their grievances against the deans that they were 'nearly all of the most violent politics'.[64]

These differences had appeared openly when Daniel O'Connell paid his only visit to the college on 12 January 1847. A Dunboyne student, James MacMahon of the diocese of Clogher, sent a detailed account the next day to his bishop, Charles McNally.[65] O'Connell's health had now broken: he was to make his last faltering speech in the House of Commons on 8 February, and to die in Genoa on his way to Rome on 15 May. MacMahon wrote that 'whether O'Connell was invited or not to the college and what the object of his visit was is a perfect mystery to the students.' The mystery still remains. A formal invitation seems unlikely, given the strength of the party opposed to him, and as for O'Connell himself the institution seems to have always existed in the margin of his mind and the indications are that he did not particularly warm to it. Fortunately, James MacMahon had a sharp eye both for what happened and for its implications. O'Connell and his son John were to arrive at half past eleven. About an hour before this the students heard of preparations being made for their reception in the parlour. This allowed them to meet them at the gate and escort them with loud cheers to the front door of Stoyte House. Here they were met by the President, Laurence Renehan—on crutches, for he had sprained his foot. The cortege of students escorted them to look at the preparatory work for the new buildings. O'Connell then addressed the senior students briefly at the door of New House. He spoke of the evils of indifferentism and infidelity, and of how 'Lutheranism' was fading in the English universities and Catholicism re-establishing itself. Shortly afterwards he addressed the Junior House students. When he returned the senior Dunboyne student through Dr O'Hanlon asked him to come for a few moments to a hall where every student in the college had been assembled, and an address on their behalf, hastily cobbled together by a few Dunboyne students, was read to him. It spoke of their gratitude to O'Connell for all his past services, their present love of him and confidence in him, their attachment to his son John O'Connell, and 'their resolution to persevere in that attachment and that adhesion when O'Connell will be no more.'

This may not have been a particularly tactful way of putting things to a man who knew he was dying, but O'Connell replied that 'the address would be remembered by him till death and would prove a source of consolation to him at that awful hour', and shortly afterwards John O'Connell expressed his satisfaction to the Dunboyne students. After this the O'Connells were passed back to the staff, presumably to be entertained to dinner, but keen eyes watched everything, noting that Murray and Crolly, with Charles Russell, professor of Ecclesiastical History, Matthew Kelly, professor of English and French, and Walter Lee, a dean, 'offered no external mark of respect', but all the others did, especially John O'Hanlon and the vice-president, Robert ffrench Whitehead. When the O'Connells left in the January dark at six o'clock it was to loud student cheers, prolonged up the town, and now strengthened by a band which was playing at the gate.

Events of that summer showed that the Trustees would not countenance student involvement in politics. Attempts to heal the divisions between O'Connell and 'Young Ireland' finally broke down on 4 May 1847. Some time afterwards it became known to the college authorities that an address to John O'Connell had been prepared and signed by all the students. Letters from two bishops expressing disquiet have survived in Renehan's papers, and there may well have been more.[66] At any rate the Trustees at their meeting on 22 June passed a resolution ordering the President to convey to the students their 'decided disapprobation' of the introduction of any political topic for discussion or any political document for signature, and threatening transgressors with their 'heaviest displeasure'. It was not easy to steer a middle course. In

February 1848 Archbishop Murray was writing anxiously to Renehan to say that his absence from the Lord Lieutenant's levee had been noted, and that it had been reported he had said he could not go because if he went he could no longer govern Maynooth. Renehan, a staunch political conservative, who had had little time even for O'Connell's Repeal movement, denied indignantly that he had ever said any such thing. He did not go, he said, because he had no idea he was expected. He had never gone since being appointed President, nor had he heard of any of his predecessors ever going.[67] However, he did appear at the levee at the beginning of August 1849. Renehan, indeed, had things to be anxious about. On 3 April 1848 leaders of the Young Ireland movement presented a fraternal address to the French Republic in Paris, where it was received in a very non-committal way by Alphonse de Lamartine, Minister for Foreign Affairs, not anxious to offend Britain or to appear to countenance violent action in any way. The mission had raised false hopes in Ireland, including Maynooth, as appears from an entry in the *Liber Poenarum*,[68] which, despite its title, is for the most part a dull book. But on 2 April nine students got themselves into trouble. It was a quarter to six in the morning. As it was now April the college had risen at five, and the first study of the day had begun. The crime of the nine was disturbing study by being 'on the corridor and singing the Marseillaise song so loud as to be heard at a distance.' During the visit of Queen Victoria and Prince Albert to Ireland in August 1849, Archbishop Murray had written to Renehan saying the Queen was visiting Carton the next day, 10 August, and that he would be there. He added 'I am far from thinking it improbable that some of the royal party will look in on the college. Perhaps even the amiable little Queen may take it into her head to do so.'[69] In the event, there appeared to have been no visitors: certainly the Queen did not come. It was the middle of the vacation, but that summer there were 115 students in residence. It is idle to speculate what welcome they might have given 'the amiable little Queen'. It was widely said at the time, so widely that it is useless seeking its origins, that at the prayer for the monarch sung after High Mass each Sunday some students replaced '*Domine salvam fac Reginam*' with '*Domine salvam whack Reginam*'. It is likely that some did; but probably equally likely that courtesy would have won in the actual presence of royalty.

It is doubtful if even the most courteous reception would have stopped the attacks on Maynooth. On 16 September 1849 there had been an attack on Cappoquin police barracks, inspired by James Fintan Lalor, and arrests followed. The local Tory press embroidered the tale, and its account was taken up by *The Times*, quoting the *Clonmel Chronicle* to the effect that 'certain students of the Romish Colleges of Waterford and Maynooth' were implicated 'in connection with the secret societies. A few of the students of the former are already fugitive, and it is rumoured, we know not how truly, that 50 or 60 of the youths at Maynooth will have to be expelled, for being connected with the secret conspiracy.'[70]

That would have made a good entry in the *Liber Poenarum*.

CHAPTER V

A NEW
ORDERING

The revolutions of 1848 marked a real transition in most of Europe. Even though in most countries they were apparently unsuccessful, everywhere they marked at least the beginning of the end of the conservative 'Restoration' regimes set up after 1815. Religion had been a great sufferer in the French Revolution, and these regimes held it in honour. The Catholic Church had been the greatest sufferer, and was correspondingly honoured. In return it allied itself with these conservative governments, too closely for its own good. In 1848 the Papal States were the only place where the radical revolutionaries were for a time successful. Their regime shocked not merely European conservatives but bourgeois liberals as well. By itself it would have ensured an end to any aura of 'liberalism' that may have surrounded Pope Pius IX (1846–78). But there was more to it than that. After 1848 Europe seemed to turn against religion in more than political matters. At the core of this development was the great expansion in what men called 'science', the physical sciences, marked, it was then believed, by rigorous deduction from exact observation. This gave the opening to 'positivist' philosophy, based on the view that the only certain knowledge was 'scientific'. Karl Marx was claiming to have the key to a reordering of society in his 'scientific' socialism. Yet the most famous clash of the times, marked by the publication of Darwin's *Origin of Species* in 1859, did give some indications that the scientists might not always fully accept the proclaimed austerities of their discipline. Darwin, however, did raise plausibly a prospect frightening to the religious mind, of a humanity totally enclosed within natural phenomena. The reaction of organised religion to all these developments was frightened and defensive. It was definitively summed up by Pius IX in the final proposition in the Syllabus of Errors in 1864, when he rejected the idea that 'the Roman Pontiff can and should reconcile himself with progress, liberalism and recent developments in civil society.'

In Ireland, the attempt at a revolution in 1848 had been a failure bordering on farce. In part this was because the leaders had the weaknesses characteristic of mid-century European liberalism almost to the point of caricature. It was perhaps unavoidable, they felt, that the revolution should bring some harm to persons, but there should be no damage to property: it was desirable to make the omelette without breaking eggs. But the failure in 1848 was due even more to the fact that the country was debilitated by the great Famine which had begun with the first failure of the potato crop in 1845. No doubt what was in many respects a new pattern of society developed rapidly in Ireland after mid-century; but it was shaped by the effects of the Famine more than by the ideals of 1848.

At Maynooth, two events in particular marked this mid-century transition. These were the building of the Gothic quadrangle and the visitation by the Royal Commission in 1853. This latter was most important in its conse-quences, and these may be particularly associated with Paul Cullen, appointed Archbishop of Armagh in 1849 and of Dublin in 1852. He was a man of the new age, Roman-trained, anxious, authoritarian. He would wish to increase episcopal control over Maynooth, and the Commission provided him with an opportunity.

Pugin's Quadrangle

As has been seen, the Act of 1845 had provided £30,000 to erect additional buildings, and to furnish and keep in repair both these and the existing build-ings. All this was entrusted to the Commissioners of Public Works.[1] Immediately after their June meeting in 1845 a committee of the Trustees met with the architect of the Commissioners. Shortly afterwards Lord Shrewsbury wrote to Archbishop Crolly of Armagh, recommending A. W. Pugin as archi-tect.[2] The Board was quite willing that there be a special architect, and that it be Pugin. He was notified of his appointment on 24 July, and asked to submit plans for the buildings as outlined by Parliament. At the same time he was warned of the tight financial restrictions: the sum of £30,000 had also to cover furniture, fitting-out, and repairs to the old buildings. These had already begun and were proving very expensive.

Augustus Welby Pugin (1812–52) was the son of a French architect who had come to England in 1798. He trained his gifted son, who became leader of the Gothic Revival. He was brought up a High Church Anglican, and his con-version to Catholicism in 1835 was a severe blow to his career, costing him many private commissions and barring him from public ones. However, he found a powerful patron in Lord Shrewsbury, who got him a number of com-missions, including some in Ireland. The building at Maynooth was his first public commission in Ireland or in England. Inevitably it would be Gothic, designed by an architect of genius, a genius showing some signs of the strains that brought his death at the early age of forty, a short time after his Maynooth buildings were completed.

Pugin had plans and suggestions for the Trustees at the beginning of September. They were impressed, and indeed the buildings proposed were impressive. There was a new ornate Gothic quadrangle, closed on the north side by the College Chapel and Aula Maxima. In addition, he proposed a heavy 'Gothic' remodelling of the old buildings, sometimes quite drastic, as with the demolition of Stoyte House and what appears to be the total rebuilding of Riverstown Lodge in Gothic style (Plate 18). The Trustees were happy to approve, but a serious problem emerged the next day when an official from the Board of Works joined the meeting, namely that Pugin had costed his proposals at a figure ultimately specified as £57,400. It was made clear that there would be no more money for building beyond the £30,000 voted by Parliament. Archbishop Crolly proposed that part of the money provided for the support of students might be added to the building fund until the work was completed, because only then could the full numbers be accommodated, but this was unacceptable to the Treasury. At the end of November the Treasury spelled out its decision. No more than £30,000 might be expended on buildings, understood as meaning not merely the proposed new buildings but repairs to the old. In the additional building priority was to be given to student accommodation and the furnishing of public rooms. The Trustees had to repay £1,200 already spent by the Board of Works on providing furniture for junior students. That decision meant the end of plans for the Chapel and Aula Maxima. The loss of the chapel was especially hard, for new Catholic churches were beginning to be built all over the country while the national seminary had to remain content with a chapel considered temporary even in 1795. But the Trustees put a brave face on things and set up a permanent building committee to confer with the Board of Works and with Pugin.

The Board wrote to Pugin on 10 January, repeating that the maximum amount that could be spent was £30,000 and that this could not include a library, chapel, infirmary, and various other amenities. In reply Pugin resigned as architect. He said that when he had been told what buildings were required he had given as his opinion that they could not be built for the money available, but that he could not cost them accurately until plans had been prepared. He was unwilling to act as architect for the Board's trimmed-down proposals, because he felt he would be blamed for the shortcomings, especially the omission of the chapel. He relinquished all claim to remuneration.[3]

The Board took it calmly, probably feeling it was acting magnanimously in proposing that Pugin be given an honorarium of £100. Jacob Owen, its own architect, was instructed to draw up plans for the Maynooth buildings. It was not taken quite so calmly in the college. On 11 March the staff wrote to all the Trustees, saying they had learned with deep regret of Pugin's resignation, that they hoped the difficulties might be overcome, and respectfully hinting they hoped the Trustees would move in the matter.[4] The Trustees did in fact have several conferences with officials of the Board of Works, though the only record of them to have survived is a pithy reference in its annual report dated April 1846.[5] But Owen continued with his plans, and at the end of April these were submitted to the Trustees. Meanwhile, contact had been made with

Pugin, either by the Trustees or, more likely, the college President, Laurence Renehan. Pugin had softened his position, but was still hesitant to accept unambiguously the restrictions spelled out to him. The Board of Works asked the Trustees to decide on the plans submitted by their own architect by 27 April. They took legal advice, and were told they might still adopt Pugin's plans if they could square them with the demands of the Treasury. It appears Pugin was persuaded to confer with Renehan before the Trustees met, and as a result he was able to give them assurance that he could build a smaller quadrangle for the money available, without the chapel and other buildings.[6] The officials of the Board of Works agreed to recommend his reappointment as architect. Pugin produced, it must have been at great speed, the drawings still extant which allowed tenders to be invited. At the end of July the Board of Works informed the Dublin builder Beardwood that his tender for £22,297 5s 9d was acceptable, and the contract was signed on 10 October.

Pugin's drawings show the buildings as actually erected, with one notable exception. When he had spoken of a smaller quadrangle he meant that the south wing would be about fifty feet shorter than the east and west wings. Even as actually built the tall buildings can still make the place fairly gloomy on winter days, and it appears this began to be talked of that winter in the college. At any rate, Renehan wrote to Pugin on 7 February 1847 saying that he now wished to extend the south wing to equal the other two, and that he felt the money should be available even though the contract had now crept up to £24,037.[7] The Trustees' building committee agreed, and guaranteed an additional sum up to £2,000. The Board of Works agreed also, and Pugin was asked to prepare new plans. Beardwood's tender for the additional work was £1,968. There is a drawing of the revised plan in the National Archives, and a comparison of his first plan with what was actually built shows that the beneficiary was the library, which expanded from eight windows to twelve.

Between one thing and another about a year had been lost, and progress remained slow through 1847, mainly, the Board of Works was convinced, because Beardwood did not have enough men on the job. He had to apply for an extension of his time to 1 October 1849, which was granted grudgingly, and in the end he did not meet this date. But, however slowly, Maynooth began to see the rise of buildings seemingly of a quality not known before, Gothic in style, the walls of high-quality rubble masonry from the local quarry, the door and window surrounds in lighter stone from a quarry at Ardbraccan.

Two plans in the college library, one signed and dated 'Robert Pierce for A. W. Pugin, April 1848', the other unsigned and undated, but also by Pierce, provide a clue to the only other substantial questioning of Pugin's plan. He had proposed to accommodate the staff in the east wing of the new building, a move they looked forward to eagerly, for they were to have three rooms each, whereas up to this most of them cannot have had more than one. It would appear—though there is no evidence in direct support—that the accommodation as at first envisaged was as later actually built, namely suites of three rooms with a western aspect on the first and second floors, with a very wide and spacious corridor facing east and occupying the rest of the floor. Pierce's undated plan, however, which must be placed early in 1848, proposes smaller suites of three rooms on the west side, a narrow central corridor, and a row of students' rooms on the east side. This led to a petition from the staff to the Trustees' building committee, also undated. They said they had only recently heard of the proposed change. They considered it unsatisfactory and, they claimed, so did Pugin. They objected to having students' rooms immediately opposite to them and over their dining room, and claimed Pugin had suggested there be no students on the professors' corridors, and that there be rooms on one side only.[8] Pierce's second plan submitted in April showed their petition had been effective.

The building still went slowly. On 28 July the Board of Works decided to give legal notice that if things did not speed up they would have to take proceedings. It does not seem to have been very effective. Writing to Paul Cullen in Rome on 21 December 1848, Edmund O'Reilly, professor of Theology, said that the new buildings were 'rising in Gothic grandeur' but that it would be some time before they were roofed, and in another letter of 3 July 1849 he described them as 'far advanced' but only partly roofed.[9] Problems were bound to arise given a dilatory builder and a building committee that met infrequently. There had been an understanding that the new buildings were to be lit by gas, but this had not been in the contract, and when the committee adverted to it in April 1848 some of the building must have been roofed and interior plastering already in progress. As things turned out, no decision was taken before building work had advanced so far that gas-piping could not be incorporated into the plasterwork, much less into the walls, so the installation had to be deferred and inevitably cost more when it was done.

On 26 June 1850 Pugin reported that the building was completed according to his contract (Plate 19). Beardwood's final bill was for £30,477 5s 6d, so that Pugin estimated, taking into account the £2,000 already guaranteed by the Trustees, that enough remained for a long list of what he called 'absolutely necessary works' still to be done. The list was a formidable one, and even so his estimate of what remained to be done was optimistic. That same day the Trustees guaranteed the Board of Works a further £1,000 to install drain-pipes and drains, and £700 for staining internal woodwork and glazing the cloister windows. It proved even harder to get a water supply to the buildings, surely 'absolutely necessary'. A form for tender had been prepared in January 1850, but nothing was done. As late as 13 December 1851 the Board of Works informed the college that it could not meet the full cost of supplying water, and it appears to have been the late summer of 1852 before the contract was placed.

Meeting on 15 October 1850 the Trustees glumly noted that the parliamentary grant of £30,000 was exhausted, and that an additional £3,700 they themselves had provided was spent also. In return they had three sides of a Gothic square, with an extension from the east end of the south side marked 'Kitchen etc.' and one from the west end marked 'Privies etc.', as indicated on a plan dated 20 August made by Pierce for Pugin for the humble purpose of indicating the considerable amount of drainage works still to be done, and which conveys rather well the gaunt character of these totally unfurnished buildings, useless until much more had been spent in fitting them out, and no money to spend. The Trustees decided that the President and bursar should draw up a petition to the Treasury, of which nothing more seems to have been heard. They also authorised the President to select the site for the coal store and other buildings the Board of Works was now preparing to erect.

There had been hopes of moving in over the summer of 1851, but the buildings were still gauntly empty. However, the bursar reported to the Trustees at their June meeting a surplus of £1,653 on current account, and he was authorised to use it to begin fitting out the new buildings. The first to be done were the rooms on the ground floor of the south wing, the great refectory to the east, the space under the extended library, now divided into three and designated as class halls, and the large room to the west, marked 'study-hall' on the 1846 plan, later promised to Nicholas Callan as a class hall, but finally set aside as an oratory to serve the new building. In November the Trustees authorised the fitting out of the kitchen, and no doubt some unrecorded progress was made on students' rooms. The hope now was for the summer of 1852, but this too passed, because the building stubbornly refused to dry out. The metal windows Pugin had insisted on to give the architectural effect he wanted unfortunately let in wind and rain, and the very walls were porous for several years until extensively pointed with mastic cement. The vice-president, Robert ffrench Whitehead, simply refused to occupy the rooms built for him in the centre of the west wing. Of the class halls under the library Professor Patrick Murray commented to the visiting Commissioners in 1853: 'they are constructed in the Gothic style; but, I doubt not, the Goths would have been greatly pleased with them.'[10] The buildings had just been occupied, in September 1853, a month before the Commission opened its inquiries, though the library was not fitted out until after 1860. The bursar, Thomas Farrelly, listed to the Commissioners what was still needed: a chapel, an infirmary, an Aula Maxima; as yet there was neither gas-lighting nor water-heating in the new buildings; there were about fifty students still living two to a room, though this was a great improvement on the five or six to a room previously. Overall, he admitted, the new buildings did mark a great improvement, and their defects, though still many, he judged not beyond remedy (Plates 20, 21).[11]

When Sir Francis Head wandered round the still empty buildings in August 1852 he was surely perceptive when he remarked that 'the fine new system—by whomsoever it may have been devised—of giving to each student a separate cell, instead of crowding, as in the old building, from 2 to 8 in a room, will undoubtedly increase the monastic severity of the education to which they have hitherto been subjected.'[12] It came about, though it took some time, and the buildings were not completely responsible.

Finance and Fabric, 1853–70

The Act of 1845 had assumed that the capital grant of £30,000 would cover repairs as well as new buildings, but almost from the outset it was clear that it would not. However, because the Act had made the Board of Works legally responsible for the repairs, 'Repairs to Maynooth College' became an item in its own annual estimates. This reintroduced Maynooth into parliamentary debate, a particularly unfortunate development in the sectarian animosities of the early 1850s, following the revival of 'Popery' as perceived in the synod of Thurles in Ireland or the restoration of the Hierarchy in England—precisely what Peel's legislation of 1845 had been designed to eliminate. No provision was included in the estimates for 1852, and the following year the sum proposed was rejected in committee by a small majority. After this the annual estimates no longer included an item for Maynooth. On 10 June 1853 the Board informed the college that all works would come to an end the following day.[13] Since 1845 it had spent in repairs the substantial sum of £7,638 10s 4d, nearly £1,000 a year. While it is clear it had done a great deal of necessary work, it seems equally clear that it was working more expensively than the college authorities had done before 1845.[14]

These authorities were now left in the awkward position of possibly being legally obliged to entrust repairs to the Board while having to pay for them out of domestic resources. While the annual parliamentary grant had been greatly increased in 1845, every penny of it was earmarked for specific purposes, and none of it for buildings. The only source available was the 'fee fund', so called because it derived principally from fees students continued to pay on entering the college. On average it came to about £750 a year, and there were other calls on it. The Board of Works may have carried out extensive repairs to the old buildings, but the fabric of the new buildings was also giving trouble and they were totally unfurnished. At their meeting in June 1853 the Trustees decided to put their problems before the Chief Secretary, but without effect. The Royal Commission of 1853 adverted to the problem, and in their Report dated 1 March 1855 had recommended that the Trustees should be empowered 'from time to time and for a time', with the sanction of the Lord Lieutenant, to divert some of the annual grant to buildings and repairs, particularly, they suggested, the annual stipend of £20 to the 250 'senior students',[15] but nothing came of this either.

By the end of the decade the situation was critical. At the beginning of 1858 the new President, Charles W. Russell, wrote to Archbishop Dixon of Armagh asking approval from the four archbishops for his making an approach to the government to have an item for Maynooth repairs again included in the annual estimate for the Board of Works.[16] It took the Trustees some time to make up their minds, but they reached a decision at their meeting in June 1859. Just before they met Archbishop Cullen had received an interesting suggestion from one of the Irish Catholic MPs, George Bowyer. Leading politicians were indicating, he said, that the annual grant might be capitalised and placed at the absolute disposal of the Trustees. The only obstacle seemed to be that the capital sum involved would be very great, and Bowyer, no doubt acting for these 'leading politicians', asked Cullen if a smaller sum would be acceptable, and if so could an indication be given of what an acceptable sum might be.[17] It is clear that some political soundings had been taking place; in addition, the general election of 1859 had just replaced Derby's Conservative government by a Liberal one, which enjoyed such a narrow majority that it could not afford to alienate the Irish Liberal MPs. On 22 June 1859 the Trustees addressed a memorial to the Lord Lieutenant in which they set out their financial position and needs and asked that an item to meet these needs be inserted once again in the annual estimates of the Board of Works.[18] Shortly afterwards the President set out for London to put the case to Gladstone, the Chancellor of the Exchequer, and the Chief Secretary for Ireland, Edward Cardwell. He found them sympathetic, but clearly reluctant to meet the Trustees' request for an annual vote in the estimates of the Board of Works. One reason for this was certainly the outbreak of war in Italy in April. Though the situation appeared to have been stabilised by the Peace of Villafranca in July, the solution proved very temporary and dramatic events of the following year led to a united Italy and the reduction of the Papal States to a small area around Rome. All this sharply polarised Catholic and Protestant, Irish and English, the one side defending the beleagured papacy, the other cheering on Italian unification. Palmerston, the Prime Minister, made no secret of where his sympathies lay, and the Foreign Secretary, Lord John Russell, was even more outspoken, not for the first time indeed, for it was he as Prime Minister who had led the attack on the 'papal aggression' in restoring the English Catholic hierarchy in 1850.

In these circumstances there was little hope of getting an annual grant to Maynooth through Cabinet, much less through Parliament. Already on 24 July 1859 Russell, in writing to Cullen from London, had said that Cardwell had made him a suggestion he should like to discuss privately with the Archbishop.[19] What this specific suggestion was does not emerge, but a number of ideas were floating around. At the beginning of June 1860 Richard More O'Ferrall, one of the college trustees and MP for Kildare, wrote to Cullen saying he had spoken to Gladstone on the matter and found him sympathetic. He had written to Cardwell, asking him to raise the matter in Cabinet, and suggested to him the possibility of an Exchequer loan of £10,000.[20] However, reluctance to make the college a further direct charge on the Exchequer appears shortly afterwards in a letter from the Irish Office in London to the under-secretary in Dublin, Thomas Larcom, enquiring if the Maynooth Trustees had been legally empowered to mortgage the land they had been legally empowered to acquire in 1845.[21]

A year had now passed since the Trustees' memorial to the Lord Lieutenant. On 14 June 1860 Russell wrote to Cardwell, saying he had been instructed by the Trustees to lay this memorial before him again, and venturing to suggest they might have an answer before their meeting on 26 June. Cardwell replied to their chairman, Archbishop Dixon, on 18 June, recalling the proposal made in the Report of the Royal Commission of 1853, to divert part of the annual grant to finance repairs by the Board of Works, saying that an Act of Parliament would be required to give effect to it, and asking if it was acceptable to the Trustees. Two days after the meeting, on 28 June, Dixon replied on their behalf. He said that the Trustees could not voluntarily relinquish their right to a parliamentary vote for repairs, but as there was no hope of this they were constrained to accept 'any reasonable expedient'.[22] Given the sectarian tensions, it was clearly desirable to get the bill through Parliament as unobtrusively as possible, but it did stir up some controversy. In the Commons, an amendment was carried excluding the Board of Works from any connection with Maynooth on the grounds that such a public body should not be tainted with Popery. The Lords, however, restored the Board, and it remained when the bill came back to the Commons.[23] The Protestant press was hostile, making the most of the alleged speed with which the measure was being got through Parliament, and asking why Maynooth could not be kept in repair by voluntary subscriptions from the Irish Catholics, who were collecting so much money for the Pope and even incurring great expense to send soldiers to defend him.[24] However, the legislation was enacted and received the royal assent on 20 August (23 & 24 Vict., c. 105). To enable the Maynooth Trustees to put up additional buildings and repair existing ones, they were empowered, with previous Treasury sanction, to use from time to time for this purpose part of the money annually provided for all free places and the £20 stipend to 'senior students'; the Board of Works, again with Treasury sanction, was empowered to advance loans on this security to be repaid with the interest legally specified for such loans (an onerous rate of 6.5 per cent over twenty-two years); and all work was to be carried out by the Board of Works.

The financial situation dictated that any work carried out would have to be financed by loan. The annual grant had been completely apportioned out between commons of staff and students, stipends to the 'senior students' (both of these determined individually), and staff salaries (determined in bulk but not individually). The £28 a year allotted for student commons in 1845 was no longer sufficient at the beginning of the 1860s. As the Trustees saw it, the student dietary had been much improved (the students might not have agreed), there had been a steep increase in prices (especially meat, up by a third since 1845), and the now enlarged college was more expensive to run. Any reserve in the fee fund had been exhausted by the burdens placed upon it. As well as financing repairs, it paid the salary of the fourth dean, appointed in 1856, and not provided for, it was agreed, in the parliamentary grant; it was the source of pensions for retired staff; and it had been used to purchase in bulk books published by the college staff, laudable in principle, but getting out of control by the early 1860s.

The Trustees imposed small charges on students, such as making them pay for their laundry, resented by a student generation that assumed everything was free. There was further student resentment when it became known that, clearly to pay interest on loans, the Trustees decided to raid the senior students' stipend[25] (by 1868 only 190 of the 250 students originally entitled to it were still receiving it). In 1862 the salary of all to to be appointed to the staff in future was reduced by 20 per cent, and twelve months later the 'fee fund' was relieved of all the charges it carried and diverted to general college purposes, the staff being advised to set up their own pension fund. Yet it was necessary to authorise the bursar to negotiate with the Bank of Ireland for a loan of £2,000, the estimated deficit for the accounting year 1863/64.

In the late 1850s, shortly after he became President, Russell had tentatively raised the question of the College Chapel. But when some money for building became available under the Act of 1860 it was clear there were other priorities, especially a new infirmary for the Senior House: the old one, built as the lay college at the very beginning, had been threatening to fall down as long as anyone could remember. This was a large undertaking, involving a loan of £10,000. By October 1863 total advances by way of loan had been £14,735, repayments only £5,304, with an interest charge of £613 a year on the outstanding £9,431.[26] Matters had come to a head after the President, on 26 June of that year, had been ordered by the Trustees, at the request of the Board of Works, to apply to the Treasury for further loans totalling £2,300. The Treasury officials took fright. In their reply, delayed until 28 August, they agreed to an additional loan of £1,099 for new works, but they refused the £1,200 sought for repairs and ordered that these be paid for out of current income, as provided for in the first clause of the Act of 1860. As has been seen, there was no such current income, and Russell approached the Treasury again, in a letter dated 30 August, which he was able to back up with a petition from the Trustees, dated ten days previously. Between them they made the points that the Act of 1860 had contemplated loans for running repairs, that this was the first application for a loan for repairs, and that these repairs represented the accumulation of ten years' neglect. The Treasury considered the matter for two months, but finally sanctioned the £1,200 requested for repairs, adding however that in future the cost of repairs must be met from the first section of the Act of 1860, that is, from current income. In a further letter it said that while regretting to see the money provided for student stipends spent on repairs, it might be so spent as it came in, but there must be no more talk of loans.[27]

Unfortunately the Board of Works found itself short of money to finish works it had begun, and it asked that a further loan be sought.[28] At their June meeting the Trustees instructed Russell to apply for £1,477 16s 8d 'to make up deficiencies in a former estimate', and £1,787 2s 4d for 'sundry improvements in the college and furniture for the new infirmary,' to a total of £3,264 19s. The Treasury replied that it would make no further loans for repairs.[29] In October the Trustees sent a memorial to the Treasury, which led to the latter enquiring from the Board of Works through the Chief Secretary if the sums sought could safely be granted under the Act of 1860, to which the Board replied, fairly predictably, that it was not competent to advise in such matters.[30] On 31 March 1865 the Treasury sanctioned a loan of £3,264.

The Chief Secretary in question was Sir Robert Peel, son of the Prime Minister of the 1845 Act. Russell now tried to use his influence to get money for a project dear to his heart, a worthy College Chapel. He had raised the matter with the Irish bishops in the autumn of 1858, and had got support from some of them, but not enough. All had numerous diocesan collections, and there was the national collection for the Catholic University. When Peel, appointed on 29 July 1861, visited the college towards the end of the year he expressed great dissatisfaction at the existing chapel, which he declared totally unworthy. He asked if his father had planned a chapel, and if Pugin had left a plan. He was answered 'yes' to both questions, and told that Pugin's plan was with the Board of Works.[31] Peel attended the visitation held in 1864, and saw to it that its report to Parliament made a very strong representation on the state of the chapel, so strong indeed that Russell took action as soon as the report had been laid before Parliament and went to London, where he planned to see Gladstone, the Chancellor of the Exchequer, and the Home Secretary, Sir George Grey. From London he wrote this news to Cullen, saying that he had been advised the correct procedure was to present a memorial from the Trustees to the Lord Lieutenant, and as time was pressing before the annual estimates were presented he took the liberty of drafting such a document and enclosed a copy.[32] As presented in March 1865 the memorial recounted the provision made for the college under the Acts of 1845 and 1860, pointed out that under the latter urgent and necessary works had to get priority, and asked for a supplementary grant to build a 'church and common hall'.

In June of that same year the Trustees instructed Russell to apply to the Treasury for sanction for further loans, £765 odd for repairs and £776 odd for 'extra foundations for the infirmary'. After two months, on 26 August, the Treasury sanctioned a loan of £700 for 'completion of works', and wrote to the Board of Works to say that no request for a loan for repairs would be considered without previous approval of the Board. On 2 October the Board instructed its architect to ascertain in consultation with the college authorities how much might be required annually for repairs.[33] There is no indication what came of this initiative, and probably nothing did.

All this would indicate that the memorial seeking a supplementary grant for chapel and hall would not get a favourable response. Russell's desire for a worthy chapel had been strengthened by Peel's interest and patronage, but Peel's term of office expired at the beginning of December 1865. Though the

Trustees had in October requested Russell to remind the Lord Lieutenant of the March memorial, the indications are that they did not push the matter. It had no great prospects in any case, and Archbishop Cullen, who had by now got a firm grip on the Trustees' meetings, did not like Sir Robert Peel, had disliked his visiting Maynooth, and had resented his pressing for a visitation in 1864, even if he used it to bring Maynooth's case for a grant for a chapel to the attention of Parliament. In addition, Cullen did not particularly like Maynooth, and certainly resented any attempt at control by civil authority which might be associated with its dependence on public money.

From all this it is clear that the college's fortunes under the Act of 1860 were mixed. When not merely the Board of Works but Parliament and Government finally severed all connection in consequence of the Irish Church Act of 1869, the Board informed the bursar on 15 February 1871 that the full extent of the loan outstanding (fortunately written off as part of the 1869 settlement) was £18,700, adding that this was as it stood in October 1865.[34] From this it appears that no repayments were made after October 1863, and no new loans approved after August 1865, though the Board continued to carry out a few minor works until advised by the Treasury on 22 November 1869 not to begin any more.

Nevertheless, over these years the college acquired some amenities which could not have been otherwise provided.[35] Chief of these was a new infirmary for the Senior House students. Serious illness and even death, especially from tuberculosis, was an element in even young lives at the time to an extent difficult to realise today: the Visitors in November 1864 noted eleven deaths among the college community in the year 1861/62, two in 1862/63 and seven in 1863/64 (not all these deaths would have occurred in the college, but many did, as the inscriptions in the cemetery and the diary of Professor Daniel McCarthy testify). A tender for £7,218 19s 9d from the firm of Carolan and Kerr of Dublin was accepted in July 1861. The architect was J. J. McCarthy, who was later to build the chapel. It is in a plain Gothic style, as befits a functional building so close to Pugin's uncompleted quadrangle, to which indeed it must have appeared as a slightly detached north side before the building of the chapel and the maturing of the splendid line of alternate green and copper beech planted in front of it. To some extent from the outside but especially inside it gives an impression of height and gauntness, faulted today as being very expensive to heat, but a generation overshadowed by tuberculosis would have approved it as well-ventilated. The building was completed with no more than the problems to be expected in any large project. The contractor's complaints about the quality of the stone available from the quarry in the college grounds which had been used for Pugin's building seem to reflect a reluctance to quarry deep enough: certainly the stone used has worn very well. Then there was the not uncommon problem of builders not completing a contract as soon as they had promised, so serious at the very beginning of 1864 that the Board of Works sought legal advice as to whether they could break the contract and finish the work themselves. Some of this delay must have arisen from the fact that the bursar ordered work outside the contract, and, worse still, without the approval of the Board of Works. At one stage it seemed uncertain if a chapel for the infirmary could be afforded, but it was built, and dedicated to the Blessed Virgin on 8 December 1866, the feast of the Immaculate Conception.[36] It is an interesting building in its own right, with a small floor space but rising to the full height of the main building, with tall windows behind the altar, everything very vertical indeed. Shortly before this—the exact date has not been recorded—the infirmary had come into use. On 3 January 1866 McCarthy recorded in his diary the death of a student, Robert O'Leary of the diocese of Ferns, on the previous day. He had, McCarthy noted, received the last sacraments on the previous 18 October, but lingered on; and he added 'he was the first, I believe, who removed to the new infirmary.'

A second major development, proceeding at the same time, was the erection of gas works. As has been noted, there had been a proposal to provide gas fittings in the new buildings, but this had come to nothing. The matter surfaced again in June 1855 when a committee set up to investigate the financial situation recommended, among other things, 'the erection of a gasometer', and the President and bursar were authorised to seek tenders up to £1,200 and make a recommendation. The matter does not appear subsequently in the minutes of the Trustees, for which financial conditions are probably sufficient explanation, but after 1860 the question could be addressed. Pugin's first plan had included a 'gas works', situated, rather inappropriately, immediately behind an enlarged junior infirmary. A site more remote from the buildings was now chosen, where a brewery had stood since 1834, when its building was ordered by the Trustees, in the spot where it is marked in the first Ordnance Survey map of 1838 (Plate 5), and occupied by 'Gas Works' in the revision of 1872 (Plate 6). From the beginning, students had been offered a choice of beer or water at dinner, as was the usual custom. But social habits began to change not long after 1834, when it had been decided it was worth while to build a domestic brewery. A turning-point came in 1840, when on 14 June Father Mathew addressed the college, from which, ironically, he had been expelled some thirty years before for inviting some of his fellow-students to a party in his room. Now, however, about half of the staff and students—8 and 250 respectively—took the total abstinence pledge. It proved quite acceptable to the students when in response to complaints from them beer was halved at dinner in 1856 in return for tea for breakfast every day, and completely abolished in 1864 in return for butter at breakfast and supper all the year round, instead of only during the plentiful months of May to November. By then, a domestic brewery was no longer needed.

The contractor for the gas-house and mains was a firm called Holloway, while the interior fittings were installed by William Daniel of 55 Mary Street, Dublin. This part of the contract in particular expanded out of effective control, from an initial figure of 615 lights to a final one of 1,293, and a cooking range in the kitchen. Under the circumstances, it was something of an achievement that the return of the students had to be postponed only from 1 September to 1 October 1864.[37] When they returned in the shortening evenings it must have been quite an experience to find how brightly the college was now illuminated, with a gas-light in every student's room instead of a guttering candle. Though the incandescent mantle was still some time in the future, the device whereby a gas-air mixture was used to give light by raising a non-combustible material to white heat had been in existence since the 1820s.

Central heating was installed in Pugin's buildings, the contract being awarded in November 1861 to the firm of Ross and Murray. This was an important step towards making the buildings habitable, to some extent a necessary one, for work still went on in 'staunching' the windows. In February 1862 the contract for fitting out the new library went to the firm of Whelan and Clancy. The design had been drawn up years before by the architect J. J. McCarthy,[38] and it was completed in January 1863. By now the Treasury was beginning to look more guardedly on loans to the college. In August 1865, when all the works mentioned above had been completed, the Board of Works gave notice that a sum of £846 11s 3d still remained and that this would suffice to put up a kitchen yard and build a boundary wall along the western road. Both were built from slender resources, the kitchen yard first, contracted for in May 1867. The total cost was £254 1s 9d, it being built mainly if not exclusively from material salvaged at the demolition of the old infirmary. Visitors sometimes shudder at the thought that it may have been Pugin's idea of a Gothic farmyard, but he is not to blame for it. Neither is he responsible for the large building to the east of the kitchen yard, put up in the early 1850s as a coal store and now full of large oil tanks. The last work to be undertaken was the boundary wall, build at a cost of £503 9s 6d, though an unspecified part of it was built by the landlord, the Duke of Leinster. It was still unfinished in September 1870; the surveyor of the Board of Works was far from satisfied with the workmanship, and the Board would have been happy to pull out leaving it unfinished. After some wrangling they agreed to supervise its completion, and presented their final accounting on 15 February 1871, with a note that the unexpended balance came to £57 10s.

In the words of a minute of the Trustees in June 1849, the effect of the new building was 'the old garden rendered useless, and the recreation-ground of the students curtailed'. A year later the President was authorised 'to enlarge the recreation-grounds in the manner he proposes, and to call in a person experienced in the laying out of grounds'. An undated plan of the college and grounds, with rough pencillings, now in the library, is certainly Renehan's musings on what might be done. There are also two other plans, one rough and one finished, inscribed 'Outline plan submitted for approval: James Frazer, 17 Lower Dorset Street, January 1851.' It shows a walk leading some distance from the west wing of Pugin's buildings, terminating in a cross-walk, from each end of which another walk runs at right angles to the far end of the grounds, one just north of 'the glade', with a balancing walk to the south, just where they are today. Financial constraint did not allow the carrying out of a proposal for a 'private garden, between St Mary's oratory and the cemetery', nor the 'proposed garden for fruit and vegetables' in the area later known as 'the high field'. The visitors in December 1851 reported that much had been done in levelling and draining the grounds, and in June 1860 noted them as thoroughly drained, levelled and planted. What later generations knew as 'the Park' had taken on an outline still familiar.

Frazer had also proposed that the cemetery be walled in. This was done, but only after Renehan's death and in part with a legacy from him. In August 1852 Francis Head had described its neglect in some detail:

> . . . a very small space of ground, surrounded by an ordinary hedge, and choke full of long rank grass and thistles. There was no cross of any sort or kind; indeed all that marked it to be a burying-ground were four flat stones, each resting on four plain pedestals about three feet high. One of these stones was surrounded by iron rails. All were to the memory of the great Dons of this College, whose distinctions were detailed at unusual length in Latin. To the graves of the students—three or four only of which I could manage to find out with my feet, so completely were they covered with weeds—there was neither epitaph, stone, cross, or any memorial whatsoever . . . [39]

Renehan had left £100 to put up an oratory in the cemetery and to place in it or elsewhere marble slabs with the names of those buried there.[40] What happened was slightly different, and cost a little more. The cemetery was surrounded by a low but handsome wall, through which it was entered by a lych-gate on which were inscribed the names of the dead. The impressive copper beeches surrounding the cemetery and the avenue of yews leading to the lych-gate obviously date from the same time. The work was finished by the autumn of 1860.

The interior of the college can still look sparsely furnished, but it must have looked bare indeed in the earlier days. Responding to another initiative taken by Russell, the Trustees agreed in June 1858 to procure portraits of all deceased staff 'of whom authentic portraits can be found', the cost not to exceed £8 each. Individual Trustees and bishops were co-operative, and Russell found a competent young artist. Unfortunately, his name does not appear to have been preserved, but the portraits, which were hung in the new students' refectory, are at least competent as art as well as being invaluable as history.

When the Act of 1845 incorporated the Trustees it specifically authorised them to acquire additional landed property to a value not exceeding £3,000 a year. In 1859 they began to rent extensive lands to the north of the college, in the townland of Laraghbryan. In 1868, in addition to the 'park, garden and pleasure grounds', and the Dunboyne legacy, amounting to 438 acres, held by a fee-farm tenant at an annual rent of £461 18s 2d, they held 123 acres lease-hold in perpetuity, and 218 acres as tenants at will.[41]

The Visitation of 1853

Peel's legislation, especially the Queen's Colleges Act (31 July 1845), had divided the Irish hierarchy fairly evenly. The archbishops divided two and two, Armagh and Dublin not being prepared to reject the colleges. The matter was taken to Rome, where the decision went against them on the issues of sub-stance. When Archbishop Crolly of Armagh died unexpectedly on 6 April 1849 it was inevitable there should be disputes over his successor. These were resolved by the appointment of Paul Cullen, rector of the Irish College, Rome, and native neither to the diocese or province of Armagh. He arrived in Ireland as Archbishop at the beginning of May 1850, and also as papal legate to convene a national synod and establish a Catholic University (the Queen's Colleges had opened the previous October).

The National Synod was held at Thurles from 22 August to 10 September. Differences emerged on some points of ecclesiastical discipline, but the real clash occurred over university education, where the bishops were deeply divid-ed, and on a completely free vote might well have accepted the Queen's Colleges. However, the matters of substance had already been decided by the Pope, and so had to be regarded as beyond debate. But there were some lesser issues, on which all Cullen had to show was a decision by the Congregation of Propaganda. Although he put intense pressure on the individual bishops, and although he got his way, it was by narrow margins, on one vote by sixteen to twelve and on another by fifteen to thirteen. This outcome annoyed Protestant public opinion, and annoyance became outrage consequent on the restoration of the English Catholic Hierarchy on 29 September.

Even before he became Archbishop of Armagh Cullen had been watching developments at Maynooth with suspicion. In letters he wrote to his vice-rector, Tobias Kirby, when he visited Ireland in 1845 and 1847, he referred disparagingly to Maynooth and its staff, speaking with misgivings of their intellectual capacity and of signs emerging that in their new circumstances they would be dangerously subservient to the civil authorities. More pragmati-cally, he added that he was finding it hard to get seminarians to go to Rome, for the free places and £20 allowance to theology students in Maynooth were a great attraction. His suspicions did not diminish when he returned as arch-bishop. He saw more and more Irish seminarians going to Maynooth rather than to other colleges, and he judged some of its professors guilty of favouring 'mixed education', which in the circumstances of the time he considered the great betrayal.[42] Even the Roman-trained Edmund O'Reilly wrote to him say-ing that while he wished the project of a Catholic University every success, and was sending a generous subscription, he had to insist on remaining anonymous, for by now everything was being seized on as an argument for restricting or even abolishing the government grant to Maynooth.[43] These fears were real. The synod of Thurles and the restoration of the English Hierarchy had led to the Ecclesiastical Titles Act on 1 August 1851, and by the time it was enacted Maynooth College was close to the top of the list of Popish institutions that English Protestantism loved to hate. In 1845 Peel had hoped to remove Maynooth from debate in Parliament, but by 1848 it had returned, because the Office of Public Works found it necessary to include in its annual estimates a sum for repairs to the college. Evangelicals and Voluntarists, led by the tireless Charles Spooner, pressed for the restoration of the college grant to the annual estimates and for a far-reaching inquiry into all its aspects, and the government had only a narrow majority when Spooner put down a motion to this effect.

Cullen, however, seemed convinced that any threat to Maynooth was only a feint from a government which really planned to enrich and pervert it. He revealed his mind most clearly in 1851 and 1852 in correspondence with Bernard Smith, preserved in the archives of the Irish College, Rome, and of St Paul-without-the-Walls. Smith, then serving as vice-rector in the college, shortly afterwards quarrelled with his rector, Tobias Kirby, and ultimately became a Benedictine. Cullen told him he was using his speech at the annual prize-giving to appeal directly to the students over the heads of both staff and Trustees, for in both groups he did not trust the majority. His relations with Archbishop Murray had become very embittered: in a series of letters in October and November 1851 Murray wrote to Cullen with real and uncharacteristic harshness. He said he could not give positive support to the plans for a Catholic University; that he was certain Cullen would trade Maynooth's grant for government support for it; and that if his attitude to Maynooth were known it would cause Irish Catholics very real dismay.[44] Cullen's letters corresponding to these have not been traced, but there is a letter to him from Smith dated 30 November, which, after a savage attack on Murray, gleefully reports that after a conversation he had had that morning with Monsignor Barnabò, the secretary of Propaganda, Barnabò had told him that the sooner Maynooth was closed the better.[45]

Political turmoil in England, to which the religious debate contributed, led to the fall of Russell's government at the beginning of 1852. His Conservative successor, the Earl of Derby, failed to get a secure majority in elections held in July, and was defeated on the budget proposals on 17 December. A new government was formed under the Earl of Aberdeen, a coalition of Whigs, Peelites and Radicals. Aberdeen consulted with the Irish MP William Monsell. He told him that the call for an inquiry into Maynooth could no longer be resisted, but he was prepared to be friendly, even helpful. His proposal was that the inquiry should be conducted, not by a Committee of Parliament, but by a Royal Commission, such as had recently held inquiries in Oxford,

Cambridge, and Dublin.[46] The warrant for this was issued on 19 September 1853.

In his subsequent strictures on the Maynooth staff, Cullen kept singling out three by name: Henry Neville, George Crolly, and Patrick Murray. Neville was a young man, ordained for the diocese of Cork in 1847 and appointed to Maynooth in 1850. His transgression was that he was reputed to favour the Queen's Colleges. This was not surprising, for Cork people, including the bishop and many of the clergy, had widely welcomed the prospect of a university college in their city. Crolly was a nephew of the late Archbishop of Armagh, and he had resented what he considered slurs on his late uncle arising out of the debate on the Colleges. His efforts to defend him drew on him the pen of Cullen's uncle, James Maher, parish priest of Carlowgraigue. The exchange quickly became vituperative.

The case of Patrick Murray raised issues of more substance. A native of Clones, Co. Monaghan, he was ordained for the diocese of Clogher in 1837, appointed professor of English and French in 1838, and of Theology in 1841. When the college statute forbidding professors to publish without permission of the President was abolished in 1848 he prepared himself to publish a set of essays each year. His first volume appeared in 1850 with the title *The Irish Annual Miscellany*. A second followed in 1851, and a third in 1852, this time with the title *Essays Chiefly Theological*. The fourth and last, in 1853, reverted to the title of the first two. Murray was already preparing a very large-scale treatise on the Church, *De Ecclesia Christi* (3 vols., 1860, 1862, 1866), but these annual collections had a different purpose in mind. In the tradition it had been hoped to establish in Maynooth's postgraduate school, the Dunboyne, they were written in English and dealt with questions of the day. Here theology was interwoven with politics, ecclesiastical and secular.

In November 1849 Murray was writing agitatedly to Propaganda in Rome. He had, he said, been one of a group of four from the staff who had publicly opposed their senior colleague, John O'Hanlon, as a candidate for the vacant see of Armagh. This had drawn on them the anger of O'Hanlon's supporters, and he feared that what he planned to publish, what was indeed already in print, on delicate issues concerning church and state might be misrepresented to the Roman authorities. He enclosed proofs of pages 56–100 of the first volume of *The Irish Annual Miscellany*, being the second half of a long essay on state endowment of the Irish Church.[47]

There is nothing in the archives of Propaganda to indicate that any of O'Hanlon's supporters made any move against Murray, but he thought it prudent to write to Archbishop Cullen when he arrived in Ireland, explaining what he was doing and seeking his patronage. By the end of the year, however, Cullen, already incensed by Crolly's attacks on his uncle, was reading Murray's second volume with a suspicious eye, notably the concluding section on 'Mixed Education'. Here he found an assertion 'that, in certain circumstances, certain forms of mixed education may be, not merely tolerated as a lesser evil, but accepted as themselves good and sinless, though a lesser good.'[48] Murray went on to explain that he was considering a situation in which the only existing institutions were actively proselytising Protestant ones, and there was no hope whatever of a Catholic college. Cullen read this as a subtle defence of the Queen's Colleges, and wrote to Kirby in Rome saying that if Murray were to approach the authorities there again he should be pulled up. He expected Kirby to pass this letter on to Propaganda, which he did.[49]

Meanwhile castigation much more swift than any Roman dicastery descended on Crolly and Murray from Frederick Lucas in the pages of the *Tablet*. Lucas (1812–55), an Englishman, had become a Catholic in 1839 and founded the *Tablet* the following year. He became more and more interested in Irish affairs, and transferred the *Tablet* to Dublin, where the first issue appeared on 5 January 1850. Sincere, impatient and tactless to a very high degree, he was rather more ultramontane than the Pope. It would not be long before Cullen would find Lucas an impossible ally, but for the moment he was welcome, as is clear from his correspondence with Kirby and Smith in Rome. To Smith on 25 January he remarked that it was curious how 'all that party' were 'Young Irelanders and government men at the same time', and writing to Propaganda on 28 September he said their position looked like 'pure Jansenism'.[50] Indeed it began to look like Polonius's cloud, like a camel, backed like a weasel, and very like a whale. But Archbishop John MacHale, soon with Lucas to be a thorn in Cullen's side, wrote on 29 January that the Maynooth writings had excited universal disgust, and that at their next meeting the Trustees must put an end to that kind of thing.[51]

Murray, who had engaged in newspaper polemics with Lucas, had reason to feel disturbed. On 12 June he wrote to Propaganda, enclosing a Latin summary of what he had written about mixed education.[52] This was handed over to Smith for his verdict, which he submitted on 9 July. It was characteristically intemperate. Murray and Crolly, it alleged, had given grave scandal; Murray had argued that the Queen's Colleges might be tolerated as a lesser evil, and his book should be put on the Index.[53] The reply of the Congregation to Murray on 12 July has not been traced, though it must have been much more measured. Smith kept assuring Cullen that it would go hard with Murray in Rome, and from Ireland Cullen kept Smith supplied with details, mostly rumour, of the misdeeds of Murray and Crolly—it was being said, he asserted, that they were going around saying there was no obligation to obey the decrees of the synod of Thurles, and commented, '*Che bravi professori*'.[54] Nevertheless, Cullen, while still providing information to Smith, was clearly not pressing hard at Propaganda. In a long letter on many things, dated 28 September, there is only a passing reference to Maynooth and its professors. On 4 October Murray, in a long reply to the Congregation's letter of 7 July, explained what he had written in almost painful detail.

He said he had been discussing a purely hypothetical case, in order to show

how the situation in Ireland was different from one in which mixed education might conceivably be accepted; that everyone was agreed he was against the Colleges (he claimed, with what seems a touch of pride, that the *Athenaeum* had called him a bigot), everyone, that is, except Frederick Lucas and the *Tablet*. He claimed that what he wrote induced many who had been wavering to reject the Colleges; and finally he professed that he would obey the Bishops and the Holy See in everything, as he had always done. His letter was on the table at the routine weekly meeting of Propaganda on 7 November. The indications are that by now the officials of the Congregation had informed themselves to the extent of feeling slightly embarrassed. Their decision is recorded in a note on the letter to the effect that no reply was necessary: *Non esige risposto. Congresso 7 Nov. 1851.*[55]

Beyond question in this letter Murray had very fairly summarised what he had written, and he was certainly badly used. Regrettably, but naturally, he was discouraged from writing theologically in English on questions of the day. In the introduction to his fourth and last volume, published in 1853, he said he had been planning six but had now decided to stop, giving as his reason the demands made on his time by his Latin treatise, *De Ecclesia Christi*. When this came it was an exhaustive work, also an outstanding one, but firmly in the 'manual' tradition; and even though it gave the first full Catholic theological treatment to the Anglican position, Irish theology was left the poorer when Patrick Murray stopped writing in English.

Visitations and Visitors

The Act of 1845 had laid down elaborate regulations for visitation. The two Archbishops were to continue to be Visitors, together with 'such other five persons as her Majesty shall . . . from time to time nominate'. Three were to form a quorum. There was to be an annual visitation, with additional ones at the request of the Lord Lieutenant. Minutes of each visitation were to be kept, on the basis of which a report was to be made to the Queen and laid before Parliament. The minutes were kept and the reports presented, but the Visitors had such limited powers that these are valuable mainly as evidence for what was happening in the college, and not as influencing its running in any real way. This was because the limitation continued that matters affecting 'exercise of the Roman Catholic religion or the religious doctrine and discipline thereof' were the exclusive concern of the Catholic Visitors, the only stipulation being that they should exercise their functions in the presence of the others.

In fact, the personnel of the Visitors changed very little over the years. The Duke of Leinster was chairman, and in addition to the two archbishops there was Lord Fingall, acknowledged senior of the lay Trustees, and of course a Catholic. The others were the Chief Secretary for the time being, the Chief Baron of the Exchequer, D. R. Pigot, who served from beginning to end, as did the seventh visitor, William Parsons, Earl of Rosse. It was Pigot

(1797–1873), a distinguished lawyer, who insisted that the minutes be first written by the secretary to the Trustees, and a separate report to Parliament compiled from them.[56] Worse, he began to insist that the students should have an absolute right of appeal to the Visitors, but though he pressed this point he did not win it.[57] When Cullen arrived in 1850 he judged it quite unacceptable that Protestants should be reporting to Parliament on the affairs of a Catholic seminary. While Archbishop Murray of Dublin was trying to smooth over difficulties so that visitation might continue, Cullen simply did not attend while he was Archbishop of Armagh. After Murray's death in February 1852 no further visitation was held until 1860. There can be no doubt that this was due to Cullen. While the visitation was formally ordered by the Duke of Leinster as chairman, the secretarial work was done by Matthew Flanagan, secretary to the Trustees and a priest of Cullen's diocese of Dublin.

The Royal Commission of 1853 was not restricted by the provisions of the legislation of 1845: it was simply empowered to examine 'the management and government of the College of Maynooth, the discipline and the course of studies pursued therein.'[58] The five commissioners named were men of strong religious convictions and with notable legal and educational interests. The chairman was Dudley Ryder, second Earl of Harrowby. 'Solid, sensible and reasonable', he was a dedicated member of the Established Church, with many philanthropic interests and in politics a moderate Peelite. The second English member, Travers Twiss, and one of the three Irish, Mountifort Longfield, were both clergymen's sons and distinguished lawyers. Then there was Chief Baron Pigot, a link with the statutory Visitors; and finally, James More O'Ferrall, a Catholic, who, like Longfield, was a commissioner of the Board of National Education and had also been one of the eight laymen appointed to the committee of the Catholic University in 1850.

The Trustees were invited to make suggestions as to what topics might be inquired into. There is no evidence that any of them did this. They were not examined by the Commission, but the whole staff was, together with past students who had left the priesthood, present students representing a 'committee of grievances', and some others, including notably David Moriarty, president of All Hallows. Beyond question, the approach of this inquiry was more understanding, less hostile, than had been the case in 1826, but it was much more rigorous than the contemporary commissions in Oxford, Cambridge, or Dublin.[59] The Maynooth inquiry held forty sessions in all, from 20 September to 26 October 1853, from 3 to 11 January 1854, and finally, to complete the writing of its report, from 1 to 8 January 1855. It was presented to Parliament on 1 March. This was certainly a weighty document, two folio volumes, in all 779 pages.[60] However, like the annual visitations, much of the report is more useful for the information it provides than for any way in which it directly influenced college policy. It did not take a Royal Commission to point out defects in the academic and disciplinary situation, though it might perhaps have been hoped that analysis by so weighty a body might have hastened a remedy. And while it exposed shortcomings clearly, on the other hand it offered nothing to those who had called for blood. On the two most sensitive issues, as far as Protestant public opinion was concerned, namely 'certain points . . . on which the spiritual and temporal authority have been, or might be, in conflict' (that is, papal authority in the realm), and 'those portions of Moral Theology which relate to purity of life' (with special reference to confessional practice), the judgement of the Commission was unambiguously favourable to the college and its teaching.

CHAPTER VI

INTO THE NEW ORDER

Staff

Cullen was in possession of the evidence given before the Commission long before its report was published: it was regularly passed to him by one of the Commissioners, James More O'Ferrall. At the end of October 1854 he left for Rome to be present at the definition of the Immaculate Conception on 8 December, accompanied by five other bishops, Armagh (Dixon), Tuam (MacHale), Clogher (McNally), Clonfert (Derry) and Cloyne (Murphy). He went with a firm determination to seek a verdict on Maynooth and specifically its theological teaching, on which he believed he had damning evidence in the testimony given before the Commission. Some time after he left Ireland the controversy came to a head between himself and Frederick Lucas and the Tenant League on the issue of 'priests in politics', when the Tenant League decided to appeal to Rome. This led to Propaganda setting up a 'special commission' to inquire into Irish problems,[1] which kept Cullen in Rome until the end of June 1855.

The six Irish bishops were invited to a meeting in Propaganda in December, which seems to have been exclusively concerned with the question of Maynooth. They divided three and three. By now relations between Cullen and MacHale had become very embittered, and he was supported in his opposition to Cullen by two other past members of the college staff, Derry and McNally. The matter was referred to Propaganda for a decision. It was at this meeting that it became known that Cullen was in possession of at least a substantial part of the evidence given to the Commission, and that he communicated this to Propaganda.[2] Inevitably, this information was relayed to Maynooth. Shortly after Archbishop Dixon returned to Ireland he reported to Cullen that three of the professors had written in protest to Lord Harrowby, who had replied, Dixon alleged, that he saw nothing remarkable in letting a trustee and a visitor know what was being taught in the college. The secret was now out, and there were plenty of hard words against Cullen, in Parliament and in the newspapers and reviews, but they broke no bones. In Rome, a decision on the question advanced slowly over the next six months, all the more slowly because it was only one of a number of issues concerning Ireland. The first session of the 'special commission' was held on 18 January, and relations steadily deteriorated between Cullen and Monsignor Barnabò, the secretary of Propaganda, on the one hand and MacHale and his two episcopal supporters on the other. The three of them left Rome abruptly early in February. Lucas remained there to oppose Cullen, but his interest was the Tenant League and he was not particularly friendly towards Maynooth.

Cullen's views were put forward in two documents, one a routine report on his diocese, presented on 27 March, the other a long document on all the Irish issues, elaborated in final form by 23 April. The authority of the bishops in Maynooth, he said, was very much restricted by the system of Trustees and Visitors. He had no complaint against the superiors, or against most of the professors and students. Some professors, however, were still unsatisfactory in the matter of Gallicanism, notably George Crolly. He also named as suspect Patrick Murray and Henry Neville. He submitted in evidence an Italian translation of a considerable part of the evidence Crolly had given to the Commission. He asked for a Roman decision because the Irish bishops were divided, and he asked that any professor judged to be offending be removed (it is clear he had been nettled by what he judged Crolly's claim that no bishop could remove him because he was teaching theology in a public college).[3]

Expert theological opinion was sought from Giovanni Perrone SJ, at this time rector of the Collegio Romano. His verdict was very hostile to Crolly, to the verge, one might suggest, of unfairness. He made four general recommendations: that the Theology textbook be changed (in fact, Bailly had been discontinued in January 1853); that the removal of certain professors might be considered; that the President or prefect of studies be given authority to supervise theological teaching and to bring any problems to the notice of the Bishops; and that the Congregation of Propaganda should issue some general declaration of disapproval. The Congregation gave its decision on 14 June. Perrone's recommendations were accepted, but there were to be no dismissals. Instead, Crolly was to be gently induced to retract his opinions and to agree to visit Rome, where, it was hoped, he might be brought to a better frame of mind. A letter was sent to the Trustees asking that no action be taken on the Commission's report at their June meeting. Cullen left Rome at the end of the month and was in Dublin by the middle of July.

Rumour and report had preceded him, but he must have felt reasonably in control of the situation. At their June meeting, the Trustees had deferred action to June 1856. But as the weeks passed and no formal communication from Propaganda arrived, Cullen began to grow anxious. Nothing had arrived when Maynooth opened on 29 August. The first good news came in a letter from Moran dated 4 September. Once Cullen had left, Moran wrote, Propaganda had dithered, some arguing that at this time it would be wrong to offend the government, others that one of the professors might appeal to the government if proceeded against. On Saturday 1 September Kirby had received a note from Cullen saying that unless Propaganda sent its decision he would cease to attend meetings of the Trustees and would let the others manage as best they could. Kirby took the letter to Propaganda, as he was meant to do, and the following Tuesday Moran could assure Cullen that the decision would soon be on its way.[4] It was dated 6 September, posted on 15 September, and arrived in Dublin in the then customary eight days. The decision was to be implemented by the four Archbishops.

Propaganda followed this up with another letter, dated 17 September, urging Cullen to proceed diplomatically. What was needed was not a triumph over Crolly but a retraction from him and a promise to go to Rome.[5] Dixon too counselled that nothing should be done until after the Trustees' meeting on 16 October, when the four Archbishops could consult informally. He wrote a few days later saying he had arranged to meet Crolly in Dublin, after which they could both meet Cullen, as it was desirable there should be agreement before the Trustees met.[6] There was naturally much anxiety among the staff in Maynooth. As early as March Murray was writing to his friend Gavan Duffy saying that Cullen was making desperate efforts to control the college, using all kinds of underhand means, and that nothing could save them except a parliamentary inquiry. These were the circumstances in which he and two others had written to Lord Harrowby.[7] In the news media this action was rapidly attributed to 'the Maynooth staff', and in a body so divided it was natural there should be a group wishing to exculpate themselves. What was claimed to be 'more than a third' drew up a document, but when it came to presenting it to Cullen only two were willing to sign it.[8] In any case, the incident showed a divided and demoralised staff. That same evening a letter of unqualified submission was received from Crolly,[9] and it was proposed that the archbishops should meet to put an end to the matter on 15 November. Now, however, MacHale raised difficulties. The Archbishop of Cashel was old and ill. He had not been at the meeting of the Trustees, and it was not to be expected he would attend the meeting of the archbishops on 15 November. MacHale pointed out that Propaganda had explicitly remitted the matter to the four archbishops, and claimed that if the four could not assemble new instructions must be sought. Dixon and Cullen decided they would proceed even if MacHale did not come, and the meeting at Maynooth went ahead on 15 November.[10]

There are accounts from both sides of what must have been a tense and painful occasion: several letters from Cullen, and a memorandum by Patrick Murray, obviously written while the wounds were raw.[11] Both sides agree substantially as to what happened. George Crolly was first interviewed separately; he confirmed his submission and his willingness to go to Rome at the beginning of Lent. The rest of the staff were interviewed together in the Board Room. Murray found it particularly difficult that as a body they should be addressed insensitively from a high moral ground by Dixon, who had been until recently one of them. Cullen he found by contrast courteous, but also insensitive to the pressures under which the staff gave evidence to the Royal Commission on the question of papal authority, and that given the circumstances their good intentions should have been presumed. The fact was that, apart from Crolly, the Roman authorities had not attached a special censure to any specific individual. There was, of course, the letter to Lord Harrowby, and on this Cullen took an unyielding position. It was, he maintained, an appeal from ecclesiastical to secular authority. He had considered withdrawing ecclesiastical faculties from the signatories, but finally decided not to. When all this was over MacHale put in an appearance. It was about half past one, and he claimed he could not have arrived any earlier, having spent seven hours travelling from Tuam by the first available transport. He had not been given any hour for the meeting, he wrote to the Cardinal Prefect of Propaganda, and he did feel aggrieved that it had gone ahead without waiting for him.[12]

At the general Bishops' Meeting on 20 and 21 June 1856 Cullen pressed home his advantage, getting formal approval for the events of the previous November, and agreement that both Propaganda's letter of 6 September 1855 and Crolly's submission of 15 November should be inserted in the minutes of the meeting. There was a long debate over inserting Crolly's letter, bishops arguing that to do this would cast a slur on Maynooth or give offence to the government, but in the end it was agreed to do so, though the meeting also recorded its confidence in the general orthodoxy of the college and its commendation of Crolly for his prompt submission. When Cullen tried to go further and press charges against Murray and Neville only Dixon supported him. Other bishops adopted the tactic of blurring the issue, and in this they were successful. There was an even longer debate when MacHale challenged a sentence in the letter of Propaganda which, he said, implied that the doctrines condemned in 1853 were the same as those advanced to the Commission of 1826, where he himself had given evidence. In the end, Cullen had to agree to the insertion of a rider in the minutes to the effect that any such charge was aimed at one person only, Nicholas Slevin.[13] But when Propaganda considered the episcopal decisions at a meeting on 9 February 1857 it insisted this rider must be deleted, on the grounds that the only point it had been making was that the Congregation's silence in 1826 had not implied approval. Further, to certain regulations the bishops had made for the running of Maynooth it added that Cullen as local Ordinary had authority in case of necessity to suspend a professor whose orthodoxy was suspect pending a meeting of the Trustees.[14]

By the time the Bishops met in June 1856 Crolly should have fulfilled his undertaking to go to Rome. Early in March, however, he had written to Dixon saying he could not go for family reasons, but promising to go in September.[15] By then he had heard of the insertion of his letter of submission into the minutes (inevitably, for the bishops were as divided as the college staff) and he resented this further humiliation. It seems to have been Dixon who finally persuaded him to go, together with his bishop, Cornelius Denvir, who was in

Rome on other business. Dixon undertook to ask that he be awarded a DD while in Rome, and Denvir supported the request. But the Roman authorities were unwilling to give him this honour in the circumstances.[16] He renewed the request in 1861. The Propaganda authorities consulted Cullen, who replied that the honour should not be granted until Crolly had personally published his retractation (in the same letter Cullen recommended for a doctorate Gerald Molloy, a Dublin priest appointed to teach theology in Maynooth immediately after his ordination in 1857).[17] Sixteen years later, in the autumn of 1877, Bishop Patrick Dorrian of Down and Connor inquired in Rome about the possibility of securing an honour, a domestic prelacy or doctorate, for two ageing priests of his diocese who had given long service to Maynooth, George Crolly and the President, Charles W. Russell, saying 'It would give satisfaction, I think, to the Irish Bishops. Any reason that ever existed for withholding it has long passed away.' Russell became a domestic prelate, but Crolly got no doctorate. In the closing days of 1877 Dorrian wrote to Kirby to tell him that Crolly was dying (he died on 24 January 1878). 'As it is now', he wrote, 'I shall keep the matter quite secret from him; but it would have given great satisfaction to the clergy of Ireland had the old errors been forgotten.'[18]

It was a bitter controversy, generating so much heat that the issues never completely focused. As has been seen, Cullen made unsuccessful efforts to find grounds to proceed personally against Murray and Neville, against Murray because he had claimed that circumstances might arise in which mixed education could be regarded not merely as a lesser evil but as a lesser good, against Neville because, like many in Cork, he had spoken in favour of the Queen's Colleges. The charges against Crolly sounded more academically theological: Perrone found him guilty, or at least suspect, of what he called 'Gallicanism' under twelve distinct heads.[19] By now, however, 'Gallicanism' was losing sharp definition. It need mean no more than a general addiction to old French attitudes to church authority, and similarly 'Jansenism' need mean no more than an extreme form of 'Gallicanism'. It would appear that Crolly was not a Gallican in any strict sense: there is, for example, interesting testimony from ex-pupils, now priests attached to the pro-cathedral in Marlborough Street, at the time that clouds were gathering in the spring of 1855: they knew from his lectures, they said, that any such charge was without foundation.[20] Yet there can be no doubt that in his evidence to the Royal Commission he provided rope enough to hang himself. It is not easy to be sure why: there may have been a kind of donnish anxiety to explain himself more fully than his listeners really wanted to hear, but it is even more likely that the polemic he had been engaged in in defence of his uncle had gradually led him into unguarded expression. After his ordeal, like his colleague Patrick Murray he turned to the manual tradition, producing treatises on justice and contracts that, like Murray's treatise on the Church, made a real contribution in that they took account of British and Irish civil law, so that students had no longer to be told by their professor that in these matters they must ignore the edicts of long-dead French kings referred to in their textbook.

As for Cullen, certainly in the early 1850s he would define 'ultramontane' simply as being a good Catholic, ready to obey without question decisions of the Pope or of his Curia. It does seem fair to say that in the 1850s, apart from the practical pressures of the education question, intellectually he was not adequately placed to grasp the way in which Maynooth reflected the subtly changing position of northern European Catholicism generally. He did believe there was an unacceptable 'Gallican' element in the theological teaching there. This conviction was reinforced by more practical issues arising from the Queen's Colleges, the Catholic University, and the Ecclesiastical Titles Bill. Neither would it be doing justice to the evidence to ignore the fact that there was an element of a power struggle in the whole affair. Cullen regarded effective episcopal control over Maynooth as essential, and as the college was exclusively concerned with preparing candidates for the priesthood this was not an unreasonable position. As will be seen in a little more detail, he did use the events of the mid-1850s to get more control for the bishops, but he regarded even this as insufficient and began to develop his own diocesan seminary at Clonliffe.

What may be regarded as a dispassionate analysis of the theological issues in the debate appeared only after Cullen and Crolly had died. It was occasioned by an article in the *Dublin Review* for October 1879, entitled 'Theology, past and present, at Maynooth', by Henry Neville, one of the three professors singled out by Cullen for censure. He had resigned in 1867 and returned to Cork, and there are grounds for suspicion that the article was written to promote his candidature as coadjutor to the ageing bishop, William Delany. It was, in truth, not a very searching article. He claimed that Gallicanism had been 'carefully cultivated' at Maynooth for the first half-century of its existence, but that afterwards the teaching staff had thought their way out of this innately weak system of theology. A much more satisfactory reply, 'The alleged Gallicanism of Maynooth and the Irish clergy', appeared in the next number (January 1880). It was by William J. Walsh, at that time vice-president of the college, soon to be President, and not long afterwards Archbishop of Dublin. He belonged to a younger generation, ordained in 1866 and appointed to the staff the following year, in fact in succession to Neville. He made two particularly telling points. The first was that before the definitions of 1870 the issues of 'theological Gallicanism', that is, papal primacy and infallibility, were regarded as matters for discussion in the schools, the arguments for and against being set out. The second was that the retreat from Gallicanism had begun before the date claimed by Neville, and that it had been a slow and gradual process. He appealed to the earlier Commission of 1826 for proof that the original Gallican position had never been part of Maynooth teaching. In particular, he adduced the evidence of Thomas Furlong, who had been examined as a student in 1826 and as a professor in 1853. Appointed Bishop of Ferns in 1857, he had been one of the four 'inopportunist' Irish bishops at the First Vatican Council, believing that the time was not ripe for a formal definition of infallibility. Asked in 1853 if the teaching in the college was the same as in 1826, he had replied: 'Yes, I am not aware of any difference, save that a more decided bias prevails generally in favour of the infallibility of the Pope and his authority in spiritual matters.' In Maynooth as elsewhere theological Gallicanism was in retreat, and the retreat had begun well before 1850. Furlong's scrupulously careful judgement echoed that of Edmund O'Reilly in 1839.[21]

Cullen pressed on steadily with his aim of getting Maynooth under the control of the bishops. As he saw it, it would not be easy: as he wrote to William Monsell MP on 1 September 1855:

> It will be difficult to make any change at Maynooth without giving some occasion to the bigots to assail us. My humble opinion is that the college never can go on properly, until it will be reduced to smaller dimensions. If the government would divide the grant into four portions, and let there be four colleges or more, things would go on much better. At present no one has in reality any control over the college and hence there is to be found in it on the one side a strong Gallican spirit and on the other a great democratic tendency which is the occasion of the great interference of priests in politics. These evils will never be corrected whilst the governing power of the college is constituted as it is, consisting of eleven bishops and seven or eight laymen. It would be very different in a college less numerous and with a more compact governing body . . .[22]

But already by 1854 he was taking steps to change the system. At the general Bishops' Meeting in May a number of regulations were drawn up for the domestic affairs of the college, thus emphasising, Cullen explained to Propaganda, that in these matters control should rest with the Bishops rather than with the Trustees.[23] This practice continued at subsequent Bishops' meetings, but Cullen had nevertheless to live with the Trustees. When the President, Laurence Renehan, died at the end of July 1857 he was unwilling to see the vice-president, Robert ffrench Whitehead, promoted, apart altogether from the fact that MacHale favoured him. He himself favoured Matthew Kelly, 'a very good holy Roman' though ordained in Maynooth, with interests in a field Cullen was much interested in, the Irish Christian past, hardworking but dogged by ill-health (he died on 30 October 1858). Most of the lay Trustees, however, favoured Charles W. Russell, who was chosen President on 20 October 1857. Russell's election was possibly the last occasion on which the lay Trustees exercised an important influence. For the most part, they were not closely in touch with the workings of the college. In almost all cases chosen on the hereditary principle, it was inevitable that some of them should not even be greatly interested. When one of them died in 1867 a proposal that he be replaced by a bishop was apparently judged worthy of serious consideration[24] even though it did not happen. The lay Trustees were losing importance well before the Irish Church Act of 1869 saw them disappear.

The annual visitation prescribed in 1845 Cullen found even less palatable: so many of the Visitors were Protestants and they were statutorily bound to report to a Parliament where so many seized every opportunity of attacking Maynooth. He dealt with this problem by seeing to it that the Visitors met as seldom as possible. On 10 June 1860 Chief Baron Pigot wrote to the under-secretary, Thomas Larcom, demanding that a visitation be held—the last had been in 1851—and complaining that the idea had been put about that the 1853 Commission had superseded the annual visitation, or at least left it with no function. It was true, he conceded, that the Visitors' statutory powers were marginal indeed, but they did have a statutory obligation to carry out an annual visitation.[25] This initiative led to a visitation on 20 June 1860, attended by the Archbishops of Armagh and Dublin, the Earl of Fingall, and the Chief Baron, and another on 4 June 1861, attended by the Duke of Leinster, the Earl of Fingall, the Earl of Rosse, and again the Chief Baron. Neither ruffled the scene very much, but an incident at the end of the year showed how the possibility of visitation was sensed as a kind of threat in the college, and why it was considered desirable to avoid it. On 10 November the funeral of Terence Bellew McManus took place in Dublin. Archbishop Cullen had refused to allow the body to lie in state in the pro-cathedral, on the grounds that the occasion was political, not religious. At Maynooth, some students held a sur-reptitious Office for the Dead. The President, Charles W. Russell, took action, what precisely does not seem to be recorded, but it may be presumed to have been drastic.[26] But as well he consulted Cullen in some anxiety to the effect that if the Lord Lieutenant came to hear of it he might order a special visitation, as he was legally empowered to do. Cullen in turn consulted Richard More O'Ferrall, one of the lay Trustees, a man who took his duties very seriously. O'Ferrall gave his opinion, with which Cullen agreed. The incident was certain to become known. The thing to do was to ask what Cullen called 'the head Visitor' if in his opinion it was necessary to hold a visitation. He would reply that it was better not to make a fuss; and this would protect the college should the matter ever come before the government. By 'the head Visitor' Cullen seems to have meant the Archbishop of Armagh, not the Duke of Leinster. At any rate Russell in his reply to Cullen said he had in fact notified Dixon in his capacity as trustee and visitor, so that the matter might be raised at the next meeting of the Trustees if that were felt useful. This was far better than submitting it to the Visitors, thereby 'inviting lay and Protestant interference'.[27]

There were no more visitations until Pigot again took the initiative in May 1864, when he wrote to Walter Lee, secretary to the Trustees, saying that Chief Secretary Peel was expecting a report from the Visitors, and that Lee should write to the Duke of Leinster and Archbishop Cullen. Lee wrote to both the same day, inviting the Duke to preside at a visitation. Cullen's reply to Lee has not been traced, but Lee's reply to Cullen indicates that it had been an angry one. The visitation took place on 23 November 1864, attended by the Duke, Archbishop Cullen, the Chief Secretary and the Chief Baron. Again it accomplished little or nothing, though Pigot did produce a petition from the Dunboyne students alleging irregularities in the administration of their stipends.[28]

Peel retired as Chief Secretary at the end of 1865, Larcom as under-secretary in 1868. There were no more visitations, though there are clear indications that Russell, for one, may have felt that not holding them was more trouble than it was worth. The issue surfaced finally in April 1869, when Maynooth's position was being probed in the debates on the Irish Church Act. The only effect seems to have been to cause Russell some uneasiness, and when the Act became law on 26 July the college had no more obligations to Parliament.[29]

Studies

It took the passage of time to improve relations with Cullen, a new broom determined to sweep clean. A major issue was the Theology textbooks used in the college, Delahogue for most of Dogmatic theology, Bailly for a little Dogma and all Moral, both of them deriving from the French pre-revolutionary Gallican tradition. In France itself a forceful Nuncio, Fornari, had been sent in 1843 to break the Gallican heritage, and he had registered major success by the time he returned to Rome as a Cardinal in 1850. Curiously, however, it was an Irish cleric who initiated the controversy that led to Bailly's works being placed on the Index. Though Tobias Kirby, Cullen's successor as rector of the Irish College, Rome, made one of his very few visits to Ireland in the spring of 1852, the person who brought the matter to the attention of the Pope, apparently by a casual remark to the effect that Bailly was the textbook in Maynooth, seems to have been Bernard Smith, at that time Kirby's vice-rector.

The result of this information was a request to the Nuncio in Paris on 31 August to make discreet inquiries. He reported on 20 October that Bailly was very widely used indeed in French seminaries, but he advised that no action be taken. While it was true that in its original form it could be described as a monument to eighteenth-century Gallicanism, substantial modifications had been made in subsequent editions, notably in 1829, when the strongest Gallican statements had been relegated to an appendix, with the suggestion that they were purely hypothetical. The book was popular with students, the Nuncio reported, because it was well written, and it was being used intelligently by their teachers. Reaction in Rome was divided, some wishing to follow the Nuncio's recommendation, but others, including Fornari, pressing for condemnation. A compromise of sorts was reached at a meeting of the Congregation of the Index, where Fornari found himself in a minority of six to two: Bailly would be put on the Index pending correction—*donec corrigatur.* But even this was strong action—public condemnation of a work so widely used, without prior consultation or even warning. It was much resented in France.[30]

From Rome, Smith in particular was keeping Cullen informed. Already on 24 November Propaganda had written to him to see that Bailly was removed from Maynooth, and on 8 December, the day after the Pope confirmed the decision of the Congregation of the Index, Tobias Kirby wrote enclosing a copy of the decree.[31] Cullen would have liked to see Bailly removed, and indeed Delahogue as well, but he could see problems, as is clear from his rather hesitant first reply to Kirby. Kirby's answer contained little comfort. The Maynooth senior dean, Walter Lee, had arrived in Rome on sabbatical leave and read to Kirby part of a letter he had received from Renehan, in which it was pointed out that that the part of Bailly read in Maynooth did not concern Gallicanism or the prerogatives of the papacy; that while the Trustees could undoubtedly order its removal this might cause an uproar and might indeed involve the government; and that it was maintained in certain quarters—including, it was said, by John O'Hanlon, Prefect of the Dunboyne—that decrees of the Index were not received in Ireland. From Paris Kirby had got news from John Miley, the rector of the Irish College, that when Archbishop MacHale had been there on visitation he had asked him to remove Bailly as a textbook because the Pope had disapproved of it and was about to place it on the Index, and that MacHale had refused, on the grounds that it had been so long in use and continued to be used in Maynooth.[32]

However, the removal of Bailly from Maynooth was inevitable. The Trustees took their decision when they met on 18 January 1853. Cullen saw to it that the decision was minuted as having been taken because in Rome it had been placed on the Index. The President, the Prefect of the Dunboyne and the professors of Theology were instructed to select another textbook of Moral Theology and submit it for approval. There were problems in finding such a textbook. As J. P. Cooke reported from Waterford to Kirby, a bit sardonically and a bit unfairly, one rumour was that the professors, none of whom, he supposed, had ever sat an hour at confessions, were planning jointly to write a Moral Theology; and Cullen, reporting on 21 February to Propaganda that there had been no problem in removing Bailly, had to admit that as yet there was no agreement on what to put in its place.[33] In this Maynooth was not exceptional: the same search for a replacement for a work that had been so taken for granted was occurring all over France.

Cullen and his friends in Rome would have liked to see Delahogue go the way of Bailly, but caution was needed. An undated note in Kirby's hand, which may however be assigned to the end of January 1853, indicated to Propaganda the danger of the expected Royal Commission probing the question of Ultramontanism, and in this context might make a fuss about the removal of Bailly, so that Cullen had decided it was prudent to do nothing about Delahogue for the present.[34] Even Smith, perhaps not noted for caution or prudence, admitted that a condemnation of Delahogue was unlikely, because he was 'within the limits of Gallicanism'. He nevertheless urged Propaganda to write asking that his books be removed in Maynooth, which the

Congregation did on 16 February, though their letter does not seem to understand the precise role the textbooks of Bailly and Delahogue had played there.[35] Cullen mulled over this for some time. He had room to manoeuvre, because the order to remove Delahogue did not have the backing of papal authority. He replied to Propaganda on 30 April, indicating that he would do as asked if pressed, but urging reasons for not doing it. Delahogue, he said, had taught at Maynooth for nearly thirty years, and had written his books for college use. He added that it was said that his works when published had been examined in Rome and that nothing had been found to fault in them.[36] (There is some support for this in an entry for 10 December 1815 in the diary of Michael Blake, the Dublin priest later to be entrusted with the reopening of the Irish College in Rome, and present there from October 1815 to January 1816 in connection with the Veto controversy. Referring to an audience with one of the officials of Propaganda, he wrote: 'He bestowed some encomiums on Dr Delahogue's book *De Ecclesia* which I had submitted to him at his request, but he repeated his former assertion that on some points he did not dwell sufficiently.')[37] And finally, Cullen urged that there was no point in making unnecessary difficulties with the now inevitable Royal Commission.

In June 1853 the Trustees sanctioned the treatise on Grace—not covered in Delahogue—by the Roman Jesuit Giovanni Perrone, and the *Theologia Moralis Universa ad Mentem S. Alphonsi* by Pietro Scavini, professor in the seminary at Novara, first published in 1841 and running through successive editions until 1901. Pressure continued to have Delahogue removed. It was resisted in Maynooth but in the end unsuccessfully. On 6 January 1856 Propaganda wrote to Cullen saying MacHale's patronage would have counted against him. There is no explicit record of when Delahogue's books were dropped. The annual printed *Calendar* begins in the academic year 1863/64, but the earlier issues do not list the Theology textbooks. A student petition in 1862, asking for the purchase of a lithographic press for the dissemination of lecture notes, may indicate that there was at the time no textbook.[38] It was in many ways a sad ending. Perrone was, of course, his natural successor in the Maynooth theological schools. *Stat magni nominis umbra.*

At their meeting in June 1856 the Bishops had required the President to keep a careful watch over teaching in the college: he was to visit classes often, sometimes listen to professors' lectures, and see to it that they used the prescribed textbooks. The following spring Laurence Renehan suffered a stroke, from which he did not recover, and he died at the end of July. The natural successor should have been Robert ffrench Whitehead, vice-president since 1845. But among other things he was considered to be dependent on Archbishop MacHale, and in 1857 this alone was nearly enough to rule him out. The name that began to emerge was that of Charles W. Russell, appointed professor of Humanity in 1835 and of Ecclesiastical History in 1845. He was a distinguished scholar, best remembered perhaps for the tribute paid to him in his *Apologia* by John Henry Newman for the key role he had played in bringing him to Rome. In the circumstances rumour shading into calumny was generated, including, curiously, the rumour that he was in secret a professed Jesuit.[39] Cullen was circumspect in supporting him as an alternative to MacHale's candidate. Three years before, in connection with the choice of a coadjutor to the Bishop of Dromore, he had dismissed him as one who was always running around, a government man and a litterateur, who gave no support to the Catholic University.[40] He made no secret that he would prefer Matthew Kelly, an admirable candidate were it not for his poor health, soon to decline very quickly. Russell was appointed President on 20 October 1857, and a little over two years later, in connection with another episcopal appointment, Cullen was urging that he could not be spared from Maynooth.[41]

Walter McDonald entered Maynooth in 1870. In his reminiscences, written at the end of his life, where in all honesty he showed himself more prone to blame that to praise, he wrote of Russell: 'He was one to be proud of, and we were proud of him . . . in many respects he was an admirable President';[42] but he adds, perceptively, 'he can hardly have been happy'. He would not have found it congenial going around listening to what his colleagues were teaching.

For all his poor health Matthew Kelly, professor of English and French, was an obvious candidate for the chair of Ecclesiastical History, having published many outstanding works on Irish church history. He was appointed the same day, 20 October, the Trustees having decided they were not obliged to hold a concursus for this chair, or for the chair of Irish and the junior chair of Theology (neither of them vacant at the time), on the grounds that in the case of these chairs the statutes did not prescribe one. Matthew Kelly, unquestionably the proper man for the post, was in fact proposed by MacHale and seconded by Cullen. But his health declined rapidly, and he died on 30 October 1858. This time there was no obvious successor, and the dangers in appointing without a concursus, or something like it, began to appear. Canvassing began —John MacHale for his nephew Thomas, Denis Gargan, professor of Humanity, with others, for himself. The argument he put forward in a letter to Cullen may have been ingenuous—he had served a long time in the junior ranks and people junior to him had been promoted over his head[43]—but the alternative was MacHale. The idea got into circulation that it was more or less promised to Gargan, and he was appointed in June 1859.

In the summer of 1863 John O'Hanlon was in Rome, where Patrick F. Moran, vice-rector of the Irish College, told him he would not be averse to an appointment to the chair of history at Maynooth. Moran, Cullen's nephew, had already made his mark by pioneering research for material for Irish church history in the Vatican Archives. By 7 September O'Hanlon was able to write to him to say that Gargan's doctors had advised him to go to a parish ('the health was never very good, but not worse than usual lately', McCarthy confided to his diary). Moran informed Cullen, Cullen inquired from Russell, who told him on 18 September that Gargan had that day publicly announced to the staff his intention to accept the parish of Duleek, where he was formally inducted four days later.[44] Almost immediately an embarrassing number of candidates appeared, canvassing support from Trustees. Bishop Walsh of Ossory had promised support to a candidate from Kildare before he knew Moran was in the field, and was very embarrassed at having to withdraw it. By the end of the month there were eight candidates. O'Hanlon was working hard to muster support for Moran, but, as Russell advised Cullen, in the situation that had developed his election was by no means certain. Russell himself was reported to be canvassing for Charles Macauley, a fellow-diocesan, appointed to the chair of Rhetoric in 1854.[45] An unpredictable situation, potentially embarrassing to a number of people, was saved by Gargan resigning his parish and returning to resume his classes before the Trustees met in October.[46] It does seem certain that he had never wanted to leave but had been put under pressure by the forceful O'Hanlon. Whatever the state of his health in 1863, he remained on to become vice-president in 1885, and President in 1894, just in time for the centenary celebrations. He died in office on 26 August 1903, aged 84.

There was, then, something to be said in favour of the concursus. However, it had its faults, and these can be assessed from the detailed descriptions of four of them given by Daniel McCarthy in his diary between 1858 and 1874. The trial took four days. On the first day the concursus board fixed the details, which could vary, though around a fixed core, in that a candidate for any chair had to show competence in every subject taught in the college. Naturally, in all cases much of the next three days would focus on the area where he was expected to show special competence because he was going to teach it. It was perhaps arguable that a candidate for a chair of Natural Philosophy in a seminary should show some knowledge of Theology, but it was harder to defend devoting one of the three days to testing him in this area, especially when nearly half of the remaining two was devoted to Rational Philosophy. It was a little harder to defend testing a potential teacher of Theology in algebra. Science was becoming more complex, and already Natural Philosophy was beginning to show signs of losing the battle to be an essential part of a general humanist education. Bishops seeking to shorten the courses of their students because they were still short of priests were tempted to ask that they might skip Natural Philosophy, especially after the formidable Nicholas Callan died in 1864.

As well as this problem about the concursus in principle there were problems in detail. Writing to Russell on 3 November 1857, just after he had become President, the secretary to the Trustees, Walter Lee, pointed out that as part of the test always consisted of candidates interrogating one another, staff members might be inhibited from applying seeing that among their rivals these were certain to be recent or even current Dunboyne students.[47] An even more serious problem arose from the statutory structure of the board. It still consisted of the President, the vice-president, the deans (now four of them), and the professors of Theology (now six), with the possible co-option of a professor from the relevant discipline, should there be two chairs in it. In October 1859 there was a concursus for the chair of Humanity, with two candidates. After it was over Patrick Murray wrote heatedly to the rising legal luminary, Thomas O'Hagan, asking if there was anything he could do to get the decision set aside. The board, he said, had consisted of seven professors (the seventh would certainly have been Charles Macauley) together with the six from the administration. Six of the professors had voted for one candidate, but O'Hanlon, 'the redoubtable Jack', had joined the 'rabble of deans etc.' to recommend Edward O'Brien of Derry, 'like most Derry people, a person of extreme violent party leanings'.[48] Whatever influence O'Hagan might choose to exercise would have been private and unofficial, and in the end O'Brien was appointed.

The pre-theology course of studies continued to follow a long-established pattern recognised to have unsatisfactory features. In 1856 the Trustees ordered that the classical texts for the entrance examination should include Christian authors, and that from the approved list candidates should select two in Latin and two in Greek, with a pagan and a Christian author in each langauge. Yet the only Christian texts in the programme set out in detail in the first printed *Calendar* for 1863/64 are described as 'voluntary', even though an anthology of extracts from Christian authors had been published in Dublin in 1858.

There was, however, a marked improvement in the pattern of the Theology course, though continuing problems in applying what had been learned are apparent from two ineffective student petitions, in 1862 and 1864, for the appointment of a professor of elocution.[49] It will be recalled that the Royal Commission in 1853 had been scathing on the structure of the Theology course, designed, they felt, to make the most inefficient use of scarce resources. The professors thought so as well: the solution they favoured was to group the four classes in two groups of two, each group having two professors, one teaching Dogma, the other teaching Moral. The solution finally imposed by the Trustees in June 1861 was somewhat different, but a great advance on what went before. Each professor was to continue to teach Dogma and Moral to one class, so that his teaching load was not lightened. The overall ground he had to cover was, however, reduced by three-quarters, in that he repeated the same course every year. This had the added advantage that the Theology course was no longer presented cyclically to the students, so that material of a more introductory nature might be concentrated in the first year. The new pattern may be seen in detail in the *Calendar* for 1864/65, when it had settled down (it should be borne in mind that the 'first class' is fourth year's Theology, and so on).

In Scholis Theologiae Dogmaticae et Moralis

In Classe Prima (*Professore R.D. Patricio Murray, S.T.D.*)

In Semestri Autumnali: Singulis Hebdomadis, a die 12mo Septembris ad diem 20um Decembris, feria ii., iii., v., hora decima cum dimidio et hora secunda pomeridiana; feria vi., hora secunda pomeridiana; sabbato vero, hora decima cum dimidio; praelegetur De Gratia; De Baptismo; De Confirmatione.

In Semestri Verno: Singulis Hebdomadis, a die 23mo Januarii ad diem 13m Maii, diebus et horis jam indicatis, praelegetur De Extrema Unctione; De Ordine; De Praeceptis Decalogi; De Praeceptis Ecclesiae; De Virtutibus et Vitiis; De Simonia; De Obligationibus Statuum.

In Classe Secunda (*Professore R.D. Georgio Crolly*)

In Semestri Autumnali: Diebus et horis jam indicatis, praelegetur De SS. Trinitate; De Incarnatione Christi.

In Semestri Verno: Diebus et horis jam indicatis, praelegetur De Matrimonio; De Jure et Justitia; De Contractibus.

In Tertia Classe (*Professore R.D. Henrico Neville*)

In Semestri Autumnali: Diebus et horis jam indicatis, praelegetur De Sacramentis in Genere; De Eucharistia.

In Semestri Verno: Praedicits diebus et horis, praelegetur De Poenitentia; De Purgatorio; De Indulgentiis; De Censuris Ecclesiasticis; De Irregularitatibus.

In Quarta Classe: (*Professore R.D. Giraldo Molloy, S.T.D.*)

In Semestri Autumnali: Singulis Hebdomadis, a die 12 Septembris ad diem 20m Decembris, feria ii. iii. v. vi., hora decima cum dimidio et hora secunda pomeridiana; Sabbato vero, hora decima cum dimidio, praelegetur De Actibus Humanis; De Conscientia; De Legibus; De Peccatis; De Religione.

In Semestri Verno: Diebus et horis praedictis, praelegetur De Locis Theologicis.

The gains from this rationalisation had to be watched, When Henry Neville resigned and returned to Cork in 1867, pleading ill-health, it was proposed for financial reasons not to replace him, thus calling the whole four years' course into question. The professors protested vigorously,[50] and their case was made easier in that there was a really outstanding candidate available, William Walsh, the future Archbishop. He was appointed, without concursus, on 22 October, the day Neville resigned. By removing the fourth chair of Theology from the concursus, the Trustes had in fact reserved to themselves all theological appointments, though this was not firm policy, for a concursus was held when Gerard Molloy resigned in 1874.

Authority to confer degrees remained elusive: *non expedit*, Cullen wrote to Kirby in 1854 as he became aware of the evidence given before the Royal Comission.[51] In 1867 the name of Maynooth did surface in a university context, but indirectly. The tortuous search for a solution of the university problem acceptable to Catholics had gone on for years. In 1866 Palmerston's government suggested that the Queen's University might get an additional Catholic college. The bishops were prepared to entertain the idea, but laid down conditions: the new college was to be autonomous and endowed, and a number of Catholics were to be added to the Senate of Queen's University. Opposition grew within the Cabinet, and what was offered was a proposal for a 'supplemental charter', which would open the degrees of the Queen's University to all comers, and this was rejected in a judgement by the Master of the Rolls.

These proposals had caused disquiet in certain quarters in the Queen's University. In a pamphlet published in 1867, *Studium Generale, a Chapter of Contemporary History*, Thomas Andrews of Queen's College, Belfast, came up with a proposal to make Maynooth into a university, indeed 'the Irish Catholic Oxford' where lay and cleric would study together, as, he claimed, had been the case at the beginning. The bishops considered this at their meeting in the middle of April. They accepted a proposal from Bartholomew Woodlock, rector of the Catholic University, to ask for an institution to be called 'St Patrick's University', to consist of two colleges, Maynooth, with schools of Theology and Moral Science, and the Catholic University College, with Arts, Science, Law and Medicine.[52] The proposal never came to anything, as there were rumours of a future state initative. The Chief Secretary, Lord Mayo, was coming to the conclusion that neither Maynooth nor the Queen's University was a suitable foundation for any proposal, though the charter he drafted for a proposed new institution, the 'Roman Catholic University of Ireland', was modelled on that of the Queen's University. This draft charter was in fair shape by the end of March 1868. It proposed a university with a number of affiliated colleges, Maynooth being one of them, with its President an *ex officio* member of the Senate.[53] The bishops again sought such extensive control over appointments and courses that it became clear agreement was not possible. Meanwhile, Disraeli had become Prime Minister on 27 February, and on 4 April Gladstone mustered a majority against him on the first of his resolutions on the Established Church of Ireland. It was no longer possible to run with Disraeli's university hare and hunt with Gladstone's disestablishment hounds, and the bishops chose Gladstone.

It was the postgraduate Dunboyne Establishment that suffered most from the inability to grant degrees. John O'Hanlon was in charge as Prefect for nearly thirty years, from 1843 until his death in 1871. The legislation of 1845 had added £700 a year to the income from the Dunboyne legacy, enough to provide twenty students with free places and an annual stipend of £40. There are indications that it was not easy to maintain the full complement, partly, no doubt, because there were still some dioceses not well enough supplied with priests to afford the luxury of postgraduate theology, partly, it would appear, because the postgraduate theology was not very exciting. It seems clear from the details in the first printed Calendars that in substance it consisted of a revision of the courses at undergraduate level. The *Calendar* for 1863/64, for example, sets them out thus:

In Schola Seniorum Alumnorum

(Professore R.D. Joanne O'Hanlon, S.T.D., Seniorum Alumnorum Praefecto.)

In Semestri Autumnali

Singulis Hebdomadis, a die 19mo Septembris ad diem 13um Decembris, feria ii. iii. v. et vi. hora decima cum dimidio, disputabitur, moderante R.D. Praefecto:—

(1) *In Sacra Theologia* De Virtutibus Theologicis; De Ecclesia Christi; De Actibus Humanis:

(2) *In Jure Canonico* De Monachis et Regularibus; De Matrimonio; De Rebus Sacris:

(3) *In Historia Ecclesiastica* De Historia iv.-v. saeculi.

In Semestri Verno: A 30 die Januarii ad diem 6m Maii, diebus et horis jam indicatis, disputabitur:—

(1) *In Sacra Theologia* De Voto et Juramento; De Gratia:

(2) *In Jure Canonico* De Rebus Temporalibus Ecclesiae; De Monachis et Regularibus; De Judiciis:

(3) *In Historia Ecclesiastica* De Historia v.-vi.saeculi.

The *Calendar* for 1866/67 prints the 'theses' to be formally defended before the Trustees on prize-day, with John O'Hanlon presiding, but the very number, a hundred and ninety-eight, is an indication that little if anything beyond what might be called 'a refined undergraduate knowledge' could be expected on any given point.

Indeed, the biggest excitement in the Dunboyne Establishment over these years seems to have been generated by a memorandum sent by the students to the Visitors in 1864, to the effect that they were suffering in the general retrenchment while part of the Dunboyne funds was diverted to general college purposes, though both Visitors and Trustees had ruled that they were to be applied exclusively to the Dunboyne. They appeared to have relied principally on the good offices of Chief Baron Pigot, who behaved very correctly and courteously throughout. When they wrote to him after the visitation he replied in a long paternal letter (sending a copy to Russell), in which he pointed out that as an individual he had no standing in the matter and sugggested a friendly conference with the President and bursar. This seems to have been the end of the matter, for the bursar had already presented the Visitors with a detailed statement of accounts from the Dunboyne since 1845, in which he admitted only to a 'balance apparently unexpended' of £16 13s 6d.[54]

The great new library remained unfurnished for over a decade: it was here, in an empty hall, that Cardinal Wiseman addressed the staff and students when he visited the college in September 1858. In 1860 the Trustees addressed themselves to a more modest but possibly more urgent problem, the restoration of some library facilities in the Junior House, where what little had existed had been taken over as dormitory accommodation in the crowded conditions after 1845. In 1861 they voted £1,000 out of the Treasury loan to fit out the new library; as already noted, the design was by McCarthy, and the contract was carried out between February 1862 and January 1863. It appears, however, that it was in the academic year 1863/64 that the books were actually moved: in October 1863 the Trustees were trying to arrange that they be catalogued, and the wording of their minute makes it clear that they were still in the old library. Meantime, Russell had committed himself to an ambitious plan of what he referred to as 'enlarging the library'. In 1863 he established contact with the Abbé Migne in Paris, and though because Migne preferred to be paid in money designated as offerings for Masses he did not get the whole collection of two thousand volumes, he did get the Latin and Greek Patrology and a considerable number of other works.[55] He drew on his contacts with British statesmen to persuade the Stationery Office to present the Public Record Office publications to Maynooth and indeed to the Vatican Library as well (regrettably, the Maynooth copy did not continue to arrive after the setting up of the Irish Free State).[56] He cast his net more widely when he received a number of French publications by appealing to the Emperor Napoleon III, and the St Petersburg edition of the Codex Sinaiticus by a request to the Tsar.[57] He was anxious too to build up the manuscript collection, recently augmented by a bequest from the late Laurence Renehan, including the Black Book of Limerick, and hearing that ecclesiastical libraries in Italy were in danger of confiscation in the troubled years of 1859 and 1860 he sounded out the possibility of getting for Maynooth the valuable collection in the Roman Franciscan house of St Isidore's. Thomas Furlong, professor of Theology, wrote to him from Rome saying that the guardian of St Isidore's had told him that no manuscript might be removed without permission from the Vatican, but he felt there was no problem if this was obtained, and mentioned Monsignor George Talbot as a useful man to approach.[58] But the Italian situation resolved itself for the moment without the occupation of Rome, and the Franciscan manuscripts did not come to Maynooth.

College Life, 1853–70

The new ordering of things inevitably extended to student life and discipline. To begin with, in the 1850s the college settled down into the three divisions that were to characterise it for over a century. The three senior classes of Theology lived in the new buildings, an oratory for them being provided in the large hall at the west end of Pugin's south wing. It had originally been designated as a study hall, then as a class hall and promised to Nicholas Callan, who protested when it was taken from him, but to no effect. The oratory was dedicated to the Blessed Virgin, so the senior division became St Mary's. The classes of first-year Theology and of Natural Philosophy were to form the middle division, St Joseph's, living in New House and Long Corridor, with the College Chapel serving also as their divisional oratory. Though they shared some facilities—the refectory and the new theology class halls under the library in particular—the two divisions were to be strictly separated. The three junior classes—or two-and-a-half, because only about half the freshmen were required to enter Humanity—came to form an even more separated Junior House. It is clear the Trustees hankered after a completely separate establishment for the freshmen, such as had existed in the buildings of the old lay college from the time it was bought in 1817 until Rhetoric and Logic Houses were built at the beginning of the 1830s. The existence of these buildings made totally separate provision for freshmen physically very difficult, and although the Bishops demanded it at their meeting in June 1856 Junior House settled down into the three classes that stamped their names on the buildings they occupied, Logic, Rhetoric, and Humanity, and survived a short-lived attempt to divide it into two.

The overall student body was over five hundred, the number maintained by the annual grant. In addition to this there was a small number of privately funded burses, and there were a few students who paid pensions, at least for a year or two. There were still some dioceses about 1860 which could not afford to leave students for a fourth year's theology, but their numbers were declining, and already there were some bishops saying they could not find places for all candidates who offered themselves for ordination. In 1861 Archbishop Leahy of Cashel described his problem almost with a note of panic. 'During the years of comparative prosperity following the Famine', he wrote, 'the farmers of these counties [Tipperary and Limerick] ran their sons into us [the college in Thurles] in great numbers, who had better many of them be in the fork of the plough.' However, he added, one fine day they nearly all walked out in protest at the quality of the food, and he vowed he would concentrate on a better type of student in future.[59]

The synod of Thurles had laid down that in all ecclesiastical colleges both staff and students should within the college wear soutane, Roman collar and biretta. Maynooth was in no particular hurry to follow this ruling. The meeting of the bishops in 1854 had ordered that the Thurles decree, and even, it seems clear, a little more,[60] must be strictly enforced, but in June 1858 the Trustees were requiring the students to provide themselves with soutanes of black cloth 'as soon as can conveniently be done.' It may have taken a few years more—a student petition of 1862, in listing reasons why new charges should not be imposed on them, referred among other things to expenses incurred because of 'recent changes in the academic costume.'[61] But about 1860 the college student body donned the soutane, thereby approaching closer to the Roman model (Plate 24).

Liturgical developments were limited by the overcrowding in the old College Chapel when the two senior divisions with the staff met there for High Mass, Vespers and Benediction on Sundays and holydays. The Junior House had a new chapel, converted from the old refectory in Long Corridor, in place of the room in Rhetoric House which had been their oratory for twenty years. In 1854 the Trustees ordered that 'the furniture of the old chapel' be removed to the new one, where it must have looked pitiful enough, for twelve months later they ordered £100 to be spent in each chapel on new furnishings. At the same time they ordered estimates to be sought for an organ for the College Chapel, up to £400, and the instrument installed survived up to the radical reconstruction of the early 1950s, though for years it was called on to perform only at the September retreat of the junior classes, and for some time it had been serving notice that even this would soon be beyond it. The Junior chapel had to content itself with a harmonium, bought for twenty guineas in 1860. In 1853 the Trustees had ordered the deans to take classes in ceremonies and chant, to be attended by all the students. This was specified as Gregorian chant by the bishops in 1854, somewhat to the disappointment of Archbishop Cullen, who would have liked to see some Roman polyphony. Gregorian chant was probably enough for the meagre resources: in 1863 the Trustees noted that one of the professors was teaching chant on a part-time and voluntary basis. A part-time organist, Mr John Keane, was engaged in October 1856 to play at High Mass, Vespers and Benediction on Sundays and holydays, and to teach students selected by the President for one hour a week. In May 1856 Cullen informed Kirby in Rome that now the whole college body attended High Mass and Vespers, and that for the first time there were public and solemn May devotions.[62] At their meeting in June the Bishops ordered liturgical processions to be held for the Purification, Palm Sunday, the feast of St Mark, and Corpus Christi. The injunction was repeated by the Trustees in June 1860, and it is to be assumed that at this time they became part of the routine of the college (Plate 66). There is little record of any changes in the personal spiritual formation of the students. Reliance was still concentrated on the disciplines of mental prayer and observance of rule. A passing reference in 1860 to the importance of maintaining silence still sets this observance in the context of public order. In the mid-1850s a fixed period was set aside each day before supper for spiritual reading, from 6.45 to 7.00 p.m. In 1852 the Trustees had ordered the printing of 1,000 copies of the *Selva* of St Alphonsus, so that each student might have his own. This work, first published in 1760, was a complete treatise on sacerdotal perfection, the pastoral work of a priest, and the substance and form of preaching.

To turn to more material things, the question of dietary figured in the student petitions of 1862 and 1864, but the matters raised seem small and marginal. In 1864, however, they did ask the Trustees to commission a report from the newly appointed college physician, Dr R. D. Lyons. They agreed, and his report, dated 10 October 1865, called attention to some shortcomings. The materials used were good, he said, but they did suffer from bad preparation: this applied especially to the staples of bread and meat. The Trustees had been trying to restrict butter at meals to the plentiful period between May and November, but Lyons was insistent that it be served all the year round. He recommended that soup be served at dinner, and that a kitchen-garden be established to provide an adequate supply of vegetables (it will be recalled that Renehan had planned this in 1853). He agreed with the students that there was need for much improvement in dinner on days of abstinence, and said the water supply was 'open to grave objections', making the tantalising recommendation that it should be mixed with 'a ration of a good wholesome *vin ordinaire*'. In his opinion, the intervals between the meals were too long: breakfast at nine, dinner at three, and a light supper at eight.[63] He concluded by referring to 'depression' and 'malaise', which he said was caused by 'bad ventilation'. In so far as it existed, the more likely cause must have been the punishing daily round. Healthy young men could cope, some quite easily, but the college was no place for people with health problems, though the new infirmary doubtless helped. The community was shocked on the morning of 20 April 1860 by the news that another student had committed suicide from the same room in Rhetoric House that had been the scene of a similar occurrence nineteen years before. This second tragedy is documented in detail by McCarthy in his diary and in a letter from Russell to Archbishop Cullen two days later.[64] The young man was Thomas Maginn, a student for the diocese of Kilmore. On his first night in the college he had been assigned this room, but the next day, as was customary, he had chosen a different room for himself. He fell into depression, however, partly because he had difficulties with his studies, partly because his brief tenancy of the room preyed on his mind. The authorities were aware of his condition, but had come to the conclusion that he was getting over it when, on the morning of 20 April, he left Mass and went to the room that filled his fears, to take his own life. He lingered until eight o'clock the next evening, when he died. The following October the Trustees ordered that the room be opened out to the corridor and fitted out as an oratory, and that Mass be said there occasionally. This seems to have been all that was remembered as recollection of the double tragedy faded. Russell's private letter to Cullen remained unknown, and McCarthy's diary went missing until it surfaced in Belfast in 1964 and was presented to the college. His account of the suicide was published in the student journal, the *Silhouette*, in 1964.

In truth, there were not many relaxations in the daily round. It was a long-established custom that on the evenings of St Patrick's Day and Christmas Day there should be an entertainment for the students, with wine served at a meal, followed by a concert. In 1860 the Trustees minuted their 'desire that in addition to this some instructive and entertaining exhibition be provided for them on these occasions.' This seems to have taken the form of a sketch composed by the students, and it was soon in trouble, apparently at Christmas 1861, when, in the words of a student petition of 1864, there was 'some exception . . . taken by our superiors to the sentiments of one of these pieces'.[65] These 'sentiments' must be linked to the trouble that had occurred in connection with the funeral of Terence Bellew McManus on 10 November. All this became public to such an extent that the authorities issued a disclaimer in the name of the students, and when one of them, discreetly signing himself 'A Maynooth Student', wrote to the *Nation* dissociating himself,[66] and the President protested to the editor, he was told that 'it was not improper for a student to express his dissent respectfully from a political declaration put forward in his name'.[67] 'Fenian sentiments' among the students continued to be a matter of disquiet to some bishops,[68] but not, it would seem, to many, and certainly no overt expression occurred. In the late 1860s, however, an end came to the Oath of Allegiance which all had been obliged to take. It was indeed increasingly an anachronism. A Royal Commission set up to examine and simplify the legislation concerning oaths of loyalty that had proliferated over the years recommended that the number of people required to take such oaths should be severely limited and the formula of the oath simplified. This was accepted and enacted. Maynooth was not specifically mentioned, but Russell, having taken advice from the Chief Secretary and the Visitors, simply did not present the freshmen to take the oath at the January quarter sessions in 1867.[69]

By the 1850s the railway system had so developed that more and more students went home for the summer vacation. At their meeting in June 1856 the bishops ruled that no student was to go without the permission of his bishop. While at home he was to teach Christian Doctrine, and at the end of vacation he was to get a letter from his parish priest, to be presented to his bishop and to the President, testifying to his good conduct and frequentation of the sacraments. These letters form an additional series in the college archives. The historian will not find a great deal in them, and it is clear that the young men behaved themselves well on vacation and that sensible parish priests were not given to dwelling on minor backslidings.

In the first fifty years of its existence Maynooth attracted many visitors, most of whom included it in the books they wrote about their travels, and these accounts are valuable at a time when domestic records are thin. The very development of the railways killed off this kind of traveller. Travel was now possible for people of more moderate means, who did not plan to write a book describing what they saw but wanted a book to tell them what to look for. The traveller had become the tourist, and markets had opened up for Thomas Cook and Karl Baedeker. Mainly, however, thanks to the diary of Daniel McCarthy, accounts have survived of the visits paid to Maynooth in the 1850s and 1860s by persons of public importance. Royalty came, admittedly of the second rank. On 15 July 1857 there was a very private visit from Napoleon III's son and heir, the Prince Imperial. Cardinal Cullen happened to be present, as it was the last day of the Dublin diocesan retreat, and, McCarthy notes, as the Prince was being shown round the grounds they conversed in Italian, which he spoke more fluently than French. The Prince of Wales came twice, in July 1861 and April 1868, and his younger brother Prince Arthur in April 1869. McCarthy noted that on the second visit of the Prince of Wales 'it poured down torrents of rain' all day, so that he had to meet the staff in the President's room and the students in the cloisters, when they had an opportunity of asking him that the end-of-year examinations be suspended. An announcement that they would 'was received with loud cheering', in which even the Fenians probably joined.

McCarthy's long account of the visit to John Henry Newman from 19 to 22 May 1852 makes it clear he knew he was in the presence of greatness. At this time Newman was actually delivering in Dublin the addresses that ultimately grew into *The Idea of a University*. His own passing reference to the visit confines itself to the fact that there was no enthusiasm in Maynooth for the Catholic University, citing his friend Dr Russell, who clearly felt that the project, however worthy, could not succeed, and the President, whom he calls 'Dr Kenehan', who was 'distinctly cold'.[70]

Newman's visit had been private, no doubt at Russell's invitation, but the next visit of a distinguished ecclesiastic, Nicholas Cardinal Wiseman, was less so. At 9.45 on the morning of 8 September 1858 he left Broadstone station by special train, and on arriving at Maynooth he was met by 'a large concourse of townspeople' with the band, who conducted him to the college. Here he presided at pontifical High Mass for the feast of the Nativity of the Blessed Virgin, and at half past two in the afternoon met the students and staff in the new library, still an empty hall, where he was presented with an address and made a suitable reply. The celebrations continued:

> In the evening his Eminence was entertained at a banquet by the President. Upwards of seventy prelates, clergy and gentry sat down. The Lord Mayor was amongst those present . . . After nightfall the College and also the town of Maynooth were handsomely illuminated in honour of the visit of the Cardinal. A band paraded the town playing favourite airs, and there was general rejoicing.[71]

Eight years later, on 20 September 1866, Maynooth welcomed another Cardinal, this time an Irish one, Paul Cullen. Cullen had not approved of Wiseman's tour in Ireland: he was meddling, he said, in things he knew nothing about. One of the things he knew nothing about, Cullen was certain, was the theological orthodoxy of the Maynooth professors, and when in his reply to the address he specifically complimented them on this Cullen wrote to Rome complaining, leaving Wiseman quite puzzled as to where he had gone wrong.[72] The programme for Cullen's reception at Maynooth as a Cardinal follows closely the Roman Pontifical and the address and reply seem to reflect the same kind of anxiety not to put a foot wrong.[73] The old wounds healed slowly: as has been seen, George Crolly went scarred to his grave. The next to die was the Cardinal, and on that occasion the surviving protagonist, Patrick Murray, confided to his diary:

> Cardinal Cullen died on yesterday, exactly nine months, by the day of the week and of the month, since Crolly's death (Crolly, Thursday, January 24: Cardinal Cullen Thursday, October 24). The Cardinal's death will, no doubt, cause a very sensible change in the affairs of the Irish church. Since he came to Ireland nearly 28 years ago, but especially since he became Archbishop of Dublin upwards of 26 years ago, his influence at Rome in Irish matters was paramount. Whether it would have continued so under the present Pope, especially since Card. Franchi's death, it is now impossible to say. He came here as Archb. of Armagh with very strong views, which he often put forward in very strong terms. Very much to his credit, however, it must be said that for many years back those views had been greatly moderated, some of them entirely abandoned. Whatever errors he may have committed, God has judged him, not according to the objective rectitude of his deeds, but according to the lights he had and the rectitude of his motives . . . we had, this morning, the office and Mass for the repose of the Cardinal's soul—I celebrating the Mass in the junior Chapel.

CHAPTER VII

THE BISHOPS' COLLEGE, 1870–95: STRUCTURES, FINANCES, BUILDINGS

The Irish Church Act

Maynooth's long-established links with the secular authority came to an end with the Irish Church Act of 1869. This in turn was motivated by developments within the United Kingdom as a whole rather than just in Ireland. These came from a growing body of opinion, given political voice in the Reform Act of 1832, which wished to see the disestablishment of the state church and the setting up of a non-confessional state. The Church of England was strong enough to survive the challenge, but the Church of Ireland was in a much weaker position, and had already suffered major state intervention in 1833. For a long time there had been wide agreement that 'something would have to be done' about the Irish Established Church, so that when Gladstone moved his resolutions on it in the House of Commons on 23 March 1868 he secured a majority which left no option but to call a general election in which the Irish Church became a major issue. What Gladstone had proposed was disestablishment—it was no longer to be the state church—and a substantial measure of disendowment, the taking away of wealth which had accrued to it over the centuries. Gladstone himself was a reluctant convert to disendowment, but he had to accept it as part of the price to be paid for the coalition he was putting together and which was to develop into the Liberal Party.

It was still very much a coalition of different interests after the election of November 1868, so that Gladstone's majority of 112 was not as overwhelming as it might appear. Absolutely speaking, the annual grant to Maynooth might be considered as a separate issue from the endowments of the Established Church, but in practice if one went the other would have to go, as would the annual subvention to the Presbyterians, the *regium donum*, because an important part of Gladstone's parliamentary group was made up of those who called themselves 'voluntarists', centred on the Liberation of Religion Society, and proponents of a view with a long history in England, that all Christian congregations should be purely voluntary bodies. Indeed, when Gladstone moved his three resolutions in March 1868 there was a 'a fourth resolution proposed by some firebrand to stop the Maynooth grant and the *regium donum*', so Cullen wrote to Tobias Kirby in Rome. Cullen viewed even the extinction of Maynooth with equanimity, believing that Clonliffe and the other seminaries could fill the gap. By contrast, a bishop in an older 'Whig' tradition, Delaney of Cork, declared that he shuddered at the prospect of disendowment of the college.[1]

Whatever individual reactions might be, it was clear from the beginning that Maynooth would be profoundly affected by the proposed legislation. As early as October 1868 the President, Charles W. Russell, initiated correspondence with Gladstone.[2] He began by saying that inevitably there would be heated and unhelpful discussions at the hustings. Catholics, he said, were agreed that Maynooth could no longer remain a charge on the consolidated fund, but he urged that some permanent provision should be made for the college, as it was, he claimed, to be considered comparable to the training of Protestant clergy at Trinity College rather than to the Church Establishment: this would be no more that the 'equal dealing' to which Gladstone had declared himself committed. In reply, Gladstone said that while it was accepted in principle that the disposable wealth of the Established Church must not be used for teaching religion, in practice there would indeed have to be equity and 'equal dealing'. Two months later he wrote again saying that after further reflection on the points Russell had made he had to warn that to treat Maynooth as an educational establishment would leave it open to unacceptable government pressures, probably in the form of an argument that its exclusively clerical character left it too narrowly based to claim state support, leading to what he assumed would be demands for a change in its exclusively clerical or indeed Catholic character. In his reply, Russell took the point: the bishops, he said, would never agree to changes such as Gladstone spoke of, and it would indeed be better to treat Maynooth as part of the general Church settlement, which he assumed, as did many others, would involve a sharing-out of the wealth of the Establishment among all the churches in Ireland. In further letters in response to a request from Gladstone for more information on Maynooth, he showed a continuing anxiety that the college's finances might be crippled, together with a perception that the hostility being shown towards Maynooth as argument developed in England made it essential to put the case where, he admitted, Gladstone had always said it should be, on a basis of absolutely equal treatment.

What of his anxieties he confided to his colleagues led to the proposal of Gladstone receiving a delegation. Gladstone demurred, preferring that personal contacts should in the first instance be with the officials in Dublin Castle, but he agreed to receive a memorial. In this, the college staff claimed that they held offices 'fixed and permanent in law', and made an 'earnest request' that they receive at least 'equal legal security' in any legislation.[3] Gladstone acknowledged the memorial, but understandably refused any comment, because the bill was then taking shape in Cabinet.

On 1 March it was introduced in the Commons and given a first reading. Russell expressed himself pleased with the proposals, and said he felt assured the real interests of Maynooth would be safely preserved. In reply, Gladstone said the case of Maynooth had received much thought and he believed the solution proposed was the right one. Consideration had been given to the possibility of legislating specifically for the vested interests involved, but it was decided that it was better to legislate for the Trust alone. The basic proposal, as contained in the bill when first presented to Parliament, went through all its stages without substantial change. It repealed those parts of the Acts of 1800 (40 Geo III, c. 85) and 1845 (8 & 9 Vict., c. 25) which established links between Maynooth and the civil authority, and on this principle repealed the whole of the short Act of 1860 (23 and 24 Vict., c. 104). What was left were those provisions of law which regulated the Trust and Trustees of Maynooth College. Again on this principle, the foundation Act of 1795 (35 Geo. III, c. 21) was not mentioned, on the assumption that what of this was not modified or abolished by later legislation concerned only the Maynooth Trust. The overall repeal involved the ending of the annual grant from the consolidated fund, which was to take place, in parallel with all the pecuniary measures of the Act, on 1 January 1871. In its place, again in parallel with the other provisions and, like them, from the wealth of the Church of Ireland, '. . . compensation shall be made . . . by payment of capital sums as follows . . . In respect of the annual sum paid during the financial year ending the thirty-first day of March eighteen hundred and sixty-nine, to the Trustees of the College of Maynooth . . . The capital sum to be paid . . . shall be fourteen times the amount of . . . such annual sum.'

This was, as Gladstone had envisaged, equal treatment with what he considered equitable adjustments to take account of how the case of Maynooth differed from that of the Established Church. The main difference lay in the fact that in the case of the Church it was vested rights of individuals which were directly provided for, with, however, a clause not merely permitting but encouraging them to capitalise their life interests at fourteen years' purchase, in this way accumulating a capital sum for the institution, while in the case of Maynooth it was the institution which received the sum capitalised at fourteen years' purchase. One effect of this was to make the compensation to Maynooth more generous, for the general principle of the Act was that it was life interests which were to be compensated, and in Maynooth by far the greater part of the life interests were the rights of students, which in the nature of the case simply could not be calculated at fourteen years' purchase. The fact that the benefits accruing to them would come indirectly through the Trustees seems, however, to have revived the fears of the staff, and Russell asked Gladstone for assurances that their rights would be legally secured. Gladstone's reply did not altogether quieten his fears. He pointed out that when a trust existed Parliament would not wish to deal directly with individuals; that the staff would do best to communicate with the Trustees; and that they should communicate with the

Attorney-General when he went to Dublin after the second reading or go to London to see Gladstone personally. It is a measure of Russell's fears that he left immediately for London, accompanied by his vice-president, Robert ffrench Whitehead.

News of their arrival was not altogether welcome, even to Irish Liberal MPs who were very well disposed to Maynooth. They feared, not without reason, that when the bill came to be debated clause by clause the Maynooth proposals were guaranteed to stir up such opposition that any appearance of differences among Catholics should at all costs be avoided. One of them, Myles O'Reilly, wrote to Cullen on 15 March, just after the Maynooth delegation had arrived. He pointed out the danger of financial loss in emphasising individual life interests, because of the necessarily short life interests of students, and that Gladstone had proposed fourteen years' purchase compensation overall on the general ground of life interests, deliberately putting it vaguely. He said that the claim of the staff to their life interests was undeniable, but they should seek assurance by a pledge from the Trustees and not from civil law.[4] However, only the day before Cullen had written to another MP, William Monsell, in terms that suggested a little civil law protection might be needed. There were, he said, no life interests at Maynooth, for staff and students could be called away from the college by their bishops at a moment's notice. He had rather less than the whole truth on his side when he disingenuously added that the grant had in the past been paid to the Trustees, not to college personnel.[5] Monsell's reply was that the Maynooth staff had an undoubted right to their life interests: the only consolation he could offer was that many of them were old men.[6]

The Maynooth proposals did provoke lengthy and sometimes acrimonious exchanges. At the debate on the second reading it was objected that the provision proposed for Maynooth was more generous than that for the Established Church, and indeed that in proposing to devote anything from church funds to general religious purposes Gladstone was contradicting the principle laid down in the preamble to the bill. However, Gladstone's party was more agreed on the need to disestablish the Irish Church than on any other issue, and the bill was carried without modification by a majority of 118. In committee Gladstone added a clause safeguarding 'any pecuniary and individual interests at present existing against the Trustees'. In writing to thank him Russell raised a further point: the staff, he said, were anxious to see some provision made for old age or sickness, such as was made for the clergy of the Established Church, and he enclosed a petition to this effect signed by all the staff. Gladstone's reaction was cautious. The Established Church clergy, he said, already had such a right: to make similar provision for the Maynooth staff would be to create a new right. His first reaction was that this could not be done, but in the end he did write in such a provision, guaranteeing to any of the existing staff a pension equal to two-thirds of his salary in the event of his retirement by reason of old age or permanent infirmity. The bill went to the

'Mr Stoyte's House' — the entrance hall

Plate 33

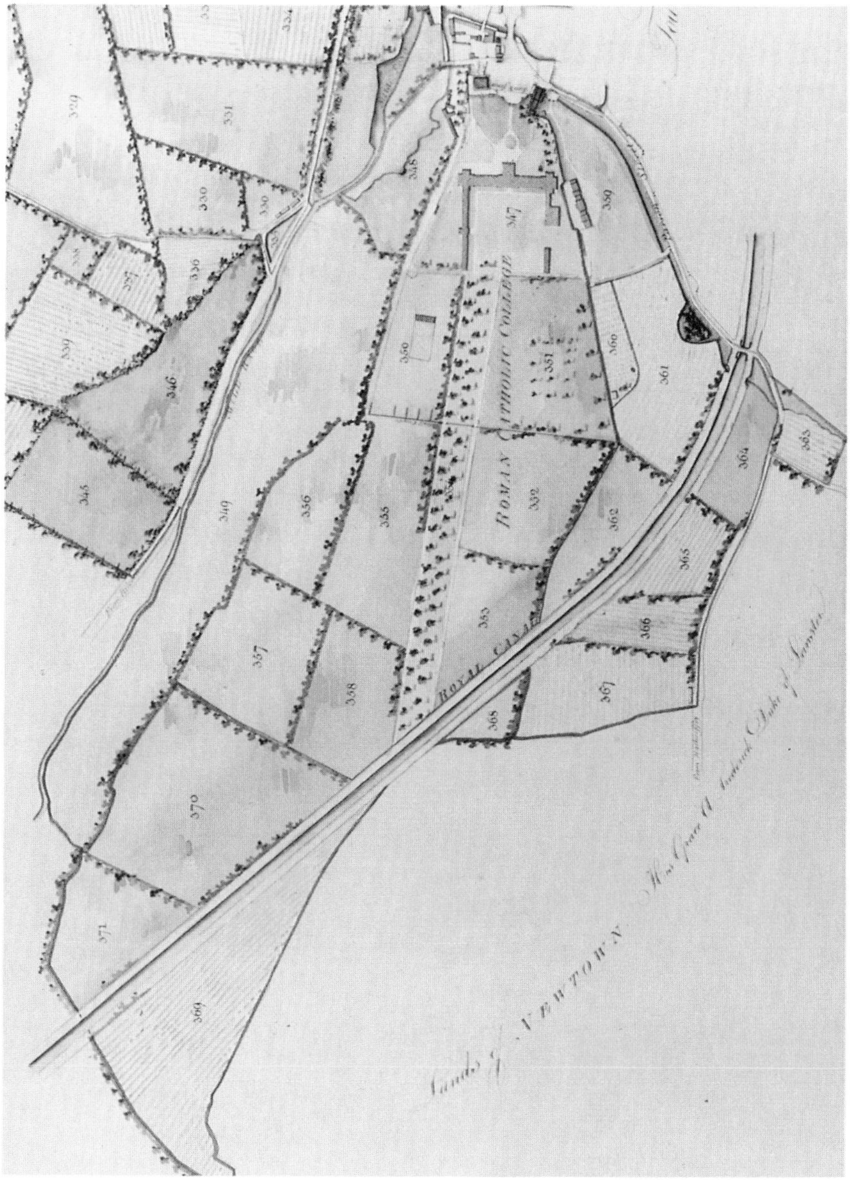

The College holding 1821 (*Carton Estate Maps, by courtesy of Mr Lee Mallaghan*)

Plate 34

Long Corridor, *c.* 1800. Water-colour, artist unknown

Plate 35

Aerial view of College and surroundings

Plate 36

Miniature of St Christopher from a French manuscript Book of Hours, late fifteenth century (*MCL*)

Plate 37

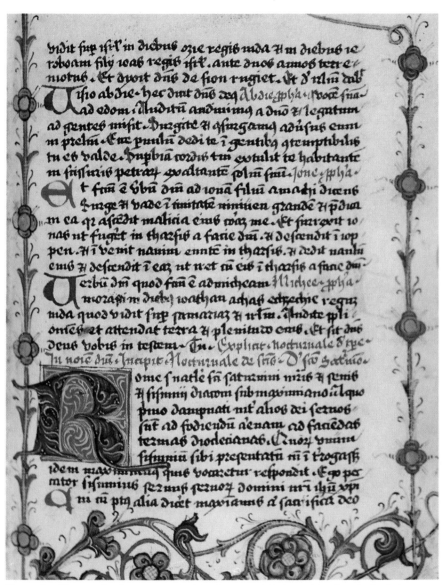

From the *Nocturnale* of a manuscript Breviary, *c.* 1490 (*MCL, Renehan Collection*)

Plate 38

Early prize stamp (*MCL*)

Plate 39

Lords on 1 June. The atmosphere was hostile, but the Lords devoted so much of their energies to amendments which would have in effect re-endowed the Church of Ireland that the Maynooth clauses escaped unscathed. The heavily amended bill was returned to the Commons on 12 July. Nearly all the changes were unacceptable to the Cabinet, and most of them were removed in the Commons on 15 and 16 July. The remaining gap between the two Houses was closed by negotiation over the next week, and royal assent was given on 26 July.

The provisions for Maynooth College, though far-reaching, represented only one clause and part of another in a long and complex piece of legislation. Gladstone's original proposals had been augmented by legal security for the life interest of existing staff and students, and for the pension rights of existing staff. A short separate clause extinguished the debt owed by the Trustees to the Commissioners of Public Works. This, about £18,000, was a considerable sum in view of the burdens of the years immediately ahead, when vested interests, admittedly diminishing, would have to be met out of reduced income. There was one curious oversight. Clause 4 of the founding Act of 1795 had obliged the Trustees to lay before the Lord Lieutenant any regulations and statutes not affecting the exercise of the Catholic religion; they were to be binding unless he signified his dissent within a month. This provision had not been repealed by subsequent acts of Parliament, and the Act of 1869 assumed that the unrepealed sections of the 1795 Act all concerned the inner functioning of the Maynooth Trust. The matter was a small one, because the power conferred on the Lord Lieutenant was in marginal matters and had never been exercised (if it did not expire at the setting up of the Irish Free State it certainly expired shortly afterwards). But, however insignificant, it was embarrassing to notice this oversight, which must have happened just after the Act became law, for on 12 August the college solicitor, John O'Hagan, in conjunction with the Solicitor-General, Sir John Coleridge, gave as legal opinion that the Trustees were no longer bound to lay any such regulations before the Lord Lieutenant.[7] But on 19 October 1870 the Trustees instructed Russell to approach the government to have the clause of the 1795 Act formally repealed, and a bill to this effect, also proposing to increase the number of Trustees, was introduced by the Chief Secretary in July 1871, but on account of this second proposal it did not get beyond a first reading. In September the Trustees again instructed the President to seek a bill repealing clause 4 of the Act of 1795. Gladstone planned to do this as part of his Irish University Bill of 1873, but this was lost because the bishops judged its general provisions unacceptable and what remained of any Maynooth obligation to consult the Lord Lieutenant was forgotten.[8]

Trustees, Visitors, Troubles

The functions of the lay Trustees had been diminishing, especially since Paul

Cullen took over leadership of the Hierarchy. The changed status of the college after the Irish Church Act made their position so anomalous that five of the six immediately resigned[9] (the sixth, Lord ffrench, refused to resign, and remained on the list of Trustees until his death over twenty years later). Five bishops were elected to fill the vacant places, but a problem remained. It had indeed been there since the early days of the college, when from time to time a bishop who was not a Trustee would express his dissatisfaction at having no voice in the government of an institution where his students were trained for the priesthood. After 1850, Cullen had encouraged discussion and even decision on the affairs of Maynooth at the general meeting of the bishops, and seems to have considered the possibility of increasing the number of Trustees by adding more bishops, for at the end of 1859 legal opinion was sought as to whether the Trustees had power to add to their number. The answer given was that they had not.[10] The question had a new urgency after 1869, when the bishops became free of control of civil law over how they ran the college. But the civil law still laid down that the governing body consisted of seventeen Trustees, while there were twenty-eight bishops, each not unreasonably demanding a voice.

As already mentioned, in the autumn of 1870 the Trustees instructed the President to ask the government for legislation to repeal clause 4 of the 1795 Act and to increase the number of Trustees by eleven. Anticipating no problem, they decided in June 1871 to invite all the bishops to their next meeting. The government was indeed ready to facilitate them, and a bill was introduced on 12 July,[11] but the proposal to increase the numbers of the Trustees ran into trouble and it did not get beyond a first reading. With the failure of the Irish University Bill, the proposal to repeal clause 4 of the 1795 Act had to be abandoned, but the question of the number of the Trustees continued seemingly intractable, as is clear from another legal opinion given at the beginning of 1875 by John O'Hagan to Bishop Gillooly of Elphin, leading spirit among the recently constituted episcopal Visitors.[12] This was to the effect that authority in the college rested with the Trustees, and that while they were free to consult others they might not agree in advance to be bound by the decision of a body consisting partly of Trustees and partly of others. This led to another attempt to secure legislation. The government was now Tory, headed by Disraeli, so it was decided to introduce a private member's bill, trusting in a wide spread among its sponsors to secure the support necessary. The sponsors did indeed represent a wide section of opinion. There was Arthur McMurrough Kavanagh, Conservative MP for Carlow, a good if paternal landlord, firm but not fanatical in his opinions (he voted against the Irish Church Act, but for the Land Act of 1870); Hugh Law, Liberal representing Londonderry County, who drafted the Irish Church Act, and was successively Irish Solicitor-General and Attorney-General in Gladstone's administration; the O'Conor Don, Home Ruler representing Roscommon, but a reluctant convert from Liberalism; and Captain J. P. Nolan, representing Galway

County, a far from reluctant Home Ruler, indeed returned as such in a bye-election in 1872, with clerical support so vociferous that he was unseated on petition, support that was equally strong, if a trifle more discreet, when he triumphed at the general election of 1874. The bill was introduced on 3 June 1875,[13] but it soon ran into trouble, not unconnected with the fact that when the matter had been raised at the Trustees' meeting in January MacHale had dissented and had insisted his dissent be recorded. Why he dissented is not clear, but what is clear is that Captain Nolan with many other Irish MPs would not oppose him—indeed it must have taken much persuasion to induce Nolan to sponsor the bill in the first instance. But reports of differences among the Irish members killed any hope the proposal might have had.[14]

However, the legally awkward relationship between the episcopate and the Trustees gradually developed a pragmatic and working solution. Finally, in June 1893 the decision was taken that the autumn as well as the June meeting should be held in Maynooth (for a long time it had been held in Clonliffe). By now, the association between 'Maynooth' and 'the bishops' was established in the popular mind, but the Trustees had always to be mindful of legal distinctions. In 1869 they were the only legally constituted Catholic religious corporation in Ireland. They were legal proprietors of the college, with tenure in perpetuity, subject only to the condition of applying the income of the Trust to its proper purposes. They were bound too, of course, to invest only in trustee securities, and to keep an eye on changing provisions of law, checking their position carefully in 1890, for example, when new investment on a large scale was called for because a number of term mortgages had matured, and there had been important legislation on trustee securities just a few years before (51 & 52 Vict., c. 59).

When the Irish Church Act was being prepared the Trustees had been particularly anxious that existing regulations for the visitation of the college should be replaced, and this was done without difficulty, indeed without question. From what has been seen of the pre-1869 visitations, their impact was very limited indeed. But shortly after 1869 the episcopal Trustees set up a visiting committee from among their number which was to have an influence far beyond anything previous Visitors would have even thought of. The leading spirit in this development was Bishop Gillooly of Elphin. He had been a Vincentian, the Congregation trusted above all others by Paul Cullen, and by Cullen promoted, very reluctantly, to the episcopate in 1856. He naturally emerged as Cullen's right-hand man as the Trustees tried to take stock of the changed situation in Maynooth when they returned from the First Vatican Council in July 1870, by setting up a sub-committee to examine and report. The early correspondence between him and Cullen shows them committed to firm and extensive intervention.[15] Cullen was ageing and no doubt exhausted after the work of the Council. He felt it would be hard to do much, because a number of people, including some of the committee, did not want to do much, and because it was far from easy even to find out what was going on in the college; he even suggested (a bit naïvely it might seem to anyone who has lived there for longer) that two or three of the committee might be delegated to live there for a month to find out for themselves. But Gillooly was already gearing himself up to sweep clean. He drew up printed 'Heads of Inquiry' for the college staff, and quickly decided that a new set of statutes was needed, which he began to draft. Even at this stage there were indications of disquiet, from some of his colleagues on the committee and from the President. At their meeting on 18 August 1871 the Trustees set up what almost immediately became a permanent committee of Visitors, consisting of the four archbishops (of these, Leahy of Cashel wanted minimum changes, and MacHale was more positively obstructive), and four named bishops, of whom Gillooly and his fellow-Vincentian James Lynch, recently returned from an unhappy appointment in Scotland to be coadjutor bishop of Kildare and Leighlin, emerged as leaders.

The Visitors did a number of things of real benefit to the college, including the setting up of long-overdue Administrative and Scholastic Councils in 1871, embodied in new statutes in 1872, which at least incorporated the many Trustees' resolutions which had the force of statute, though the same process continued and soon made the new statutes in turn out of date. But in many respects it was not a happy time. Gillooly might have done well to pay a little more heed to the wise advice given to the abbot by St Benedict in the Holy Rule, 'not to be too suspicious, or he will never be at rest'. The moves to 'tighten things up' antagonised many in the college, students, staff and the President himself, who in his declining years was left in a very painful position. Daniel McCarthy, professor of Scripture, wrote to Cullen on 15 April 1872, saying that a searching visitation of the college was long overdue.[16] McCarthy emerges as another suspicious abbot: when James O'Kane retired as dean in 1871 he offered to take on his duties while continuing to teach, and the Trustees, conscious of their diminished revenues, agreed (in fairness, it should be noted that Walter McDonald, who entered as a student in 1870, though critical of what he judged grave limitations in his biblical scholarship, regarded him as 'a pious and able man').[17] But his letter must have encouraged Cullen to accept Gillooly's pleas for a general visitation, which Gillooly in turn set out to prejudice by a tactless letter to Russell, saying 'that information has been conveyed, to my own personal knowledge, to several of the bishops, and I believe directly from the college . . . that the rules lately made by the bishops for the government of the college, have been rather evaded than honestly carried out by some of the superiors.' This drew an angry reply from Russell, denying the allegation and asking him to name his informants, a reply indeed so angry that it ended up on Cullen's desk, as such things had a habit of doing.[18] It was in this atmosphere of confrontation that the committee of Visitors was made permanent and the new statutes approved, both at the June meeting of 1872.

These 1872 statutes are, of course, not altogether new.[19] They rest on previous statutes, as modified from time to time by resolutions of the Trustees. It has already been suggested that for some time these modifications had been steadily directed towards tightening discipline, and this is very clearly embedded in the revised statutes. The most significant overall change was the extensive powers given to the episcopal Visitors: 'In the intervals between the meetings of the Board the Visitors shall enjoy the administrative powers of the Trustees in matters of discipline.' Within the college, the authority of the President is spelled out in detail, but it is strictly subordinated to that of the Trustees and Visitors. In 1853 the Royal Commission had urged the setting up of two statutory councils, 'one of Discipline and one of Studies'. The 1872 statutes bring two councils into existence, but their competence is not so clearly defined, and in some respects they only give a statutory position to what is already happening, and, as has been seen, grave objections had been urged against this. The Administrative Council, consisting of the President, vice-president, deans and bursar, had a very wide remit: 'all matters affecting the studies, discipline, finances and material conditions of the college'. That would not appear to leave much for the Scholastic Council, all the more so as it was to consist of the Administrative Council, together with the professors of Theology and Scripture, while other professors attend only 'when the arrangements for their respective classes may be under consideration'. Studies, indeed, are placed under the close supervision of the disciplinary authorities. Every year the detailed programme for the following one is approved by the Scholastic Council and submitted to the Trustees. Individual professors are to report to the President every month, oftener if required or if necessary, and to report in writing twice a year. The statutes, not unreasonably, envisage dismissal of staff members for grave misconduct, but there is no statute explicitly setting out conditions of employment; the assumption seems to be that they hold office at the Trustees' pleasure. They are explicitly reminded of their obligation to edify; and once again they are forbidden to publish without permission of the President.

In September 1872 the vice-president, Robert ffrench Whitehead, resigned. He had spent an unbroken fifty-two years in the college since he entered it as a student in 1820. He had been appointed vice-president in 1845, but in 1857 had been passed over in favour of Russell for the presidency. To no-one's surprise, he was succeeded by Daniel McCarthy. McCarthy continued to teach his classes after his appointment, the first vice-president to do so. The absence of recorded trouble would suggest that the following few years were peaceful, but it did not last. The Visitors, led by Gillooly and Lynch, held a searching inquisition before each Trustees' meeting, in the course of which they summoned a number of students before them in addition to the college administration. This contributed to trouble on all sides: trouble among the students; a complaint from one of the deans that he had ben unjustly accused to the Visitors (in both cases the vice-president seems to have had an active role); and complaints from the staff that students when interviewed by the Visitors were encouraged to tattle about them.[20] On 16 May 1877 Russell was thrown from his horse and seriously injured, and though he lived until 26 February 1880 he took no active part in the administration of the college. On 7 June 1878 McCarthy was promoted to the see of Kerry. Cullen was more than usually well informed in advance, for he had been in Rome since early in the year for the conclave consequent on the death of Pius IX and the election of Leo XIII. On 8 June he wrote from Paris to Gillooly, giving him the news and discussing the problems of Maynooth, where there was now an incapacitated President, a vacancy in the vice-presidency, and other vacancies because there had been a slowness in filling posts since resources had been diminished. The obvious candidate for the vice-presidency was William Walsh, priest of Dublin and professor of Theology, and already at thirty-seven years of age showing exceptional capacity. He did not view his prospects with great enthusiasm. The college had serious problems and he did not approve of the methods of Gillooly and his fellow-visitors, so he asked for some assurances before letting his name go forward.[21] He was appointed vice-president on 25 June.

Whatever assurances he received, the troubles he had anticipated with the Visitors did in fact happen. Within a short time Gillooly was complaining that Walsh was going behind his back, with Walsh making exactly the same complaint against Gillooly.[22] Walsh's hand was strengthened when he became President in June 1880, consequent on the death of Russell the previous February. Evidence of tension dies down, but it seems to have been a wary armistice. On 23 June 1885 Walsh was appointed Archbishop of Dublin. At their meeting on June 1886 the Trustees laid down detailed regulations for college visitation which seem obviously inspired by him. Their aim is to ensure that visitation is done in order and that there is constant contact between the Visitors and the college administration. Visitation is to begin at 2.00 p.m. on the Saturday before the Trustees' meeting. The Visitors first go over his report with the President, then over the minutes of the college councils with their secretary, the vice-president. On Sunday at 10.30 a.m. one group of Visitors inspects the college, accompanied by the President and bursar, while a second group examines the accounts; both groups report back at twelve noon. In the afternoon from 2.30 to 4.30 p.m. they 'see such members of the college staff as it may seem advisable to summon or may desire to present themselves' (there is no mention of students being interviewed). Finally, on Monday the Visitors meet to prepare their report for the meeting of the Trustees the following day. It was certainly an exhaustive inquisition, in which the eight bishops functioned as much as a sub-committee of the Trustees as in the traditional role of Visitors, and they certainly wielded much more power than any previous Visitors of the college, but now that things were being done in order the system worked.

Assets and Liabilities

In principle, what was available to the Trustees as a result of the Irish Church

Act was a capital sum calculated at fourteen years' purchase of the previous annual grant of £26,360, that is, £369,040.[23] There had been some fears that it might be slightly less, but they came to nothing except the generation of correspondence between the college, the Chief Secretary, the Treasury and the Auditor-General.[24] Of more consequence was the undoubted fact that the Church Commissioners as constituted under the Act were entitled to pay out the lump sum in up to eight half-yearly instalments. In fact they paid it all at once, on the date the Trustees selected as most convenient for themselves, 4 April 1871, and added interest from 1 January, when the annual grant stopped. The bursar, Thomas Farrelly, reported that they acted throughout with 'prompt attention and obliging kindness'.

It was important to get as much money as possible as soon as possible, for after 1 January 1871 the college still had heavy commitments to existing staff and students. These commitments were set out in detail by the Trustees' legal advisers in the autumn of 1869.[25] Existing staff were clearly provided for in the Act: they were entitled to their present salaries and benefits while they continued in office, and thereafter to a pension at the rate laid down. Students admitted to the college before the Irish Church Act became law on 26 July 1869 were entitled to a free place until they finished their course, and also to the stipend payable to Theology and Dunboyne students. This entitlement extended to those whose stipends had been suspended to service the debt of the Commissioners of Public Works, as this was now cancelled, and to those who were pre-theology students when the Act was passed, as they had a 'deferred interest' in receiving the stipend. The income from the Dunboyne estate remained, as always, at the absolute disposal of the Trustees. Students admitted after 26 July 1869 had a right to all these benefits until 1 January 1871, when the provisions of the Act came into effect and the annual grant ceased; thereafter they had no legal claim on the college, like the students admitted after that date. It was a potentially heavy burden, but was greatly eased by the Church Commissioners paying the compensatory sum in one instalment at the earliest possible date, and by the Trustees reducing the number of students with claims on the college by temporarily suspending the fourth-year theology and Dunboyne courses.

The money received had to be invested in trustee securities. The rate of interest on government consols was only 3 per cent. East India stock paid up to 5 per cent but inevitably was in short supply. Legislation of August 1870 greatly extended the range of real property in which trustee funds might be invested. In February 1871 the Earl of Granard was offered a mortgage, and the following June the amount was agreed: £91,592 7s 2d. It was a lot of eggs in one basket, but in principle mortgages on land were considered good investments, paying from 4.25 to 4.75 per cent, well above the average for trustee stocks. At the time the Church Commissioners were freely investing in mortgages, and the Maynooth Trustees fairly soon had approximately three-quarters of their capital in them. But in practice a mortgage was a good investment only if certain conditions were fulfilled; above all, the estate should be reasonably well managed and the rents promptly paid. When these mortgages taken out in the early 1870s fell in twenty years later relations between Irish landlords and their tenants had changed considerably. Yet all the loans, with one exception, repaid the capital after regularly paying the interest, though not without problems in some cases. The one exception was the Granard mortgage. The estate was not well managed; it contained much poor land in Leitrim and Longford and, fairly inevitably, there was much trouble with tenants in the 1880s. The outstanding loan was a long-running anxiety to college officials and Trustees and in the end a considerable part was not recovered.

The archival deposit left is substantial: five large boxes of documents, together with lengthy reports and much in the way of minutes. It is a very interesting story, but the details concern the history of the Irish land question rather than of Maynooth College, where only a summary is called for. Complaints of overdue interest begin in 1882, and when the Ashbourne Act of 1885 opened the way to land purchase it was soon being said that only the sale of land could recover the capital and even the overdue interest. Granard was naturally reluctant, and he found himself a devious solicitor. There was poor communication between the Trustees and the President, Robert Browne, made worse by the fact that they faced the problem only reluctantly, even the Visitors. Inevitably, individuals began to take initiatives,[26] and equally inevitably this was resented by others, even if not altogether reasonably. By 1891, when the mortgage should have been redeemed, arrears of interest alone came to over £10,000. Land was being sold—in 1892 the Trustees received £30,000—but inevitably the tenants were getting difficult: having announced an intention to buy, some stopped paying the rent and in consequence felt no great urgency in concluding the sale. In June 1893 the Trustees set up a commission consisting of the college President and bursar, with two local priests, Canons Hoare and O'Farrell, 'to confer with the tenants of unsold lands'. Though they reported that they 'made a promising start' it is clear that at their June meeting in 1894 the Trustees decided to cut their losses. By then they had received a total of £40,439 7s 6d. What their overall loss was is not easy to calculate exactly, partly because of the complexities of the long-drawn-out affair, partly from an understandable reluctance to look it in the face; as the bursar, James Donnellan, wrote to the local bishop, Bartholomew Woodlock of Ardagh, on 15 October 1894: 'As far as I know the sale of the residue of the Granard Estate is left in the hands of Dr Walsh. The bishops have been very reticent about the matter, so that I really do not know what conclusion they came to.'[27] It could not be in safer hands than those of Archbishop Walsh as far as competence and knowledge of the Land Acts was concerned, but even he would have been defeated by the sheer intractability of things. The final overall loss, counting unrepaid capital, arrears of interest, and legal costs, was in the region of £40,000.

Indeed the college could hardly be said to be fortunate in its transactions where land was concerned. When Archbishop John MacHale died on 7 November 1881 he left to his nephew Thomas his estate at Milltown, Co. Galway, held in fee simple, with a yearly value of about £200. Thomas MacHale wrote to the college authorities to say that though his uncle had made no mention of it in his will it had been his intention to bequeath the lands to Maynooth. He now offered them, but with elaborate conditions attached. The annual income was to be used to provide prizes of £10 each for students. Detailed conditions and orders of preference were laid down, and the recipients were to recite choral Requiem Office for the late Archbishop on his anniversary or the next convenient day. The Trustees were to undertake not to sell the property for less than £5,000, and if they sold it to devote the proceeds to the same purposes.[28] In his President's report for June 1882 William Walsh warned the Trustees of possible legal problems, but they decided the bequest should be 'gratefully accepted'. Walsh asked MacHale to have a deed of assignment drawn up. His solicitor sent it to the Trustees' solicitor, who subsequently admitted to having received it on 18 June 1883, but did not forward it until 19 November, after two meetings of the Trustees, in summer and autumn.

Meantime the property was deteriorating. Some tenants had not been paying rent even before the archbishop died. After his death their number increased. Some tenants went to the Land Courts set up in 1881 and got large reductions in their rents virtually unopposed. By the beginning of 1884 ten of them, representing between them half the income from the estate, had had their rents reduced by a third. For his part Thomas MacHale was understandably perplexed at receiving no reaction from the Maynooth Trustees. As well, he was distancing himself from the diocese of Tuam because of differences with the new Archbishop, John McEvilly. He kept adding new conditions: the Trustees were to undertake not to sell the land for less than £6,000; while he himself lived they might not appoint or dismiss a land agent without his approval; and they were to put up a marble slab in the college chapel commemorating the bequest. When the Trustees met in June 1884 it was clear to them that under the conditions now proposed they could neither manage the estate nor sell it. They instructed the President to write to MacHale to ask if he would transfer the property unconditionally or make over a sum representing its real value. This was rejected indignantly, and when another approach was made in the autumn there was no reply. It is impossible not to regret the imbroglio, not to regret 'MacHale scholars', the annual choral office, and the commemorative inscription. The Lion of the West may not have been the easiest of men, but his unbroken connection with the college, which ended only with his death, had begun when he entered as a student in 1806.

The trouble which arose over the college farm at Laraghbryan was much more serious. In 1849 the Trustees had taken this farm of 135 Irish acres, 218 statute, from the Duke of Leinster as tenants-at-will at an annual rent of 45s an acre. Though there was no doubt that a lease could have been got on request none was asked for. Relations with the Duke were good: when a complaint was made to Cardinal Cullen that one of the deans, Thomas Hammond, was coursing hares with greyhounds with a 'poaching tailor' from Maynooth village, it had to come from the gamekeeper and it is a reasonable inference that the Duke himself would at least not have taken this line.[29] But he died in 1874, and the next Duke installed an agent who clearly planned to increase rentals. His first demand, in January 1877, was for an increase in rent to £3 an acre, on the grounds of improvements made to the lands since 1859. In reply, the college authorities pointed out that the improvements had been done at the tenants' expense, mainly since 1867, when a slight modification of boundaries agreed with the Duke between the college grounds held in fee simple and the farm held in a yearly tenancy had produced a verbal assurance which the Trustees understood as guaranteeing the rent would not be raised.[30] But the only reaction was a fresh demand in March 1878 for a rent further increased to £3 10s an acre, which it was claimed was based on current valuation, together with an acceptance of what had come to be known as the 'Leinster lease', by which the tenant agreed to opt out of most of the rights conceded by the Land Act of 1870, including the right to compensation for improvements. This demand was accompanied by a threat of eviction. The Trustees first offered a rent of £3 an acre if they were granted a lease for thirty-one years without the 'Leinster' restrictions, and then £3 an acre as tenants at will. Neither was acceptable, and they withdrew from the farm before eviction actually took place; they were awarded £1,000 compensation for the improvements they had made. Personal relations with the Duke remained good, and with the development of land purchase the Trustees were in the 1890s beginning to think in terms of buying the farm back.

A sizeable addition to college resources had come with what came to be called the 'Belgian Burses'. In the country which became Belgium in 1830 relatively good endowments in favour of Irish students had survived the French Revolution, most of them in Louvain. They were administered by various local authorities, and were enjoyed in some instances by foreigners of Irish descent under the claim of being 'founder's kin', and in others by young Irish students who presented themselves with letters of recommendation. In both cases the administration was almost necessarily loose, sometimes perhaps bordering on the irregular. After the establishment of the Belgian state attempts were made to have the revenues applied to the benefit of the Irish College in Rome, reopened in 1826, but almost nothing was achieved, in spite of the patronage of Archbishop Murray and the formidable internuncio in Brussels, Raffaele Fornari. The rector of Louvain, when the university had been restored in 1834, was particularly inflexible.

In 1864 the Belgian government introduced a new law regulating 'bourses d'études' generally. This opened new possibilities that the Irish burses might be enjoyed by Irish students outside Belgium, and because the United Kingdom government would be involved this would certainly be envisaged as being in Ireland rather than in Rome.[31] The bishops would have preferred a simple transfer of the revenues to the Maynooth Trustees, but a much more complicated scheme emerged. It involved the competent Irish ecclesiastical authority (for Maynooth, where the burses were soon concentrated, the President and the secretary to the Trustees), the Foreign Office, the British Embassy in Brussels, and the Belgian Commissioners of Administration set up under the law of 1864. This inevitably meant a complicated procedure, producing much but repetitive documentation containing some, but disappointingly little, individual detail. When a burse became vacant, the Belgian authority notified the Foreign Office, which notified the Maynooth authorities through the Irish Office, and in agreement with them advertised the vacancy. Applications were sent to the President of Maynooth and by him sent to the Foreign Office, with his recommendations, which were then passed on to the Belgian authorities. Notice of awards made came back through the same complex channels. In addition, at the close of each term individual certificates of intention to continue studies or to resign the burse had to travel the same ground, as had the necessary certification of completion of studies at the end of an individual's course.[32] Matters were sometimes even more complex, leading to difficulties and delays. These arose in part from a well-meant attempt by the Belgians to lump small burses together into a sum able to support a student. They arose also from the fact that because the burses could still be enjoyed in Belgium claimants turned up there from time to time, and while the Foreign Office gave generous co-operation its generosity did not extend to providing legal assistance in Belgium to contest dubious applications. Irish bishops who might have students in Louvain or elsewhere in Belgium might apply for them to enjoy a burse there, and they at least occasionally did this.[33] In 1867 the British Embassy in Brussels published a list of the available burses.[34] The total revenue came to the equivalent of £1,072 18s, a sizeable sum, giving support to about forty students. These revenues were naturally subject to some fluctuation. A report presented to the Trustees by the President and vice-president at the end of 1898, voicing objections to a proposal to transfer the funds to the Irish College in Rome, gave the income at that date as sufficient to provide thirty-seven burses averaging £25 10s, that is, a total of £943 10s. A further attempt to have the burses transferred to Rome was made in 1906,[35] but at their October meeting the Trustees reiterated that they were all to be held in Maynooth.

Thomas Farrelly, college bursar in 1870, had been appointed in 1845, two years after his ordination. His considerable capacity is shown by such things as how he handled the Royal Commission in 1853 and the problems arising from the Irish Church Act. Between 1845 and 1870 he had enjoyed a fair measure of independence of the Trustees. In 1862 they had imposed on him the obligation of presenting an annual financial statement, where, however, he had shown a kind of patrician unwillingness to be precise, while giving the impression that it cost a great deal more to run the college than the Trustees could possibly appreciate. He was set in his ways in 1870, but now he was much more vulnerable to Trustees who were understandably feeling harassed and impatient.

The College Administrative Council set up in 1871 functioned through two committees, one concerned with student affairs and the other with finances.[36] A resolution of the Trustees in October 1874 suggested that the bursar might be considered an executive of the Finance Committee, but it is clear Farrelly was not content to so regard himself, and the following June much more far-reaching arrangements were made. An assistant bursar was to be appointed, to be in effective control of the domestic areas, where money was spent, and the members of the Finance Committee were to sign the annual accounts. Henceforth it was to consist of the President, vice-president, bursar, assistant bursar, and a member elected by the staff from among themselves (a year later, in June 1876, one dean to be elected by the staff was added). Over the coming years the Finance Committee gradually developed into an independent body, the Finance Council, while the Administrative Council, consisting of the President, vice-president and deans, dealt with student affairs.

The assistant bursar, Andrew Boylan, appointed on 30 June 1875, was characterised by Walter McDonald as 'good-humoured, honest, weak'.[37] It seems certain he was unable to stand up to Farrelly, who in turn was reluctant to share authority. The situation deteriorated after Russell's disabling accident in May 1877. After long years of hope deferred the building of what would be a worthy chapel had begun in March 1876, but within a few years the problem of financing it was giving real concern. In November 1878 a fire gutted a notable part of Pugin's building: fortunately, it was well insured; and, as noted above, serious trouble with the Leinster estate over the college farm began in January 1877. In June of that year the Trustees referred back the accounts as presented by the bursar, because they had not been signed by the members of the Finance Committee (Farrelly retorted that they had refused to sign them because they claimed they did not have enough detailed information).

An episcopal Finance Committee was set up on 16 October 1878, but it may be that the real turning-point was the appointment of William Walsh as vice-president the previous June. He produced a detailed report to the Finance Committee and after consideration by them to the Trustees, which analysed problems and remedies fairly starkly. Farrelly resigned on 29 June 1881. His pension was guaranteed and he stayed on in the college until his death over nine years later at the age of seventy-six. There was some delay before Boylan was appointed bursar, and some talk of seeking a layman with commercial expertise that could not be presumed in a priest, but he succeeded to the post in October 1882. Times were still difficult, and in 1886 professional advice was sought to help towards a new system of keeping accounts. By now the interest on the Granard mortgage was seriously in arrears, and there were real fears for the capital. Each year between 1887 and 1891 the bank had to be approached for overdraft facilities. By then Andrew Boylan had gone—he left in October 1887 to join the Redemptorists, where, it may be suspected, he found a more congenial existence. His successor, James Donnellan, was appointed the day he resigned. The fact that he held the office until 1923 would in itself suggest a firmer hand.

Student accommodation was still austere. As the centenary year came in sight the students' rooms were still whitewashed; there was heating only in the Pugin buildings, from 12 November to 12 April. The authorities were always concerned about how much the heating system cost in return for what little it gave. At their meeting in November 1880 the Trustees declared that students' health had been harmed by overheated buildings, and that henceforth heat be turned on only at regulated times, and in the bedrooms only 'occasionally'. Recurring complaints about the system might suggest doubts if it was capable of raising water to a dangerously high temperature, but the installation of new boilers in 1891 together with the incongruous red-brick chimney did bring improvement. Gas, as already seen, had been supplied to the whole college in the 1860s—a great expense, Farrelly considered; and in June 1874 the Trustees decided that students' rooms were no longer to be lit by college gas but by candles they themselves had to buy. Farrelly was proud of the 'great water-wheel pump' which came into use in November 1864 and through roof tanks gave a supply through the buildings, though William Walsh in his survey on becoming vice-president was critical of the expense of what he called 'this elaborate system of hydraulic apparatus'. Neither was the staff accommodation luxurious, though when giving a detailed description of Dr Patrick Murray's quarters Walter McDonald makes it clear he regarded them as more spartan than most:

> Dr Murray's room was quite bare of all but books, which were stored all round, in plain deal cases, well glazed. There was no carpet; nor pictures, that I remember, except one of Suarez such as may be found in the frontispiece of some old folio edition of his works . . . There was a rather long, narrow, deal table in the middle of the room; with a plain board-seated arm-chair at the head, towards the fire, where he sat at study. Plain unbacked forms ran at each side of the table; I do not remember any other chair.[38]

The earliest record of damage to Pugin's buildings is in 1868, when a great January storm stripped the lead off the whole roof of St Mary's wing and seriously damaged the roof of St Patrick's. Ten years later, however, they suffered a disastrous fire. Small fires were recorded in the college in 1867, but they did little damage and the bursar could congratulate himself on the effectiveness of the 'large fire-engine' he had bought at the Dublin International Exhibition of 1865. However, it proved too small to deal with the conflagration that broke out on the morning of 1 November 1878.

Dr Patrick Murray wrote a long graphic account of the catastrophe in his diary, now in the College Library; and there can be little doubt that he was also the author of the detailed account published in the *Freeman's Journal* the following day and reprinted in the *Calendar* of 1879/80. The trouble started in a furnace-flue beside the staircase outside St Mary's Oratory (its companion, long disused, may still be seen beside the staircase at the other end of the wing). About half-past eight in the morning smoke was seen at roof level and the fire had soon taken a firm hold. Help was summoned from Carton House, but it was decided to ask for a fire engine from Dublin as well. As seems nearly fated in a crisis, the local telegraph failed to work, and there had to be a rush to Celbridge to send the message. Meanwhile, what apparatus the college and Carton House could muster between them, manned by workmen, students and volunteers who quickly gathered, concentrated on stopping the fire spreading to the library. As an additional precaution, all the books were removed: fortunately the door was at the end furthest from the fire. In what must have been a much more hazardous operation, for the door was within a few feet of the flue where the fire had started, quite a bit of the furnishing of the oratory was saved also.

The request for a fire engine from Dublin got an immediate response, and a special train to take it down was laid on. The train arrived in Maynooth at twenty past ten, but the fire engine then had to be drawn to the college and get up steam. It is described as having been 'set-up' by eleven o'clock, and concentrated on the west wing itself, where it brought the fire under control, but not before it had consumed half the building, including the centre block. A sketch made the next day and published in the *Graphic* on 16 November is a striking record of the destruction (Plate 25). The debris smouldered all night and the fire brigade continued to keep watch, leaving only the following afternoon at half past three.

Fortunately, the building was very well insured. Inspection showed that the walls were substantially undamaged, so it was possible to restore it as it was before.[39] The insurance money indeed allowed for the introduction of what were considered improvements. The interior lath-and-plaster partitions were replaced by more solid structures. The windows inserted in the north side of the oratory and refectory for additional ventilation also date from this rebuilding. Pugin no doubt would not have considered them very Gothic, but additional ventilation was badly needed. Three interior walls in the west wing and the east wall of the oratory were carried up to the roof as additional firebreaks. The interior of St Mary's Oratory was given a more ecclesiastical appearance: it will be recalled that it began life as a study hall, then became a lecture hall promised to Nicholas Callan, and when finally designated as an oratory remained a plain box of a room until the fire gutted it. New and safer external chimneys were built for the heating furnaces. A staircase was constructed to what had now become the dean's rooms in the central block, and it was even possible to do some work on the north gable of the building. This had not been damaged by the fire, but, together with the north gable of St

Patrick's, it had been left unfinished in anticipation of the completion of the fourth side of the square. Fairly extensive masonry pointing was carried out, and the three windows, one on each floor, also date from this time. Their Gothic style would probably have been enough to win Pugin's approval.

By now too buildings which in general had been built cheaply were beginning to show signs of age, sometimes at a fairly early age indeed. In 1883 the Finance Council called attention to the need for 'urgent repairs, amounting in several cases to the reconstruction of the roofs, walls, parapets . . . absolutely necessary for the preservation from ruin of the front house and of the buildings of the old quadrangle'; and a detailed specification of the work actually carried out indicates the tendency of repairs of this kind to expand once actually begun.[40] Sagged beams and floors over the Junior Chapel were to be lifted, settlements in the walls of both chapels to be underpinned, and four hundred feet of parapets to be taken down and rebuilt. And even the new buildings called for attention; not just desirable developments like new tiling in the students' refectory or the construction of a Muniments Room, but substantial repairs to buildings as yet only thirty years old: defective pointing on the east side of St Patrick's to be attended to, and, even more serious, the re-slating of the south side of the library.

At Last, Chapel and Aula Maxima

The long-drawn-out frustrations in building the chapel have already been noted. In 1858 the President, Charles W. Russell, approached individual bishops. Many expressed themselves in favour, but a number were lukewarm or even opposed. Pugin's son too wrote a number of times to Russell, arguing that he should be the automatic choice as architect because his father had done a design for which he had never been paid. Even at this stage Russell seems to have had another man fairly definitely in mind, J. J. McCarthy, Professor of Architecture at the Catholic University. His estimate that a chapel for five hundred students, with 'a simple and noble exterior and a presentable interior' would cost 'every penny of twenty thousand', does not seem to have been meant to be discouraging, but in fact it was.[41]

As the years went by with new churches going up all over the country Maynooth's makeshift College Chapel became more and more anomalous. The matter was taken up seriously in the autumn of 1873, when the Administrative Council wrote to the Trustees suggesting the time had come. The Trustees said they agreed cordially, and asked the President to present proposals to the June meeting. Finance was naturally the greatest problem. For quite a while Russell seems to have believed it could be done by simply inviting public subscriptions, encouraged perhaps by the fact that Dean James O'Kane, who had died on 16 February 1874, had left the bulk of his estate towards building the chapel, a not inconsiderable estate, most of it deriving from royalties on his *Notes on the Rubrics of the Roman Ritual*. There was, however, talk of a national church collection, and already some bishops were beginning to express reservations. However, the Trustees set up a building committee at their October meeting. It consisted of the four Archbishops, the Bishops of Clogher, Ferns, Kerry and Elphin, the President, vice-president and bursar, with power to co-opt, and was empowered 'to make all arrangements'. It met on 20 January 1875 and appointed J. J. McCarthy architect. On legal advice, he was instructed to prepare preliminary drawings as soon as possible, and, again on legal advice, to be careful to use none of Pugin's sketches. He presented two designs to the committee on 10 February. He included a spire and Aula Maxima, but the spire did not survive his first costings, and the Aula does not seem to have been more than an aspiration. The designs differed only in their proposals for the east end. In one it was plain, as it had been in Pugin's proposal, while in the other it was surrounded by a cluster of five apse-chapels. This second design won unanimous approval (Plate 26). At their summer meeting the Trustees agreed that the foundation-stone should be laid on 20 October.[42]

In his June report, which detailed much of this for the Trustees as a body, Russell also gave details of the progress of his appeal for funds. However, doubts were growing as to whether this alone would be enough. On 15 September the bishops, gathered at Maynooth for the national synod from 30 August to 20 September, held a special meeting at which they awarded the building contract to Thomas Hammond and Son of Drogheda, and individually pledged themselves to forwarding a collection in their respective dioceses 'by every means in their power'. They also removed 'the tower and two bays' from the plans presented to them, thereby reducing the cost from just under £35,000 to just under £25,000.

Problems arose with both architect and builder, about how his fee should be paid to the architect, and about the securities provided by the builder. In both cases they were satisfactorily dealt with, but they did reveal serious reservations with some powerful bishops. The recently appointed Archbishop Croke of Cashel was quite sharply opposed, urging that the whole project be reconsidered, that many did not approve of the plans or of the site, that £20,000 would be quite enough to spend, and that in view of the state of discipline in the college Maynooth did not deserve to have £20,000 spent on it. For his part, Bishop Gillooly of Elphin, while ostensibly confining himself to the concrete issues, would clearly have been happy enough to see the project dropped.[43] But the work went ahead. The builder arrived at the beginning of March, but it was a wet spring, the quarry was flooded, and he finally got under way only at the beginning of May. A surviving detailed progress report from the clerk of works dated 10 October notes the foundations sunk to 'hard compact gravel' at nine or ten feet, and the masonry foundations nearly completed.[44] The walls rose rapidly, in building stone from the college quarry, with limestone from a quarry owned by Hammond at Sheephouse near Athy being used for carved and finer work.[45] The building had its own momentum, and was not affected by Russell's incapacitating accident of May 1877. William Walsh's reports after his appointment as vice-president in 1878 chronicled the steady progress towards completion, though they were filled with growing concern as to how it could be paid for. It was almost completed when at the beginning of 1881 the architect, J. J. McCarthy, was in turn incapacitated by illness, and it was his son Charles who on 4 April issued the final architect's certificate that the building was completed.[46]

Internally there was still everything to be done, just plain walls and clear-glass windows. But externally it was completed, and it was apparent that it would be a worthy College Chapel. The basic style is 'French Gothic' of the fourteenth century, contrasting very well with the plainer thirteenth-century Gothic used by Pugin (Plates 27, 28). On each side is a cloister, communicating with the main church through the entrance-porch at the west end. The five apse-chapels give it a more ornate appearance than Pugin's design, but on the other hand it does not have the flying buttresses he had planned. The dimensions alone make it impressive, the great choir and sanctuary measuring 188 feet by 40, 70 feet high from floor to ceiling, while the overall exterior dimensions are 221 by 71 feet, with a height from ground level to roof ridge of 95 feet. To furnish it in a way worthy of the structure was a challenge, but before this could be thought of there was a problem of debt to be faced. Russell's accident had not interfered with the progress of the building, but it had left no-one in overall charge of collecting money. As has been seen, in September 1875 each bishop had pledged himself to hold a diocesan collection, and St Patrick's Day 1876 had been suggested as a suitable date. However, only fifteen bishops, a little over half the total, held it on that day, and even here in some dioceses the collection was postponed to the autumn in some parishes. The other dioceses spoke of holding the collection the following year. When he reported progress in June 1876 Russell showed no sign of concern. Between diocesan collection and private subscription about £15,000 had been raised, of which £13,000 had been actually received.

The year 1877 saw Russell's accident and no further diocesan collections. At their October meeting the Trustees urged that outstanding collections be held as soon as possible, referring, ominously enough, to the need to pay the builder as various stages of the work were certified complete by the architect. In June 1878, at the meeting at which William Walsh was appointed vice-president, authorisation had to be given to seek a bank overdraft to make these payments. Shortly afterwards, in a curious way, another calamity afforded temporary relief. On 1 November 1878 a large part of Pugin's building was destroyed by fire. As has been seen, it was very well insured. At a special meeting to review the serious problems, held in February 1879, the Trustees decided to borrow from the insurance money rather than from the banks to meet the recurring demands of the chapel. Of its nature this could only be a temporary respite, during which the real indebtedness of the chapel continued to mount. When the rebuilding of St Mary's was completed the chapel overdraft stood at £12,845, and measures suggested by the Trustees in 1882 indicated real alarm: a resolution that outstanding diocesan collections be made before the end of the year, and a proposal to choose priests to collect funds in America or Australia. Nothing came of these proposals over the next two years, and at the summer meeting of 1884 the President, William Walsh, was authorised to sell as much stock as would meet the debt and so end the crippling interest charges. In October Walsh presented the final account. The overall cost had been £30,575. Of this, £12,488, approximately 40 per cent, had been subscribed in diocesan collections and £5,921, approximately 20 per cent, by private subscription, and there was a bank overdraft of £12,734, again approximately 40 per cent, to eliminate which securities were sold. However, the Trustees envisaged this loss being made good by the defaulting dioceses holding their collections, and they agreed fairly draconian measures. The overall cost was to be assessed on each diocese in proportion to the free places it enjoyed from college funds; its contribution to date was to be first deducted, and interest of 4.25 per cent charged on the amount outstanding. Until its liability was cleared, free places were to be withdrawn from the diocese in question. This was indeed a strong incentive to clear the debt, but it was a time of economic depression when even the better-off areas might well hesitate in asking for money for a non-diocesan purpose. There is no doubt the scheme was heatedly debated: an amendment was proposed by Bishop Duggan of Clonfert, seconded by Bishop MacCormack of Achonry, asking that the sum be raised by a public appeal by the President, recalling that this had been Russell's original intention, but it was lost, and in October the Trustees, having learnt their exact liability, confirmed their decision.

Even after this painful decision, what stood there was an empty shell, very different from today, when the dim religious light persists, though the quiet is perhaps not what it once was. Especially if one looks up at the ceiling, more particularly on the rare occasions when it is lit to meet the demands of television, the word that springs to mind is 'pre-Raphaelite': the blessed do indeed lean out from the gold bar of heaven (Plate 56). The President who achieved this transformation over about six years was Robert Browne of the diocese of Cloyne, appointed in October 1885. The result is a tribute to his persistence and indeed to his taste, for many things have come right and the overall blend is harmonious. A first impression might suggest that money was no object, which indeed is not necessarily a guarantee of a happy result. In fact money was always tight, and the pennies had to be counted. Robert Browne was good at counting pennies, which was fortunate, as he had no other option.

In June 1880 William Walsh had estimated that it would cost £8,000 to £9,000 to fit out the interior. The bishops took the first steps towards this at their June meeting in 1884 when, having taken a painful decision on the outstanding debt, they agreed that funds must be quickly raised to complete the church, and put the President, William Walsh, in charge. In the circumstances of the time it could not have been easy for him to get started, and indeed nothing seems to have been done by the following summer, when he was appointed Archbishop of Dublin. In his first report to the Trustees the following June, the new President, Robert Browne, had some good news to give them. Six dioceses had paid off their arrears and there were seven donors of large stained-glass windows. This nerved him to ask for the launching of an appeal for approximately £10,000 to complete the chapel. The Trustees responded by urging the dioceses still in default to clear their arrears, and set up a committee of the Visitors with two other bishops to organise collections throughout Ireland and in America and Australia if necessary. In October they were more precise. They authorised a collection for £6,000; by June 1887 each bishop was to make his contribution, proportioned to his college free places; but, they warned, in no case were funds in the college to be used to supplement deficiencies; and finally, the President was to make arrangements with the individual bishops. When June came Browne could only characterise the overall response as 'fairly satisfactory', but he was able to list a number of individual donors as well. The Trustees decided to invite architects to submit proposals to their October meeting.

The contract went to William Hague, the man who had succeeded to much of McCarthy's practice. He and Browne were both strong-minded men, and his letters to Browne record clashes that sometimes generated peppery exchanges,[47] as when Hague retorts to Browne's complaint that he does not visit the site often enough by saying he is the architect, not the clerk of works, or when he asks to be given notice should Browne fulfil his threat of taking their differences to the Trustees. But they learned to work together, and this was important, for Browne was the consistently active member in a committee consisting of himself, the Archbishop of Dublin and the Bishop of Elphin, authorised in October 1887 to enter into contracts according to the architect's specifications up to maximum of £6,000. This was extremely tight budgeting, as things turned out impossibly tight budgeting, even though much helped by the fact that Browne worked tirelessly and with success to get individual donors for such major items as windows, altars and Stations of the Cross, but made worse by the fact that not all the money promised was subscribed. Bishop McGivern of Dromore may, as he claimed, have been speaking for others when he wrote in 1888: 'That a few bishops at the Maynooth Board can impose a tax on each and every diocese for such object greatly surprises me. Indeed I share the opinion of many others that Maynooth College and its students have been spoiled with too much money.'[48] Shortly after this letter was written Browne was reporting that contracts had been entered into to a total of £8,988, while £1,635 was still outstanding from the promised £6,000, leaving a considerable shortfall, and as well many dioceses had not cleared their arrears from the 1876 collection. He pointed out that the college accounts had shown a surplus of £3,000 over the past three years, and asked that that be put into the fund as a kind of 'college contribution' (the staff had subscribed about £1,000 between them, most of it towards a balcony over the high altar: this was never built, and the money seems to have gone into the general fund). The Trustees agreed, but twelve months later, in view of worsening general finances, they declared that they had meant it only as a loan, to be repaid as diocesan arrears came in.

The first ceremonies took place in the new chapel with ordinations to the priesthood on 24 June 1890 (it is possible, but not certain, that a small group of first-year Dunboyne students had been ordained there on 5 June, the feast of Corpus Christi). After Prizegiving on 25 June there was a *Te Deum* and benediction. The President suggested that the solemn consecration take place in twelve months' time, though the overall deficit on the chapel was still £9,812. It was £8,642 when the consecration took place on 24 June 1891, but in June 1893 Browne was able to report to the Trustees that though four windows and five Stations of the Cross still awaited donors, and though three dioceses were still in arrears, and there was not a penny left in the chapel fund, it was not in deficit.

The consecration was a public occasion, extensively reported in the press. Much of the reporting consisted of description of the details of the chapel. Perhaps the best way of giving some overall impression of so many things is to take the main features in turn, and the best beginning is the stained-glass windows, which determine the quality of light and will also introduce the firms who left the greatest overall mark on the interior (Plate 56). William Walsh had been seeking ideas and sketches for windows as early as 1880, all from English firms, with the exception of Earley and Powell of Dublin, but finances did not allow anything to be done. This was just as well, for attention seemed to be concentrated on figures of Irish saints, first six of them to a window, later reduced to three. Even this was not very promising: it would be hard to avoid monotony in a row of windows each portraying three unconnected figures. In 1886 talk began of 'scenes', first envisaged as two to each window, one from the life of Christ above and one from the life of St Patrick below, but this later refined itself into a large scene from the New Testament, with a pediment below and a canopy above, with a small depiction of a related topic at the apex, in the choir windows an Old Testament 'type' of the New Testament scene, in those of the apse one of the priestly sacraments.

The windows were supplied by three firms: Mayer of Munich, Lavers and Westlake of London, and Cox Buckley, likewise of London, who set up a branch at Youghal during their work in Maynooth. The great west window is a rose depicting Christ in glory surrounded by saints and angels. It was erected by Westlake in 1890, and was the joint gift of Gerald Molloy, rector of the Catholic University and formerly a professor of Maynooth, and Denis Gargan, vice-president of the college. The other windows depict the life of Christ in a succession of scenes from the New Testament, from the mysteries of his Mother to the sending of the Holy Spirit. The one directly at the back of the high altar is out of series. It very suitably shows Christ sending his disciples, with the Holy Trinity depicted above. It was the gift of the deceased Cardinal

McCabe and erected in 1885. The others may be listed in series, beginning next the sacristy door on the south side, noting for each the themes; the supplier; the donor; and the date.

Assumption, Annunciation, Visitation; Vision of Abraham: Mayer; Patrick Canon Kearney, PP, Moate; 1890.

Nativity; Moses in the bullrushes: Mayer; Bishop and clergy of Clogher; 1890.

Presentation in the Temple; child Samuel in the Temple: Mayer; Bishop and clergy of Ossory; 1890.

Holy Family; family of Tobias: Cox Buckley; Bishop and clergy of Raphoe; 1891.

Christ among the doctors; Daniel before King Belshazzar: Cox Buckley; in memory of James Ryan, coadjutor bishop of Killaloe; 1891.

Baptism of Christ; Noah's Ark: Cox Buckley; Patrick Canon Clifford, PP, Fintona; 1891.

The marriage at Cana; Moses striking the rock: Cox Buckley; Michael Canon O'Keeffe, PP, Coatbridge; 1891.

Christ and the Samaritan woman; Solomon and the Queen of Sheba: probably Westlake; 'ab alumno oblatum'; 1905.

Christ heals the man at the pool of Siloe; Naaman cleansed in the Jordan: Stephen Montgomery, 'patronus collegii fidus'; probably Westlake; 1905.

Christ raises the widow's son; Elijah raises the widow's son: probably Westlake; 'collegio amicus'; 1897.

Mary Magdalen washing the feet of Christ; Ruth at the feet of Boaz: probably Westlake; Canon Donovan, PP, Dunlavin; 1895.

Peter puts out into the deep; the Tyrian sailors take Solomon's ships to Ophir: Westlake; Bishop, coadjutor bishop and clergy of Clonfert; 1892.

Miracle of the loaves and fishes; miracle of the jar of meal and cruse of oil: Westlake; Elizabeth Nelson, Cooldrinagh, Leixlip; 1892.

St Peter receiving the Keys; Moses receiving the Law: Westlake; James Nelson, Cooldrinagh, Leixlip; 1892.

Transfiguration; the three children in the fiery furnace: Westlake; Bishop of Galway; 1892.

Palm Sunday; Baptism: Cox Buckley; Bishop Clancy (Elphin) in memory of Bishop Gillooly; 1895.[49]

Last Supper; Holy Communion (with small figures of St Thomas and St Benedict Labre): Cox Buckley; Archbishop Croke; 1900.

Descent from the Cross (after Rubens); Holy Orders: Cox Buckley; Archbishop Logue; 1890.

Resurrection (after Pieter Pourbus); Eucharist: Cox Buckley; Archbishop Walsh; 1890.

Pentecost; Confirmation: Cox Buckley; Archbishop McEvilly; 1890.

The same information for the small windows in the apse chapels is as follows:

St Brigid instructing her companions: Cox Buckley; Michael Fogarty (college staff); April 1892.

The Flight into Egypt: Cox Buckley; Joseph McRory (college staff); April 1892.

The Presentation: Cox Buckley; Brigida [damaged] Manutiana; March 1891.

The Sacred Heart: Cox Buckley; Bishop Flannery (Killaloe); April 1892.

SS Flannan and Lua: Cox Buckley; Bishop Flannery; April 1892.

The first three choir-windows were erected by the German firm Mayer of Munich. Browne kept urging them to put more 'richness' of colour into their designs, and they resisted, saying that if they darkened the glass any more there would not be enough light in the church. When the three windows were installed in 1890, unluckily for Mayer in the summer months, Browne immediately protested that the colours were too light, as he had always claimed. Mayer replied that the effect could not be judged until more stained glass was installed in the nave, and indeed a look at their windows today would suggest that they were right, but they got no more commissions.[50]

Another firm was working on the windows in the apse and sanctuary at the same time, the London firm of Cox, Buckley and Co. Despite his name, the Irish origins of the head of the firm, Michael J. C. Buckley, do not seem to have been recent. However, the fact that he opened an Irish branch in Youghal in 1889, including a glass-making kiln, certainly suggests some existing link with the locality. This helped him to secure orders from Browne, who was under some pressure from the Home Manufacture Movement. Buckley was probably also helped by the fact that he began work in the more confined space of the apse, where the erection of even a few windows could produce the 'rich' effect Browne so hankered after. From the records surviving in the college[51] it is not possible to say how much of the glass he installed was actually made in Youghal, but some almost certainly was. Browne, as was his custom, kept hounding him, but Buckley could give as well as he got, except perhaps in the matter of prices, though even here there is evidence of a shrewd business judgement that it was worth while to cut prices because the job was not only a big one but also very strategically placed before the eyes of young men who were potential future customers. It was not a good period for stained glass. Artists were content to imitate past works of art, not only windows but also canvases: two of the apse windows in the chapel are copies as close as the medium will allow of paintings by Rubens and Pieter Pourbus of Bruges (c. 1510–84). Yet Buckley prided himself on striving to produce what he kept referring to as 'true stained glass . . . the richest, thick "antique" glass of the finest colours, not painted on, as some foreign modern glass is done . . . thousands of pieces, exactly as in a fine mosaic'.[52] On his own initiative, he supplied and installed in the chapel cloister the mounted cartoons of his windows, at a token price.

The third major firm supplying stained glass, and which shared with Cox Buckley most of the other decorative work, was Lavers and Westlake of London. They had installed the great western rose window in 1890 and won the contracts for the four windows erected on the north side of the choir in 1892. They are probably responsible for the other windows on this side, though in the absence of documentation it is hard to be certain, because the work of neither firm was particularly distinctive. The firm's earliest commission, however, was the decoration of the ceiling. Browne wished the work to go to the Dublin artist Robert Mannix, but William Hague was very insistent that it be N. H. C. Westlake: Mannix, he said, was a highly competent workman but not in the same class as Westlake as a designer.[53] The acceptable compromise was that Westlake designed the panels and sent the designs to Maynooth, where Mannix executed and installed them. The work was begun in March 1888 and finished by the end of the year. The panels are canvases attached to a wooden ceiling. They depict saints and angels in a heavenly procession to the high altar. When the work was finished Mannix claimed for gilding beyond what was in his contract, done, he said, at Browne's urging. If this is what happened it was worth it, and the niggling nature of the dispute may be forgotten, for the Westlake-Mannix ceiling is a splendid thing and has worn well.

Westlake was also the artist of the life-size Stations of the Cross (Plate 29). They give the impression of being frescoes, but again are canvases attached to the wall. The general effect is striking, and the gold background suggests, admittedly at some remove, Siena and the quattrocento. Eight spaces are available on each side. The extra space on the south side is occupied by the pulpit, flanked by figures of St Peter and St Paul, while on the north side the first station is preceded by a panel depicting the Messianic prophets. Each station had to await an individual donor, and priority seems to have been given to the windows, for at the consecration only the four nearest the high altar were in place, two on each side. The work was completed in 1894.[54] Every station except the last three carries a donor's name.

As has been seen, it was the firm of Cox Buckley which installed the windows in the apse and sanctuary. The same firm was responsible for the wall and ceiling decoration of the whole area. It does not come up to the level of Westlake's ceiling, and one area in particular, the large unbroken wall facing the sacristy door, is fussily overdecorated, though the fault may lie more with Browne than with Buckley. The most ambitious work here is a series of six paintings, five over the arched entrances to the apse chapels and the sixth over the blank space just mentioned, again giving the impression of being frescoes but in fact canvases attached to the wall. It was decided that the series depict the Irish saints, and after some discussion agreement was reached on the scenes to be portrayed. Beginning on the north side and working clockwise they are: St Laurence O'Toole remonstrating with Strongbow's soldiers; St Brigid receiving the veil; St Malachy leaving Clairvaux for Rome; St Patrick preaching at Tara; St Columbanus founding Bobbio; and St Colmcille sailing from Derry. Detail is not easy to pick out, for they are high up and the background is dark and the colours muted. Needless to say Browne was disappointed when he saw them, declaring they were not sufficiently 'elaborately' painted, but this drew the tart retort from Buckley that if he wanted more elaborate work he should have been prepared to pay more.[55] But all the work in the apse was finished for the consecration. This was not the case with the apse-chapels, where again Cox Buckley was the contractor. Each was floored, but not all as yet had a marble altar. Only the central Lady Chapel had its stained glass and wall-painting, which was afterwards replaced by the mosaic which is there today. The other four chapels had their stained glass and painted walls by the end of 1892. The painting, it has to be confessed, is not very inspired, and fleeting impressions from old photographs suggest that the original painting in the Lady Chapel was not very inspired either.

The carved oak choir-stalls are a feature of the chapel of which Maynooth can be unreservedly proud. There is a persistent tradition, committed to paper nearly fifty years ago, that this work was carried out by a family of woodcarvers named Moonan from Dundalk, who lived in Maynooth while the work was being executed, apparently over a number of years, in the large house just over the bridge on the right-hand side as one leaves the college. Sadly, the records, though fragmentary, do not sustain this version of things, even though it is the version, recalled through the blur of fifty years, of a man who was a student, admittedly in the ghetto of the Junior House, at the time the work was being done.[56] In the obviously supplied newspaper notice on the occasion of the consecration, it is explicitly stated: 'This work, it is a pleasure to be able to state, has been done in the city of Dublin, the contractors being Messrs Connolly and Son, Dominick Street.'[57] This firm was the main contractor for the joinery work in the chapel. In March 1889 the President reported to the Trustees that the supports for the stalls were completed, and in September the architect reported that 'Mr Connolly seems to be progressing fairly with the stalls',[58] which may well refer to work in progress in his

Dublin premises. There is no explicit record of when they were erected in the chapel, but they were in place for the consecration in June 1891. Six months later, in connection with the furniture of the sacristy, there was correspondence with a firm called Bryan Moonan of Drakestown, Ardee, Co. Louth.[59] The firm, a father-and-sons team, had carried off awards for woodcarving at the Irish Artisans' Exhibition in Dublin in 1885, and proudly carried a commendatory letter from William Hague on its business stationery. Among the matters raised was the possibility of the Moonans coming and living in Maynooth to speed up the work. The father was willing but not enthusiastic; he admitted it would speed things up, 'should the President see to put us up and board us while doing the work', but he added that he and his sons 'would prefer to do the work at home'. They certainly do not appear as a team who had recently spent a considerable time working on the chapel and living in Maynooth. That they did work in Maynooth and lived there while doing it seems proved beyond question by the roll-book of the Presentation Convent school. This shows the enrolment of a girl whose father was named Moonan, and described as a woodcarver from Ardee, into the sixth class. What the work was seems proved equally beyond question by the fact that she was enrolled in the year the sacristy was being fitted out, after the choir-stalls had been finished. As a final tease, the vesting bench carries a small brass plate identifying the maker as 'Moonan and Sons, Bolton Street, Dublin'. One would like to have more information about the individuals who actually carved the stalls, 454 of them, more than anywhere else in the world, for the chapel is effectively one huge choir. The American oak timber is of high quality: regrettably, Irish oak of that quality was not available. The overall work is very fine, and there is some good detail, the arms of the Irish dioceses carved in the panels at the back, where there are also carved figures of Our Lord, the Blessed Virgin and the saints, while there are exquisitely carved finials which very seldom repeat themselves.

As the chapel moved towards completion, Browne began to think of an organ and an organist. Beyond doubt, the provision so far made would have to be improved. Walter McDonald noted that when he was a student in the 1870s Liturgy was taught by the deans, and church chant by students, when it was taught at all. James O'Kane had taught Liturgy well, but those who came after him taught it badly. There was a part-time organist, but when he died in 1877 it was not easy to get a successor. When William Walsh was appointed vice-president in 1878 it was decided to look for someone who could teach church music as well. In fact, such a person proved easier to find, for professional organists tended to be busy at weekends (Walsh himself had to play the organ during the academic year 1878/79). However by June 1880 two people had been found, a part-time organist and a part-time choirmaster, but Browne decided that for the new chapel only a resident priest would do, and when he discussed it with Archbishop Walsh and his coadjutor Nicholas Donnelly they agreed with him. Donnelly wrote to the Director of the College of Church

Music at Ratisbon, who recommended a priest, Henry Bewerunge, and obtained for him three years' leave of absence from his diocese. He was appointed on 26 June 1888, and spent the rest of his life in the college, dying there on 11 December 1923. He was a demanding perfectionist, but he was appreciated for it (Plate 31). The musical training of the Maynooth student reached a new level of professionalism that through the professor and his students reached out through the country. Highlights were fondly remembered, like the Palestrina tercentenary in 1894, with an augmented college choir and a memorable lecture from Bewerunge in the Aula Maxima.[60] Naturally he took over the business of getting the organ.[61] A contract was signed on 28 July 1889 with the firm of Stahlhut of Aachen, and the work was finished twelve months later. It had some features which made it unique in Ireland, though there were some similar instruments in Europe; unique especially in the electrical connection between the keyboard and the pipes, which made it possible to site the keyboard anywhere in the chapel (it was installed immediately below the organ-loft at the west end of the stalls on the south side). A clause in the contract had provided for a committee of experts to report on it, and they tested its capacities on 6 August 1890.[62] They expressed some reservations: in particular, the innovative electric connection, they said, 'cannot, as yet, at least, be pronounced to be anything more than a highly interesting but only partially successful experiment', where, it would seem, time was to prove them wrong. The organ, finally, was enclosed in a handsome case, designed and built by Cox Buckley.

It is impossible to enumerate every detail that went into the chapel. The altars, made by the firm of Ryan of Dominick Street, did incorporate some Irish marble, but most of it was white Carrara. The names of the donors are inscribed on four of the five altars in the apse chapels: the high altar (Plate 30) was presented by Archbishop Walsh, though before long it was replaced by the very ornate structure which still stands there and which those who knew both were inclined to compare to its disadvantage with the earlier one, especially in that the new structure was so large that it obscured the pattern of the apse chapels. Caen stone was used for the interior groining, and where the groins were sprung from the walls the corbels were carved into angels holding the liturgical instruments handed over at the conferring of the various orders. Browne would have liked marble flooring, but he had to settle for a mosaic, supplied by the firm of Burke Brothers of Paris and London and made in their Paris workshops. Even relatively mundane matters such as gas lighting produced some fine brasswork: the heating was concealed, under the choir-stalls. The spring and early summer of 1891 saw a flurry of minor furniture, vestments and so on from Cox Buckley, and all was ready for the consecration on 24 June. It was a national event and got wide coverage.[63] The consecration was carried out by Archbishop Logue of Armagh, and Archbishop Walsh of Dublin sang the Mass. The sermon was preached by John Healy, like the two archbishops a past member of the staff, appointed coadjutor bishop of

Clonfert in June 1884. He took his text from the first letter of St John: 'This is the victory that overcomes the world, our faith.' To modern ears it might sound a bit triumphalistic, but that is the way people were feeling at the time.

The other long-felt want, the Aula Maxima, was met shortly afterwards, and in an unexpected way. McCarthy, like Pugin, had sketched a building to the west of the chapel completing St Mary's Square, but this never seems to have been more than an aspiration. Browne seems to have toyed with the idea of converting the old chapel when the new one was ready, but this had a double function, being also the oratory of one of the three divisions of the college. He detailed what happened next in his report to the Trustees in June 1891. He had seen in the papers that an Irish-born priest, James McMahon of New York, had donated no less than $400,000 to the Catholic University of America. He established that he was a nephew of Michael Montague, the President who had built so much of the early college, and had himself spent some time as a student in Maynooth. However, he had gone to America and lived his life as a priest in New York. His considerable wealth derived from land he had bought in Manhattan while the area was still open country. Browne wrote to him asking for help to build the Aula Maxima. McMahon's reply arrived towards the end of May. He told Browne that it was a pity he had not written even a year earlier. By now he had given almost everything away, but 'for Maynooth's sake' he undertook to enter into a bond to provide £3,000 over three years, and more quickly if he could. To execute such a bond he needed the agreement of the Trustees.

At their June meeting they decided that his offer should be gratefully accepted, and that a permanent record of his generosity should be placed on the building: they added, however, that the cost must be strictly limited to £3,000. Architects were invited to compete with designs, but it seems no great excitement was generated. What appears to have been a preliminary sketch by William Hague, representing substantially what was actually built, was sent by Browne to Michael Buckley for comment. Buckley replied that nothing could be done to improve a building which showed such utter absence of taste, reflecting 'the gloomy ugliness of the old house'. It was also, he claimed, very wasteful of materials, so much so that he believed a very handsome and most useful hall (in the Gothic style, apparently) could be built for the money.[64]

In this he must have been wrong, as appears when tenders were invited for a building to accommodate 800 people ('from 900 to 1000' is crossed out in a surviving draft specification),[65] and to cost no more that £3,000, less the architect's fee of £150. In fact nobody tendered, and when Hague tried to interest builders he found only one agreeable, Stephen Lalor of Kilkenny, described, optimistically as it turned out, as being 'known not to be of much means'. He was willing to tender for £2,750, and the Bishop of Ossory. Abraham Brownrigg, spoke well of him, saying he had done good work locally and the sureties he offered were reliable.[66] There was some discussion about the site, for clearly it could not form a part of Pugin's square. Browne proposed the still vacant site between Dunboyne and Rhetoric, probably because it would be a convenient assembly point for the strictly separated divisions of the college, but Hague said it was too closed in, and it was agreed to build between New House and the wall of the quarry field. Here Patrick Lalor arrived to begin work on 18 February 1892.[67]

By the end of March it was apparent that he was in trouble. To begin with, he did not have the cash to pay his own workmen; and the people who had supplied him with materials for his masonry work were writing to complain that they had not been paid, and the stage had been reached where it was necessary to bring in sub-contractors for such things as roofing-timbers and furnishing.[68] By June Browne, who had been subjected to pressures amounting to at least mild blackmail, was paying these bills directly. Yet he concealed his anxieties in his June report to the Trustees, merely chronicling progress: Lalor had accepted a contract within the limits specified, and had promised to be finished by November; the walls were now within a few feet of their full height, and the roof was made and ready for delivery; and the first £1,000 had been received from Monsignor McMahon. By August the walls were finished and the roof-beams erected, but it was now clear that Lalor could not continue unless Browne paid the weekly wages and for all materials—in effect, build by direct labour. He turned to Hague, who consulted Thomas Connolly, head of the firm who had done so much work on the chapel. After they had visited the site, Connolly offered to complete the building for £1,875, provided Lalor handed over at once. Lalor jibbed at this, saying that when the news got around he would never get another contract, but he had little option, and after some by now perhaps inevitable horse-trading the building finished with nobody feeling particularly happy about it. It is good to record that despite the financial stringency two handsome memorial plaques to McMahon were not forgotten, though the official title of the building, 'The McMahon Hall', is not often heard nowadays. What has traditionally been reputed his portrait hangs outside St Mary's Oratory (Plate 40). That it is seems confirmed by the fact that in October 1895 the Trustees reimbursed the President for £46 5s expended on 'a portrait of Monsignor McMahon and two memorial slabs'. The overall cost had been £3,634 13s 1d. McMahon had honoured his commitment and sent £3,000, but when asked if he could add something replied he had no more to give. It was Connolly who had to press for the £634 13s 1d owing to him, and at one stage Browne had to borrow £200 on his personal security, but in June 1894 he was able to report that Connolly had been paid, but he himself was still owed £204 5s 1d.

The first function in the Aula Maxima was held on 19 April 1893, a reception for the Archbishop of Armagh, who had been created a Cardinal in Rome on 16 January. He had returned laden with honours for Maynooth, a domestic prelacy for Denis Gargan, the vice-president, and doctorates in Divinity for all the members of the theology faculty, which was soon to be empowered to confer degrees, and also for Francis Lennon, the professor of what was still some-times called Natural Philosophy. The honours were conferred in the new chapel, and the college then adjourned to the Aula for speeches. It is to be pre-sumed that Francis Lennon went with them, though tradition had it that he never entered the building, saying that by all the laws of nature it should fall down. It looks a bit better today that it did then—the illustration in Healy's *Centenary History* has been described, not unfairly, as showing it looking rather like a large boot-box (Plate 41). Buttresses had to be built about seventy years ago, at a substantial cost, and other amenities were added more recently. And yet the list of functions held there in its first year as detailed by Browne in his report in June 1894 showed clearly how much it had to contribute; and over the years it became clear that the cheap and rather graceless building had a quite outstanding acoustic.

Just when he made this report, on 26 June 1894, Browne was nominated bishop of his native Cloyne, where he died on 23 March 1935. He left the col-lege in good shape to prepare for its centenary.

CHAPTER VIII

THE BISHOPS' COLLEGE, 1870–95: STAFF, STUDIES, COLLEGE LIFE

Staffing in Hard Times

Maynooth had less money, so there had to be economies in every possible direction. One economy was to cut back on the number of students entitled to free places. Those students who had been admitted to Humanity passed directly to Logic at the end of the year, bypassing Rhetoric, and students in Logic were given the option, which most of them took, of bypassing Natural Philosophy and beginning Theology. Students of Fourth Theology were ordained at the beginning of 1871, and the fourth-year theology and Dunboyne classes were suspended until finances should improve. That left some of the staff unemployed or under-employed, but their position was safe-guarded in the Irish Church Act. Discussing possible economies in a letter to Cullen in June 1869, Bishop Moriarty of Kerry considered that a rearrange-ment of classes could make three or four professors redundant, or put to teaching things not taught at all, preaching for example. In sentiments that did not fit well with the Sulpician spirit he had professed such admiration for in the Visitation of 1853, he concluded: 'The whole system might be made more absolute, and better calculated to foster humility and obedience.'[1] John O'Hanlon, Prefect of the Dunboyne, died on 12 November 1871. When Daniel McCarthy became vice-president in September 1872 he continued to teach his full course in Scripture, and the courses in Catechetics and Bible History with the junior classes, traditionally the responsibility of the vice-president, passed to the junior dean. In June 1873 the Trustees ordered Patrick Murray, whose fourth-year theology class had been suspended, to take a class in Sacred Eloquence with the senior theology students; and when Gerald Molloy left in March 1874 to a post in the Catholic University, William Walsh had to take on his classes as well as his own. James Tully, the professor of Irish, was old and feeble (he died on 2 October 1876), and his classes had to be entrusted to a student, not even a Dunboyne student, for there was no Dunboyne.

The Visitors, through the Trustees, tightened control over the staff. The 1872 statutes allowed the Trustees to make appointments after either concur-

206

sus or examination, or without either of them provided all the Visitors had been consulted. The salary for future appointments was to be reduced by a third. Each professor was to have his programme for the coming year in the hands of the President in time for it to be posted before the end of the current one, and subsequent changes needed the consent of the newly constituted Scholastic Council; and the statutes required each professor to submit a monthly report on each student in his class. At this the Scholastic Council protested unanimously and called for two reports, one on 1 February and the other at the end of the year. This came to be accepted, but relations between the staff and the Visitors were very low. Then in 1877 George Crolly's health failed (he died on 24 January 1878) and the President had the accident from which he did not recover. Resources were being spread very thin. When Bishop Moriarty of Kerry died on 1 October 1877 it was an open secret among those who knew that his successor would be Daniel McCarthy, vice-president and professor of Scripture at Maynooth. The obvious successor as vice-president was William Walsh, and it was suggested he might perhaps be induced to continue teaching with the lighter load of Scripture. But then someone would have to be found to take his theology classes, and Patrick Murray, now teaching the restored fourth-year course, was coming to the end of his days. Perhaps, Gillooly suggested to Cullen, an eminent German or Italian theologian might be found: 'the Maynooth staff is below par: it needs to be renovated.' Cullen however had to reply that there was no hope of getting a theologian in Rome; and he had been there for some time, for the conclave that elected Leo XIII.[2]

McCarthy's appointment as Bishop of Kerry was delayed until the end of the academic year, and William Walsh became vice-president on 25 June 1878. There was then a rather undignified hiatus because McCarthy refused to resign as vice-president, and a crestfallen Gillooly had to inform Walsh at the end of August, with the new year beginning, that he had managed to consult the majority of the Visitors and on their authority he might begin to discharge the duties of vice-president.[3] Walsh indeed needed all the authority he could get. The President was incapacitated, and two of the four deans had just been appointed, a third only three years before. Michael Logue had been appointed dean in 1876, being also required to teach Irish; in 1878 the Trustees appointed him, grudgingly enough, to one of the vacant chairs of Theology. He was to continue to teach Irish until other arrangements were made, but the terms of this question were changed when he was appointed Bishop of Raphoe in 1879. Hugh O'Rourke, professor of English and French since 1862, got leave of absence for health reasons in October 1878, and his classes were taken by one of the newly appointed deans, Patrick O'Leary. Edward O'Brien, professor of Rhetoric, got similar leave of absence in December: his classes were taken by a Dunboyne student and, Walsh reported to the Trustees, 'Dean Browne helped with Greek'. Then in February 1879 Charles Macauley, professor of Rhetoric since 1854 and newly appointed to Scripture, got leave of absence. Walsh taught Scripture, and Thomas Carr, appointed in 1874, took classes in third and fourth Theology, while his own classes in first and second Theology were taken by a fourth-year student. Discontent was simmering among the staff and students generally. Small wonder that Walsh had serious reservations when the presidency came up after Russell's death. At the Trustees' meeting in June 1881 he set out twice to call on his archbishop, Edward McCabe, but twice his courage failed him and he slipped a note under his door. In this he said that in 'the extraordinary condition of affairs . . . now grown almost inveterate' he felt that a solution as dramatic as that in 1812 was called for, that a bishop should take over for a while; that he had discussed this with John McEvilly, coadjutor archbishop of Tuam, and Bartholomew Woodlock, bishop of Ardagh, and would be happy to see either President; he suggested his colleague Thomas Carr as vice-president.[4] Walsh was appointed President that same day and Thomas Carr vice-president

There was a hand at the wheel, but the staffing problems continued. Two of the four Theology chairs were vacant, even though Logue's place had been filled by the appointment of John Healy. The number was made up by the appointment of Patrick O'Donnell in September 1880 and Walter McDonald in September 1881: until this was done there had to be further patching, courses being taken by Walsh and by Dunboyne students. Then in June 1883 Thomas Carr was appointed Bishop of Galway, leaving two vacancies, the vice-presidency and a chair of Theology. There was no obvious candidate for the vice-presidency, and there was talk of an outsider. Walsh felt however that if a good candidate could be got inside the college it would be preferable to a slightly better one from outside. In the event, the successful candidate was the very capable dean, Robert Browne of the diocese of Cloyne. Denis Gargan of Meath, professor of Ecclesiastical History, a member of the staff since 1845, had been strongly supported by a group from the northern ecclesiastical province, and he and they were disappointed. The third candidate was Dean Thomas Hammond of Limerick, twelve years senior to Browne. He took his defeat in good part, but it was understandable that he soon returned to a parish in his native Limerick.[5] Two years later William Walsh became Archbishop of Dublin, Browne succeeded as President, and this time Gargan became vice-president. In his first report to the Trustees in June 1886 Browne listed the classes which had to be supplied because chairs were vacant or professors ill. The extent of the problem appears when he says that nine students began the Dunboyne course; during the year two were called out to serve in their dioceses; five lectured for nearly the whole year, one for part of it; and only two of the nine took the end-of-year examinations.

Arranging lectures in a subject so complex as Theology was not made easier by the substitutions which had to be made so often. The single professor in both Scripture and Ecclesiastical History took the classes allotted to him, and if he was for one reason or another not available the best possible substitution was made. The core subjects of Dogmatic and Moral Theology presented more complex problems. There were four chairs, though in the 1870s one was frequently vacant and at times two. A fourth year's Theology had been introduced in 1834, but even in the 1860s about half of each class was ordained at the end of their third year of Theology, and about half the remainder before completing their final year, so much so that in 1860 and 1861 the Trustees discussed the possibility of reducing the course to three years, a step they took because of financial stringency in 1870, restoring the fourth year in 1875, when things had eased.[6] In 1861 they did, however, in response to repeated requests from the teaching staff, replace the bizarre system whereby each professor taught the complete course of Theology over four years with one in which each taught a single year's course of both Dogmatic and Moral Theology. The staff had urged that an even better use of resources could be made by dividing the Theology classes into two groups and allotting two professors to each, one teaching Dogma, the other Moral. Even with the doubled classes, they felt, there would still be enough opportunity for class interrogation, while the professor, with his lectures halved, would be able to take more written work from the students, a necessity if the new statutory demand of monthly reports was to be met.[7] It was possibly this consideration which led the Trustees to accept the view of the staff with what seems surprising ease considering their previous resistance. The revised division of lectures was agreed in principle in June 1871, and the new courses were worked out and phased in over the next two years. With them new textbooks were definitively prescribed: in Dogma that of Giovanni Perrone SJ (1794–1876), the distinguished theologian of the Collegio Romano, and in Moral the treatises by Jean-Pierre Gury SJ (1801–66). His *Compendium Theologiae Moralis* (1850) and *Casus Conscientiae* (1862) had come to be widely adopted in seminaries because of their real virtues of moderation in judgement and careful clarity. Patrick Murray's epitome of his *De Ecclesia* (1874) was also used.

When these new courses were adopted Theology ran for three years, and every student did the full three-year course. It seems to have worked well, despite what the staff regarded as meddling by the Visitors, especially Gillooly. The practice of interviewing students as part of the visitation proved particularly questionable. Naturally at least some of them expressed dissatisfaction with their courses, because, the staff claimed, students now had to work harder and submit more written essays.[8] Real problems arose only when in October 1874 it was decided to restore the fourth-year course. As it was assumed—rightly—that not all would remain for this course, and as students of third and fourth years were to attend class together, there was a serious problem in devising an overall course which might be regarded as substantially complete after three years. An obvious solution was to restore the old system of each class having its own professor, and the Trustees would have preferred this, but the staff held out, hoping that the bishops would allow more of their students to remain for the full four-year course, because, it was alleged, students were called out by their bishops for ordination even when there was no urgent need for their services. In fact the new system worked well only when it became the norm that students were left in the college to complete four years of Theology, and in the interim things were not eased because one and even two chairs of Theology might at times be vacant.[9]

Over these years there was a real transition from one generation to another. It was noted by Walter McDonald, who entered as a student in 1870 and was appointed professor of Theology in 1881. O'Hanlon died in 1871, Crolly in 1878, Murray in 1882, all more or less in harness. With their deaths, McDonald considered, whatever theological tradition was in the college was broken. Those who might have acted as bridging figures, Walsh and Carr, appointed professors of Theology in 1867 and 1874 respectively, were absorbed into administration. The old professors he saw as men of 'great, strong, childlike faith', well suited to form missionary priests, but not what he liked to call 'scientific theologians'. They were in any case slaying foes disabled or killed long ago, and not facing current problems; and yet as a student he had carried away the impression that they were greater theologians than John Henry Newman.[10]

The taunt of 'Gallicanism' which had so vaguely and to an extent unjustifiably clung to them was disposed of just as they were dying. In a draft memorial, probably never forwarded, drawn up by Tobias Kirby, rector of the Irish College, Rome, after the death of Paul Cullen, he instanced among the reasons why Patrick F. Moran should be the new archbishop the need to keep a vigilant eye on Maynooth. He does mention the Gallican imprint given by the first professors and the troubles of the 1850s, to show the need for continuing vigilance in spite of all Cullen had done.[11] Then an article, 'Theology, past and present, at Maynooth' appeared in the *Dublin Review* of October 1879. It was by Henry Neville, one of the three professors singled out for censure in 1855. In all conscience, it was not a very searching analysis, and was possibly written to support Neville's hopes of being appointed coadjutor bishop of Cork. William Walsh decided to answer it. Some interesting reactions came his way while he was putting the answer together for the next number (January 1880). A Passionist priest, who had spent his life giving parish missions, wrote to say that his personal experience was that almost every priest ordained in Maynooth up to forty years ago was very severe in confessional practice (this he describes as a 'a taint of Gallicanism, perhaps even a taint of Jansenism'), while those ordained up to about fifteen years ago were 'anything at all but enthusiastic regarding papal infallibility'.[12] Walsh picked up useful guidelines from the dying President, who was indeed the person who suggested he should answer Neville. In the context of an article in the *Saturday Review* after Russell's death, which among other things asserted that no-one really knew his mind on papal infallibility, Walsh recalled that the only time he heard Russell speak at table in a way that could be called severe was in connection with Neville's article. It was he who stressed the distinction between Gallicanism in dogma and rigorism in morals. Rigorism was taught in Maynooth, he freely admitted, but on principles described as the very reverse of Gallican. Walsh's article, 'The alleged Gallicanism of Maynooth and the Irish clergy', was a very competent analysis of the college's position on theological Gallicanism, in which he showed how developments there paralleled those in northern Europe generally, in that there was a gradual move away from the French *ancien régime* position towards what was defined at the First Vatican Council.

'What is wrong with Maynooth, and has been wrong with it while I know it', Walter McDonald wrote, 'is that we aim at producing good average men.'[13] The 'good average man' is indeed what Maynooth may well be proud of. His eyes fixed on parish ministry, he tried faithfully to mould himself in the Tridentine pattern, to preach and administer the sacraments. He learned to preach from his Dogma lectures; to administer the sacraments he learned from the deans' instructions and, most specifically, from his course in Moral Theology, which taught him to be a good confessor (in 1871 the Trustees introduced a special pre-ordination 'faculties' examination in the theology of penance, justice and marriage); and anything over and above this he was content to leave to the academic minority of his time. The weakness of the system lay in the poor provision for teaching practical, 'pastoral' skills. For the most part the programme here was 'make do and mend', with one exception. In October 1874 the Trustees decided to ask Father McGowan CM to give lectures in Sacred Eloquence to the senior classes. Walter McDonald, then a student, was deeply impressed by him.[14] After a year he proposed an extensive programme to the Scholastic Council, providing for lectures on preaching, catechesis of children, reading and declamation, and the composition of sermons. Unfortunately his health broke down during the academic year 1877/78, and though for a few years there were hopes he might come back, by 1880 it was back to 'make do and mend' again, until 1904, when Patrick Beecher of Waterford was appointed to a full-time post with the formidable title of Professor of Pastoral Theology, Sacred Eloquence and Elocution.

The study of Philosophy struggled with the growing problem of fitting a credible course in both Mental and Natural Philosophy into two years. The demands of both were growing—Natural Philosophy because of the explosion of scientific knowledge, and Mental Philosophy under the stimulus of Pope Leo XIII's concern to encourage a Christian philosophy (it is hardly accidental that the first of his great encyclicals, *Aeterni Patris*, issued on 4 August 1879, was a call to develop this Christian philosophy on the basis of the *philosophia perennis* of high Scholasticism). It was perhaps inevitable that Natural Philosophy should in the end fail in its claim to be an essential part of a general liberal education, but even in the 1890s the Trustees were still accepting its right to half the available time, though the Roman authorities had a decade before insisted that a one-year course was utterly inadequate for Mental Philosophy.

Walter McDonald did not look back on his Philosophy course with enthusiasm.[15] The professor, Richard Hackett, he regarded as uninspired, ploughing his way in Latin through the textbooks, the *Logicae seu Philosophiae Rationalis Elementa* of William Jennings, published in 1863, with, in the background, though usually in the form of the heritage of 'a good set of notes' rather than the work itself, Anglade's book published in the early days of the college. A new textbook, the *Institutiones Philosophicae* of Salvatore Tongiorgi SJ, published in 1862, was adopted in 1880. This is regarded as having made a major contribution to the manual tradition of neo-scholasticism, but the impact a textbook could made was necessarily limited as long as the essential problem was getting a quart into a pint pot, and though efforts to do this continued it just would not go. The fact was that no other seminary institution had a course of Mental Philosophy lasting for one year only. A further change of textbook in 1884 seems only to indicate a continuing lack of direction, for whereas in 1882 the Trustees decided that a second professor be appointed for the academic year 1883/84, this was not done, and indeed the right of Natural Philosophy to a full year was reiterated. In 1884, however, under stimulus from Rome the Trustees again decided to appoint an extra professor. The problem still remained of finding time for the extra lectures and indeed of finding someone to give them.

Traditionally, there had been two years before the course of Philosophy began, Humanity and Rhetoric, the core content of each being the Classics. About half the entrants were judged sufficiently advanced to be admitted to Rhetoric, and this number tended to increase as the secondary education system improved. In consequence, the chair of Humanity was an obvious target as the Trustees naturally sought areas for economies in the 1870s. They did indeed resolve to abolish it in June 1873, but it continued for a number of years, because of recurring complaints that students who had been allowed to pass into Philosophy after one preliminary year were sometimes seriously deficient in Latin, though in the late 1870s the numbers matriculated into Humanity were very small, ranging between twelve and twenty a year. It finally went in June 1879. By now it was becoming possible to apply external standards. The Intermediate Education Act of 1878 had led to the establishment of public examinations. In June 1879 the Trustees decided that a pass in Middle Grade should admit a student to Rhetoric and a pass in Senior Grade to Logic. This could be no more than tentative, for the standards for those examinations had yet to be established. In 1879 there was further legislation leading to the establishment of the Royal University with its matriculation examination. In 1886 the Scholastic Council ruled that a pass matriculation or Middle Grade should admit to Rhetoric, an honours matriculation or Senior Grade to Logic. The situation might be summed up by saying that Maynooth required a good secondary course, ending at university matriculation level, before admitting a student to philosophy, the beginnings of his studies for the priesthood.

Irish, English and French fitted in as best they could. English and French were still the responsibility of one lecturer, Hugh O'Rourke, appointed in

1862. The position of Irish had deteriorated during the long incumbency of James Tully, appointed as far back as 1828, and it did not improve for quite a while after he died on 2 October 1876. When Michael Logue, who had taught Irish in addition to his other duties, was appointed Bishop of Raphoe in 1879 Irish was for years entrusted to a Dunboyne student, after an abortive attempt to get a layman on a part-time basis for less money than he was prepared to take. It was indeed a low point for the language: in 1884 the Trustees made it clear they envisaged it continuing on a part-time basis, and that it should be taught by a student 'until a professor appointed to some other chair be found competent to take charge of it', and three years later the Scholastic Council actually put to a vote the question whether Irish should be continued; and though they decided it should they agreed no better provision should be made for it and that it should be optional for all students except where individual bishops directed otherwise. Part of the problem was that no-one really wanted to give his life to teaching Irish; indeed, according to Walter McDonald, tradition had it that James Tully was not interested in Irish because he felt it had no future.[16] Then in 1891 Eugene O'Growney was appointed and a reasonably ambitious programme took shape: two classes weekly to both Rhetoric and first-year Philosophy, one weekly to second Philosophy and one, optional, to the three senior Theology classes. He was also to deliver six public lectures annually in Irish literature and antiquities. In July 1893 together with Eoin MacNeill and Douglas Hyde he founded the Gaelic League. But his body was not strong enough for his spirit. In October 1894 he got his first six months' leave of absence for 'threatened consumption', the disease that was to kill him on 18 October 1897. A conspicuous mausoleum marks his resting place in the college cemetery (Plate 47).

To read through the minutes of the Trustees' meetings in the 1870s gives a sense of what is almost an obsession with securing minute exactness and uniformity in teaching and examining, down to detail which would appear much better decided by those who were closer to the problems, especially given that a Scholastic Council had been established in 1871. Because the Visitors' minute-book for these years is missing, it must remain an inference—but a very strong one—that these developments were initiated by them. In 1872 the professors of Theology and Philosophy were required to take monthly essays from their students, and the new statutes published in that year demanded a formal monthly report on each student, which was later reduced to three reports a year, and finally to two, after the Christmas and summer examinations. It is hard to know what happened to a laudable attempt to introduce a tutorial system for students of first-year Theology. It was decided to introduce this in the academic year 1874/75, the tutors to be the fourth-year Theology or Dunboyne students, but as neither of those groups existed at the time it is hard to say what happened. In 1878 the President was instructed to take every care to investigate and report to the Visitors on how professors discharged their obligations at the informal daily class interrogation of students and the more formal monthly revisions, these revisions being extended from the classes in Theology and Philosophy to all other subjects. One's first reaction is that Russell of all men would have found this very distasteful, until one remembers his incapacitating accident of the previous year. Some of the decisions—the twice-yearly reports, for example—became permanent, but others were allowed to lapse. The piled-up detail of regulation indicates that the 1870s were indeed an unhappy decade in the history of the college, with resentment among staff and students mounting against what was seen as excessive regimentation by the Visitors, led by Lynch and Gillooly. As will be seen, the regimentation of student discipline produced particularly dangerous flashpoints.

Towards a University

It has been seen that Maynooth had made a number of attempts to get authority to grant degrees, and that all had failed, the latest being the 'St Patrick's University' proposal of 1867, which would have linked the college with the Catholic University and given the joint institutions the support of a civil charter. In 1875 the proposal to unite them was renewed, this time as a private venture, and the Trustees set up a joint committee to consider how to make the programmes common to both institutions 'as far as possible identical', and to report to the next meeting in October. It was a year before the committee reported, in June 1876. The report said it was impossible to draw up identical programmes, because of the different nature of the two institutions, and more specifically because Maynooth was reluctant to change the wide-ranging character of its pre-theology course and its facility to matriculate students into classes ranging from Humanity to first-year Theology on the basis of its own entrance examination. The committee went on to detail how the programmes might be assimilated as far as possible.[17] On this basis the Trustees at their meeting in June 1876 decided that Maynooth should become a college of the Catholic University, with Faculties of Theology and 'Philosophy and Letters', the professor of Natural Philosophy to be aggregated to the university Faculty of Science. The full range of Theology degrees was to be awarded, with the doctorate at the end of fourth year, and baccalaureates in Philosophy and Science at the end of the Philosophy course. Maynooth was to keep its existing courses and entrance examination. It is hard to see how this plan could have worked, apart altogether from the fact that the Catholic University was now in a very weak state, and though in June 1880 the Trustees called for Maynooth programmes leading to Catholic University degrees in Philosophy and Theology, the situation had been changed by the University Education (Ireland) Act, passed into law on 15 August 1879 (42 & 43 Vict., c. 65). This opened the way to the Royal University, which offered new opportunities and searching tests to both institutions.

The Royal University of Ireland, incorporated by charter on 27 April 1880, was an attempt to give an indirect subsidy to teaching for degrees in institutions the Catholic Church could approve of. Its governing body, the Senate, in the first instance nominated, was to be composed equally of Catholics and Protestants. The Senate nominated the examining body, the Fellows, again preserving the religious balance, thirty-two as originally proposed, but later pared down to twenty-six. Half the fellowships were to go to the Queen's Colleges, which retained their existing grants. Fellows were to receive a salary of £400 a year, and it was not merely allowed but envisaged that they should teach in affiliated colleges, in this way helping Catholic institutions to raise teaching standards to a level allowing them to present their students for degrees of the university. Prizes and exhibitions would be awarded on the results of the examinations. It was anticipated that Maynooth would be one of these institutions, and indeed a favourable eye was cast on proposals to mesh university and seminary courses. In effect the new university, an examining body, offered modest financial help to allow Catholic students to obtain in Ireland degrees recognised by the state without having to attend institutions condemned by the church.

In September 1881 the Trustees approved the connection of the Maynooth courses in Rhetoric and Philosophy with the Royal University and unfortunately if perhaps inevitably commissioned the Visitors to make detailed arrangements. The first thing to be done was to submit students to the university matriculation examination. In all, 128 were presented, and though they were selected from the three junior classes, being in all about 55 per cent of an overall total of 236, the results were more than encouraging given the fact that the candidates had to attend the existing college courses and got only such special coaching as some of a small staff might be willing to give. Only six failed to matriculate, 122 passing. Maynooth students won four of the twelve first-class Exhibitions, two of the twelve second-class, and the two scholarships in Ancient Classics, worth £50 a year for three years, both going to Kerry students in second-year Philosophy.[18] The question now was how many of these should continue to study for degrees, and who was to teach them. This became entangled with the question of who was to enjoy what fellowships might be allotted to Maynooth. Matters were further complicated by the fact that overall Catholic policy on the Royal University was discussed at the general episcopal conference, not at meetings of the Maynooth Trustees, and while communications of the Maynooth authorities with the Trustees were not good, with the general conference they did not exist at all. At their meeting in September 1881 the Trustees, having approved the connection of Maynooth with the Royal University, reached an informal agreement that what fellowships might be allotted to Maynooth should go to those teaching the subjects in which students were being prepared for examinations. A meeting of the general conference on 11 January 1882 decided to divide the 'Catholic' fellowships between Maynooth, the Catholic University and St Malachy's College, Belfast (no doubt to establish a counterweight to the Queen's College there). Even this could not be final, for allocation of the fellowships rested with the

Senate, and not all its Catholic members wanted the bishops to make the decisions for them.

Inevitably, there was a good deal of lobbying for fellowships. Through 1881 Walsh had been working hard to secure fellowships for Maynooth, especially since Henry Neville, rector of the Catholic University since Woodlock became Bishop of Ardagh in 1879, was pressing to have them all concentrated there (it will be recalled that Walsh and Neville had recently clashed over the alleged Gallicanism of Maynooth). Walsh was handicappd by the fact that he had no official liaison with the bishops, and it was apparently only after their meeting on 11 January 1882 that he was informed, probably by Woodlock, that they proposed to seek fellowships for Maynooth and allot them to those teaching 'university' subjects.[19] There were only four of these, and they had their problems. Francis Lennon, though not averse to a university fellowship, was conscious of the gap between Maynooth's Natural Philosophy and a university Faculty of Science. Richard Hackett, a hard-working, exemplary man, does not seem to have been greatly interested in Mental Philosophy beyond taking his students through an elementary course. Hugh O'Rourke, professor of English and French, had poor health, was often on leave of absence, and was not really interested: 'though specially urged by his most intimate friends' he had simply not turned up at the meeting of the Scholastic Council held on 21 September 1881 to prepare a case to induce the Trustees to allow the college to enter the Royal University. There was a young enthusiastic professor in the key chair of Rhetoric, Malachy Scannell from Kerry, appointed in 1879 after O'Brien resigned. His enthusiastic coaching had contributed greatly to the successes in the matriculation examination, but it is clear he quickly became disillusioned, for he resigned his post in July 1883. While at that date both staff and student numbers in all universities were quite small and one professor to a department the norm—it would be misleading to think in terms of today's numbers—Maynooth's teaching resources were slender even by the standards of the time, and it was hard to see university teaching being sustained unless they were strengthened.

Walsh was working hard to get as many fellowships as possible, but it was also necessary to get credible people to fill them. The matter was urgent, for the students who had matriculated might be presented for the First University examination in September 1882. He persuaded Lennon to allow his name to go forward, but other initiatives being taken in the college did not make the work of assembling a teaching body any easier. Two members of staff, John Healy, professor of Theology, and Robert Browne, one of the deans, canvassed for fellowships and seemed likely to get them. This was quite in order, as the Fellows were in the first instance university examiners and only secondarily college teachers: Laurence Gillooly, Healy's bishop, assured him not only of his own support but that of Archbishop McCabe, and Walsh too seems to have regarded his appointment as quite acceptable.[20] However, when the decisions on the Maynooth fellowships were taken at a Bishops' meeting held in Dublin at the end of March it was clear that they did not favour the claims of Healy or Browne, and indeed clear that other members of the staff might be passed over in order to bring in outsiders; so Walsh seems to have been able to gather, though he complained to Woodlock that though he had been officially invited by Gillooly to attend, he was not called before the meeting, while representatives from other colleges were.[21] Healy expressed himself aggrieved, and Walsh began to fear that once again Gillooly was arranging things he did not know enough about, and he began to express doubts, first of the wisdom of connecting Maynooth with the Royal University on terms Gillooly might negotiate, which developed into growing suspicions of the whole university project, which he began to fear might result only in giving respectability to the Queen's Colleges. Many bishops were beginning to become suspicious also: indeed only McCabe, Woodlock and McCarthy of Cloyne were positively in favour. It was unfortunate that relations between Walsh and McCabe were cooling, not only on the university issue but because he had inclined towards Croke in the public altercation between the two archbishops over the Ladies' Land League in March 1881. The Maynooth Visitors were to meet in the college on 16 April 1882, and before they met Walsh was writing to Woodlock urging caution over a decision on Maynooth fellowships, saying it would be a disaster if university obligations were undertaken without resources to provide teachers. He need not have worried: in the absence of McCabe (in Rome to receive the Cardinal's hat) the Visitors decided nothing and there was a definite air of opposition to Maynooth being connected with the Royal University.[22]

May and June passed in a three-way correspondence between Walsh, Gillooly and Woodlock in an attempt to square the circle. Statutorily, the Fellows were distinguished scholars constituting a university Board of Examiners who *might* (and normally did) teach university courses. Multiple poverties forced Maynooth to reverse these priorities. Income from fellowships was essential to fund a sufficient staff, at least four, hopefully five, more if possible. Even with that, it was suggested, things might have to be cobbled to fund more staff, reducing salaries of individual Fellows to £240. But was this compatible with the university statutes, and would outsiders accept it? Walsh did not want to bring these in, but it was hard to see how a staff could be provided without them. And writing to Gillooly as early as 24 April he had put his finger on a very serious problem. The Fellows were in the first instance nominated by the Senate from among existing teaching staff in institutions, but this was for a period of seven years only, after which there would be open competition for fellowships among all graduates of the university. Though he saw the Queen's Colleges casting a long shadow, Walsh was still prepared to take the risk provided Maynooth got five fellowships. This looked increasingly unlikely. The university Senate was getting impatient, and not all its Catholic members were content to be put in a position where they seemed to be awaiting the bishops' orders. Yet no Catholic member wanted to lose Maynooth, for the sheer size of its potential student body offered the only real counterweight to the Queen's Colleges.

The decisions, however, were being taken by the general Bishops' Conference. At a meeting on 6 June they had set up a sub-committee to examine the question. Its members could not be considered particularly favourable to the connection of Maynooth with the university: it included neither McCabe nor Woodlock, both members of the Senate. Another indication of how things were going was provided at the Trustees' meeting on 27 June, in the shape of a grudging permission to the two students who had won classical scholarships to finish their degree, 'but without any right of special help from the college professors'. When the sub-committee reported to a meeting of the bishops on 17 July it mustered the arguments for and against, but there was no doubt of its conclusion. It would be difficult, they said, to match a seminary with a university system, especially one new and untried; seminarians would be attracted to secular pursuits; two streams of students would develop among them; theology as a subject would be downgraded; in future professors would be appointed by the university Senate; and it was clear the experiment would cost the college money, which it did not have. They unanimously rejected the proposed link, and a majority of the bishops agreed with them. McCabe was appalled. He had discussed the question with Simeoni, the Cardinal Prefect of Propaganda, when he was in Rome earlier in the year, and he now wrote to him urging that he ask the bishops to reconsider their decision. Simeoni wrote the letter, but a Bishops' meeting at the beginning of October reaffirmed their decision of July, and by a bigger margin.

In so far as this may be regarded as an opportunity lost, the staff must share the responsibility with the bishops. At the beginning of October the college councils were consulted by the episcopal education committee, though it might be said it was now late in the day and the outcome already decided. The staff as a whole was asked its opinion on the advisability of the college participating in the Royal University courses, provided '(i) that there is question only of an experiment, to be abandoned if found injurious; (ii) that any additional teaching power considered necessary by the Council of Studies will be provided.' The first thing the staff in council did was by an unspecified majority to add a third proviso: 'that such changes should be made in the R.U. programme as the College Council might consider necessary to guard against neglect of the ordinary studies and class-work of the college.' After some hours' consideration, a vote was taken. Of thirteen present and voting, seven considered a participation on these terms not injurious; three considered it injurious; two were doubtful and one could make no choice at all. It was now irrelevant that the Administrative Council voted, by three to two, that while there was some risk to discipline and spiritual interests the experiment might be tried if adequate safeguards could be devised. When McCabe reported the outcome to Propaganda, the Cardinal Prefect suggested, in a letter of 11 November, that the issue might be raised again, but in fact it was now dead. The student body had shown itself ready for an intellectual challenge, but the leadership failed them.[23]

It seems clear that by now some at least of the bishops never wanted to hear the word 'university' again. The Catholic University was down to a handful of students, and the annual collection, in so far as it was still made, was an embarrassment. In October 1882 the bishops decided to hand it over to Cardinal McCabe, and concentrate in it the thirteen fellowships finally allotted as the 'Catholic' share. In the circumstances of the times, this represented riches, and when McCabe reached an agreement with the Jesuits in October 1883 it got new life as 'University College'. Some seminaries presented candidates for Royal University examinations, but the way ahead was rocky, shown by a minute of the Bishops' meeting held on 1 October 1884, deploring 'the dangers to which Irish Catholic students are exposed in the Royal University, as revealed by the questions set for their examination at the recent examinations in Metaphysics—questions practically necessitating the reading of anti-Christian works, most dangerous to the Catholic faith.'[24]

The whole incident had exposed serious weaknesses in the Maynooth staff. Over the years ahead it was to get some modest strengthening. The resignation of an obviously disillusioned Malachy Scannell in 1883 must have been a loss to classical studies: his successor was Edward Maguire of the diocese of Clogher. When Hugh O'Rourke died in 1885 John F. Hogan was appointed to a chair of Modern Languages and John Clancy to a chair of English; when Richard Hackett died in 1877 two chairs of philosophy were established, one, designated as a chair of 'Higher Philosophy', filled by a foreign Dominican, Thomas Esser; and finally, in 1891, the chair of Irish was filled by Eugene O'Growney. One of the reasons for these developments was promptings from Rome.

When Leo XIII became Pope in 1878 one of his concerns was the state of studies in Catholic institutions, particularly in seminaries. The problems arising from the Royal University certainly brought Maynooth before the Roman authorities, who reacted, as they normally did, by seeking information from someone they trusted, who, now that Paul Cullen was dead, was his nephew, Patrick Francis Moran. Moran's reply to 'a list of questions about Maynooth' sent to him through Tobias Kirby 'a few weeks ago' is dated 30 April 1882. He had no doubt, he said, of Maynooth's general orthodoxy: 'French ideas' were long dead. But there were what he called 'college traditions' leading to 'a general spirit of independence', and he felt these should be looked at. He regarded the Theology course as in general sound and serious, but the other courses were not, especially Philosophy and Latin, and pastoral training was very deficient. In regard to seminary discipline, the size of the institution posed a problem, but the deans were vigilant; he suggested that a spiritual director should be appointed. Asked whether the bishops took an interest in the institution, he replied that as a body they were possibly too interested, in that the Trustees at every meeting kept chopping and changing things. He believed that a college rule should be drawn up and submitted to Propaganda for its approval, and not changed afterwards without the Congregation's consent.[25]

In March 1884 the Pope decided to summon representatives of the Irish bishops to Rome. The matters to be discussed were wide-ranging, for there were serious political issues on which they were divided, but Maynooth seems to have headed the list. The bishops, meeting there on 1 and 2 July, were agreed that philosophical and theological studies needed to be improved and prepared themselves for a meeting in Rome in October; some still expressed regret that Maynooth had not linked itself to the Royal University. However, when they met again in Clonliffe on 1 October it was agreed they were not ready for the Roman meeting, and McCabe wrote to ask the Pope to defer it to a time he considered suitable the following year.[26] Meanwhile the Romans continued to seek information. On 28 August Kirby wrote in response to a query from the Cardinal Prefect of Propaganda. The Maynooth courses, he said, were thin and restricted, and nearly all the professors had been prepared simply by passing through them. He considered spiritual formation deficient, saying that the real goodness of Irish priests came from their family background rather than from the college formation. The numbers of the students posed a real problem: Cullen had subdivided the existing two divisions into four, but after his death they had been reduced to three. Propaganda studied the Maynooth situation at meetings on 11 and 14 September, and sketched out the positions to be taken on problems,[27] only to find that the meeting was now postponed at the request of the Irish bishops.

On 2 January 1885 McCabe wrote to say he had consulted all the bishops and they had agreed to be in Rome about 20 April. He added that his own health was much improved and that he hoped to be with them,[28] but he died on 11 February, thus adding the contentious issue of the succession at least to the background of the agenda (William Walsh was appointed Archbishop on 23 June). At the end of February the Pope set up a commission of cardinals to prepare for the meeting with the Irish bishops: Simeoni, the Prefect of Propaganda, Jacobini, one of the secretaries at the Vatican Council and now Leo XIII's Secretary of State, and Franzelin, the distinguished Jesuit theologian, papal theologian at the Council.[29] They met the Maynooth committee of the Irish bishops on 1 May. This consisted of the Archbishops of Cashel (Croke) and Tuam (McEvilly), the bishop of Elphin (Gillooly) and three bishops who had been members of the staff, Healy (coadjutor in Clonfert), Carr (Galway) and Logue (Raphoe). It is probably significant that they began with Philosophy, for this had been the subject of the first of Leo XIII's great encyclicals, *Aeterni Patris*, dated 4 August 1879. The cardinals asked for a full two years of Mental Philosophy, taught in Latin and designed as an introduction to Theology; they considered the Maynooth course, in effect one year of Mental Philosophy, to be much too short. The issue seems to have been hard argued, and the final decision was that there should be a three-year course, one year of Natural Philosophy followed by two of Mental; in individual cases bishops might petition Propaganda to allow a shortening. The issue of the Royal University filled all of Saturday 2 May and spilled over into Monday. In this matter Propaganda had decided the previous September to take no line until the Irish bishops should be heard. They now explained the situation, and informed the cardinals that most of the bishops were against Maynooth seminarians presenting themselves for Royal University courses. The cardinals agreed but suggested that newly ordained priests might attend them, not in Maynooth but in another Catholic college, for example University College in St Stephen's Green, and this was agreed unanimously. The cardinals raised the possibility of a 'Pontifical Institute of Maynooth' with power to grant its own degrees; the final decision was that application should be made to the Pope for authority to confer degrees in Theology after the system now worked out had been tested.

Seminary discipline did not prove very contentious. The Propaganda briefing to the cardinals had been that there should be four divisions, with a dean and spiritual director in each. It was finally agreed that the existing three divisions should remain, and that there be two spiritual directors, to have no other duties and to be chosen by the bishops. A college rule was to be drawn up, to be submitted to Propaganda for its approval and not to be subsequently changed without its consent. A Roman proposal that students spend vacation in a 'villa' in the Italian style was withdrawn. The cardinals insisted that there be no vacation on any plea at Christmas and Easter, and when they asked that a report be sent after the summer vacation by the parish priest of each seminarian they were told that this had long been the practice.

Because time was pressing and because there appeared to be general satisfaction with the Theology course, this was remitted to a sub-committee of the bishops and Cardinal Jacobini, and when they presented agreed proposals on 15 May they were accepted. Dogmatic and Moral Theology were to be, as hitherto, the core, but substantial changes were proposed in the way they were to be taught. The first theology year was to be taught separately, the other three classes together, and there were to be eight hours of Dogma each week, with three professors, and only one professor of Moral, with four hours. The courses in Scripture and Ecclesiastical History at two hours a week for three years were confirmed, as were two classes a week for two years in Canon Law, now stabilised as a distinct subject in the curriculum. Overall, there were not to be more than eighteen classes a week, the academic subjects being distributed over five days, to leave time for the pastoral and practical aspects.[30]

Particularly in view of the change of emphasis between Dogmatic and Moral Theology, it would appear that some pressure may have been put on the Irish bishops. However, it was accepted that what had been agreed in principle might have to suffer some modifications when applied in practice. In fact the modification turned out to be substantial. The Scholastic Council held a series of meetings over the academic year 1885/86, giving itself terms of reference which suggest that Moran was perceptive when he referred to 'a general spirit of independence'—'to give effect, as far as we believe it practicable, in the circumstances of our college, to the suggestions of the Propaganda scheme.' Their proposals were submitted to the Trustees in June 1886, and adopted for one year as an experiment, which proved lasting. Very substantial modifications were made in the matter of teaching Dogmatic and Moral Theology. The students remained divided into two groups of two classes each, each group with one professor teaching Dogma and one Moral, and the number of lectures in Dogma, while greater, was only marginally so. They remained very much at the core of the programme, and the other subjects had to struggle to assert themselves. An elaborate setting-out of the concursus programme for the future, adopted by the Trustees in September 1886, shows this basic test for a professorship still centred on a grilling in the college textbooks of Philosophy and Theology. Yet when Joseph McRory was appointed professor of Scripture in October 1889 following the death of Macauley, this subject at least begins to be discussed at the Scholastic Council, with proposals to extend the course, include more of the Old Testament, and provide lectures in Introduction to Scripture where the critical questions of the day could be dealt with. Leo XIII's encyclical on Scripture studies, *Providentissimus Deus*, came in 1893.

The problems of Philosophy were more intractable. A course of three years overall had been accepted in Rome, but this was in practice overturned when the Trustees decided they would in no circumstances extend the college course as a whole beyond seven years. They accepted the proposal of the Scholastic Council that there be two years' Philosophy, Natural and Mental Philosophy being taught in each, the latter getting the larger share. This was no great improvement on a system acknowledged to be deficient, and it is not surprising that it proved hard to do anything about the teaching of 'higher philosophy', mooted in 1884. When Richard Hackett died in March 1887 a newly ordained priest, Thomas Judge, was appointed to succeed him in June, but it was clear that a professor of 'higher philosophy' would have to be sought abroad, and Thomas Esser OP was appointed in October. However, he was frustrated by the scant lecture time that could be allotted to him, with Natural Philosophy actually fighting back, claiming an equal division of time in 1888, and getting it. The excellent proposal was made that he lecture to the two senior Theology classes on modern philosophical errors, but here too no time could be found for him. No suitable textbook could be found to teach the History of Philosophy, and in the end a truncated course of about twenty lectures was agreed. In June 1891 Esser resigned to take up a professorship in Fribourg, and though two professorships of philosophy were now established it was clear that the subject had not escaped from its problems.

If lecture time was too short for those trying to draw up programmes and timetables, it looked quite different for those attending lectures. The old pattern had been two lectures a day. Now it was three a day, eighteen or even nineteen a week, with a lecture spilling into Sunday to allow for the

Wednesday half-day. Naturally the students did not like it, but a petition to the Trustees in 1890 for a return to the old system, claiming that three lectures a day were injurious to health, met a predictable response.

As has been seen, the Dunboyne course was suspended as an economy measure in 1870. John O'Hanlon, Prefect since 1843, died on 12 November 1871. Towards the end of his days the institution must have stagnated, and indeed under him it never gave the impression of being very dynamic. He himself taught Ecclesiastical History and Canon Law as well as Theology. Theology he taught by having students debate theses, culminating in a 'public defence' before the assembled Trustees, staff and students at prizegiving. Some changes were made in the rigidity of this programme when the Dunboyne course was reconstituted in the autumn of 1879. Henceforth the Prefect would teach Theology only: the professor of Ecclesiastical History would take two classes every three weeks, the professor of Scripture one class every three weeks in Hebrew, while William Walsh, even though President, would teach Canon Law. The students were also to have one class a week in 'Physics and Higher Mathematics'. The course was to run for two years, not three as formerly, with five students in each year. They were to be ordained at the end of the first year of their course, and were bound by the general seminary discipline except where specifically exempted. The vice-president was to live with them (in the centre of the south wing) and be responsible for their good behaviour. In this respect things seem to have worked reasonably well: there are some indications of young men finding it hard to settle down to two further years of a punishing grind, but on the whole not many. What was more serious was the round of additional duties: they were required to supply the place of absent deans or professors, and to act as tutors. In some years this seems to have left little time for their own studies.

Patrick Murray, as the senior professor, was appointed Prefect, though he was now very close to the end of his days. He was succeeded by John Healy in 1883, by Patrick O'Donnell in 1884, and by Walter McDonald, who was then just six years on the staff, in 1888. The reason for the rapid turnover was simple: of the twelve appointed professors of Theology between William Walsh in 1867 and the centenary year of 1895 eleven were subsequently appointed bishops, the solitary exception being Walter McDonald. From one point of view this was helpful, in that the college had on its governing body a number who knew it from inside, unlike Cullen the Roman or Gilloly and Lynch the Vincentians. It was not so happy, however, in regard to the teaching of theology. Even Walter McDonald, Dunboyne Prefect until his death in 1920, found it hard to introduce changes, increasingly as his judgement, if not altogether his orthodoxy, came more and more under suspicion. When Murray died William Walsh, the President, begged the Visitors not to appoint a successor until the institution could be reorganised. As he wrote to Cardinal McCabe on 21 March 1884, 'the Dunboyne establishment was always an ill-conceived organisation'; 'but', he added, 'of course Dr Gilloly had his way'[31] and Healy was appointed. Walsh now pinned his hopes on the forthcoming conference in Rome, but, as has been seen, when that took place McCabe was dead, Walsh was poised to succeed him, and the proposal for a Pontifical Institute was deferred. Earlier there had been a proposal that Maynooth confer Theology degrees of the Catholic University, but this was not really a serious option. Robert Browne, Walsh's successor as President, was keen on a public display like the defence of theses, and so were the Trustees, so that McDonald had little room for innovation. Later in life, after considerable experience in the conducting of postgraduate courses, he was to write: 'I have sometimes thought that the Dunboyne Establishment is a mistake altogether; that a college or university, however excellent, in which one has already spent six years or more, is not the place in which one would derive most profit from a postgraduate course—of Theology or any other science.'[32]

A thriving university institution has certain distinguishing features, among which are a good library and at least one learned periodical. Maynooth was not really well served under either head. The periodical which soon came to be associated with the college was the *Irish Ecclesiastical Record*. This had been founded by Paul Cullen in 1864, with the specific object of fostering links between the Catholic Church in Ireland and Rome. It ceased publication in 1876, principally because its editors kept being promoted to bishoprics. William Walsh revived it in 1880, and from then onwards it was edited at Maynooth. Its contents reflect the interests of the Catholic clergy at the time. A strong interest in ecclesiastical history was imparted to it by its first editors, especially Patrick F. Moran. From the beginning it carried a feature headed 'Liturgical Questions', and Theology and Canon Law duly came to be added, the answers to the questions being contributed by members of the Maynooth staff, though there were in addition quite substantial contributions on wider theological issues. It had a wide circulation, Irish priests in general believing that it kept them in touch with any developments they needed to know of. It came to an end in 1968, a time when many traditional things were dying.[33]

In an institution poorly funded overall a well-funded library could hardly be expected. Traditionally, accessions to the Maynooth library had depended heavily on the collections made by professors over their lives. These sometimes came free—Murray is recorded as having already given generously during his lifetime—but sometimes they did not. When O'Hanlon died in 1871 the Trustees authorised the selling of stock up to the value of £1,600, or even more if necessary, to ensure that his library was not lost to the college. Some money was paid too when Russell died in 1880, but not on this scale. His books were kept in a special collection under his name, and a portrait was commissioned to hang there. This was exceptional: all other such acquisitions went into the general shelving, and while there was no overall principle that duplicates be sold some of this was inevitable given the tiny funds available for purchase.

The office of librarian was traditionally united to that of Prefect of the Dunboyne. He had overall responsibility, but the daily routine devolved in two student 'sub-librarians', traditionally Dunboyne students, but senior students during the 1870s, when there was no Dunboyne. Given this level of staffing, access was necessarily restricted, and the fact that there was no artificial light there until the 1960s was for long not a serious additional handicap: in 1872 professors only were admitted, between the hours of twelve and three, and after 1880 students of the reconstituted Dunboyne. Working libraries were provided for students in each division of the college. Walter McDonald is scathing on their inadequacies, and there is no reason to disbelieve him—'of some use' for Ecclesiastical History, 'of very little use' for Theology, and 'of none, practically, for general reading'. He adds, however, that the students had among their own body some who acted as book-agents on a system that provided 'a fair supply' of general reading, 'poetry, history, essays, but not novels'.[34] It was worked on a credit system, and the possibly inevitable trouble with money occurred. In 1893 the Trustees ordered that an additional servant be engaged to act as book-agent.

In 1887 the Trustees agreed that students in their final two years of Theology be allowed to use the main library, 'on vacant days and in such way as may not interfere with the students' preparation for class'. The Scholastic Council broadened this to include those in their final three years, and others with individual permission, but not until the library was catalogued, on which the Library Committee was to make recommendations. (This appears to be the first reference to this body, which split off from the Scholastic Council much as the Finance Committee had from the Administrative Council: the fact that it developed statutory responsibility for the library reflects the weakness of the librarian rather than the strength of the Library Committee.) The problem of cataloguing was not easily solved. Russell's books were catalogued by Patrick Grogan, who went on in 1884 to become librarian in Capel Street Public Library until his death in 1915. Proposals for cataloguing by students seem to have come to little, and a proposal in 1889 that a competent person be engaged may well have come to nothing. The cataloguing was very defective until the work of Dr Thomas Wall in the 1930s. That shy and gentle book-lover gave it a very practical system, related, as the library should logically be related, to the teaching programmes of the college. It was he too who wrote of its treasures, inevitably modest ones, but real.[35] (Plates 37, 38)

The teaching staff in Theology was somewhat stronger than that in the junior classes. It amounted to seven in all. The senior by appointment was Prefect of the Dunboyne, withdrawn from general teaching to preside over the Dunboyne, an institution even then perceived as uncertain. There were four professors of Theology, one of Scripture and Hebrew, and one of Ecclesiastical History. The fact that appointment to a chair of Theology in Maynooth was the fairly immediate prelude to a bishopric greatly weakened the teaching staff. As has been seen, there were notable departures from the scheme of studies agreed in Rome in 1885, but the Roman authorities nevertheless continued to have a good opinion of theology teaching in Maynooth, so that it was natural that steps should be taken to seek authority to confer degrees as the centenary of the college's foundation approached.

In June 1893 the Trustees set up a committee of the President, vice-president and Theology professors, and asked them to report to their next meeting in October. This was not realistic, and it took the whole of the scholastic year 1893/94 to hammer out a scheme for degree courses. As presented to the Trustees in June 1894, it proposed examination for the baccalaureate in Theology at the end of the fourth year, by oral and written examinations on the year's course; the licentiate was to be taken at the end of a two-year course as a Dunboyne student, with oral examinations to a total of over one-and-a-half hours in Dogmatic and Moral Theology, Scripture, Canon Law and Ecclesiastical History, with an hour's defence of twenty-five theses and an essay in English on a set topic; and the doctorate after a further year, by a Latin dissertation of about a hundred pages, to be defended orally, together with a defence of seventy-five theses, for a total time of four hours. The Trustees suggested some modifications, added some of their number to the committee, and accepted a final report at their October meeting. This was sent to Rome, accompanied by a request for authority to confer all degrees, including the doctorate, in Theology, Canon Law and Philosophy.

Not surprisingly, Rome asked for more information. When this was sent, Monsignor Salvatore Talamo, ex-rector of the Seminario Romano, or as it was called from its location, the 'Apollinare', was asked to examine the proposal. He gave his verdict on 5 June 1895. He had no problems with the proposals for degrees in Theology. He regarded the standards required as high; the only rider he added was that the candidates should be required to read more than the basic textbooks. He made no mention of the proposal to confer degrees in Canon Law, and he was very critical of the proposals for degrees in Philosophy. He noted that a doctorate was requested after a course of only two years, based on elementary textbooks, and shared with Natural Philosophy. Again he sought more information. The reply from Maynooth, while it pointed out that the statutes of some Roman ecclesiastical institutions did provide for a doctorate after a course of only two years, made clear that authority to confer a baccalaureate in Philosophy would be acceptable. Talamo's further report, dated 7 July, indicated that this was acceptable to him too, adding that institutions empowered to confer a doctorate after two years should be eliminated, not added to.[36] Propaganda accepted his reports, and the faculties to confer degrees were granted at a papal audience on 13 March 1896. Statutes were to be drawn up and submitted for approval within twelve months. The news was transmitted to Cardinal Logue as chairman of the Trustees on 29 March.[37] An extension of the term had to be sought, and when Logue forwarded the draft statutes to Rome on 25 June 1898 they envisaged doctorates in Theology, Philosophy and Canon Law. Rome yielded, only adding that the third year of Philosophy, after which a doctorate could be conferred, was to be postgraduate in character. Final approval of the statutes, in the first instance for a period of seven years, was given on 9 June 1900.[38]

Commenting on the academic courses in Maynooth, Walter McDonald wrote with some perception:

> What is wrong with Maynooth, and has been wrong with it while I know it, is that we aim at producing good average men. The worst of it is that we succeed; for, while our average man is very good, our best men are poor—as compared, that is, with those who are trained elsewhere; or if you object to that, as compared with what might be made of our best men if they got a training to raise them above the average.[39]

He was not the only person whose thoughts were running along these lines. Patrick Canon Sheehan (1852–1913) had been a student between 1869 and 1877, obviously a man of good intellect who was not happy with the system. His verdict is to be found in his portraits of priests in his novels. There are plenty of 'good average men', parish priests and curates, men who have conscientiously prepared themselves to preach and hear confessions, without regarding either Perrone or Gury as filling the whole of life. The earlier rigorism appears, notably in *The Blindness of Dr Gray*, and the Maynooth intellectual is etched in *Luke Delmege*: Luke the leading prizeman of his class, the 'first of first', a young man of real intelligence but narrowed by his training into believing that the whole of life had indeed been distilled into the textbook, into Perrone and Gury. Gerald O'Donovan, a student from 1889 to 1895, is more vindictive, less reflecting, but at times uncomfortably close to the bone. He had certainly never settled into the system: even his scanty student record indicates him at odds with it. His first novel, *Father Ralph*, published in 1913 after he had left the priesthood, is to a great extent autobiographical. The account of his years in Maynooth pillories almost every institution and person in the college. A few of the staff escape his wrath, but not many; and his 'first of firsts' is a complete blockhead with a photographic memory. The novel closes with him president of the diocesan college and comfortably on the road to the bishopric. Gerald O'Donovan and Patrick Canon Sheehan would probably agree that success as a priest and a man owed little to Maynooth formation, especially Maynooth intellectual formation. It is time now to turn to the other formative element in the college, the daily round of rule.

College Life

In a number of ways life got more rigorous for the seminarian in the 1870s. One very obvious one was that now more often than not he had to pay a pension of £30 a year. When the claims of pre-1869 students diminished, and finally ended in June 1874, it was possible to make some of the college resources available for student support. Indeed the problem now was to raise student numbers, given that overheads were more or less constant. There had been 533 in the academic year 1869/70, 500 of them enjoying free places. In the years 1873/74 and 1874/75 the numbers reached a low of 372, because of restrictions imposed by the Trustees, but afterwards climbed steadily, topping 500 again in 1881/82. The Trustees used all available resources to re-establish diocesan free places, and the number increased steadily:

1873	1874	1879	1880	1894	1907
166.66	200	216.66	250	300	270

Indeed, as the figures indicate, resources were overstrained in the euphoria of the centenary, and the number had to be cut back from 300 to 270, where it remained. The free places were divided among the ecclesiastical provinces in the traditional proportions, 30 per cent each to Armagh and Cashel, 20 per cent to Dublin and Tuam, and within the provinces among the dioceses according to population, each bishop being free to allot his share among his students as he saw fit. It was of course no more than just that as much of the college resources as possible should go to student support, but the residue was so small that it left general financing very tight indeed.

As had been seen, the initiative in reshaping the college was taken by the episcopal Visitors, especially the two Vincentian bishops, Lynch and Gillooly, and the professor of Scripture, Daniel McCarthy, who took on the duties of senior dean in 1871 and became vice-president the following year. A series of letters from him to Gillooly reveals the new programme: 'We need no change, and we never needed any, except active, unceasing and general supervision.' To that end a new students' rule was approved in 1871, and to ensure it was carried out the obligations of the deans were spelled out in minute detail. Over 1874 and 1875 a battle was waged between the Trustees and the Administrative Council over the extent to which students were to be obliged to go from one place to another in a long procession walking two by two, the Council trying to temper principle by a consideration of the long and often rainy distances to be traversed. The separation into four divisions, introduced by Cullen, was even more rigidly enforced. Walter McDonald has left his impressions of his time spent in the senior section of the Junior House, St Brigid's Division, in the early 1870s. They were only about forty-five students in all, living in Logic House, where one of the class halls had been converted into an oratory. For recreation grounds they had only the small field at the back. Even the space under the trees along by the wall was surrounded by a hedge and out of bounds until they petitioned to be allowed to use it, and a few rough walks were made rather than laid out. It was known irreverently as 'the pound'.[40]

Division into groups as small as this made little sense: dividing the five classes who now made up the Senior House made some, but it still had problems. There were two oratories, St Mary's in the Pugin buildings, and what was still the College Chapel but doubled as a divisional oratory, St Joseph's. But there was only one refectory, and the classes of the students of St Joseph's Division, second-year Philosophy and first-year Theology, were to a great extent shared with other divisions. Everywhere the walls went up, physical and psychological (Plate 32)—walls in the grounds with gates always to be kept closed, walls in the senior infirmary, and in the senior refectory a movable division four-and-a-half feet high, which gave rise to a problem of how to make it possible for the supervising dean to see both parts at once. Above all, the gate to the outside world was always to be closed. Students were no longer to go there to meet tradesmen; instead, the old kitchen, long disused, was fitted out as a 'mart', where necessary business might be done. Gillooly's correspondence with Russell keeps insisting that, despite the shortage of money, all the building necessary to make these physical divisions and changes be put in hand, and without delay.[41]

For recreation there was, according to Walter McDonald, handball all the year round and cricket in the summer. Football and hurling were not allowed, because, he says, the authorities feared provincial rivalries (in fact, when they came to be allowed, the rivalry that developed was between class and class). He recalls that he and a few others bought a football and began to kick it around, but were told it was not allowed, and when they persisted their ball was confiscated. He notes that games like dominoes, draughts and chess were permitted 'whenever the halls were open during recreation hours',[42] but in December 1877 McCarthy tried unsuccessfully to have such recreations forbidden even to students in the infirmary.

By now, all students went on vacation in summer: a testimonial from their parish priest was rigidly required when it was over. There were about ten days free in January after the mid-year examinations. Students from Dublin and Meath were allowed home, others only for 'medical reasons', which, however, were broadly interpreted. This produced a situation very difficult to control, but the Trustees were reluctant to grant a formal Christmas vacation, which had been forbidden in Rome in 1885. Yet it had to come, for the situation was getting out of hand. In 1896 the Administrative Council sought sanction for a holiday of fourteen days, because more than half the students were in fact allowed home, and because they went on the plea of health they left irregularly and returned irregularly. In 1899 the Council gave statistics to support a renewed plea: 77 per cent of the students had gone home the previous Christmas, and they straggled back slowly indeed, the last returning on St Patrick's Day. In these circustances, the demand for an official Christmas vacation could no longer be resisted.

Food is a perennial and predictable grievance of students in institutions, but there would seem to be foundation for such a grievance in Maynooth in the

1870s. The basic reason was that the bursar, Thomas Farrelly, distanced himself from details, leaving these to untrained and unsupervised servants, according to Walter McDonald, and content if the books balanced.[43] And, as has been seen, a state of hostility developed between him and the Visitors and Trustees, one consequence of which is that reliable evidence on the dietary is hard to come by. There is an impression of rough plenty with basics such as bread and meat; concern is expressed several times about vegetables, and there seems to be a growing realisation that the college would have to grow them, but the first reference to 'vegetables from the college garden' occurs in 1896. The basic problem was the untrained, all-male servant body. To quote Walter McDonald again, writing in happier days after the Daughters of Charity had come, 'two or three good women placed in authority in refectory and kitchen as at present, would have saved all the trouble', and when serious trouble broke out in December 1875 it started in the refectory with complaints about soup and tea.

The minute-book of the Administrative Council gives a detailed account of the tense following days.[44] The refectory had been disorderly for some time, and the authorities decided on a fairly stiff response. The vice-president, McCarthy, went round the study halls to address the students. He got a hearing, but some expressed their dissatisfaction by 'scraping', dragging their feet on the ground. All eleven students at one table were brought before the Council and solemnly warned. One member of the Council, unnamed, thought this excessive, and the story went around and, true or false, came to be accepted, that this group was in fact the most unoffending of all. A few very uneasy days followed, unparalleled since December 1809, perhaps even worse in 1875 because the students had learned to look beyond the college superiors to the episcopal Visitors. Disorders continued and after four days, on 21 December, the authorities picked out five declared to be ringleaders, senior students, one a deacon, declared them rusticated for the rest of the year and ordered them to leave by twelve o'clock the next day. At first it looked as if this would make matters even worse. Disturbances, so far largely confined to St Mary's, now threatened the St Joseph's and Junior divisions. A collection was taken up for those leaving, two monitors being treasurers, ostensibly on the ground that some of them did not have their fare home. The mood is well caught in a letter written by a student on 21 December. No-one, he said, felt safe. None of those punished (for 'scraping' McCarthy) got any real chance to defend themselves. He admits the disturbances had to be put down, but not so severely. No study was taking place in the college, though examinations were coming up. Everybody was asking 'Who next?'[45]

There was always a day's retreat on Christmas Eve. The authorities believed that this calmed the situation, and it must at least have helped. By the end of December the truce might be said to be holding. At the June prize-giving the students were addressed on the problems, but the Trustees did agree that complaints respectfully made by students through monitors should be considered by the Administrative Council and entered in its minutes. The whole incident must have been very painful for Russell. In 1877 his accident removed him from the scene, and in 1878 a bishopric removed McCarthy. William Walsh stepped into what was a very large gap. He could be severe if he felt it necessary, but a number of incidents showed a hand that was judicious as well as firm. Traditionally, students had studied in their rooms only at the beginning and end of the year, and in study halls heated by fires during the colder months. In 1873 the students of St Mary's asked to be allowed to study for the whole year in their rooms, as they were now heated. The Administrative Council approved, but the Trustees said no. One of Walsh's first acts on becoming vice-president was to repeat the request. This time the Trustees agreed to give it a year's trial, the students 'supplying candle-light at their own expense'. At the same time he asked for an end to the division of the Junior House, detailing the unnecessary and expensive duplication and the inconvenience in having all the freshmen totally isolated from any other group of students. The Trustees asked him how these inconveniences might be avoided while maintaining the division, and on being told fairly tartly that they couldn't because they were part of it they surrendered a year later in June 1880, at the meeting at which Walsh was appointed President. The most revealing document is a letter from him to Bartholomew Woodlock, Bishop of Ardagh, dated 20 June 1883.[46] It concerned a student in his final year, whom Walsh had decided should not be ordained to the priesthood. The names of those called to Orders were read out before the whole body, beginning with the lesser orders and going on to priesthood, so that a student like this one with many steps still to climb could face repeated disappointments before finally learning his fate. Of course, Walsh wrote to Woodlock, he will be informed privately beforehand:

> I have always felt that it is an inconvenience to be obliged to use the Order List as in any sense an instrument of punishment. But there is clearly no need to make it an instrument of torture and this is the result when a student at the end of his course is brought to the Prayer Hall or Chapel with all his companions to hear the long list read out, beginning with the *tonsurandi* and in the end find himself passed over in the list of priests.

An approach like that, instead of the over-suspicious abbot, would have saved such things as the unsigned articles by a past student which appeared in the *Whitehall Review* in September 1880, complaining that 'the domineering spirit with which we were ruled was an intolerable yoke', and going on to say, nostalgically even if on slender evidence, that things were better when there were lay Trustees, for 'of all governments episcopal government is the most tyrannical.'

For a long time, decisions as to which students to call to Orders had been taken by a non-statutory group of the President, vice-president and deans. When the Finance Committee of the Administrative Council developed an independent existence the Seminary Committee inherited the name of the Administrative Council. Over the 1870s the Trustees tried to do two things, in neither of which they were successful: to involve the teaching staff in general student formation, by sharing at least by invitation in the weekly conferences and the retreats given by the deans, and to add a number of professors to the Administrative Council, at least two, it was suggested. These issues came to a head in 1878, but nothing was done in regard to either of them, because the deans jealously guarded their monopoly; in October 1878 the Administrative Council decided unanimously that any such development would be prejudicial to the spiritual interests of the college.

Within a few years the deans had to share these responsibilities when spiritual directors were appointed. In September 1884 Propaganda had decided to press for four spiritual directors, one in each division in the college, but when the Bishops and Cardinals met in May 1885 objections were raised, not to the principle but to the numbers proposed. It was agreed in the end that the college should retain its three divisions (Junior House had been reunited in 1880) with three deans and two spiritual directors. These were to be ordinary confessors to the students, but the staff as a whole were to remain confessors as well. The spiritual directors were to be chosen by the bishops, and to have no college duties outside their specialised ones.[47] It was natural that the bishops should turn to the Vincentians, asking for two men 'for at least one year'. When they arrived in October 1886 there was still a good deal to be decided. The deans were clearly anxious that their office might be restricted to 'purely external observation and the application of punishments', and these fears, that the students might see the deans and the rest of the staff differently in comparison with what might be called professional holy men, seemed to get some foundation when students decided to become Vincentians, as many as five in the academic year 1887/88, but this figure was not maintained. Rooms were provided for the two spiritual directors on the top floor of Dunboyne House, which had lain vacant since the library was moved from there twenty-five years before. It took some little time to reach agreement on a division of work. It was spelled out in detail in the President's report in June 1889. Both were to give instructions to the students, the spiritual directors once a week in each division at the time for spiritual reading, the deans on Sunday mornings and 'frequently' at the time of spiritual reading as well. The spiritual directors were to be in charge of the sodalities which the Trustees had ordered set up in 1884, if only to let the students know how to run them, for they were becoming very common in the parishes. They were also to be available for confessions for about four hours a day two days a week in each division, but all priests in the college were to continue confessors at the traditional times on Saturday evenings. The retreat at the beginning of the year was to be conducted by a priest invited from outside, as had long been the practice, but all other retreats, including the ordination retreat, were to be given by the spiritual directors. There are indications that the deans had been very reluctant to give up all responsibility for retreats, especially the ordination retreat, indications too that the Administrative Council regarded itself as retaining overall direction of a spiritual formation that did not change its shape easily, being solidly based on observance of rule and the practice of mental prayer.

Daily life at Maynooth was settling into a routine which remained substantially undisturbed until the 1950s or even the 1960s. The opening of the college after the summer vacation shifted from late August to early September to suit the examinations of the Royal University, when students began to sit them shortly after the turn of the century. The position was defined in 1922, with Theology students returning on the first Tuesday in September, the freshmen a week later, and the two remaining classes the following Thursday. The end of the year was determined by ordinations at the end of June. Complex liturgical rules governed the dates on which orders might be conferred. Rome was slow to dispense in this matter, but rescripts dated 26 May 1883 and 17 May 1885 allowed enough flexibility to have ordinations on the days that suited best. In 1899 the Trustees fixed the prize-day and their summer meeting for 'the Tuesday nearest the feast of St Paulinus' (22 June). This meant that ordination to the priesthood was on the Sunday falling between 17 and 23 June, both days inclusive.

Despite the growth of externally recognised tests, the Royal University matriculation and more particularly the Intermediate examination system, the student on entering faced a college examination. This probably took up more effort than it was worth. The Scholastic Council would spend much time elaborating a programme only to have the Trustees chop and change. Again it was William Walsh in October 1878 who persuaded the Trustees to leave things to the Council. Interspersed with written examinations on Wednesday and oral examinations on Thursday, the neophyte had to think of furnishing his room. It is hard to be certain what he found there when he first opened the door, but it was probably not much more than a Board of Works bedstead and palliasse dating from the 1850s. For anything in addition he had to negotiate with the servants, whose role as dealers in furniture seemed very objectionable to William Walsh, though the Trustees were willing to put some kind of uniform furniture into the students' rooms only if it could be done 'without pecuniary loss to the college funds'. Most students had little furniture and the rooms were cheerless and untidy, and not even very clean. But things improved slowly: in 1888 the Trustees were talking of installing shower baths, and decided that fibre mattresses should be gradually introduced, and crucifixes and religious pictures provided.

After the entrance examination there was the retreat, followed by the long grind of class-days, beginning with the rising-bell, now at six o'clock, and ending with 'lights out' at ten. In 1887 the long wait for breakfast was reduced, but the earlier breakfast opened a yawning gap until dinner at a quarter to four, and a light lunch of soup and bread at a quarter past twelve was introduced in the following year. The discipline as stiffened in the 1870s settled into a regime acceptable to superiors and students: as the President put it in his annual report in 1887, the balance had been achieved by the constant application of the deans and their Sunday instructions, by the fact that students were encouraged to make known their grievances through the monitors, and because any insubordination was firmly dealt with.

Tuberculosis continued to be a plague, not helped by the fact that to admit to it was regarded as somehow shameful: victims sent home for 'a change of air' would insist on returning without a medical certificate, obviously no better and sometimes much worse. There were the usual threats of epidemics—typhus in Maynooth village in 1880, scarlatina in 1885, both kept out of the college, which since the disciplinary tightening was now a very closed community. But the large gaunt infirmary always had a number of young men dying of tuberculosis, and it was a step forward when it was decided in 1889 that the nurses there should be sent for some training to St Vincent's or the Mater hospitals. There had been baths in the infirmary since it opened in the 1860s, but though there was general agreement in the Administrative Council and the Trustees that enough should be installed to give each student a bath once a week it proved difficult to get the work done. Heating the whole complex was also mooted, and this was in fact carried out during the summer vacation of 1894.

Medical provision improved in various ways. A dentist had attended, but only when sufficient patients had built up. In 1880, however, arrangements were made to have a dentist come on fixed days. The college had its own surgeon and consultant physician, but it was the local medical doctor who was the first line of defence. This office remained in the same family for a century. Edward Talbot O'Kelly, born at Carrick-on-Shannon in 1779, had in 1804 entered into partnership with Edward Magann, medical attendant to the college; when he died shortly afterwards Dr O'Kelly took up the post, and in due course he was succeeded by his son, also Edward Talbot, though the father remained active almost until his death in sight of his ninetieth birthday.[48] When the son retired he was in turn succeeded by his son, Thomas Edward Talbot, who was in office in the centenary year, 1895. The surgeon and consultant were distinguished Dublin professionals. A problem arose in 1880 when the consultant, Robert S. D. Lyons, was elected a Liberal MP for Dublin City. He proposed to discharge his duties through a substitute, which might work for his statutory visit on the first Monday of each month, but not so well if the local doctor wanted a consultation in an individual case. The awkward situation arose of a student dangerously ill, Dr O'Kelly asking for a second opinion, Dr Lyons in Westminster, and William Walsh not sure who by medical etiquette should be consulted. Lyons was asked to resign, and when he refused his employment was terminated in September 1882. The appointment of his successor was contentious. He was Joseph E. Kenny, well known as a radical Parnellite. It was said that he was not outstandingly distinguished as a physician, and that he had been appointed by the vote of the bishops who favoured Parnell.[49] He was denounced by George Errington in Rome as the man who was admitted to Kilmainham to smuggle out the 'No Rent Manifesto' and publish it.[50] He was elected an MP for Cork South in 1885, and supported Parnell in the 'split'. It comes as no surprise to find the Trustees calling on him to resign in June 1891, 'his pronouncements on several public occasions being grossly offensive to the clergy.'

With politics among the bishops and politics among the staff, as Walter McDonald describes in some detail, it would be surprising if there were not politics among the students; indeed, as Moran explained to Propaganda in 1882, that a priest be involved in politics in Ireland to some degree was inevitable.[51] The Fenian priest, Father Lavelle, had visited the college and addressed the students in the spring of 1870 while the bishops were absent in Rome at the Vatican Council. Cullen, who had used his visit there to get a decree from the Holy Office formally condemning Fenianism, wrote angrily to his secretary George Conroy in Dublin, denouncing the weakness of the authorities who had allowed Lavelle to become 'the idol of the students'.[52] The incident seems to have died, however, or perhaps to have been absorbed into the general tightening of discipline in the 1870s. By the beginning of the 1880s the Irish bishops were dividing on the new political developments, and William Walsh was becoming estranged from his Archbishop, Edward McCabe. After McCabe's death, George Errington, in a memorandum presented in Rome to discredit Walsh, alleged that after McCabe and Croke had publicly disagreed over the Ladies' Land League in March 1881 the Maynooth students had cheered Croke noisily at the annual prizegiving (which indeed is likely enough), and that when McCabe complained to Walsh he was snubbed (which seems very unlikely indeed, if only because at this date the two men were working closely together).[53] Another long memorandum of about the same time, from C. R. Stewart with an address at 44 Great Cumberland Street, London, exhorts the Pope among other things to 'reform Maynooth, which is a hotbed of anarchy and rebellion'.[54] This might well be described as strong language, but things were stirring. The diary of a student ordained in 1888, Laurence O'Kieran, contains an interesting account of the 'long walk' of Easter Monday to Wolfe Tone's grave at Bodenstown. He says that it was a long-established custom that this was the destination every third year. There is a vivid description of the trek across the fields to Clane, 'singing, shouting, laughing and running'. When they arrived, there was a slight hesitation in kneeling to pray for a Protestant, but it was overcome, and they stood around singing ballads, 'God Save Ireland', 'The Memory of the Dead', 'In Bodenstown Churchyard' and others.[55]

Young men need escape-valves, and the minutes of the Administrative Council allow glimpses of those officially sanctioned. As well as the 'long walk' in Easter Week there was a duly supervised excursion for the college choir, first mentioned in 1889, no doubt the result of the appointment of Henry Bewerunge as professor of Church Chant and Organ the year before. For long years it had been the custom to have 'amusements' on Christmas Day and St Patrick's Day (when a Christmas vacation was sanctioned the festivities of that day were transferred to 1 November). Traditionally they had been provided by a professional entertainer, but in 1887 there is the first reference to a play staged by students. Inevitably it was in one of the student divisions, but in a few years the play was being staged, still by one of the divisions but for all the students and staff. It took place in the Senior House refectory, which must have been quite awkward, but the Aula Maxima became available in 1893, and with the gradual erosion of the physical division between St Mary's and St Joseph's the pattern of Senior House and Junior House plays became established.

Information on the domestic life of the staff comes from Walter McDonald. It was not very exciting. There was little intercourse between them, except when they met at table or walked in provincial 'batches' after breakfast and dinner. They rarely visited one another's rooms. When he was appointed in 1881 port and sherry were served at table; claret came later. He goes into some detail, but it appears that domestic life had not changed greatly since Sir Francis Head's visit in 1852. Politics, perhaps, had developed a bit, but not greatly. The younger staff had the politics of their time, the older men were Gladstonian liberals. He noted that Patrick Murray detested all revolutions because of the strength of his ultramontanism.[56]

Gladstone himself visited the college on 5 November 1877, arriving at half past eleven and staying for two hours. That evening Daniel McCarthy, the vice-president, wrote a long account to Cardinal Cullen, and Gladstone made a brief entry in his diary. McCarthy noted the presence of 'the media', seven or eight reporters, from England as well as Ireland—for what seems the first time in the history of the college—and one of them, J. B. Hall, later recorded his impressions.[57] Gladstone was accompanied by his wife and daughter ('both very unpretending ladies', according to McCarthy), his secretary, the Duke of Leinster, and Mrs Barton from Straffan House. Of Gladstone himself, McCarthy noted that he appeared 'most affable and anxious to please', but 'some of our staff did not receive him, not wishing, I suppose, to countenance in any way his *Vaticanism*.' (This was the pamphlet, for Gladstone quite intemperate, published in 1875 and counter-attacking those who had attacked his earlier criticism of the First Vatican Council.) The students were respectful but silent. Gladstone himself noted: 'It produced on the whole a saddening impression: what havock we have made of the vineyard of the Lord.' This last cryptic phrase would appear to refer to buildings and equipment rather than theology, for he added immediately 'they are honourably beginning a rich chapel'. Hall, the reporter, has the eye of a man looking for a story, and may not be trustworthy in all detail. He said Gladstone took a special interest in the library, examined the catalogue and had a flood of questions. He strode rapidly round the grounds, and was shown the yew tree, declared to be eight hundred years old. 'Mr Gladstone walked round it with what I thought a hungry look, and when shown two noble chestnuts further on, he instantly said he would "dearly like to cut one of them down".'

Archbishop McCabe was a good friend, and his two formal visits to the college, his first as an Archbishop on 10 June 1879 and his first as a Cardinal on 25 June 1882, were relaxed and happy occasions. The visit of the papal envoy, Archbishop Persico, on 16 October 1876, was obviously different, and both he and the President, Robert Browne, were straining for 'political correctness' in every word of address and reply.

But the most famous visitor was the Empress of Austria. 'Sissi' (1837–89) was a Wittelsbach from Bavaria. Of quite striking beauty, she married the young Emperor Franz Joseph of Austria in 1854, when he was twenty-three and she seventeen. A family heritage of neurotic restlessness, coupled with a distaste for the stiff court etiquette of Vienna, urged her to a life of activity and travel. When she visited Maynooth in 1879 she was in her early forties. The great tragedy of her life lay ahead—the suicide of her only son, Crown Prince Rudolf, in 1889. She herself was assassinated by an Italian anarchist while on a visit to Switzerland in 1898. She had been staying at a house of Lord Longford in Summerhill, Co. Meath, and had been out with the staghounds when quarry, hounds and hunters broke into the college grounds. The august visitor was invited back by William Walsh, the vice-president, and she came a few days later, on 2 March, at eleven o'clock. By her own wish, she attended Mass in the simplicity of the Junior Chapel, the celebrant being Patrick Murray, now a kind of father of the house, a generous gesture on Walsh's part. Benediction was imparted after Mass by Bishop McCabe, who a month later would be named Archbishop of Dublin, and the Empress had a *prie-dieu* in the sanctuary. After Mass she was shown the buildings, including those recently devastated by fire. She was then shown 'the spacious recreation grounds', and returned by the new chapel, where she particularly admired the west window. The students got three free days, and everyone was happy. On her return to Vienna, she sent a gift of 'a small statuette, representing St George', in the belief that he was Ireland's patron saint. She certainly liked the college, for the next year she was back again, on 15 February 1880. This time the Mass was in the College Chapel (the old College Chapel, of course). She again occupied a *prie-dieu* in the sanctuary, and again the celebrant was Patrick Murray. After Mass she was conducted through the front square, the central walk lined with students; 'unfortunately the day was dark and damp'. Someone must have told her tactfully about national patrons, for this time when she went back to Vienna she sent a set of High Mass vestments, stiff with gold and festooned with shamrocks—too good to use, really, so a replica was made, and they are conserved in the Museum.[58]

The Centenary

At their meeting in June 1894 the Trustees decided that the forthcoming centenary should be 'duly celebrated', and set up a committee of the bishops, the college staff, and two priests from each diocese, to arrange it. John Healy, coadjutor bishop of Clonfert, was commissioned to write the centenary history, and it duly appeared, all 711 pages of it. It does bear marks of the speed of composition: there is too much padding, and the material is assembled in blocks thrown together rather than in a reasoned narrative. But given the short time in which it was written it is a remarkable piece of work, a real storehouse of information. For its part the committee, though it might seem to be unwieldy by its very size, had produced a report for the October meeting of the Trustees, which they considered, modified and accepted. To keep numbers under some control it was decided it should be almost altogether a clerical occasion, and that the completion of the College Chapel and the building of the spire were to be its permanent memorial.

The President was Denis Gargan. He had entered as a student fifty-nine years before, in 1836, and had been appointed to the staff in 1845. The institution had greatly developed within his memory. In the centenary year there were 650 students, more than ever before, and in one respect 1836 was repeating itself, in that they were doubling up in rooms and it was necessary again to turn class halls into dormitories. There was even talk of putting up a new building, between Logic House and the Junior Infirmary, but it was just as well the plans came to nothing. The atmosphere of forthcoming celebrations increased as the year went on, and it was only natural that as the great day approached the students felt they might be allowed to share in an appropriate way by the cancellation of the summer examinations. They probably overplayed their hand. On 6 May they put their request to the college councils, saying that the teaching staff had been consulted individually, and were 'all but unanimous' in favour, and that the 'professors generally' were even willing to prolong lectures through the time normally set aside for examinations. This news seems to have come as a surprise to many of the professors, but the students were told they could petition the Trustees. On 17 May they were told the Trustees had refused their request, and they could display their feelings only by 'scraping', 'shouting and hooting', as it was minuted by the Administrative Council, 'disorderly manifestations' as the President put it in his end-of-year report.

The celebrations were held on 25, 26 and 27 June, chronicled by Bishop John Healy in the 247 pages of the *Maynooth Centenary Record*, and more succinctly, but still running to fifty-four pages, in the *Calendar* for 1895/96. Letters of congratulation came from the Pope and the Cardinal Prefect of Propaganda and from many bishops and Catholic educational establishments round the world, many bishops and educators attending in person. A centenary sonnet was written by Aubrey de Vere. It appears that something longer had been expected. This gave an opening for an 'Ode on the College Centenary' composed by a student, William Byrne, and recited by him in the Aula Maxima to a distinguished gathering. To today's taste it is unbearably verbose and cloying, but 'the applause was rapturous' and 'all felt that it was a very remarkable poem for a student to write, and was not unworthy of that great occasion.'[59] The three days were filled with liturgical events, concerts, banquets and addresses. On 26 June Bishop Healy gave a long lecture on the history of the college. The next day Walter McDonald, looking more to the future, suggested the establishment of a Maynooth Union of past pupils, meeting annually in the college. The bishops had in fact approved this beforehand, and the Union was established that day and a committee set up to run it. On 22 October there was a public appeal from the hierarchy for funds to complete the church and build the spire. It would be fair to say that overall there were few doubts: people knew where they were going, and some might have the feeling that after the spire was built they might well have arrived. Yet Walter McDonald's paper concentrated on work still to be done, and in all fairness there must have been much in the general mood quite conscious of what the French sociologist Louis Paul-Dubois would shortly describe as characteristic of the Irish of the time, 'the fatalism, the lethargy, the moral inertia and intellectual passivity, the general absence of energy and character, of method and discipline' (this is a recurring theme in the novels of Canon Sheehan), 'distracted by denominational struggles, sectarian fanaticism, and the first phases of anticlericalism.'[60] The tone of this incipient anticlericalism could be seen in such works as Michael J. F. McCarthy's *Five Years in Ireland 1895–1900*.[61] He described the celebrations as 'The most remarkable body of men in the country, the Archbishops, Bishops and Priests of the Roman Catholic Church, with many ecclesiastical dignitaries from other lands, including Cardinal Vaughan, were assembled at Maynooth engaged in the elaborate, ritualistic, oratorical and gastronomic celebration of the centenary of that College'. There were many others writing in the same strain.

CHAPTER IX

UNIVERSITY STATUS ACHIEVED

The Pontifical Charter

Beyond question, the greatest single development in the college at the beginning of its second century was when it finally received the power to confer degrees. What had seemed justified hopes in this matter had been disappointed in the past. Now, however, university status came in generous measure, first ecclesiastical degrees with a Pontifical charter, and shortly afterwards degrees in Arts and Science, in association first with the Royal University and then with the newly founded National University of Ireland.

As has been seen, faculties to confer degrees—all degrees in Theology, including the doctorate, and the baccalaureate in Philosophy—were granted by the Congregation of Propaganda on 13 March 1896. Draft statutes were sent to Rome in June 1898, with a request that the college be empowered to confer all degrees, up to and including the doctorate, in Theology, Philosophy and Canon Law. The final Roman reply came on 9 June 1900. It granted the request, and approved statutes for the three faculties for a probationary seven years.[1]

Propaganda had given detailed guidelines for the drawing up of the statutes, and added that 'Regulations and Courses' were to be incorporated, substantially as submitted in the original petition. The committee set up to draft the necessary documentation consisted of five trustees, the President (Denis Gargan), the vice-president (Thomas O'Dea), the Prefect of the Dunboyne (Walter McDonald), the senior professor of Theology (Daniel Coghlan), and of Mental Philosophy (Michael Barrett). Though the first deadline of March 1897 had to be extended to June 1898, the original rescript had given authority to proceed at once to the granting of degrees, and in June 1897 the BD was awarded to twenty-one candidates, drawn from the fourth theology year and Dunboyne. (A light diversion was provided by the fact that the printed diplomas had not arrived in time, and the one specimen copy available had to pass from one candidate to another.) The first licentiate was granted, exceptionally, to one of these, Patrick Dineen of Cloyne, on 3 February 1898, with approval to continue his studies for the doctorate (he was now a second-year Dunboyne

Monsignor James McMahon, donor of the Aula Maxima

Plate 40

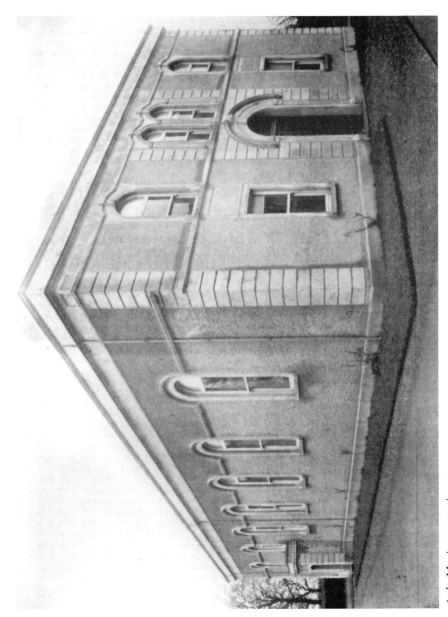

Aula Maxima: exterior

Plate 41

Aula Maxima: interior

Plate 42

Spire and Chapel

Plate 43

John Flood, 'for 50 years a devoted College servant: died 26 September 1933'

Plate 54

One year after, as seen by James Cassin

Plate 55

student). He defended his dissertation, a hundred pages of Latin on the theme of 'Probabilism', for three hours on 21 January 1898, with a further hour given to the defence of seventy-five theological theses, and was acclaimed as Maynooth's first doctor of divinity. That same year six candidates were awarded the licentiate; one of them, Patrick Sexton of Cork, was awarded the doctorate in June 1899. There were no doctorates for a number of years afterwards. The standard was certainly not being set too low; arguably, it may have been set too high. The new status did present challenges to the staff of the college, as they tried to meet the requirements laid down by the Congregation of Propaganda, requirements that grew stiffer when things passed under the more professional eye of the Congregation of Seminaries and Universities following the changes in the central administration of the Church introduced by Pope Pius X in 1908. The Scholastic Council, which, by a decision of the Trustees in October 1889, had been expanded to include the whole teaching staff, now became an overall supervisory body, meeting infrequently, in contrast to the faculties, which met monthly, Theology, Canon Law and Philosophy. Philosophy included Natural Philosophy, and 'Arts', though referred to as a faculty, was for the moment a bit out in the cold, but its turn was to come very soon. Of the Pontifical faculties, the best-equipped was Theology, though even Theology could find itself stretched; Philosophy had more modest equipment, but also more modest goals; while Canon Law must stand as Maynooth's recurring problem of making a little go a long way indeed.

The teaching staff in Philosophy was modest, indeed below the minimum Roman demand: it consisted of two professors of Mental Philosophy and one of Natural. It was allowed to confer a baccalaureate after one year's study, a licentiate after two. Fourteen candidates received the baccalaureate in 1900, drawn from both first and second year. Thereafter a small number of second-year students received the licentiate, and a small number of first-year the baccalaureate: there were four of each in 1901, the first year both awards were given. The third year or 'higher course' was envisaged as postgraduate in character, with a doctorate awarded at the end. Here the demands were more stringent. The basic texts had to be the *Summa Contra Gentes* and philosophical *opuscula* of Aquinas, and an absolute minimum of four lecturers, with two distinct chairs in Natural Philosophy, one in Mathematics and one in 'natural science'. The Scholastic Council did not foresee any problem in students at that level using Aquinas as a textbook; as for building up the strength of the faculty, they noted it was reasonable to hope that this might be done by the earliest date a doctorate course could be envisaged, in six years' time. The teaching strength was indeed built up, but by then the main interests of Philosophy were pointed in a different direction, for its students were preparing for degrees in another institution, first the Royal University and then the National University of Ireland. Indeed, apart from a few given *honoris causa*, only one Pontifical doctorate of philosophy has been awarded, in 1944. Yet

241

Philosophy continued to give a good account of itself, and in 1907 its charter to confer all degrees was confirmed *in perpetuum*, together with that of Theology.

Theology was better equipped to attempt a more ambitious programme, though even here resources were stretched. There were five professors of Theology, one of Scripture, and one of Ecclesiastical History. The senior professor of Theology was Prefect of the Dunboyne, an increasingly anachronistic position, in that he was cut off from undergraduates, and the others cut off from postgraduates, so that there was no structural contact between postgraduate and undergraduate teaching. Even with this limitation on scarce resources, the traditional bias heavily in favour of the 'manual theology' in Dogma and Moral remains clear. Scripture, as has been seen, had taken second place in this scheme of things, the assumption being that sufficient proof-texts could be gleaned from the manuals. New horizons in biblical study had just been opened up by Pope Leo XIII in the encyclical *Providentissimus Deus* in 1893, and in 1897 the Trustees decided to appoint a second professor of Scripture. For the moment, however, Dogma and Moral were still at the centre, both in Maynooth and in Propaganda at Rome, though the Congregation's response to the draft statutes, given on 15 May 1899, contained a few things that needed thinking over. It demanded that in the degree courses, both Dogma and Moral, the textbook be the *Summa Theologica* of Thomas Aquinas. This the Scholastic Council was prepared to accept, though in practice the old manuals remained. A demand that special attention be given to Patrology and the History of Dogma was answered by saying that these matters were sufficiently well catered for in the general course. There was some justification for this attitude, for in a subject so vast as 'general theology' there is always the danger of fragmentation into a multitude of courses. Pressure in this direction could not be altogether resisted. A separate course in Patrology was introduced in 1907, but though the Trustees decided on a course of Ascetic Theology in 1921 it did not in fact materialise, seemingly becaue it was considered that this area was sufficiently well covered by the deans in their well-structured conferences given to their students. The demand that there be a separate professor for what Propaganda called 'Casuistic and Pastoral Moral Theology' raised questions about the nature of Moral Theology that do not seem to have been really addressed. When Patrick Beecher was appointed first professor of Pastoral Theology in 1904 it was not envisaged that he would be responsible for taking future confessors through the manuals: this was the task of the professor of Moral Theology; and indeed it is not unfair to say that in student eyes Beecher never seems to have been quite perceived as a professor of Theology (Plate 45). So, the Scholastic Council petitioned that Moral and Casuistic Theology be taught together, as hitherto. Preoccupations are further revealed when the petitioners went on to say that in Moral Theology especially they trusted it was permissible to use other books in addition to the *Summa Theologica*. The same preoccupation can be seen from what happened when it was decided to strengthen the teaching staff by appointing newly graduated doctors of divinity as temporary lecturers, for the duties assigned to them were to coach the weaker students in Moral Theology in the first and second years. The experiment in temporary lecturers did not last long. One reason, already noted, was the fact that no doctorates were awarded for several years after 1899, but at least a contributing cause must have been the nature of the work allotted.

Initially, then, the BD degree was awarded at the end of the traditional Maynooth theology course. Students as a body were divided into pass and honours streams. There was little difference in the courses, except that honours students had to attend lectures in Hebrew (it appears to have been assumed that they would already have sufficient knowledge of Greek) and pass students were excused what must have been regarded as the more dispensable parts of the course, Old Testament and the more abstract questions in Canon Law. Every year, however, students in the honours stream were closely scrutinised before being allowed to continue as candidates for the degree. A final selection was made at the end of the third year, and about twelve accepted as candidates for the BD examination a year later. The standard required, it might be fairly said, was a stiff honours one. The examination was basically on the year's course, in Dogma, Moral, Scripture and Ecclesiastical History, with, however, some topics from earlier years. Examinations were oral and written, the oral examinations totalling at least one hour, the written at least six hours. And at the back of this lay the weekly grind of five lectures in Dogma, five in Moral (despite Roman reservations it had re-established parity with Dogma), three in Scripture, and two in Ecclesiastical History. Propaganda would have liked to see the whole faculty acting as an examining board, but this wasteful proposal had to be abandoned because there were so many non-degree students to be examined. For orals the staff divided into boards of two, while the written examinations were normally graded by the professor acting alone, though it was envisaged that a colleague might be called in in doubtful cases. No provision was made for extern examiners for either the baccalaureate or the licentiate.

The best of the graduates were allowed to enter Dunboyne to study for the licentiate, a course of two years, those to be allowed to present themselves for the degree being chosen by examination at the end of the first year. The licentiate courses consisted of three parts: universal Theology, where, however, a degree of specialisation in Dogma, Moral or Scripture was allowed (it may have some significance that few opted to specialise in Moral); a small number of postgraduate-type courses; and an extended essay in English on a set topic. The examination lasted for two-and-a-half hours, one-and-a-half on course work and one on twenty-five theses selected from universal theology. Candidates for the doctorate were selected on the results of this examination—very sparingly, as has been seen. A further year was spent in studying for this final distinction. The principal work was the preparation of a dissertation, based on original research, of about a hundred pages. The first statutes demanded that it be written in Latin, but a derogation from this was sought, and the definitive (1905) statutes allowed presentation in English. The first English dissertation, 'Penance in the Early Church', was submitted that year by Michael O'Donnell, later professor and Prefect of the Dunboyne. As well, seventy theses had to be prepared, drawn from universal theology, though allowing for a measure of specialisation, as with the licentiate. The examination was a gruelling four hours' defence, the written dissertation against members of the faculty, the theses against an invited extern examiner.

Some things had not changed, but overall these were more demands on a staff that needed to be more professional. First steps were taken in this direction in October 1895, when John Harty, appointed professor of Theology, and Michael Forker, appointed professor of Mental Philosophy, were given a year's leave of absence on full salary to study in Rome and Louvain respectively. Archbishop Walsh was mainly responsible for this, according to Walter McDonald. McDonald himself believed they should attend as students, sit examinations, and take a degree. Others opposed this as 'unworthy of a Maynooth professor', but it soon came to be accepted.[2] When a few years later it was decided to add a second chair of Scripture a specially qualified person was sought in Reginald Walsh OP. It was accepted on both sides that the appointment was temporary. His successor was Patrick Boylan, a Dublin priest ordained in 1903. He went to Berlin to study oriental languages, and was appointed professor of Scripture in 1905. His appointment was a serious blow to the traditional method of concursus, that is, examination of the applicants by a board drawn from the college staff. Walter McDonald summed up the situation with some acerbity but not unfairly. The old system, he admitted, did have some advantages. The votes were cast honestly, and the Trustees in making the appointment normally followed the recommendation. The drawback was that the members of the board sometimes were not equipped to form a professional judgement—necessarily in the case of the many posts where there was only one chair; and even in Theology the assessment was inadequate, being, he claimed, no more than an oral examination in 'twelve marginal questions' from Gury's *Theologia Moralis*, to the neglect of Dogma.[3] The new statutes allowed for appointment without concursus, and in 1905 this was availed of, possibly fairly gladly, and no replacement formality was needed as there was only one candidate. In August 1915 the senior professor of Scripture, Joseph McRory, was appointed Bishop of Down and Connor. His successor, Edward J. Kissane, was appointed in June 1917. Ordained a priest of the diocese of Kerry in 1910, he was already a graduate of the Biblical Institute in Rome, very recently founded by Pope Pius X. He undertook responsibility for the Old Testament, which he taught until his appointment as President in 1942. A detailed report on the teaching of Scripture accepted by the Scholastic Council in October 1917 is especially impressive and imaginative in its proposals for the Old Testament, and shows him already as the gifted teacher remembered by a whole generation of students. By then too Ecclesiastical History had secured its modest niche among the degree subjects. Traditionally, it had straddled awkwardly between the senior Philosophy class and the junior classes of Theology. Now it had a professor with professional training, James MacCaffrey, appointed in 1901 and awarded a PhD at Freiburg-im-Breisgau in 1903. Four years later he was allotted courses spread over the whole BD course, two lectures a week in the two junior Theology classes, two more in the two senior ones, and one a week to the Dunboyne postgraduates.

Originally, his had been the only subject envisaged as being taught in English. In approving the faculty statutes in 1907, Propaganda had expressed the wish that Dogma, Moral, Canon Law and Scripture be taught in Latin, though, not altogether logically, at the same time it allowed doctorate dissertations to be presented in English. The proposals of the professors of Scripture in 1917 contained a recommendation that the language of instruction be English. This was accepted: the advantages to the future preacher were very obvious. Elsewhere, a certain unease persisted: the Trustees, with some prodding from the Congregation of Seminaries and Universities, continued to worry if the students' oral Latin was adequate, or if they neglected their Latin textbooks and relied exclusively on class notes in English. The implication of this is that lectures were delivered in English and students were expected to answer in Latin—possibly the worst of all worlds. The case for Latin rested on an assumption that the average student had reasonable facility in the language. This was not always true: indeed it may not have been true of all professors. Dean Mulcahy, a student of theology from 1890 to 1895, remarked of one of his professors, Richard Owens, professor of theology from 1884 to 1894, that his lectures were 'a quaint mixture of English and Latin'. A sample sentence has been preserved in the private notebooks of none other than Peter Coffey, remembered by his generation of students as a philosopher of formidable austerity (Plate 46). He did not begin his theology until 1896, but the sentence he gives would have been of very recent currency, though, students being students, some measure of embellishment may possibly be allowed for: 'if the homo doesn't enter into the occasio of the peccatum and if the voluntas doesn't vult peccare then the homo commits no peccatum.'[4]

The Canon Law Faculty was truly bricks with little straw. Before codification, with the issue of the Code of Canon Law in 1917, the subject was taught at undergraduate level from textbooks ('institutiones') while postgraduates studied legal texts in the original ('decretales'). A great deal of the material covered in the 'institutiones' had been incorporated into the Moral Theology course. In 1899 Propaganda had granted authority to confer all degrees; it had gone further, and had allowed both baccalaureate and licentiate to be studied concurrently with the corresponding degrees in theology. To meet this heavy commitment the Trustees appointed a separate professor of Canon Law in October 1897, the first in the history of the college. He was a distinguished

Roman canonist, Salvatore Luzio, and he began his teaching in January 1898. He must soon have found that what was expected of him was more than he felt he could give. He taught an undergraduate course for two years, and the degree class of 1900 sat concurrently for the BD and BCL. Faced now with the prospect of a postgraduate course as well, he decided he could not do both. The Trustees referred the matter to the Scholastic Council, which reported on it in June 1901. The problem was twofold: one lecturer could not give both courses, and few or no students might be expected for the postgraduate course. All the Council could do was make what it accepted was an unsatisfactory suggestion, that the professor take the postgraduate course and also examine in the undergraduate one, which would be taught by a lecturer. In fact no postgraduate course developed, no lecturer was appointed, and down to 1908 degree students in the fourth theology year sat the BD and BCL concurrently. In 1907, when the charter for Theology and Philosophy was granted permanently, that for Canon Law was only renewed for a further seven years, and the appointment of a separate professor of Public Ecclesiastical Law was demanded. In October 1909 Professor Luzio retired. No doubt he was to some extent disillusioned, but he had also found the Irish climate trying and had constantly been in poor health: in February 1902 he had had to return for a while to Italy, so ill that a companion had to be sent with him.

At their meeting in October 1907 the Trustees had decided to meet the statutory requirement of three professors by one full-time appointment, with the two professors of Moral Theology helping in a part-time capacity, and that on this basis they would request Propaganda to allow the BCL to be examined at the end of the second theology year and the LCL after the fourth, concurrently with the BD. There are indications that Propaganda may have had some reservations, but it approved the proposal on 5 November 1909. A student of the fourth theology year, Jeremiah Kinane of Cashel, was designated to go to Rome to be trained in Canon Law, and was appointed professor in October 1911. No degrees in Canon Law were conferred in 1909 or 1910, but from 1911 to 1916 the BCL was conferred on candidates from the second theology year. In 1913 and 1915 there was one LCL in the fourth year, and in 1916 there were four. By now it was necessary to seek a renewal of faculties to confer degrees, this time from the Congregation of Seminaries and Universities, and the Congregation proved difficult. On 30 May 1915 it had renewed the faculties, but for three years only, and subject to new conditions. Courses in Theology and Canon Law must be completely separate, and not just the professor but all examiners must have the appropriate doctorate. A period of grace of three years was allowed.

In October the Trustees considered a report they had commissioned from the Scholastic Council. There were, the Council said, two possibilities: to ask that at least the BD and BCL be allowed to be taken concurrently, or that the faculty should be allowed to lapse, with an arrangement whereby Canon Law be accepted as part of the BD programme, or at least as an obligatory qualifying subject for BD candidates. They favoured this second alternative, saying fairly bluntly that 'the establishment of a really successful Faculty of Canon Law is almost impossible of attainment.' However, the Trustees decided to appeal directly to the Pope over the head of the Congregation.[5] The upshot of this was a reply from the Congregation, dated 8 February 1917, allowing candidates to present themselves for the BD and BCL concurrently, but insisting that after this there had to be one year of special studies for the licentiate, with a further year for the doctorate, insisting too that all examiners have a DCL or at least proven competence, demonstrated by publications or otherwise. It might have been better to have left it at that, but further probing brought a stiff letter saying that an appropriate doctorate was not merely required in university examiners but that the Code of Canon Law just published had extended this obligation to seminaries. Existing staff in Maynooth might continue, but all new appointments must meet the legal requirements. With it came a covering letter, dated 9 October 1917, from the rector of the Irish College, Rome, Michael O'Riordan, who had been agent for the Trustees in the business.[6] The rescript, he said, represented all he could get and it had been rather reluctantly given. The danger was that things might be tightened up later. He begged respectfully to repeat a suggestion he had made, that the Congregation be approached to confer a DD on two members of the Faculty of Theology who did not have this technical qualification. Both were otherwise distinguished scholars, qualified in their respective fields, and no application was made. Future professors of Moral Theology seconded to Canon Law were, however, required to have a double doctorate, beginning with Patrick O'Neill (1918) and Michael Browne (1921). The BCL continued to be conferred concurrently with the BD at the end of the fourth year of theology. In 1920 there were two doctorates, Neil Farren of Derry and Edward O'Brien of Dublin, surely not unconnected with the new Code of Canon Law promulgated on 15 September 1917 to come into effect on Pentecost Sunday, 19 May 1918. There were two more in 1921, one in 1925 and one in 1927. Thereafter there were none until the exceptional days of the second World War.

Maynooth's new status was marked by the appearance of a periodical in January 1907, the *Irish Theological Quarterly*. Its editors were five professors of theology—McDonald, McRory, Harty, MacCaffrey and Toner. Daniel Coghlan, a very senior figure, was a notable absentee. Walter McDonald claimed to have originated the idea in 1905, and there is no reason to question this. He says some were encouraging, but some were suspicious—he names explicitly Cardinal Logue and John Healy, now Archbishop of Tuam. Archbishop Walsh insisted that the journal must submit to the normal ecclesiastical censorship and carry an *Imprimatur*, and at their meeting in January 1906 the standing committee of the Hierarchy had expressed surprise that the publication of a theological journal should have been undertaken without the approval of the Trustees. This was conveyed to the editorial board by Daniel Mannix, the President. McDonald replied on their behalf to say that they had acted as five individuals, not in any official or statutory capacity, and that they were not conscious of any obligation to consult the Trustees, either in obedience or reverence.[7] The tone was uncompromising, and after a few years he decided it was best for the *Quarterly* if he severed his connection with it. Harty became a bishop in 1913; Toner resigned from the staff the same year; in 1915 McRory became a bishop. For some years the editorial board was down to three, but there were good young men coming along: Garrett Pierse, William Moran, Edward Kissane. Contributions from the staff fell off a bit, but for the first three years they had been at the unsustainable level of nearly 70 per cent, and at the end they were still a respectable 40 per cent; prestige names from abroad were still being attracted, and the Irish contribution from outside Maynooth suggested that the periodical was in fact stimulating theology in the country. Nevertheless, it came to an end with the issue of October 1922, and in the absence of documentation it is hard to be certain why. Tradition, such as it is, would rule out trouble with authority, financial constriction, or any lack of material to publish; there may be a suggestion that the routine editorial work fell to too few of the editors, but this is by no means certain. Anyway, the *Quarterly* was in abeyance until its revival in 1951.

In its early years the Maynooth Union sponsored a number of projects in the college. The committee meetings of 1910 and 1911 led to the setting up of the Catholic Record Society of Ireland, for the purpose of 'collecting and publishing documents which have not been published hitherto, or which, if published, are not generally available, and more especially those documents which have some bearing on Irish ecclesiastical history'. The membership soon rose to over five hundred, clergy and laity, the latter including such distinguished figures as Eoin MacNeill and M. J. McEnery of the Public Records Office. An annual subscription was fixed at ten shillings, ample to publish an annual journal—the first number, of 383 pages, cost, including postage, £117 12s 4d. It appeared in 1912, entitled *Archivium Hibernicum*, and was edited by James MacCaffrey, professor of Ecclesiastical History.[8]

In June 1919 the Trustees established the 'D'Alton Endowment', investing a sum of £500 received from Dean D'Alton, parish priest of Ballinrobe. He directed that the income be used for the encouragement of Irish historical studies, primarily by making grants towards publication: his only regret was that he had not the means to endow a chair. The fund was to be administered by the President and the professor of Ecclesiastical History.[9] It was another help to Maynooth to take on some of the lineaments of a university institution in Theology and related sciences.

Theological Conflicts

The privilege of granting degrees in 'the theological sciences' came to Maynooth just before the Modernist crisis came to a head. A summary of 'Modernism' is quite simply impossible. Even the perspective of a century is of limited help in understanding what happened at its beginning, but at least a few words are necessary. As the name implies, it was an attempt, well-motivated, to relate Christianity to a contemporary world which seemed to have increasingly little time for it. Inevitably, it was fascinated by all that passed under the name of 'science', evolutionary biology, the new psychology, critical history, what were beginning to call themselves 'the human sciences', anthropology, sociology. It came late to Catholic Christianity, but for that reason with all the more fury. Leo XIII had held back from formal condemnation, believing the line could be held by the teaching he enunciated in his great series of encyclicals. But to the Modernist theologians these were not enough to deal with the pulsating, constantly developing world the Church now lived in: religion as lived in the individual consciousness could not be measured by scholastic formulas. The next Pope, Pius X (1903–14), decided that confrontation was necessary. The decree *Lamentabili* of 3 July 1907 singled out sixty-five propositions for condemnation. Hostile critics would claim that thereby the Pope created a movement which he called 'Modernism', for no theologian assailed as a Modernist held them all. This may have some truth, but the main points made in the encyclical *Pascendi*, issued shortly afterwards on 8 September, indicated clearly where the movement was heading, and where numbers of its followers had already arrived. These points may be summarised somewhat as follows: a denial that certain knowledge of the supernatural was possible; an assertion that God was immanent in the individual soul to the extent that the Church was no more than the social organisation of those who believe; and a strict compartmentalisation of Church teaching and 'scientific' theological research. An oath against Modernism, to be taken by all professors and priests with the care of souls, was imposed on 1 September 1910. By then the movement was broken. There had been excommunications; to a regrettably unChristian extent there had been houndings and denunciations. Beyond question there was a slowing down of scholarship; but what had been excised was a wild growth, not unreasonably seen as life-threatening. Walter McDonald, commenting on the misfortune he and his colleagues had in starting the *Irish Theological Quarterly* in 1907, summed up his reactions:

We were unfortunate in the time at which our project was commenced, as the Modernists not only lamed but killed us. They aimed at progress, so did we; therefore we were Modernists. It was of no avail to disclaim Modernistic views: were not our whole aims Modernistic? If we were not Modernists, should we not be content with the *I.E. Record*? Is it not a strange, sad thing that I, who not only hate Modernism, but feel a contempt for it, should be classed as a Modernist by so many, even high-placed ecclesiastics—as I know I am? The Modernists have set back the hands of progress in the Church, dear knows how many years—far beyond my time, I expect . . . It was hypocritical and mean of Loisy and Tyrrell to pretend to remain in the Church.[10]

249

This was the troubled background against which Maynooth had to bend its theology to university ends. At the day-to-day level, the problem expressed itself as the teaching of academic theology to candidates for the priesthood. The long-tested Tridentine tradition had aimed at producing pastors rather than theologians, men trained to preach the diocesan programme of catechetical instruction and to hear confessions, distinguishing sins by number and kind. The tradition of the manuals had developed to realise these aims. As has been seen, after 1895 it was still envisaged that the great majority of Maynooth students would not aspire to a university degree in Theology. But what of those who did? Should they not be asked to probe a little deeper, at least at postgraduate level, possibly at undergraduate level too?

These were the questions now facing their teachers. Inevitably, these were of mixed capacity. Their training had conditioned them to believe that Theology did not change. As late as 1945 a highly intelligent man, and a professor of history to boot, could say, speaking of someone who had complained that Maynooth theology was 'out of date': 'He was referring, of course, primarily to dogmatic questions: for unless one has the eccentricity of the ostrich, it is more, rather than less, difficult to be out of date in matters of Moral Theology, Sacred Scripture, Canon Law or even Church History.'[11] That there could be some kind of development he was prepared to concede only in matters of Dogma. No matter what allowance is made for tongue-in-cheek writing, the years that followed have commented on what he said with an irony rough at times; and there really does not seem room for much tongue-in-cheek quality, for these remarks about the immutability of Theology are set in a context of the immutability of Maynooth of which he clearly approves.

The issues were fought out between the two senior professors of Theology, Walter McDonald and Daniel Coghlan (he later spelled his name Cohalan). They were men of real capacity, if in different ways. The quality of the Maynooth student had already been commented on unfavourably, by Canon Sheehan and, with more acerbity, by Gerald O'Donovan. An even more acerbic comment on the whole Maynooth system, from first-year student to Cardinal, is contained in a letter written on 1 April 1916 by Michael O'Flanagan to John Hagan, then vice-rector of the Irish College, Rome (O'Flanagan's political activities had already led to trouble with his bishop, and it was to get worse). He wrote:

> With all that you say about the pettiness and parochialism of clerical life in Ireland and especially Maynooth clerical life I am in entire agreement . . . In Maynooth the classes are very big—a thing that in itself tends to depress the development of personality. In each class there is a first prizeman, who is worshipped as a demigod. In selecting the first prizewinner the professor is the sole examiner. The natural result is that the student who is meekest in his admiration of the professorial oracle, if he is industrious, comes out first on the list. Once in twenty or thirty

years any given diocese produces this boy-prodigy. He gets a chair at the end of his course, and there his glory is embalmed for twenty years until his native diocese becomes vacant and then the men who have grown up in the Maynooth atmosphere vote him in as Bishop. At present the four Archbishops are Maynooth class-leaders. Two of them are Archbishops entirely and the other two largely because they were leaders. And all the leaders are leaders largely because of the want of those qualities that lead to breadth of view and the capacity to get out of a rut.[12]

It is easy to point out the exaggerations, and even to counter by noting Michael O'Flanagan's propensity to get out of a rut by digging deeper, but there are disturbing flashes of perception.

Daniel Coghlan, appointed to teach Theology in 1886, became senior professor in 1894, yielding only to the Prefect of the Dunboyne who was, of course, Walter McDonald. He was a guardian of orthodoxy, a man of the manuals. Before his lectures he distributed lithographed notes to his students so that there might be no occasion for error. They were known to the students as 'blocks', and the name passed from the notes to the man. They ended as substantial Latin treatises, strictly in the manual tradition. He himself ended as bishop of his native diocese of Cork. By contrast Walter McDonald was the only professor of Theology between William Walsh (1867) and Patrick McKenna (1904) who did *not* become a bishop. Appointed to the staff in 1881, he became Prefect of the Dunboyne in 1888, and held this post until his death in 1920. He was a controversial figure as a theologian, but there was no controversy about his qualities as a man and a priest. Elderly priests, who would have had only the most general contact with him as students because their theological aspirations did not rise to his heights, constantly spoke of him in tones of respect and affection. He appears as 'Dr Donaldson of the Dunboyne' in Shane Leslie's account of his visit to Maynooth in 1911 in his thinly fictionalised autobiography *Doomsland*, published in 1923, 'a keen face full of the milk of unsoured kindness', but with a disconcerting habit of breaking into a discourse on metaphysical theology, ending with the claim 'Now grace and motion were possibly identical.'[13] Speaking of him as a colleague, Dean Mulcahy recalled that

> it was a joy to know him: the most sociable of companions, with the liveliest enjoyment of every sport and pastime, hospitable as a prince, and always kindly. Original and progressive in thought and expression, often startling in his theories, he was always tolerant of reasonable contradiction though it might not change his outlook. He had reverses in his career that would have soured another, but his charity was proof against temptation; he fought his corner fairly and was always an amiable opponent.[14]

The theological phenomenon that was Walter McDonald does seem to demand a more thorough examination than what for many reasons is all that can be attempted here. There can be no reasonable doubt that when he angrily denied any association with Modernist views he was speaking the simple truth. His academic credo is fairly set out in an address he gave during the Centenary celebrations, on 27 June 1895: 'In Philosophy and Theology, as these sciences have traditionally been taught in the Catholic schools, is found the surest refutation of even the most modern forms of error.' But he did not see these 'sciences' as a static inheritance: they were something to be worked on (like so many of his contemporaries, he was fascinated by all the overtones of the word 'science'). Why his approach should have led him to theories that Dean Mulcahy often found startling is not to be resolved in any facile way, but by trying to hold a just balance between the possibility that Irish theologians at the time were easily startled, and the possibility that faced with Walter McDonald's theology they may sometimes have had good cause to be. One factor worth reflecting on is the degree of isolation in which he worked. Naturally, he read extensively, but otherwise he was very much circumscribed by Maynooth. As well, in his time every theologian on the staff of Maynooth had of necessity to have a wide field of expertise, none more so than the Prefect of the Dunboyne, a post he succeed to at the age of thirty-four.

His first conflict with Daniel Coghlan erupted in June 1894. The highlight of the prizegiving ceremony had traditionally been an academic 'disputation' held by the Dunboyne students in the presence of the Trustees. McDonald had for some years printed the propositions for debate in the college *Calendar*. On 24 June he received a letter from Coghlan stating that he considered the doctrine on grace which had been enunciated in some of them to be 'clearly opposed to the faith', and that he had formally referred the whole matter to the President. A meeting of the Scholastic Council was called. The meeting was not minuted, but it was agreed that the contentious propositions would not in fact be debated, and would not be printed with the others in the *Calendar*. Nothing was said to the episcopal Trustees (the President, Robert Browne, was himself nominated bishop of his native diocese of Cloyne two days later, on 26 June). McDonald had not gone to the meeting, but apparently Coghlan had. For this reason McDonald may have felt himself a little hard done by; at any rate, he approached Archbishop Walsh and proposed that the matter be referred to Cardinal Satolli, Prefect of the Congregation of Seminaries and Universities, and implied he would like Walsh to make the approach. Walsh put out feelers, from which it appeared that Satolli would not like even to be asked; and so for a few years the matter rested.[15]

McDonald continued his researches into the theology of grace. At the beginning of 1898 he published a book on the subject, entitled *Motion: its Origin and Conservation*. It was certainly a book for the specialist. He himself said, reflecting on the storm which arose out of it: 'Neither the book nor the opinions would set the Liffey on fire. Why not then let them be discussed among the select few who would take any interest in them?'[16] What he was trying to do was to examine the theology of grace in the light of contemporary scientific ideas on motion. He complained of his isolation while writing it, isolation from theologians as well as scientists. Scientists since, while deferring to him as a theologian, are less kind about his understanding of science. Before publication he submitted the text to a number of people as well as the official ecclesiastical censor. He was a Dominican, Louis Hickey, and he later told Archbishop Walsh that he saw nothing censurable in it and advised publication, anticipating an interesting discussion. The archbishop commented that while the Dominicans did go pretty far in their idea of *praemotio physica* McDonald seemed to go far beyond them.[17]

The matter came to the attention of the bishops immediately because Coghlan rushed hot-foot to John F. Hogan, editor of the *Irish Ecclesiastical Record*, with an article which he wanted printed immediately. Hogan was appalled when he read it, and almost everybody else who read it shared his view. He sent it privately to Archbishop Walsh, in whose diocese the *Record* was published. The archbishop agreed with him: whatever the theological issue, on which at this stage he was ill-informed, he judged 'the whole tone and scope of the paper . . . so objectionable' that on this ground alone it should not be published. He consulted Cardinal Logue, who agreed with him, writing 'I think it would be a ruinous scandal to have it published in the *Record*. The tone is bellicose from the beginning, and the revelations regarding matters which took place in the college anything but edifying.' In this and subsequent letters he expressed his fears that should the book prove unorthodox it might pose a threat to Maynooth's new university status, adding that the author's name had just been submitted to Rome by the Trustees for the prestige post of Prefect of Studies.[18] Walsh wrote immediately to a relieved Hogan telling him not to publish. Hogan had shared his anxieties with other bishops. His own bishop, Thomas McRedmond of Killaloe, admitting he had not read the book, counselled that it was 'essential that your Theology professors wash their dirty linen at home'. This was essentially the view of John K. O'Doherty, Bishop of Derry. It was true, he wrote, that McDonald was 'said to be fond of new theories which he sometimes carries to a dangerous length', but he judged this violent assault in which an individual professor sought publicly to accuse another of heresy to be so motivated by personal spleen that it was right not to publish it. Even Bishop John Healy of Clonfert, though he felt the bishops would have to take action about McDonald's book, and that Coghlan's reply was 'an able paper', said he was glad it was not published. Only Edward Thomas O'Dwyer, Bishop of Limerick, himself no mean fighter, expressed the view that with some emendations it might be published: 'Personally I like to see this heat amongst the professors. It always existed in the Catholic schools.'[19]

Already in his first letter to Logue Walsh had suggested the line to be followed if there was any suspicion of the book's orthodoxy: it should be submitted to the judgement of the Holy See, preferably by McDonald himself. This was in fact the advice conveyed to him by the standing committee of the Hierarchy on 26 April: there was no questioning his good intentions, but in his own interests he should submit his work to Rome for judgement as soon as convenient. This he did, sending copies of the book and other documentation he judged relevant to Cardinal Ledochowski, Prefect of Propaganda.[20] It was referred to consultors of both Propaganda and the Congregation of the Index. On their report the book was condemned in a decree of 15 December, forwarded through Archbishop Walsh on 20 January 1899. The decree was not to be published, out of respect to Maynooth and in recognition of the author's 'right dispositions of mind', but he was to withdraw the book and renounce the opinions put forward in it. He had only one problem in giving the internal assent required and which he was willing to give. What precisely were the opinions he was required to renounce?[21] Archbishop Walsh could hardly be faulted for referring him to the Roman authorities. McDonald took him up, and wrote to Ledochowski, enclosing a list of theses defending his doctrine. Ledochowski replied in May, saying that it was unusual to make schedules of erroneous propositions in individual books, but he was sending the reports of the consultors of both Propaganda and the Index. They did not satisfy McDonald, who was reading and thinking furiously, and he said so in a letter to Ledochowski dated 28 May. It must have given scant comfort to him when the Cardinal replied that if he felt aggrieved he should place the matter before the Irish bishops, who at their October meeting referred it back to Rome. In November McDonald addressed three agonised letters to Archbishop Walsh (the replies have disappeared, but their substance can be inferred from the side of the correspondence that has).[22] He said he had just had printed a little dissertation in Latin, giving his view of the vital activity of created being, which he now saw as the core of the difficulty. He was sending copies to Propaganda, and suggested he should go to Rome to discuss the matter with a few people there, in particular the consultors. It is clear that Walsh put him off, prudently judging this would only make matters worse, for his next two letters are pleas from a man who knows he is defeated to the effect that he knows he will not be taken seriously unless he goes and puts his case in person.

Ledochowski wrote to Logue on 17 April 1900, a carefully worded letter in which he suggested that the Irish bishops might take very drastic action should the doctrine of the book not be in conformity with Catholic teaching, and yet at the same time managing to suggest that this might not be necessary. This was communicated by Logue to McDonald in June, with a verbal injunction to confine himself in future to expounding to his students the theology of grace of the Thomists and the Molinists. There was fight in him yet. He countered by saying that he was in charge of postgraduate students, and that statutes approved in Rome obliged him to give them 'a more ample and profound knowledge' of theology. The only result was that the oral prohibition of June was repeated in writing in October. McDonald's perceptive final comment is perhaps more sad than bitter:

> As my book was condemned and my theses animadverted on officially, it was necessary, to save the face of authority, to enforce the condemnation in some way; but it was no less necessary to do this vaguely, so as not to involve in my condemnation a number of others whom it was not so convenient to condemn . . . I felt that the Bishops of Ireland . . . turned against me to save the face of the Propaganda consultors . . . everybody was content and even glad to let sleeping dogs lie.

Neither protagonist could have been happy with the outcome, and they tried to continue a sniping battle in the *Irish Ecclesiastical Record*. Coghlan got more of a welcome, and as the Modernist crisis matured he contributed a number of articles in this particular area: a careful investigation might show that a very local target was not altogether out of his sights. The editor, John F. Hogan, would have refused space to McDonald if at all possible, but it was not easy to exclude altogether the Prefect of the Dunboyne, and though his contributions seemed to be on fairly non-controversial topics he was anxiously watched.[23] In 1903 McDonald had another book ready, *The Principles of Moral Science*. Archbishop Walsh was not enthusiastic, but it did appear with his *Imprimatur* (no doubt he kept recalling the same authorisation he had given to *Motion* five years before). He seems to have yielded when the book was vouched for by a senior Maynooth professor, Michael Fogarty, who gave the *Nihil obstat* as theological censor.[24] Daniel Coghlan still felt that a dangerous man had not been adequately dealt with. There seemed to be no limits to where he might break out, or on what topic. In January 1908 a short article by McDonald appeared in an obscure enough journal, *C.Y.M.*, edited by a member of one of the Dublin branches of the Catholic Young Men's Society. Entitled 'The Hazel Switch', it was primarily an examination of the practice of 'cattle-driving', men with no land or only a patch of land driving away graziers' cattle, not harming them, but making grass-farming difficult. It raised the moral question of how far pressure may be used to secure rights. Boycotting, McDonald said, 'had been answered by the people in the affirmative, against the teaching of practically all the official lawyers and of many of the Bishops, and of other lights of the Church.' Pope Leo XIII had been hostile, stopping just short of outright condemnation. If such hostility was shown to the farming class, there were real fears of what might happen to landless farm-workers; not to speak of the fact that the wage-earners would be the next to apply pressure. The article was a slender contribution to an obscure journal, and it did not go further than a plea to the clergy not to rush to condemnations,[25] but it served notice that the author was turning his mind to contemporary moral and social questions, developed at more length, and sometimes disconcertingly, in *Some Ethical Questions of Peace and War* (1918) and *Some Ethical Aspects of the Social Question* (1920), both published in London with a Westminster *Imprimatur*.

Late July and early August are quiet times in academic institutions. The editor of the *Irish Ecclesiastical Record* was on holiday in Europe in the summer of 1908. When the August number of the journal appeared it carried an article by Daniel Coghlan, ostensibly a notice of a book published in Paris in 1898, *Le mouvement*: it was all too clear that it was a review of a book published in Dublin in that year. The conflict came to a head in 1913, over the doctoral dissertation of William Moran, *The Government of the Church in the First Century*. This had been directed by McDonald, and, as was normal, handed to two readers from the faculty. They had pronounced favourably and it was admitted to defence. Coghlan had not been one of the readers, simply because it was not his turn. The first overt sign of his dissatisfaction came when he called the attention of the Visitors, meeting on 20 June, to one of the propositions Moran had chosen to defend, expressing the opinion that it was not 'clearly safe'. It was hard to see what could be done about it at this late stage, especially as there was an assurance from the candidate that he 'meant what was true'. He had a successful doctorate defence on 23 June and his degree was conferred the following day. That same morning McDonald had an article in the *Freeman's Journal*, giving an account of the dissertation and doctoral defences generally.[26] Its contents, together with Coghlan's urgings, led the Trustees to set up a committee to report to their October meeting. When they met they had before them a memorandum from Coghlan.[27] Moran's dissertation, he said, had been duly published after the degree was awarded, and people were now holding him responsible for its contents although he had had nothing to do with it. He believed the views expressed in it raised problems in the context of what the Council of Trent had defined in regard to the institution of the monarchical episcopate, and indeed tended towards Presbyterianism.

The episcopal committee had to be careful in its criticism of a dissertation which had been awarded a doctorate. Their criticism was in the first place directed against McDonald's letter to the *Freeman's Journal*, especially his remarks on the use of Latin and of the syllogistic method in the teaching of theology. They objected too to what was represented as claims that 'the Bishops have gradually appropriated all . . . jurisdiction'. This was 'unseemly and incorrect', conveying the impression that Presbyterianism and prelacy were each half right and half wrong, and in so far as this represented Moran's work fairly it could not be accepted. The verdict was read to McDonald by the secretary to the Visitors. He said he accepted it fully and said nothing more, but there was no rancour.[28] The chief sufferer was Moran, who had to wait for the theological chair he so richly deserved, Garrett Pierse being appointed in preference to him when Patrick Toner resigned in June 1913. There were two further appointments, John Blowick and Patrick Cleary, before Moran's turn came, but they left very quickly to become founders of the Maynooth Mission to China. Moran was appointed in October 1917 and had a long and distinguished teaching career until he resigned in 1943 to become parish priest of Trim. Daniel Coghlan had been appointed auxiliary Bishop of Cork on 25

May 1914, and Walter McDonald died in Maynooth, painfully, on 1 May 1920. He left a lengthy memoir of his life and struggles, entrusting it to Denis Gwynn as his literary executor. It appeared in 1926, entitled *Reminiscences of a Maynooth Professor*.

Royal University, National University

The subjects taught in Maynooth in addition to Theology and Mental Philosophy had concentrated on the traditional 'core subjects', offering what had long been regarded as a rounded education centred on the Classics ('Rhetoric') and mathematics and physical science ('Natural Philosophy'). The resources for teaching even this programme were slender, and looked even more slender when tested against the demand for growing specialisation in the short and bruising experience with the Royal University in the early 1880s. This had led to the establishment of separate chairs of English and Modern Languages, but they still retained their subordinate position, and for some time no-one considered Irish could be anything more than a practical training needed by priests in certain parts of Ireland. The grant of the Pontifical charter weakened these subjects still further, because it siphoned off Natural Philosophy into the Pontifical Faculty of Philosophy. Even Rhetoric now seemed consigned to an auxiliary role: this is certainly implied in the request of the Trustees to the Scholastic Council in June 1897 for a report 'on the reform of studies in the Junior House, with a view to raising the standard of knowledge of the classical languages.' Despite a hint that a second professor might be provided, the concern clearly was that students should be equipped to pursue their Theology and Philosophy studies in Latin, and have enough Greek to study Scripture to degree level.

Though the report of the Scholastic Council in October widened the terms of the debate, it still did not break out of the context of 'core subjects'. The situation was that of the three pre-theology years the first was devoted to 'Rhetoric', followed by two years' philosophy, 'Mental' and 'Natural'. The Scholastic Council proposed the years should be called First, Second and Third Philosophy, with Rhetoric, Mathematics and Philosophy being studied concurrently in all three, with courses at pass and honours level. Other subjects were to be optional, each student to select one (elementary Irish, of course, was still obligatory on all students in the junior classes). This was small comfort to the professors of English and Modern Languages, and it was clear that tensions were developing between Natural Philosophy, anxious to keep its place as an essential part in humanistic education, and Mental Philosophy, which would favour the development of the other discipline in principle, but argued that pressures on time dictated a subsidiary role for it in the Pontifical programme. The professor, Francis Lennon, was not a young man—he had been appointed to succeed Nicholas Callan in 1864—and faced with these pressures and a new obligation to sit on examining boards in Mental

Philosophy he began to see advantages in association with the professors of 'Arts'.

The breakthrough came in October 1898 when the Trustees received what they called a 'very important statement from the Arts professors', J. F. Hogan, professor of Modern Languages, Henry Bewerunge, professor of Church Chant and Organ, Cornelius Mulcahy, professor of English, Michael O'Hickey, professor of Irish, and Michael Sheehan, professor of Rhetoric. Who were the principal instigators can only be inferred, but it is a reasonable inference that they were Hogan, appointed in 1886 from a totally Continental background, and perhaps even more especially Sheehan, appointed only in October 1897, a Maynooth student but with a brilliant preparation for his post which had taken him to Bonn and Oxford. The proposals were indeed far-reaching. In effect, they were that courses should be designed to allow students to take the degrees of the Royal University at pass and honours level in all subjects. Because only some students had university matriculation at entrance, it was envisaged that the others be given an opportunity to matriculate in their first year. They were then to take the first and second-year university examinations, and so it was necessary to postpone the final degree examination to a year spent as a Dunboyne student after ordination. It was requested that scholarships be set up for this, to parallel the provision for postgraduates in the Pontifical faculties. Because of the demands of Philosophy, and the fact that by a college regulation Irish was compulsory for all their students, they suggested that they choose one 'optional subject', in effect a choice between English, a modern language (Hogan was teaching courses in French and Italian), and a 'Natural Philosophy' that was inexorably parting into Mathematics and the experimental sciences.

The Trustees referred the matter to the Scholastic Council, and asked the professors of Philosophy and Arts to prepare a timetable for the changes proposed, on the assumption that a second professor of Classics would, and a separate professor of Mathematics might, be appointed (the chairs were established in 1901, but the actual appointments came only under new pressures a decade later). Tensions surfaced at the Scholastic Council: specifically, the proposal for Dunboyne scholarships was rejected, on the grounds of expense and because it would distract students from 'the studies of their sacred calling' during their Theology years. The decisions of the Trustees were even more restrictive. They allowed students to be entered for the university examinations, but insisted they still take two 'optional subjects', in addition to compulsory Irish, and deferred the proposal for separate honours courses. They also deferred the proposed Dunboyne course, and rejected the proposal for scholarships. But the momentum towards university degrees proved unstoppable. In 1901 the first students sat university examinations, and in October 1902 the Trustees sought a report on how to make more subjects voluntary 'without detriment to the essential studies of the college'. The following June they called for the preparation of courses for university degrees on the basis of existing staff, making this at least more possible by envisaging that within a few years university matriculation would be required of all at entrance.

Until this was implemented, and as long as the old teaching programme remained in place, sitting university examinations demanded much extra work and therefore very special commitment. In June 1903 the Trustees decided that the courses in the first three years be modified to meet the requirements of degree courses of the Royal University. This cleared the way for a notable increase in the numbers registered as university students in the next academic year—twenty for matriculation, eleven for First Arts. It also meant that the interests of Mental Philosophy turned more to the Royal University than to Pontifical degrees: seminary requirements demanded that much of the pre-theology years be devoted to 'philosophy'. For its part, Natural Philosophy had rather thankfully thrown in its lot with Arts in 1900, while not altogether severing ties with the Pontifical Faculty of Philosophy.

The experience of the 1880s had surely shown that university courses could not be taught by the existing staff, and any strengthening since then had been modest. Fortunately, the structures of the Royal University provided a solution. It will be recalled that all the 'Catholic fellowships' had been allotted to the successor of the Catholic University, now known as 'University College', and that the Fellows, while they taught courses there, were not primarily college professors but university examiners. This meant they were free to teach university courses in another institution as well. As early as 1897 Denis Coffey had been appointed to give in Maynooth a course of fifteen lectures on 'Biology and other natural sciences bearing closely on Psychology', clearly against a background where Natural Philosophy was still regarded as an adjunct to Mental. But in 1902 and 1903 Fellows of the Royal University were appointed to help with the new courses established in 'Arts'. Michael Sheehan took the honours courses in what was no longer described as 'Rhetoric' but 'Classics', and he had the assistance of Patrick Semple for the pass courses. Mulcahy and Hogan were still alone in English and Modern Languages. 'Natural Philosophy' had split into three: Francis Lennon taught the course in what was now described as 'Physics'; Mathematics was taught at honours level by J. J. Gibney (succeeded by Arthur Conway) and at pass by Patrick Dowling; and Chemistry by Hugh Ryan in a laboratory fitted out in what had been 'St Joseph's Library', the big hall in Long Corridor to the left of the right-hand arch as one faces into the square.[29]

These developments took place against a background of rising expectations that the long-running 'university question' might at last be solved. On 1 July 1901 a Royal Commission was set up, usually called from the name of its chairman the Robertson Commission, to examine and report. In Maynooth the Scholastic Council gave their views to the October meeting of the Trustees. For the university to be acceptable, they said, it must have a Faculty of Theology; Maynooth should be associated with it at least as one of its theological colleges; and while the faculty sought no endowment it would expect recognition of its Pontifical charter, regulations and courses. This heavy pre-occupation with theology reflects the balance in the Scholastic Council at the time, but when the standing committee of the Hierarchy directed the vice-president, Thomas O'Dea, to give evidence to the Commission on behalf of the college it is clear they gave him a wider brief.[30] Others who gave evidence seem to have had even wider views: Bishop O'Dwyer of Limerick and John F. Hogan seem to have led the Commission to believe there was a possibility of all Maynooth university students living in a hostel in Dublin and attending courses there. O'Dea's brief stopped short of this, but it was far-ranging and imaginative. It was, he claimed, in everybody's interest to provide university education for the Catholic clergy. As things stood, this could not be done without bringing Maynooth into the scheme, but this in itself would not be enough: a hall of residence must be set up for ecclesiastical students at the seat of the university. Undergraduate university courses in theology, arts and science would be taught to Maynooth students at Maynooth; the university hall would serve more specialised purposes. It would cater for postgraduate Arts students who had completed their theological studies, and presumably had been ordained; undergraduates who wished to take courses not provided at Maynooth, or exceptionally gifted students even where Maynooth courses were available; and postgraduate students of Theology. The Maynooth Faculty of Theology should be the university faculty, but its postgraduate branch, the Dunboyne Establishment, should be located in Dublin, this having the double advantage of maximising university influence on theology and theological influence in the university, which was to include the provision of a university course of religion for lay students.

The Commission's report was published in February 1903, and proved a great disappointment. It rejected out of hand the idea of a Catholic university. All it proposed was the reorganisation of the Royal University as a teaching body, with four colleges, a new institution acceptable to Catholics and the three existing Queen's Colleges. Maynooth was positively excluded. The report was signed by all the commissioners, but so many of them added such substantial reservations that it was clear there was no real agreement except that the situation was unsatisfactory and something should be done. In the circumstances no government could be expected to do anything.

In Maynooth, there was at least a working arrangement under the Royal University. Daniel Mannix had been appointed vice-president in June 1903 on the nomination of O'Dea as Bishop of Clonfert, and succeeded as President in October on the death of Gargan. As professor of Theology he had not been particularly favourable to the aspirations of Arts in the Scholastic Council a few years before. It was he who had on 13 March 1899 proposed a motion to defer the establishment of Arts scholarships in Dunboyne. It was seconded by Michael Fogarty, likewise a professor of Theology, appointed vice-president to Mannix in October 1903. It was carried, but it surfaced again at meetings of 21 March and 14 April 1900, being defeated each time, clearly amid some rancour. When however he became President at thirty-nine years of age, the *wunderkind* of his generation, the courses were established and he bent his formidable powers to see that the system worked.

The problems he faced were equally formidable. The teaching system depended heavily on part-time staff, of their nature temporary, and given the hopes that a new system of university education would soon be introduced likely to prove temporary in fact. But there was little that could be done immediately, for there were no priest-candidates, and everyone assumed that permanent appointments would be priests. The problem of the mix of matriculated and non-matriculated students was less intractable, for enough young men of the necessary calibre were in fact offering themselves. In June 1904, at the end of his first year of office, Mannix recommended to the Trustees that university matriculation should be required for every freshman, and in the next year only one course was taught in each of the three junior classes, directed towards the examinations of the Royal University. In June 1905 forty-three students out of eighty-one took the First Arts examination at a centre set up in the college. At the same time the Trustees made university matriculation mandatory, and from June 1906 all students sat the examinations; it was many years before this regulation gave rise to serious problems.

Other problems and dissatisfactions were still lurking. Traditionalists were unhappy that subjects hitherto regarded as part of a general education would no longer be studied by all students. Latin was still compulsory, but Greek was felt to be under threat. In 1910 a college regulation prescribed a knowledge of Greek for entrance, though the standard required was pared down in 1914 for students proposing to take Science subjects. Nostalgia for 'Natural Philosophy' inspired the idea of giving all students short courses in 'General Science'. And whereas the Roman Congregation required oral examinations in Latin, the Royal University demanded written examinations in English, detrimental for students preparing to go on to the study of Theology, and particularly difficult for students presenting Philosophy in the Royal University, in this case not just because of language but because of content. Modifications were introduced, and in 1908 a third chair of Philosophy was established, and John O'Neill, a Cashel priest, was appointed. Like Peter Coffey and Michael Forker, he studied in Louvain. There was the further problem of how candidates for an honours BA in other subjects could make time for the philosophical studies required of them as seminarians. This remained intractable, and a resolution of the Trustees in October 1907 that these students take an extra year to study philosophy seems to have died at birth. Finally, there was the problem of 'compulsory Irish'. In June 1901, when a university Arts programme was taking shape, Denis Gargan as President recommended to the Trustees that they revert to the old system, where Irish was compulsory only for pastoral reasons, that is for students from dioceses with Irish-speaking congregations. There was the further complication that despite all this teaching very few students had a knowledge of Irish good enough to be presented for university examinations. In June 1905, as has been seen, forty-three out of eighty-one students sat First Arts. Of these, only two presented Irish, and they got special coaching. There was pressure from the Gaelic League to make Irish compulsory for entrance, and when in June 1905 the Trustees decided that Irish be obligatory in the first two years only, and only until it was sufficiently well taught in the secondary schools to be presented as a university subject without disadvantage, they were in fact taking a step that had risks attached.

The Government tried another commission, the 'Fry Commission', appointed on 2 June 1906 and issuing its final report on 12 January 1907. This was perhaps even more inconclusive than that of the Robertson Commission. In fact there were two sets of recommendations, a majority favouring a 'University of Dublin' including Trinity College, the Queen's Colleges, and a new college acceptable to Catholics, a minority recommending that Trinity keep its independence, with a new university to include the Queen's Colleges and the new 'Catholic college'. Despite the disagreement certain areas of consent were emerging: it would have to be 'hands off Trinity'; there would have to be a college acceptable to Catholics; and some provision would have to be made for the student body in Maynooth, if necessary in the college itself. Maynooth indeed was proving one of the major obstacles to a solution. Its very size made it easy to say that it would be a great episcopal Trojan horse inside the university. Within the college and elsewhere numbers felt there were good reasons why Maynooth students should attend Arts courses in Dublin. On 20 July 1906 the President, Daniel Mannix, wrote to Archbishop Walsh. He recalled that Thomas O'Dea had made a good case to the Robertson Commission for Arts teaching at Maynooth, but he went on: 'When everything is said, unless all the talk about the advantages of university teaching and equipment and university life be lacking in substance, it is in Dublin our Arts students ought to be, if we ever have there a Catholic university or a Catholic college in an acceptable university.' In any other system, he said, Maynooth students would be at a serious disadvantage because of lack of resources. He had no doubt that resources actually to make the transfer could be found: the boldest policy was possibly the best policy. 'If we are to make the university work, why not go in to it thoroughly and on even terms with others? If we do not, we may later have to regret that we came out of our splendid isolation at all.'[31] The Maynooth episcopal Visitors considered the proposal at length, but decided against it. The most they would envisage was that honours students in Science or Modern Languages might be sent to 'the seat of the university' after First Arts. The Maynooth staff should be strengthened to offer genuine honours courses in at least Philosophy and Classics. In January the Faculty of Theology again urged on the Trustees the proposals O'Dea had put to the Robertson Commission, namely that the Maynooth faculty should be the university faculty and that postgraduate studies should be transferred to Dublin, with the establishment there of 'a systematic course of higher scientific

Theology'. It did not look any more likely than in 1903.

The government decided to tackle the question. The initiative was taken by James Bryce, Chief Secretary from 1905 to 1907, but the job was done by his successor, Augustine Birrell (1907–16). His bill went through Parliament and became law on 1 August 1908 (8 Edw. VII, c. 38). There was real debate on only two topics—the lack of provision for residential accommodation, and the proposal for 'affiliated' or 'recognised' colleges, which had in mind Magee College in Derry and, of course, Maynooth. The idea was not new—power to 'affiliate' colleges had been more or less standard in nineteenth-century 'red-brick' charters, normally, however, with a stipulation that part of the course be attended in the university. What was now proposed was to affiliate a seminary, whose name still stirred fears and resentment at Westminster, with no obligation to attend any courses in the university itself. Its very size, it was feared, would make overall clerical control easier. But in the end this clause was carried by a large majority, many, however, supporting it as the lesser evil, and cherishing some hopes that over the years Maynooth Arts students would slowly trickle to Dublin because provision could not be made for them at Maynooth.

For many of the Irish bishops, too, the new legislation was no better than the lesser evil. It dissolved the Queen's Colleges and established two new universities, the Queen's University in Belfast, and the National University of Ireland, with three constituent colleges, a new college in Dublin and the former Queen's Colleges in Cork and Galway. The Senate of the university was to have power to grant recognition to other colleges. The new institution was quite positively undenominational. There was some provision to protect the faith of students, but many would consider it vague and insufficient. There was little, if any, advance on the Queen's Colleges in regard to Theology: chairs of theology might be set up by private endowment, and the university buildings might be used for teaching. There would be no grant for the erection of a university church. One big difference was that the Catholic authorities were fully consulted, and Archbishop Walsh was cautiously in favour where his predecessor Archbishop Cullen had been implacably hostile. The biggest difference, however, was less tangible. It rested on the simple fact that in the sixty years between the Queen's Colleges and the National University the Irish Catholics had grown immeasurably more self-confident, assured that they had the capacity to mould the institution into what they wanted.

In June 1909 the Trustees authorised Mannix to apply to the university Senate for recognition for Maynooth, and he applied on 11 July. At its meeting on 25 February 1910 the Senate agreed, for a period of four years in the Faculties of Arts, Philosophy and Celtic Studies (the backdating of recognition to 1 November 1909 was for the practical reason of taking in the current year's course, and the limitation to four years was in the hope that Maynooth's students might yet migrate to Dublin). At the end of the four years recognition was granted *in perpetuum* to these three faculties and also to a Faculty of

Science. Theology, to pick up Mannix's phrase, remained in 'splendid isolation'. The first conferring of degrees of the National University took place in Maynooth on 8 December 1911.

'Recognition' was in the first instance acceptance of the teaching staff by the Senate on the nomination of the President. The university claimed no authority in the appointment of staff or the composition of the governing body; conversely, the college had no statutory right to representation on the Senate. (Mannix had been a member of the first, nominated, Senate, and with his successor the custom began that the Maynooth President was co-opted as a pro-vice-chancellor.) The college was free to develop its own courses, subject to general university regulations, and recognised teachers could be and in fact were nominated to the General Board of Studies. Despite this limited status Maynooth bulked large in the university scene—how large will be clear from the numbers of candidates from each college entered for examination in 1912, the first year for which the figures are not complicated by a carry-over from the Royal University.[32]

Summer Examinations

	Dublin	Cork	Galway	Maynooth
First Arts	150	34	10	78
BA (Pass)	104	23	6	36
All Faculties	399	141	93	114

Autumn Examinations

BA (Honours)	107	18	6	21

The first examinations, in 1910, were conducted by the Maynooth teaching staff and the extern examiners of the university. Nobody in Maynooth had any doubt that this met every legal requirement, but it was now pointed out that the charter required that examinations be conducted by professors of the university, not by recognised teachers alone. Legal opinion was sought and confirmed this. At Maynooth both the President and teaching staff were dumbfounded. This, they claimed, had never been contemplated when recognition was applied for. It was even asserted that 'the worst features of the old Royal' were back (this was an exaggeration, for Maynooth could now draw up the courses on which its students would be examined, and its staff had a defined if limited function as examiners).[33] It was decided to petition the Senate to seek an amendment to the charter allowing the Maynooth staff to examine in conjunction with the extern examiners, and the Senate agreed.

Experience had shown that in a number of areas amendments to the charter were desirable, and a consolidated list was forwarded to Dublin Castle after the meeting of the Senate on 16 May 1913. In regard to the Maynooth petition, more information was sought, on the grounds that it was bound to cause controversy. The Senate did no more at its October meeting than to amplify slightly the grounds for the request. The reply of the Chief Secretary was before its meeting on 27 February 1914. Writing on 20 December, Birrell said he had given the request long and careful consideration. When in drafting the bill consideration was given to examinations in recognised colleges it was felt necessary to establish the authority of the university over its degrees, and it appeared that the only distinction between a constituent and recognised college was the third examiner. He expressed surprise that the Senate should wish examinations for its degrees to be conducted with no representative of the university present, but if it insisted he would agree, but with two conditions: there must be two extern examiners in recognised colleges, and there must be a new statute defining the status and qualification of extern examiners.[34]

The Maynooth request now looked as if it might well affect all the colleges, and the President, Mannix's successor John F. Hogan, had little option but to agree to postpone it for the present. He had taken up the matter privately with Birrell, and had received a courteous but firm reply. Birrell asked him to try to see the Government's point of view. He acknowledged the great help he had received from Maynooth in the anxious months when the bill was going through. When it had become known during the debates in Parliament that Maynooth students would be allowed to take their degrees without any obligation to attend courses outside the college, it looked as if this might wreck the bill. He had relied on the provision for examining in recognised colleges as a guarantee of the university's control over its degrees, and also expressed his belief that Maynooth students would soon be attending courses in Dublin. This had not happened, and if at the request of the Senate the remaining safeguard were withdrawn he judged there would be serious trouble. When Hogan tried to take the matter up with him again later he received a much sharper reply. Birrell said curtly that he had had to think of the good of the university as a whole. To have removed the safeguard on Maynooth examinations would have lost the bill, he said, and added 'but even so that would have broken no one's heart but my own'.[35] So the Senate, which had appointed the Maynooth staff examiners for the year 1912, appointed for 1913 the corresponding professors of University College, Dublin 'to assist in conducting' the examinations at Maynooth. It was a gracious formula that worked well.

In preparing students for degrees of the Royal University the courses taught in Maynooth had been the same as those in Dublin, a sensible arrangement because so much of the teaching was done by Fellows who also examined. It was on the basis of these Dublin courses that the first general regulations for degrees in Maynooth were introduced in 1910. It was repeated that matriculation was required of all entrants, and all students had to have a National University degree before being admitted to theology. Five subjects were to be presented at First Arts: Latin; English; one subject chosen from Greek, Irish, French, Italian, German, Hebrew; one chosen from

Mathematics, Mathematical Physics, Experimental Physics, Chemistry and Logic; and a fifth subject not already chosen from those listed. For the pass BA the course was: Logic and Psychology; Metaphysics; and two additional subjects. For the honours BA there were courses in Philosophy, Classics, Modern Languages and Mathematics, students being required to take college courses in philosophy if they were not presenting it for their degree. There was to be a college Second Arts examination, and a course in Irish language and history for all students not presenting Irish at matriculation (Irish became a compulsory matriculation subject in 1913). 'Science' made its separate appearance when recognition became permanent that same year. At first there were only pass courses in experimental science, partly because of the expense and partly because it was believed there would be few candidates at honours level. In 1914 a lecturer in Welsh was appointed, and this made possible a degree in Celtic Studies. In February 1916 the Board of Studies approved the first distinct Maynooth courses. In this proliferation of subjects Philosophy appears to have been feeling the pressures: at any rate there are suggestions to the Trustees that some more promising students might be directed to it.

The staff was built up to replace the part-time lay lecturers who could no longer give their services under the new system. The last of them, Henry Kennedy, tendered his resignation as lecturer in Mathematics in the middle of the academic year 1912/13. This resulted in Maynooth adding to its list of teachers a name that later became well known indeed: the President reported to the Trustees in June 'I secured the services of Mr Edward de Valera'. He continued to teach the following year, while the priest-professor, Patrick J. Browne, appointed in October 1913 (in the Faculty of Philosophy), completed his studies at Göttingen. There was now a second professor of English, Patrick MacSweeney, appointed in June 1912, and in Classics, John F. D'Alton, lecturer in June 1910, professor two years later. All three were priests of the diocese of Dublin, and, unusually, none had been a student of Maynooth.

CHAPTER X

THE NEW CENTURY: THE FABRIC OF LIFE

Finances and Farms

In 1895 the college finances were in good shape to meet increased expenditure. Yet a report to the Trustees by the Finance Council as early as June 1903 called attention to threatening developments (in 1896 the 'Finance Committee' of the Administrative Council, for some tine in fact independent, was finally given recognition as a separate, autonomous body). The extensive mortgage loans were being repaid, as part of the land purchase schemes that had begun with the Ashbourne Act of 1885. For the most part, these mortgage loans had proved good investments. They yielded 4.25 to 4.7 per cent, whereas the trustee stock that replaced them gave only 3 per cent. The process was gradual—the last small portion of the last mortgage was repaid only in December 1937—but it was cumulative. This shrinking income had to bear charges that were on the whole rising. The biggest single charge was the subsidisation of students. The Finance Council pointed out that in 1903 each student cost £45 a year, £29 maintenance and £16 tuition. Of the 565 students in the college, 300 were entitled to 'free places on foundation', which meant they paid nothing. Of the remainder, some enjoyed burses of diocesan foundation, and even students paying the full pension of £30 were in fact getting free tuition. Tuition costs were rising sharply, because of the extra staff required to meet university commitments. The 'free places on foundation' had been steadily increased since they had been restored in 1875: a final burst of generosity at the Centenary had added 50, bringing the total to 300. The Finance Council argued that this increase was unsustainable, and should be withdrawn. The Trustees were naturally reluctant, but in October 1907 they agreed to a temporary withdrawal of 30 free places, until the overdraft, now standing at about £5,000, should have been cleared. It proved intractable, and there was still a debt when war broke out in 1914. This ensured that the withdrawal of the 30 free places was permanent. They were, however, soon effectively replaced by the 'Mooney Bequest'. In his will, dated 21 May 1915, Canon Mooney, the parish priest of Ringsend, left his whole estate to the Trustees for the support and education of students for the priesthood. The estate was substantial. It was enough to establish one free place for every diocese in Ireland, twenty-seven in all.

One reason for the increased expenditure has already been examined, namely the extra staffing. The other, to be examined in detail shortly, was a number of substantial physical improvements to the college fabric. These were summarised in reports of the Finance Council in June and July 1913. Over the previous twenty-five years, the council said, there had been extensive purchase of lands; the installation of electric light; the extension to the whole college of central heating, previously confined to the student rooms in the Pugin build-ings; a new sanitary system; a swimming pool; together with many minor improvements, to an overall total of about £40,000. The minor improvements were normally financed out of current income, but stock was sold for the big-ger projects. Initially at least the college was well placed to do this. The 1890s had been a decade of low prices, and there was an annual surplus of four or five thousand pounds, which was invested. But prices rose after 1900, and the 1914 pound had been worth £1 8s twenty years before. This was followed by a war-fed inflation such as had not been experienced before, and, as has been seen, even in 1914 the financial position was not altogether satisfactory.

In October 1914 the Trustees set up a committee to examine the problem, consisting of three of their number together with the Finance Council. It reported to the Trustees in June 1915. Despite the calls which had been made on it, the investment portfolio was still greater than twenty-five years before, by about £34,000. Income, however, was slightly down, because of the repay-ment of mortgage loans. Farm profits were up, both because of increased holdings and of rising prices, and the annual student pension had been increased by £5 a year in October 1914. Overall, the annual surpluses of twenty-five years ago, which had been succeeded first by deficits and then by a balance achieved by careful management, now faced a deficit that seemed to demand even more drastic correction. 'It seems obvious', said the report, 'that the college income had been weighted with more burdens than it can safely bear.' It went on to recommend that the suspended free places be not restored (they were not), and that the £5 increase in pension be considered permanent (here, far worse was to come); it suggested that the Irish bishops should bring the needs of the college to the attention of the Catholic laity (this they agreed to do, but in fact did little or nothing about it in the troubled years ahead); and finally, it suggested that consideration be given to limiting the National University courses to 'professional' ones (they did not specify these, but they would have had Philosophy in mind and probably Classics, and in any case the Trustees regarded this proposal as 'totally undesirable').

Though the pension was raised to £40 in 1919, and to £60 in 1920 (this now being the equivalent of only £24 in 1914), and though farm prices remained high through the war years, by this date the annual deficit was, in the words of the Finance Council report, 'serious and recurring'. A bad situa-tion was made worse by two heavy items of capital expenditure: one, morally irresistible, in 1918, when at last the opportunity arose to purchase the Laraghbryan farm from which the Trustees had been evicted in 1878; and another, physically unavoidable, in 1919, when the Aula Maxima, erected far too cheaply in the 1890s, threatened to collapse unless repaired for more than it had originally cost to build. The ending of the war also saw a collapse in farm prices. The reports of the Finance Council in 1921 and 1922 border on panic. Not merely were they appealing to the Trustees not to reduce the pension, they were asking them to distribute the accumulated debt proportionately among the dioceses, in the way the debt on the chapel had been finally cleared. These, however, were the worst years. While there was some recovery in farm prices, prices in general fell fairly rapidly. By 1923 the annual account showed a small surplus, and after that a reserve fund was slowly built up. By 1930 it was just about strong enough to discharge the debt incurred in buying the Laraghbryan farm. Prices continued low during the 1930s, but in 1938 the reserve fund was again exhausted to pay off nearly £9,500, the part of the cost of a new farmyard that could not be met out of revenue. The next year a new and even more destructive war began.[1]

This account of finances will have suggested that farm profits now played a greater part than before. Earlier involvement in farming had been relatively modest.[2] The large farm of 432 statute acres, which had come to the Trustees in the compromise with the heirs of Lord Dunboyne in 1809, had always been let to a tenant. After the Act of 1845 had empowered them to do so, the Trustees had taken land from the Duke of Leinster, some 115 acres leasehold in perpetuity, and 218 acres as tenants at will. As has been seen, they were evicted from this latter holding in 1878.[3] The eviction soon became an embarrassment to the Duke, but even when he was willing to restore the Trustees he could not, as by now he was unable to dislodge the existing tenant.

In 1903 the Trustees bought the leasehold interest in a farm of nearly a hundred acres in Newtown and Greenfields, bordering on the few fields to the south of the Royal Canal which had been college property since the Riverstown holding was bought in 1817. This and the original holding bought in 1795 had been held under a lease for lives renewable for ever (most of it had been designated the townland of 'Collegeland', 136 acres, 3 roods and 35 perches, by the Ordnance Survey in 1837). On 22 February 1904 it was bought outright under Balfour's Land Act of 1896, the advance being £1,552, subject to an annuity of £50 8s.

The college had not taken its eye off the lost acres of Laraghbryan. It was not being well farmed, but the tenants could not be dislodged. Ultimately the widow of the last of them, an absentee living in England, decided to set the land for grazing, and the college took over most of it. There were compulsory tillage orders during the war years 1914 to 1918, and this caused serious problems. Then in the autumn of 1918 the long-awaited opportunity to purchase finally presented itself. The college finances were fairly desperate, land prices were high, and though farm prices were also high they would not hold up much longer. But this opportunity could not be missed, even though it cost dear. Most of the purchase price was still outstanding when the reserve fund had grown strong enough to pay it off in 1930.

As early as 1904 the college had become the leasehold tenant of a very large farm at Killick, a few miles west of Kilcock. Documentation going back to early in the nineteenth century shows this had always been a single holding, a non-residential grass farm of 490 acres. It came on the market in 1904. At this time the Finance Council had been authorised by the Trustees to negotiate for the leasehold interest of Laraghbryan as prospective tenants, and with the tenant of their Dunboyne farm as his landlords. In neither case were they getting anywhere, and when Killick came on the market they held a rapid consultation with the Visitors to urge that it be taken instead. It had, they argued, many advantages. It was convenient to the railway station at Ferns Lock. One herdsman could run it as a grass farm. It was held on a lease renewable for ever at a very low rent for one of the best farms in Meath or Kildare, and as it had been for some time badly farmed and deteriorating the leasehold interest might be expected to fetch less than the £8,100 it brought when last sold in 1887. In fact it was secured for £6,800 on 16 March 1904, and the college was still in a position to sell stock to pay most of this. It was only natural in those times that thought should be given to buying it outright. A bid to do this was made in 1917, but the bursar considered the terms 'exorbitant', even for wartime. Negotiations began with the Land Commission in 1930, under the Hogan Land Act (1923), and the farm was finally vested in the Trustees on 29 December 1933, subject to an annuity of £322 1s 9d against an advance of £6,991. At the same time the Dunboyne estate was sold. The tenant was anxious to buy, and after Birrell's Land Act (1909) the landlord was in no position to refuse. The farm, 432 statute acres, passed out of the hands of the Trustees on 1 December 1933, when it was vested in the Land Commission. In return they received £7,154 New Land Bonds at 4.5 per cent, representing a loss of income of £139 19s by comparison with the rent previously paid.

In October 1934 the President, James MacCaffrey, raised with the Visitors the problems of the farmyard. It was still on the same site as John Stoyte's farmyard in 1795, in a hollow behind the gate-lodge, and it was showing its age. It was a public nuisance for which the college had been brought before the courts, and a real health hazard according to medical opinion. The Visitors agreed, and in June 1935 they authorised the building of a new farmyard at a site just off the Galway road, to the west of the college and further removed from it than the old one had been. In January 1936 the contract was signed with the firm of P. R. Fearon for £17,541; equipping and fitting out was estimated at another £7,000 to £8,000. The work was completed by September 1938, with no more than a due share of hazards—a strike in April 1936, and a borehole that went down three hundred feet before it found an adequate water supply. Of the expense, all except £9,414 came from current resources; the residue was met from the Reserve Fund, leaving it fairly well exhausted. The relocation of the farmyard and the compulsory tillage of wartime made the Newtown farm hard to work. Physically, it was tantalisingly close to the new farmyard, but the canal and railway lay between. On 5 March 1943 the college bought out the leasehold farm it had long held in 'Laraghbryan West'. The two holdings in Laraghbryan were not contiguous, but the land in between, part of the Crew Hill holding of the Chamberlain family, was now in the hands of the Land Commission. Through the Commission the Newtown farm was exchanged for an equivalent acreage of the Crew Hill property. The college now had a consolidated holding across the road from the new farmyard, 454 acres in all, 218 acres of the original holding in Laraghbryan East with 115 acres in Laraghbryan West, and in between 121 acres of the former Crew Hill property. Add the 490 acres at Killick, and it owned nearly a thousand acres of agricultural land, as well as the 'College Park' or 'Collegeland'.

The Completion of the College Chapel

It had been decided that the permanent memorial to the Centenary should be 'the completion of the College Chapel', by which everyone meant the building of the spire, regretfully struck out of McCarthy's original plan because money would not stretch to it. The spire was, of course, not to be a charge on college funds but to be built by public subscription. Walter McDonald proposed that any money collected to mark the Centenary should rather be devoted to improving the library, but he appears to have got little support. It was hard enough to drum up enthusiasm for the spire, or, more precisely, for collecting the funds needed to build it. In a joint pastoral issued in October 1895 the bishops commended the project, but committed themselves to no practical steps to get it under way. It would never have been built were it not for the exertions of the President, Denis Gargan. He was seventy-six years of age in 1895, but he threw himself into the task with an energy and singlemindedness that he sustained until his death eight years later at the age of eighty-four. By then the spire had been built but in spite of all his efforts not yet fully paid for.

In his annual report to the Trustees in June 1896 Gargan had to inform them that money was coming in only very slowly; twelve months later he noted less than £100 received since his previous report, and he urged that an organised collection was essential. The Trustees received this suggestion with no great enthusiasm, agreeing only to postpone any consideration of the best way to raise funds. Twelve months more passed and nothing happened, and finally in October 1898 Gargan proposed that he would make himself responsible for raising the funds required to begin work in March 1899. The Trustees could hardly say no, but their response was indeed cautious. All they authorised Gargan to do was to hold a collection in each parish with the consent of the parish priest. The architect, William Hague, was to be asked to provide specifications for McCarthy's design. He was so to arrange things that the work was divided into three sections and might be halted after any one of them was completed. Tenders were to be sought, but no contract was to be signed for more than the money actually in hand at the time of signing. A committee of the Trustees was set up to oversee all stages of the project.

A less enthusiastic man might have drawn back, especially if he was in his eightieth year, but Gargan accepted and began his journeys all over the country, appealing and preaching. Work began in March 1899, the main contractor being the firm of Thomas Connolly and Son, which had done a good deal of work on the chapel. In June 1900 Gargan reported to the Trustees that the first section was virtually complete. Its total cost would be £5,921, and finances were still on a knife-edge: to date he had collected £5,630 and paid out £4,811. Doubtless repeating what was being said to him by architect and contractor, he pointed out that it was in practice impossible to leave the work partly built with the intention of finishing it later. Once begun, the choice was simple—finish it or abandon it. The overall cost was £14,000, and the shortfall could be met by a small collection from the parishes which had not already contributed. It is clear the Trustees were uneasy and divided; it had possibly been a mistake to have mentioned the sum of £14,000. In any case, they drew back from a mandatory collection. The President was authorised to borrow £3,000 on the security of the Trustees, but there was to be no further borrowing until this was repaid. Recalling how they had been forced finally to clear the debt on the chapel by sequestrating diocesan free places, they ruled that in no circumstances were these to be touched to finance the spire. They requested all members of the staff to preach a charity sermon during the summer vacation. Twelve months later, in June 1901, the problems had not been resolved. Gargan reported that half the third section was now finished, and it was absolutely impossible not to complete the work. To date he had spent £11,034. His assets were £11,103, but these figures concealed a quite alarming situation. He had borrowed the full £3,000 authorised by the Trustees. Total cash received came to £7,103, which means that he had raised only £1,473 over the preceding year. He had made up the deficit by borrowing £1,000 on his personal security. The division among the Trustees may be gauged from the very unusual fact that not merely was there a vote on an amendment but the fact was recorded. It was finally agreed that a further £3,000 might be borrowed on the security of the Trustees to complete the work. The defeated amendment had demanded that there be no further borrowing until full accounts were submitted with a firm estimate of the final cost.

The spire was completed early in 1902, and the staff celebrated the occasion by entertaining the President to a dinner. As remembered by Dean Mulcahy, it was a slightly boisterous affair, but not beyond what was in the circumstances due to a man of eighty-three.[4] But in reporting to the Trustees in June he had to return to the problem of finances. He had paid out £13,885 and an estimated £900 was still due, a total, say, of £14,775. Against this he had assets of £14,361, but of this only £8,361 represented cash received, this implying receipts of £1,258 over the previous twelve months, a small decline in the year before, as is the way with these things. £6,000 had been borrowed on the security of the Trustees, but this, with its interest charges, was in fact a debit in the college accounts. He pleaded that a small parish collection would be enough, but the Trustees still held back from imposing one, deciding only that the bishops of dioceses where so far there had been no collection should 'take such measures as each may deem expedient' to have one held. Twelve months later, in June 1903, he reported that he had spent £15,155, and about £150 was still due. Against this, he had collected in all £9,145 (£784 over the past year), and the borrowed £6,000 was still outstanding, with interest piling up. He pleaded pathetically for 'a small collection', which he did not get. He died on 26 August.

The tower and spire will be his lasting memorial, both because without him it would not have been there, and because it is the visual image of Maynooth left even with those who pass by on the road. Just after recording his death it may seem churlish to say that his spire must excite mixed feelings. As a structure it is a piece of Gothic revival that manages to be both graceful and massive, but there can be little doubt that it dwarfs the west end of the chapel (Plate 43). It certainly perpetuates the memory of Denis Gargan. He should also be remembered for the west window of the chapel, presented jointly with Gerald Molloy, and the stone statue of the Blessed Virgin, executed by the Dublin firm Earley and Co. of Upper Camden Street, which stands at the south entrance to the Infirmary, also his gift. He left all he had to liquidate the debt on the spire. It came to £250.

As has been seen, Gargan's death brought a complete change in the top administration of the college. Daniel Mannix, who had been appointed vice-president in June, became President in October. He immediately began to apply pressure to liquidate the debt incurred in building the spire. Some bishops had imposed collections in their dioceses, but others had not, and the debt still stood at £5,522 in October 1904, when the Trustees authorised Mannix to present a report distributing the total cost among all the dioceses in proportion to the number of free places each enjoyed, and noting the contribution of each diocese to date. Each was to be responsible for its shortfall, and the President was to contact bishops individually. It is clear that any reference to diocesan free places could still stir memories of how these had been temporarily sequestrated to clear the debt on the chapel, for the Trustees added that there was no obligation on any bishop to sacrifice his free places, and noted that this was inserted at the request of Edward Thomas O'Dwyer, the formidable Bishop of Limerick (1886–1917). However, the following June Mannix was able to report that the response of the defaulters had in general been 'prompt and generous', and the debt was substantially reduced. What was left of it in the end—a small amount—seems to have been absorbed into the general liabilities of the college. A bishop of one diocese was still discharging his liability in the presidency of Mannix's successor, John F. Hogan, and even in October 1920, in the presidency of Hogan's successor, James MacCaffrey, the

Trustees were calling on dioceses still in default to clear their obligations. This minute refers to 'a large debt' on the college: by 1920 the monetary stability it could count on since its foundation had been shattered by the Great War.

In 1895 the chapel itself was in some respects incomplete, but Robert Browne when President had more or less established the principle that stained glass windows and the like should depend on the generosity of individual donors, and the problems of financing the spire meant that this had to be rigorously adhered to. This lends a certain poignancy to the decision of the Trustees in October 1897, approving the completion of the west façade by statues 'as soon as they are supplied by the generosity of college benefactors', for the niches for the statues are still empty (Plate 27). Maynooth has had generous benefactions since then, but there were always more pressing needs. There were still some windows without stained glass at the time of the Centenary. In the autumn of 1895 the bishop and clergy of Elphin donated a window to replace that given by Bishop Gillooly in 1885, which with its theme of the Immaculate Conception was out of harmony with the scenes from the life of Our Lord depicted in sequence in the other windows (the 'Gillooly window' was taken to Elphin). The remaining windows on the north side were glazed during the next ten years, presented by Canon Donovan, PP, Dunlavin (1895); 'collegio amicus' (1897, unidentified except as 'a lay gentleman' in the President's report of that year); Stephen Montgomery, 'patronus collegii fidus' (1905); and a window 'ab alumno oblatum' (1905, unidentified). The two windows at either end of the organ-gallery remained plain, but their position makes them inconspicuous. There is no record in the college to indicate what firm executed the windows erected between 1895 and 1905. It was either Cox, Buckley or Westlake, but their style is so similar that in the absence of evidence it is impossible to say which with certainty, but the more probable of the two is Westlake.

The high altar in the chapel had been designed by J. J. McCarthy. There is an illustration in Healy's *Centenary History* (Plate 30), where indeed it does look small but has the merit of not obscuring the apse chapels behind it. There was, however, a general feeling that it should be replaced, and the opportunity was provided by the will of Gerald Molloy, who died in 1906. He left the residue of his estate for charitable purposes in Ireland. It was a considerable sum, and Archbishop William Walsh agreed that portion of it might be spent on a new altar for Maynooth. Notwithstanding its flamboyance of Italian marble, design and execution are Irish—the design by the architects Ashlin and Coleman, the execution by Earley and Co., including the remarkable reproduction in marble of Leonardo da Vinci's 'Last Supper' (the illustration in Healy's *Centenary History* shows the first altar similarly adorned). The new altar was solemnly consecrated on 6 February 1913 by Archbishop Mannix before he left for Melbourne. It was also about this time that the great sanctuary lamp was installed.[5]

The decoration of the apse chapels had been the place where Robert Browne's ambitions had been most severely thwarted by lack of funds. When John F. Hogan became President in 1912 he expressed his hope that something better might be found to replace the stereotyped stencils, but there was first a problem of damp in the ceilings. Though he did not find the Trustees very co-operative he pressed ahead, and in his report in June 1917 claimed to have solved the problem. In this he was over-optimistic, for the damp proved persistent indeed, because it was caused by the porosity of the roof-tiles. And when the chapels were redecorated in 1931 it was still, with one exception, in the unimaginative stencil-work. The exception was the Lady Chapel, where Hogan was able to achieve something more ambitious. In June 1914, just before the world of the nineteenth century exploded, he sought permission to decorate the chapel, for which he claimed to have funds in hand, though it is not altogether clear where he got them from. The architects Ashlin and Coleman had prepared a plan to decorate the walls in 'glass Venetian mosaic', the predominant colour to be blue, preferably with scenes from the life of Our Lady. The Trustees agreed. Not unexpectedly, things turned out to cost more than anticipated. A proposal to embellish the altar with white Carrara marble and lapis lazuli had to be dropped, but the walls were decorated with an elaborate glass mosaic, the architect's design being carried out by Earley and Co.[6] No work was done on the ceiling, which must have looked a little shabby faced with the new magnificence. In 1927 the firm of J. Clarke and Sons of North Frederick Street executed the highly successful scheme in a cool blue with restrained pictorial panels.

Additions, Renewals, Living

When the glitter of the centenary celebrations had faded, it began to come to people's notice that there was a great deal of scruffiness and even dilapidation about. In October 1895 the Trustees requested a report on improvements the college authorities felt were needed, and when this was presented in June 1896 they sanctioned a number of works, especially in the infirmaries, where, as will be seen, things were not good. And even though major improvements took place within a quite short period the problem of very large and ageing buildings proved intractable.

The first problem to be tackled was heating. Up to this, central heating had been limited to students' rooms in the Pugin building: elsewhere they studied during the winter months in class halls heated by fires. In October 1893 the Trustees commissioned the heating of the whole college, and this was completed in a little over two years, the contractors being Musgrave and Co. of Belfast. Now all could study in their rooms. This was made more attractive by the installation of electric light. Coal gas had been available for lighting since 1864, but in the economies after 1870 supply to the students' rooms had been discontinued, and these were lit by a single candle, bought by the student himself. (It must of course be borne in mind that during the dark months many of them studied in the halls.) The professors did have a supply of gas for lighting in their rooms, but they provided at their own expense the incandescent mantle introduced in the 1880s.[7] It was only to be expected that the Trustees would approach the provision of electric light cautiously. In June 1897 they sanctioned the expenditure of £7,000 on the project, but opinion must have been divided, for twelve months later everything was postponed until a more rigorous costing should be done. However, work began in the spring of 1900 and was finished in 1902, but even while it was in progress the Trustees showed repeated concern at the possible cost, even though the students were to pay a special fee of thirty shillings a year 'for electric light and other purposes'. The installation was well done: it continued to function until the early 1950s, though it was limping a little towards the end, and by then the ration of a single 25-watt bulb to each room did not seem quite so shining as it had half a century before.

Though the Trustees hesitated over electric light, they seem to have been quite large-minded in improving the sanitary services. In 1864 a hydraulic system that some thought extravagant had been installed through the buildings, but the separate toilet blocks remained earth closets. In 1898 this was remedied. As well, bathing facilities were installed on a truly generous scale. Before this they had been limited indeed—a bath in each of the infirmaries. The initiative in making improvements seems to have come from the college doctors, but they received immediate support from the President, the Administrative Council and the Trustees, even though their proposals included 'a large swimming-bath, such as is found in Clongowes and other colleges'. The Trustees sanctioned the work in October 1898, and the swimming-pool and ten reclining baths were completed by June 1901. Fifty years later there were improvements and additions, but the original building is still fulfilling its purpose.

All these were large-scale projects, comparatively easy to carry out once the decision had been taken. Stock was sold to pay for them, and the finances were able to bear it. The problem of what might be called running repairs was more difficult; it began to emerge that an important reason for this was that permission had to be sought from the Trustees for almost anything, and it was some years after the Finance Council became juridically an independent body in 1896 that there was any change. In June 1898 the Trustees again requested a report on the college fabric, and particularly on the condition of the students' rooms. The report, presented twelve months later, pointed out that there were real problems, for the rooms had for a long time been in what it called (in clear understatement) 'an unsatisfactory condition'. It was not that nothing was being done but rather that sizeable sums had been spent to little effect. Over the previous twenty years £3,613 had been spent in the furniture for students' rooms, of which student charges had repaid £2,600. Yet this furniture was by now badly damaged 'by wear and tear and by rough usage'. As well, there was not enough college furniture to allow students to store their books and clothes. The rooms were not clean, the floors especially being discoloured by mud and bootblacking. The council recommended that the walls be kept properly coloured and the floors well washed; that the furniture supplied by the college should be put into repair immediately, and students held individually responsible for damage to it; that additional furniture be supplied—'a small bookcase, a small dressing-table with mirror, a wash-stand with a towel-rail, instead of the present iron one'; and that uniformity be required in any additional furniture supplied by students themselves.

The Trustees agreed, but little if anything seems to have happened, except that at their request all the rooms were gradually equipped with a Crucifix, a picture of the Blessed Virgin, and a holy water font. That so little happened was not only because the Finance Council had such limited powers but also no doubt because all the energies of an octogenarian President went to building the spire. In June 1904 the Trustees were again complaining of 'notable want of cleanliness' and again commissioned a report. The President now was Daniel Mannix, and the first recommendation of the report prepared under his supervision and presented in June 1905 was that the Finance Council should have authority to order routine repairs and maintenance. It went on to say that the servants should black the boots in a room specially set aside and that standard furniture should be agreed and purchased in bulk, freshmen being obliged to buy the furnishings of their rooms, arriving to find their rooms furnished, at less expense than the existing system, or rather lack of a system. It requested specifically that a small strong bookcase be supplied to each student, and that the woven wire mattresses, already existing in some rooms, should be extended to the whole college within two years, replacing what at least in some instances must still have been the beds supplied by the Board of Works after 1845.

The Trustees accepted, and this time something was done, the furniture being financed by a fee of £1 10s paid by each student at entrance 'for the use of furniture during the college course'. As well, the Council embarked on an extensive refurbishing of the whole place, set out in its Report to the Trustees in October 1905. Keeping up the buildings, this said with an incisiveness that surely came from Mannix, was 'a matter of outlay; first to put things in order and then to keep them in order'. The rooms of the Junior House had been painted during the summer, oil paint from floor to ceiling, which it was proposed to extend to the whole college—in the short run more expensive than the previous distemper, but a saving in the long term. Work had also been done on Long Corridor, 'always the despair of anyone interested in training our students in the habits of neatness, cleanliness and good order'. The ventilation was bad; there was no natural light in the central corridor; the woodwork had perished and the walls were dirty. 'We have, therefore', the Council reported, 'in the past vacation, by the construction of lanterns and skylights (Plate 44) introduced . . . an excellent system of lighting and ventilation; the floors, staircases and window-sills have been renewed'; and in the summer of

1906 the interior walls would be repaired and painted. Ten years later these were fears that the new skylights, each heavily clad in lead, might be the cause of a sagging in the floors. The architect's report was rather less reassuring: the floor-beams were sagging from the general weight of years. The remedy adopted was to support them in the centre with iron pillars. That prolonged the life of the building for another generation.

It was perhaps only to be expected that the oldest building should be showing signs of decrepitude, but it was more alarming news that the newest threatened a much more dramatic collapse. In June 1919 the President reported that the Aula Maxima was in a 'highly dangerous' condition; in fact, it was threatening to cave in, and the threat would become reality unless something were done quickly. The college finances were under strain, and estimates of the cost mounted as the inadequacies of the building became clearer and clearer. It was necessary to bind the walls together with steel ties; and, as things turned out, a complete new roof was needed. It should be remembered to the credit of the authorities that in the rebuilding they added a proscenium arch, a serious omission in the original plan (Plate 42). The work was completed shortly before Christmas 1921. The bill was frightening, nearly £12,000, much more than the original cost, even allowing for wartime inflation. It was decided there should be an annual levy until the bill was paid: £1 10s from each student, and a further £1 10s from the college for each student on roll.

There had been repeated student complaints about dirt and bad food in the kitchen and refectory. They were not without foundation. Dean Mulcahy gives the impression of a certain rude plenty.[8] The senior refectory was an austere and uncomfortable room, roughly and poorly furnished, but at least with some heating by the end of the century. In 1908 it was painted, and floored and wainscotted in terrazzo, as the Finance Council reported, 'the last of the extraordinary expenditure . . . inaugurated with the painting of the Junior House.' There were important developments too in the area of food and service, important because though the food was plenty preparation and service were rude. The first breakthrough came when the Daughters of Charity, who had arrived to take charge of the Infirmary in 1905, took over the general supervision of kitchen and refectories two years later, and, as Mannix said in his President's report in June 1908, 'what seemed one of the most difficult and hopeless tasks in the college is now on the way to a perfectly satisfactory solution.' The Sisters were able to put their ideas more fully into practice when Patrick Connolly was appointed assistant bursar in 1917. The light midday lunch of bread and soup introduced to bridge the gap between breakfast and dinner had been a particular grievance. Some students did not take it at all, and there were persistent demands for tea or coffee to replace the soup. Connolly now proposed a lunch of tea, bread and butter. For dinner he reduced the quantities of soup and meat, but added an 'aftercourse'. It was wartime, of course, and he had to show that costs would not rise because of the changes, but he was able to do this and they were introduced. In 1919 he resigned, much regretted, to join the Maynooth Mission to China.

The Infirmary was a very important institution in the days before speedy transport to hospital, before modern developments in drugs, and when tuberculosis was widespread. (The 'ice-house' behind the gate-lodge was built in 1897, ice being considered good treatment for tubercular haemorrhage.) There were manifold problems, and the situation was not improving. The male nursing staff was not professionally trained and not even in full control. There were repeated complaints that students were frequently admitted for short stays without any illness at all, and that some students on one pretext or another spent long periods in the infirmary, even for the whole academic year, while still managing to sit their examinations. A room had earlier been fitted out where what were called 'minor operations' could be carried out, but this practice had stopped because, so Mannix believed, conditions had so deteriorated. The college physicians were pressing for skilled nursing staff, and in 1902 it was decided that nuns should be asked. The first approach was made to the Bon Secours Sisters, but difficulties emerged, and it was three Daughters of Charity who arrived on 28 March 1905, a date that surely deserves to be remembered precisely. It is also the place to recall the affectionate tribute of Neil Kevin some thirty years later to their ministrations to hard-pressed students in the Infirmary, or 'on the List', as it went in the colloquial phrase:

> There was something defiantly solid, stony and stern about the outward form of this building . . . Inside the air was soft and welcoming, there were flowers in all the windows; and friendly smiles on the faces of the Sisters under those wide linen caps that flapped like seagulls' wings on a windy day (Plate 48). The Sisters were our indispensable friends. They readjusted the limbs and renewed the features of those who came, maimed and scarred, to them from the perils of a class-match. They were mothers to those whose ills were worse; to those who might be passing forever beyond the sphere of class-matches, to those who did. Even we, who were always sound in wind and limb, and our bucolic health a joke among our companions—even we must not fail, in passing, to salute the List as an old friend. For the Sisters gave a wide meaning to the law; and though the best we could ever do was a questionable cough, helped along by a well-timed sneeze, these symptoms of our debility were accepted, and the ease and peace of a stay 'on' the infirmary were granted to us.[9]

Mannix's account in his President's report in June 1905 of the improvements being carried out in the Infirmary gives some idea of how much needed to be done. He speaks of a kitchen being fitted out there. What existed before would appear to have been very rudimentary, with some cooking at least being done in the main kitchen. He speaks too of fitting out a theatre for simple operations, and of providing bed-linen for patients, who up to this had to bring their own with them. In 1907 two Sisters took charge of the kitchen and refectories; in 1909 another came to the Junior Infirmary; and finally, in 1918, one took charge of the sacristies.

Medical care was now greatly improved, but it was, of course, overwhelmed by the great influenza epidemic of 1918. The disease appeared at the end of October, and the college was forced to close on 8 November. Nearly all the students were ill, and no extra nursing staff could be got. The sixty worst cases were kept as patients in the infirmaries, and the rest sent home. None of those who stayed died, but of those who went home eleven did not come back. There was another outbreak in February 1919, but it was less virulent. Additional nurses could be got, and only about 160 students were attacked. The class halls in Junior House were turned into hospital wards, and after about a week there were no fresh cases.

In various small ways overall health care was modernised. It was very much with tuberculosis in mind that the college physicians kept insisting that students should have a medical certificate of health at entry, but when this was introduced it was not fully satisfactory, so in 1924 it was decided a medical examination should be carried out after the student had arrived. It was for medical reasons too that pressure began for 'telephonic communication with Dublin', and in 1910 this was installed.

There was little change in the layout of the grounds, the division of the students into three bodies dictating their use. In the general refurbishment at the turn of the century two groundsmen were hired to keep the walks and grounds, and in particular to keep the grass in the squares neatly trimmed. In the great storm of 26 February 1902, as Gargan has put it in his President's report the following June, 'irreparable damage was done to the avenue of limes in our noble park, and many of the patriarchal elms were uprooted'—indeed, allowing for casualties on a smaller scale before and since, there must be few if any trees left that were there in 1795. The centre of the grounds, what is at present the large football field, was then and for years to come part of the farm. St Joseph's division had recreation grounds to the north of it, St Mary's to the south, both a little cramped given the numbers of the students, but not so cramped as the grounds of Junior House, these to be further limited when in 1902 the bursar successfully objected to field games in front of Rhetoric House and Riverstown, and a ball-alley was built in the centre of the pitch, leaving only the cramped playing field at the back of Logic. There were repeated requests for an extension of the Junior House grounds, but in truth there was nowhere to expand to. The abolition of the rule of division between St Mary's and St Joseph's in 1901 stepped up demands for the big centre field as recreation ground, but the bursar fought a long delaying action in the interests of the farm, and it was only in 1938 that he yielded what he was said to have described as 'the best field in Ireland'.

The existing playing-pitches were a little cramped for Gaelic games. In the field at the back of Logic House a local rule said that the hurling puck-out had to be a drop-shot, for otherwise it would be too easy to score a point direct at the other end. As might be expected, Gaelic games were increasing in popularity at this time, though soccer and rugby were also played (Plate 50). Cricket, a traditional summer game, was on the decline, as it was in Ireland generally. Croquet was widely played up to about thirty years ago, each diocesan group having its own court. It is not possible to say when it was introduced, for it does not figure in regulations made by authority, no doubt because it was considered to have a decorum suited to aspiring ecclesiastics. Lawn tennis made its appearance in 1903, when, Dean Mulcahy recalled, as a young staff member he laid out a court where he played with his Limerick diocesan students; and, he went on to say, there were soon ten more.[10]

For long years one of the first signs of spring was the beginning of the preparations of the tennis courts and croquet courts. It was a wet year that did not allow the lawnmower to be brought out on the free day in honour of St Thomas Aquinas, on what was then his liturgical feast, 7 March. The tennis courts in particular did not give good value for the work put into them, simply because the students left in June, but it was the late 1930s before the first hard courts were laid down. A passing reference in the minutes of the Administrative Council in 1905 to a petition from the Junior House (refused, of course) to be allowed to attend the sports in St Mary's in Easter Week shows the Senior House sports already in existence, and presumably the Juniors organised their own shortly afterwards.

The authorities would look on tennis and croquet more benignly than on field games, which gave more openings for roughness and frayed tempers, and might also revive provincial rivalries, though as things turned out it was between classes that rivalry developed. It will be remembered they were not allowed when Walter McDonald was a student in the 1870s: he recalls he was one of a group that bought a ball and began to kick it round only to have it taken from them. The seeming absence of any formal permission for field games may suggest there was a time when a ball was introduced and simply not taken away, possibly after the rules for hurling and football had been codified by the Gaelic Athletic Association, founded in 1884. There were, inevitably, such anxieties as that students would press to wear shorts as well as jerseys—a photograph of what is described as a 'hurling group' from St Mary's division in 1903 shows a mixture of jerseys, shirts, and even a waistcoat, but black trousers are *de rigueur* (Plate 49). In what sounds a desperate compromise, the Administrative Council in March 1906 allowed dark jerseys and trousers cut short, but prohibited 'drawers, white or striped jerseys, white or coloured hats'. The compromise did not last long: in September 1907 permission was given for 'black jerseys and black football drawers reaching below the knee'.

Among the staff, the great recreation was horse-riding, and, after the National Synod of 1900 had relaxed the previous absolute prohibition, riding to hounds (Plate 51). Dean Mulcahy recalled that in his early days on the staff there were eight horses in the stable. Daniel Coghlan he described as 'a splendid horseman, always well mounted', a dashing rider if a cautious theologian, who trained the younger riders like himself and Peter Coffey.[11] The staff too participated in the general improvements about 1900, though a cook hired especially for them in 1899 was dispensed with two years later, and talk of improvement of the pantry from which their dining-room was served came to nothing until 1925. The large suites of rooms in St Patrick's continued to be without central heating, it was said because the professors living there had feared that if it were installed they would lose their right to a fire. Various amenities float through minute books at the beginning of the century—a chop at breakfast, 'if requested', an 'aftercourse' at dinner. It added up to what would later come to be seen as a kind of 'baronial discomfort', but the discomfort was probably not so obvious at the time.

CHAPTER XI

THE NEW CENTURY: TENSIONS AND ENTHUSIASMS

Changing Patterns

The events described in the last two chapters might give the overall impression that the college was settling down to a kind of 'establishment' respectability. This is misleading, at least to the extent that it is far from being the whole story. When Bishop John Healy of Clonfert was appointed to Tuam in February 1903 Archbishop Walsh wrote to the Cardinal saying that Thomas O'Dea, the vice-president, should be appointed to Clonfert, as he felt he could not handle 'the present shockingly disorganised condition of the college, owing to the absence, for a number of years, of any real head.'[1] This is strong language, even allowing for Gargan's years and his almost total preoccupation with building the spire. The official relaxations had been small—talking allowed at dinner on Sundays and holydays in 1900, at lunch every day in the following year—but when Daniel Mannix became President in 1903 it was clear that he was expected to 'tighten things up'. This he did, and even though he ruled with a hand of enlightened authoritarianism there is evidence of a degree of general restiveness among students, much though not all of it caused by over-tight discipline. In January 1907 Maynooth had its third student suicide, Thomas Burke of the diocese of Killaloe, a third-year theology student, who on the night of 19/20 January left his room and made his way to the vegetable garden, where he took his life, to the great shock of everybody, for nobody, superior or fellow-student, could note the slightest sign of disturbance even the previous evening. Most disturbances were more mundane— grievances about food, which were well-founded, and a real clash between students and authorities in the matter of smoking, by now a socially accepted habit, but where the rule was to be rigorously enforced until 1918. It did not even figure in the long list of student petitions which filtered up to the Visitors in June 1906, most of which were granted. There was a marked liberalisation too in allowing students newspapers and periodicals. A large number of Catholic periodicals, Italian, French and German, as well as English, were sanctioned in 1903, and, after some hesitation, the *Athenaeum*, the *Saturday Review* and *Nature* two years later, in 1905. For reasons not altogether clear, it took a further two years before the *Tablet* was sanctioned, and then for senior students only. The professors had formed a 'Reading Association' to pool their periodicals, and they co-operated by passing on sanctioned publications to the students. Approved novels were allowed in the libraries, but for a student to have a novel in his room meant trouble.

In a number of ways the institution was slowly opening up. Ordination to the priesthood, the great climax to the college year and to the student's whole course, was becoming more and more a family affair. That attendance was still limited in 1900 seems clear from a decision of the Administrative Council that the organ-gallery and the space beneath it be reserved for students' guests and that local people not be admitted until the guests were all in. Growing attendance is reflected in the Junior Refectory being set aside for ordination breakfasts in 1904, these being moved to the Senior Refectory in 1906, and in a regulation in 1917 that each student be limited to four guests, which implies that by now all were inviting their immediate families.

Tensions over tightening discipline might be expected to be worse with the postgraduate or 'Dunboyne' students, all the more so as for some years they had been ordained to the priesthood with their class-fellows at the end of the four-year theology course. The official attitude was that they were bound by the full student rule except where specifically exempted, though if the exemptions were too strictly limited discipline might be in practice unenforceable. The first decade of the century is full of discussions of the problem by the Trustees and the Administrative Council, and a set of regulations was finally sanctioned in October 1909. It was a tense time, as will be seen in detail later, but the tensions can hardly be seen in the regulations. The general principle was re-stated—they are bound by the general rule except where specifically exempted. The principal exemptions concerned permission to take recreation outside the college and the regime within Dunboyne House itself. They might leave the college for recreation on the afternoons of Saturdays, Sundays and holydays, when they might use that new aid to mobility, the bicycle, though they were to pay no visits locally, and they were not to visit Dublin without special permission. Within Dunboyne House they were exempt from the rule of silence, they might enter one another's rooms, and read in their rooms permitted newspapers and periodicals. There was no reference to smoking, though everybody knew it went on.

The pattern of the daily round showed few external changes. One topic which comes up regularly in the discussions of the Administrative Council is the use of the Irish language. In 1899 it was noted that for some time past the Rosary had been recited in Irish in the Junior House (the Rosary after night prayer had been introduced as a voluntary devotion, but by now everybody remained for it). That there was continuing pressure to extend the use of Irish is clear from a decision of the council in November 1906 that permission was needed before students replaced English with Irish at official college functions. A month later they accepted a student request that the book read at supper should be in Irish. There was indeed growing enthusiasm for Irish language, history and culture.[2] In 1894 the Administrative Council sanctioned for St Joseph's division a 'Gaelic Literary Association', to meet once a week during recreation, but that is the last that is heard of it. An initiative in 1897 left a much more lasting legacy, when a student, John Hynes (later president of University College, Galway) read a paper to St Mary's Literary and Debating Society in which he proposed a student society to foster esteem for Irish culture and history. This won approval from the authorities and the Trustees' sanction in October 1898, including permission to receive *Fáinne an Lae*, at that time the official journal of the Gaelic League. The new society soon became better known by the Irish version of its name, 'Cuallacht Chuilm Cille', though its constitution was drawn up in English:

1. The League shall be called the League of St Columba.

2. The object of the League is to foster in the students a due appreciation of the value in the cause of Religion, and upon the consequent claims upon the attention of Ecclesiastics, of Studies (i) In National Literature and Language, (ii) In National History, especially Ecclesiastical, (iii) In Irish Hagiology, Archaeology, Social Manners, and Customs; and to encourage among its members the cultivation of these various departments in order that they may be more zealous and qualified to labour in promoting, extending and controlling movements connected with these objects, and so perpetuate the truly religious and Catholic nationality represented by and identified with them.

3. The League aims at attaining its end by means of papers and discussions.

The first meeting was held on 3 November 1898, and events soon proved that the time was ripe. Within a few years there was an impressive string of publications, primarily the work of the students themselves, beginning with *Irisleabhar Muighe Nuadhat*, sanctioned as the 'Record of the Columban League' by the Trustees in October 1902. Publication, however, was never seen as the primary aim. Rather, it was proficiency in the language, and this was seen not as an end in itself but as the key to the Irish Catholic religious experience. This was fostered among the bulk of the students by the formation of Irish-speaking 'batches' or '*buíonta*'; these developed to the extent that Donnchadh Ó Floinn could claim that when they were strongest, about 1920, little except Irish was spoken during recreation (he himself entered the college in 1924).

Secondary it may have been to the purposes of the Cuallacht, but the publications over the early years must be hard to match as a student effort at any time in any place. They were not, of course, working in isolation. In the background the Council of the Maynooth Union was at hand with subsidies. The

Union, as has been seen, was a kind of by-product of the Centenary celebrations. Here much of the planning had not been carried out. One of the proposals had been for an elaborate Catholic Congress, spread over many topics and involving the laity, which got no further than a list of topics.[3] This developed under other auspices when the Catholic Truth Society of Ireland, founded as a result of a paper read to the Maynooth Union in 1899, launched the Catholic Truth Conference in 1903. It continued until the outbreak of war in 1939, though for some years it had not been thriving; the papers delivered were published in the *Catholic Truth Annual* until 1919.[4] The Maynooth Union meeting, then, had been a clerical occasion, when ecclesiastics delivered papers to ecclesiastics on ecclesiastical topics: ecclesiastical in a broad sense, for, according to Walter McDonald, the papers soon became 'political' rather than 'academical', the work, he believed, of the first secretary of the Union, Daniel Mannix. He did not object to this, though it was not what he had in mind when he read the paper which launched it.[5] The pattern developed of having two papers, one in English, one in Irish. For a few years they were printed in the college *Calendar*, and for a few years more there was a brief report of the proceedings. They were printed separately as part of the annual *Report* of the Union until the 1950s. A full set might be hard to come by.

The Union sponsored and subsidised the 'Maynooth Manuscripts Publication Committee', active from 1906 to 1915. Its original members were John Harty, James McGinley, James MacCaffrey and Michael O'Hickey; Peter Coffey and Patrick MacSweeney were co-opted in 1912. Michael O'Hickey undertook to arrange the O'Curry manuscripts in the library for binding; this work was completed in 1913 by Patrick MacSweeney. In 1907 James MacCaffrey's edition of another library manuscript, *The Black Book of Limerick*, was published, paid for by the Council of the Union. Attention then turned to the manuscript of the unpublished section of Canon O'Hanlon's *Lives of the Irish Saints*, but in 1913 MacCaffrey had to report that it was in such a state that no-one could be expected to edit it. The last meeting of the committee was held on 22 June 1915. There was no indication that it would not meet again, nor is there any explanation why it did not.[6]

It was through this committee that the Union channelled funds for the impressive student publications, which can be only listed here: *Seanmóirí Muighe Nuadhat*, from the manuscripts in the library (4 vols., 1906–11); *Éigse Suadh is Seanchaidh* (1909) and *Mil na mBeach* (1911), collections of poetry and prose, this last described as 'sliocht do shein-leabhraibh an meud so idir prós agus filidheacht, iar na chur in eagar agus in ordughadh maille le gluais agus sonas ag comhaltaibh do Chuallacht Chuilm Cille atá ag Maigh Nuadhat'; and *Gadaidhe Géar na Geamh-oidhche* (1915), a volume of tales from the Fenian cycle from manuscripts in the library.

It is perhaps possible to see a certain irony in the fact that it was in these years of growing nationalist fervour that the college had its two visits from reigning monarchs, Edward VII with Queen Alexandra on 24 July 1903 (Plate 52), and George V with Queen Mary on 9 July 1911. A speculation too might be permitted that for many of the students there was no great sense of loss because the visits took place during the summer holidays when they were away. Both visits were reported in detail in the press, and the accounts were reprinted in the college *Calendar*. Edward, of course, had visited years before as Prince of Wales. On 24 July 1903 the royal party drove from the Viceregal Lodge to Ashtown and took a train to Maynooth, where they drove through the decorated town to the college, where about a hundred guests had gathered. It was noted that the royal party wore 'discreet mourning' as a tribute to Leo XIII, who had died on 20 July. The Pope's death also meant that the Cardinal had left for Rome, so that Archbishop Walsh headed the welcoming party at the President's Arch, with the other two archbishops, fourteen bishops and members of the college staff. They passed through St Mary's Square into the College Chapel; 'God Save the King' was played as they entered. From there they went to the students' refectory, where predictable addresses were exchanged. Tea was served and the college inspected, and the royal party left at a quarter past five. George V and Queen Mary came on 9 July 1911, and it was a more elaborate affair. The party motored down from Dublin Castle and were received by a 'vast gathering' in the grounds, with music from the Artane Boys' Band. Again they were formally received by the Hierarchy and staff, and the address of welcome was signed by Logue and Mannix. Queen Mary visited the Infirmary, where the sisters were presented to her. Again the royal party was greeted with 'God Save the King' as it entered the chapel, and again there was tea, for royalty in the President's room, and in the students' refectory for nearly eight hundred invited guests.

On 2 August 1904 the college had another visitor who ranked with royalty, Cardinal Vanutelli, Papal Legate at the consecration of the cathedral in Armagh; he was accompanied by Cardinal Bourne of Westminster, Archbishop Smith of Edinburgh, and the Duke of Norfolk. But the most solemn reception of all had taken place the autumn after the visit of Edward VII, and it was for a priest who was dead. Eoghan O'Growney had died in Los Angeles on 18 October 1897. In 1903 the American Gaelic League wrote to Douglas Hyde suggesting that his remains be ceremoniously re-interred in Maynooth. Indeed ceremony attended every step of the long journey from Los Angeles, from where the funeral set out on 5 September. On 25 September the remains arrived in Queenstown, to be received by representatives of the Gaelic League, led by Douglas Hyde, and, representing the college, Daniel Mannix, now effectively President, Michael O'Hickey, professor of Irish, and Peter Coffey, professor of Philosophy and language enthusiast. After the body had lain in state in the cathedral overnight the funeral went by train to Dublin, and from Kingsbridge station to the pro-cathedral, for another overnight lying in state. On the morning of Sunday 27 September after High Mass, 'the funeral through the streets to the Broadstone station was the most imposing that ever passed through Dublin.' There was a special train, arriving in Maynooth at half past four, and another funeral procession, led by the staff and students; on the terrace 'they chanted the "Lament for Father O'Growney" in Irish, recently written by a Dunboyne student'; and a sermon was delivered from a pulpit in the middle of St Joseph's Square. Once more a lying in state, and after Office and Mass for the Dead on Monday morning the remains were given a temporary resting place in the ground floor of the newly built spire, until the mausoleum to receive them should be built in the cemetery (Plate 47). To this they made their last journey on Tuesday 28 February 1905.[7]

The Case of Michael O'Hickey

In a charged atmosphere there is always danger of explosion, and the Maynooth explosion centred on the dismissal of Michael O'Hickey. A generation ago there was a dispassionate survey by the late Leon Ó Broin.[8] He noted that O'Hickey's side of the story had got considerable publicity, notably from his colleague, Walter McDonald.[9] A probably better-known account, based on McDonald, but taking a good measure of 'poetic licence' with the facts, is in the third volume of Seán O'Casey's autobiography, *Drums under the Windows*. This volume is dedicated to Michael O'Hickey, and the following one, *Inisfallen Fare Thee Well*, to Walter McDonald. Leon Ó Broin used Michael O'Hickey's papers, now in Mount Melleray, but not any archival material from the side of the Trustees, commenting that from their side 'there has been silence, but that silence is perhaps justified because, apart from somewhat legalistic points that were made by O'Hickey, the bishops do not seem to have anything to answer.' In the Maynooth archives there is some material in the papers of Daniel Mannix and his successor as President, John F. Hogan, but far more important is a large collection of documents sent from Rome when the confrontations were over, some of them having been sent out from Ireland, some worked up by the legal advocates of both parties in Rome. Hogan sealed them in a bundle, dated it 14 May 1915, and deposited it in a locked strong box where it remained until the box was opened a few years ago and the contents put into the archives.[10]

One of the great merits of Leon Ó Broin's study is that he fits Michael O'Hickey's career as professor in Maynooth into the background of the Irish revival and the Gaelic League. He had been ordained in St John's College, Waterford, in 1884. Like a growing number of newly ordained priests, he spent some time abroad—nine years in Scotland—before getting an appointment at home. After a very brief spell as a curate, he became diocesan religious examiner, in a diocese which had sizeable Irish-speaking districts. When it was decided to advertise the chair of Irish in Maynooth his interest in the language was strong, but his interest in teaching in Maynooth was roused only because of a rumour, in fact unfounded, that an appointment might not be made. Characteristically, once he decided to apply he canvassed vigorously. Eoin MacNeill wrote him a glowing testimonial, and Peadar Ó Laoghaire commended him as a native speaker, which, he later discovered, did not seem to be the case. O'Hickey was appointed in October 1896. He soon proved both an enthusiast and a difficult person. A reference to his still living predecessor in a letter to Eoin MacNeill shortly after his appointment is ungracious, even in a private letter—he dismisses O'Growney as 'not the man to enthuse our young men here'. His public lectures appeared as the first Gaelic League pamphlet, *The True National Ideal*; 'on this subject', he wrote to Father Maurus of Mount Melleray on 11 February 1898, 'I feel strongly, fiercely, savagely.' He became vice-president of the Gaelic League after O'Growney's death, but severed his connection with it in 1903, for reasons never explained, but certainly because of clashes between a number of bickering personalities.

A radical enthusiasm for all things Irish and national was certainly not lacking among the students. In 1906 the Administrative Council was very concerned at the radical tone of speeches at the Debating Society and the Cuallacht. O'Hickey gave himself credit for the radical enthusiasm but he was only one factor. Much of it was self-generated, led by gifted, hot-headed young men, like Larry Murray of Armagh, to whom was attributed the saying 'What this college needs is a proper spirit of insubordination', predictably in constant trouble with the authorities, expelled in his final year at Easter 1908, ordained by an American bishop, to return to Armagh in 1918 and to have a life of distinguished scholarship. Even more distinguished as a scholar, less hot-headed, but also in trouble, was Paul Walsh of Meath; as a leading figure in the Cuallacht in the crisis year of 1909 he was refused ordination to the priesthood, but was ordained in All Hallows. Much of his future scholarship was to be generated as a professor in Maynooth. He has left an unflattering verdict on Michael O'Hickey as a teacher—'painstaking, industrious, minute and methodical', but lacking 'that light touch and liveliness which keeps a class awake'.[11] His scholarship must of course be judged by the standards of the time, when the Irish language was just beginning to find a niche in learning; and, necessarily, he was self-taught. Finally, it must be remembered that the students were subject to many other exciting influences: an address from Peter Yorke, the prominent Irish priest from San Francisco, was said to have 'set the college ablaze', and newspapers were widely read, some circulating legally, others illegally but it would appear fairly freely.

After O'Growney's appointment in 1891 Irish classes had been made compulsory for the junior students, two a week in the first two years, one a week in the third. As well, there was a voluntary class once a week for all students of theology. This programme came under pressure as more and more students in the junior classes began to present themselves for the examinations of the Royal University, and naturally tried to cut back on non-degree subjects. The pressure applied to all subjects, but was felt especially in regard to Irish because of its emotive associations and because only a very small, even if growing, number were able to present it at university level. In October 1904 the Trustees ruled that Irish was to be a subject at the entrance examination, but that bishops might dispense in individual cases, and that as far as possible Irish should be taught as a university subject.[12] This meant the end of compulsory classes in elementary Irish, which O'Hickey would not accept. He approached Archbishop Walsh to get the ruling changed, saying he had already clashed with Mannix on the subject.[13] The archbishop was a language enthusiast, and his influence must be seen in the decision of the Trustees to restore compulsory Irish in the junior classes, with, however, the option to dispense in individual cases. The number of dispensations given was leaked to the press in great detail, so much so that in October 1906 the Trustees stigmatised as guilty of 'a grave violation of duty' anyone who 'communicated to the press the domestic secrets of the bishops and of the college', and ordered that this ruling 'should be read for the professors and other members of the staff.' The students were warned in the same terms by the Administrative Council. The leaks continued, and when Mannix taxed O'Hickey with one for which he believed he was clearly responsible O'Hickey denied it but added that he did not accept that the Trustees had any authority over him in this matter. After the entrance examinations in September 1907 the organ of the Gaelic League, *An Claidheamh Soluis*, ran a number of articles complaining that Irish was clearly no longer compulsory at Maynooth and that degrees of the Royal University were being preferred to the language, and on 23 November Arthur Griffith's paper, *Sinn Féin*, not over-friendly to the clergy, published detailed lists of students dispensed from the Irish class that clearly must have been supplied from inside the college. Possibly to drive the point home, it published on 4 January 1908 an exchange of letters between Mannix and the secretary of the Coiste Gnótha of the Gaelic League, in which Mannix refused to do more than send a copy of the college *Calendar* in reply to the query about the exact numbers dispensed.

A debate already hot was brought to the boil by the Irish Universities Act, which became law on 1 August 1908. The first, nominated, Senate began its work of drawing up detailed statutes. From the beginning the Gaelic League was determined that Irish should be compulsory for matriculation. O'Hickey had had no contacts with the League for five years, but when asked by a member of the Coiste Gnótha to come out of his isolation and help he agreed readily, and, characteristically, once he agreed he joined in with passion and enthusiasm. Great numbers of meetings were being organised all over the country. He was invited to these but did not attend. Instead he sent a letter, to be read at the meeting and given to the press. At these meetings the Gaelic League was pulling few punches, and O'Hickey was pulling fewer than most. His first letter was to a great meeting in the Rotunda on 7 December. Among the many telegrams of support received was one from the students of Maynooth. In the college he was approached by the Debating Society, and he addressed them on 13 December. Immediately afterwards he sent the text of his paper to *Sinn Féin*, where it appeared word for word on 19 December. He had turned to examine the Senate of the university, and concentrated on the five clerical members, Archbishops Walsh and Healy, Daniel Mannix, William Delaney

SJ, and Andrew Murphy. Archbishop Walsh he believed was to be trusted, but as for the others 'I shall say nothing further than to recommend them to your earnest prayers.' He was not the man for the light or jocular touch, and that he was in deadly earnest is clear from what, in the words of Leon Ó Broin, 'we must describe as a hysterical peroration':

> Our first duty is to make it [the university] Irish, and, if we cannot make it Irish, to abandon it to its fate. The treachery of those who show themselves false to Ireland at this juncture must never be forgotten whilst a solitary fragment of the historic Irish Nation remains. Sir Jonah Barrington has preserved for us a blacklist of those who voted for the infamous Union passed—
>
> > by perjury and fraud
> > by slaves who sold their land for gold
> > as Judas sold his God.
>
> A similar black list of the recreant Nationalist Senators must be preserved that, in after times, all men may know who were the false and vile, in a supreme crisis of Ireland's fortune, and who the leal and true.

The standing committee of the Hierarchy addressed itself to the increasingly shrill debate at its meeting on 20 January 1909. They could be forgiven an over-riding anxiety that the regulations of the new university should not positively exclude Catholics, and compulsory Irish might be one such regulation. There were, they said, reasons against it as well as for it, and they deplored the tone of the debate in what should be, they said, 'a matter of fair argument'. They asked O'Hickey's bishop, Richard Sheehan of Waterford, to write to him privately saying that while the bishops accepted his right to express his views they took exception to his language. The letter was sent on 29 January. O'Hickey's reply, dated 31 January, was in no way conciliatory. He said he understood the letter as an instruction to take no further part in the controversy. He was prepared to do this, but he defended what he had done, said the language he used was justified, and reserved his right to explain his silence should he at any time in the future feel it necessary to do so.

On 8 February 1909 there was a great meeting of students in the Mansion House in support of compulsory Irish. It was fully reported in the *Freeman's Journal* the next day, including the texts of many telegrams received from colleges all over the country. Two were from Maynooth. One read 'Columban League Maynooth are in complete sympathy with fellow-students' demands for compulsory Irish in the National University', while 'Dunboyne priests Maynooth' telegraphed 'Uncompromising we stand for compulsory Irish.' A week or ten days later a pamphlet appeared, *An Irish University . . . or Else*. It was a collection of all Michael O'Hickey's letters to the press. Walter

McDonald later said O'Hickey had told him the pamphlet was published without his authority. This is hard to credit, for it carries a prefatory note signed 'Michael O'Hickey' and dated 'Maynooth 22 January 1909'. More fuel was being added to the flames by the fact that some bishops were treating their priests in a way suggesting they did not regard the question as 'a matter of fair argument', especially Archbishop Healy of Tuam. Through February and March Healy was regularly attacked in *An Claidheamh Soluis* and *Sinn Féin*. A particularly bitter attack on him in *Sinn Féin* on 20 March stigmatised him as 'a bully' and 'an Archbishop rampant'. The word 'bully' cut close to the bone. Mannix may have been authoritarian, but Healy was worse, and conflict seemed more and more unavoidable.

Matters came to a head in June. The Administrative Council decided not to call to Orders the students who had signed the telegram to the Mansion House meeting in February, and to refer the case of the Dunboyne priests to the Trustees. When the Visitors met they asked the council what further disciplinary measures should be taken. They recommended that the Dunboyne priests be withdrawn by their bishops; that all newspapers be removed from student libraries; and that the activities of student societies be suspended until their rules were revised. These recommendations were approved by the Visitors and enacted by the Trustees. In October, however, the societies were allowed to function again under new regulations, not markedly more restrictive. The newspapers would have gone soon in any case, as part of the reaction to Modernism. Dunboyne, however, was emptied of its postgraduates. There had been eight of them: Garrett Pierse of Kerry, a third-year student who completed his DD and was to be appointed to the staff in 1914; two who received their licentiate at the end of second year but were then withdrawn, Edmund O'Donnell of Cashel and Cornelius Cremin of Kerry; and five withdrawn at the end of their first year, John O'Connor of Kerry, Henry Tohall of Armagh, Francis Breen and Timothy Harris, both of Kerry, and Andrew O'Kelleher of Cloyne.

Michael O'Hickey was called to the meeting of the Visitors on 19 June. He consulted Walter McDonald before he went. Passages from his pamphlet were read to him, and he was reminded of his obligations under the college statutes, confusingly dated 1907, by their latest printing. His attention was drawn in particular to Statute VIII, 2:

> The professors shall endeavour with the utmost zeal to impart to their pupils a thorough knowledge of the subject-matter of their respective classes, and, for that end, to incite the students to conscientious application to study. Whilst zealously endeavouring to inform their minds with useful knowledge, the professors will still more earnestly labour to edify them by holiness of life, gravity of manners, and exemplary fulfilment of duty; to guide them by prudent and timely advice; and to assist the superiors in promoting order and piety in the college; thus convincing the

students that their spiritual training is the first and clearest object of the
professors and of their superiors . . .

He was then asked if he wished to make a statement. He did, but it was completely intransigent, and the Visitors, after consultation with Mannix, recommended to the Trustees that he be asked to resign. The Trustees met on 22
June. Before they came to any decision, the Bishop of Waterford offered
O'Hickey an appointment in the diocese, telling him that if he did not accept
his resignation would be called for. O'Hickey consulted McDonald, refused to
resign, left the college that day, and did not return.

Walter McDonald acted as a kind of legal adviser to O'Hickey through the
whole confrontation. He felt the issue had to be fought, otherwise 'the
Trustees would base on this case a claim to dismiss professors of the college
for any cause whatever—or even none . . . Might it not be my turn next—and
soon? The position of the whole staff was at stake.'[14] In this he was quite
wrong, and there is much to the charge formulated by Leon Ó Broin that in
planning O'Hickey's strategy he 'fed fuel to his discontent from his own sense
of grievance'. In mitigation, it might be urged that he was never slow to put
himself at risk when he believed a principle was at stake, though he did draw
back before final confrontation, out of something like a deep sense of the
Church. It might also be urged that no counselling could have held Michael
O'Hickey back from confrontation. But McDonald certainly added fuel to the
flames, and equally, a certain sense of grievance distorted his judgement.

It was decided to hold a special meeting of the Trustees on 29 July, when
O'Hickey would be confronted with the choice of resignation or dismissal. His
bishop and his diocesan on the staff, Michael Sheehan, urged him to resign,
but unsuccessfully. Behind the scenes, Eoin MacNeill tried to use his influence
to help his friend.[15] The newspapers, as was to be expected, were ablaze with
indignation, apart from the *Leader*, where D. P. Moran argued that much
indignation was being based on little fact. *An Claidheamh Soluis* reprinted a
scathing attack by Peter Yorke in his own paper, the San Francisco *Leader*; and
in a letter in the *Irish Independent* on 4 July O'Hickey himself declared that the
charges against him were based on extracts from his pamphlet, where he had
only given his views on what the bishops themselves had said was open to free
discussion. This indeed came to be so taken for granted to be what was at issue
that the Trustees felt it necessary to issue a statement from the meeting of 29
July protesting against serious misrepresentation and saying that action had
been forced on them in the interests of ecclesiastical discipline in their seminary. O'Hickey's reply to the summons to this meeting was drafted by
McDonald. It said that if dismissed he should consider himself aggrieved; and
as he was advised that dismissal by the Maynooth Trustees was an act of civil,
not ecclesiastical, jurisdiction, he asked for leave to appeal from it to the civil
courts. He did not attend the meeting of 29 July, and was formally dismissed.
He was told that leave to appeal to the civil courts could only be granted in
Rome.

The ecclesiastical authorities nevertheless braced themselves for such an appeal,[16] but none was lodged. Then O'Hickey announced he was taking his case to Rome. Again the advice came from McDonald. An 'O'Hickey testimonial' had been launched at a meeting in the Gresham Hotel on 3 August 1909, and though it did not bring in as much as had been hoped it left him with enough funds to bring his case. He went to Rome in April. Here there was a possibility that the decision might be an administrative one, given by the Congregation. However, on 6 June the Pope referred the case to a judicial tribunal, the Rota, sitting as a court of appeal. Here the case was to drag on for two whole years. Walter McDonald's angry reaction was that the delay was deliberate on the part of the Trustees. It does not seem really necessary to posit this. No legal process is speedy, and the Rota, like all courts, had a waiting-list. The proceedings were unfamiliar to those more used to the courts of common law—'the whole procedure is amazing', Mannix wrote to Archbishop Walsh on 10 July 1910—and unfamiliarity shading into incompetence was no doubt a factor in the delay. In contrast with the 'adversarial' process of the courts of common law, the canon law courts, in common with the civil courts deriving from Roman law, were 'inquisitorial'. The court of the Rota had three judges, called a 'turnus'. The parties were first called together to determine precisely the point at issue. When this was agreed a date was fixed for the trial. Each party was to present its evidence thirty days in advance, printed and translated into Latin. The summoning of witnesses to court was not envisaged, much less their examination and cross-examination there, but at the request of either of the parties a 'judge instructor' could be appointed to take evidence from witnesses, their testimony being translated and incorporated into the general evidence. Each party got a copy of the other's evidence, and on this basis the advocate prepared his plea, also printed, and, naturally, in Italian. The judges of the 'turnus' deliberated their verdict, reached either unanimously or by a majority.

As soon as it became clear there would be a legal process in Rome the Trustees ordered their solicitors to draw up a statement of their case for the instruction of their legal advocates there. This was despatched on 30 June 1910, together with the college statutes (those of 1872, still current, reprinted in 1897 with a view to a revision never in fact carried out), a copy of a college *Calendar*, and Michael O'Hickey's pamphlet. It was not helpful that the solicitors, in order to make the case as good as possible, should also have singled out Statute XI, 11: 'No member of the collegiate body shall publish any book or writing without the approbation of the President, who shall be accountable therefor to the Trustees . . . ' This should have copperfastened the case, except that this particular statute had been an ill-judged attempt by episcopal authority in 1872 to revive an earlier draconian regime. It seems that before long there had been tacit agreement to ignore it. Older members of the staff could not recall it ever being invoked, and some younger ones had never heard of it. Neither did it help when some time afterwards a demand arose for the terms of O'Hickey's appointment, for all this said was that he was appointed 'subject to the usual conditions', and nobody could say what these were, except that presumably they included an undertaking to observe the college statutes.

The Trustees had as their agents in Rome two experienced men, Michael O'Riordan, rector of the Irish College, and Salvatore Luzio, who had returned to Rome in the autumn of 1909 after twelve years teaching Canon Law in Maynooth. They engaged advocates who proved efficient if expensive. Michael O'Hickey was perhaps not so fortunate. Certainly as the time went by there were suggestions that his advocate might be dragging out the case,[17] though in truth he was dealing with a difficult client. On 8 November 1910 the points at issue were agreed: whether O'Hickey had been unjustly dismissed and if so what damages should be awarded him. The trial was fixed for late March 1911. In reply to a request from the Rota the Trustees' solicitors on 17 February sent further documentation from Ireland: various minutes of the Visitors and Trustees, including the minute of O'Hickey's appointment; a copy of the President's report for June 1909; authenticated copies of the letters between O'Hickey and his bishop in 1909; and many copies of newspapers judged relevant. Naturally, these first went to the Trustees' agents and advocates, not to the court. O'Hickey would have had fewer documents to present, and he concentrated on making sure the Trustees would present everything. He began to press for 'minutes and votes of the bishops', alleging that the decision of the Trustees as recorded was merely a rubber-stamping of a previous decision by all the bishops, of which, he asserted, there existed minutes recording not merely individual votes but expressions of individual opinion. These demands made the Trustees' representatives slow to deposit their documentation in court: as O'Riordan wrote to Mannix on 11 March, 'each side having measured the ground are [sic] loading our pistols.'[18]

No particular pressure seems to have been coming from the Rota, which had a full load of other cases. In June O'Hickey asked for the appointment of a 'judge instructor' to take evidence from witnesses in Ireland. This was granted, but it inevitably delayed the case further. It was planned that one of the judges of the Rota, an Englishman, should take the evidence while on holiday. Cardinal Logue protested, personally to the Pope it was said, got himself appointed 'judge instructor delegate', and took the evidence in October. One can sympathise with Walter McDonald's reaction that this would hardly encourage O'Hickey's friends to speak up for him. His own testimony amounts to a plea that the punishment was disproportionate to the admitted offence. Only the ever-courageous Peter Coffey spoke out, in words O'Hickey himself would have endorsed, praising his 'candid, intrepid, strong and energetic language'. The evidence of the witnesses was handed to the parties in Rome on 4 December. O'Hickey complained that it did not contain everything he had asked for. On 3 February 1912 the Rota fixed the hearing for 21 March. On 14 February the Trustees' documentation was deposited in court and a copy was communicated to O'Hickey's advocate. By now he had come to believe his client's contention that substantial evidence was being withheld, and he advised that they should refuse to proceed. Walter McDonald was consulted, but he judged this too dangerous. The Trustees' advocates twice asked for postponements, first to 4 May, then to 20 May, to allow their plea to be translated and printed. Their work was completed when O'Hickey's advocate asked for a further postponement for the same reason. He got it: the trial was fixed for 28 June, the documents to be deposited by 1 June. When they were not the court judged O'Hickey to have abandoned the case. He turned to the court of appeal from the Rota, the Signatura, which rejected him.[19] He next took the very unusual step of appealing to the full College of Rotal judges, which was reluctant to give him a hearing. Then, at the end of May 1914 the Pope, surprisingly, sent the case back to the Rota, to preclude an appeal to the civil courts, it was surmised, but withdrew it again shortly afterwards, the Rota being apparently unwilling to take it up.

Michael O'Hickey lingered on in Rome until the summer of 1916, when he returned to Ireland. There had been great changes since he left. Relations between the Gaelic League and the bishops had been mended by moderate men led by Douglas Hyde. The country had been shaken by the great confrontations of 1913, by the formation of the Volunteers, the outbreak of the Great War, and the Easter Rising. Pearse was dead, MacNeill in prison. Late in August O'Hickey called on his bishop, the Redemptorist Bernard Hackett, appointed on 29 January 1916 in succession to Bishop Sheehan. He received him kindly and promised him the first suitable appointment that presented itself. But O'Hickey died unexpectedly in November, aged fifty-five. The Maynooth students paid him the tribute of putting his photograph in their 'class-piece' beside that unlikely hero of 1916, Bishop Edward Thomas O'Dwyer of Limerick. From the staff, Walter McDonald and his diocesans Sheehan and Beecher attended his funeral in his native Carrickbeg.[20]

After all the conflict and pain the verdict must surely rest along the lines set out by Leon Ó Broin. The Trustees, he said, 'were entitled to be aggrieved at the leading part one of their priests and professors took against them and at the intemperate language he used in the course of the debate. In particular, they could not have been expected to tolerate his address to an immature and highly inflammable group of students. That they dealt drastically with him under provocation is defensible in the light of what would be done, even today, in similar circumstances both within the Church and elsewhere.'[21]

Old Constraints, New Horizons

When Michael O'Hickey returned Daniel Mannix had also left the scene and was in Australia, half a world away. On 6 October 1912 he had been consecrated, in the College Chapel, coadjutor to Archbishop Carr of Melbourne. Carr had also been a member of the college staff. Ordained for the diocese of Tuam in 1866, he had been appointed professor of Theology in 1874, vice-president in 1880, Bishop of Galway in 1883 and Archbishop of Melbourne in 1886. Inevitably, there have been suggestions that Mannix's appointment was side-tracking rather than promotion.[22] This is the kind of thing that is not easily susceptible of proof. Archbishop Carr's career is an indication that Melbourne was regarded as promotion from an Irish see, and Carr was seventy-three when Mannix was appointed. He died less than five years later, in May 1917, while Mannix lived on to a legendary old age, dying in his hundredth year on 6 November 1963. The case of Michael Sheehan makes it very clear that ten years later appointment as coadjutor to a great Australian see was still regarded as promotion for even an outstanding member of the Maynooth staff. Sheehan's brilliant career was very much on an upward curve when in June 1922 he was appointed coadjutor to Archbishop Kelly of Sydney. Sheehan returned to Ireland in poor health in 1937, still coadjutor, for in Sydney it was Kelly who lived to the legendary old age, dying only in 1940.

At the meeting in June 1909 when the Trustees approved of disciplinary action against the students and emptied the Dunboyne they also gave some consideration to the lack of social communication between students and teaching staff and asked the staff to report to them in October as to how they could have better intercourse with the students, special reference being made to the possibility of a common table. It is not easy to know how things developed. All that has survived is an undated draft report, in Mannix's hand.[23] This said the staff set a high value on close relations with the students and would do all they could to promote this. They pointed out that they attended meetings of student societies from time to time, that they were ready at reasonable times to receive students and advise them on their studies and other things. They did not, however, recommend any change in the existing situation; specifically, they were not in favour of a common table. There can be little doubt that this would reflect the feelings of many if not most of the staff; at least equally, however, it would reflect the traditional attitude of the college administration. The fact that the draft is in Mannix's hand may be significant.

His last years as President of Maynooth were still dogged by serious problems of student discipline. These do not seem to have arisen, at least directly, from the crisis of 1909: as has been seen, the measures then taken in regard to students were on the whole moderate and seem to have been accepted. A careful reading of the minutes of the Administrative Council between 1909 and 1912 allows some inferences to be drawn with a fair measure of certainty, even though a good minute-book does not exactly wear its heart on its sleeve. What does seem clear is that there was a measure of tension in the college, and at the day-to-day centre of it was the rigid prohibition of smoking. The time had come when the students simply would not accept this, and the authorities, while still determined to enforce the rule, had growing doubts if it could be done. The penalty for smoking was not expulsion, but a 'solemn warning': in June 1911 the Trustees gave discretionary power to rusticate culprits for six months as well. But the offence of smoking came to be endorsed on the records of a growing number of students. As well, attempts to enforce the rule placed the deans in the position of policemen, lurking around toilets or demanding admittance to rooms where two or more students had gathered for a forbidden smoke. Pressure was put on the bishop of a Dunboyne priest to withdraw him for the offence. Ironically, the priest in question later became a bishop himself.

It is clear too that there were (as indeed there always were, though now the situation was worse because of the underlying tensions) numbers who by any standards were not serious ecclesiastical students, no great sinners indeed, but careless, happy-go-lucky, and, of course, smoking. They included some who afterwards became prominent in other callings. The best-known is probably the young man who then called himself Kevin Higgins, a student of the diocese of Kildare, expelled at the end of his first year after being in serious trouble since the previous mid-November. His lack of any real application not only to the college rule but also to his studies for a university degree seems a fair indication that he had not seriously decided to bend his talents towards becoming a priest. How real those talents were was made clear by the political career of Kevin O'Higgins, as vice-president of the Executive Council of the Irish Free State and as Minister for Justice, where he had the remarkable achievement of setting up an unarmed Garda force while the gun was still in politics, as was tragically shown by his own death in 1927.

That Mannix undoubtedly felt the tensions cannot have helped him. His annual report in June 1911 refers to 'a large number' of students expelled (there appear to have been nine, including four on the occasion of the end-of-year 'Order List'). He adds 'One is sometimes tempted to think that students find it increasingly difficult to bear the restraints of college rule.' Minute-books, as already noted, are not prone to give motives for acting, but a minute from the meeting of the Administrative Council on 19 March 1911 may be revealing. It noted that a custom had grown up of making a collection for expelled students. The decision was taken that all collections in the college must be authorised, and the reason for it taking this form was that 'it was thought well to make a general rule.'

No doubt he was authoritarian, and inevitably he had his critics. Shane Leslie in his account of his visit to Maynooth recognises the complexity of the man but presents him as 'a consecrated ramrod in purple-fringed cassock', adding that as he entered the dining-room 'no glance was shot from the book-weary line of professors, though one or two backs unconsciously stiffened as the President passed.'[24] Dean Mulcahy paid him a tribute when both were old men. No-one could ever accuse the dean, now celebrating his golden jubilee, of lack of courage, or of being greatly enamoured of authoritarian figures. What he had to say of Mannix, his colleague on the staff for seventeen years, was not just praise but warm praise: 'His whole career in the college was a record of brilliant success . . . He taught Moral Theology . . . for nine years. His students outvied one another in his praise. As President, he was wise, with large views, generous and progressive. He did much for the college in the sphere of studies, and in general improvement.'[25]

The apparent ambiguities in regard to the statutes which appeared during the O'Hickey case gave new impetus to producing an up-to-date version which should be in the hands of all college officials. As has been seen, a beginning had been made immediately after the Centenary, but it had not been carried through. All that was done was to reprint the 1872 statutes and to classify and print all the relevant resolutions of the Trustees since then, the assumption being that all these should be incorporated in the new version. It seems that the sheer difficulty of incorporating the multitudinous resolutions was one reason why the revision did not materialise. During the O'Hickey troubles it appeared that not every member of the staff possessed a copy of the statutes, but by 1914 the only advance was a resolution of the Trustees to the effect that the 'standing resolutions' printed in 1898 should in their turn be brought up to date and presented to every staff member on appointment, presumably together with the 1897 reprint of the 1872 statutes. Revision finally got under way in 1915, and by October 1916 the new draft was ready to be submitted for counsel's opinion. The counsel, James A. Murnaghan, was instructed to confer with a committee of Archbishop Harty of Cashel, Bishop Gilmartin of Clonfert (both former members of the staff), the President, John F. Hogan, and the vice-president, James MacCaffrey. Counsel's opinion, dated 1 October 1917,[26] made some interesting suggestions. He advised that it was a mistake to treat Trustees' resolutions as 'statutes', needing regular incorporation into the text (Patrick F. Moran, it might be recalled, had said the same thing in 1882).[27] Statutes, Murnaghan said, should be only 'such enactments as are important, and at the same time capable of being enforced'. He suggested a division into Acts of Parliament, statutes, and bye-laws. In regard to the governing body, he pointed out that a proposal to give all the bishops a right to be present at meetings of the Trustees was illegal and must be omitted, but he felt he could probably support the authority of the Trustees to delegate Visitors from their body, though he felt it necessary to add a clause to make it clear that they could not act independently of the Trustees. He pointed out that the Trustees had accepted an Instruction from the Congregation of Seminaries and Universities dated 30 June 1896 insisting on the importance of securing for the professors permanence of appointment and dignity of status. It was up to the Trustees to decide if this was a counsel to them or if there should be a formal contract of employment. In 1910 he had advised Mannix on the need of 'a clear and binding contract . . . that would have legal effect and leave no room for doubt', a fact which came as a surprise to his successor, John F. Hogan.[28] This question was discussed at some length with the college solicitors. Various drafts of possible conditions of employment were drawn up,[29] but in the end the idea of a contract was not accepted. Neither was Murnaghan's suggestion that statutes as distinct from bye-laws should be few, enforceable, and deal with the more important things. There was a final delay while they were checked against the new Code of Canon Law, but they were promulgated by the Trustees at their June meeting in 1919, with effect from 15 August.

A new student rule was approved in June 1918. The changes were not great, and certainly not as important as the decision finally taken the following October to abolish the rule against smoking. It was allowed out of doors and as far as possible from buildings; what was grandiosely called a 'verandah' was to be provided as soon as war-time restrictions on building were lifted. The debating societies recovered their vitality after the crisis of 1909. It would appear that this vitality, which tended to boil over about 1905 and the years following, was a heritage form the vice-presidency of Thomas O'Dea (1894–1903). Patrick Beecher was appointed first professor of 'Pastoral Theology, Sacred Eloquence and Elocution' in 1904, so O'Dea was the last vice-president to give up his previous classes and devote himself to such matters, a practice which in substance went back to the beginnings of the college. Student dramatics took a great turn for the better with the appointment of M[a]cHardy Flint as lecturer in English Elocution in 1895. The Aula Maxima had opened only a few years before, but the stage entertainment continued to be 'chiefly comedies of a rather foolish type, the acting indifferent but always well received'. McHardy Flint, a gifted professional actor, changed all that, and Shakespeare, Goldsmith and Sheridan became the staple stage-fare.[30] The big night, or rather nights, were the Sunday and Monday of a mid-term break at Shrove. The administration retained the right to approve the play, and was anxious to see that rehearsals were not an excuse for wasting time. The 'Christmas feast' had been transferred to 1 November after a Christmas vacation was granted in 1899, and this became the focus for another mid-term break and another play. A play in Irish came to dominate the entertainment on St Patrick's Day, sometimes no light matter, for example the translations by Dr Patrick Browne of *Rí Oidipús* and *Oidipús i gColón*, published by An Cuallacht. Some 'non-political' papers in Irish seem to have made their way back, but the ecclesiastical ban arising from Modernism kept newspapers in general out. Novels too were rigorously proscribed, except for the carefully screened ones in the library; among those confiscated between 1917 and 1921 were *Lavengro* ('very hostile to Catholicism'), *Anna Karenina*, and *Eltham House* by Mrs Humphrey Ward. But there was scope for mental relaxation, a good thing, as there was still much youthful enthusiasm trying to get out. Some of it surfaced in political nationalism, some in other ways.

One striking manifestation of this idealism was the 'Maynooth Mission to China', as it was popularly known, formally and canonically instituted on 29 March 1918. A quality that might well be called Pentecostal had gone to its making. The Irish had been latecomers to missionary activity to peoples who were not Christian, in modern times at any rate. The reasons lie in the history of Ireland. During the centuries when peoples of European origin were opening up the world, the Catholic Church in Ireland was forced to lie low and not advertise its activities. During the nineteenth century the country produced priests beyond its needs, but their energies came to be directed to the Irish emigrants. It was only exceptionally that these priests came from Maynooth. They came rather from the regional seminaries, Carlow, Kilkenny, Wexford, Waterford, Thurles, and from All Hallows, Dublin, founded in 1842 exclusively for this purpose. The mission of Bishop Patrick Carew to India in 1838 was not a sustained effort, nor was it sustainable at the time. Some time later French missionary congregations established themselves in Ireland, the Holy Ghost Fathers (CSSp) in 1859 and the Society of African Missions (SMA) in 1877. Through them Irish priests made their entry into the 'foreign missions', men like the legendary Bishop Shanahan. Where Ireland lagged especially was in societies of secular missionary priests. Here France had led the way with the Société des Missions Étrangères de Paris, a seventeenth-century foundation. The English-speaking world came in with the Mill Hill Missionaries in England in 1866 and the Maryknoll Missioners in the United States in 1911. Ireland was to join with the Maynooth Mission to China.

It began when Father John M. Fraser addressed the students in June 1911. Canadian-born, he was working as a missionary in China, and was in Ireland seeking funds and volunteers. He got the funds immediately, the staff subscribing one burse, the students another. The volunteers were a little delayed, but not for long. Prominent among them would be three young men who had become members of the college staff: Patrick Cleary of Killaloe and Patrick Connolly of Clonfert, both ordained that same year, and John Blowick of Tuam, ordained two years later, in 1913.

On his way back to China in January 1912 Fraser met in a Brooklyn presbytery a young Irish priest on temporary mission there, Edward Galvin, ordained for the diocese of Cork in 1909. The thought of offering himself as a missionary in China had been in Galvin's head for some time, and Fraser's visit decided him. The two left together on 28 February. As they worked together in China, Fraser fired him with his vision of the foundation of a seminary in Ireland to supply priests for the Chinese mission. Galvin wrote home indefatigably to priests, to sisters, to seminarians, and to the papers. These letters aroused interest and enthusiasm, especially in Maynooth. In December 1915 two Irish diocesan priests arrived in China to help, and they pressed Galvin to go home to urge his case. He was diffident but finally agreed, and reached Dublin at the end of August 1916. Central to his plans was the hope that one of the Maynooth professors would surrender his chair and head the new venture. He arranged to meet with John Blowick, appointed professor of Theology in 1914, because he had heard he might be interested. It was a decision Blowick thought hard over, but he agreed. A committee was set up, headed by Galvin's bishop, Daniel Cohalan of Cork, to draw up a memorial to be presented to the bishops at their October meeting. Episcopal approval came on 10 October, and Blowick, Galvin and three companions, Edward McCarthy of Cork, ordained in 1915, James Conway of Kildare, ordained in 1916, and John Heneghan of Tuam, ordained with Galvin in 1909, set out to preach their vision around Ireland. There was no shortage of volunteers, priests and seminarians. The community moved to Dalgan Park near Galway in January 1918. On 29 March it was canonically erected by the Roman Congregation of Propaganda as the Society of St Columban. The first five seminarians to be ordained were in fact ordained in Maynooth, on 20 April, in the rushed 'conscription ordination'. But by now the Society was firmly launched on its independent way, symbolised by the first group of twenty setting out for China in March 1920.[31]

It was only to be expected that the outbreak of war in 1914 would, with clergy as well as laity, and in Maynooth as elsewhere, rouse hopes among some that England's difficulty might be Ireland's opportunity. Bishop Gilmartin of Clonfert, dean in the college from 1891 to 1909, and appointed vice-president in 1904, wrote to the President, John F. Hogan, on 1 March 1915, saying he had heard there was a good deal of pro-German feeling in Maynooth, and that some of the young priests were 'disaffected'.[32] The following spring the Administrative Council had to deal with a request from the recruiting officer, who claimed the right to come into the college and interview students and employees. He was told that on no condition would he be allowed to speak to students, and he might speak to the workmen only if he could produce specific authorisation. He appealed to higher authority, which inclined to support the college. In the end he had to be content with what for him must have been an unsatisfactory compromise, that he might stand at the gate at the time the workmen were going out, and speak to them if they were willing to listen.

Easter Week was a time of high tension with the student body, especially as the town of Maynooth sent its own body of Volunteers to the Rising, and on Easter Monday, 24 April, seventeen in number, led by Donal Buckley, they came into the college to seek a blessing before setting out. There are three detailed accounts of what happened. The best-known is probably that of Walter McDonald, but he had it only on hearsay, for he returned to the college only on Tuesday.[33] In June the President, J. F. Hogan, gave a detailed account in his annual report to the Trustees. Fifty years later a priest who had been a student at the time, Michael Casey of the diocese of Elphin, put his reminiscences on record.[34] When the contingent knelt before the President's Arch and begged his blessing, Hogan told them he could not bless their 'foolish and most ill-advised expedition', and urged them to go home. (He had, of course, been brought up and educated in France, and right-wing French Catholicism shuddered at the very thought of revolution.) They told him they would not go home, repeated the request for his blessing, and said that if he didn't give it they would go without it. He then told them that he would bless them as far as their spiritual needs were concerned, but was totally opposed to what they were doing. He then suggested that they should not leave by the front gate, where, as he graphically described it, there was an excited crowd, 'some cheering and others hooting, some women crying, with a few policemen on duty', but that instead he would let them out by the goods entrance on the canal. They agreed, and marched on the canal bank to join the insurrection in

302

Dublin (Plate 74). Hogan reported diplomatically to the Trustees that the college was otherwise quiet during Easter Week, glossing over things that he knew and probably conscious that there were things he did not know. Making all allowance for the tendency of legend to grow in people's minds, it seems clear from Casey's memoir, and other contributions to the 1966 number of *Vexilla Regis*, that many students passed the week in a tension of excitement. He mentions in particular that drilling took place all the week in the comparative seclusion of the back of Logic House. One squad had ventured into more open ground in front of Rhetoric when the President turned the corner. The drill-sergeant had the presence of mind to step into the ranks, and Hogan contented himself with saying 'You'd be well advised to disband, gentlemen.' At the prize-giving in June there was loud cheering for the rather unlikely nationalist hero, Bishop O'Dwyer of Limerick. Hogan took the occasion to address the students on the need to show proper respect for authority. It was a tactical mistake, for the student body showed its disapproval noisily, and—an indication of how delicately the situation was poised—the Trustees took no action, and therefore the college authorities could take none.[35]

Tensions continued in Maynooth as in the country. In June 1917 nearly all the students put their names to the address to President Wilson drawn up by the surviving 1916 leaders immediately they were released from prison, though a few did not, still supporting the Irish Parliamentary Party. But as Sinn Féin began to contest elections the signs grew that the end was coming for the Parliamentary Party. When the government passed a law introducing military conscription to Ireland on 18 April 1918 all the political parties came together at the Mansion House Conference, and all agreed to oppose it. A delegation was sent to the Bishops, meeting in Maynooth. According to Father Casey, there were great student cheers when Eamon de Valera appeared. Some of those in their final years would have been earlier taught Mathematics by this man recently elected President of Sinn Féin; as well, perhaps, holidays were beginning unexpectedly, for the Trustees had decided to ordain the students in their final year and to close the college. The students returned on 6 August to sit their examinations, which the Senate of the National University had postponed to autumn in all the colleges. Tension did not slacken over the next few years. As in other institutions, shelter was given to men 'on the run', some being taken on as workmen by the assistant bursar, Patrick Connolly. In general, the authorities had to tread warily. In December 1920 the Administrative Council decided to demote the chairman of the Debating Society 'for having allowed a sensational advertisement of a political debate to appear on the notice-board', adding prudently 'it was thought inadvisable in these exciting times to inflict a severer penalty'; and in November 1921 the council, noting that a Dunboyne student, Michael Troy, had read an address purporting to come from Maynooth at celebrations organised by the National University in honour of its chancellor-elect, Eamon de Valera, was content to express indignation, but took no action.

The staff were divided, mainly by age. When the students had shown their dissatisfaction at the prize-giving in June 1916 they had claimed, according to Bishop Morrisroe, that they had the support of a professor. The unnamed professor was certainly Dr Patrick Browne, appointed to the chair of Mathematics in 1913, taking over from Eamon de Valera. He was deeply involved in nationalist politics. As the split developed between Sinn Féin and the Parliamentary Party the bishops tried to control the political activities of the clergy. In June 1918 the Trustees issued a special mandate to the Maynooth staff: they needed the permission of the President as well as the local bishop before taking an active political role. The occasion for this was certainly Browne's activities in the East Cavan by-election. This was the last to be held before the general election in November. Arthur Griffith, standing for Sinn Féin, inflicted a heavy defeat on a long-sitting Nationalist candidate, first elected as an anti-Parnellite in 1892. This result, it was widely felt, indicated that the future belonged to Sinn Féin. Browne was reprimanded by the Visitors. In reply he said he had attended no meeting without the permission of the local parish priest, and had at once obeyed the bishop's ruling to desist, but that he nevertheless admitted the impropriety of what he had done and promised it would not happen again. However, he remained active in politics. He took the anti-Treaty side, and again embarrassed the authorities by being arrested on 26 February 1923 in the company of Miss Mary MacSwiney, Mrs Tom Clarke, and Miss Barry. The arresting party claimed that many treasonable documents were seized. They were clearly anxious to be rid of this awkward prisoner, but he was not co-operative, using, it was alleged, unpriestly language, refusing to give the undertaking 'normally required of all suspected prisoners', and giving his name as 'Father Perry of Maynooth' (it was later agreed that one of the women had referred to him as 'Father Paddy of Maynooth').[36] For this he could hardly hope to escape a severe carpeting. In June the Visistors told the President to notify him that 'in view of the impression which prevails among the clergy and people of the country that you have been associated with the activities of the Irregulars the Bishops deem it their duty to direct your attention to the terms of the College Statute II, 16.' This forbade any official of the college to 'take any public part in politics by presence, word, or writing without the approbation of the President, who shall be accountable therefor to the Trustees.' They went on to stress the necessity of his complying strictly with the statutes as long as he remained an official of the college. The caution had however been overtaken by events. On 24 May de Valera had called an end to the fight, and an exhausted country had turned wearily to contemplate the rather tarnished fruits of victory.

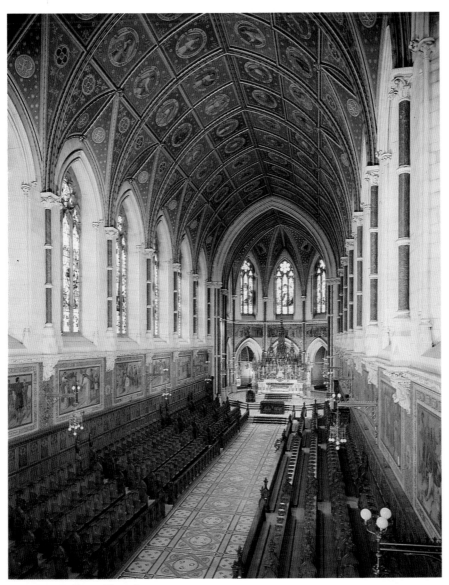

Interior, College Chapel

Plate 56

Pope John Paul II addressing seminarians in the College Chapel, 1 October 1979

Plate 57

Presentation of gifts to the Pope with Cardinal Ó Fiaich and (*back to camera*) Monsignor Michael Olden, President

Plate 58

The John Paul II Library, opened 7 October 1989

Plate 59

President Cossiga of Italy with Monsignor Ledwith, 8 June 1986

Monsignor Ledwith, President Hillery, King Juan Carlos of Spain, Queen Sofia, Mrs Hillery, 2 July 1986

Plate 60

'Our Lady Queen of the Angels', dedicated by Cardinal Roger Mahony of Los Angeles as 'a gift from the people of Los Angeles to the seminarians of Ireland', and commemorating benefactors from the west coast of the USA, 3 October 1991

Plate 61

'The Heritage Wall', dedicated by Cardinal Cahal B. Daly to commemorate benefactors from the east coast of the USA, 23 May 1993

Plate 62

Aerial view of the hostels complex (1970-72) and the University Village Apartments (1991)

The University Village Apartments

Plate 63

PEACE—THEN WAR

The Irish revolution had been fought hard, fought even bitterly, very bitterly in the Civil War. Yet the outcome was marked by no social upheaval, but rather by a conservative government in a conservative society, where the Catholic Church proved to be the principal defining element. Maynooth College followed this national pattern very faithfully. The previous two decades had been marked by stirrings and troubles of many kinds. These now gave way to an era in which rule and law were certain and were normally obeyed without question. This pattern came to be accepted as the norm by the students of the time, though the experience of the generation before them had shown that the overall pattern was clearly more complex. Yet in 1945 John F. O'Doherty, professor of Ecclesiastical History, ordained in 1926, could assert that it was difficult to write the history of the previous fifty years because history implied change and Maynooth did not change: 'Maynooth is something which not even the puniest mind can change. So, at least, it has been. So, we hope, it will always be.'[1] There may possibly have been a measure of tongue-in-cheek, but it was a remarkable statement none the less.

The Material Fabric

Even though farm prices fell sharply after the ending of war in 1918 the financial situation was relatively easy. In October 1921 the annual pension was reduced to £50 from its war-time £60, and further reduced to £45 two years later, at which level it remained, 50 per cent above the pre-war figure of £30. General costs and prices settled down at about this level (the last to get an increase in salary were the teaching staff, in their case 40 per cent). So the comparatively comfortable pre-war situation was in effect restored. There was a surplus on current account every year, and in time a reserve fund was built up. Prices were at their lowest in the mid-1930s, though against this must be balanced the fact that the reduction was in large part due to the collapse of agricultural markets, and the college was now farming extensively. Even now, however, it was felt that the reserve fund was strong enough to bear heavy capital expenditure. The new farmyard, as has been seen, was financed out of the reserve fund; and, as will be seen, the new Theology class halls were to be substantially financed from it too. The unfortunate outcome was that the fund was exhausted in 1939, at the outbreak of a new and even more destructive war.

As well as these major projects, buildings and installations that were getting older made constant demands. In 1928 there was a large-scale overhaul of the College Chapel organ, carried out by Messrs Willis of London, since no suitable Irish firm could be found. The overall cost was in the region of £5,500.[2] The college served as a hostel for a large number of clerical visitors to the International Eucharistic Congress in Dublin in June 1932, all the rooms in New House and Humanity being occupied. The preparations showed up how shabby parts of the complex were; St Mary's Oratory was repainted, and a new sacristy built, with a passage from sacristy to oratory under the stairs, presumably removing the last traces of the furnace and flue that had caused the disastrous fire of 1878. In 1936 the Junior Chapel and St Joseph's were refurbished, the altars in both being remodelled, as was the altar in St Mary's in 1938. There is a curious lack of documentation on a real glory of St Mary's, the two stained-glass windows in the west end. These depict four scenes from the life of the Blessed Virgin: the Annunciation, the Visitation, the Nativity and the Coronation. Inscriptions name the date (1939), and the donors, Daniel Mageean, dean in the college in 1919, Bishop of Down and Connor in 1929, and John F. D'Alton, professor of Classics in 1912, and President in 1936. The glass is brilliant, particularly effective in the evening light, a striking tribute to the advances in the art of stained glass, and especially in Irish glass-making, since the work done in the College Chapel half a century before. The windows were made by the Dublin firm Earley and Co. of Camden Street. A later refurbishing of the oratory in the name of liturgical renewal consigned them to a less prominent position, but they remain splendid things and their day will come again. Liturgical renewal was less kind to another embellishment of St Mary's, a carved oak pulpit presented in 1941 by Walter McDonald, then curate in Fairview, in memory of his uncle and namesake.[3] The time came when the pulpit had to yield to the ambo, and Walter McDonald's pulpit lay neglected in a storeroom until another use was found for it, liturgical at least after a fashion, as a base for the huge wax candle presented to the college on the occasion of the visit of Pope John Paul II in October 1979; where, as well as serving a purpose liturgical only after a fashion it is also ignominiously upside-down. The new benches, acquired a few years later through the generosity of Canon O'Keeffe, PP, Dunamaggan, Co. Kilkenny, have ridden the tide of liturgical change rather better, and still serve their purpose in the oratory (Plate 73).[4]

Certain amenities came the way of the teaching staff. Their dining-room was awkwardly placed in relation to the main kitchen, where all the cooking was done, the food being brought to the table through an underground passage, dark and hard to maintain. In 1925 the area was reconstructed, by the building of folding doors between the dining-room and the adjacent parlour and the construction of a substantial pantry beside the dining-room, where much of the cooking could be done. (This has had an extensive refurbishing recently, in 1989.) In 1932 an internal telephone system was installed, prompted no doubt by two sudden and unexpected deaths, that of Malachy Eaton in November 1929 and of Garrett Pierse in March 1932. It was, however, to be many years before this domestic system was linked to the public telephone. In 1936 baths were installed for the exclusive use of the teaching staff, four of them in St Patrick's, or more precisely three, for in 1923 Beecher and Bewerunge had raised the matter with the Finance Council, and had been allowed to fit out a bathroom, but at their own expense.

There were minor modifications in odd corners, such as the building put beside the swimming-pool in 1928 on the proposal of the bursar, to serve as a tradesmen's workshop with a linen-room above. The workshop is now the bookshop, the tradesmen having migrated to refurbished buildings in the old farmyard, while the linen-room has passed from one use to another, mainly academic, in recent years. The two most obvious changes, however, were the improvements in the grounds and the building of the new Theology class halls.

The old class halls had never been satisfactory. 'They are constructed in the Gothic style', Dr Patrick Murray had told the Royal Commission in 1853, 'but, I doubt not, the Goths would have been greatly pleased with them.' Eighty years later they were as dark and cramped as ever, and inevitably even dingier. New class halls were made possible by a bequest from Michael Loftus. He had been born in Dublin in 1845, became a civil servant and transferred to England during his career. On retirement he settled at Bournemouth, where he died on 6 February 1929. He had no apparent connection with Maynooth, but by his will, made in 1923, he left his whole estate, except his books and furniture, to the college, with the sole condition that the income for the first three years be devoted to improving the library and having it professionally catalogued. The legacy came to just over £20,000, in bank deposits and investments. These details, biographical and financial, were put to the Trustees by the President, James MacCaffrey, in his annual report in June 1929. He went on to say that the library badly needed professional cataloguing. It was, however, so overcrowded that it would be very difficult to catalogue unless some elbow-room were provided. Underneath it were the Theology class halls, which, he said, 'must have been designed by the architect as store-rooms'. He proposed that they be incorporated into the library and that new class halls be built. He appreciated the danger of their 'being unnecessarily expensive or an eyesore', situated as they must be beside the Pugin buildings, and he submitted two alternative plans drawn up by the architects, Ashlin and Coleman.

As has been seen, the financial situation was easy, and the Trustees accepted the more expensive plan. They further decided that the Loftus bequest be added to the college capital, in the belief that the halls to be erected in his memory could be largely financed out of the annual surplus, as in fact they were. They added a block to contain lavatories and a gymnasium. Pugin's 'privies', even as refurbished at the beginning of the century, certainly needed replacement; and MacCaffrey was anxious for dry-weather accommodation for the gymnastics he had introduced. The only thing to do in regard to this block is to express the hope that all those responsible for it have been forgiven, for indeed it is hard to forgive, unadorned and aggressive concrete closing off so much of the finest façade Pugin left the college, indeed one of the finest he did anywhere. As a final irony, the proposed gymnasium turned out to be so poorly ventilated as to be unusable; the long-mooted Museum was just now looking for a home and gratefully moved in. Building work had begun in 1930, and the class halls came into use in October 1932. This building is not in the disaster category of the other block, but not even its friends would call it distinguished. The overall cost, £27,000, was substantially met from the reserve fund, supplemented by the annual surpluses in current accounts. It was not exactly cheap—as has been seen, the Trustees accepted the more expensive of the two plans before them—but it looks an uneasy compromise, though between what and what is not altogether easy to say (Plate 64).

The embellishment of the grounds was the work of MacCaffrey's successor, John F. D'Alton, appointed President in June 1936, and of the gardener he engaged, James Murray, remembered for the amount of work he could get through while always ready for a chat he seemed in no hurry to bring to an end. St Joseph's Square is naturally an attractive place, but now it was further embellished by flowering shrubs, roses and bedding-plants. Where the greatest changes were made was, however, the Junior House. This had always been cramped, in contrast with Senior House, where there was great spaciousness when the 'middle field' had been finally granted to the students in 1938, in exchange for the 'high field' recreation ground of St Joseph's in the days of a strict rule of division. The attempt to divide Junior House had been short-lived, but its grounds remained very cramped. The new President set out to provide a reasonable playing pitch by removing the ball-alley built in the middle of Rhetoric field precisely to stop the playing of team-games there. This still left a very narrow pitch, so he turned to the great trees that lined the 'Dark Walk' beside the boundary wall, replacing them by macrocarpa and flowering shrubs, which have not lasted well. He coated with tarmacadam the walks in Junior House, and laid down two hard tennis-courts, the first such amentities, though they had to be removed in 1993 after some years of disuse. His proudest achievement was, however, the renewal of 'Tony's Garden', a name the students of the time believed immemorial, but which derived from so recent a figure as Father Tony Boyle CM, spiritual director from 1905 to 1926. It was in fact the walled garden clearly depicted in the 1809 map of the Riverstown property (Plate 2), probably the vegetable garden of Dean and Martha Craddock. Now it got new splendours, herbaceous borders and a rock garden. It has managed to retain some of them into more financially constricted times.

Routines and Idealisms

James MacCaffrey, appointed President in June 1918, died in office on 1 November 1935. In his earlier years there were tensions with both staff and students, but by the mid-1920s his annual reports to the Trustees depict a student body where there appears to be little disorder, no unwillingness, and no complaint. It is only occasionally that a student is brought before the Administrative Council, the offence being usually the possession of newspapers, magazines or novels. The lifting of the ban on smoking had removed a great source of tension, but new issues kept raising themselves—on 27 March 1939 the council reprimanded a student for 'possession of a wireless set and some newspapers'. Yet 'the modern world' kept making its way in—as far back as 1921 there had been permission for a 'cinema lamp' with a generator to power it, and in 1936 the college advanced a loan for 'sound picture apparatus', to be paid back by a student levy of half-a-crown a year. In November 1942 Edward J. Kissane, appointed President the previous June, sanctioned the standard Catholic weeklies, together with the *Times Literary Supplement*.

James MacCaffrey was a disciplinarian. It seems symptomatic that in 1925 he should have asked the Trustees for authority 'to secure the services of a competent drill master'—he often complained of the slouching carriage of too many students, though a brilliant student cartoonist, James Cassin of the diocese of Ossory, ordained in 1921, recorded his verdict that any uprightness and polish imparted by the end of the course might be expected to deteriorate quite distressingly after as little as twelve months free of institutional constraint (Plate 55). He would like to keep the staff drilled as well as the students—at the end of October 1927 the Administrative Council noted that there was good reason to believe that a few members of the staff had again introduced card-playing, which the Visitors had strongly censured some years before. It was decided that the President take steps to put an end to it, and that if they were ineffective the matter should go to the Visitors. There can be no doubt who took the initiative at the council, and there is no record of the Visitors having to intervene.

Student members fell during the 1920s, perhaps, it was sometimes surmised, because of better prospects of employment for young Catholics. The college roll never rose greatly above 500, and once, in the year 1928/29, dipped marginally below it. But by the mid-1930s the numbers were rising. In September 1936 a small group who had been students at Salamanca was admitted, on a temporary basis, pending the reopening of their college. A much larger group came from Paris in September 1939, again temporarily, pending reopening. In fact neither college reopened, and from about 1946 the 'Salamanca student' was a regular legal fiction, there being nearly always one or two allowed to continue on this title without a university degree. With this artificial boost the student roll once (1939/40) topped 600, but it settled down at something over 550 on average.

It is not easy for administrative records to penetrate the secret of a community of young men pursuing a vocation through dedication to the daily round. In many ways the ethos of these years was caught in his book *I Remember Maynooth*, published in 1937 by Neil Kevin, student from 1922 to his ordination in 1929, and appointed professor of English in 1932. This is how he summed up the student's day:

> Though we were up at a somewhat unearthly hour of the morning the rule did not allow us to speak until after breakfast—that would be about nine o'clock. The short period of recreation before the first lecture was generally too well filled . . . With a short interval for lunch, it was all class-work and silence until dinner. All through dinner—as during the other meals—a student read to us from a great rostrum, or tub . . . When we were next allowed to speak, after dinner, the day was already far advanced; and if we were going to get seriously into any game during this time of recreation, there was little time for parley . . . the time flew. An hour went by, a little more, and then a bell rang (Plate 65). In five minutes another bell would ring, at which time, the rule prescribed, every student should be in his room, sitting at his desk, studying . . . After study we went to the chapel, then supper followed, and after supper the only other break in the day's silence, when there was a short recreation ending with night-prayer at nine o'clock. When that bell rang for night-prayer the silence that was called 'solemn silence' fell upon the whole college.[5]

Neil Kevin is here describing a long-established horarium, indeed in substance going back to the beginnings. In 1937 the President, John F. D'Alton, introduced considerable modifications which represented real improvements. The day was rearranged to allow for badly needed extra class periods, while at the same time the students' main meal was advanced from 3.45 to 3.00 p.m., with the consequence of advancing the long recreation period, which up to this, from 4.15 to 5.30, had been in the dark, or at least in the gloom, during the winter months. The traditional hour's study before breakfast was replaced by an hour after supper, this leaving 'lights out' fifteen minutes later at 10.15.

For some time, the final year's class had staged a light-hearted 'Old Fourths' Concert' just before Christmas. This year it included a parody of Shakespeare's *Julius Caesar*. D'Alton had taught Classics before becoming President, and Caesar displayed some of his more marked mannerisms. To drive the point home, the final accusation against Caesar, the reason for his death at the hands of an angry Senate, had to do with the later hour of 'the evening services in the temple', in other words, night prayer. The concert was banned for a year or two, but on neither side does there appear to have been much resentment. But if this passed for excitement, things had changed very much from thirty years before—or thirty years after. 'Maynooth College',

Neil Kevin explained, 'never gets into the news. In the newspaper sense of "happens", nothing ever happens there.' He went on to think the unthinkable:

> In order that Maynooth College should force its way into the headlines and come to be universally talked about, a far different state of things would need to prevail there. Something in the nature of a general strike among the students would be necessary, a refusal on their part to leave the lecture halls until certain specified demands of theirs were met, such as the reduction of all lectures by half. During the second week of the stoppage it would be discovered that the 'outlook was serious', that 'there was danger of the strike spreading to all educational establishments in the country'; and daily the college would cut a big figure in the news. The publicity would be assured and intensified by pictures of the college from every angle, if it could be said that a 'feature of the strike was that a large number of senior students had now retired to the roofs of the principal college buildings, and signified their intention of not coming down until a final settlement was reached'. Further, the whole affair could be called a 'sensational' and 'amazing student strike', if it could be added that the strikers were now refusing the food sent up to them by the college authorities, and were whiling away the time playing musical instruments and singing popular songs.[6]

On the contrary, the time showed a great sense of moral earnestness. In his presidential reports of the mid-1920s MacCaffrey gave much of the credit to what he called 'the excellent work of the spiritual fathers and the deans'. In the nature of things, the work of the former is not easily documented, but what the deans were doing may be assessed from their weekly spiritual conferences. From the 1880s the Trustees had demanded to be informed on the subject matter of these conferences,[7] and from there they moved on to prescribing it. In October 1919 the Administrative Council was considering a request from the Trustees for a report on the teaching of Ascetic Theology. The council noted that the deans were trying to co-ordinate their Sunday morning conferences to cover such a course and advised that they should consult with the spiritual directors about possible overlapping, and that the Faculty of Theology should also be consulted. In fact, the giving of a course of lectures as prescribed by the Trustees devolved on the deans. As printed each year in the *Calendar* during the 1920s and 1930s, a two-year cycle for the two classes in Junior House and St Joseph's, a three-year cycle for the three in St Mary's, the course covered broadly the practice of the Christian virtues, with special reference, of course, to the vocation of a priest. It affords an interesting comparison with the academic course in Moral Theology, whose approach was rather from the standpoint of law, the law of God and the law of the Church. During the Roman reform of studies initiated in 1931 by the constitution *Deus Scientiarum Dominus* the Maynooth theology faculty pointed out that 'Ascetical Theology' was taught by the deans, but received a tart reply that this was not enough—there had to be an academic course as well.[8]

The guidelines towards the priesthood were indeed firmly marked out. In 1924 a list of spiritual books to be supplied to all students when they arrived was drawn up, firmly rooted in the developed Counter-Reformation, and certainly far from novelties—the Bible, an English Missal, the *Imitation of Christ*, *The Spiritual Combat* by the Italian Theatine Lorenzo Scupoli (1530–1610), *An Introduction to the Devout Life* by St Francis de Sales (1567–1622), the *Meditations* of Richard Challoner (1691–1781), a life of Christ, *Christ the Son of God* by Henri Constant Fouard (1837–1903) and *Christian Politeness and Counsels for Youth* by the Christian Brothers. The President also noted with satisfaction that each student now had supplied himself with a textbook from the start of the year, which ensured 'that the young priest leaving the college has something more in his library than the four quarters of his Breviary' (hopefully, this must be to some extent an exaggeration, though it is strongly implied it was not altogether so). An Instruction on testing candidates for Orders issued by the Congregation of Sacraments on 26 December 1930 tied further loose ends. An undated and unsigned memorandum, in John F. D'Alton's papers, clearly by one of the deans, summarises how it was put into practice in Maynooth. The Instruction was read to the students every year; each student individually petitioned clerical tonsure and the minor orders, stating specifically that he did this of his own free will; each was carefully assessed by the Administrative Council, taking full account of detailed reports on studies from each professor; each bishop required the parish priest of each student to submit a report on his conduct during holidays, which was then sent to the seminary authorities. There was a fresh scrutiny before admission to major orders, when each individual submitted an autograph statement to the effect that he was putting himself forward absolutely freely and with a clear understanding of the obligations he was taking on.[9] It should come as no surprise that in the worldwide visitation of seminaries ordered by Pope Pius XI the Apostolic Visitor, Monsignor Arthur Ryan, should have had an easy task. He addressed the community in the College Chapel on 22 March 1939 and interviewed the staff and representative students over the following days. There appear to have been few complaints and little to complain about. In any case, the visitation programme had lost its impetus when Pius XI died on 10 February, and his successor had graver problems when the world plunged into war in September.

One possible danger in this closely disciplined regime was a development of a kind of external conformity. That some probably existed must be assumed, but there existed also a predominating moral earnestness, where one might expect a continuation of the idealisms of the more exuberant years earlier in the century. This in fact was the case. Two instances may be singled out: a new missionary movement, and a social concern, this being particularly associated with one of the teaching staff, Dr Peter Coffey.

In February 1920 Joseph Shanahan CSSp, an outstanding missionary in Africa, addressed the students, seeking volunteers for his mission, suggesting that they spend 'the normal period of their temporary mission' working with him (it was now three to five years on average before a young priest could expect an appointment in his native diocese). There was an immediate response, with eleven volunteers during the 1920s, the first two being P. J. Whitney of Ardagh, ordained in 1920, and Thomas Ronayne of Dublin, ordained in 1913. There were problems: the Maynooth volunteers felt they should have some recognition as a group, and Shanahan, the Vicar Apostolic (he had been consecrated bishop in the College Chapel in Maynooth on 6 May 1920), saw serious problems in doing this with a small and changing group. It was finally decided that the best way of carrying on the work was the formation of a new missionary society. Here the guiding role was that of the Maynooth President, James MacCaffrey, who had been a constant friend and adviser to the volunteer missionaries from the beginning.[10] The embryo society was presented with a home, High Park House, Kiltegan, Co. Wicklow, in the diocese of Kildare and Leighlin, and on 10 January 1930 the bishop agreed to a foundation there. Roman canonical erection came on 17 March 1932 as the Society of St Patrick for Foreign Missions. The Maynooth connection remained strong. Indeed the number of temporary volunteers grew—forty-four in the decade of the 1930s, dropping to twenty-one in the 1940s, in large measure because of the war. In addition, ten newly ordained Maynooth priests spent some time teaching at Kiltegan.

A social conscience among the Irish clergy had been aroused by Pope Leo XIII's encyclical *Rerum Novarum* in 1891 and stimulated by the labour troubles twenty years later, the lock-out in the Wexford foundries in August 1911 on the issue of the right to join a union, and the troubles in Dublin two years later that began with the tramwaymen's strike and developed into a general lock-out. The leading social conscience in Maynooth was one of the professors of Philosophy, Dr Peter Coffey, a Meath priest ordained in 1900 and appointed to a chair of Philosophy in 1902. To the students he appeared as a quite formidable academic philosopher (Plate 46), which beyond question he was, both in his lectures and in the weighty works he published as textbooks for his courses, referred to by his students, not always perhaps with the respect they merited, as 'the volumes'—*The Science of Logic* (2 vols., 1912), *Ontology* (1914) and *Epistemology* (2 vols., 1917). But behind this intimidating façade there was an idealist: as he confided to a private notebook about 1900, 'for the last year or more my heart has been in the Gaelic movement, because I see in it a powerful means of preserving the simple faith and saintly piety of our ancestors among the Irish people. I fear I am a dreamer.' It was for the same reason that he turned to the social question. In a pamphlet published by the Catholic Truth Society of Ireland in 1906, *The Church and the Working Classes*, he argued that the remedy for the undeniable fact of poverty was not to be found either in the degrading Poor Law or in private philanthropy. Instead he pinned his hope on the trade unions, their legitimate object being to secure by every fair and lawful means that just and equitable treatment that would lead to social peace. Among these fair and lawful means he was prepared to include a just strike, and he spoke with some approval of 'Christian Socialism'.

This was strong language for the time, but his thought became even more radical. This emerged clearly in a lengthy series of contributions to the *Catholic Bulletin* in 1920.[11] A number of the Maynooth staff had contributed to the *Bulletin*. Peter Coffey was the last to sever the connection, in 1922, partly beyond doubt because of its increasingly unbending attitude on political issues, but also again beyond doubt because he himself was in trouble. The sources for his social thinking appear here: *Rerum Novarum*, of course, Chesterton's 'distributist' ideas as formulated in *What's Wrong with the World* (1910), and Belloc's *The Servile State* (1912), but as well he goes a long way with Connolly's radicalism. At the centre of human dignity, he argued, is the right to own. In the past this had been ensured by the guild system. Disaster struck with the new capitalist landowners in sixteenth-century England. It was their centralised wealth that gave the industrial revolution the 'capitalist' form it took. But while capitalism greatly restricts ownership, socialism denies it. Neither is Pope Leo XIII's concept of 'a living wage' enough. Ownership must be more widely diffused through 'vocational organisation' and 'subsidiarity', and, however regretfully, with the measure of violence that the capitalist resistance will make inevitable, his Meath farming background coming through in that the violence that had accompanied the Land League was clearly in his mind.

This was indeed strong language in a war-torn country and in the immediate aftermath of the Russian Revolution. The trouble came to a head when the ecclesiastical censor refused him permission to publish two pamphlets, *The Financing of Industry* and *The Labour Question*. He tried to appeal to the President under the college statutes, but MacCaffrey told him he did not have any function against the decision of an ecclesiastical censor, but that if he wished he might appeal the case to the Visitors; and he tried to persuade him that it was imprudent at this time (December 1922) for such views to be put forward by a member of the Maynooth staff. Prudence was low among Peter Coffey's priorities, and he appealed to the Visitors, asking if the difficulties could be met if he published anonymously. They turned him down in June 1923, and again twelve months later when he renewed his request.[12] In 1929 he again appealed to the Trustees for permission to publish *The Financing of Industry*. They referred him to the diocesan censor, who again turned him down. Over the next few years he did succeed in publishing a few pamphlets on social problems in Ireland that avoided his radical critique of capitalism: *Between Capitalism and Socialism: Some Landmarks for the Guidance of Irish Catholics* and *The Social Question in Ireland: Some Principles and Projects of Reconstruction* (both published by the *Irish Messenger* in 1930), and *The Christian Family and the Higher Ideal* (Catholic Truth Society of Ireland, 1931).

In October 1929 Dr Michael Forker resigned as professor of Ethics. Peter Coffey was among the applicants for the post, but it was hardly surprising that he did not get it. For the next few years he had brushes with the Visitors over the three pamphlets he finally succeeded in publishing, at one stage appealing to Rome through the recently appointed Nuncio, Archbishop Paschal Robinson.[13] After this the fires may have been banked down, though he remained passionate as an advocate of total abstinence. He died in harness, suddenly, still professor of General Metaphysics, on 7 January 1943. In 1944 the Coffey Memorial Prize in Sociology was set up, the funds coming from the manager and editor of the *Irish Catholic*, and a third person who wished to remain anonymous.

Courses and Studies

For by now Maynooth did have a chair of Sociology. The gestation period had been long. In 1914 the Trustees with the Scholastic Council had agreed to arrange for a course of thirty-five lectures, to be given to students of the third theology year (Peter Coffey and Patrick Boylan, professor of Scripture, drew up the report presented by the Council). Unfortunately no suitable lecturer could be found, and the project fell through. A student request to the Administrative Council in 1919 likewise came to nothing—the council favoured a course of lectures as already approved, but again no lecturer was available; they did not favour the proposal that the students engage in social work outside the college. And the academic staff seem to have had second thoughts when in 1924 the Visitors again raised the question as a result of an initiative by Bishop Cohalan[14] of Cork: both theologians and philosophers claimed that their courses were already too crowded, and suggested that Sociology might better be studied after ordination in a special institute, as they understood to be the case in a number of Continental centres, including the Gregorian University at Rome.

The breakthrough came in 1930, when the Trustees accepted an offer from the Knights of St Columbanus to endow a chair. Pending its establishment, the President was authorised to engage part-time lecturers and build up the nucleus of a library. It took some time to put the endowment together, but this was accomplished by 1937. A committee consisting of Bishops Kinane of Waterford and Browne of Galway, the President, vice-president and the professor of Ethics, Cornelius Lucey, recommended in a report dated 15 December 1937 that the chair be attached to the Faculty of Theology and that a programme be worked out in consultation with the professors of Moral Theology.[15] The previous October Peter McKevitt, an Armagh priest ordained in 1925, had been appointed professor of Catholic Sociology and Catholic Action. The term 'Catholic Action' had been first used by Pius X, but had been developed by Pius XI from the beginning of his pontificate, notably in the encyclical *Ubi Arcano Dei* (1922). It involved for the Pope 'the participa-

315

tion of the laity in the apostolate of the Church's hierarchy', and was to assume great importance because of the rise of Fascism. McKevitt spent some time in Louvain, where he completed his doctorate and studied Dutch Catholicism, then acclaimed as the model of church organisation; and he then went on to Rome to study Catholic Action in Italy. When he began his lectures on his return to Maynooth his courses aroused great interest, both because of their 'practical' nature and the institution of 'study circles', held on Thursday evenings after supper, where a student paper was followed by general discussion. This was indeed something new.

As already noted, the Pontifical University meant in practice the school of Theology, with, in a subsidiary position, the school of Canon Law, because Philosophy, while it continued to grant Pontifical degrees, was in practice much more oriented to degrees in the National University. The undergraduate course leading to a joint BD and BCL degree at the end of the fourth year pursued an uneventful way during the 1920s. In October 1921 the Trustees asked to be supplied with a list of the textbooks every year; from this it may be seen that while Aquinas is among those named for Dogmatic Theology, Moral appears to be taught exclusively from the manuals. Postgraduate theology ('the Dunboyne') had rather more problems. The grind was a long one—two years for the licentiate, with a further year for the doctorate. Over the whole decade of the 1920s only two doctorates were awarded, and only eleven licentiates. Then in 1926 a totally different possibility in postgraduate studies was opened up, the Higher Diploma in Education.[16] In 1927 the Faculty of Theology asked to be empowered to grant the licentiate after one year and the doctorate after one more, and this was agreed by the following year. It was only part of a programme of far-reaching changes, at the centre of which was the office of Prefect of the Dunboyne. There had been reservations about this office almost since it was set up in 1823: it did not seem a good idea that one man should have total responsibility for postgraduate teaching while having no contact with undergraduates, these being taught by the rest of the faculty, who lost contact altogether with those who passed on to postgraduate studies. The office became even more anomalous when degree courses were introduced, in particular a doctorate demanding specialised research, while the prefect could have no function at all in postgraduate courses in Canon Law. Radical change was in practice impossible in the time of Walter McDonald, prefect from 1888 until his death in 1920, while the very length of his term of office made it all the more difficult to succeed him. Michael O'Donnell was appointed Prefect in October 1920, and after him Garrett Pierse in June 1923. By 1927, however, it was clear that change would have to be considered. The Trustees consulted with the faculty. A minority were still opposed to change, but the majority felt that while the title and emoluments of the post should be retained all faculty members should share both undergraduate and postgraduate teaching, and the Trustees accepted this at their June meeting. In October 1929 students were invited to prepare for the advanced degree of Master in Theology, such students to be paid an annual salary and to be regarded in most respects as members of the staff. The first, and as things turned out the only, candidate was Gerard Mitchell of the diocese of Tuam, awarded his DD in June 1931. He had not completed his master's degree when he was appointed to the staff in October 1932. By now the mastership was destined to disappear in consequence of a far-reaching reform of studies promulgated on 24 May 1931 in the Constitution *Deus Scientiarum Dominus*. This also further weakened the office of Prefect of the Dunboyne. Garrett Pierse died on 31 March 1932, and was succeeded by William Moran as senior professor. In October 1939 Moran resigned the prefectship and also the post of librarian, which had been linked to it since 1823. The office of Prefect, he pointed out, was a total sinecure and not mentioned at all in the new faculty statutes. In the circumstances, there was no successor.

The Congregation for Seminaries and Universities followed up *Deus Scientiarum Dominus* with detailed regulations or *Ordinationes*, dated 12 June 1931, and Pontifical institutions throughout the world were ordered to revise their statutes in the light of these and submit them for approval by June 1932. When the Maynooth faculties got down to work in the autumn of 1931 it began to appear that there might be serious problems. However, draft statutes were submitted to a special meeting of the Visitors in Low Week 1932. No minutes of this meeting have been traced, and in any case the Visitors had no power to decide, but only to make recommendations to the Trustees. Neither Trustees nor Visitors met in June, because of the International Eucharistic Congress being held in Dublin in that month. In October the Trustees considered draft statutes for Theology and Philosophy. No statutes had been drafted for Canon Law, because the new Roman regulations raised insuperable difficulties for the procedures hitherto followed at Maynooth. These had permitted a composite BD and BCL after four years' undergraduate study, a licentiate after another year and a doctorate after one more. Now concurrent degrees were not to be allowed. Even though the baccalaureate in Canon Law might be taken after one year's study, the licentiate after one more, and the doctorate after one more again, all courses had to be taken independently of the Theology course, in practice after ordination. It was further laid down that a minimum of five professors was required for a faculty. The Trustees decided to send a special delegation to Rome, led by the Cardinal, accompanied by Archbishop Harty of Cashel and Bishop Codd of Ferns. They were to petition for a continuation of the existing pattern of Canon Law courses, that is, the BCL with the BD, as hitherto, and the licentiate and doctorate after a further one and two years respectively, and for the acceptance of three 'ordinary' professors with two lecturers or 'extraordinary' professors. After some consideration the Congregation granted this second request, for the time being, and expressed the wish that the Faculty of Canon Law should continue at Maynooth. It would not even discuss the question of 'concurrent degrees', finding it totally unacceptable that even four years of Canon Law taught as part of a general course in Theology should count as an academic year for a degree in Canon Law. Though the Trustees in June 1933 ordered the

President to have the names of two 'extraordinary professors' to be appointed at their October meeting, in fact the last degrees in Canon Law, at least for the time being, were conferred in June 1932.[17]

The Congregation gave its general reaction to the draft statutes in a lengthy reply dated 31 August 1933.[18] In general, it felt that university affairs and seminary affairs were not sufficiently distinguished. In particular, it insisted that the only criterion for the promotion of professors should be academic merit, and took serious exception to any suggestion that students otherwise qualified might be excluded from degrees on the grounds of seminary discipline. In this matter too the degree course in Theology must make up its mind: it could opt for a course in parallel with the four-year seminary course but distinct from it, with the baccalaureate after two years, the licentiate after four and the doctorate after five, or for a three-year course after the full seminary course, each degree taking a year. The courses proposed were not sufficiently academic, there were too few 'special subjects' (*disciplinae speciales*), and it simply was not good enough to say that Ascetic Theology was taught by the deans; there were too few lectures in Introduction to Scripture and too many in Moral Theology; while English as the medium of instruction and examination was too heavily favoured over Latin.

As might be expected, Canon Law and Philosophy came in for even severer criticism. In both faculties the number of professors was insufficient, but this was not the sticking-point, for it was agreed that Canon Law might be strengthened by civil lawyers and Philosophy by the natural sciences. In the statutes proposed, however, the Congregation considered that they scarcely appeared as separate faculties—indeed, no statutes had been submitted for Canon Law. The criticism of the Philosophy courses followed predictable lines—insufficient in many ways, too few *disciplinae speciales*, one lecture a week for one year to cover 'the history of philosophy'. The situation was not helped because the Congregation was far from clear on the interlocking of Pontifical and National University courses in Philosophy.

Overall, it was severe criticism, amounting almost to a rejection, as MacCaffrey put it in his President's report in June 1934. In October 1933 it had been considered by the Faculty of Theology, which expressed a preference for the first choice given by the Congregation, that is, an overall five years' degree course parallel to but distinct from the seminary course, but pointed out that this raised issues that must be discussed with the Trustees. In October a joint committee was set up with an unenviable commission that could look like squaring the circle, for even in Theology the number of students dictated that extra staffing be kept to a minimum. Agreement on draft statutes was reached in January 1934, after many meetings. In Theology, it was agreed to propose separate 'university' and 'seminarist' courses in Dogma and Moral, each to be taught cyclically over the three senior years. This would involve two extra staff. The other subjects, including Moral and Dogma in first theology, would have to devise degree supplements without extra staffing. The BD would be granted after the second year and the licentiate after the fourth, while the DD might be awarded after a further year as a 'Dunboyne' student, though it was expected it would more commonly require two. Philosophy would grant the baccalaureate after the second university year, the licentiate after the third, and the doctorate after a year's postgraduate studies. (In June 1934 the Trustees ruled that henceforth the normal BA course should be Philosophy, only a limited number being allowed to take other courses, enough to meet the needs of the diocesan colleges; in practice, however, this ruling seems to have made little if any difference.) As for Canon Law, it now had to be three years totally distinct from the Theology course, and a faculty of five had to be assembled. Approaches to civil lawyers met an unenthusiastic response,[19] and after three years without students the faculty was suspended, to be revived some years later to meet quite unusual demands.

The draft statutes were sent to Rome on 7 March. It was judged best to follow them with a delegation, Bishop Cohalan of Cork, and Boylan and Kissane, the professors of Scripture. They arrived in Rome about Easter and met the Secretary of the Congregation. He did have certain further modifications to suggest, but none that caused problems, and final approval was given on 29 June 1935. The two extra Theology professors were appointed, and the 'university' and 'seminary' courses began in October 1936. It was regarded as particularly helpful for the weaker students, especially in Moral Theology; and while the separate 'university' course inevitably did not quite live up to all the initial hopes, together with the reforms introduced in 1928 it gave a real stimulus to academic theology, the 1930s producing two, three and even four doctorates a year, compared with two over the whole of the 1920s. Most of these doctorates involved two years' 'Dunboyne' study; in June 1940 it was decided that the BD be postponed to the third theology year, with the licentiate two years later, that is, one year after ordination, because the licentiate together with ordination proved an impossible burden at the end of the fourth year, involving revision of the four years' course together with an extended essay, whereas the BD with BCL previously awarded at the end of fourth theology had been examined on one year's course only.

During the years of war between 1939 and 1945 much of the English-speaking world was cut off from Pontifical Institutes empowered to confer a doctorate. In October 1942 the Trustees agreed to accept postgraduate students other than Irish diocesans on the nomination of their own ecclesiastical superiors and with the sponsorship of an Irish bishop. The following year they agreed to revive the Faculty of Canon Law, and Roman approval was sought and given, even though it was hard indeed to muster the necessary teaching staff. Over the next few years there was a considerable influx from dioceses outside Ireland and religious orders and congregations:

Year	Theology		Canon Law	
	Irish diocesan	Other	Irish diocesan	Other
1943/44	4	12	5	10
1944/45	5	10	4	13
1945/46	2	10	4	13
1946/47	5	11	7	11
1947/48	3	3	7	5

Numbers continued to taper off as the schools in Rome and elsewhere again became available, and indeed postgraduate numbers on this scale were unsustainable except as an emergency measure, particularly in Canon Law.

With the approval of the new Pontifical statutes the suggestion was made that they should be incorporated into a revision of the general statutes of the college. Much work was done on this between 1936 and 1938, but it came to nothing, which was possibly just as well.[20] In particular, as the college solicitors pointed out to the President, it seemed inadvisable to conflate general statutes, over which the Trustees had full control, with Pontifical academic statutes, over which their control was limited. In general, it was hard to see any need to change a system that was admittedly working well, except on the assumption that the resolutions passed at meetings of the Trustees needed to be incorporated into the statutes as quickly as possible.

About seventy-five students each year presented themselves for the National University examinations. They continued to do well, as a few sample statistics on honours show (the figures for I University represent the total number of honours achieved, not the number of students achieving honours: many students would have gained an honour in more than one subject).

Year	I University		BA		BSc	
	I Hons.	II Hons.	I Hons.	II Hons.	I Hons.	II Hons.
1920	15	24	3	7	0	0
1921	21	42	10	12	0	2
1922	22	38	6	7	1	0
1932	18	38	13	7	1	1
1933	16	42	5	14	0	0
1934	24	47	7	18	2	5

The degrees were spread over several schools, and, as has been seen, the decision favouring Philosophy taken by the Trustees in 1934 appears to have had little effect in practice. These schools differed from one another in levels of achievement. The BSc courses probably raised most problems, though here as elsewhere the modest demands made by university staffing everywhere at this time must be remembered. The Maynooth science departments had few staff—two in all, offering three subjects, one an experimental one—but they also had few students, principally because in the diocesan colleges science was taught poorly or not at all, and the chief remedy for this situation was for Maynooth to produce more science graduates. In his annual report in June 1929, MacCaffrey said that because of the need for secondary teachers he was 'more or less forcing' what he judged suitable candidates to take a BSc course. But even with their few students the professors had to have assistance: they could get this from Dunboyne students after the course for the Higher Diploma in Education was set up in 1926. In 1934 Dr John Keane of University College, Dublin, was engaged to give a course in Chemistry and a laboratory was fitted out in Logic House. Ironically, the immediate stimulus for this development would appear to have been the need to strengthen the Pontifical Faculty of Philosophy. But Chemistry students were few and even intermittent, and the course ended in 1939.

Modern Languages was another weak spot. There was only one professor, Jean-Louis Rigal, appointed in 1914 in succession to John F. Hogan. Like Hogan, he was a polyglot, being also fluent in German and Spanish, and indeed was nearly trapped in Germany in 1914 because he was lecturing in the University of Breslau. His students, however, were decreasing. As MacCaffrey reported in June 1925, twenty years earlier every student entering Maynooth had a good knowledge of French, 'and a fair proportion of them had a working knowledge of Italian or German'. That had all changed, and now modern European languages had 'almost completely disappeared' from the secondary schools. In the current year in Maynooth only five had taken French in the First University examination out of an unusually large class of ninety-three, and none took German or Italian, though courses in both could have been provided. Things had come to such a pass that a course of two hours a week in elementary French had to be provided for all Junior House students.

The Celtic Studies course had many students, and insufficient staff—one full-time professor with a part-time lecturer in Welsh. Paul Walsh was appointed to this post in 1916, and he continued to give the lectures in Welsh after he was appointed professor of Ecclesiastical History in 1919. When he retired in 1928, the professor, Gerald O'Nolan, lectured in both Irish and Welsh. When he himself retired in 1940 his successor, Donnchadh Ó Floinn, lectured in Modern Irish only, having assistants for Old Irish and Welsh. English, with two full-time staff, offered a course in Language and Literature, given by Patrick MacSweeney and Cornelius Mulcahy, Mulcahy being the last of the old school, appointed in 1896 without, of course, any degree, and retiring in 1932 similarly unadorned. The strong department was, inevitably, Classics, with three full-time staff, the senior being the brilliant and gifted Michael Sheehan, who taught Greek. He was lost too soon, being consecrated coadjutor Archbishop of Sydney on 28 May 1922, an unhappy appointment from which he returned in 1937 in poor health, dividing his time between a nursing home and his beloved Irish College in Ring until his death in 1945. An unsigned tribute, almost certainly by the man who as a young Dunboyne priest had been appointed in 1922 to take his lectures until the end of the year, Christopher O'Neill of Kerry, himself later a celebrated Classics teacher in Killarney, records a remark attributed to the extern examiner, Professor Harrower of Aberdeen: 'You have the best Greek school here in the British Isles. And I don't think there is anything better in Europe.'[21]

The reorganisation of secondary education in the Irish Free State led to the introduction of the Higher Diploma in Education. It was urgent to decide what might be done in Maynooth because so many of the teachers in the diocesan colleges were priests. A special meeting of the Trustees in May 1926 authorised the President to arrange lectures for the coming year, as a circular to the bishops had indicated that there would be enough candidates. Some reservations were expressed, notably that what could be done in Maynooth, then far from secondary schools and the necessary teaching practice, might be markedly inferior to what the other colleges could do. However, Timothy Corcoran SJ, the driving force behind the new diploma, on being asked to examine the Maynooth proposals, replied: 'The whole plan, if I may say so, would be as good as the best we can ever secure in Dublin.'[22] The course opened in October, with six students, being given by William J. Williams of University College, Dublin. He continued to lecture until 1931, when Martin Brenan, a priest of the diocese of Kildare and Leighlin, was appointed professor, with the further responsibility of instructing students of the theology classes in Catechetics, both English and Irish. Catechetics was a long-standing problem, and though truly native speakers of Irish were still declining the demands of the new state were summed up in a resolution of the Trustees in August 1927: that a competent lecturer be appointed, preferably a Dunboyne student, to train selected theology students to preach, catechise, hear confessions and recite public prayers in Irish.

The munificence of Michael Loftus had made possible the cataloguing of the library. This was badly needed, both because of the way the library had grown and because it had never been properly catalogued. It had been built on donations. Book-purchase funds were at first intermittent and at best totally inadequate, but the donations had been substantial. Because it is not easy to trace the gifts of individual donors it may be no more than just to try to list the principal ones.[23] At the head of the list is Edmund Burke, who presented some of his son's books immediately after his death. The nucleus of the library, however, was the gift of Andrew Dunne, who died in the college as librarian in 1823. Then there was 'the magnificent library' of Bartholomew Crotty,

President from 1813 to 1831, who died as bishop of Cloyne in 1846. Laurence Renehan, who died as President in 1857, left a complicated will, but from his library there came his valuable manuscript collection and many of his books, some of which must have been bought at his auction. There followed Nicholas Callan (1864), C. W. Russell (1880), the books of the Catholic University with the magnificent 'Newman bookcases' (1900), Gerald Molloy (1906), Henry Bewerunge (1923), James MacCaffrey (1935), Peter Coffey (1943), E. J. Kissane (1959)—and this list, apart from Burke and the Catholic University, includes only major donors who were members of the college staff.

The library was so understaffed that it was hard to keep it in order, much less to find the time to impose on it the order of a good catalogue. Since the appointment of Nicholas Slevin in 1823 the Prefect of the Dunboyne had also been librarian, and tried to run it with a servant and some student help. This lasted until 1939, when William Moran, in resigning from the prefectship, resigned also as librarian. After that it devolved on a junior staff member, who also carried on with student help until the appointment of Seán Corkery as first full-time librarian in 1951; his support staff, however, was for long no better than that of his predecessors.

By the 1930s the physical space of the library was badly overcrowded, so much so that cataloguing was just not possible until more space could be found (Plate 85). Because of the way it had been built up there was much duplication of standard works, even in identical editions (the University of Louvain was to be a great beneficiary here, as it tried to build up its library from the rubble of war after 1945). The Loftus bequest allowed the cataloguing of the Maynooth library to begin, providing both the money and the extra space that made it physically possible, the former theology class halls on the ground floor, which were fitted out with shelving, even if in a rough and ready way, from 1933 onwards. The cataloguing was done by Dr Tom Wall (1906–85) between 1936 and 1940. His method was to arrange the books according to the subjects in the curriculum, according to the teaching pro- gramme, and those who have had to adjust from it to Dewey will recall its many merits. As well as being a skilful cataloguer, he was a true bibliophile, and he took care to collect the rare books and treasures in a special locked bookcase. The collection of precious things is relatively small, but should be all the more treasured as the fruit of relative poverty.[24] The collection of incunabula may not be large, but it is very representative. There are illuminat- ed Latin manuscripts (Plates 37, 38), a good collection of the 'classical' six- teenth-century printers, and from the seventeenth century much Irish Continental printing. There is a massive array of classical theologians, arranged chronologically, not as much consulted as in the past, for they wrote in what is increasingly an unknown language, Latin. There is a very large pamphlet collection. Its origins are obscure, and it is only now being satisfac- torily catalogued.

There are three major collections of Irish manuscripts, as well as minor collections and single pieces. The first of the major collections is that of Dr Murphy, Bishop of Cork, a great collector, presented by his brothers after his death in 1847. In Renehan's large collection of manuscripts there are about twenty volumes in Irish. Finally there are the O'Curry manuscripts, which came from the Catholic University in 1900. They have all been catalogued. The first volume was begun by Paul Walsh and completed in 1943 by a group of students under the direction of Donnchadh Ó Floinn, with seven more volumes published by Pádraig Ó Fiannachta between 1965 and 1973.

A museum was several times spoken of during the nineteenth century, it being generally agreed that it was the kind of thing a centre of learning should have, though in the later part of the century universities were inclined to think of a museum in terms of geological or biological specimens. Maynooth thinking, in so far as it was focused, naturally tended to be directed to the Irish religious heritage. The closest it had come to focus was in 1903, when the Trustees ordered that a room for a museum be selected and appointed Michael Sheehan curator. That, however, was as far as things got until 1931, when in a paper to the Maynooth Union Canon Patrick Power, professor of Archaeology at University College, Cork, proposed a museum for Maynooth. Hopes were expressed that it might find a home in the new Loftus building, but its location in the rejected gymnasium was the result of good fortune rather than planning. It really got under way when William Moran was appointed curator in October 1934. His appeal for donations[25] brought in a great deal of material, some of it valuable, some valuable if miscellaneous, like the huge gift of T. W. O'Ryan, parish priest of High Street in Dublin. The modest catalogue lists the major acquisitions: the vestments used by Geoffrey Keating, vestments embroidered by Marie-Antoinette and her ladies, the vestments from Salamanca, the magnificent gold vestments presented by the Empress of Austria, chalices and crosses, especially 'penal crosses' of the seventeenth and eighteenth centuries. All these have been very depleted as a result of two robberies. The first was on 19 September 1972. Most of what was taken was by great good fortune recovered, though some of the items were considerably damaged; but in spite of improvements in what had been manifestly insufficient security there was another raid on the night of 28/29 November 1980, and this time nothing was recovered. Some of the smaller pieces may have found a buyer, but there is reason to fear that some others— one thinks of some of the chalices in particular—may have been barbarously melted down, a thought all the more painful because the heritage they represented was so slender. Finally, in one way anomalously, in another way not so anomalously, there is a collection of nineteenth-century scientific instruments, at the centre of which are those made by Nicholas Callan (Plates 22, 23). These were placed in the Museum by his successor as Professor of 'Natural Philosophy', by now become Experimental Physics, who became curator of the Museum in 1943 when William Moran retired.

'The Emergency'

The late 1930s were overshadowed by a war that seemed to grow more inevitable with every week that passed. It finally came in September 1939, and was to last for nearly six increasingly bitter years. It spread first to almost all of Europe, and then to almost all the world. The physical destruction was on an unparalleled scale, ending in August 1945 when, like Prometheus long ago, humanity brought fire from heaven not greatly to its profit, to destroy two Japanese cities and lead to the immediate surrender of Japan, leaving a legacy that has haunted the world ever since. On the other side of the globe, American and Russian troops had met on the Elbe, each army with the ruins of half a continent behind it. Ireland managed to maintain a military neutrality, though it was inevitably affected by the global disaster. Yet there was a curious detachment, summed up in the way the word 'war' was avoided in favour of the euphemism 'emergency', borrowed from the declaration of a national emergency in 1939 and the 'emergency regulations' issued in great numbers by the Government. The time was seen, essentially, as one of shortages and deprivation. The fact that so many found work in labour-hungry Britain was a social safety-valve, and, in a muted kind of way, life went on.

Maynooth was not in good financial shape to face this crisis. As has been seen, money had not been short in the years between the wars, but the 'reserve fund' had been heavily drawn on in the 1930s for many capital projects, including two major ones, the Theology class halls and the new farmyard. In June 1938 the Finance Council reported that the fund was 'almost exhausted', and twelve months later, in the last report of peace-time, it had to announce an overall deficit of £3,663, a deficit that grew quickly as prices rose in spite of Government controls. It was not a good time for a major fire, but that was the misfortune that happened. New House was gutted in the afternoon and early evening of 29 March 1940.

The college *Calendar* for 1940/41 contains an account described as being 'from reports in the Dublin press Saturday March 30th', and there is a vivid description from 'A former student of the college', clearly an eye-witness, in the *Standard* of 17 March 1949. It was the Friday of Easter Week, and at mid-afternoon St Joseph's Square was deserted. Easter Week was holiday-time: most of the staff were away, and those who were not were at dinner. The students were not allowed home, but most of the week was taken up with the annual sports, and they were all out in the recreation grounds. The people closest to the fire were those in the College Chapel, where the Forty Hours Adoration had begun that morning. So, there was no death or injury, nor ever any danger that there might be. Some time about four o'clock it began to be noticed that smoke was drifting round the college. Soon it was all too clear that the source was New House. Fire had already spread the whole length of the roof, and was burning its way down the wooden staircase in the centre of the building. The cause was never established beyond doubt, but was almost certainly defective wiring. The timber roof, a hundred and thirty years old, burnt like tinder. There was fire-fighting equipment in the college, long lengths of hosepipe and a hand-pump, but it had not been maintained and was quite ineffective (Plate 67). The only thing to do was to summon professional help from Dublin, and until this arrived little could be done. There was a possible danger that the fire, driven by a westerly wind, might spread to Long Corridor, and a team of workmen led by the bursar cut a gap in the slated roof over St Joseph's chapel (Plate 67). There was even talk, though not very serious talk, of blowing up the archway in Long Corridor should the fire spread so far, but in fact there was never a real threat it would extend beyond New House. However, St Joseph's chapel and its sacristy were cleared of everything, and in New House for a time students worked through a building blazing above them, throwing anything that they could out the window, necessarily unselectively, ignoring calls from understandably anxious deans below. Even the sacrosanct rule of division collapsed: after watching the excitement in frustration from the corridors of Humanity for a little while, the Junior House students surged across, and helped in salvaging things from Long Corridor, which was never in any real danger. One of the professors living there was asked when he returned if he had lost much in the fire, and was reported to have replied rather acidly: 'Nothing except what the Junior House students saved.'

The professionals took over when a unit of the Dublin Fire Brigade arrived some time after five o'clock. The college water-mains were inadequate, but it was easy to pump water from the large reservoir conveniently close to the back of New House. By now it was clear the fire would not spread to Long Corridor, and New House was brought under control about seven o'clock, though the firefighters remained overnight, being relieved by a new unit shortly after midnight. In the chapel, though it was filled with smoke, the Forty Hours went on, students and villagers slipping in and out all the time. At half-past seven, the usual time, the bell was rung for supper and the deans appealed for 'business as usual'. Naturally, it could not be quite as usual. About seventy students were homeless, in a college that had taken in the Paris students the previous September and was bursting at the seams. For the night they were bedded down in the Aula Maxima, and the next day they were quartered a little more comfortably in various places around the college, the Senior Infirmary, the upper floor of the Loftus class-halls, the ground floor of Dunboyne and various nooks and recesses in the attics of Long Corridor. Then quarters had to be found for the six professors living in New House. For Maynooth of those days it was high excitement indeed. Rumours circulated among the news-starved students that the fire had been an item in the midnight bulletin of the BBC and, rather less credibly, that a German English-language broadcast had boasted that 'HMS Maynooth is blazing in mid-Atlantic', though even this was possible, as it was still the days of the 'phoney war'. Maynooth returned to the routine of lectures on the day prescribed, Monday 1 April. On 9 April the Germans invaded Norway and the war began in earnest.

The interior of New House had been destroyed, but the architect reported that the exterior walls were still serviceable, apart from the parapet and a small portion immediately below it (Plate 68). Rebuilding began soon and it went quickly. New House was roofed again by November, and reoccupied in September 1941, but a number of students and staff had to live in makeshift quarters during the very bitter winter of 1940/41. The initial tender for rebuilding (including concrete floors) came to £15,750, but various modest improvements, including running water (cold water only) added several thousand, and in the end the costs were greater than the insurance money. As well, by now materials were getting scarcer, more expensive, and of poorer quality, especially the electrical fittings, which, though the best that could be got, were to give trouble in the future. Much more immediate trouble arose as a result of the old stone walls being exposed to the weather for some time. This led to a fungus infestation, which cost time and money to clean up. In his report in June 1944 the President reported final success.

The abiding memory of those who were students during 'the emergency' must certainly be that of the cold. There were indeed many suffering from cold in these years, the older among them more vulnerable than the young men who formed the Maynooth student body. But the huge unheated buildings of the college were very cold, and very damp. There was simply no means of heating them. Coal had doubled in price by 1941, and soon it was not to be had at any price. And each wing of Maynooth had its own voracious furnace, built to take only the best coal. The President's report in June 1942, that 'some restrictions on heating may be necessary', proved to be an understatement. Fortunately the bitter winter of 1940/41 was succeeded by average or mild seasons that lasted until 1946/47, the worst of them all, with war-time shortages still persisting. Much of the credit for bringing the large community through must be given to Daniel Hourihane. Appointed assistant bursar in 1938, and bursar six years later when his predecessor John R. Maguire retired, he had responsibility for domestic affairs from his first appointment. The fact that he bought a lorry—the last, he claimed, for sale in Dublin—assured the college of some fuel at least, for anyone who could turn up at the bog with his own lorry stood a better chance of getting a load of turf than if he had to scrounge round Dublin. It also allowed him to buy trees, haul them home, and invite the students to attack them with cross-cut saws, urging that in this way they would warm them twice, though some of them looked so unhandy that others felt he should have been more worried about insurance than he appeared to be. At best, their labours provided the occasional hour's heat from the furnaces. It proved possible to fuel the central powerhouse with turf, though it was expensive, but without it there would have been no electricity. The old plant was nursed through with a kind of loving care by the engineer, Peter Kelly. Food was strictly rationed—tea, sugar, butter, and for a time bread, the quality of which soon became very bad because the flour was milled exclusively from the soft Irish wheat, and no offals were removed from it.

Meat alone appeared plentiful; when young English and Scottish priests came to study they could hardly believe their eyes as they contrasted what they saw in Ireland with their meat-starved homelands. The cooking equipment was old, and had been fuelled by gas generated in the college, generated from coal, and soon there was no coal. Again the bursar had, just in time, bought a large Aga cooker, choosy indeed in the matter of its fuel, but demanding far less than a gas-plant. It saw the institution through 'the emergency'.

Shortage of fuel meant shortage of transport. Not that Maynooth students had ever been very mobile, but there were two occasions when mobility was important, going home to their families on vacation, and having their families to their ordination to the priesthood. From Christmas 1941 onwards they had to go home in batches. There was only one train a day, which normally arrived, but when could be uncertain: for a time there were trains only two days a week. One bus a day was provided on the principal routes, but the demand for places was heavy, and several hours' queuing was needed to be sure of one. Restrictions on transport came suddenly at the beginning of 1941, and soon private motoring was banned altogether. In a hasty decision it was ordered that the ordinations in June 1941 be altogether 'private', with no visitors, because, it was said, there was no transport to bring them. It should not have been matter for surprise that the families turned up, and it was surely matter for regret that they had to wait outside the gate until the ordination was over. Things got much worse, but this mistake was not repeated. In 1943 ordinations to the priesthood were held on Saturday, because there was no public transport at all on Sundays. The traditional ending of the year was partly restored in 1945, with first Mass as well as ordination in the college, and fully in 1946, when the conferring of degrees and prizegiving, held in the autumn for several years, reverted to the Tuesday after ordination Sunday. It looked as if 'the emergency' was over; at least so it seemed at the time.

CHAPTER XIII

STIRRINGS

Budgets and Buildings

One area where the emergency certainly did not come to an end was the financial one. In war-time, prices inevitably rose in spite of strict controls. When these began to be relaxed with the ending of hostilities prices rose even faster, and this time, unlike the 1920s, they did not settle down after slipping back somewhat. By 1948 prices were double what they had been ten years before, three times what they had been in 1914, and they continued to rise. By June 1943 there was a cumulative deficit of £24,306, and three years later this had risen to £40,156. The annual pension was raised from £45 to £70 in October 1945, and to £80 two years later. The President was authorised to make an appeal on behalf of the Trustees 'to the clergy and laity of Ireland and to friends abroad'. It brought in £26,678, but by now (1946–47) the annual operating deficit was £9,262. Two years later it had risen to £12,119, and the cumulative deficit was £39,953, almost exactly what it had been three years earlier, before the President's appeal. More radical remedies were clearly needed.

To make matters worse, problems were arising in various parts of the college buildings. The oldest, Long Corridor, had been sending out signals of tiredness for some time. During a patching operation in the spring of 1944 it became apparent that both roof and walls were, as the President reported to the Trustees in June, 'in a rather serious condition'. This was soon shown to be an understatement, but for the moment nothing could be done except patch. The more the building was examined the more serious its condition was seen to be, and in June 1947 the President reported that total replacement now seemed inevitable. Then the roof of Pugin's great library began to leak in several places. An architect's report was commissioned, and tenders for repairs sought. They seemed frighteningly high to men whose sense of the value of money had been fixed before the war of 1939–45, indeed to some degree before that of 1914–18.

In October 1947 the Trustees set up a committee of four of their number, 'to consider the financial position of the college, especially with regard to possible economies, with power to employ competent professional advice.' For this they turned to the Belfast firm of accountants, Magee and Hillan. Edward J. Hillan spent some time in the college in the beginning of 1948. His report, dated 12 March, was based on a very detailed examination, and showed that no conceivable economies could meet the problem; indeed, though he did not say so explicitly, necessary modernisation would make increasing demands.[1] The picture he painted revealed a situation that, though not unique for the time, except perhaps in the size of the establishment, had certain characteristics of the 'Big House', perhaps even echoes of a medieval monastery. Meat, milk and vegetables still came from the farm and garden. When in 1945 it was decided to supplement what in the conditions then prevailing was necessarily a meagre student diet by providing eggs occasionally for breakfast, this was seen as necessarily establishing a poultry farm (in practice, it almost certainly did). So, there had to be a large number of servants, domestic, groundsmen and farm workers (high tillage quotas were imposed by government regulation as a wartime measure); and while there was much real paternalism there was a measure of what in retrospect would certainly be described as exploitation.

A poster headed 'Instructions to Servants', issued under the name of Andrew Boylan in 1883, just after he had been appointed bursar, illustrates what may truly be called an *ancien régime* (Plate 53). Its severity it all the more notable because Boylan personally was no martinet. The house-servants were known colloquially as 'navs', for a reason never quite satisfactorily explained. Many of them came and went, but quite a number gave a lifetime of loyal service. Some of these might reach a position that made them more feared than the bursar, like Michael McBrine, the long-serving house-steward, who died in 1945. The sterling qualities of others were set in a more gentle mould, and some had achievements of real quality, like John Flood the harper (and also, if tradition be trusted, the master of perceptive comment). He is described on his tombstone in the cemetery as 'for 50 years a devoted college servant' (Plate 54).

Hillan first assessed the income of the college. Its portfolio of trustee stocks had shown a small increase in overall value but an actual decline in income. For the year 1946/47 investment income had been £14,741, but this modest amount was subject to heavy charges. What he bluntly called a direct subsidy to student pensions amounted to £8,696, namely £8,100 a year for 'free places on foundation', and, in the current year, £596 for Dunboyne 'free places and stipends'. To make matters worse the number of students was falling: in 1946/47 it was 487, the lowest figure since 1930/31. Turning to expenditure, he judged that overall it was reasonable. There had, however, been a great increase in wages and commodities, with what he modestly described as 'somewhat greater comforts' to students, such as, though he did not mention it, the poultry farm. Then there were ageing buildings, which he described as cheaply built and every year calling for greater maintenance. In view of what was known of the condition of Long Corridor by this date this was an understatement, as was what he had to say of the main power-plant, now over forty years old, worn and obsolete and therefore costly.

His first recommendation was that

> the investment income is insufficient for any appropriation whatever for the provision of free places . . . I therefore feel obliged to recommend that the free places on the foundation be withdrawn . . . the college requires all its income (plus additional sums) to maintain the pension as low as £80, and so the first use of college moneys should be to keep the pensions at their published level.

He suggested tentatively that the college might have a claim to state assistance, for, as he pointed out very definitely, even the total withdrawal of free places would still leave an operating deficit. He was equally definite in his judgement that the only solution was a public appeal. He clearly favoured an annual collection rather than a single appeal to raise a capital sum, for, as he said with characteristic reticence, money was 'tending to fall'.

His report and recommendations were considered by the Trustees in June and October 1948. With some reluctance from some of them, they accepted that there could be no meaningful economies and that there would have to be a public appeal, to bring in at least enough to liquidate the debt and create a fund for rebuilding. That they had something more in mind would appear from their decision regarding Hillan's recommendation on the free places: it was 'left over for consideration until the result of the general appeal becomes known'. An appeal was to be directed to corporate institutions, and there was to be a general collection on the Sunday after St Patrick's Day 1949. The target was set at £300,000, though some felt this was impossibly high. Archbishop D'Alton of Armagh, chairman of the Trustees, announced the appeal in a radio address on 21 November 1948. The academic staff bent itself to what was an unfamiliar task of publicity, beginning on relatively familiar ground, an address to the priests of Ireland. From there they moved to less explored territory, preparation of publicity papers, writing for the newspapers, acknowledging money received. Acknowledging contributions of necessity devolved on the academic staff, for while the bursar had traditionally had an office staff of two the President up to this had no-one at all. Even the students had to learn a little of the arts of publicity: on 3 February 1949 the provincial press arrived in force, and students had to give their views and have their photographs taken, to impress the people of their own localities, many of whom knew little about Maynooth except, it was sometimes said, that it was in China, through a probably pardonable confusion between the college and its missionary offspring.[2]

Reporting to the Trustees in June 1950, the Finance Council gave the amount collected as £652,663 14s 6d, which must be very close indeed to the final total. Everyone had been generous beyond expectation, but there can be little doubt that the main force behind this great effort was the widespread loyalty of the diocesan priests of Ireland, many of the younger among them products of the MacCaffrey regime, the older ones with memories of Mannix, not many of them, apparently, cherishing much in the way of resentment.

In October 1949, though by now the great success of the appeal was known, the Trustees decided on an approach to the Government for an annual grant. The Taoiseach was John A. Costello, who had taken office as the leader of the inter-party Government in February 1948. He showed himself most sympathetic and got unanimous support from his colleagures. The President of the college then prepared detailed memoranda for Costello and his Minister for Finance, P. J. McGilligan. He claimed that the annual deficit still stood at about £7,000, and that the greater part of the collection would be required for rebuilding and re-equipment. He pointed out that a grant voted annually in the estimates could not be considered an endowment of Maynooth, much less an endowment of religion, and—though he did not rest his case in this—he mentioned the college's role in the training of secondary teachers.[3] The Government agreed to include Maynooth in institutions sharing the university grant, and allotted £15,000 a year, with a promise to raise this to £20,000 if needed. It was raised to this level in 1957, and raised further to £27,500 in 1964.[4]

By 1949, then, it was possible to address the problems of reconstruction and renovation. It was some time before the size of the task became apparent. As early as October 1946 the Trustees asked the President to inquire from the Royal Institute of Architects about the possibility of holding a competition for the rebuilding of Long Corridor, but he had to report that the cost of this would be prohibitive—this, of course, was well before the decision to hold a collection. A more modest beginning was made by commissioning a builder's report on the structure. His report, dated 6 October 1947,[5] came down heavily against what was regarded as the least expensive solution, namely taking off the roof and demolishing the top floor only. Wider horizons seemed to open up in the second half of 1949, when it was clear that the collection would be successful beyond anyone's expectations. In June 1950 the Visitors recommended that there be a completely new front building, and this was accepted by the Trustees. The architects Robinson Keeffe and Devane were asked to prepare plans, the new building to have one chapel, in place of the two in the old Long Corridor, for the thinking was that the college in future would have two divisions only. The plans when submitted called for an imaginative prolongation eastwards of the north and south sides of St Joseph's Square, leaving Stoyte House islanded in the centre. The estimated cost, however, was prohibitive—£538,000.

The plans had been submitted in January 1951. In April a special meeting of the Trustees was held in conjunction with the meeting of the Hierarchy called to consider the Government's 'Mother and Child' proposals. The Trustees had little option but to reject the architect's plan. Instead they asked him to continue his inspection of the building, suggest remedial measures, and prepare a new plan, the overall cost not to exceed £400,000. This figure would suggest they had by now come to realise that renewal of the buildings would require a very sizeable part of the money collected. The architect presented his proposals in June. They contained some alternatives, but the Trustees adopted a scheme for 'repairs to Long Corridor and Stoyte House, building a new storey, necessary repairs to the two oratories'. In due course detailed plans were prepared, and the tender of George P. Walsh, the Dublin firm of builders, was accepted. It was for £271,481 12s 10d, but given the nature of the work it inevitably escalated. It was not just that additions and alterations were made—including two large changes, a lecture theatre and a granite cornice—but that when part of the old walls was taken down it proved necessary to do more demolition than the architect had anticipated, and to take more precautionary measures—including an expensive copper roof—to lean as lightly as possible on what was left of the 1795 building.[6]

The college simply could not give up at one time all the accommodation provided by Long Corridor, so the work was done in three stages, first the southern half with the Junior Chapel, then the northern half with St Joseph's Chapel, and finally Stoyte House. The attic storeys were raised to full height, and the whole building raised to an even three storeys right across its whole length (Plate 70). This provided more and better accommodation, but largely, though not exclusively, because the builders were tied to the old ground plan, not always really good accommodation. The top floor was given over to the students' rooms, much better than those in the decaying old building, immeasurably better than what had been in the attics, but the layout of the building dictated that they be double rooms. The middle floor was for professors' quarters and visitors' rooms. They were strung out along a single corridor noisily and unimaginatively. The professor had two rooms only—in the 1840s Pugin had provided a third room as a book store—and there were communal toilet and bath facilities, a great improvement on what had gone before but soon dated in a country of rising expectations.

The first section came into use in September 1954, though the Junior Chapel was not quite finished. The old chapel had been one-storey—it had, it will be recalled, been originally built as a refectory—and though intimate and prayerful it was undeniably stuffy. Now the centre aisle was raised to two storeys. It had been decided to retain the choir seating and install new benches, but these turned out to be very uncomfortable. Indeed the overall effect was, and continues to be, rather gaunt and cold (Plate 71). In 1963 it got a pipe-organ, built by the firm of John Compton of London. Dissatisfaction with the new Junior Chapel was sufficient to lead to a decision to reproduce St Joseph's exactly, and specifically its fine plasterwork. The chapel was turned round on its axis, the high altar being moved from the west end to the east, but as the building was totally symmetrical this gave rise to no problem in achieving an exact reproduction, and had the advantage that students from both New House and Long Corridor could enter the chapel without having to go out in the rain. Pressings were taken of the plasterwork before the building was demolished, and it was reproduced exactly. Yet a certain patina was lost. The old building, the main College Chapel for a hundred years, had developed into a period piece, difficult to recapture and not completely recaptured (Plate 72). In the work of demolition the grave of Peter Flood, the second President, was discovered in the north aisle, where it is now marked by a plain cross in the floor. The work was completed and the building occupied in September 1956.

Stoyte House remained to be tackled. It had been rather better built than Long Corridor, but now it had to fit into the overall plan, so it was gutted and rebuilt. With recent memories of the troubles encountered in rebuilding New House in the early 1940s, fears had been expressed if what was to be left of Long Corridor's walls could stand exposure to the weather, but in fact it was those of Stoyte that gave trouble. The roofing was almost completed when a fungal infection broke out in the walls, and extensive precautions had to be taken to eradicate it and prevent its recurrence. As with the end blocks, the attic storey was raised and the heavy granite cornice added. It is useless to pretend that the result is anything other than incongruous, and indeed the overall verdict on the rebuilding must at best be lukewarm, a sense of opportunity missed (Plate 70). The old building had many and obvious drawbacks. Even in its youth it had been designed to enclose as much space as possible as cheaply as possible, but exteriorly at least it retained a certain period charm to the end. Its replacement has a functional, slightly aggressive quality, which time has done little to tone down, and it is reasonable to suspect that time will not have great success for quite a while to come. In June 1954, when the southern half had been completed, the Trustees ordered the cutting down of the 'two large drooping trees' in the interior angles, outside the two chapels, Junior and St Joseph's. These were magnificent fully grown weeping beeches. They had softened the lines of the down-at-heel old building, and the softening effect would have been even more welcome with the new one. The corners still look empty.

New House, the north wing of St Joseph's Square, had been rebuilt after the fire in 1940, but the south wing, Dunboyne and Humanity, had to have extensive rebuilding and restoration. When the external plaster was removed it became clear how the building had been done in two parts. The first, Dunboyne House at the western end, built in 1812, stopped two window-bays short of the central block, which, with Humanity, was filled in ten years later to complete the third side of the square.[7] When the stonework was revealed one glance was enough to show that money was much tighter in 1812 than in 1822. The Humanity end was structurally sound, but Dunboyne, as the President reported when the restoration was completed in 1952, was 'apart from some sections of the walls . . . effectively a newly-built house.' A large subsidence in the south wall had to be cut out and rebuilt from the ground up. The massed row of chimneys, so apparent in old photographs (Plate 32), reflecting the fact that before central heating had been installed each

Dunboyne student had a fire in his room, was reduced to those necessary to service the staff living on the top floor. The other end of the wing, though well built and structurally sound, needed 'extensive jobbing work in repairing dilapidations', mainly in the form of the replacement of wormed woodwork and defective plaster. In the end the whole building was refloored, with many joists replaced. It was the kind of work where costs inevitably escalated, as more timber was found defective and hammering the new floor often brought down the ceiling below.[8] But the whole wing was refurbished by 1952. In 1956 the much bigger job of Long Corridor was finished, and four years later all the walks in St Joseph's Square got a new tarmacadam surface. In the College Park only the central walk, known to the students as 'Graf' (short for 'Grafton Street') had enjoyed this comfort. In 1950 all the walks there were surfaced, not very well indeed, for forty years later extensive resurfacing was necessary.

Michael Montague had built Humanity in the 1820s, and had built well. He built Rhetoric, Logic, and the Junior Infirmary in the 1830s, equally well. But, like Humanity, these buildings now required 'extensive jobbing work in repairing dilapidations', repairs to the roofs, to plastering, and to flooring. This was carried out between 1952 and 1955. The oldest building in the college, Riverstown Lodge, required rather more. Reporting to the Trustees in June 1955, the President said that the walls had been found to be sound, but nothing else was. Extensive repairs were completed in the autumn of 1955, with, it was noted, 'some improvement' in the servants' quarters, though this work was cut short by economies ordered by the Trustees as the final bill threatened to overtake the amount collected.

The Pugin building had been better built than Montague could afford, but it was now over a hundred years old and in need of some attention. Half of St Mary's had, of course, been totally reconstructed after the disastrous fire of November 1878, and all in all the building had lasted well. The whole of the exposed west side, however, had to be pointed, and earlier encouraging reports on the condition of the roof proved optimistic and more work had to be done than anticipated, though it turned out to be a stop-gap solution even if it lasted forty years until the building was completely reroofed in 1992. Internally, there was the usual extensive reflooring, and a new door was opened at the east end of St Mary's oratory. The library roof had already been dealt with: after Long Corridor, it had given the second warning of problems on a large scale. Extensive work had to be done on the kitchen roof, and the stonework pointed. New equipment was installed in the summer of 1954, electric now, to replace the obsolete gas cookers, but Pugin's great Gothic hall turned out to need much greater adaptation in the years ahead. St Patrick's was in a somewhat worse state than these other buildings, but again all it demanded was a patching job—repairs to the roof, pointing of the west face, internal refurbishment and reflooring, repair of the leaded lights in the cloisters. The extension of the library stairs to the roof to serve the students' quarters was a real new amenity. Before this the only stairs had wound round and round inside the bell-tower, in practical terms dangerous even for the young men who used it, in architectural terms, to borrow a phrase from a closely related context—Dr Paddy Murray on the theology class halls—something that would no doubt have pleased the Goths, and by the standards of modern fire regulations enough in itself to close the place down. Toilets were built into the bell-tower after the old staircase had been removed, the necessary pointing was done, and it was given a copper roof. It was necessary to renew completely the roof over the refectory, which was an extension of the library roof. Finally, the continuous cloister running round three sides of the square was refloored. The existing stone flooring had been rough granite on the south and west sides, rather more refined flagstones on the east. A wide trench had to be excavated all round to carry the heating mains. The flooring was put back, but it had suffered a good deal of damage. What had been possibly acceptably shabby in an old and shabby setting was now so much worse as to be totally unacceptable, and it was decided to have a complete reflooring. The stone used was fine travertine from near Tivoli in Italy: it was difficult to get an Irish stone in any way comparably suitable, and quite impossible to get one in any way comparable in price.

The Senior Infirmary, built in the early 1860s, required the same kind of attention to roofs and stonework. Inside, it got some long-overdue modernisation of its amenities. The College Chapel too was calling for attention, for it had problems with the roof and walls, and long-standing difficulties with damp in the cloisters and apse-chapels. Three of these were repainted, as were both cloisters, the northern one being also replastered. The southern one has since given constant trouble, and it is clear that here too complete replastering is the only solution. Finally (in so far as the word can be used) in 1958 plans were sought for a new entrance and porter's lodge. The lodge was a crumbling building of indeterminate age, damp and granite-flagged. It had adapted itself only grudgingly to the intrusion of the telephone. The curved entrance railings were rusted and demanded a great deal of maintenance. The entrance gate, planned for Mr Stoyte's house, was narrow, but on the side of the Protestant church there was a wide 'tradesmen's entrance'. The decorative lions and sphinxes were in a bad way. They were of soft stone, Bath or Caen, and over the years had been so split by the winter frosts that extensive repairs were called for every spring: indeed one of the sphinxes was reputed to be mostly the work of the college mason. In June 1958 the Trustees commissioned plans for a new entrance, with 'a wide central gate, a wide service gate, railings and pillars', that is, a reproduction of what was there, apart from the widening of the central gate. The estimates proved expensive, and in October it was decided that there was to be a one-gate entrance, with a stone wall in place of the service gate, 'the lions and sphinxes to be retained'. In the event they were not retained; the stone wall looks heavy and overpowering by contrast with the gate it replaced; and with every day that passes there must be increasing regret that the second gate was not included, as a maelstrom of cars, cyclists and pedestrians struggles with the—admittedly a little widened—single entrance. The porter's lodge also turned out expensive, and earlier ambitious plans were cut back. Gate and lodge were completed by June 1960.

As well as all this, services were renewed right through the college.[9] Heating had been supplied by twenty-three separate hand-stoked furnaces, which functioned only when fuelled with the best coal. Electricity was generated by boilers that were also hand-stoked, powering 70-kilowatt generators installed in 1901, supplying 200-volt direct current in limited quantities even when well stoked, and venting the exhaust steam to the atmosphere. Water was supplied from filter beds by water-wheel to roof tanks, in what an earlier generation had thought to be prodigal quantities, but the distribution points were confined to a few taps and toilets in each corridor, apart from the northern wing of St Mary's and all of New House, where there was cold running water in each room. The water, though filtered, was not of drinking quality. Water for drinking and cooking came from a number of hand pumps. The swimming pool was filled directly from the river, and though the water was changed frequently it had a deep brown colour that would hardly satisfy public health authorities of later years. It received an occasional trickle of heat from the power-house, but the trickle was meagre and the frequent changing of the water prevented heat from building up.

It was decided to centralise all these services in the power-house. Electricity was to be generated by two new alternators, each of 140-kilowatt capacity. It would have to be alternating current, because, among other considerations, it was by now almost impossible to get equipment for direct current supply, as local generating plants in Ireland and elsewhere were replaced by a national grid. That left the problem of what to do after a quarter past ten, when the main load disappeared as each student's light obediently went out. The ESB was for a time reluctant to act as a 'supplementary supplier', but it did agree to come in with a 'transitional' supply while the college renewed its own plant. Somehow this supply-line remained after the plant was renewed. It delivered only a very limited amount of electricity, and when the time came when every student's light was not extinguished obediently at 10.15 p.m. there could be, and too often was, a complete black-out as the overloaded system gave way. All this is very much past history. It is long years since electricity was generated in the power-house except by emergency stand-by machinery, and there have been extensive renovations and expansions of the machinery and boilers for the hot-water systems. The college was connected to the public water supply in 1951, and to public sewerage in 1952. That made easier the ambitious plan to provide a new centrally fuelled heating system, and hot and cold running water in most of the rooms. The heating and plumbing contractors were the firm of Matthew Hall and Son. This was the second-biggest contract after that of George P. Walsh the builders, and again the contract was several times extended while it was being carried out. It was a massive operation, with inevitable misunderstandings—for example, it had been assumed that water for heating and plumbing could be supplied by the waste steam left after the generation of electricity, but this proved to overestimate the power of waste steam and was the beginning of cumulative demands on the boilers that were more than they could meet. But the work was substantially completed by 1955. The most tangible sign of the new world was probably the swimming pool, with an extension containing new shower baths. The pool itself, unheated during the war years, received its first trickle of heat from the old power-house as early as November 1945. Ten years later the heating was more generous, and what was heated was clear and sparkling chlorinated water.

By now it was clear that the great renovation would prove costly indeed. In contrast with what happened when war ended in 1918, prices did not fall after 1945. Instead, there was a continuing inflation with a tendency to accelerate, with a looming threat that it might get out of control, as it nearly did in the 1970s. Prices rose by 33 per cent over the decade of the 1950s, and by 48.5 per cent over the 1960s. By 1955 the Trustees were seriously concerned as the bills continued to mount, and began to order cut-backs. This caused tensions with the bursar, Daniel Hourihane, who as the man on the spot may have felt that it was easier to order cut-backs than to carry them out. A dedicated worker for the college, who had seen it through the grim days of 'the emergency', if he had a fault it may have been a tendency to think beyond his means. He was seriously injured in a road accident in August 1955, and though he recovered sufficiently to take up an appointment in his diocese he did not resume as bursar. One of the deans, James Cosgrove, took over as acting bursar, and was appointed bursar in October 1957. The following June he was asked by the Trustees to submit to their October meeting a 'final and complete report on the whole reconstruction and repair work in the college'. This is contained in a report from the quantity surveyor, undated, but clearly compiled in reply to this request.[10] It said that the original contract with George P. Walsh and Sons, the builders, had been 'very much extended', and now stood at £456,000, later slightly reduced to £444,000. The bill of Matthew Hall and Son for heating and plumbing was £87,325. Smaller contractors, for the power-house, electrical installations and kitchen equipment, brought the overall total to £592.000. This meant that most of the collection (£652,663) had been spent on the fabric of the college. And it was not as if everything was now secure for the foreseeable future. In October 1960 the Trustees had to consider what the architect called matters of 'immediate urgency'. The Finance Council judged some of them false alarms, as indeed they turned out to be, but money had to be spent on reinforcing sagging wooden beams over the professors' and students' refectories, on further pointing of the walls of the senior infirmary, and on an extensive (and expensive) refurbishing of the area of the Mart, in an attempt to provide amenities for servants (curtailed as part of the economies of 1955).

At that same meeting the Trustees decided that the Bishops' Appeal Fund would be closed in twelve months' time. A plaque commemorating benefactors was commissioned. It was in place by June 1961, where it could be admired by visitors during the Patrician Year, proclaimed by the Hierarchy to mark the fifteen hundred years since the death of St Patrick. It is indeed admirable, the graceful Latin phrases of Thomas Finan, recently appointed professor, being matched by the graceful lettering of Michael Biggs (Plate 69). But the Trustees were left with a financial situation that was far from satisfactory, with nearly all the money from the great collection spent and increasing difficulty in matching expenditure to income. As already noted, the government grant was raised to £20,000 a year in 1957, and it was further raised to £27,500 in 1964. In 1957 the Trustees were allowed by the Holy See to retain half the annual collection for the Propagation of the Faith for a period of five years. In 1959 they decided to set up a reserve fund. The principal component was £60,000 from the Bishops' Appeal Fund: from what has been seen it is clear that this must represent more or less what was left in it. Costs mounted inexorably as inflation continued and more elaborate equipment demanded higher expenditure. The request for rates from Kildare County Council was unexpected. The reason given was the need for a revaluation of the premises in consequence of alterations and improvements, though up to this the college had not paid rates at all. This was in September 1953, and led to a claim for an annual payment of £5,000. Though this was later reduced by agreement to £1,500 the Trustees decided to contest it, first with the county council, later by appeal to the courts. First the Circuit Court and then on appeal the High Court rejected various pleas put forward on behalf of the Trustees, and ruled that before 1870 the college was not subject to rates because it was 'a state institution', but that it should have been rated after the passing of the Irish Church Act.[11] At least there was no demand for arrears, but the rates bill was an additional burden on what were becoming scarce resources.

Student Life

It is tempting, in the light of what happened later, to look for signs of change in the 1950s, and in fact they are there. Yet even in countries which had suffered the desolation and destructiveness of war it would appear that the great social upheaval came only when a generation of youth had grown up to whom the war, much less what may have happened before the war, was in no way a personal memory, nor indeed much of any kind of memory, for they lived in a world of such bewildering technological advances that the human past seemed less and less relevant to present human experience. In Ireland, there was stronger continuity with the past, for its people were conservative and for them the shock of war had been blurred into the hardships of 'the emergency'. In addition, the framework of existence in Maynooth was so rigid and so seemingly immemorial that it took a good deal of shaking to move it, and this made the moving all the more unsettling when it came.

Yet there is a unity in the years between the late 1940s and the early 1960s.

An important element in this unity was Edward J. Kissane, President from 1942 until his death in February 1959. He had been a student in the strained years at the beginning of the century, from 1902 to 1910, had taught in St Michael's College, Toronto, and studied in the newly founded Pontifical Biblical Institute in Rome before being appointed to Maynooth in 1917. He developed into an Old Testament scholar of quite formidable capacity and reputation, and was an attractive and lively lecturer who caught and held the attention of his hearers. He was genial by temperament, large-minded, a lover of the arts. He must have been frustrated by the 'emergency' conditions of the 1940s and the attention that had to be given to repair and rebuilding in the 1950s, but he was open to change beyond the average of Irish society, and in so far as change occurred in Maynooth he had a part in it.

Another element worth noting was the appearance of a student magazine, the *Silhouette*, the first number in 1946, with two or three issues a year until 1965. There had been nothing quite like it before. There had been a kind of 'rag mag', if the comparison is thinkable, the *Echo*, that appeared intermittently, circulated surreptitiously, and was a mixture of poking fun and voicing grievances. But the *Silhouette* lasted for twenty years, and had successors when it ended in the mid-1960s. It was also a serious magazine, maybe too serious, or at least too earnest. At the time it was unthinkable that it should appear without the supervision of authority, but this was exercised indirectly, through a professor who accepted responsibility for general guidance, as had long been the case with student societies in general. The full file of the *Silhouette*—if one could be assembled—would certainly repay detailed study, for, with allowance for all necessary and obvious reservations, it does represent a 'grass-roots' voice not available in this form before.

The *Silhouette* revealed photographers and cartoonists among the student body. Among the latter there was one who recalled James Cassin of Ossory in 1921, both for his skill as a draughtsman and for his powers of observation. He was Joseph Dunn, ordained for the diocese of Dublin in 1955. His groups of students are lively depictions of individuals, obviously still themselves in spite of rule and soutane, whether they are sitting outside in the sunshine, chatting over the books brought in for sale by the firm of M. H. Gill on Wednesday afternoons, or making one another up for the play in the 'green room' of the Aula Maxima (Plates 75, 76). Another student group (Plate 76) may need a little more explanation. It carries a caption in the form of a clerihew:

> Only swots
> Collect pots
> Although there have been cases of crocks
> Who were mentioned as prox.

The clerihew needs a little commentary. 'Swots' is fairly universal student slang, and it may not be necessary to explain that 'pots' are prizes. A 'crock' is a person who is frankly not very gifted in any particular area in the whole range of student accomplishments, from theology to hurling. And a 'prox' is a *proxime accessit*, that is, someone who did not make the prize-list but was included in a list of those who nearly did.

Fifteen years before Neil Kevin had depicted a 'crock' who had done a little better, even if not much:

> An annual event in the Aula Maxima was prize day, with all the bishops attending in state for the reading of the list of premiums. Naturally a student would like to appear a greater intellectual force in the eyes of his bishop than he actually was. But it was difficult to find a place in the sun. The same ten or twelve names in the class were read in one subject after another; it was even difficult to force an entry among those who were honoured under the generic title of *proxime accesserunt*. And even to be *proximus*, what did it count towards convincing the bishop of one's powers of mind and habits of study? When all has gone unfavourably for him (and he has begun to wonder according to what criteria professors *do* correct examinations) like a bolt from the blue, a student hears his name called for a prize in Rubrics. In the hope that the bishop may have lost touch with the proceedings, and think that this is a distinction obtained in Moral and Dogmatic Theology, he goes on to the stage carrying his award of books to be greeted by the bishop, and kiss the episcopal ring. But His Lordship has been following closely the printed list. His Lordship: 'Thank you, Mr —, I see you specialise in Rubrics'. Student: 'Yes, My Lord'.[12]

Student numbers were low in the years after 1945, but they rose dramatically in the 1950s, though there were already indications that a higher proportion of entrants did not complete the course to ordination.

Years	Total student body (average)	Entrants (average)	Entrants as percentage of total
1944–51	504	75	14.85
1952–59	544	92	16.91

Indeed, no decade in the history of the college saw the number of entrants so consistently high as in the 1950s. The Junior Infirmary had to be closed as a separate institution in the year 1956/57, the first small dent in the sacrosanct 'rule of division'. It was closed simply because by now there was a chronic shortage of student accommodation in Junior House. But the 'drop-out' rate continued to increase, so much so that the Trustees sought a report in 1964. This stated that between 1948 and 1957 the rate varied between 17 and 24 per cent a year, but with no discernible overall tendency to climb. After this it seldom dropped below 30 per cent and was 37 per cent in 1959 and 1963. Quite exceptionally, a spiritual director was asked to advise the Trustees. He could do little more than state the obvious: there was increased prosperity and better opportunities for all; young people were enjoying a full round of social activities at an earlier age; and in the eyes of their generation the life of a diocesan priest could appear dull and unattractive. By now the signs of change were undeniable. What was not so clear was how to cope with them.[13]

At their autumn meeting in 1952 the Trustees had declared that they would welcome 'extern' students, that is, priests and seminarians not attached to Irish dioceses. As has been seen, there had been a big influx of postgraduate priests during the war years, but their members dwindled quickly as the European centres opened again to the English-speaking world. After the war there was a scattering of refugees from Catholic eastern Europe, Poles and Lithuanians, and a small number of Americans, which never really grew (Plate 79). Among them was an ex-navy chaplain on a 'war veteran' grant, John D. O'Sullivan of Boston. He brought with him a large American car, and no-one in authority seemed quite sure what should—or indeed could—be done about it. Then in May 1960 there was an application from the Premonstratensian Abbot of Kilnacrott, asking for permission to send students from time to time for National University degrees, under the patronage of the Bishop of Kilmore, to prepare themselves to teach in St Norbert's College, which was to open in September. The college did not prosper, but the students continued to come in small numbers, remaining for their theology course, though they are hard to find in the official records, where they are listed among the students of the diocese of Kilmore. A much more far-reaching application was received in November 1963 from the Society of the Divine Word, for the admission of about twenty students a year to the four theology classes in the college. This would involve the building of a separate house of studies, but is also raised domestic problems, such as the adequacy of lecture-hall accommodation. The Faculty of Theology welcomed the prospect, pointing out that in England the Jesuits at Heythrop had already opened their doors, and the Trustees granted the application in June 1966.[14] In fact, the first students had begun to commute the previous year, and land for the house of studies had been bought in December 1964. Building commenced in May 1968, students were able to move in the following January, and work was completely finished two months later (Plate 80).

By this date signs of change were multiplying, but change came slowly for seminary life in Maynooth. A feature of the *Silhouette* was a student chronicle of events headed 'Ourselves'. There are constant signs of the frustration of the chronicler at there being so little to record, though there are memorable gems that make something out of a little: 'They are cutting the grass for the

Bishops', for example. As well, the traditional reticences and silences were still strong: as the diarist noted in the issue for Christmas 1954, 'Not all that we experience in Maynooth can be made articulate. Not all that we articulate can be printed. Over seminary life, so much of which is lived inside ourselves, in prayer and study, all of which is lived inside a rigid daily order within four walls, hangs a heavy curtain of privacy and reticence.' Another diary entry a few years earlier, for 17 February 1949, may reveal something of the 'average man': 'Today a grand free day. Long sleep, eggs for breakfast, glorious weather, two good matches. Simple ingredients—but then, we're pretty simple people.' (Here it may be recalled that it had been necessary to establish a poultry farm to provide the occasional egg for breakfast, and it may be necessary to explain that 'long sleep' meant that this was Thursday, and on Thursday morning the rising bell was at a quarter to seven instead of six o'clock.)

Changes came slowly, but they came. Students took responsibility for keeping the grounds of the senior infirmary and the cemetery. In the autumn of 1955 they began serving at table for one another—'a new departure and a good one', the diarist of the *Silhouette* recorded on 10 October. And for a number of years there was at least one autumn free day to allow the students to help in picking potatoes. There was never a shortage of volunteers, though some took a few days to regain a fully upright position. In the year 1947/48 an indoor recreation room was provided in each of the three divisions, and in these, in January 1957, there appeared the unthinkable: copies of the daily papers, the *Irish Independent* and the *Irish Press*. A reliable tradition records that one of the deans made the announcement at the short after-dinner visit to the Blessed Sacrament, led his division proudly to see the manna provided by a benevolent administration, only to find the room empty, some students having arrived there before him, seen the papers, reached the only possible conclusion—that they had been left there by mistake—and fled with their spoils. More soberly, the diarist in the *Silhouette* thanked the President in person for this new boon in an entry for 19 February. At Easter another taboo went— sweets and chocolate appeared in the college shop, which up to this had nothing more exciting than stationery, textbooks and cigarettes. The ban on sweets and chocolate had been something like the forbidden fruit of Paradise, except that it was theologically somewhat more difficult to see what all the fuss was about. The profits were enough to provide four very welcome hard tennis-courts in the Senior House by the spring of 1960. Just at the same time there is a revealing entry in the minutes of the Administrative Council, to the effect that students were not to take holiday work in England. This implies that some of them had been doing this, and it is reasonable to infer that some continued to do so. Many Irish people had gone to England to work during the war years, and the exodus continued and possibly increased in the 1950s, when western Europe was rebuilding after the war and every economy seemed to be booming except Ireland's.

The year 1964 saw the introduction of a week's vacation outside the college during Easter Week, an indication, among other things, of an increase in the mobility that had first allowed students to go away in summer and then at Christmas. And if increased mobility let the students out it also let outsiders in, as Ireland turned from the immobility of the war years to a society in which greater and greater numbers owned a car. As already suggested, it was the collection in 1949 that aroused a general awareness of Maynooth. In the early 1950s the Administrative Council was very concerned at the increasing numbers of visitors, deciding successively that unaccompanied lay visitors might visit the chapel only; that there should be a notice displayed in the porter's lodge that the college was open to lay visitors only during the vacation; and that they might be admitted to the chapel and museum between two and five o'clock on Sunday afternoons. Even if rigorously enforced, this represented a real change from the previous monastic seclusion, where the only exceptions were visitors for individual students, and it now became necessary to lay down fixed times when these might come, for the earlier practice of admitting them whenever they turned up was becoming too disruptive. At the same time concern was expressed at the growing numbers of priest-visitors who took their cars into the students' recreation grounds, and it was decided to build a gate to discourage them. The gate when built was substantial enough to discourage much more than a car, but it was wide enough to let a car through and so had only limited success in fulfilling its purpose.

When Neil Kevin published *I Remember Maynooth* in 1937 a student who had left before ordination suggested to him that this group represented a notable omission on his pages. So the second edition in 1938 carried an additional chapter entitled 'Ad vota saecularia', the official title for students who did not complete their course. There were many of these, some of them in influential positions. Some naturally preferred to forget what they regarded as a mistake, but there were others who treasured the years spent at Maynooth and the mental and moral formation they had got there. The idea of forming an association began to take shape. Little could be done during the war years, but steps were taken shortly afterwards. The leading spirit was Joseph O'Connor, who had entered Maynooth as a student for the diocese of Kerry, and spent a few years there, as he put it in his autobiography, 'not attuned to its religious tempo and its semi-monastic austerity'.[15] An article by him in the *Capuchin Annual* for 1948 led to the meeting of an organising committee on 26 March 1949, and to the inaugural general meeting of the society of those who had left Maynooth *ad vota saecularia*, held in Maynooth on 29 June. The stated aims of the society, to be called 'Vexilla Regis' in honour of Christ the King, were to help and befriend students leaving the college and to foster a sense of identity among themselves as a group. They had a general meeting once a year, and published an annual journal, *Vexilla Regis*. In time the general upheavals in society put an end to their activities but the idea that inspired them seems worth reviving. They were, it is surely not necessary to add, good friends to the college.

Edward J. Kissane, as has been said, was a lover of the arts. The college over which he presided had never been a great patron, less out of philistinism than out of poverty. The poverty had not turned to riches, but he did manage to do a few things to ornament walls that on the whole were bare except for the dining-rooms of staff and students and the Pugin cloisters, with the 'class-piece', the composite photograph of each class, along one side and portraits of bishops on the other, a few of these having artistic merit, but not many. In 1936 the college had received on loan from a Dublin priest, Francis Sheridan, a fine set of Arundel prints, which were put up in the new Loftus class-halls; when he died in 1963 they were made over to the college by Archbishop McQuaid as residuary legatee. Some of these, notably the great van Eyck Polyptych of the Mystic Lamb, are almost works of art in their own right. What was indubitably such was the Christ Mocked by the Soldiers by Georges Rouault (1871–1958). In his later years Rouault had concentrated on the themes of human sinfulness and the Passion of Christ with a smouldering religious creativity that was too strong for some Irish tastes immediately after the war, but when the painting came to Ireland Kissane took it on loan for Maynooth, where it hung until inevitably the loan was called in. The same happened later to a selection of biblical papyri from the Chester Beatty collection, given on long loan in 1957 for display in the library. From the closed Irish College in Salamanca there came back some paintings of Irish historical interest. One was of Dominic Collins, Jesuit lay brother, one of the seventeen Irish martyrs beatified on 27 September 1991. It is an idealised portrait, not a likeness. What is a likeness, however, is a large portrait of Donal O'Sullivan Beare (1560–1618) who went into exile after the defeat at Kinsale and the surrender of O'Neill and O'Donnell. The portrait, by an unknown artist, depicts him as the very figure of a Spanish nobleman, but when he became a knight of Santiago his title was Count of Bantry and Berehaven. Then there was the collection of Italian paintings and furniture put together in the 1930s by the Cashel priest Thomas O'Connor, who left them to Maynooth when he died as parish priest of Doon in 1952. It is regrettable that the surviving documentation on things like this is scrappy, strangely scrappy for a man who died in office, making all allowance for the fact that he was the kind of man whose scholarly files were probably better kept than his administrative ones.

He was a devotee of music, with a good voice and some skill on the violin. It was with pleasure then that he saw the first College Chapel broadcast High Mass at Easter 1949. These Holy Week and Easter broadcast ceremonies continued: in 1956 the college choir give a broadcast performance of the polyphonic motets arranged for male voices by Bewerunge and thereafter the choir's chief glory. Kissane was always seeking an opportunity to invite artistes to give performances in the college, such as the Bentheim String Quartet in 1953 or Geraldine O'Grady in 1958. A search through the student diary in *Silhouette* would reveal other such occasions. The records here are quite fragmentary. The Radio Éireann Symphony Orchestra gave its first concert in the

Aula Maxima on the evening of Holy Saturday in 1950. This became an annual event, changing to Shrove Tuesday in 1964 when the Easter vacation came in and liturgical change decreed the ending of Lent not at midday but at midnight. In 1966 the college choir accompanied Bernadette Greevy as soloist in the Alto Rhapsody by Brahms, to such good effect that it was invited to take the same part in a repeat performance at a public concert in the Gaiety Theatre on 6 November.

Neil Kevin had died at the age of fifty in August 1953. He did not live to see Maynooth becoming 'news' in a way he had judged impossible not many years earlier. Illustrated articles on the college appeared in the *Irish Tatler and Sketch* in July and August 1959, and a short contribution, illustrated by line-drawings of St Patrick's and the chapel interior, in the *Times Education Supplement* of 1 January 1960. And the most persuasive and invasive of the media was poised for entrance. In 1953 the BBC had begun television transmissions from Belfast, and Dublin and the east coast picked them up gratefully. Irish television broadcasting began on 31 December 1961. In the atmosphere of the time, a programme on Maynooth was inevitable: 'Men for the Harvest' was transmitted on Easter Sunday, 14 April 1963. Indeed interest was not confined to the national station: three years later, on 27 April 1966, Ulster Television and Television Wales and West broadcast a programme, 'Men in Black', in which Maynooth figured prominently.[16] The world had indeed broken in.

Studies

A first impression of theological studies in the 1950s might suggest that it was a fairly uneventful time and that the round of studies as reorganised by *Deus Scientiarum Dominus* went placidly on. A slack period in postgraduate studies followed on the ending of the war-time influx: in the first half of the 1950s doctorates averaged less than one a year. By the end of the decade, however, numbers were back to what they had been in the late 1930s, two or three a year on average. As well, there are indications of topics being chosen for dissertations that reflected the contemporary concerns of the Catholic world, and that were to surface when the Second Vatican Council opened on 11 October 1962. But at the level of undergraduate teaching there was little evidence of change.

It might be argued, indeed, that new ideas tended to emerge outside rather than inside the lecture halls, even though almost all of them came from the Maynooth Faculty of Theology. In January 1951 the *Irish Theological Quarterly* was revived after a lapse of nearly thirty years. In a prefatory note to the first number the editors spoke of the time being 'a period as critical as any for the maintenance of spiritual and supernatural values'. By now the time might well be ripe for an attempt to assess the relevance of the periodical to the developing problems of this 'critical period'. In a general survey such as this, it is hard to do more than call attention to the fact that, whatever the relevance, the college staff would again appear to have played a major role: over the decade of the 1950s they contributed a very respectable 42 per cent of the major articles, most of a sometimes lengthy section entitled 'Notes and Comments', and made a considerable contribution to the book reviews.

Plans were still being formulated for the revival of the *Quarterly* when a new journal appeared, the first number in February 1950. The *Furrow* was the brainchild of J. G. McGarry, appointed professor of Pastoral Theology in 1939. His manifesto in this first number pledged loyalty to 'the mind and spirit of the Church', and specifically to 'the traditions of the Irish Church' when calling for a 'pooling of experience' and 'exchange of views on new pastoral methods' in 'branches of pastoral work to which our times have given a special importance . . . preaching, pastoral organisation, the liturgy, the church, its art and architecture'. There were challenges to be faced, especially with priests, but McGarry was a man of gritty courage, and his venture was, at the time, a quite remarkable call to 'break out of the sacristy'. The 'pastoral' bent of his journal was certainly a factor in tempting some of the college Faculty of Theology to contribute more to the *Furrow* than to the *Quarterly*, conceived as more abstract, more a purveyor of 'theological science', to take up the phrase of Walter McDonald.

The origins of the Maynooth Union Summer School of Theological Studies are indicated in its title. The Union had indeed been the origin of many things: the Catholic Truth Society of Ireland from a paper by Michael O'Riordan in 1899, the Catholic Record Society of Ireland from a paper by James MacCaffrey in 1911, the College Museum from a paper by Patrick Power in 1931. The striking publications by the Cuallacht early in the century would have been impossible without subvention from the Union, though later more ambitious proposals for a publications fund never really got off the ground. The idea of a Theological Summer School originated with the Council of the Union, who asked Bishop Philbin to launch it at the diamond jubilee meeting in 1955. William J. Philbin, appointed professor of Theology in 1939, had been named Bishop of Clonfert in 1953, where he bent his keen mind to an intellectual analysis of Irish problems. His paper to the Union meeting recalled the aspirations of Walter McDonald in 1895: that the Union should have social aims, fostering friendship among its members and their continuing association with the college, which he judged to have been achieved; and intellectual aims, the fostering of serious study among the clergy, where he ventured to be more doubtful. This was now urgent, he said. In contrast with the problems of the past, 'we have to consider the difficulty associated with education and comparative prosperity and freedom . . . the secular alternative to Christianity is being propagated in this country'.[17] His proposal for a theological summer school was taken up, and it was decided to canvass clerical opinion in the country in preparation for a discussion at the meeting in twelve months' time.

This canvass showed that almost all the clergy were in favour of the proposal, but faced with a choice only 21 per cent opted for 'strictly theological topics' against 79 per cent for 'pastoral topics'. Faced with a choice between the branches of Theology, 35 per cent wanted Moral, 22 per cent Liturgy, 22 per cent Dogma and 18 per cent Scripture. The Union meeting of 1950 may give relevant background. The paper, read by Bishop Beck of Brentwood, had called attention to serious lapses among Irish Catholics in Britain. It provoked a heated and heavily defensive discussion. There was, then, agreement that there was a task to be done. The heavy preference for 'pastoral' over 'strictly theological' topics, and of 'moral' and 'liturgy' over 'dogma' and 'scripture', may indicate a belief among the priests that the theory they had got in the lecture hall seriously needed guidelines for its practical application. What does not seem to have been called into question was that this was a problem facing the clergy and them alone.

Irish clerical sociology also found it hard to shake off the same presumption. The class ordained in 1941, the golden jubilee of *Rerum Novarum*, founded the Christus Rex Society with guidance from Peter McKevitt, professor of Sociology, and Cornelius Lucey, professor of Ethics. Little could be done during the war years, but the first of a series of annual conferences was held in Galway in 1946, and the *Christus Rex Quarterly* began publication in 1947, edited by McKevitt and Lucey. The society justly claimed to be a pioneer in the invitation of laymen to lecture to priest-audiences, but despite a growing sense of the need for more lay involvement it remained a society for priests, finding it hard to shake off the conviction that there was a specifically Christian vision for civil society, and that if it were implemented all problems would be solved.

Apart from what had been contributed by the Union there had been in Maynooth little or no money for things usually taken for granted in university circles, things like postgraduate scholarships and travelling expenses to conferences, and libraries and laboratories had always been poorly provided for. The Maynooth Scholastic Trust, set up in 1963, was an attempt to meet needs of this kind. The founding Deed of Trust is dated 30 April 1963, and the first meeting of the committee was held on 3 August. The committee has consisted of lay professionals and representatives of the Trustees and staff. The work of the Trust may be traced in its annual reports. A review of activities in the report for 1991/92 indicated an income and expenditure of about £20,000 a year, not riches indeed, but riches in comparison with the poverty that had been there thirty years before.

By the early 1950s it was clear that the courses for degrees in the National University were facing new kinds of problems. In 1910 Maynooth had student material for an impressive Arts Faculty, and the staff had been strengthened to a level quite adequate for the times. Science students had been few in number—too few, everybody was agreed, but for most people sights were raised no higher than the provision of teachers in the diocesan colleges. The problems faced by science courses in Maynooth in the early 1950s were fairly straightforward: a staff of two permanent professors was insufficient to provide courses for an honours degree, but even more so the laboratory equipment that Maynooth could afford was increasingly inadequate as demands became more sophisticated. The problems with the Arts degree were somewhat less tangible but equally real. Here the problem was not at honours level but at pass. It was not just that the standards required for a basic degree were rising, though this was in some sense true. Neither was it simply that the quality of the student who was expected to just reach pass standard was declining, though this was possibly true even in the early 1950s and was certainly true later. The problem must rather be seen against a general background of a kind of 'professionalising' of the arts degree, as student and faculty numbers grew everywhere and the degree moved further away from being something a gentleman picked up on his way through youth, with even the possibility of an *aegrotavit*, and became something that young people having to make their own way through life could regard as a qualification.

In this new situation Maynooth's basic problem was that it was now simply too small, with its traditional student body not capable of expansion and so unable to afford sufficient staff. The admission of students other than candidates for the diocesan priesthood in Ireland was indeed mooted—in 1952 the Trustees, in response to urgings from the staff, decided that the university facilities of the college should 'be brought to the notice of bishops outside Ireland, and others who may be interested', but the idea was not taken up with any energy, and little came of it. The pass BA course was further bedevilled by the fact that it had to incorporate the philosophy component required of seminarians. This was not good for the humanities, but neither was it good for philosophy. No special postgraduate school of philosophy developed, and though the faculty was responsible for what was probably the most rigorously professional journal Maynooth produced—*Philosophical Studies*, which began publication in 1954—there was little link between what appeared in the journal and what went on in the lecture hall. As the 1950s advanced it became clear that it would be difficult to provide extra staff on any great scale, because so much of the money collected in 1949 was needed to repair the buildings. A lecturer in Modern History was appointed in 1953. This had been an obvious lacuna in Maynooth courses, but it soon became clear that the establishment of another one-man department added to overall problems. The lecturer appointed was Tomás Ó Fiaich, later President and Cardinal Archbishop of Armagh. He was also a distinguished Irish scholar, but the only strengthening in this admittedly understaffed department had to wait until 1959, when Pádraig Ó Fiannachta was appointed lecturer in Welsh.

After the examination results had been published in June 1952 the President drew up a memorandum for the Trustees on 7 July concerning the failure rate in First Arts.[18] There had been 72 candidates. Of these ten had failed, and of the 62 passes only 38 had passed in all their five subjects. Twenty-four had passed 'by compensation', that is, they had passed four subjects with sufficient marks to spare to lift the other subject to pass level. In one subject 43 per cent had failed. He commented that this implied either defective teaching or too high a standard, or, if this was the standard required, serious consideration must be given to the requirement that all take a university degree. The first step in this direction was taken in 1956, possibly prompted by a decision taken two years earlier to admit no further 'Salamanca students' until the position of the college there should be decided by the Holy See. What was decided in 1959 was that all must attempt the degree, but that those who failed might go on to their theological studies. Problems continued with most subjects, and they were most serious in the traditional heartland, Classics. In 1953 it had been necessary to admit students who had no Greek, with the stipulation that they pass an examination in Greek before entering theology. This was not going to be an easy line to hold, especially as the numbers admitted without Greek kept increasing. They were taught Greek by a Dunboyne student and examined by the professor of Greek. The situation had so deteriorated by June 1962 that it was decided that Greek should no longer be required except for degree candidates in theology, whose capacity would be tested by examinations in that faculty. All others were to be examined in elementary Greek, but there was to be no penalty for failure.[19] By this date too there were problems over pass standards in Latin and Irish, which, with three obligatory philosophy subjects, constituted the most favoured course for the pass degree. Latin was being subjected to the same pressures as Greek, though they came more slowly. However, they were coming rapidly enough to have Pope John XXIII's encyclical *Veterum Sapientia*, issued on 22 February 1962, greeted with considerable reservations, because it insisted that not merely a reading knowledge but also a speaking knowledge of Latin was essential in seminary studies, and to those on the ground this seemed curious from a Pope who had summoned a general council because of a perceived need of facing up to modern problems, of what he was to call *aggiornamento*. In Irish studies too enthusiasm seemed to be declining: the student society, Cuallacht Cholm Cille, would appear to have been at a fairly low ebb at the time. The professor, the gifted Donnchadh Ó Floinn, spent himself in trying to reverse this. He had a fine mind with broad humanist interests; he had taught philosophy in All Hallows College for ten years; and he had a deep religious commitment. He fused all these together in his work with An Réalt, the Irish-speaking section of the Legion of Mary. They appear in his pamphlet *The Integral Irish Tradition*, which, he said, was a lecture given to various student societies in 1953–54. He himself summed up his conclusion: 'The thing about the old Irish world it is most needful to revive is its holiness', but in Maynooth as elsewhere in Ireland the sixth decade of the century found it harder than the first decade to live with this as an ideal, though under Donnchadh Ó Floinn's inspiration the fiftieth anniversary of Eoghan O'Growney's death was celebrated in 1949, and the centenary of his birth in 1963 (Plate 81).

The science student had always belonged to a kind of elite, because an honours course in Mathematics was required for entry. But two professors with a part-time assistant, usually a postgraduate from University College, Dublin, were overstretched in their efforts to provide the courses needed. An extra full-time lecturer was appointed in 1954. He had full responsibility for Mathematics, leaving his two colleagues Mathematical Physics and Experimental Physics respectively. The faculty had pressed for an additional appointment, for more equipment for the 'totally inadequate' Physics laboratory, and, in a curious echo of the claims of 'Natural Philosophy' in days gone by, that a general course in experimental science be part of the ordinary course for all students. This course was set up, taught by Michael Casey OP, professor of Chemistry at the Dominican College, Newbridge, and there was what in Maynooth terms was a sizeable grant for equipment for the Physics laboratory. But the aims of Maynooth science could not rise too high. In April 1957, in response to a request from the Trustees concerned about science teaching in the diocesan colleges, the faculty proposed the organisation of a 'teacher's degree' at pass level, within the reach of an intelligent student coming to it with pass Mathematics only. They urged that a full course in Chemistry be restored, as it was the most popular experimental subject in secondary schools.[20] This was done in October 1957, Michael Casey OP being appointed lecturer and three years later professor. The small Chemistry laboratory in Logic House was refurbished, and two years later the adjoining large lecture hall was fitted out as an extension. A government capital grant of £6,000 was sought and given for this work. Chemistry had been brought in at both pass and honours level, but a few years later it had to be accepted that Maynooth did not have the staff or facilities for an honours degree in the experimental sciences, particularly as the other colleges had extended the course to four years.[21] In October 1961 the Trustees agreed that for the present there would be an honours degree in Mathematics and Mathematical Physics only.

It was now approaching a hundred years since the death of Nicholas Callan, master of the experimental sciences in his day. The large lecture theatre in the restored Long Corridor was named the Callan Hall in his honour—over the protests of the philosophers, who pointed out that they were its principal tenants and that the laboratories had been moved to the other side of the building. No doubt the fact that the professor of Experimental Physics had been appointed vice-president a few years before was an element in the decision. The Nicholas Callan Society, formed in 1962, prepared to celebrate the centenary of his death. This was duly done on Union Day 1964, and a suitably inscribed marble plaque unveiled in the Callan Hall (Plate 82).

By the early 1960s the problems associated with courses for degrees of the National University were plain for all to see. The teaching staff, who had to live with these problems, could do little without the approval of the Trustees, but were frustrated by the difficulties in establishing contact with them. However, in October 1961, in response to a memorandum from the President, the Trustees set up a committee from among their own body to investigate and report. The committee consulted widely with the teaching staff, and presented their report twelve months later. Some professors, they said, felt that up to a third of entrants were not really of university standard, pointing out that this was the current failure rate in First Arts at University College, Dublin. By various means the failure rate had been kept low in Maynooth, but a crisis had now been reached. The staff recommended that while all should sit First Arts those who failed might be allowed to go on to two years' philosophy, not taking a degree, and that the number of subjects might be reduced, especially in the BA. The recommendations of the Trustees' committee were somewhat different. It should be possible, they felt, to keep failures at Maynooth decidedly lower than in Dublin, because the students lived a more regulated life. Failures could be lowered further by the introduction of a 'tutorial system'. There should be a supplemental autumn examination, as in the other colleges. The number of subjects should not be reduced. Turning to the provision of courses, they accepted that it was no longer possible to have an honours degree in the experimental sciences, nor a single-subject honours degree in English Language and Literature. They accepted too that the introduction of a Modern History Department with a staff of one had led to problems, in that it was a popular subject at First Arts but could be taken for the BA only at honours level, thereby leaving a number of weaker students with diminished choice of subjects. They proposed that courses in History be provided for the pass degree with the assistance of a part-time lecturer. The state of Greek they regretfully accepted.

Concern was expressed at deficiencies in the library, at the fact that the college was too small to provide an adequate staff, and that the facilities to prepare staff for teaching posts were inadequate. The staff too had expressed considerable frustration at the difficulty in making contact with the Trustees, and this, the Trustees' committee reported, would have to be remedied. Particular frustration had been expressed, the committee said, at the inability of the staff to have the question of the future of the college raised with the Commission on Higher Education, established in September 1960, and it was forced to comment that 'they seemed to be unaware that these matters had already been decided by the Trustees in June 1961.'

In June 1963 the Trustees reached their decisions. Terms, already long by university standards, were to be lengthened further by pinching at holidays and at free days given during term. A supplemental autumn examination was to be introduced and a tutorial system set up. There were to be four subjects instead of five in First Arts, only Logic being compulsory, 'and the philosophy subjects [to] be sufficient for the BA'. The Academic Council was to supply a memorandum on the development of a tutorial system. The idea of a pass BA in philosophy alone without any arts subject proved unacceptable, and the Academic Council was wary of a 'tutorial system', pointing out that what the Trustees had in mind was not 'tutorials' but rather 'grinds' to bring up to pass level people who should not be attempting a university degree at all. Besides, there simply was not the staff to give 'tutorials' on the scale envisaged. The final decision was that the First Arts course was to have five subjects, only Logic being compulsory, and the pass BA to have four subjects at the choice of the candidate, with the obligation, however, of passing a college examination in any of the three philosophy subjects not presented for the degree. It was sensed that it was an uneasy compromise, and that the debate had uncovered more radical questions. What was also becoming clear was the great problems in bringing to a conclusion a debate between the Trustees and the academic bodies, especially in view of the fact that any agreement that might be reached had then to be put through the complex procedures of the National University before it could come into effect. And the signs were that the days of leisurely change were ending.[22]

The insufficiencies of the library were another nagging question. The office of librarian had been a part-time one, and there was one untrained assistant. Help was given generously by the students, but they too were untrained in the skills of library management. The annual purchase grant was quite inadequate, though in the light of resources not ungenerous. These had been very tight in the 1940s, and tightened again in the mid-1950s when it became clear that the necessary building programme would absorb most of the money collected. In October 1951 the first full-time librarian was appointed, Seán Corkery of the diocese of Ardagh. A dedicated bibliophile, he put in long hours at what should have been the work of support staff, for he did not have any. The annual grant was supplemented in one way or another. He organised the sale of duplicates. A donation from Dr Edward O'Brien of Dublin bought books in canon law; one from Canon O'Keeffe of Ossory, donor of the benches in St Mary's oratory, bought a microfilm reader and a document copier. In 1952 a number of valuable antiquarian books of Irish interest were received from the Irish College in Salamanca, together with its valuable archives, these including archives of other Irish colleges in Spain that had closed in the eighteenth century. Regrettably, Maynooth's resources could give them only poor accommodation. In the late 1950s and the 1960s very valuable help came from European embassies in Dublin, especially those of Germany and France. They gave books on various subjects: the Germans were especially generous towards theology. Most valuable of all was the number of periodicals supplied.[23] These were essential for anything claiming to be a research library, and they were very expensive. But taking everything into account the resources of the library remained unequal to its needs. A report of the Library Committee in 1957 spoke of defective cataloguing, much of it the admittedly willing work of students, the 'prohibitive expense' of binding, and of the need to shelve the largest of the rooms on the ground floor.[24] This was done, but symptomatically in very cheap steel shelving. Presses to hold the Salamanca archives were constructed of the same material.

This was the unsatisfactory state of the main library. For the bulk of the students the divisional undergraduate libraries were more important, apart altogether from the fact that there was as yet no artificial lighting in the main library. These divisional libraries, as might be expected, had many deficiencies: they were shabby in appearance, and the new books put into them were few indeed. Modest requests for improvement were made at the beginning of the 1960s, and they were met, though it appeared that while all the students demanded more books some admitted they did not make use of books very much.

So there were admittedly problems. In a report to the Trustees in October 1964 the Academic Council reiterated its view that a number of the students were 'not well fitted for university courses', especially if these had to combine 'a pretty comprehensive course in Scholastic Philosophy' with two other subjects.[25] The changes finally agreed by the Trustees—a five-subject First Arts with only Logic compulsory, and a four-subject pass BA, with a college examination in any philosophy subject not presented—might help to reduce the problems but would not eliminate them. In an addendum the council went on to wider considerations. Maynooth, it claimed, no longer had the resources for university courses in view of the expansion of other colleges, especially since 1945; and increased help should be sought from the Government, to meet the needs of the library and to pay salaries of lay professors should priests not be available. There had been four staff appointments in 1958, and five in 1959, one of them to a new post. A few others followed in the early 1960s. There was, then, a considerable young element, with its promise of renewed vitality. This concentration of fresh resources had happened before in the history of the college, but this was the first time misgivings had been expressed that it might not be sustainable.

In the background lurked the question not just of structures but of spirit behind structures. Pope John XXIII had convoked the Second Vatican Council on 25 January 1959. It had opened with high expectations on 11 October 1962, expectations much strengthened when it closed on 8 December 1965. Yet the Irish National Synod of 1956 did not seem to have lifted its sights much above making new rules and enforcing old and new rules more rigorously. Its decrees took a slow path through church bureaucracy, being approved in 1959 and promulgated in 1960. By then *aggiornamento* was in the air. The college too got new statutes. They were well debated in meetings of the drafting committee between October 1960 and May 1962. There was consultation, though on a very limited scale, and the new statutes still left that communications void between Trustees and staff which was now showing up and which was to be more serious in the years ahead.

CHAPTER XIV

OPENINGS AND UNCERTAINTIES

There are special problems in writing 'contemporary history', for history by its nature demands perspective. When the historian is writing from within the scene he is describing, there is always the danger of an analysis that is parochial and partial. There are some safeguards in painting the picture with broader strokes and in constantly recognising how hesitant judgement has to be. All this is true even if the framework of the present is substantially that of the past, or if there is at least a demonstrable continuity. What makes 'contemporary history' difficult to the point of impossibility at the present time is the marked cultural discontinuity that manifested itself a generation ago. Yet the attempt has to be made, for it would be ludicrous to stop at the seminary of the early 1960s in a 'bicentenary history' of Maynooth.

The Second Vatican Council

It is necessary first to try to put some shape on the new order that came so suddenly and unexpectedly. For the first time in the history of Maynooth College it is necessary to ask radical questions, questions that literally go to the roots of things. Before this, there had been a discernible and agreed framework, that which had been provided by the Council of Trent. True, it was beginning to show the scars of time, beginning to look its age. It had been shaken by the Enlightenment, the French Revolution, and the many issues, intellectual and social, raised by what passes under the general name of 'the scientific revolution'. Then there had been the horrors of the twentieth century, centred on its two hideously destructive wars: but even in 1945, when the dust settled on the world, and especially on what even a moderate pessimist might fear was the ruins of Europe, it began to appear that even amid the ruins the framework was still there. This seemed dramatically true in regard to the papacy: in Rome, Pope Pius XII emerged as a kind of 'saviour of the city' from the red rake of war that had been drawn up in the Italian peninsula, and the Holy Year of 1950 showed how central the papal office was to Catholics all around the world.

Nevertheless, it had for some time been apparent that there were basic questions not being adequately faced, that the Church was in some danger of being engaged in a kind of dialogue with itself, that questions thrown up by developments in science and over a wide field of scholarship were not being satisfactorily answered. The Church reaction in many cases had been defensive and authoritarian, and it seemed to become even more defensive and authoritarian. It could be plausibly maintained that Pius IX in 1864 had closed the Church's door on the world when he declared that the Pope could not come to terms with 'progress, liberalism and recent developments in civil society'. His successor, Leo XIII, attempted to break out of the impasse by calling for an updating of the *philosophia perennis* which had been built into a great Christian system by Aquinas. It would be hard to think of a more solid foundation, and 'neo-Thomism' found some brilliant practitioners and had some real successes. Yet the rapidly developing world always seemed to be just outrunning it: it kept showing signs of being not quite enough. Then catastrophe came on Europe. In 1945 proud nations had to suffer the indignity of being rescued by the Americans, for the second time indeed, while others had to suffer the much greater indignity of not being rescued by the Americans. From 1945 until his death in 1958 Pope Pius XII consciously set out to guide the Church into the new age with the means immediately at his disposal. His successor John XXIII (1958–63) took a different approach. The new Pope recognised that an increasing and increasingly unsustainable burden had been laid on the papacy in the years since the First Vatican Council in 1870, a kind of 'creeping infallibility' that no institution could sustain, not even the mighty institution of the papacy. Angelo Roncalli had been elected Pope as John XXIII on 28 October 1958. The very fact of his age—he was seventy-seven—inevitably suggested a 'Pope of transition', a kind of stop-gap appointment after the long and impressive pontificate of Pius XII. That judgement began to be queried when on 25 January 1959 he made the first and completely unexpected announcement of his plan to convoke a General Council.

True, the signals being sent by the new Pope were not without ambivalences. On the same day as he declared his intention of calling the Council he also convoked a diocesan synod for Rome, and pointed it in the direction of 'ancient forms of affirming doctrine and of wisely ordering ecclesiastical discipline', and the Roman synod was to be followed by an updating of the Code of Canon Law. Yet subsequent papal messages seemed to communicate a different vision: he spoke of renewal, of a new Pentecost, in charismatic exhortations that roused high expectations. The word *aggiornamento* summed up the mood and the Pope. In his opening address to the Council on 11 October 1962 he chided what he called 'the prophets of doom', and opened up a vision of guarding the deposit indeed but also of stepping boldly forward, meeting the pastoral needs of the Church, using 'methods of research and literary forms of modern thought'.

Preparatory work for the Council had begun in 1959 with the setting up of various commissions. There was a considerable measure of control by the offices of the Roman Curia, and the documentation prepared by these commissions was challenged when the Council opened on 11 October 1962. New commissions prepared heavily revised documentation, which was ready for the opening of the second series of sessions on 29 September 1963. By now there was a new Pope, Paul VI, for John had died on 3 June. The new Pope had immediately on his election declared his intention to continue the Council, and reiterated his predecessor's emphasis on its 'pastoral' nature and on the need to begin dialogue with the contemporary world. When it closed on 8 December 1965 there had been only marginal opposition to the decrees proposed and passed. The general mood was of euphoria and optimism, which the world's Catholic bishops shared with others who had been present, observers from other Christian churches, Catholic laity, men and women, and the priest-theologians who had played a very important role. Regrettably, the opportunity to attend was measured out only very grudgingly to the theologians of Maynooth. The Faculty of Theology had been asked for its views as part of the work of the 'antepreparatory commissions', but once the Council opened it appeared that for Maynooth staff the episcopal Trustees were primarily concerned that they should not be absent from lectures. It was a genuine concern, but showed little appreciation of the fact that they might have much to learn from the Council, possibly even a little to contribute.

The Vatican Council of 1870 had been the first to be covered by journalists of the daily press. Now nearly a hundred years later the news media were much more complex and sophisticated, with the addition of radio and television. They took a lively interest in the spectacle of a great religious community in the process of a renewal that appeared to be very far-reaching indeed, symbolised by the order of the opening chapters of the key document, that on the Church. Christians were invited to consider the Church first as mystery, then as 'the people of God', and only then 'the hierarchical structure of the Church with special reference to the episcopate'.

Pope Paul VI dedicated himself to realising the vision of the Council: 'from now on', he said, '*aggiornamento* will signify for us a wisely undertaken quest for a deeper understanding of the spirit of the Council and the faithful application of the norms it has happily and prayerfully provided.' It proved for him a *via dolorosa* in a world gripped by change, a world of rising expectations, even though they might come from Pandora's box. In this kind of world it was inevitable that the decrees of the Council should come to be regarded only as a kind of springboard for further change. It has been well said of church councils in general that they close one debate only to open another. Never was this more true than of the Council that closed on 8 December 1965. For the most part, the continuing debate seems to have come as a surprise. Those going home from the Council had a very pardonable pride in work well done, and could be forgiven a belief that there would be no more change, at least for some time. As things turned out the great debate was only beginning. To an extent it proved bitter and divisive, but in retrospect it must be seen as inevitable in the world of the mid-1960s. It is necessary now to take a look at this world, to try to understand the shape of developments.

A World of the Impermanent

In the 1960s the world exploded, or so it seemed to many. 'Explosion' may be an exaggeration, but at the very least there was the emergence of a sudden discontinuity with what had gone before. When it came it took nearly everyone by surprise. This was true not just of Maynooth, where thirty years before Neil Kevin had seen students on strike as an unimaginable absurdity. Paris was equally surprised when students proclaiming a new dispensation tried to make common cause with the workers at the Renault plant or tore up the paving-stones in the Rue Soufflot and had to be scattered by desperate police charges. These put an end to the rioting, but something new had revealed itself, not a new order perhaps, for it was not clear what if anything had come in place of the old. If analysis could explain it it would have been explained long ago, for there has been a real torrent of books. Many of them are excellent probing indeed: to select just a few in the English language, there is Allan Bloom, *The Closing of the American Mind* (1987); George Steiner, *Real Presences* (1989); and Jaroslav Pelikan, *The Idea of the University : a Re-examination* (1992). The rough and ready path hacked from 'structuralism' to 'postmodernism' in the following few paragraphs obviously leans heavily on them. It will concentrate on two aspects of our discontents: firstly higher education, with special reference to theology; and secondly, the consequences for religion, with special reference to vocation to religious life and the priesthood.

As with so much in today's world, America appears in some sense to be at the centre. In the bilingual preface he wrote to the English translation of *Le soulier de satin*, Paul Claudel spoke of 'dark America'; in his French text it was 'l'Amérique ruisselante': in both languages the imagery was of a giant emerging from the ocean. The year was 1931, and European intellectuals were conscious that America had already rescued Europe once from its follies, conscious too on their uneasy continent that the American Revolution might have worked in a way French Revolution had not. Added to this was the American leadership in applied science and technology. This was to shape the world in ways undreamt of even in 1945, the year of the second American rescue, though the shadows of Hiroshima and Nagasaki lay across the path of Promethean man, who had stolen fire from heaven and found it brought him little comfort. Nevertheless, the great American achievement had its roots in Europe. Even a highly selective list of the Europeans who are at the roots of the world we live in will be a long one—Bacon, Descartes, Locke, the Philosophers, Kant, Nietzsche, Freud, Weber. Of the twentieth-century figures, Freud died in London in 1939. In this he was exceptional, for America was the destination of nearly all the refugees from the uneasy continent.

If there is one thread running through the modern European philosophical inheritance, it is a kind of critical chipping at the human condition. There is nothing constructive or creative about it, such as the criticism of Homer made by Virgil when he wrote the *Aeneid*, or of Virgil by Dante in the *Divina Commedia*. The road from 'structuralism' through 'deconstruction' to 'post-modernism' has been a trail of destruction, and sometimes it is possible to sense a kind of mourning for the house that has been destroyed. The European roots of the movement have been traced to France. Its introduction to the English-speaking world is sometimes pinpointed to a lecture given by Jacques Derrida at Johns Hopkins University in 1966, but this is introducing a precision foreign to a slow and complex process. What is certain is that about this time the world of criticism was speaking a common language. The central assertion was that the only thing writers do is to confide to paper words to which the reader supplies the meaning. In consequence, the 'text' can mean pretty well anything the reader wants it to mean.

One of the keys to this approach is what is known as 'historicism'. It is a chameleon concept, but at its core is the assertion that all thought is consciously related to its own time and cannot transcend it. The only 'history' is the history of the present. In truth there is no past, for the 'text' comes to life only when the reader breathes upon it. So, for example, a refusal to do the hard work at the Bible and the Classics traditionally believed necessary in order to understand Milton does not spring from sloth, pride or stupidity. The key lies in Marxism if the critic is a Marxist, as were a number of Europeans, especially the French. Across the Atlantic Marxism was indeed an un-American activity, but there were substitutes in aspects of the American dream. For the committed Marxist the collapse of Soviet society had to raise probing questions. Was anything left except a kind of ironical detachment— *cogito ergo sum*? If one reader creates one 'text' and another creates another 'text' what human relationship is left? There would seem to be no possibility of attachment to particular things, no possibility of religious commitment, or indeed of any commitment. The buck stops nowhere. Yet these were the people who assumed that as 'intellectuals' they had a kind of right to rule. It is possible that the wave of 'deconstruction' is passing, but it may be leaving a wasteland behind.

Theology could not but be affected by the milieu in which it lived: indeed the Council had encouraged it to try to speak to the world about it in a language the world understood. It was, in fact, not the most promising of worlds for theology, not a good time for 'God-talk'. It was a far cry from the fifth century, when the great patristic figures became the heirs of classical culture, or the thirteenth, when the scholastics made theology the *regina scientiarum* in the universities. For those who believe in God there may be the feeling that at the end of the twentieth century the cutting edge of human encounter with Him may not be in theology so much as in certain branches of science, such as biochemistry or cosmic physics. True, only a small minority of scientists live in these heights of 'natural philosophy', and not all of them are believers. The need to make a living steers most scientists towards applied science, how to make ever more ingenious things.

Theology has been struggling for its place among the 'intellectuals' since the age of Enlightenment thought began. Specifically, it has to face the question of how a faith conceived as 'given' can fit into a system that proclaims its dedication to free inquiry. The answer is difficult and nuanced, and the question has not always been faced with total honesty. In the abstract, the answer is fairly clear: the role of Church authority has been seen as proclaiming that something 'given' in revelation may mean *this* or *this*, but not *that*, while reflection on the choice between *this* and *this* was rather the field of the theologian. Particularly since the first Vatican Council in 1870 there had been a temptation for authority to try to extend its competence by a kind of 'creeping infallibility'. Predictably, the second Vatican Council released the theologian, and perhaps predictably in Germany, where Catholics had worked in close proximity to their Protestant colleagues and had envied them their much greater freedom. Again predictably, the new Catholic university theologian could feel a certain unease in combining the role of theologian and churchman, and in the university scene of the 1960s this could tempt endless discussions with deconstructionist leanings, increasing doubt as to whether religious authority, be it Scripture or Church tradition, could prescribe doctrine or practice for the modern world. Can one be more than a kind of twentieth-century *vicaire savoyard*? In this world it is hard to sustain the sense of there being some authority in the historic experience of the Church. But if this is so is theology any more than the individual's reading of his 'text', the latest theological fashion?

Inevitably, the cry of 'heresy' was to be raised by those who still clung to older theological forms. It was at times raised too easily, but the whole of the new theological process did leave itself open to the charge. As George Steiner so well put it, 'heresy can be defined as eternal re-reading . . . the heretic is the discourser without end.'[1] And indeed it did seem at times as if the discourse was without end. There had been perceptive theologians who had insisted on voicing the great concerns that prepared the way for the Council, and in some cases had suffered in their own lives for their courage, but they were relatively few in number. Now theologians multiplied: theology emerged as a kind of profession. In some respects however it emerged in a cold climate. The world's attention may have been caught by the Council, but there was still great indifference, even derision. As theology grappled with the intellectual framework of the age it was, as already noted, tempted along the deconstructionist path. As well, it was led into the sheer proliferation of the secondary and the parasitic, with even the electronic database struggling to keep the bibliography up to date. One seemed to be living amid the ruins of past systems, with even Scripture providing only a kind of 'pre-text' for the commentary, with nothing grounded in temporality, in cumulative Church experience. To quote Steiner again, 'the genius of the age is that of journalism',[2] what is written for the day.

Speaking of journalism even in his day, John Henry Newman had noted in his Preface to *The Idea of a University*, dated 21 November 1852:

> The authority, which in former times was lodged in universities, now resides in very great measure in that literary world [of journalism], as it is called, to which I have been referring. This is not satisfactory, if, as no one can deny, its teaching is so offhand, so ambitious, so changeable . . . Even when they are known, they can give no better guarantee for the philosophical truth of their principles than their popularity at the moment, and their happy conformity in ethical character to the age which admires them.

Commenting on this almost a century and a half later, Jaroslav Pelikan noted:

> The situation Newman lamented has deteriorated still further, with the result that we would have to paraphrase him to say that 'the authority which in former times was lodged in universities and then was transferred to newspapers as the successors to universities, now resides in very great measure in the non-literary world of television.'[3]

And television, he went on to say, so much more potent than its predecessors, has a tendency to reduce everything to entertainment. One might add confrontation, except that television confrontation may be only a form of entertainment.

With young people indeed it would seem that in rock music television has to face an even more powerful rival for their attention. Here, anyone not young enough to have thrilled to it in the 1960s comments at peril because from a position of incomprehension at this new growth filling what Plato called the 'enthusiastic' part of the soul. Whether the commentator's mind is at home in the lands of classical music or the hauntings of such places as country or traditional folksong, there is a disquiet which will not go away. The enthusiasms tapped by rock are raw indeed—the assault of electronic magnification, the undisguised eroticism. The loud jingle of cash is not drowned out, and as the performers strive to outdo one another they can become very weird indeed. In many respects the 'industry' has all the moral dignity of drug-trafficking. That it was so widely adopted as the first mark of freedom after the collapse of Russian Marxism must give rise to very mixed feelings indeed.

The culture of the book appears to be in real danger. Young people, and indeed some people not so young, are so impressed with the power of the electronic database to gather information that they may ignore the validity of the dictum 'garbage in, garbage out'. It is not easy really to learn to read in a world where rock and television are at best always flickering at the edge of perception. The attention span is shortening. A professor in the University of Southern California, as quoted in the *Los Angeles Times*, remarked that were Lincoln delivering his Gettysburg address today he might have to content himself with: 'Read my lips: no more slavery.' Quality suffers too. In one of his novels, *That Hideous Strength*, C. S. Lewis introduces a character depicted as being in real danger of losing his soul. He had, said Lewis, an 'education neither scientific nor classical—merely "modern". The severities both of abstraction and of high humanist tradition had passed him by.' He had 'neither peasant shrewdness or aristocratic honour to help him'; he was 'a man of straw, a glib examinee in subjects that required no exact knowledge'. But now pop culture is even making its way into the syllabus, to the detriment of 'the great books'. Malone dies, waiting for Godot. Pindar had said that mankind was a creature of a day, the dream of a shadow. But he went on, and like other great classical writers in similar circumstances—Virgil is a striking example—he tended to stop speaking about Zeus or Jupiter and talk of God: 'But when a God-given brightness comes a radiant light rests on humankind and life is gladdened.'

People today grow up in a world of impermanence; the concept of 'a job for life' is disappearing. It is no wonder that the concept of a lifetime commitment gets more difficult, whether it be to marriage, priesthood, or the religious life. The search for wholeness is haunted by the ghost of Rousseau, claiming that man is born free and therefore born whole. Freud confirms this: it is the demands of civilisation that give rise to neuroses. Freedom and wholeness come from rejecting them, 'doing one's own thing'. A few years ago, Allan Bloom wrote:

> I chatted with a taxi-driver in Atlanta who told me he had just gotten out of prison, where he had served time for peddling dope. Happily he had undergone 'therapy'. I asked him what kind. He responded 'All kinds— depth psychology, transactional analysis, but what I liked best was *Gestalt*'. Some of the German ideas did not even require English words to become the language of the people. What an extraordinary thing it is that high-class talk from what was the peak of Western intellectual life, in Germany, has become as natural as chewing gum on American streets. It indeed had its effect on this taxi-driver. He said that he had found his identity and learned to like himself. A generation ago he would have found God and learned to despise himself as a sinner. The problem lay with his sense of self, not with any original sin or devils in him. We have here the peculiarly American way of digesting Continental [i.e., European] despair. It is nihilism with a happy ending.[4]

But the cast of mind is not confined to America. The escape route is, of course, illusory. Academic freedom should be the right to follow reason wherever it leads, whatever the cost. But if there is no real 'text', only a multitude of interpretations, what defence has the individual against the tyranny of the majority? Or, in a century which has seen so many grisly dictators working through tightly organised parties, what defence against the tyranny of the thrusting minority, the 'politically correct'? There is a real urgency in considering the role of centres of higher education in restoring the human house, which is in some danger of being left to us desolate. Surely higher education must maintain the permanent questions at the centre, the great philosophies, the high points of literature. Add to these the heights of science as 'natural philosophy'. Add further the great revelations, with some sense of repentance, even with some sense of trepidation, conscious that religion when tainted by power has proved a source of inhumanity in the world, more so than when it was repressed by tyrannies. But if the world is to be saved it will not be saved by the *vicaire savoyard*, by reducing theology to 'religious studies'. Yet while there are strong arguments that real theology can only live within a church and a credal tradition, the university theologian has to live in a world inclined to accept him only on quite other terms, if at all.

Developments in Irish Higher Education

A Commission on Higher Education was set up by the Government in September 1960 and held its first meeting on 8 November. Its report was presented on 22 March 1967. It had broad terms of reference: 'To inquire into and to make recommendations in relation to university, professional, technological and higher education generally.' Its membership naturally included a number of university academics. No-one from the Maynooth staff was a member, but it did include two former professors who were now bishops: William J. Philbin, appointed Bishop of Clonfert in December 1953 and of Down and Connor in June 1962, and William J. Conway, appointed auxiliary to the Archbishop of Armagh in May 1958. He became Archbishop in September 1963 after the death of Cardinal D'Alton, and resigned from the Commission in February 1964.

The Commission regarded Maynooth as an integral part of the Irish university system, and it was among the institutions invited to make submissions. It visited the college on 10 March 1961, having been supplied by the President with a general memorandum, the request for submissions having been referred to the academic bodies in the college for more detailed consideration. These were presented to the Commission in October.[5]

The Faculty of Theology wrote on the assumption that its Pontifical status lay outside the remit of the Commission and concentrated on trying to secure for religion a more general presence in university education as a whole. It opened with a plea for the traditional humanities and for the continuance of Latin as a compulsory subject for university matriculation. It went on to ask that religious education be part of the course for all university students, arguing that it was an essential element in a necessary general cultural formation, and that this was the pattern in many institutions in the United States and Germany and in Louvain. The lectures in Catholic theology already established in the National University might, it was suggested, be extended and even made mandatory.

The Academic Council, representing the faculties in the 'recognised college', took a more pragmatic approach, using the opportunity to call attention to problems it was already quite conscious of. There was need to widen the scope of teaching in the college and improve its juridical position; it should, it was suggested, apply for the status of a 'constituent college' within the National University. Whatever the outcome, something had to be done to improve the quality of university courses at Maynooth, because courses everywhere were improving. It would be difficult to do this without opening up to a wider student body, though the phrase used, that Maynooth should become 'an open ecclesiastical centre for higher studies', would indicate that at this time the Academic Council was not thinking in terms of admitting lay students. An increase in students, it argued, would allow the increase in staff now demanded by university courses, though admittedly there would be need for more state aid.

The President, Gerard Mitchell, gave oral evidence to the Commission on 23 March 1962. It might not unkindly be described as unambitious and pessimistic. He prefaced his remarks by saying he could only offer a personal view. This might seem a curious statement, but was no more than the truth, underlining the fact that the President of the college had no statutory position on its governing body. He would, he said, be satisfied if the status of the institution was not diminished. It was too small to make a realistic claim to independent or even constituent status, and, as he saw it, the scope for expansion was very limited. It is clear that he had envisaged the possibility of lay students, but he had envisaged it only to dismiss it, saying that the whole constitution of the college would have to be changed to admit them. He added that nearly all the religious orders and congregations had already committed themselves, by building in the vicinity of the constituent colleges. His conclusion was that Maynooth should not seek to better its status; and if the National University were to be dissolved it should seek the relationship of 'recognised college' with the institution that would succeed to University College, Dublin.[6]

The report of the Commission was presented only on 22 March 1967. As widely expected, it recommended that the three constituent colleges of the National University, together with Trinity College, should become independent universities. These universities would be supplemented by a number of 'new colleges', the first of these to be set up in Dublin and Limerick. They were envisaged as having limited faculties, limited fields of study, and teaching to pass degree level only, but the idea was never worked out in detail, and a number of members of the Commission expressed reservations or even outright disapproval.

By the time the Commission issued its report the Maynooth Trustees had in June 1966 announced their intention of developing the college as 'an open centre of higher studies'. No doubt this influenced the final report of the Commission, but the indications are that even before June 1966 it was envisaging an enhanced role for Maynooth—in a number of places this seems quite clear from the actual wording. To begin with, it was accepted that its students should continue to have access to university degrees on the basis of courses conducted in the college. The report went on to express the view that despite the evidence given by the President the extension of its university facilities to religious orders and lay students would at least 'require examination in the future' and, in what seems an obvious insertion, it noted the decision of the Trustees the previous June to develop Maynooth as 'an open centre of higher studies'. This, the report concluded, warranted ambitions higher than the status of 'recognised college', particularly when the potential for theological studies was taken into account. Maynooth might indeed legitimately aspire to the possibility of becoming an independent university, or at least a 'new college'. If it wished to have some arrangement with the institution that was to succeed University College, Dublin, this should not be in terms of a 'recognised college'. The term 'associated college' was suggested.[7]

In a later section the report went on to discuss theology in the university.[8] It noted what it called 'a considerable surge of opinion' that the restrictions imposed on the study of theology by the 1908 Act should be lifted. It chose its words carefully in regard to how theological studies might develop:

We believe that theology is a proper subject of university study and should be allowed to take its proper place in the university system . . . we do not, however, recommend the establishment of departments of theology in every university as a matter of course . . . we are not in a position to recommend the organisational form of theological studies, whether they should be wholly on a denominational basis or whether some branches might not be dealt with on a broader basis . . . our recommendations are made on the basis that the universities would not be denominational, while recognising that St Patrick's College, Maynooth, is a special case.

This amounted to at least a guarded and indirect signal to Maynooth to plan a school of Catholic theology within the state university system; but in the general context it came as no surprise that the Commission had reservations about the proposal that there be a mandatory element of philosophy and theology in all courses: 'We readily agree that the student should be encouraged and enabled to develop an intellectual grasp of his religion. But we hesitate to endorse the proposals for the mandatory inclusion of courses of philosophy and theology in every course.'

It was from their June meeting in 1966 that the Trustees had declared their intention to develop Maynooth College as an open centre of higher studies and to extend its faculties and courses so as to meet the requirements not merely of priests, diocesan and regular, but also of brothers, nuns, and laity; to set up a committee of representatives of Maynooth and other possibly interested parties to examine the feasibility of this proposal and to report at an early date; and to examine thoroughly the possibility of an institute for non-clerical religious. They added that a statement be issued to the press signifying the Trustees' 'general approval . . . in the light of the decrees of the Second Vatican Council and the present-day needs of the Church.'

What precisely brought this matter to a head at this precise time remains uncertain. There are suggestions that some Trustees were hesitant, some possibly very hesitant. But the time seemed ripe. The Council had closed on 8 December 1965. Beyond question, some of the developments had taken some people by surprise, but the real storms lay ahead, and the mood in general was one of enthusiastic optimism for *aggiornamento*. Several meetings of the college staff, chaired by the President, had been held in the first half of 1966. There was widespread agreement that for Maynooth this was 'a moment of historic opportunity'. In its decree on the renewal of the religious life the Council had laid down specifically in regard to non-clerical religious, nuns and brothers, that their formation should continue after the novitiate, particularly their doctrinal formation. The decree on the laity envisaged theological formation for them also. The message from the staff to the Trustees was that a public statement of policy was urgent; that various religious bodies and the Commission on Higher Education should be informed; and that a small working party should be set up to get things into focus. So, there was strong recommendation from the staff, fairly well along the lines of the Trustees' statement. By now too the Trustees would have a good idea of the recommendations for Maynooth being formulated by the Commission on Higher Education; and in fact the college was, even if as yet modestly, expanding its student intake beyond candidates for the diocesan priesthood. The laity, while mentioned, seem to have as yet existed only on the margin of planning, and to have been near the centre of some of the hesitations. Was a large new educational establishment in the neighbourhood of Dublin necessary? If it turned out to be predominantly clerical, was it desirable? If predominantly lay, did it not involve a radical change from the college's traditional purpose? And would it not involve financial problems, as yet far from thought out?

The Advisory Committee set up by the Trustees consisted of the President, two staff members, two provincials of clerical religious orders, both with close connections with Maynooth, one Christian Brother, two religious sisters, and one layman, Dr Patrick Masterson. It held ten meetings at monthly intervals, between July 1966 and June 1967, gathering information and trying to relate it to the developments proposed for Maynooth. The interests of religious education were naturally central, and a number of topics did come into some focus —courses for non-clerical religious, an Institute of Catechetics, and recognition of theological subjects for the BA degree of the National University. Other things proved harder to focus—there was talk of 'formation', of 'integration of sacred and secular learning', of 'theology as a general preparation for a career'. The information coming in was not altogether encouraging on this point, for it appeared that theology would be a minority interest among prospective students, and that in science and arts subjects there was a demand for courses not currently provided. There was much talk of Anthropology.

Neither was the information coming in on prospective students altogether encouraging. By and large, the clerical religious had made their options. They had built their houses of study, most of them in Dublin. They were taking the first steps to centralise their theologates, many of them already looking to the Jesuit house in Milltown Park as a base. At this stage the congregations of religious brothers seemed by far the most promising, especially the Irish Christian Brothers and the De La Salle Brothers. As for the religious sisters, those of pontifical rite with a centralised administration had for the most part already opted for an educational base in Dublin, while those of diocesan rite were so fragmented that common action was not in practice possible.

The Advisory Committee put these points to the Trustees in June 1967. Getting off the ground, they said, would involve much work, planning, and, above all, decision. It was necessary to prepare and publicise a general plan of development as soon as possible. Maynooth was badly lacking in many material things, from class halls, libraries and laboratories down to more basic social amenities such as a canteen and rest-rooms. The need now was not for advice but for decision, and the Trustees, a large and cumbersome body then meeting twice a year, was not the best placed for quick decisions. Finally, the committee said, it could hardly be possible to begin without hostel accommodation, initially for two hundred male and two hundred female students, and—here surely failing to read the signs of the times—for a hundred and fifty religious sisters.

Meantime, plans were advancing on another front. At their meeting in October 1966 the Trustees decided to petition the Senate of the National University to accept theological subjects for an arts degree at the recognised college, Maynooth, to establish a faculty of theology in the National University, and to accept the Faculty of Theology at St Patrick's College, Maynooth, as a faculty in the National University. A committee of the college staff was to draw up the petition, with an outline of the proposed courses. The text emerged from joint meetings of the Faculty of Theology and the Academic Council. It was agreed that until the teaching staff was strengthened theology could be proposed for a degree only in conjunction with another subject, and draft courses were prepared on this basis. This shortage of staff was an even greater concern to the Arts departments: the scientists, while not immediately involved here, were still more concerned about their staffing levels. Structural difficulties were felt to pose lesser problems, even the consideration that statutory faculties existed only in the constituent colleges, not in the university itself.

In fact when the Maynooth petition came before the Senate of the National University in January 1967 it got a favourable reception, and a committee was set up to examine it, consisting of the presidents and registrars of the constituent colleges, the registrar of the university, and the president of Maynooth. When this committee met on 10 February it had just been announced that a summary of the report of the Commission on Higher Education would shortly appear, so it was to an extent inevitable that the committee, after a general discussion, decided to await publication of the report, which in fact happened on 22 March. Meanwhile the committee of presidents and registrars was finding serious problems in accepting the Maynooth proposal within the structures of the National University. The matter finally came before the July meeting of the Senate. It had before it a report from its committee. This recalled the proceedings in the Senate concerning Maynooth between 1911 and 1914, which made it clear the Senate then accepted that an amendment to the charter was needed to allow recognised teachers to act as full university examiners. The committee recommended that a decision be postponed in view of the far-reaching changes being proposed in university education, and this was agreed.

When the report of the Commission on Higher Education had been published at the end of March there was general expectation that its recommendations had so wide a measure of support that there should be no great difficulty in bringing them about. By July this was by no means as certain. On 18 April, a bare four weeks after the Commission had reported, Donogh O'Malley, the Minister for Education, announced what was to be contentiously discussed as 'the merger', the Government's intention to combine Trinity College and University College, Dublin, in a single institution. This was contentious by its very nature, as well as being a rejection of a major recommendation of the Commission on Higher Education. The minister restated Maynooth's options, including that of independence, and gave general assurances on the place of theology in the university. But the seas were becoming uncharted, and this underlined the fact that Maynooth simply did not have a body able to take quick and flexible decisions.

In April the Standing Committee of the Hierarchy had set up a 'liaison committee' to negotiate with the Government. It consisted of their chairman, Cardinal Conway, their secretary, Bishop Fergus of Achonry, and Bishop Lucey of Cork. In June the Trustees instructed the committee 'to see the Minister as soon as possible to initiate discussions on the place of Maynooth in the new university system', and issued a statement to the press expressing the hope that 'within the new university system there will be recognition of the full university status of Maynooth, and that its peculiar strength as a world-renowned centre of Catholic theological studies will be fully utilised.' Under pressure from a teaching staff frustrated at being left so much in the dark they also agreed in principle to an 'advisory board' consisting of representatives of the Trustees and of the staff, but nothing came of this. Instead, three staff members were nominated in November 'to explore various possibilities' with the Minister 'with a view to a scheme whereby Maynooth would be associated

St Patrick's, Chapel and Spire

Loftus Theology class halls 1932

Plate 64

'I Remember Maynooth': obedient to the bell

Plate 65

'I remember Maynooth': Corpus Christi procession

Plate 66

New House fire 1940: a threat to Long Corridor?

Philosophers analysing fire-fighting equipment

Plate 67

New House after the fire: Patsy Malone, Paul Weafer RIP and Joe Gillen RIP

Plate 68

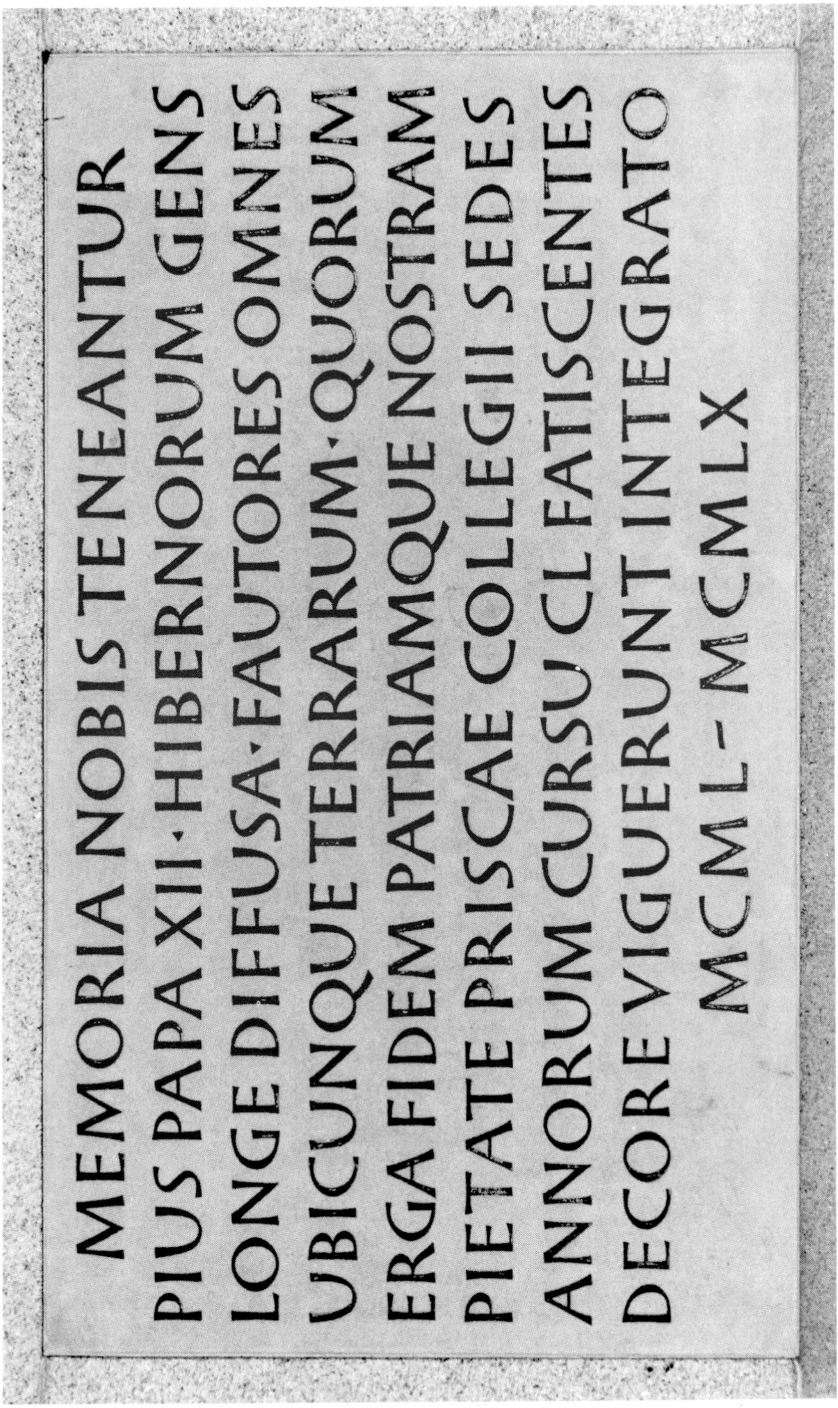

MEMORIA NOBIS TENEANTUR
PIUS PAPA XII · HIBERNORUM GENS
LONGE DIFFUSA · FAUTORES OMNES
UBICUNQUE TERRARUM · QUORUM
ERGA FIDEM PATRIAMQUE NOSTRAM
PIETATE PRISCAE COLLEGII SEDES
ANNORUM CURSU CL FATISCENTES
DECORE VIGUERUNT INTEGRATO
MCML – MCMLX

Plaque to the Benefactors of the 1950s

Plate 69

Long Corridor rebuilding

Long Corridor rebuilt

Plate 70

The old Junior Chapel

Junior Chapel rebuilt

Plate 71

Archbishop Michael Ramsey of Canterbury, with Patrick J. Hamell, vice-president, Monsignor Mitchell, President, and Archbishop George Otto Simms of Dublin

Plate 78

Isidore Eyo and John Paul
Essien, Nigeria 1963

John Mulvihill and James
Haddad, Boston 1964

Plate 79

with the new university with effective provision for certain safeguards.' What seemed to be emerging was an insistence by the Trustees that in the last analysis they should have final control over all aspects of any institution that might emerge at Maynooth, and that this might not be acceptable to the Minister, Donogh O'Malley. Then, on 10 March 1968, he died, suddenly and unexpectedly.

His successor, Brian Lenihan, announced the Government's blueprint for higher education on 5 July. The National University of Ireland was to be dissolved. Cork and Galway would become independent universities. Trinity College and University College, Dublin, were to be combined in one University of Dublin, but each was to retain its own identity. As for Maynooth and theology,

> statutory provision will be made for the teaching of theology and divinity, but particular arrangements in regard to them will be subject to consultation with and the agreement of the appropriate church authorities. In that regard it is envisaged that Saint Patrick's College, Maynooth, would as an Associate College of the University of Dublin be in a position to play the fullest part in the teaching and study of Theology as well as fulfilling a distinguished role in the realms of Arts and Science.

Brian Lenihan's statement was no more than an opening salvo in what was to be a protracted engagement between the two Dublin colleges. Maynooth and its theology were not forgotten, it is true. In his statement of July 1968 Lenihan had announced the setting up of a Higher Education Authority, and in a report in 1972 that body stated:

> Because of Maynooth College's tradition, facilities and standing in the teaching and study of theology, it expects to play a particularly important role in this field and will continue accordingly to maintain a centre of excellence there . . . Finally, it is to be assumed that the position of Maynooth College, a Pontifical University, as the country's main centre for Catholic theological training and research, is likely to be seen as accentuated when, in accordance with the government's decisions, statutory provision is made for the recognition of the subject of theology throughout our university system.

But the date when this would be done seemed to recede indefinitely, and Maynooth College seemed to have only a very small voice in influencing higher education policy.

CHAPTER XV

THE CHANGING
SEMINARY

Great Expectations, Winds of Change

On 28 September 1965 the Council issued its Decree on Priestly Formation, *Optatam totius*; it was to come into effect on 29 June 1966. Priestly formation, the Council declared, was still to be centred in the seminary, but this venerable and tested institution needed to be revitalised. This it envisaged as happening under three broad heads. First, the seminary would still be a place of formation by discipline, but it would now be consciously directed to the end that the seminarians 'can gradually learn to discipline themselves'. Second, there was need for a renewal of studies—a course was envisaged which would integrate the study of philosophy and theology, and the students were to be actively involved in learning through seminars and other work in small groups. Finally there was to be a conscious promotion of pastoral training, both during term and during vacation. This was a matter in which the old-style seminary had taken only a limited interest. Signs were multiplying that it now needed more, and a number of things—the reactions to the proposal for a theological summer school, for example—showed that by the 1950s the clergy working in the parishes were already conscious of this. A set of detailed regulations or *Normae* was promised by the time the decree was to be implemented, 29 June 1966. In fact these were issued only in 1970, following the Synod of Bishops in 1967, and they were in turn referred to local episcopal conferences, as was now the practice, so that any adaptations judged locally desirable might be made. The version for Ireland was approved on 24 August 1972, with only marginal changes from the Roman exemplar. By now the rapid pace of change had passed it out. The necessary further new impetus came slowly, initiated at the Synod of Bishops in 1990, followed by the papal exhortation *Pastores dabo vobis*.

The proceedings of the Council had raised high expectations in seminaries world-wide even before the publication of the Decree on Priestly Formation. Maynooth was no exception. A new outgoing mood was exemplified by the college's first participation in an inter-university debate when it faced University College, Dublin, on 1 March 1964. At the end of the following academic year there was a perceptive comment from the President in his report to the Trustees. Among seminarians there was, he said, 'some evidence of a new attitude to authority, revealed chiefly in a greater ease and freedom in their dealings with superiors', which, he went on, 'we think is something to be welcomed', because, together with it 'there continues to be a true spirit of obedience. As far as we can see, there is no sign of any unrest or insubordination of the kind reported from some seminaries in other countries.'

He was correct in this, but there was expectation and the beginnings of impatience. In the student magazine, the *Silhouette*, the issue for Easter 1965 had carried an exceptionally long preface to the standard feature, 'Ourselves', a normally light-hearted commentary on day-by-day student activities. Early on there was a truly purple patch:

> Vatican II has done much to prise open Maynooth's windows on Europe, be the opening ever so little. The winds of change emanating at gale force in the regions of the Rhine, sweeping tornado fashion across Germany, whirling between the battlements of curial walls, and emerging again but with diminished force and slightly out of breath, came to us in Maynooth like a gentle breeze whispering such strange and uncanonical words as *encounter* and *dialogue* . . .

It went on more soberly:

> We hail the day when the professor in the oral examination (we fear that Vatican II with all its helps, visible and invisible, won't shake this last Inquisitorial institution of antiquity) will, in the name of democracy and common sense, change his questions from the long-established format of *Quid sit* this and *Quid sit* that and *Quid dicit Codex?* to something more conducive to natural communication. Why not, for example, a question like 'How would you explain to the man in the street the difference between *ex opere operato* and *ex opere operantis* effects of the sacraments? . . . Maynooth has changed over the years—and for the better. We do appreciate these changes, even though we might not be so enthusiastic as to kneel beneath the windows of the Administrative Council Hall and sing 'Well over to you' to the delight or otherwise of the responsible body within. But we would like to let them know we appreciate the new loaf (it is better than no bread), the improvement of facilities in the library, the making available to us of fairly modern books . . . of newspapers, and radio, and occasional—very occasional—view of T.V. . . . .

The *Silhouette* was coming to the end of its life after twenty years. In 1966 there appeared *Maynooth*, 'formerly the *Silhouette*', but it ran to one number only. However, it did reflect the urges of the time in that it was devoted to seminary renewal. Many of the contributions were perhaps predictable, but two might be singled out: 'The new theology and the Christian life' by Donal Murray, ordained in June of that year, and later auxiliary bishop in Dublin, and 'The new theology and the modern Church' by Donal W. McClatchie, a student of the Church of Ireland Divinity Hostel, who had visited Maynooth the previous January as part of the newly instituted Church Unity Week. Something more far-reaching was in the air, however, and in spring 1967 there appeared the first number of *Agora*, describing itself as 'a university-seminary magazine'. It did not last as long as the *Silhouette*, but that was the nature of the times. The editor was Michael Ledwith, ordained priest of the diocese of Ferns the following June, and subsequently President of the college. There was an editorial group in Maynooth, and also associate editors in the regional seminaries, together with the Irish College, Rome, the seminary at Oscott, and the Irish universities, the National University colleges at Dublin, Cork and Galway, Trinity College, Dublin, and Queen's University, Belfast. That spring it was good to be alive, and to be young was very heaven.

It was only to be expected that the Trustees would move cautiously. At their June meeting in 1965 they authorised the Maynooth administration to have annual informal discussions with rectors of regional seminaries on matters of common interest. The Decree on Priestly Formation was issued in September, and on 25 October there appeared from the students in the final or fourth theology year a paper which gave indications that slow change might easily be left behind. (The exemplar in the college archives has the autograph signature of every student in the class, and it is hard to imagine such a document being produced without some encouragement from authority.) The document asked in the first place for more personal responsibility, and specifically that deacons be given more opportunity to exercise their order. It went on to seek a freeing-out of social life among the students—the abolition of fixed places in chapel, lecture hall and refectory; an end to reading at meals; the provision of more recreation rooms; and an improvement in the 'remote, formal and impersonal relationship' with the college staff. It spoke of defects in the presentation of philosophy and theology, and called for the supplementing of the rigid lecture system with seminars and discussion groups, with the large increase in staff and library facilities necessary for this. Thought should be given to an additional 'introductory year', which might not in fact be additional for some if it was accepted that an Arts or Science degree should not be required of all. Finally, permission was sought to affiliate to the Union of Students in Ireland, and to set up 'a university-seminary magazine'. This last request resulted in the publication of the first number of *Agora* in the spring of 1967. Permission for student organisation had already come. At the beginning of 1960 the USI had asked for the affiliation of Maynooth students, and had been told that there was no place for ecclesiastical students in their organisation, but in December 1965 the students of Maynooth were allowed to affiliate, through an elected Students' Representative Council. That there were perils ahead become plain when a report appeared in the *Irish Press* on 4

February 1967 describing enthusiastically the visit of Maynooth students to Trinity College to link up with Catholic students there. This drew an acerbic protest from Archbishop McQuaid of Dublin, to which there could be no defence in existing circumstances. He pointed out that the prohibition on Catholics attending Trinity was still in force; that the visit of the Maynooth students had been made without any reference to himself; and that he was not aware that any permission had been given to them to join the undenominational USI or to associate themselves with Trinity 'in regard to the magazine *Agora* or other activities'. As he had been authorised, the President of Maynooth invited the presidents of the other seminaries to a series of meetings, between November 1965 and May 1966. These were envisaged as informal conferences, primarily to share experiences, but in the course of them it came to be generally accepted that no cobbling up of the old seminary rule was going to be adequate. It was assumed, however, that the Roman directives, promised for 29 June 1966, would prove to be sufficiently detailed guidelines. In Maynooth, attempts were made to involve the teaching staff, for the Council had laid down that

> directors and teachers need to be keenly aware of how greatly the outcome of seminary formation depends on their own manner of teaching and acting. Under their rector's lead, they should create the strictest harmony in spirit and behaviour. Among themselves and with their students they should constitute the kind of family which answers the Lord's prayer 'that they may be one' and which intensifies in each student the joy of his calling.

Given the Maynooth tradition, such involvement of the whole staff would represent a substantial innovation, presenting real difficulties. In the event, the staff were consulted individually, and there was no follow-up to this. Of the surviving replies, there was only one which did not approve of radical change but instead spoke of the need to take steps to counter what it called a crisis of faith and a crisis of obedience.

During the academic year 1965/66 changes were being introduced by the Administrative Council. There was less reading at meals; the outside contacts of students were extended, contacts with other institutions, affiliation to the USI; deacons were sent to minister in their native parishes in a Holy Week liturgy now to a great extent in the vernacular. A very substantial change in the student horarium had been introduced for a year's trial in this year, and it proved permanent. The greatest changes were the moving of the main meal from mid-afternoon, where it had been since the foundation of the college, to one o'clock, with four lectures in the morning and one in the afternoon; and the changing of the rising bell to 6.30 every morning of the week, this replacing a 6 o'clock rising with the concession of 6.45 on Thursday. In detail, the new horarium read:

6.30 rising; 7.30 Mass; 8.15 breakfast; 9.10–12.45 four lectures; l.00 main meal; 2.00–2.30 study; 2.30–3.20 lecture; 3.20–5.00 recreation; 5.00–7.00 study; 7.00–7.30 spiritual reading; 7.30 supper, followed by recreation; 8.30–9.45 study; 9.45 night prayer; 10.30 lights out.

In June 1966 the President laid before the Trustees the document submitted by the students of the fourth-year theology class the previous October. He said that the suggestions in it were made by young men who took their vocation to the priesthood seriously. He summarised the consultations held with the heads of other seminaries, and outlined the changes already introduced by the Administrative Council. But, he said, the council felt that on its own authority it could make only marginal changes. Much more was needed, and it was desirable that the Trustees draw up a programme quickly, for it was essential that changes should not appear to come from pressure from below (which was indeed a real factor, and a growing one).

The President made a number of requests on which he asked for immediate action. The 'rule of division' should be abolished, for it had long been an anachronism. The Trustees agreed, for one year, as an experiment, which fairly predictably became permanent. He asked for a reconsideration of the rule of silence, proposing it be associated with prayer and study only (this, it may be recalled, was the concept of seminary silence Laurence Renehan had propounded before the Royal Commission in 1853). The Trustees made piecemeal changes, with no really discernible pattern. The President had also asked for a number of minor freedoms: that students might do their spiritual reading in their rooms, a concession already enjoyed by the senior division, St Mary's; that there be lights out at choice (granted to St Mary's division only); and that students be free to choose their own times for study (here a decision was deferred).

A number of decisions were needed in liturgical matters arising from the Decree on the Renewal of the Liturgy, promulgated on 4 December 1963, the first to be completed by the Council. Again, the changes introduced were gradual, even slightly hesitant. It was agreed that night prayer should be the liturgical office of Compline, but morning prayer was to be the office of Lauds only occasionally. Low Mass on Sunday morning was to continue, in addition to 'High Mass' in the College Chapel. Here too the vernacular was advancing inexorably, not really delayed by a Trustees' decision in October 1970 that the Mass be fully Latin and fully vernacular on alternate Sundays. They agreed that St Mary's oratory be reconstructed to bring it into conformity with the new liturgy, and accepted proposals from the firm of Robinson, Keeffe and Devane for a 'simple, logical layout', where 'the nave arrangement is replaced by an assembly gathered round chancel tabernacle and altar', these last being by Benedict Tutty OSB. The idea was a good one—that there should be one oratory in the college that might stand as an exemplar—but it is hard to be enthusiastic about its execution (Plate 73). However, the work was put in hand in the summer vacation of 1966, and came into use for the year 1966/67.

Finally, the Trustees set up two committees—one of four bishops, all of them with seminary experience, and the other of the presidents of Maynooth and the other seminaries. Though the two were instructed 'to keep in close liaison', it was an unnecessarily clumsy way of dealing with a situation demanding quick decision. Further delay was caused when the promised Roman guidelines did not appear in June 1966, nor indeed for years after-wards. The results were predictable. In June 1967 the President had to report what he called 'disturbing tendencies'. Some relaxations had been granted, but others were simply being taken. Even the hallowed 'solemn silence' between night prayer and morning Mass was being ignored. He repeated his conviction of the urgent need for a planned and far-reaching reform. What in fact was happening was like a pressure-cooker lid too long screwed down giving way under the pressure that had built up. For generations of students the college rule had been sanctified as the fundamental source of character development. There may have been mutterings that it was better suited to develop monks, but they were necessarily muted ones. Things considered sacrosanct for gener-ations just went. The soutane, introduced into a reluctant Maynooth after the Synod of Thurles in 1850, was abandoned in the national colleges in Rome in 1966, and Maynooth followed. The approved replacement was the suit, but this could not hold out against the very informal dress in sudden favour with youth. The 'diocesan system', which had developed from a natural association between young men from the same diocesan college and destined to serve in the same diocese, had for a long time been in practice obligatory, and any laxi-ty here was regarded by authority as a serious example of the grave fault of 'singularity'. It went with little resistance, though not altogether without regrets, some students claiming that it had simply been replaced by cliques, others arguing that it was surely a natural basis for the 'small group' organisa-tion now so fashionable, though this was not as convincing as it seemed, for the student intake for a diocese no longer came exclusively from the diocesan college.

The committee of presidents of seminaries met on 13 November 1966, and very sensibly decided to seek a joint meeting with the episcopal committee. It is clear that they were already finding that the relaxation of rule often led to disturbing developments; reservations were expressed about involving the whole staff in seminary administration; and while it was noted that most semi-naries now had some form of student councils, and this was judged on the whole a good development, certain moves in English seminaries should be treated with caution. Similar reservations were expressed at the joint meeting of the two committees on 11 December. However, five subcommittees were established, which got through enough work to allow the episcopal committee to present a report the following June. Again there was a decided hesitation at the idea of involving the whole staff in administration, especially in Maynooth because of the big number involved. There should be regular meetings between student representatives and administration. The rules should be few, should deal with essentials, and be firmly insisted on: they should include a 'carefully limited' rule of silence. The aim was the development of a progressive personal responsibility under a code of discipline freely accepted. The course of studies was to be carefully integrated with spiritual and pastoral training. There was to be an introductory year, mainly of a spiritual nature, followed by a six-year course of integrated philosophy and theology. It was noted that the degrees of the National University at Maynooth might cause problems, but even here the background was still the introduction of theology courses into university studies generally.

These were excellent ideas, but still far from 'a code of discipline freely accepted', and student ferment went on. In the year 1967/68 the Students' Representative Council was busy circulating questionnaires and drawing up reports. There would need to be, they said, better contact with the Administrative Council and, of course, with the professors. One of the spiritual directors should be a diocesan priest, and all should have pastoral experience. Above all, there should be more trust. It was claimed that 'most students do not honestly want things made easier in a material way', though coffee machines and television sets were welcomed, and smoking in the common-rooms. At the end of the year the Administrative Council was still apprehensive. Change, it was repeated, was urgent. The present situation was wholly unsatisfactory, in that piecemeal changes had eroded the old system, without putting any system in its place. There was a crying need for something clear, definite and enforceable. They proposed certain measures to be adopted for an experimental period of two years. These were based on a principle that as a student advanced through the house he should have progressive freedom to choose the time and place of study and personal devotions; that silence should be confined to the hours of prayer, lectures and study, with solemn silence extending from night prayer until after breakfast next morning. Students should be free to take recreation outside the college as individuals every day during the long afternoon recreation, and for longer periods on Sundays, free days, and the weekly Wednesday half-day.

The Trustees agreed. At the end of the two-year trial period the Administrative Council reported in June 1970. The report said that while final assessment would take longer, the results to date were encouraging: on the whole, the new freedom had been responsibly used. The Council submitted for approval a draft 'Information and Rules for Students'. This document included the elected Students' Representative Council, and in addition provided for a 'Joint Board', consisting of the President, one other member of the Administrative Council, one member of the teaching staff, one Dunboyne student, and three students elected by the Students' Representative Council. The Board was to meet at least once a month, for general assessment, supervision of society finances, approval of the constitutions and rules of student societies, and approval of statements proposed by the Students' Representative Council for publication. The Trustees agreed, but seem to have made no response to a further proposal made to their March meeting in 1971. This was for the establishment of a 'Seminary Executive Council', to consist of three Trustees, the President, the vice-presidents (two in number since October 1968), the three deans and the bursar, to hold ordinary meetings every two months between September and June. However, at least the 'Information and Rules for Students' was distributed to all students, including lay students, when term began in the autumn of 1970. The lay students were still few in number, and they did have a separate section of the document, but even this soon became outdated. There remained the problem of getting the seminarians to accept their section of the rule-book, which was in fact a quite reasonable provision for their lives.

Because of its size, it had always been difficult to create in Maynooth the kind of community traditionally accepted as the ideal of a seminary. The difficulty was increasing, even though the number of seminarians was declining. A few sample figures will indicate the extent of this decline:

Academic year	Total seminarians	Departures during year	Departures as percentage of total
1962/63	546	50	9.15
1968/69	395	57	14.45
1974/75	280	42	15.00

The rise in the proportion of those who left was worrying, especially as it inclined to be higher among those more gifted intellectually. Another destabilising factor was the number of priests leaving the priesthood and seeking 'secularisation'; the first from the Maynooth staff did so in 1974. While departures increased, intake declined. In September 1968 there were only fifty-eight entrants, and though this would later have been regarded as riches it led to a decision the following year to admit a limited number of unmatriculated students. At the same time the number of lay students increased, and it was not long until they outnumbered the seminarians. This had happened well before any new library or class hall facilities were provided, so that physically and psychologically lay and cleric intermingled. Indeed, as seminarian numbers fell the old Junior House was progressively handed over to Science and Arts. Even the two main squares were hard to keep defined as a seminary area. Even after the opening of the new Arts Building in 1977 St Joseph's remained the only link between the new developments and those in what had been the Junior House. St Mary's was wide open as long as there was only one library, but the opening of the new library in 1984 relieved pressure here. The sudden disappearance of the 'diocesan system' tended to atomise the seminary body. There were regrets, but all attempts to revive it failed. The fourth theology year had in the past posed certain problems even for the old disciplinarians, and it was some time before a suitable solution to the new circumstances began to take shape. The sense of each class as a community was further weakened by the growing numbers ordained individually in their native localities. In 1970 there was no-one left for ordination in the college, and this proved a permanent development.

It was, inevitably, a time of troubles, with ups and downs, and the occasional worrying problem. Maynooth, of course, was by no means unique among seminaries. Everywhere there was the need to damp down the changes that had come so suddenly, almost violently, in the 1960s. In the nature of things the passage of time was a necessary element, but there also had to be people able to see the opportunity and to seize it. Here the far-reaching changes in personnel in the college administration in the mid-1980s was a decisive factor. In his report in June 1985 the new President, Monsignor Ledwith, spoke of a considerable improvement in discipline, leading to better morale. There was more framework to life, especially among the junior classes. Shape was given to an introductory 'spiritual month' for first-year students in 1986, for the second year in 1987, and for those entering second-year theology in 1989. The deans saw each student individually, at least once a month in the junior classes. The night 'solemn silence' began to have a meaning again, there seemed to be more shape to things, an attempt to build a real community. Unfortunately, numbers showed some signs of slipping again after remaining stable for a decade.

A School of the Service of the Lord

The Decree on Priestly Formation had stressed the importance of 'catechetics, preaching, liturgical worship, the conferring of the sacraments, works of charity, the duty of seeking out the straying sheep and unbelievers, and other pastoral obligations.' Some of this had had its place in the Maynooth curriculum, but not all of it, and it was firmly subordinated to detailed study of the theological manuals. Indeed in a stable society there was only limited need to provide the equivalent of the 'internship' of a young doctor. This was to be provided in the parish, where the older priest knew what to do and how it should be done, and the neophyte accepted his authority. But now these foundations were being shaken, and 'pastoral training' in the wide fields envisaged by the Council was a necessary part of the seminary course. Here especially the delay in the promised Roman *Normae* was badly felt. How were these extensive developments to be integrated into what was regarded as an overloaded course? A beginning was made in the year 1969/70, under the direction of the senior dean. There were to be courses lasting a fortnight at the beginning of the year, 'Communications' for the second theology year, and 'Pastoral Training' for the third and fourth years. This was followed up by work through the year. As outlined by the director in his report in June 1970, it included the exercise of deacon's orders in neighbouring parishes for all, with other work by invitation—hospitals, reformatories, the Legion of Mary, the Society of St Vincent de Paul, and some house visitation. He added that it would be a great advantage if work like this could also be offered during vacation, and that in fact arrangements had been made to place about fifteen deacons in the diocese of Westminster in the coming summer.

Extramural pastoral projects naturally gravitated towards the senior classes, but no class was excluded. They could not but be fashionable, and the traditional curriculum could not but suffer some downgrading, with some danger of the pedagogical methods of Wackford Squeers, that a boy would be sent to clean the 'winder' as soon as he had learned to mis-spell it. Yet from an early date there were some student complaints that these activities were excessive. In any case, if there was to be a stable programme there was beyond question need for a full-time director. The situation was still fluid when one was appointed on 27 September 1971, with instructions to submit a report and recommendations in June 1972 on how to integrate academic and pastoral formation.

In spring 1972 the Faculty of Theology took the momentous decision that the academic course should be reduced to three years, the fourth year being given over to 'planned pastoral work', elements of which were also envisaged in the other years. In fact, if only under timetable pressure, an academic element made its way back into fourth year. The director's report in June 1972 set out his plans for a detailed programme, and not surprisingly revealed many tensions. These were inevitable if there was to be anything like what he envisaged, a Department of Pastoral Training within the college or a Pastoral Institute outside it. This raised the fears of the Faculty of Theology, but even more of the hard-pressed Academic Council (representing Arts and Science), facing an influx of new students, long conscious of its deficiencies, for quite a while under pressure because of what the Trustees considered an unacceptable failure rate, and inevitably wondering how this might be affected by evenings spent, say, at youth work in Ballyfermot. While activities naturally tended to concentrate in the more senior years, even here there were problems, especially in drawing up a summer programme. It was very desirable that students be involved in summer pastoral work from the end of the first year of theology, building up to a specific diocesan appointment as deacon after the third year. By now, however, many seminarians were taking vacation work like other students.

On 29 January 1975 the director wrote to the President saying he was resigning in June. At their meeting the Trustees had a number of reports before them. In his, the outgoing director stressed the need to link pastoral, academic and spiritual training. He pointed to defects in the traditional systems, notably in Catechetics. The reports of the Administrative Council and of the Faculty of Theology were widely agreed. Both urged caution. The emphasis should be on pastoral courses within the college, with correspond-ingly less outside involvement during term. By now everyone, including the director, was agreed that student enthusiasm for this outside work had notably lessened, though they were not agreed why. The episcopal Pastoral Com-mission, reporting through its chairman, said they had had consultations with a number of priests in close touch with Maynooth students, and found them on many points in agreement with what the college bodies were saying. These priests also expressed reservations about deacons working in parishes during term. The commission concluded by raising the possibility that it might be enough to have work and courses mainly within the college, supervised by the deans.

In every report, the director of pastoral training had been severely critical of the provision made for Catechetics. When Peter Birch was appointed bish-op in July 1962 there was no successor in the chair of Education and Catechetics. Instead, Philip Walsh CM was appointed on a part-time basis to lecture in Catechetics. The course he inherited consisted of one lecture a week to combined classes of first and second theology, and of one lecture also to the combined third and fourth years. There was difficulty in getting teaching practice, because student numbers were so big and local schools small. A devoted professional, he decided to concentrate the course in one year, and with much ingenuity devised a scheme by which students went to schools in pairs, one to teach and one to observe, followed by a discussion group of the whole class once a week. He resigned in 1974; for some years the course was continued under Sister Nora Connolly and Sister Antonia Curran, but from 1979 to 1984 there was no formal provision. It was then incorporated into a revitalised programme of pastoral training, courses in Catechetics extending over the three senior theology years, with part-time lecturers to help the director.

In June 1975 the Trustees adopted the programme for pastoral training submitted by the Administrative Council and the Faculty of Theology, to be carried out once again under the direction of the senior dean. He reported on the year's experience the following June. The three senior classes had had courses lasting a fortnight at the beginning of the year, in Catechetics, com-munications and counselling. The programme during the year concentrated on the fourth-year theology class. Courses were organised within the college. These were experimental, and there was admittedly room for improvement. With the generous co-operation of the parish priests of eight neighbouring parishes, a 'team' of deacons had been assigned to each, to preach and to do any other work the parish priest might request. Two years later, however, the senior dean, now President, was expressing misgivings about the problems of the fourth theology year in his annual report to the Trustees. These needed, he said, serious consideration. For some at least it was a kind of 'petering-out' year, with much time spent arranging petty details of their ordination. It would help, he urged, if the traditional group ordination in the College

Chapel could be restored. Three years later the Trustees agreed, but they were divided, and those opposed to the group ordination got the decision reversed.

In June 1978, however, they did agree to a new programme for the fourth theology year, to begin in September, described as 'heavily academic' up to mid-February, when it terminated with a 'serious examination'. After this there was a 'pastoral programme' directed by the senior dean, with limited extramural activities. After a year's trial it was claimed that there was much improvement, precisely because of more study and less going-out. The assessment was optimistic. A successful course would need a full-time director. But what should his qualifications be? What should his programme be? In particular, the need for firm overall direction established itself only very slowly. Here again the mid-1980s were a time when things settled, with the appointment of a full-time director with a new programme 'academic with a strong pastoral emphasis', spread over the whole year. The traditional examination in Moral Theology for the grant of diocesan faculties to hear confessions was extended to include Dogmatic Theology and Homiletics, and deacons continued to preach in the neighbouring parishes. Finally, a diploma in pastoral studies was instituted, first awarded in 1989.

The post of 'Maynooth professor' had always been given high respect among the clergy and laity. However, it had its human problems. Above all, it was a lonely life. A priest living in Maynooth was normally far from his native place, and cut off from the society of the clergy of his diocese. Several times there had been proposals to give the teaching staff an active role in the seminary community at Maynooth, but this had not happened. These problems arose primarily from the very size of the place, but there had also been a deep-rooted suspicion of 'the method of Saint-Sulpice', which tried to involve everybody in everything, even back in the days when there was complete agreement about what a seminary should be. In consequence, the professors lived a lonely existence. Numbers of them filled it with research; many found their teaching duties sufficient; and there were some who went down under the strain.

In the new world of the 1960s it was only to be expected that 'the remoteness of the staff' should be a constant plaint of the students, but, as has been seen, particularly in Maynooth but not only in Maynooth, both governing body and college administration were reluctant to involve the whole staff, as the Vatican Council had suggested. In 1971 there were hopes they might be involved in a revival of the 'diocesan system', but the system did not revive, and it is hard to say who, if anyone, was to blame. The fact is that in the 1970s Maynooth was becoming a different kind of institution. The members of staff and students in no way attached to the seminary was growing, but while not organically attached they interpenetrated with it in an unstructured way. The college statutes drawn up in 1962 were becoming less relevant to the institution as a whole, to some degree even to the seminary aspect of it. And just as the students felt the remoteness of the staff, so the staff felt the remoteness of the Trustees, inevitably feeling from time to time that they were acting harshly or even arbitrarily in the new problems that constantly arose, while the Trustees for their part had to be content with pragmatic solutions where there were no firm guidelines.

In the years after the Council priests began leaving their ministry, and Maynooth could not hope to be unscathed. The first case occurred in 1974, and between that and 1981 there were seven. For men middle-aged rather than young it was a serious step with many possible hardships. They were too young to benefit from any pension arrangements, and while *ex gratia* payments were normally made they were small, because the resources of the college were limited. But at least they went out into a world where the university system was expanding, and almost all found a place in it, though even with this the transition must have been psychologically disturbing. It was disturbing too for those who remained. The priest-members of the staff had been raised in the belief that a priest was a priest for ever, while to the student seminarians the experience must have been very unsettling.

The departure of priests was one of the many problems that Pope Paul VI (1963–78) faced in the wake of the Council. He offered them an honourable release from the obligations of priesthood, a process knows as 'laicisation'. In return for this release they had to give certain undertakings. One was that they would not teach in 'a seminary, theological faculty or similar institution', and priests from the staff had accepted that 'laicisation' involved leaving their teaching posts in the college. When this was resisted, two were removed by the Trustees in 1977, and they appealed to the civil courts. The verdict of the High Court was given by Mr Justice Hamilton on 14 August 1978. The next day the *Irish Times* printed verbatim his lengthy judgement, which cited all the documents in the case and summarised all the arguments. The real issue, he said, was the consequences of seeking a rescript of laicisation. This did involve giving an undertaking in regard to teaching in certain types of institution, and 'if the Trustees in fulfilling their function as the governing body of the college take the view that the continued employment of priests who have been laicised is contrary to the interests of the college as a seminary it seems to be a view they may reasonably take', and so he found against the plaintiffs. There was an appeal to the Supreme Court, where on 1 November 1979 the five judges gave a unanimous verdict, in which they confirmed the judgement of the High Court. They went on to consider two subsidiary issues. One was a charge under the unfortunate college statute requiring the staff to have the permission of the President before publishing 'books or articles'. In spite of the experience in the case of Michael O'Hickey, this had been retained in the 1918 revision of the statutes, and again in 1962. The judges did no more than circle it circumspectly, clearly unwilling to give a ruling on regulations made by bishops about writings by priests; they did, however, note that this statute seemed to be obsolete. They did give a ruling an another matter, the wearing of clerical dress, and said that a deliberate refusal to wear it in the college, knowing the order to have emanated from the Trustees, 'could be reasonably regarded by the Trustees as being a grave delinquency against clerical obligations.'

In the judgement of both the High Court and the Supreme Court, therefore, the Trustees had behaved like that final arbiter of the common law, 'the reasonable man'. This did not prevent the whole issue becoming bitterly divisive in the college community. The focus of opposition within the college was the Academic Staff Association, and in the university world generally the Irish Federation of University Teachers.[1] These bodies had grown out of the educational ferment of the 1960s, and had sought and got trade union status. It was claimed that the issues could be reduced to one of 'academic freedom', an issue, as has just been seen, which the courts were not to regard as particularly relevant but which was pursued in academe as a kind of test of 'political correctness'. The pressure culminated in the calling of a one-day token strike, leading to even greater polarisation.

When the debris settled there were many people who were very drained. It had been a very painful reminder of the instability of the situation in the college, for which a lasting remedy could be provided only by new university legislation. Until this came it was not possible to think of more than interim solutions, and any attempts to update the 1962 statutes could hardly expect to succeed. With hindsight, one can see that it might have been wise to have produced a simple document for the priests attached to the seminary. The civil courts had recognised them as a distinct body, and there was the example of the 'Information and Rules for Students' first drawn up in 1970. There was much to be said too for an interim document for the staff as a whole in the context of wider university interests. Negotiations between the Trustees and the Irish Federation of University Teachers were necessarily difficult, and were conducted in an atmosphere of increasing suspicion. On 27 January 1979 an advertisement from the Federation appeared in the daily papers, when the dispute in Maynooth was before the Supreme Court on appeal. It concerned a number of hard-won additional teaching posts which had been advertised, and prospective applicants were advised 'that the Federation is dissatisfied with the standards of academic freedom and security of tenure which obtain in the college.' It is hard to accept this as any kind of cool and critical intellectual judgement, and it should come as no surprise that negotiations with the Trustees did not survive the judgement of the Supreme Court on 1 November. Instead, community structures were established more by trial and error, by guess and by God, as legislation was deferred and deferred again. No-one could claim that it was the best way of doing things, but it reflected the hard necessity summed up in the old Italian proverb that Voltaire clearly thought a lot of: 'The best is the enemy of the good.'

As the world opened up, it was natural that Maynooth should host important occasions, the first big gathering being the Fifth Conference of the

European Society for Rural Sociology in August 1966, and the most prestigious of all the Conference of the Heads of the Universities of Europe in May 1993. Not long before there had been a visit by the King and Queen of Spain, and another by the President of Italy (Plate 60). It was natural too that the college should from time to time see the visits of high ecclesiastics. There had been Archbishop Ramsey of Canterbury in June 1967 (Plate 78). There had even been a future Pope, Cardinal Montini of Milan, in August 1961 (Plate 77). Now on 1 October 1979 there was a reigning Pope, John Paul II, who came to the college as part of his Irish visit. His audience here was to consist of priests, religious, seminarians, the staff and students of the university, and the local people. Through the preceding night people were gathering to take part in an all-night vigil in the College Chapel and the grounds. The Pope was due to arrive at 7.45 a.m., but it was a murky morning and the arrival was delayed, and he finally arrived only after repeated scares that his helicopter might not be able to land at all. He went first to the College Chapel to address the assembled seminarians and candidates for religious orders and congregations (Plate 57). It was very crowded—invitations had been sent to 874 in all, and not many of them can have been absent—and the Pope was greeted with a very loud cheer, at which he was reported to have frowned. He spoke to them of fidelity, fidelity to the word of God as expounded in the teaching of the Church. He urged them to follow the example of St Patrick: as God counted on him, so he also counted on them, and he told them that the decade of the 1980s could be decisive for the future of the faith in Ireland. He then went to the President's Arch, where he signed the visitors' book and accepted specially bound copies of Healy's *Centenary History* and the Polish translation of Walter Macken's historical trilogy (Plate 58). Lastly he addressed the general body from a podium erected at the back of St Mary's and blessed the foundation-stone for a planned new library that was to bear his name.[2] He then left and there was concelebrated Mass at the podium. John Paul II stressed, and continues to stress, that his visits round the world are 'pastoral', aimed at the good of religion. In assessing the effects of his Irish visit one might reflect sadly on his appeal to 'the men of violence' at Drogheda: 'On my knees I beg you to turn away from the paths of violence and to return to the ways of peace.' His visit to Maynooth came at an edgy time, with the verdict of the Supreme Court still pending. For a time afterwards there was some rise in vocations, but it was not maintained. It was going to be a long haul and even so charismatic a figure as Pope John Paul II could have only a limited effect (Plate 95).

Finance and Fabric

The number of seminarians fell rapidly in the 1960s, but then stabilised at about 300. The fall was concealed for a few years by the presence in residence of about seventy students of the Society of African Missions, but they left when their own house of study was completed in October 1972. The shortage of students was made worse by the inflationary crisis of the 1970s and 1980s, when in the worst period prices could rise at over 20 per cent a year. There was still no sign of public funding for the teaching of theology, always a large element in Maynooth. Salaries of professors of theology fell far behind salaries in other subjects, but they were a heavy burden on slender domestic resources. By 1960 it was clear that repairs and rebuilding had almost exhausted the 1949 collection. Mainly from what was left of it the Trustees had created a small reserve fund of £60,000. In June 1967 they directed that all income from investments and all net profits should go into it. This was optimistic; the fund grew slowly for a while, but then net profits became losses and investment income had to be used to offset rising costs that made a mockery of phrases like 'depreciation account' or 'contingency reserve'.

In April 1948 Edward J. Hillan had already pointed out that the income of the college was simply unable to bear the charges it had to carry. Student pensions traditionally had been low and heavily subsidised, mainly from the 'free places on public foundation'. Hillan had pointed out that the college could no longer afford this subsidy, but it was quite some time before his advice was followed. It was only in 1980 that it was finally decided to discontinue the free places, and by then the stable door had been locked a little late. The burden did not weigh as heavily as might have been feared. An increasing number of students came with university scholarships, which saw them through the first years—indeed were frequently worth more than what was charged for pension and tuition. There was a certain irony in the fact that scholarships were continued through the theology course only for students from Northern Ireland. But overall, bishops had to find considerably more money to pay for their students, and they were naturally unwilling to agree to a rise in pension. The Maynooth pension remained low—£440 a year in 1979, compared with £1,120 in the Mount Oliver Catechetical Institute; the tuition fees were £190, compared with £615 in Mount Oliver and £540 in the Mater Dei Institute in Dublin.

The realisation in 1960 that the collection had been spent concentrated attention on the investment portfolio. Investments for diocesan burses were, of course, only administered by the college. The portfolio proper derived substantially from the capital sum of just over £369,000 received in 1870. The income from this was devoted to the 'free places on public foundation'. Even allowing for this absorption of income, and for the limitations imposed on investors in trustee stocks, growth over the years had been modest: the value in the early 1960s was just over £1,000,000. A couple of good equities were responsible for nearly all the growth, and most was invested in fixed-interest stocks, many of them long-dated, some even undated; it was estimated that 60 per cent of the holding actually showed a loss. It was quite unsuited to the era of continuing inflation now coming to be accepted. The advice of stockbrokers consulted was that the weak fixed-interest stocks should be sold and the proceeds invested in good Irish and British equities. The aim should be to move to a 50 per cent holding in equities over three years. Inevitably, the transaction would begin by showing a loss, but this, they claimed, would be soon recovered. The Trustees moved cautiously, wishing to be quite sure of what stocks they could invest in, and perhaps having a narrower view of what was a 'good equity' than stockbrokers had. Finally in June 1966 they authorised the conversion of £200,000 of fixed-income stocks into equities. Of its nature this was a slow process, and in fact there was only limited switching to equities, for one consequence of inflation was a sharp rise in the yield of new issues of fixed-interest stocks. Within a few years the portfolio was being raided to cover current deficits. Some Bank of Ireland stock was sold as early as 1973, and later there were truly massive sales for this purpose.

The college, as has been seen, had built up large holdings of land. As consolidated in the 1940s they comprised two large holdings—454 statute acres at Laraghbryan and Crew Hill and 490 acres at Killick west of Kilcock. The farms did not yield large profits: the net income in 1977 was £31,429. It was not so much that the land was being badly farmed as that it was not being commercially farmed, and the day had come when 'a little bit of everything' no longer spelled profits in farming. Entry into the European Economic Community in 1972 brought a farming boom that lasted for a few years, and it was estimated that to let the Killick farm might bring in £50,000 a year. As the financial situation worsened it was decided to sell it. It was hoped it would bring in £1,200,000, but the farming boom was passing and in fact it went for £900,000. £500,000 was devoted to reducing the overdraft and £400,000 invested to revitalise the portfolio.

From 1973 onwards there were increasing annual deficits, part of which were caused by expenses in the development of the college rather than in its traditional role of training students for the priesthood. There was no public support for the education of theology students. It appeared not inequitable that the unsubsidised institution should make some charge for the use of its buildings, often including expensive conversions, as space in them became available because the seminary was contracting and funds to provide new purpose-built accommodation remained altogether insufficient.

Improvements continued in provision for the students, but this remained essentially basic in a society of rising expectations, and there was no great scope for economies here. The salaries of the resident staff, administrative and teaching, had always been low, and tended not to keep up with the continuing high inflation, though by stages the actual figure did rise. By 1977 the salaries of all staff teaching National University courses in Maynooth had been equalised with those in other colleges, and it seemed reasonable that resident clerical staff should pay the full cost of their maintenance. Agreement was reached on a figure put forward by a firm of accountants, with provision for an automatic annual increase based on the cost-of-living index. In November 1980 the Trustees, faced with a financial crisis, introduced a substantial increase. Their action, as the President noted in his report in June 1981, caused 'some resentment'. It was impossible to arrange a satisfactory discussion, but in November 1983 the Trustees did accept the need for better communication and promised that in future any change 'in the basis of the charge' would be introduced only after consultation. The problem of communication was not new: Louis Delahogue had been speaking strongly about it in 1813.

If the salaries of the academic staff had traditionally been low, the wages of domestic staff had been 'shameful' (the word comes from the President's June report in 1964, announcing substantial increases during the preceding academic year). Maynooth, not uniquely among institutions, had been to an extent run on the pattern of the 'Big House', and now shared many of its problems. The 'Big House' had depended on cheap labour. How could it pay reasonable wages, especially if it was slow to realise that there must be a different level of service, possibly a lower level of service, and definitely fewer employees?

The catering situation was, quite frankly, bad. In June 1961 the Finance Council sent the Trustees a detailed report, occasioned by a student complaint the previous October. The report revealed a situation more and more out of date. Bread and groceries were put out to tender, but meat and vegetables were still supplied directly from the farm. The real problems, however, lay in the kitchen facilities and staff. New cooking equipment had been installed in the early 1950s, but Pugin's cavernous hall, the stores, the washing-up facilities and the kitchen yard were untouched. The staff were largely untrained and poorly paid; as the Council admitted, 'with the existing kitchen and refectory staff things are as good as one had a right to expect'. A way out seemed to offer with the hotel training organisation, CERT, which it was said had been very successful in Rockwell College. Here they supplied kitchen and dining-room trainee staff, with their instructors, with the college making a contribution to their maintenance. An agreement on these lines was drawn up with Maynooth, though, it was later admitted, it was not altogether precise in places.

Neither side was satisfied after the first year's experience. The trainee chefs expected to prepare hotel food, not exactly what the college wanted. The Maynooth authorities too complained of waste of food and misuse of equipment. For their part, the hotel school authorities demanded modernisation of the whole kitchen complex, much improved accommodation for trainees, both residential and recreational, and a new study, teaching and administrative area. This would involve heavy financial outlay, but a more serious issue was beginning to emerge: that the interests of the college and of the hotel training school were so different as to be incompatible. Yet it had also become necessary to begin to think of extending facilities to such things as a canteen for non-resident students. Various proposals surfaced, the most expansive—and expensive—being to turn the great refectory, kitchen and attached buildings into an extension of the library and build a new catering centre for all on a 'green field' site in the 'Long Meadow', near where the John Paul II Library now stands. Ironically, one argument in the report made to the autumn meeting of the Trustees by the Finance Council was that the 'Long Meadow' was quite unsuited for any building. The Trustees agreed to modernisation of the existing kitchen at a cost of £61,000, based on proposals from the architects Robert Creedon and Associates.

This fell far short of what CERT had asked for. Negotiations continued, the college insisting on a substantial building grant, CERT holding out the inducement that if all the facilities they required were provided there would be a large increase in the annual grant; but as time went on it began to appear that conditions unacceptable to the college would be attached to any such increase. While admittedly student food improved, complaints continued from a new and more demanding generation, who, as the catering authorities pointed out, now had freedom to go in and out of the college, which gave them access to 'junk' food. The Trustees decided to go ahead with the necessary modernisation of the kitchen whether or not CERT remained. In fact they left in June 1973, before work in the kitchen was finished. This work had begun in January 1972, the contract being for £138,697. Inevitably, such extensive work in an old building led to unpredictable rises in costs, and the work dragged on from its planned completion date of May 1973 to the very end of the year. It seems hard to justify all the work done—the extra kitchen, for example, or the huge self-service areas. It is impossible to justify the appalling plastic-topped tables and plastic chairs introduced into Pugin's great refectory hall. Fortunately, they were ejected in 1992. The final cost was between three and four times the figure of £61,000 originally mooted, and if there was one thing certain about future catering facilities it was that they would cost more than envisaged under the CERT plan, and very much more then they had cost under what now appeared almost as the *ancien régime*.

This expense, coming on top of a fairly heavy programme of conversions and adaptations made necessary by the expansion of the college, left little spare money indeed. However, reminders multiplied that Pugin's buildings were now well into their second century and that restoration work on the earlier buildings in the 1950s had not solved all problems for all time. A report requested by the Trustees in October 1967 and presented the following June listed major refurbishments required. An attempt was made to establish priorities, and in January 1970 a 'domestic bursar' was appointed. His 'Report on the College Fabric', dated 9 February 1970, extended the list of things to be done, and pointed out that what was at the core of a problem of dilapidation was that the college had too few maintenance workers paid too little. The solution reached was that maintenance work be contracted out, and it was centred in a 'college maintenance unit' set up in the buildings of the old farmyard. This resulted in better routine maintenance, which inevitably cost more. Only a few samples of the work needed can be given. The convectors installed in the rebuilt Long Corridor only twenty years before had to be replaced by radiators, for the convectors gave out very little heat. An elaborate safety system had to be installed in the museum, after it had been robbed in September 1972. What was stolen was recovered, intact and largely undamaged, three-and-a-half years later, but the safety system did not prevent a second robbery, and this time nothing was recovered. Extensive work had to be done in the College Chapel in 1975/76; necessary extensions to the Aula Maxima were done in 1982/83; and the poor-quality electric wiring, which was the best available when New House was rebuilt in the early 1940s, had to be replaced in 1983/84.

These were the years of the great inflation, and as costs spiralled annual deficits were allowed to build up to what appeared chilling figures as people accustomed to think in hundreds struggled to think in thousands, or, unbelievably, in millions. A few figures for annual deficits will bring home the size of the problem:

Year	Deficit	Year	Deficit
1970/71	£72,000	1973/74	£150,000
1971/72	£120,000	1976/77	£235,000
1972/73	£125,000	1979/80	£344,000

In April 1979 the accumulated deficit was £959,000, and the situation was getting worse as inflation ground on. Yet it was at this time that the proposal was accepted to build a new library, to be financed by public subscription. The library was desperately needed indeed, but in the circumstances the proposal was a very bold one. In June 1980 the Killick farm was sold for £900,000, as already noted, £500,000 going to reduce the deficit, £400,000 to strengthen the investment portfolio. It was a sign of the times that even these sums did not relieve the situation. The accumulated deficits continued, so did inflation, and this meant crippling interest rates. It began to look like the nightmare of the sorcerer's apprentice.

This was the problem faced by the new President, Monsignor Ledwith, when he took office at the beginning of 1985. As he put it starkly, 'the indebtedness of the Trustees already exceeds by far their disposable assets'. The debt on the recently opened library was 'by far the most serious problem', but there was also the inexorable mounting up of running deficits. This, he said, simply could not continue to be tolerated. Economies could be introduced, but the principle had to be accepted that the current account must be balanced year by year, any deficiencies being made good annually by the Trustees. The principle was adopted, and economies and good management saw the accounts in credit for 1986/87, interest payments excluded. But it was a battle hard to win, as inflation continued, even if at a slower rate, and seminarian student num-

389

bers, which had held steady at about 300 since 1970, again began to show signs of decline.

Enormous problems remained: the accumulated running deficit, the library debt, the need for substantial work, especially on the Pugin buildings. A Maynooth Development Programme had been launched in connection with the building of the library. It was now given a new and fresh focus, with the appeal to the corporate sector in Ireland and the United States backed up by a national church collection which it was hoped would bring in a substantial sum to underpin the appeal to business. It was a broad vision of a 'Bicentenary Fund', with debt eliminated, buildings and facilities renewed, the investment portfolio rebuilt—in a word, such stability as is possible in the world of the impermanent at the end of the twentieth century.

An approach to the German hierarchy yielded a free gift of £987,000 in January 1987. Later that spring the national church collection brought in £2,202,000. An Irish Corporate Group was formed, the chairman being Niall Crowley of Allied Irish Banks. In November the appeal was launched in the United States. In June 1988 the President was able to report that the accumulated debt had been eliminated, and the library debt, as he put it, 'absorbed'. But while the crippling interest charges were gone, the demands on resources seemed insatiable as he set out a programme of things that had to be done. It is possible only to list the larger items. Extensive—and expensive—protection systems were demanded by the Co. Kildare fire officers, and were installed. The power-house had been refurbished in the 1950s to provide heating and hot water for all purposes to the whole college, and also to provide it with electricity. This was asking too much of the machinery installed. As well, funds ran out before running hot water could be installed in the Pugin buildings, and although it gradually became necessary to take all electricity from the public supply only a grudging amount of hot water could be spared for student rooms anywhere. Now the power-house was renovated and upgraded, and hot water supplied to all student rooms, with other amenities such as showers more widely installed. The roofs of the library and refectory had been replaced in the reconstruction of the 1950s; now all the remainder were replaced. It was expensive work, because there were rows of dormer windows that complicated it. Even smaller works were expensive: in the summer of 1989 offices for the non-resident staff were removed from Humanity House to Rhetoric at a cost of £104,000, partly because more offices were needed, partly to rationalise the layout of the seminary. In 1986/87 a new board-room was constructed from one of the storerooms under the library, appropriately named the Renehan Hall to recall the President in whose term of office the buildings had been erected. It also housed as a unit the extensive art collection of Bishop William J. Philbin, left to the college when he retired from the see of Down and Connor in August 1982. Lastly, even if not finally, there may be mentioned the redecoration of Pugin's great refectory, which had been degraded by walls of battleship grey and terrazzo flooring in the late 1920s, and further degraded by plastic tables and chairs in the 1970s. Now the walls and floor were given warmer colours, the old oak tables gathered from round the college and reconditioned, and a set of new oak chairs provided. The physical fabric was being put in worthy shape for the Bicentenary. On 3 October 1991 a statue of Our Lady Queen of Angels was unveiled and blessed by Cardinal Mahony of Los Angeles as a memorial to benefactors from the west coast of the United States (Plate 61). Those from the east coast are commemorated in the Heritage Wall, part of a complex surrounding the sculpture of Pope John Paul II and the children in front of the new library (Plate 62). This was dedicated by Cardinal Cahal B. Daly of Armagh on 23 May 1993.

CHAPTER XVI

THE NEW COLLEGE: STRUCTURES

Maynooth College had been declared an 'open centre' in the expectation that there would soon be new legislation, in which its general status would be enhanced, and specifically that its theology school would be recognised as the principal one in the university system of the nation. More than a quarter of a century has passed, and nothing of this has happened, though there were a few times when it might be said to have nearly happened. The fact is that sweeping new university legislation was not high among the pressures on successive governments. It was increasingly seen as a complex and intractable issue; the system was working, and financial demands were controlled by the Higher Education Authority. The Maynooth Trustees, for their part, were slow to accept that they had pointed college development in the direction of a very complex institution where a number of separate interlocking interests could be discerned: first, the seminary; then two university bodies, the Pontifical University and the college of the National University; and, hopefully linked to both institutions, but an issue in its own right, the teaching of Catholic theology. At the beginning they were, understandably enough, very reluctant to envisage more than one institution, over which at all levels they would expect to have ultimate control. Again understandably, they were reluctant to accept any dilution of their existing control except in the context of firm legislative proposals, even though they had had repeated assurances in regard to the specific powers they might reasonably claim, especially in the teaching of theology. But firm legislative proposals were delayed. First there were long negotiations between University College, Dublin, and Trinity College, ending in April 1970 in an agreement that fell far short of the 'merger' announced by Donogh O'Malley two years before. What was agreed was a certain allocation of faculties between two independent universities in Dublin. Both negotiations and outcome had made it clear that any new legislation would be a tortuous process.

The consequence for Maynooth was that its student body increased rapidly and changed in character without any legislative change in structures, while theology, regarded as its strongest faculty, was to all intents and purposes excluded. As has been seen, the college had for some time been in receipt of a government grant. Increases were agreed, slowly; more significantly, a capital grant was given in 1970/71 and was continued every year afterwards (such a grant had been made only once before, to fit out a chemistry laboratory). It would appear that the Department of Finance was hesitant, but the Department of Education and the Higher Education Authority were friendly, appealing successfully to stated government policy; to the fact that there was a place for Maynooth in a rapidly expanding university system; and perhaps significantly, to the fact that while degree courses at Maynooth were being duplicated elsewhere, places there were being provided 'very cheaply'. But with legislation deferred it was a continuing battle and a confused one to provide structures at Maynooth. This chapter will try to summarise what happened under two broad headings: structures in the sense of physical structures, and structures in the sense of structures of government.

The Building of the New College

It was perhaps a sign of the times that first consideration was given to the building of hostels by religious congregations. This, however, involved a decision as to where the development should take place physically. None of the land owned by the college was considered suitable. It was not envisaged that the seminary should share any of the land within its surrounding walls, and the farm at Laraghbryan was just a little too far away. Fortunately, the Lanigan-O'Keeffe holding, directly to the north, just across the main road to Galway and the west, came on the market, and it was bought, the plan being to share it between academic and residential buildings.

Student accommodation was at that time a pressing need. Development was beginning at Leixlip, but Maynooth was still essentially a rural village. Religious congregations were still at the centre of planning vision (the first student sisters lodged in the Presentation convents in Maynooth and Clane) and a number of them expressed an interest in building hostels. At their October meeting in 1968 the Trustees ordered that an architect be engaged to draw up an overall development plan. The architect, Robin Walker of the firm of Michael Scott and Partners, prepared a draft plan for the overall development of the site with specific reference to the building of hostels: this was accepted in principle in March 1969, and a committee of the Trustees and college authorities was set up to work out the legal and architectural details. In June the President reported satisfactory meetings with the prospective builders, their architects and legal advisers. The plan he proposed was that the college would lease developed sites, recouping the cost of development by entry fines payable over a number of years. This was accepted by the Trustees, and in a series of meetings in the second half of 1969 agreement took shape on the layout of a hostel complex. Work on site development began in May 1970, including the site marked out for an academic building. Contracts for hostel sites were signed with six religious institutions, and work on the first hostel began in October 1970, and on the last in February 1971 (Plates 8, 63). The planning permission included the stipulation that there be an overpass connecting the new development with the old college, with a tall lighting mast at the general entrance to the complex. These were installed in the early months of 1972.

There were two clerical religious orders among those who built, the Salesians and the Society of African Missions. The Salesian Sisters built a hostel for lay women students. Three diocesan religious congregations of sisters took on the heavy responsibility of building a hostel. Of these, that of the Kildare and Leighlin Presentation Congregation was the last to keep serving its original purpose as a hostel for religious sisters. The house of the Tuam Mercy Sisters became a hostel for women students, while that of the Mercy Sisters of the diocese of Kildare was taken over by St Patrick's Missionary Society (Kiltegan). As already noted, the congregations of religious brothers had in the beginning shown considerable interest. The Irish Christian Brothers had acquired a site beside the main development; it was bought by the college when they withdrew. The Marist Brothers built on a similarly adjacent site, but later sold it to the Society of St Columban (the Maynooth Mission to China); and later the Paulist Congregation built its own house.

As it became clear that the number of students would keep increasing to an extent that would leave existing accommodation quite inadequate, discussions on 'a new Arts building' began with the Higher Education Authority in January 1970. The college authorities proposed a building of 63,000 square feet, and preliminary sketches, at this stage inevitably little more than 'ideas', were prepared by the architects, Michael Scott and Partners. In July 1970 the HEA approved a building of the size proposed by the college, and on this basis the architect prepared three different plans. In October the Trustees chose the proposal for a three-storey building, developed around hexagonal units and lending itself easily to possible future expansion. It was the most practical of the three proposals; it was also the most impressive and, perhaps inevitably, the most expensive. The architect and the Department of Education began to work out details, and then in May 1971 the bombshell fell. The general financial situation was worsening, and the proposals from the college were possibly a bit more expansive than the Department had had in mind. Anyway, in May it declared that it would sanction a building of 39,000 square feet only. The HEA intervened on behalf of the college, and the Department raised its offer to 44,000 square feet, with a strict cash limit of £8.50 a square foot. The HEA strongly advised the college to accept this, saying that otherwise it was highly likely it would get nothing. The college accepted.

The architect now had to address a quite different problem, and it soon became obvious that a three-storey building would be impossible within the new constrictions. It would simply have to be spread out as one storey, especially as the revised plan was expected to contain canteen and library accommodation as well. The Trustees accepted this idea reluctantly, and there was much dissatisfaction in the College Executive Council, but it was the Government that was calling the tune.[1] In discussions with the architect it became possible to introduce some improvements, the most notable being the provision of two lecture theatres, each with a capacity of 250. In March 1974 the President reported that the plans for the building were now completed, and that final approval was expected shortly. He emphasised the need to go ahead with such vehemence as to suggest the existence of continuing serious dissatisfaction, but the fact was that it was this or nothing and the pressure on existing facilities was becoming insupportable. In May a revised costing was approved by the Department of Education. It was considerably in excess of the £374,000 representing 44,000 square feet at £8.50 a square foot, considerably in excess of the £400,000 provided in the Book of Estimates, but the reason was inflation rather than improvements in the design. Then tenders had to be sought, and when that of John Sisk and Son was finally accepted on 19 August 1975 it was for £685,758.

The contract was signed a month later, and the first sod was cut by Archbishop Ryan of Dublin on 1 October (Plate 87). The building was completed in April 1977, and fitted out for October, when it was occupied (Plate 8). For a number of reasons the opening was muted. The exterior was unprepossessing, to say the least. The architect's proposal for a 'sculpture in steel' at the main entrance was not accepted, in the circumstances possibly wisely. The proposal for an interior mural was replaced by something much more modest. Though the building had been put up so cheaply that problems of future maintenance might be anticipated, the facilities it provided were in the main good, with only a few exceptions, such as the 'seminar space', unenclosed and totally impracticable, which was mercifully converted into a number of separate tutorial rooms. The need to provide space for library and canteen cut in on what was available for academic purposes, and space for lecture rooms and offices still had to be provided on a large scale in the old college, and this continued to be the case even when the library space became available in 1984 and the canteen space in 1991, because student numbers continued to grow.

Securing the New Arts Building had been a long and sometimes bruising battle. The library presented an even bigger problem. Even before the college opened its gates there had been continuing dissatisfaction with library facilities. All the inadequacies arose in one way or another form underfunding. Funds improved steadily as government financing grew, but they did not improve fast enough to keep up with new needs, such as the establishment of new academic departments or the need to have multiple copies of many books. For a long time also there had been pressure on space, only temporarily relieved by the shelving of the large ground-floor room in 1960, cheap shelving indeed, even for a place described at different times as pleasing to Goths or obviously designed as store-rooms. At least lighting had been installed with the shelving, and the expansion of the college introduced library opening hours that meant lighting had to be installed in the large reading-room upstairs.

To say that the library had been always inadequately staffed would be an understatement. The first full-time librarian had been appointed in October 1951. He had one untrained assistant, no more than a porter. It must be remembered that at the time even institutions such as the Public Record Office were also shamefully understaffed, but clearly the Maynooth situation could not measure up to an influx of new students. A beginning was made with the appointment of one full-time assistant and secretary in April 1968, but for a long time the staff grew more slowly than needs, and it was scattered in various offices wherever they could be found. And the college authorities found that more was needed than just professional and support staff: the need for library security was one of the not quite expected problems that kept surfacing in these years. Traditionally, anyone who took a book out of the college libraries incurred a 'reserved excommunication'. There is no certain record of the origins of this weighty threat, but it was clear it had now lost its power to deter, clear too that until the problem of security was tackled there would be a serious loss of books; and in the year 1970/71 the library was open to students from 8 a.m. to 10 p.m. seven days a week.

The priest-librarian, Seán Corkery, retired in 1973. It did not help that a full successor was appointed only in 1980, and there were many other problems as well. The New Arts Building opened in October 1977. It provided 250 readers' places, and space for 27,000 volumes, which had been transferred during the summer. There was, however, still pressure on space in the old library (Plate 86). There was no hope of public finance for a new one, and domestic resources were meagre, to the extent that thinking could not rise above some extension to the existing library. As has been seen, there had earlier been expansive ideas about taking over Pugin's great refectory and kitchen complex, but these had not been followed through and were now ruled out by renovations made in the kitchen area.[2] The ideas that surfaced about 1975 were more modest. They took the form of an extension of the library southwards, with a new entrance (this was important, for the existing library entrance was at the residential heart of the seminary). Some aspects of these proposals could give rise to reasonable misgivings. There was talk of 'two-storey pre-fabs', which, it turned out, would be as expensive as permanent buildings. Surviving drawings for proposed permanent buildings do not look markedly better, even allowing for the damage already done to Pugin's great south façade by the insensitivities of the 1930s and, admittedly to a lesser extent, by the newly completed extension to the kitchen.

The President, Tomás Ó Fiaich, was appointed Archbishop of Armagh in August 1977. It was a very difficult time in the college, but in March 1979 his successor, Michael Olden, laid what was indeed a very bold proposal before the Trustees. The pressure on existing library facilities, he said, had become intolerable. The staff had increased rapidly to nineteen, but they were divided over four offices. The total holdings were now over 200,000 volumes. The shelves in the main library were over 95 per cent full, which in practice meant impossible overcrowding. It had places for 400 readers, but they were really too many for the space available, and the whole place was necessarily noisy. There were 250 readers' places in the New Arts Building, with shelving for 27,000 volumes—a welcome but marginal relief. What he proposed as a remedy for a desperate situation was to build a new library, 'largely financed by the college itself'. The prospect of a grant from the Higher Education Authority was, he said, 'totally remote'. He had taken advice from an American fund-raising firm, Community Counselling Service Co. of New York, who had said that professional help in fund-raising was essential. He added that many of the staff had declared themselves eager to co-operate. In June he presented a more detailed report from Community Counselling Service. They expressed very little doubt of the feasibility of a campaign for a far-reaching programme in which the proposed new library would be only one component. They set the achievable target at £1,000,000 to £1,500,000, and asked to be retained for a year, at a fee which with expenses looked formidable enough.

The Trustees, however, agreed, and as has been seen the foundation-stone of what was to be the John Paul II Library was blessed by the Pope when he visited the college on 1 October. Over the next year a group took shape in the Irish corporate and business sector. In December 1981 they were constituted the 'Advisory Council of the Friends of Maynooth'. They were committed friends indeed, as was shown by their fund-raising efforts in Ireland. The American firm remained optimistic, as it was their business to be. In May 1980 they spoke of a 'reasonable hope' of achieving £2,000,000 by autumn; in June they spoke more realistically of nearly £1,500,000 already pledged. Most of this, however, was by way of covenant, and the cash in hand was much less, and, as mentioned, their fees were high. Yet the situation was considered sufficiently encouraging to begin consultations with a firm of architects in Newcastle-upon-Tyne that had designed many university libraries in England, which were visited by the vice-presidents and librarian.

By October the hoped-for pledges of £2,000,000 had been nearly achieved. The inflation rate was crippling, and the President urged that it was now safe to begin, even necessary, and that the college should build from its resources. He inclined to the English firm of architects, though he realised this might cause problems. He pointed to the perennial problem of the need for a small committee with real powers of decision, and asked that a Maynooth Development Office be set up. As anticipated, the proposal for an English architect did raise a problem. It was solved by a Dublin firm, Delaney, MacVeigh and Pike, being appointed associate architects. In June 1981 the Trustees authorised the building of the library. The development office was set up, and a full-time director appointed. In October 1981 he, together with the President and Cardinal Ó Fiaich, visited the United States, where they made many contacts and consulted with experts in college fund-raising, so that they were able to mount a campaign there, and, as already mentioned, the Irish 'Advisory Council of the Friends of Maynooth' was set up in December. The main contract was signed on 30 November, the amount being £3,150,125 and the contractors McLaughlin and Harvey Ltd of Dublin, and the first sod was cut by the Cardinal on the site agreed on, at the old college side of the Galway road, beside the overpass to the new college and the existing gate (Plate 8). This site in the 'Long Meadow' had some obvious disadvantages. It had a stream running through it and had always been subject to flooding. This necessitated extensive—and expensive—preparatory work and ruled out the possibility of a storage basement. A totally detached building had a number of inherent disadvantages, not least the age-old Maynooth problem of having to go out in the rain. On the other side, there was the need to keep alive the hope of integrating the teaching of Theology into the Arts courses of the National University. On 18 April 1982 the site was blessed by the Cardinal, and the foundation stone was laid by the President of Ireland, Dr Patrick Hillery.

It is in the nature of building projects that costs tend to keep mounting, but by far the greatest reason why costs increased was that these were the worst years of inflation. By the late summer of 1982 the final bill was estimated at £4,000,000, and given the continuing inflation it could not but be more in the end, while the amount pledged came only to £2,700,000. There was then a shadow over the formal opening on 7 October 1984. Again the function was performed by President Hillery, and the blessing was given by Cardinal William Baum, Prefect of the Congregation for Catholic Education in Rome. A bronze bust of Pope John Paul II, the gift of Colm Barnes, by the sculptress Marjorie Fitzgibbon, stands in the main concourse over the inscribed foundation-stone which, possibly with memories of the lost foundation-stone of Long Corridor, was given this prominent position inside the 'John Paul II Library'. Later a large bronze group, depicting the Pope with Irish youth, was set up opposite the main entrance, and was later backed, as has been seen, by the 'Heritage Wall' (Plate 88).[3] The sculptress was Imogen Stuart. It is an impressive piece of work, though there have been mixed reactions, apart from the fact that it cost nearly £50,000, which could be ill afforded.

The John Paul II Library was undoubtedly a magnificent asset, and it would have been impossible to have carried on much longer without something like it. Externally, it is a large and pleasing modern building (Plate 59). The functional interior is finished in soft shades: the extensive elm panelling is a bonus from the disease that killed all the elm trees at this time. New cataloguing on the Dewey decimal system began in 1984, and computerisation in 1991. The great transfer of books took place in the summer of 1984. When it was over the old library still looked full. Now named the Russell Library, in memory of the great President in whose time the books were first moved there from the top floor of Dunboyne House, it is now a research library with limited opening hours, a place of refreshing quiet. In 1986/87 the 'Newman bookcases' were erected there, ornate baroque shelving which had come from the

Catholic University. They had been in St Mary's theology library, and when moved to the Russell Library were re-erected as a free-standing structure in the middle of the floor near one end, where they do not really look out of place against Pugin's Gothic. As for the John Paul II Library, it looked full the day it opened, and with an annual intake of about 6,000 volumes pressures soon built up. Theoretically, what was built was only the first phase, but the financial situation dictated that the second phase must be distant, probably not before developments in electronics will have completely changed the concept of a library.

The library debt was a major element in the problems facing the new President at the beginning of 1985, though, as has been seen, by no means the only one.[4] He spelled out the problems in his report to the Trustees in June. He stressed that the work had been completed slightly ahead of schedule and at no cost over-run. The difficulty had arisen because not enough provision had been made for the overall cost adjusted for inflation and interest payments. Taking these into account, the total had come to nearly £6,000,000, plus £600,000 for furnishing. Against this £4,500,000 had been pledged, of which £3,400,000 was in hand. The shortfall would be in the region of £3,000,000, with interest payments even at the best rate coming to £400,000 a year, and fund-raising expenses at about £150,000. An approach to the Higher Education Authority brought an 'incentive payment' of £1,050,000 spread over seven years. The Irish corporate sector had been generous, but by now its resources had been for the moment tapped. Hopes must rest in the United States, where, however, nothing could be taken for granted. Over the coming years, nevertheless, a very successful campaign was mounted there. The library debt as a separate item proved intractable, for the interest charges were crippling. In 1989 it was still over £2,500,000. By then, however, the general fund-raising had been so successful that it was possible to offset the library debt 'on a temporary basis by funds from other sources'. In fact the temporary basis proved permanent.

The ordering of the college archive was a necessary preliminary to any attempt to write the bicentenary history. There were two main domestic sources, the papers of the President and of the bursar. In both cases the material was in some disarray, and also in some danger from the advance of computers. When the archive was taken in hand in 1989 some material from the bursar's office had already been deposited in the Russell Library. A research assistant in 1989/90 located and copied relevant material in Ireland, mainly in diocesan archives, and material in the Congregation of Propaganda in Rome was also copied; the following year an archival assistant completed the cataloguing of the assembled material down to about 1960, and there has been a preliminary cataloguing of later papers. Archive storage-rooms were fitted out convenient to the Russell Library, where reading space for researchers was courteously made available. The material is now stored in acid-free folders and low-acid boxes. As far as possible it has been arranged under presidencies, though there is need of a separate series for topics spanning more than one presidency, the building of the College Chapel for example. In the nature of things, the material for the later years is more extensive; indeed, the first substantial collection is from the presidency of Laurence Renehan (1845–57), and it is surely no coincidence that he was the first to live—and die—in the President's rooms in the Pugin buildings. Then there are the minute-books—of the Trustees since the foundation, of the internal administrative bodies since 1870; and long rows of account-books from the bursar's office.

The hope is that in time the archive may expand to become one of general Irish ecclesiastical interest. By far the largest accession to date is represented by the Salamanca Papers, which came in the 1950s. The bulk of them relate to the Irish College in Salamanca, but there is material from the other Irish colleges in Spain. It is clear that an attempt was made to gather their holdings into Salamanca after they had closed, almost all of them in connection with the suppression of the Jesuits in 1769. In the early 1870s the then rector, William McDonald, had some order put on the archives. They were tied up in bundles or *legajos* and a descriptive list drawn up, very general for the most part. Their first storage in Maynooth was highly unsuitable. They were then moved to the old muniment room: it would be hard to find better storage conditions, but conditions for consultation were execrable—there was no artificial light in the room, and the bundles of documents were stored on deep shelves. Then there was the material subsequent to McDonald's time, some indeed dating from before it which he had overlooked. This was in miscellaneous boxes and parcels. All has suffered some disturbance and loss, some of it from the unsupervised researches of historians, in this matter surely the natural enemies of archivists. Material from the highly acidic *legajos* has been put into acid-free folders and low-acid boxes. The descriptive list has been translated and checked against what is actually there. As is to be expected, there is material unaccounted for. Material later than McDonald, or overlooked by him, has been collected under rectorships and given acid-free storage. It will be clear there is still much work to be done.

Maynooth had a long and distinguished tradition of 'Natural Philosophy', mathematics, mathematical physics, and experimental physics. Chemistry came in the 1930s, and again in the late 1950s, this time to stay. A demand for biology came very shortly after the college opened up in 1966. The first computer centre was installed in 1977 and 1978 in Rhetoric House, in what had been the Junior library and the Junior oratory, known to generations, with affection rather than irreverence, as 'the synagogue'. Finally, a Department of Computer Science was established in 1988.

Experimental physics expanded out from Callan's old quarters in Long Corridor into prefabricated buildings to the north. The other subjects expanded out of the old chemistry laboratory in Logic House, and took over the whole building, with a swelling village of prefabricated buildings at its back. The Higher Education Authority was understandably slow to commit itself to an inevitably expensive science building. It did declare its approval in principle for such a building when the college undertook a library from its own resources, but principle was very slow in becoming practice. Finally, however, it was announced in September 1989 that a new science building for Maynooth would be included in a submission to the European Structural Fund. The project was supported, and on 24 June 1992 the Taoiseach, Albert Reynolds, laid the foundation stone of the Nicholas Callan Science Building. He opened it on 28 September 1993 (Plates 8, 90). It houses the departments of biology and computer science, and is more or less half-way to the needs of the experimental sciences. It is a handsome building, purpose-built and well equipped: indeed the 'New Arts Building' looks insignificant and quite shabby beside it (Plate 92).

Student life in Maynooth had traditionally been spartan. More amenities were being provided in the 1950s and 1960s, but the opening up of a closed community raised the new problem of provision for non-residents. At the beginning this was admittedly meagre, with canteen and recreational facilities housed in one fairly small prefabricated building. Non-resident student numbers grew quickly: in 1973/74 there were about 550 in the arts and science courses. This caused great pressure on resources that naturally led to student discontent, and in March 1974 the Trustees decided to give £50,000 to build a 'suitable recreation centre'. This was a fairly modest sum, but generous considering the resources available, generous too by comparison with what was being done elsewhere. The proposals did not please everyone. There were objections to what was seen as necessarily a noisy development from the hostels and from local residents, objections which continued even after planning permission had been given. In the end there was a compromise agreement to build it on a site as isolated as possible. The college architect also felt aggrieved. At the request of the Trustees he had laid down regulations for uniformity in the external appearance of the hostel development. The New Arts Building was conforming to it only marginally. But now the Trustees were breaking the regulations they themselves had asked for, because the money available would only be enough for 'system-building'—prefabrication, even if of a reasonably high quality. The students too thought the building inadequate and sought improvements, but these were limited by the money available, and architect and students had to live with the building until it was demolished and replaced in 1993 (Plates 8, 91). The difficulties and disputes had delayed construction, but it had been completed in the spring of 1977 and formally opened on 11 May. The contract had been for £52,431.

Minor amenities were added over the next few years. A donation of £10,000 from Allied Irish Banks provided a squash-court in the old ball-alleys at the back of Logic House, though it was soon so surrounded by science buildings as to be hard to find. Grants from the Higher Education Authority provided football pitches, dressing-rooms and tennis-courts in the new complex, and renovations, alterations and additions in the Aula Maxima, expanded green-room facilities, a foyer and cloakrooms. They were modestly done, but the architecture of the Aula did not lend itself easily to spoiling.

There was little or nothing for over a decade. Then it became possible to put together financial packages that led to three major developments. The biggest was the University Village Apartments, accommodating 240 students in modern well-designed apartments in an attractive collection of buildings in pleasant surroundings in a corner of the new developments (Plates 8, 63). They were completed in June 1991. Shortly before, on 24 May, the Minister for Education, formerly a student of the course for the Higher Diploma in Education, Mary O'Rourke, had laid the foundation-stone of a building complex to contain a student restaurant and a fully equipped sports centre. The speed of construction should not be allowed to give a false impression of the magnificent facilities made available. The restaurant was ready for the opening of term at the beginning of October and the sports centre shortly afterwards (Plates 8, 91). And finally, as already noted, the student social centre of 1977 was demolished and replaced in 1993. What in 1968 had been 'the Lanigan-O'Keeffe farm' was beginning to look quite full of buildings.

The 'Interim' Structures

It was clear that the expansion of the college would call for powers of internal decision-taking such as had not existed before. The Trustees moved with perhaps pardonable slowness into what for them was unknown territory, being willing enough to envisage bodies to advise them, but slow to delegate any power of decision. Yet this step could not be put off indefinitely. It was not just that the Finance Council was ill-equipped to decide the flood of minutiae now coming before it, things like student lockers, typists and telephones. There were many things that needed both assessment and decision, related to the preparation of an academic budget based on proposals for academic development from the Faculty of Theology and the Academic Council, and possibly the appointment of junior staff in accordance with recognised university proceedings.

In June 1971 the Trustees established the College Executive Council. It was to have nine members, three representatives of the Trustees, the President, a vice-president, the bursar and three academics, one elected by the Faculty of Theology, one by the Academic Council, and one by the whole staff. There was to be an election every two years, and members were eligible for re-election. The council was to meet monthly during the academic year. The powers delegated to it were limited but important: to prepare an academic budget on a five-year projection, as required by the Higher Education Authority, and to determine priorities in the allocation of state funds on the basis of submissions from the academic bodies, all this without prejudice to the final authority of the Trustees. And the council, through elected representatives, was to report back to the Faculty of Theology and the Academic Council at least every three months. This was a kind of attempt to have everybody consulted on everything, a kind of secular 'system of Saint-Sulpice'. Only one meeting was held, on 6 March 1972, and it was a disaster, with disparate views being urged by too many people on representatives of a body still feeling its way, and protests from members of the full-time staff who were not members of the two academic bodies because they had not been invited.

In the nature of things, the powers of the council tended to expand as it grappled with a mountain of detail there was no-one else to handle. The Trustees were reluctant to expand the powers of what was seen, not just by them but by all, as a temporary body, filling the gap until the promised legislation brought more permanent solutions. In June 1973 the existing council was continued for a year under the same terms of reference. This led to protests in the autumn, to the effect that the three nominees of the Trustees were junior figures among the bishops and not themselves Trustees; that there was no representative of the non-resident staff, or of the students; and that repeated recommendations from the council had been ignored or even refused. The Trustees replied that while they were in general agreement that the powers of the council should be enlarged, the present transitional period was not the time for decision. However, changes were introduced in the autumn of 1974, when the council was continued for a further 'experimental period' of two years. It was given more extended powers of financial management 'in the public sector', where it was also empowered to appoint junior lecturers. The membership was considerably enlarged: now it was to consist of the three representatives of the Trustees, the President, both vice-presidents, the bursar, the secretary of the Trustees, two representatives of the Faculty of Theology, two of the Academic Council, two elected by full-time lecturers not members of either of these bodies, a representative of the seminarist board (in charge of the studies of unmatriculated seminarians), and a student representative (increased to two in 1977). Even with the increased membership the considerable and growing work to be done meant a very heavy administrative burden imposed on relatively few people chosen from a small staff, though, as it appeared, this was so much to the liking of some that it was not easy to prevent an atmosphere of cliques. Nevertheless, it was the hard work of the College Executive Council that really set up university structures in Maynooth.

The changes introduced in 1974 represented a cautious advance that did not satisfy the more radical voices. On the other hand senior academic staff felt they were not being given the influence they believed was their due. In October 1980 the President sent the Trustees a memorandum in connection with a review of the council which was now pending. The main issue, he said, was the representation to be given to the Academic Council. There were, as he saw it, good reasons why the Academic Council should be more strongly represented. However, he did not agree with those who said that academics of the College Executive Council should come from the recognised college only, as some were urging: there were, in his judgement, good reasons why all interests should continue to be represented. His advice was that as the times were uncertain and not best suited to drastic changes the existing council should be continued for a year, until more thought was given to the problem. This is what was done.

In May 1981 a frustrated Academic Council sought and obtained a meeting with the Visitors. A lengthy memorandum was drawn up and presented. There were academic problems, but worse, there were serious structural problems. It instanced the 'Academic Planning Unit', set up in 1972. The Academic Council had no representative on it, and not all its members were members of the College Executive Council. The Academic Council likewise had no representative on the 'Campus Planning Committee', set up in 1979. A Promotions Board had been set up in 1974, at the request of the Academic Staff Association. It was quite wrong that there should be on such a body a preponderance of junior staff, themselves potential candidates for promotion. The memorandum ended by saying that the Academic Council 'is meeting extraordinary difficulty even in finding out what is going on . . . more and more the council finds itself talking to itself.' In his own report to the Trustees the President concurred: 'As I see it, the problem really lies in the fact that many of the academic structures set up in the last decade were seen as interim pending new legislation concerning universities. Nobody thought they would last very long . . . senior staff feel they deserve more voice.'

In many ways the episcopal Trustees were getting into an unenviable position. They were remote from the lay staff, perhaps increasingly remote from the dwindling clerical staff, and increasingly out of touch with much detail. Yet they had to take the decisions, for there was no-one else to decide. The new College Executive Council had an element of squaring the circle about it. Membership was expanded to twenty-four: the President; the two vice-presidents; the two registrars (of the Pontifical and National Universities); four representatives of the Trustees (including their secretary); one student from the Pontifical University, one from the National; the bursar; the librarian; seven representatives of the National University, four of them members of the Academic Council elected by it; three representatives of the Pontifical University, two of them full professors elected by full professors; and one representative of the seminarist board. It was to have 'general charge, subject to the undiminished rights of the Trustees, of current expenditure for academic purposes' and overall responsibility for the harmonious development of academic life and the maintenance of close liaison between the two university bodies. It was to have a consultative vote in all appointments, but no power of appointment to any post, a wise decision for a body where senior academic staff were still under-represented. And the new College Executive Council proceeded to set up a number of committees, picking up such outliers as the Academic Planning Unit and instituting two Promotions Boards, one for promotion to lecturer, the other to senior lecturer. Inevitably the committees multiplied, and there were complaints that some of them should more fittingly be committees of the Academic Council. It was a cumbersome way of doing business, but here again the best was the enemy of the good.

Staff organisations developed in the Irish universities as part of the ferment of the 1960s. In Maynooth an association grew out of joint discussions between the Faculty of Theology and the Academic Council during the year 1967/68, when the staff was still exclusively clerical. This Academic Staff Association became quite important, for a number of reasons. It was the only forum for the non-resident staff who began to be appointed, all at first to junior positions and nearly all of them lay. As well, it was the only academic co-ordinator between two university bodies with no statutory link. There was much friendly academic discussion, the newcomers expressing a particular admiration for an institution where the two cultures had not yet separated, where theologians, humanists and scientists could meet on a personal level. A kind of populist ethos was in favour, 'people power' against the remoteness of the Trustees. These had consulted the staff individually on the appointment of a vice-president in June 1970. The Academic Staff Association demanded the right to express its mind collectively, and when this was not granted it organ-ised its own ballot for the appointment of a vice-president in October 1974, using a complicated system of proportional representation that not everyone agreed was free from defects.

The Irish Federation of University Teachers grew out of a series of infor-mal meetings held between 1962 and 1964. By March 1966 it was possible to hold the first annual general meeting, and rules for the Federation were approved. Maynooth staff had played an active part in these developments, indeed a very substantial part given the size of the college. A decisive change was introduced in February 1974, when the Federation decided to seek negoti-ating powers as a trade union. It did this by a large majority, but the minority had grave misgivings, conscious of the many potential problems in unionising a liberal profession, realising too that if university teachers felt the need of union protection there were a number of existing unions they could join. In fact many had already done just this. The unionised federation pressed with university authorities for agreed procedures on consultation, negotiation and grievances generally. In the autumn of 1978 the Trustees ordered the President and vice-presidents to begin negotiations. The following June they reported that things were going slowly.[5] The background was, of course, the court cases arising from the dismissals. The federation would make no allowance for the fact that Maynooth regarded itself as a unique institution comprising different elements and was refusing to consider explicit recogni-tion 'of the binding force of Canon Law in so far as it applies to the institution and to its members, with particular reference to the canonical obligations attaching to clerical members of the staff.' On this issue the parties were poles apart, and the judgement of the Supreme Court on 1 November 1979 effec-tively ended dialogue for the time being.

All these developments had left the President of Maynooth subject to severe pressures from all sides. He was not a member of the ultimate governing body, the Trustees, and was present at their meetings by invitation only. Tomás Ó Fiaich outlined the problems in a memorandum to the Trustees in May 1976. The President, he said, 'has to fall back on tradition, custom, advice from others, and ultimately his own judgement . . . the powers of the President with regard to non-resident staff and students have never been defined.' He said it was fortunate that no major issue had arisen in this sensitive area, and pointed out the need for a complete revision of the college statutes. He was right to fear trouble, even if to an extent mistaken in the direction he expected it might come from.

Planning and Waiting

As has been seen, the report of the Higher Education Authority in July 1972 still held out to Maynooth the option of becoming an 'associated college' or an independent university. At their meeting at the beginning of October the Trustees decided to hold 'a private seminar' in November, 'to discuss the future development of the college as a seminary and as a university institution'. All members of the Irish Episcopal Conference were to be invited, together with all members of the teaching staff in Maynooth, the college administration, and student representatives. They added that three or four from outside the college might be invited. Submissions from individuals or college bodies were to be circulated in written form in advance.

The President's submission began by saying that the formation of priests remained the basic task of the college. This, however, was quite compatible with the development of an 'open university' within a single institution. He favoured the option of becoming an 'associated college', and proposed a structure of government which, though completely logical, was so complicated as to indicate that the unity of the institution would not be achieved easily. But this unity he considered essential, pointing to a number of examples from Canada of universities which had developed from seminaries (Ottawa, Laval, Quebec), where very recent changes had reduced the role of both theological studies and the seminary to a marginal one.

The Administrative Council reported that it had considered the possibility that only the students of theology should live under a seminary regime, the rest of the college being converted into hostels where students for the priesthood would live together with lay students, but in the end it had decided it was better to keep the seminary for all seven years. There should be a single head for the whole institution (the seminarians themselves preferred a clearer distinction, with a separate seminary head).

At this stage the Faculty of Theology had little new to add, except to repeat that theology needed a wider university background, and that anything that might develop at Maynooth would be impoverished without theology. It did raise the question of possible difficulties regarding appointments, but did not go beyond saying that a satisfactory system was possible and that there were models for it. It spoke too of the need for new structures of government and of the need for more academic autonomy, but again made no detailed recommendations.

Significantly, the other major submission came from the Academic Staff Association, not the Academic Council. This was agreed on little more than statements of aspiration, and admitted that there was wide disagreement on many points, with 'individual submissions diametrically opposed in outlook'. There was agreement that an independent university was the better option. There should be one overall group of trustees (of whom nine, presumably out of seventeen, were to be bishops), with 'wide' but unspecified functions in the institution as a whole. It was implied, though not exactly stated, that they would form the governing body of the seminary, which was to have a separate rector. The university was to have its own governing body with an academic majority and a substantial minority—over a third, it was suggested—representing outside interests. This would leave room for little more than marginal representation for the episcopal Trustees. There was a separate submission from non-resident staff, six of them, almost all who had so far been appointed. It spoke with much approval of the 'complete integration' of everybody, students and staff, both academic and academic support staff, with domestic staff as well, a vision of the Utopian democracy that philosophers from Plato onwards—and indeed from Plato backwards—had viewed with the gravest misgiving.

The seminar opened on the evening of 3 November, and continued all the next day. There were twelve student representatives, elected by the Students' Representative Council, and from outside the college Professors T. D. Williams and John O'Meara of University College, Dublin, and Professor George Dawson of Trinity College. In the nature of things there could not be much more than a general discussion, and the meeting was not minuted. It ended by setting up a 'Working Party on the future of Maynooth', with four sub-committees to report back to a further meeting: one on studies and external relationships; a second on internal structures; a third on the relationship between the seminary and the university; and the fourth on the place of theology. The Trustees held a special meeting on 11 November to consider the more urgent points raised at the seminar. They decided that, given the present level of resources, there should be a ceiling on admissions to Arts and Science, with priority for clerics and religious (overall numbers of non-residents had grown from 82 in 1968/69 to 507 in 1972/73). They decided further that the College Executive Council should submit to their March meeting documented requirements for additional staff in these areas, and that the Academic Council should report on the possibility of offering courses in Biblical Sciences for the BA degree; and that a special group be set up to report on the future of the physical sciences.

It will be recalled that in 1962 it had been decided that resources in the teaching of science would reach to general or pass degree level only, except for a 'joint honours' degree in Mathematical Science. What was at issue then was the teaching of experimental subjects, to honours level, or possibly even at all. In 1972 there were five academic departments in the Faculty of Science, three of them being experimental subjects (physics, chemistry and biology), with in all ten full-time staff. The position was considered by the Maynooth heads of departments, with Professors Nevin of University College, Dublin, and Dawson of Trinity College. The latter was not keen on a 'joint honours' BSc, but he was in favour of some kind of link between the experimental subjects and what were coming to be called 'the human sciences' for an honours BSc degree at Maynooth. Professor Nevin also wanted an end to the 'joint honours' degree, but what he favoured was to provide additional resources to strengthen courses for the general degree. Neither of these pleased the Maynooth representatives. Professor Nevin's proposals, they said, would reduce their role to teacher-training—which is what it had been for ten years past.

The working party held five meetings between May 1973 and January 1975. The agenda at each meeting consisted of reports from its sub-committees. The first of these, dealing with status and external relationships, reported that it 'would tend to favour' independent status for Maynooth as a university, and inclined towards a separate seminary administration, with its own president. The recommendation of independent university status was made very tentatively, probably most influenced by the fact that the staff as a body was strongly in favour. There were strong arguments against, the principal one being the small size of the college and its limited range of faculties. A meeting of the working party on 14 September 1974 commissioned a paper on 'The future of Maynooth as a University'. This was ready for the meeting of the Trustees at the end of the month, which forwarded it to the Minister for Education, Richard Burke. It recapitulated events since the 'merger' proposals in April 1967, and went on to request that if there were to be only one university for Ireland, Maynooth should be an equal college, with special arrangements to preserve the status of the Pontifical University, and that if there were to be several independent institutions, even with only one university in Dublin, 'having carefully considered the advantages and disadvantages of both independence and association, we are convinced that the arguments in favour of independence are much stronger.' By the time the document came before a full meeting of the working party on 10 January 1975 it had been passed out by events, for the Minister had given his decision on 16 December. There were to be three independent universities, including both Trinity College and University College in Dublin, with Cork and Galway united in a 'National University'; National Institutes for Higher Education (the first, at Limerick, had opened in the academic year 1972/73) were to be recognised colleges; and Maynooth was to be a constituent college in the university of its choice. And there matters rested, more or less, for longer than anyone might have foreseen.

The second sub-committee, on internal structures, recommended two governing bodies with two presidents, one for the university and one for the seminary. The university governing body was to have twenty-one members, eleven from the academic staff, three from the episcopal Trustees, and seven others. There were other recommendations, none of them very notable, in general following the pattern in other institutions. The work of the third sub-committee, on relations between university and seminary, opted for a single institution and a single president, with a separate 'seminary board'. But at a general meeting in May 1973 it appeared that agreement was clearly moving in the direction of independent status as a civil university; a clear distinction between the seminary and the civil university; two bodies of Trustees and two Presidents; with, however, 'the preservation at the same time in this new setting of the unity of the historic Maynooth'. This was slightly refined at the November meeting: one set of Trustees, but two governing bodies for two university centres. The difficulty was now becoming clearer: how can 'the unity of the historic Maynooth' be preserved if it is divided into two totally separate bodies? By what proved to be the final meeting of the working party in January 1975 the seminary and the Pontifical University were edging closer together, but no firm decision was possible 'pending clarification of the future role of the Pontifical University'.

This is a clear indication of unresolved difficulties at the fourth sub-committee, on the place of theology in the university. Polarisation appeared at its very first meeting, on 22 February 1973, between what was put forward as the voice of authority and as the voice of university theology. For authority, it was suggested that all theological degrees be degrees of the pontifical university; that civil recognition be sought for them; and that professors in the pontifical university be 'recognised teachers' of the civil university (this last was not the most fortunate of phrases, designating as it did what had long been regarded as a badge of inferiority). Against this the view was put forward that the pontifical Faculty of Theology be also a faculty of the 'civil university'. The meeting could only record that 'the basic difference of opinion was not resolved'. In fact, this second view corresponded fairly closely to what the Trustees had asked of the Senate of the National University in 1966. In the years between, however, theology and theologians had wandered into wild frontiers, and it must be regretted that no attempt was made to explore the real situation in detail. Important questions were not merely unanswered but unasked, notably whether the 'undergraduate' seminarian was to be prepared as a 'theologian' or, more basically, as a 'catechist'. The argument was directed at the frontiers of knowledge, bypassing the wise reflection, extending far beyond theology, that it is not good for undergraduates to be constantly operating at these heights. Further discussion only seemed to increase the polarisation between 'doctrinal orthodoxy' and 'academic freedom'. On the one hand, there was emphasis on the 'duty of teachers of theology to keep within the bounds of the word of God as traditionally preserved and as taught and interpreted by the living *magisterium* of the Church and especially by the Vicar of Christ', and that in regard to recent pronouncements '"Just liberty in investigation and teaching" is in these documents strictly circumscribed in a way that is foreign to the natural sciences and to the teaching of the secular university'.

The other point of view, it was claimed, was summed up in comments of the Irish Theological Association meeting on 15 May 1969. Here, it was urged, there were few limits to the 'academic freedom' of Catholic theologians: it extended even to 'the freedom to make mistakes'—at best, again, an unfortunate phrase; and in the appointment of teaching staff authority was restricted to a negative role, with power only to reject candidates from a short list submitted. The final report of the sub-committee, presented to the last meeting of the working party in January 1975, had to content itself with setting out the arguments for and against the rival options, namely that theology should become an organic part of the 'civil university' or continue its distinct existence while offering the 'civil university' students access to its 'recognised teaching'. These, its report said, were argued at length, but without agreement. Eight documents were appended setting out the irreconcilable views. The working party could do little except agree that the documentation be passed to the Trustees. Its total lack of agreed positive recommendation did not augur well for the future of theology in the university.

For reasons already suggested, governments did not give high priority to university legislation. As well, political instability was growing, and a government might have got a certain distance with the problem—sometimes indeed a considerable distance—but then it fell. There is a certain pointlessness in recapitulating proposals which came to nothing, but a summary will at least serve the purpose of underlining the dangerous vacuum within which Maynooth continued to exist. Early in 1975 a delegation from Maynooth met the Minister to discuss his scheme of the previous December. It consisted of the Cardinal, Archbishop Ryan of Dublin, Bishop Philbin of Down and Connor, and the President of the college with its academic vice-president, Dr Kevin McNamara. They had what was described as a 'wide-ranging discussion', covering a detailed examination of the implications of constituent status, Maynooth's preference for independence, the role of theology, and the need to preserve a 'distinctive character'. At the end of July 1976 the Minister issued revised proposals: five independent universities, two in Dublin, one each in Cork, Galway and Maynooth. But even independence still left unresolved the position of the Pontifical University, especially, but not exclusively, its Faculty of Theology. The Trustees were inclining to the view that the pontifical faculties, Theology, Canon Law and Philosophy, should 'while remaining pontifical faculties, become also three faculties of Maynooth University.' It was noted that this was already in fact the case with Philosophy, but continuing hesitation is evident in the anxiety that the 'incorporation or recognition' of the three faculties should be with their existing statutes explicitly embodied in any proposed civil legislation. It is also possible to sense that academic anxieties were being compounded by current troubles in the college, raising the question of the necessity (or feasibility) of seeking guarantees as to the obligations in canon law of priest staff as members of a seminary community. At their meeting in October 1976 the episcopal conference deputed their university commission to conduct negotiations with the Minister 'in the forthcoming university reorganisation'. It looked as if urgent decisions were required, because it was accepted that the details of legislation for independent multi-denominational universities, all with the same basic structure as far as possible, were being busily worked out in the Department of Education. The episcopal commission agreed that Maynooth should have one set of trustees, leasing the necessary facilities to the 'secular university', and having four or five representatives on its governing body. They felt it desirable, but possibly not easily attainable, that the episcopal trustees should have some supervisory rights 'in regard to overall policy for the development of the university in accordance with the special character, associations and traditions of the college.' In regard to the pontifical university, they felt the best solution was state recognition for the existing institution with its three faculties. These would also be faculties of the 'secular university', on equal terms with the others. Courses in theology for the Arts degree should be in 'Roman Catholic theology', and it was hoped that in what had been the colleges of the National University there would be departments of 'essentially Catholic theology' within faculties of Arts. At Maynooth, philosophy was to be taught through the pontifical faculty, and the final choice of appointments in all its three faculties would rest with the episcopal Trustees. This, it was felt, was not unreasonable: academics in subjects such as medicine, architecture and engineering had to be 'recognised and registered members of their professional bodies', and there had been even instances of the withdrawal of the right to teach. Negotiations were continuing when the Dáil was dissolved in May 1977. The elections resulted in a change of government, with a new Minister for Education, who in his youth had been briefly a seminarian in the college.

The spring of 1977 was, as had been already seen, a time of troubles in Maynooth, added to by the death of the Cardinal on 17 April, still only in his mid-sixties. These troubles divided the staff, and meant that if an independent university were set up it would be in an atmosphere of contention, with some doubt if its ethos would be Catholic or even Christian. Some form of association with University College, Dublin, began to look attractive, and there was even some talk, admittedly desperate, of trying to rely exclusively on the pontifical charter. Further, given the divisions among the staff, it was in a sense inevitable that policy-making should be more and more confined to the Trustees. They inclined to the view that 'in the light of recent happenings' the college might not yet be ready for independence, though they would not rule

411

out independence as a goal to be aimed for. An 'associated college' of University College, Dublin, was mooted, with—the term earlier jettisoned now returned—'recognised status' for the Pontifical University. It was accepted that Dublin should be involved 'in a serious way' in the governing body of the associated college, but there should be no Dublin examiner. It was recognised that difficulties might arise under both heads. How was Dublin to ensure academic standards in an associated college that was granting its degrees? And how could the Trustees, 'while not being immediately involved in the running of the associated college . . . still have considerable and final control over its development'?

The new Government took time to feel its way into the university question, but on 14 March 1979 the Department of Education informed Archbishop Ryan of Dublin that John Wilson, the Minister, anticipated 'proceeding with legislation at an early date', and requested observations concerning Maynooth from the episcopal commission on universities. The decision which emerged was that the Trustees should proceed with negotiations leading to Maynooth becoming an independent civil university, the legislation to provide

> that on an appointed day the serving academic staff of the recognised college at Maynooth shall hold equivalent positions in Maynooth University, and that on the same day the faculties of Theology, Philosophy, and Canon Law shall also become faculties within Maynooth University . . . The terms of appointment to positions in the University which could come within the jurisdiction of Canon Law shall be governed by such law . . .

There was to be one set of Trustees for the institution as a whole, and they were to have 'strong representation' on the governing body of the 'civil university'. This would have its own President, with a separate President for the seminary and pontifical university. Negotiations were to be continued by the episcopal commission on universities.

The negotiations did indeed continue, but it was not easy to reach a conclusion. Serious delay was caused by the extraordinary political instability at the beginning of the 1980s, with a coalition Government taking office in May 1981, Fianna Fáil in January 1982, and a coalition again the following November. For reasons already outlined, the episcopal Trustees had been keeping negotiations in their own hands, but as time stretched out indecisively this gave rise to frustrations within the college. In May 1981 the Academic Council had sought and obtained a meeting with the Visitors, but this had no permanent results. By 1983 other bodies, the College Executive Council and the Academic Staff Association, were urging that as there was no indication there were any plans to dissolve the National University Maynooth should seek improved status as a matter of urgency, constituent status if possible, for the number of recognised colleges was growing and Maynooth's place lay more with the constituent colleges by reason of both its seniority and the scope and diversity of its academic programmes. The theology issue, the College Executive Council said in March 1983, should be held back until constituent college status had been first achieved.

It was indeed beginning to look as if the colleges of the National University, after all the debate, were beginning to come round to the view that their best interests lay in continuing association. There would be greater autonomy for the colleges, with an upgrading of Maynooth, but the National University of Ireland would still remain as an overall body, and in particular as the source of university degrees. Here the story is beginning to enter the area of current affairs and unfinished business. One reason it is still unfinished though consensus has been more or less in place for a decade is that new legislation is hard to focus. One reason arises because the state is now to such a great extent the paymaster, though the days when it was assumed that it would provide everything seem to be passing. But it is so heavily the paymaster that it feels it has the right to see that an efficient use is being made of resources. This leaves the existing constituent colleges anxious to keep legislation to the necessary minimum, judging, not without reason, that the atmosphere at the beginning of the century was more congenial to university autonomy and the traditional academic freedoms than is the atmosphere at the century's end. What changes will come may be expected to be greater at Maynooth. The college has existed in a kind of limbo between one life and another for a quarter of a century, and it may be that it is no mean achievement to have survived. Its central problem is still a difficult one—the union of the historic seminary and the Pontifical University with a 'civil university' which though large by comparison with them might look small and vulnerable without them in comparison with other university institutions. It may be the material for a kind of marriage of convenience, but in human experience such marriages are not necessarily the least durable, even when at times they may seem to verge on marriages of inconvenience.

CHAPTER XVII

THE NEW COLLEGE: STUDIES, STAFF, STUDENTS

The Pontifical University

The Pontifical University meant, in practice, the Faculty of Theology. Philosophy retained its pontifical status, but it had always leaned towards the National University, and this increased with the new developments, while Canon Law became no more than a shadow faculty. Theology was further marked off from the rest of the institution by the seemingly endless delay in producing the university blueprint so confidently expected—and so confidently promised—in the late 1960s. This led to many damaging developments.

There were damaging developments from other quarters. Even the most enthusiastic proponents of theology would have admitted that some concentration of resources was desirable, for the available academic talent was not unlimited. What happened was rather the reverse, with such developments as the Institute of Pastoral Liturgy in Carlow, the Catechetical Institute at Mount Oliver near Dundalk, and the Communications Centre in Dublin. Holy Cross College, Clonliffe, had traditionally shared its large number of students between Clonliffe, Maynooth and Rome for their theology courses, but some time after the college was extended in the 1950s theology students for the diocese of Dublin ceased to come to Maynooth but instead received a BD degree validated by the Angelicum University in Rome on the basis of the courses they had followed in Clonliffe. It has been already noted that in the late 1960s a number of the clerical religious orders were pooling their resources. They centred on the Jesuit house at Milltown Park, where there were limited faculties of Theology and Philosophy, open to Jesuits only and only as far as the licentiate. It was reasonable that some provision be made for the other institutions now congregating there, and they felt aggrieved when in November 1968 Maynooth sought and received from the Cardinal Prefect of the Roman Congregation of Seminaries and Universities approval for the proposal that Maynooth be part of the projected 'University of Dublin' and supply its Catholic theological faculty, this to be the only such faculty in Ireland. Negotiations began between Maynooth and Milltown Park early in 1969, seemingly at the latter's request, and proposals were formulated in

February 1970. The two were to be 'aggregated' into one institution, with a single chancellor and board, two-thirds of which would be drawn from Maynooth and one-third from Milltown. Milltown would have full control of its studies, courses and staffing and would confer degrees up to and including the licentiate in philosophy and theology. Studies for the doctorate would be in Maynooth only, but professors at Milltown might be invited to participate in the programme. Milltown was to be limited to its existing student body, that is, the orders and congregations which had already settled there (by now about ten), and the situation would be reviewed in three years. The Roman Congregation was very much in favour of the proposal. The Jesuit provincial agreed on 3 March, but withdrew at the end of the month. There were, it seems, strong elements in Milltown unwilling to accept what was regarded as a subordinate relationship, some perhaps not greatly in favour of any relationship. The two institutions went their separate ways, and Milltown developed inexorably into 'open faculties'. At the end of the 1970s discussions reopened, but in an unpropitious atmosphere worsened by the fact that it was in part carried on in the newspapers, and, fairly predictably, no agreement was achieved.

The 'core course' of theology at Maynooth remained, then, that designed to prepare students for the priesthood. There was a general decline in vocations, but for a time this was balanced by students of the religious congregations who settled in Maynooth, the Society of the Divine Word in 1965, the Salesians in 1968, the Society of African Missions in 1970. (As a matter of interest, it might be noted that the Salesians had approached Maynooth in May 1914 seeking admission of a number of students to qualify as teachers for schools in India. The proposal came to nothing, possibly because of the outbreak of war in August.[1]) These three congregations made a substantial contribution to the student body. In the late 1960s the resident seminarian students of theology were rather more than two hundred. The non-residents peaked in the mid-1970s, when for a few years they numbered about 130, but afterwards there was an increasingly rapid decline.

The delay in university legislation meant that theology courses could not be offered in the Faculty of Arts. It also meant that the Pontifical University had to be financed exclusively from the tuition fees of students. This in turn meant it was difficult to increase staff, and impossible to pay them at the same level as other university teachers. An example may be given of the Department of Moral Theology, admittedly troubled rather above the average. Traditionally it had three full-time staff. A fourth was added in 1971, but from 1970 to 1976 one staff member was seconded to the post of director of postgraduate studies. A full-time substitute for him was appointed in 1972, and an extra statutory post created in 1976. However, the filling of this led to such an imbroglio that both the professor of 1976 and the full-time substitute of 1972 departed in June 1977. This left four. One retired in 1980, and another resigned in 1982 to become a parish priest. There were only two full-time statutory staff until October 1983, when two appointments restored the number to four.

Approaches were made to the Higher Education Authority seeking public funding for the Pontifical University, on the grounds that it was arguably not subject to the limitations on funding theology contained in the Irish Universities Act of 1908. The HEA was sympathetic, but felt it could not recommend funding until new legislation was enacted.

A more serious development was that the general post-conciliar euphoria towards theology cooled, and cooled fairly quickly. In the late 1960s it had been generally agreed that the absence of theology from the Irish universities was 'a strange anomaly' to be remedied as part of the imminent changes. That university theology should be confessional theology was agreed in 1967 by the Commission on Higher Education and by the Minister for Education, Donogh O'Malley, and by his successor Brian Lenihan the following year. This general good will was to some extent based on a lack of advertence to very real problems, the nature of 'university theology' and more specifically the nature of 'university confessional theology'. The question of the nature of 'academic freedom' of university teachers in a confessional faculty of theology was no new one, but it was substantially new in Ireland. Here as elsewhere, however, the issue exploded in the summer of 1968 with the publication of the papal encyclical *Humanae Vitae*. This was compounded at Maynooth by a controversial appointment, or rather non-appointment, to a chair of theology. The theological issue resolved itself into the question of church authority. The temper of the times, with its demands for a theology that should be 'living' and 'relevant', ensured a discussion that became polarised and tended to find its forum in the mass media. The Irish Theological Association had been founded in January 1966, with Maynooth staff naturally playing a leading role. In 1969 it produced a paper on 'Theology and the University'.[2] There was a frank evaluation of the problems that might arise as between the freedom of the confessional theologian and Church authority, but the solutions proposed seemed to rest heavily on mutual good will. It was doubtful if this would be enough in the thorny questions surrounding appointments to posts in confessional theology, or (though this was inclined to hover discreetly in the background) the criteria for dismissal from such a post.

Finally, as the years went by, Irish society became more questioning and even more secularised, at least in what people were coming to call 'the chattering classes'. The issues being raised were whether a 'living' and 'relevant' theology was compatible with a Church that claimed to speak authoritatively, and indeed whether religion was particularly relevant to the human condition. The 'troubles' in Northern Ireland began in the autumn of 1968 and seemed to present a spectacle of 'Catholics' and 'Protestants' so opposed that they killed one another. The passing years showed that confessional hatred was not confined to Northern Ireland, nor indeed to Christianity. If assent is withheld from the verdict of the pagan poet Lucretius, that religion was the source of great evil, 'Tantum religio potuit suadere malorum', it might be tempted some distance with that of Ambrose the Christian bishop and theologian, that it was not God's will to save his people through disputation, 'Non in dialectica complacuit Deo salvum facere populum suum.' Of course the media had a legitimate interest in what was going on at Maynooth, and there were a number of incidents to provoke comment. The comment, however, was in large part (there were honourable exceptions) marked by a hostility that was sometimes mindless, sometimes hard not to describe as vindictive. The suggestion made more than once that the only lay students who opted for Maynooth were those who could not get admission elsewhere was a particularly mean one (a survey of students' reasons for choosing Maynooth over the years 1987 to 1992 ranked 'quality of courses' very high among them). The onslaught began in 1968. The theology students' 'strike' in 1971 gave the press a field day, watched no doubt by Neil Kevin's puzzled ghost. The college was in fact an uneasy institution, with rippling tensions from such bodies as the Students' Representative Council, the Academic Staff Association and the College Executive Council. From the conservative side an onslaught came in the October 1973 issue of the Scottish periodical *Approaches*. The editor, Hamish Frazer, was a convert from communism and a true *zelante*. The whole issue was dedicated to what he called 'the scandal of Maynooth'. The scandal in question was the pronouncements of some members of the staff on the papal encyclical *Humanae Vitae* and the failure of the episcopal Trustees to take strong corrective action. The encyclical had indeed caused painful polarisations. The theological issue which became central, rather curiously to the near-exclusion of all others, was that of church authority. The context was delicate and painful, but everybody seemed to feel entitled to rush into a fray where so much depended on the professional capacity of the contributor, together with such things as the tone of the intervention and the forum in which it was made. Frazer did indeed have a case to argue, but he tarnished it by overstatement, exasperation and invective. The 'liberal' media came back in 1976, with the contentious appointment to the chair of Moral Theology. This led to agitation and continuing pressure from some sections of the staff and students, resulting in a stream of articles and reports in the daily press, reminiscent of Watty Cox's *Irish Magazine* long ago, and now Watty had a telephone. The worst year was 1977, with the grave internal troubles and the differences with Milltown Park giving rich pickings to the media. Something of a calm descended after the judgement of the Supreme Court in November 1979. At least Maynooth was no longer alone in the front line of battle. Morale crept back. Two typical incidents may be cited. In January 1988 the Pontifical University of Maynooth conferred its first honorary doctorates. The recipients were Patrick Hillery, President of Ireland, and two leading benefactors, Niall Crowley, chairman of the Irish Corporate Group, and Thomas McCarthy from California (Plate 93). The ceremony was held in the College Chapel, and the academic staff wore the full splendour of the toga and 'epitoga' of the eighteenth-century Sorbonne. Two years later it became possible to provide some funds for postgraduate studies in theology. The funds were modest, as was the increase in degrees awarded, for finance was not the whole problem with theological studies.

One area where the pontifical university was ahead of other college bodies was the question of its statutes. These needed approval by the Congregation for Seminaries and Universities, and it was accepted that they could not be finally formulated until the expected civil legislation was in place. But a start was made quickly. The congregation sent a preliminary questionnaire dated 7 October 1966. To this a reply was sent on 26 January 1967. It envisaged theology in a university context, and was optimistic in tone, though some signs of uncertainty might be detected as to how 'university theology' might be squared with the 'pastoral training' of a priest. In November, Maynooth was represented at a ten-day conference held in Rome, which resulted in the issuing the following year of *Normae quaedam*, a tentative document, as its title indicates, but replacing *Deus Scientiarum Dominus* of 1932. The college was now under pressure from Rome to produce a set of statutes quickly, if only in the form of 'unfinished and schematic drafts'. Such a draft was in the hands of the Trustees in June 1970, but the definitive Roman document, *Sapientia Christiana*, was not published until 1979. A revision of the draft statutes in the light of this document was completed in December 1980 and sent to the Trustees. A final version was sent to Rome to what was now styled the Congregation for Catholic Education in March 1982. The congregation returned several pages of 'observations' dated 6 August 1983, and consideration of them was almost completed when, it was reported, the long-awaited reorganisation of Irish university studies might be expected 'shortly'. Work was suspended pending developments.

It may be useful to offer a short comparison between the two Roman documents, *Deus Scientiarum Dominus* of 1932 and *Sapientia Christiana* of 1979. It might be fairly said that while they have the same goal they approach it differently because circumstances have changed. *Sapientia Christiana* shows a more conscious desire to situate the work of ecclesiastical faculties within the whole mission and pastoral activity of the Church. It shows a greater awareness of the contemporary requirements for the advancement of the sacred sciences and a broader view of the necessary connection between them and other human achievements and branches of knowledge. It clearly acknowledges that the exposition of revealed truth must, without change of the truth, be adapted to the nature and character of every culture. More practically, it recognises the need to take account of changes in university life and pedagogical methods since the 1930s. And lastly, it sets out the aim to make more widely available the benefits of higher education in the sacred sciences.

These were the guidelines for the new problems being opened up by the experience of the Vatican Council and the rapidly changing world. Traditionally, the theological formation of the seminarian had centred on a grinding course of lectures based on Latin manuals. 'Catechetics', or the skill to impart this knowledge, existed at the margin, as did 'pastoral training', notwithstanding the appointment of a professor of Pastoral Theology and Sacred Eloquence as far back as 1904. James G. McGarry, appointed to this post in 1939, left to become a parish priest in 1969. Long ago Walter McDonald had spoken disparagingly of Maynooth's typical product as 'the good average man'. The 'good average man' trained himself conscientiously in the Tridentine pattern, to hear confessions and preach the diocesan programme of religious instruction, as laid out in detail Sunday by Sunday. The rest of his theology course he inclined to think marginal to his vocation, some of it perhaps irrelevant. He may have been occasionally troubled at the seemingly limited contact between the lecture hall and the chapel, but the equivalent of his medical internship he had been prepared to put off until he was appointed to serve in a parish, where he would learn from elders who, he accepted, knew what they were doing in a traditional society.

Suddenly all that framework began to dissolve at frightening speed. All theology was now to be 'pastoral'. There was a new emphasis on the ability to communicate knowledge. It was decided to set up a School of Communications, within the general university complex, distinct from the Faculty of Theology, and with three professors. What happened, however, was the Communications Centre in Dublin. What happened in Maynooth was the appointment of a professor of Homiletics in 1970. It was regarded as the first step in setting up the School of Communications, but it was not followed up. The Council had opened up further horizons when it pointed to liturgy as a source of theology, to many a new dimension to 'saying Mass'. 'The study of sacred liturgy', it said, 'is to be ranked among the compulsory and major courses in seminaries.' Patrick McGoldrick, Maynooth's first professor of Liturgy, was trained in Paris and appointed in June 1965. Then there was the question of Latin. In Maynooth, the lectures had been in English, but the textbooks—and the examinations—were in Latin. It had come as something of a surprise when Pope John XXIII in *Veterum Sapientia* had demanded that all seminary instruction should be in Latin. The Maynooth faculties reacted by saying it was 'not feasible in our circumstances'. In theology, a lone voice was recorded expressing anxiety at the lost values that must accompany the loss of the Latin language. By 1969 English textbooks were being envisaged, but the trouble was that there did not seem to be any.

Philosophy, like theology, had been taught to seminarians within a 'neoscholastic' framework. This had originated with the Jesuits immediately after the Council of Trent, and Pope Leo XIII had set out to give it new life at the end of the nineteenth century. The traditional requirement had been two years of philosophy before beginning theology, but it had always been difficult to fit this into the Maynooth curriculum. Philosophy had first been pinched between the demands of the classics ('Rhetoric') on the one side and of Natural Philosophy on the other. Then when university degrees in arts and science came in philosophy had to compete with quite a number of rival subjects. It was subdivided into three: Ethics, General Metaphysics, and Special Metaphysics, a kind of catch-all subject that, curiously, included Natural Theology at honours level only. An honours degree was offered in philosophy alone. For all others there were two lectures a week in each subject, and they were compulsory for all pass BA candidates together with two other subjects. Honours BA and all BSc candidates had to take the same course, with a college examination each year. In 1965, however, the pass BA degree was reduced to three subjects. No philosophy subject was compulsory, but candidates (at this date all of them seminarians) who did not take a philosophy subject had to attend lectures in it, now four a week, and pass a college examination. A student taking no philosophy subject could then face twelve lectures a week and three examinations on top of his university course. This simply did not happen at pass BA level, but it affected honours BA and all BSc candidates. It was just too much. Attendance was poor, and so were achievements. Moreover, students were beginning to question the traditional requirements, asking what philosophy was supposed to be and how it related to theology (itself under questioning), and, in a document dating from 1968, sweepingly dismissing much of scholasticism as 'irrelevant'.

The courses were revised in the 1970s under the stimulus of a broader intake of students. There was still a three-fold division of subjects, but they did sound more relevant—Moral Philosophy, Metaphysics, and Philosophy of Religion. The problem remained, however, of devising a philosophy course for the seminarian who was presenting other subjects for his degree. There was a proposal for a special course of one lecture a week in each of the three subjects, but it was impossible to devise a satisfactory course within such narrow limits and impossible to timetable it to suit all students, and attendance and achievement continued poor. Then there was a proposal for a series of thirty-six lectures, to run concurrently with the theology course. On its own this was slender indeed, but it was hoped that it would be supplemented. The scheme finally worked out was as follows. All seminarian candidates for First Arts were required to take the course of Introduction to Philosophy which had replaced a course in formal logic in 1968, and all candidates for the pass BA had to take one of the three philosophy subjects. For honours degree candidates, room could be found only for the 'concurrent course' during their theology years. The case was even worse with all candidates for the BSc. Unless a year was added to their course—unacceptable to their bishops—all that could be asked of them was that they take the equivalent of the First Arts Introduction to Philosophy over their degree course, and the 'concurrent course' during their theology. Finally, two-year courses in which philosophy was dominant had to be set up under the supervision of a seminarist board for the unmatriculated seminarians who were first admitted in the autumn of 1969.

But it was the students of theology who were the more restive, being older and engaged in studies more immediately related to their calling. Many stirrings were following on the great upheaval of the Council. In 1965 the students had been allowed a Students' Representative Council affiliated to the Union of Students in Ireland, and in 1966 the Trustees had declared the college 'an open centre of higher studies'. For its part, the Faculty of Theology was addressing itself to the need to modify and adapt courses, though inevitably too slowly for the student opinion now rapidly forming. Much of this opinion was sound, though it could hardly hope to escape current 'political correctness', such as the emphasis on 'discussion groups', apparently expected to produce information effortlessly out of thin air, or a demand that both staff and students attend courses in 'group dynamics' as a matter of urgency. In the academic year 1967/68 the Students' Representative Council circulated an elaborate questionnaire and tabulated the results. While admitting that developments to date were worth while, they were, it was claimed, too limited. The report was widely critical of the course as a whole—fragmented into too many subjects, leading to overlapping and duplication. A 'pastoral aim' was missing. There should be fewer lectures, and more work in seminars and discussion groups. Especially since the 1930s, there had been a proliferation of minor subjects, each with one lecture a week. These, the students urged, should be consolidated, with two weekly lectures for a semester, or possibly absorbed into major subjects. There should be more continuous assessment, with oral examinations in particular being abolished. It was desirable there be one day a week completely free for study, as was the case in ecclesiastical institutions in Rome. Predictably, there was criticism of the poor contact between staff and students. Finally, a general framework of studies was proposed. There should be an introductory year, its courses corresponding substantially to those being offered in first-year theology. This would be followed by a National University degree, followed in turn by three years' theology, ending with a BD degree, to be offered at pass as well as honours level.

The Faculty continued to discuss the problems and introduce changes, even though these did not come easily when dealing with an intractably complex course. The most important change was that in the first three years in both Dogmatic and Moral Theology a single professor took responsibility for a single year's course. The fourth theology year became more 'pastoral' in character, though it still had a considerable academic content. There were more seminars, from which more student essays developed. A pass course for the BD degree was introduced in the academic year 1969/70, and a diploma for those who failed to reach this level in 1971/72.

The teaching staff, no matter how distributed, were few in numbers to deal with this new programme, which was made necessary, they claimed, by the increasing complexities of theology. In March 1969 they asked the Trustees for the employment of temporary part-time lecturers 'in such subjects as ecumenism, mission studies, philosophy of religion and scripture'. This was granted and led to the offering of quite a spread of 'elective courses' in 1971/72. The Trustees were understandably slower to establish full-time statutory posts, though in June 1970 they agreed that one of the Faculty should be appointed full-time director of postgraduate studies, even though this meant his undergraduate courses had to be taken by a part-time substitute. They also agreed to set up two new lectureships, one in Patrology and the History of Dogma and one in Scripture, but they refused two lectureships in 'general systematic theology' ('systematic' was emerging as a more acceptable replacement for 'dogmatic').

Students expected more. A course of studies is relatively short, and when students want anything they want it now. There was much talk of 'integrated studies' and 'inter-disciplinary courses', and flash-points threatened. On 15 February 1971 the students of the second-year theology class boycotted their lectures. The next day there was a general meeting of the theology students, who delegated a six-man 'action committee' to communicate with the teaching staff, administration and Trustees on the basis of a document setting out their grievances. This document claimed that the current system was entirely inadequate to form the kind of priest envisaged by the Vatican Council. There was very little personal contact. The 'small groups' which functioned were too few, and in fact too large. There was need for more tutorials and projects, and for an active interest in students' prayer life as well as in their studies. Both staff and students would benefit greatly from a preliminary course in group dynamics. Nothing would do except 'the radical overhauling of the present curriculum both in content and methodology'. There should be 'one concentrated lecture per subject per week', which should form 'the springboard and stimulus for discussion'. 'Students should have some consultative right in determining courses, and the communication of these courses', because, it was claimed, 'this is recognised in all truly responsible universities and seminaries today.'

The statutory spring meeting of the Visitors had been fixed for 19 February, and, as always, it would be held in the college. The student meeting decided to ask the Visitors to place a discussion of their document on the agenda for the meeting of the Trustees, which was fixed for 9 March. They threatened that if this were not agreed by 6 March there would be an indefinite 'strike' from the following day. They demanded further that the Trustees agree to call an immediate meeting between their representatives and representatives of teaching staff, administration and Trustees, and threatened an immediate and indefinite 'strike' if the following points were not on the agenda: that the staff, administration and students should begin to meet from September 1971 'to bring structures into line with normal university practice'; that advertisements be placed immediately for as many new staff as might be necessary; and that immediate steps be taken to raise the necessary funds from Church and Government sources. Two hundred and fifty students had voted for this approach, with one against and five abstentions. They added that their action should not be seen as a threat (though indeed it would strain language to see it as anything else) and pledged loyalty to the Church and their bishops. It was added that 'the meeting agreed overwhelmingly to keep all mention of its discussion out of the press': not, however, unanimously, and the first press notices appeared on 19 February, the day of the Visitors' meeting.

It was an unenviable situation. In fact, elements of revolt had been simmering since 1966. While the students admitted that there had been moves towards change there were, they felt, too many things still unchanged. There was much good will among the staff, but there was a shortage of resources together with a genuine uncertainty about how a very complex set of courses might be adapted. It was certainly not a situation it was wise to keep meeting head on. It had now escalated into a very intractable emergency, with truculent tone, precipitate action, threat of strike, all the elements of 'just and non-negotiable demands'.

Contacts between the Visitors and student representatives on 19 February led to a student meeting that evening at which the strike threat was withdrawn. This opened the way for meetings between representatives of the Faculty and of the students. Five meetings were held between 26 February and 16 March. The lengthy minutes indicate an edgy and confrontational atmosphere, but it was possible to present a report, adopted by the Faculty on 6 May and approved by the Trustees at their June meeting. At this meeting they also agreed to appoint a director of pastoral training and five additional lecturers—one in Patrology and the History of Dogma, as already sanctioned; two, not one, in Scripture and two in 'general theology'. The Faculty sub-committee continued its work firming up these outlines, which took final form in March 1972. In each year all students had lectures in common, with distinctions between the various levels being catered for through work in small groups. Since 1970 students proceeding to the licentiate had done the first year of the course in their fourth theology year. For other students this year moved closer to being a 'pastoral' one, treating 'theological questions as they arise directly out of pastoral experience'. It was, however, not easy to shape. The first tendency was to remove all academic work from it, but as the problems of 'pastoral activity' came into focus there was a tendency for such work to slip back.[3]

It has been seen that the conditions imposed by the Second World War had led to a great expansion of the college postgraduate programme. The expansion had overstrained the available resources, and did not outlast the reopening of the Continental centres when peace returned.[4] After the Council there were, as might be expected, hopes of a new flowering. A full-time director of studies was appointed in October 1970, in the first instance for one year, but he was re-appointed until 1976, when the filling of the post was 'deferred' and instead a member of the Faculty was to be asked to co-ordinate postgraduate studies on a part-time basis. Experience over the six years had shown that the hopes of 1970 had not been fulfilled: there had been only one doctorate, and licentiates averaged five a year. In the years since 1977 there have been nine doctorates, and an average of between three and four licentiates annually. Any dream of gathering students from the English-speaking world, European, American or missionary, had not materialised. Indeed Maynooth's own graduates showed a tendency to go elsewhere for further studies, mostly to Rome. While in principle it is very good that a student should go afield for his doctorate, any such drain was a severe impoverishment in a small institution.

The most important new development was the Baccalaureate in Theology and Arts. In Dublin, Archbishop McQuaid had established the Mater Dei Institute to train teachers of religion for secondary schools. There was a three-year course leading to a diploma, with a fourth year leading to a master's degree. Both were validated by the Angelicum University in Rome, and graduates were admitted to the register of secondary teachers, but as teachers of religion only. His successor, Archbishop Ryan (1972–84), sought affiliation to Maynooth for a degree which would allow an application to be made that graduates be placed on the 'open' teachers' register. What was proposed was a 'Baccalaureate in Religious Science', a four-year integrated teacher-training course, 50 per cent Theology, 25 per cent Education and 25 per cent a 'secular subject', English, History or Music. The application was of course granted.

By this time the Maynooth Faculty of Theology was beginning to think along similar lines, for the wait for new university legislation was beginning to seem interminable. What was in mind was a teacher's degree with a heavy theological content. Discussion and planning led to a request to the Trustees in February 1978 for a meeting to discuss undergraduate theology as part of a course for a National University BA or a degree of the Pontifical University. It was noted that the problems in regard to a degree of the National University had not changed, so they proposed to introduce such a degree in the Pontifical University the following October, 'and *pari passu* to engage in negotiations concerning the introduction of theology and allied subjects into the National University courses for the BA'. It had to be accepted that there was no real hope for this latter in the context of the existing National University, and October 1978 proved optimistic for the introduction of the pontifical degree. In the spring of 1979 the Faculty reported to the Trustees saying their plans were now finalised and they were submitting courses for approval. What was proposed was a three-year course, because the education component was not incorporated, as it was in the Mater Dei Institute. For Arts subjects, students would be sent to attend the courses in the recognised college. Here at this time students took four subjects at First Arts, continuing with three for a pass degree and with two for honours. For the first year in the Baccalaureate in Theology and Arts the course proposed was 50 per cent theology, with two arts subjects making up the remainder. In the second and third years, theology would be two-thirds, with one-third for one arts subject, taken at pass level for both honours and pass degree. Later a choice was offered of an honours degree with 50 per cent each to both theology and an arts subject. (Two full subjects was always regarded as something of an overload for an arts degree, and the recognised college has since introduced a 'BA special' with one subject at honours level and one at pass.) Intake was to be limited to forty a year, neither of the contracting parties being over-endowed with resources. After their degree students would take the Higher Diploma in Education, and qualify for the 'open register' of secondary teachers.

Pressure was mounted to have these duly matriculated students made eligible for standard university grants. At first it was argued that this would have to await new legislation, but in February 1987 it was accepted that there was no legal obstacle to giving grants. By now it was also accepted that anything further would have to await new legislation, the pot of gold at the end of the rainbow that offered the integration of theological studies into the general university system and the funding of them on an equal basis. What had been achieved in 1979 fell short of this. Moreover, through the 1980s the BA degree, losing appeal at the beginning of the decade, returned to favour as young people sought to prepare themselves for a changing world where more specialised courses might close options rather than open them. It was regrettable that theology could not have an honoured and useful place in the new developments, but here as elsewhere the best is the enemy of the good.

A feature of the return to favour of the BA degree had been the development of diploma courses to complement it. Diploma courses also developed within the pontifical university of Maynooth. The setting up of the diploma in pastoral studies and of the diploma in theology based on the seminarians' course have already been noted in other contexts.[5] When the opening up of the college was first discussed, the theological poverty of the education of non-clerical religious was noted as a need that might be supplied, and a one-year diploma in religious studies was set up for this purpose in 1969. Even at the time, however, religious sisters tended to identify their requirements as 'a non-university juniorate-type course'. Enrolment peaked at 121 in the academic year 1976/77. After that it declined sharply, following the decline in vocations. Further, the character of the student body changed, and it came to consist more of people of mature years, taking the Maynooth course as one of the many on offer, with a relatively small percentage sitting the examinations for the diploma.

A diploma in mission studies developed from the fact that the clerical religious who settled in Maynooth were missionary in character. As well, the Vatican Council had put before the Church a new concept of 'mission': the opening sentence of the exposition of doctrinal principles in its decree on the Church's missionary activity (*Ad gentes*, 7 December 1965) had stated simply: 'The pilgrim church is missionary by its very nature.' At an early date the President of Maynooth, Jeremiah Newman, had raised the idea of a Mission Institute in the college with the Columban Society and the Irish Missionary Union taking shape at the time, in which the Columbans were playing an important role. He was able to put concrete proposals to the meeting of the Union on 4 December 1973, and they were favourably received. Discussion between the Union and Faculty of Theology in the spring of 1974 led to agreement to set up a chair of Mission Studies, to be funded by the Union. A professor was appointed in autumn 1974. The introductory course offered proved a popular innovation and attracted large numbers of students. It proved harder, however, to attract students to the full diploma course, which had to compete with courses being offered in various missionary institutes. Then difficulties arose between the Trustees and the Irish Missionary Union, and these were unresolved.

The Faculty of Canon Law had been reactivated in the academic year 1962/63. There were, however, few students, and when in 1968 *Normae quaedam* did not allow anyone to be a full professor in more than one faculty it was clearly impossible to continue, and the year 1969/70 saw the last three students in the Faculty of Canon Law. There was some talk of reviving it, but it was almost necessarily half-hearted and came to nothing. Students in the honours theology course in the third and fourth years had previously studied a rigorous course in the canon law of judicial processes. It was hard to justify this in a course for a theology degree, and in June 1966 the Trustees ordered it replaced with a more practical and less academic course on the topic. In December 1975 there was a proposal to establish an 'Institute of Canon Law' within the Faculty of Theology. This would offer three postgraduate diplomas: a diploma in the theology and canon law of marriage, a diploma in the philosophy and theology of law, and a diploma in law in relationship to liturgical and religious life. Part of the motivation for this step was a desire to keep some kind of specialised study of canon law in the Maynooth curriculum. On a more practical level, there was the rapidly growing need for qualified personnel to staff marriage tribunals. It is possible that all three courses would have been beyond the resources of the college, and more than doubtful if an adequate student body would have materialised. Anyway, the proposal went to the Trustees in March 1976. What was agreed was to set up the first diploma, to train officials for the diocesan tribunals. The course would combine lectures at Maynooth with practical work locally. As well as meeting the needs of the moment, this decision might be said to reflect the Maynooth legal tradition— weak on the philosophy of law, strong on its practical application. But inevitably the intake of students declined as the marriage tribunals became adequately staffed, and this did not take long.

In the academic year 1990/91 there was established a diploma in communications and a postgraduate diploma in communications and development, with the Society of the Divine Word playing an important role. As already noted, the proposal made in 1969 to establish in Maynooth a School of Communications distinct from the Faculty of Theology came to nothing, and hopes rested rather in the Communications Centre set up in Dublin.[6] This, however, proved too expensive to maintain fully, and a study of communications came back to Maynooth twenty years later in the form of the two diplomas.

A further development was the affiliation of the regional seminaries. In June 1972 Waterford, Thurles, Carlow, Wexford, Dalgan Park and All Hallows were affiliated for the grant of a Maynooth diploma in theology on the basis of the courses taught in them, and the college of the Holy Ghost Missionaries at Kimmage Manor was affiliated for a BD degree as well as a diploma. In 1975 the All Hallows affiliation was extended to the BD, and Kilkenny was affiliated for the diploma. In 1989 all the seminaries asked to be affiliated for a degree. There were problems—they were small institutions and getting smaller, with correspondingly small staffs. It was finally agreed that a degree to be known as 'BTh' (not BD) might be sanctioned provided they agreed to a certain pooling of their academic resources. The first BTh was awarded in October 1992.

Affiliation spread outside Ireland. Indeed, it almost began outside Ireland. On 12 October 1965, in the closing days of the Council, a group of Irish missionary bishops in Africa approached the Irish bishops with a request that their regional college, Bigard Memorial Seminary, should be placed 'in a position of tutelage' to Maynooth, envisaging 'permission at some future date for selected students to sit the Maynooth BD and STL examinations.' The project was received very sympathetically, and it was agreed there seemed to be no insurmountable difficulties.[7] Nevertheless it came to nothing. Even without detailed investigation it is possible to surmise some reasons. The proposal had a certain quality of being premature, with unexpected problems lurking, and both Ireland and Africa faced changes on an unexpected scale. In Ireland the changes included the settling of missionary congregations at Maynooth, among them the Society of African Missions. It was only in the academic year 1987/88 that the first foreign affiliation came into effect, that of Chesters College, Glasgow. It was followed in 1990/91 by the Maryvale Institute, Birmingham.

The National University College

The student body of the National University college rapidly outgrew that of the Pontifical University, until it approached ten times its size. If the account of the Pontifical University seems disproportionately long, one reason may be that the very diversity of the National University courses makes it harder to go into detail. Another may well be that it is problems that make history, and the Pontifical University had perhaps more than its share of these. Indeed in the late sixties there was a certain irony in the fact that it was confident theology that was struggling to get a niche, while students were thrust on the staff of the recognised college, who had for some time been expressing reservations about their capacity to handle degree courses for the existing student body of resident seminarians. In this student body lay students came to outnumber seminarians and religious fairly quickly. In the stirrings after the Council seminarians were beginning to question the relevance of a degree in arts or science. The majority were still in favour, but there was widespread questioning of the existing courses, and all seemed agreed there should be an alternative non-degree course in the first years in the seminary. This in fact imposed itself very soon, first when religious congregations nominated seminarians who did not have university matriculation, and when very shortly afterwards Maynooth itself was forced to accept the same situation in regard to its own resident seminarians for Irish dioceses.

The first large-scale development at Maynooth was the Higher Diploma in Education. The chair of 'Education and Catechetics' had been vacant since Peter Birch was appointed bishop in July 1962. It had been repeatedly advertised, but there were no applicants, and indeed there seemed to be no great sense of urgency. There had never been more than a few candidates, all of them priests. They seemed adequately catered for, living in Dunboyne House and attending lectures in Dublin. The President had been authorised to appoint a lecturer if numbers warranted. This situation seemed clearly to have arisen when the decision to open up the college in June 1966 was quickly followed by the promise of the Minister for Education, Donogh O'Malley, that there would be free secondary education from September 1967. An Irish Christian Brother, Séamus Ó Súilleabháin, was appointed lecturer in Education in October 1966 and professor in June 1968. Numbers soared: 65 in 1966/67, 149 in 1967/68, 202 in 1968/69, 228 in 1969/70, 270 in 1970/71, 286 in 1971/72 and again in 1972/73, rising to 302 in 1973/74. It was an evening course to which students commuted, some from quite a distance, so it had a limited effect on general college life, apart from its demands on library facilities. But it had rapidly outgrown the traditional small Maynooth departments, with a small number of staff, commonly only one. By 1973/74 it had a professor, two full-time lecturers, four supervisors of schools and many part-time lecturers. It was competently organised and offered a good course that was highly regarded.

In June 1967 the President had listed the problems in admitting lay students. There was no accommodation for them, and no facilities, and in any case applications from religious bodies were likely to exhaust capacity. A memorandum from the Academic Council in March 1968 envisaged an ultimate student body of about a thousand, with 'lay-students commuting from the immediate surrounding hinterland' (in 1968/69 there was a total of 785 students, 202 being in the Higher Diploma course, 554 seminarians or religious, with 29 lay undergraduates, 25 of them in the first university year). The number of arts and science undergraduates grew rapidly and inexorably, and the great majority were non-resident. There were over five hundred in 1972/73. In 1976/77 the overall numbers of laity equalled those of seminarians and religious. Two years later there were 654 arts undergraduates, 156 in science, a total of 810. For a few years after this there was a worrying decline in arts candidates, but the arts degree returned to favour, especially when followed by a career-oriented postgraduate diploma. In 1993/94 the disproportion was great indeed:

National University college: postgraduates	412
Undergraduates: Arts	1,884
Undergraduates: Science	677
Diplomas	572
Total	3,545
Pontifical University	363
Total university	3,808
Unmatriculated seminarians	38
Total student body	3,846

Yet the development of facilities meant that it was no more difficult to cope with these numbers than it had been with the smaller numbers of twenty years before.

The development of physical facilities has been outlined in the previous chapter. They did not come as rapidly as the growth in numbers warranted, and there were intermittent expressions of dissatisfaction. The dissatisfaction in the early days did not arise solely from the shortage of physical amenities. Maynooth had had a long tradition of being a seminary. By 1970 what had been a fairly iron discipline was being relaxed, but even the most relaxed seminary discipline could hardly meet all the needs of lay students—facilities for holding dances, for example. Yet the 'Information and Rules for Students', circulated by the Administrative Council in September 1970, while a very sensible provision for contemporary seminarians, did have a kind of appendix dealing with non-resident students. At the time many of these were seminarians and religious, and all teaching activities took place in the historic seminary, so that it was not altogether unreasonable to regard them as some kind of appendix. Yet even in the academic year 1970/71 the majority of undergraduates in the National University college were lay, young men and women who could not be expected to have seminary ways imposed on them. The question was not resolved without tensions. The student magazine *View* was regarded by many as timid to the point of absurdity. A rival appeared, *Maynews*, and no doubt by way of reaction it could be brash to the point of being offensive. It soon came to be recognised that there would be two student bodies, the seminary and the university, between whom there could not be total integration. This was incorporated into a new constitution for the Students' Representative Council, and adopted by student referendum held on 27 April 1971. Things naturally took some time to fit into this pattern. Frustrations built up to another crisis in the spring of 1974. One outcome was the student recreation centre, which gave the non-seminarian students a *pied-à-terre* they had so far lacked.

One early development had been the establishment of a 'joint board' of the Students' Representative Council and the college authorities, which met once a month. The disciplinary committee of the joint board met infrequently, not necessarily a bad thing, but because there was no really agreed disciplinary framework it was hard for it to be other than toothless. In the spring of 1982 the administrative buildings were occupied as a protest against fee increases. There was participation by people from outside the college, members of the Union of Students in Ireland, and much publicity. A High Court injunction was needed to have the building vacated, and there was no internal disciplinary action. The administrative buildings were again occupied, again as a protest against fee increases, for two weeks at the end of January and beginning of February 1985. This time the administration flatly refused to negotiate under duress, even in the face of a one-day blockade of the college gate and support from some seminarians. In the end the offices were vacated, without concessions and without recourse to the civil law, and with an agreement that the students would pay for any damage. Finally, after much serious consultation, an agreed disciplinary code came into effect in the academic year 1988/89.

Various services had to be provided for the rapidly growing body of non-residents, especially the lay students, who soon became by far the biggest element in this body. There was Mass every Sunday in St Joseph's Oratory, with a concelebrated Mass every day in St Mary's at twelve o'clock. Many lay students in the arts and science courses attended lectures in introductory theology, which were provided with them in mind. A Dunboyne priest-student was appointed chaplain, and priest staff members provided pastoral care on a voluntary basis. A full-time chaplain was appointed for the academic year 1973/74.

The College Executive Council had been set up for the academic year 1971/72, and as has been seen, faced very many problems. One of the first to which it turned its attention was that of the medical and psychiatric needs of lay students. It was clarified that under the 1970 Health Act, the Eastern Health Board had responsibility for hospitalising student patients in a public ward. In September 1972 a free dispensary service was made available. A 'capitation fee' was introduced to finance it, and this fee was later extended to cover other student services and activities. In 1985/86 Higher Education Authority funds became available for a part-time psychiatrist and counsellor, and in 1990 the Students' Union provided funds to employ a nurse to attend on a part-time basis every day.

Career guidance was an idea of its nature non-existent in Maynooth in its seminary days. Again it was the College Executive Council which took up the problem, leading to an appointment on a part-time basis for the year 1973/74. Here the college and its students received years of devoted service from Dr D. A. Scholfield, especially since his retirement from University College, Dublin, in 1990, since when he gave Maynooth three days a week during term and two during vacation. The student body, too, began to take on a distinctive character, perhaps predominantly country rather than city, or at least if city first-generation rather than long-established Dubliner. An Alumni Association held its first meeting in March 1990. Just as 'the Maynooth priest' had arrived in the early nineteenth century, to a critical reception, the Maynooth lay graduate made a distinctive appearance towards the end of the twentieth.

A memorandum drawn up for the Trustees and dated 23 May 1967 had spoken of the desirability of concentrated development within a selected area, theology, philosophy, the humanities, involving the strengthening of existing departments and the fostering of 'centres of excellence'. Unfortunately it soon turned out that the traditional strengths—theology, philosophy, and within the humanities classics—were not what was most in demand. The memorandum made a further request: that there should be staff representation on the governing body and that it should meet more frequently. The request seems to have been made confidently, but in 1967 perhaps a little prematurely, though in 1967 there can have hardly been anyone who foresaw that such a development would be so long delayed. The memorandum was sent to the June meeting of the Trustees, with a detailed list of extra staff considered to be immediately required. Theology, from a base of twelve, asked for three extra lecturers—in Scripture, long regarded as understaffed, in Philosophy of Religion, curiously neglected by Philosophy, as already noted, and in a new area of interest, Ecumenical Theology. Philosophy, from a base of three, claimed it was very badly understaffed, so badly that time was needed to work out details of reorganisation; one additional post was sought as an interim measure. Classics, from a base of three, asked for at least one; English from two sought one extra; Modern History, with one, wanted one full-time with part-time assistants, and Modern Languages, likewise with one, asked for one lecturer and one *répétiteur*. Celtic Studies, with a full-time staff of two, asked that the courses be limited to Irish studies only, and that a language laboratory be established (it came in 1969). The science departments, with a total staff of three, had been forced to cut back on their courses over the years just passed. They asked for the restoration of the honours degree courses in the experimental sciences and for the introduction of Biology, with the appointment, as an urgent need, of two part-time lecturers.

In retrospect it appears a modest programme, but it reflects the current uncertainty about where the college might be going, what student body might be attracted, and to what courses. The problems of theology have been noted in some detail already. In the years immediately ahead, the expansion programme bore heavily on academic departments already in some anxiety about their ability to cope, now faced with much heavier commitments and far less additional help than they needed. Classics soon had to abandon any hope of becoming a 'centre of excellence'. The days were clearly past when Thomas Gaisford, dean of Christ Church, Oxford from 1831 to 1855, felt he could in no better way exhort his congregation, even in a Christmas Day sermon, than to say: 'Nor can I do better, in conclusion, than impress upon you the study of Greek literature, which not only elevates above the vulgar herd, but leads not infrequently to positions of considerable emolument.' Latin too was losing its allure, not just in its classical form but even as the simplified Latin that had been part of the schools of theology and philosophy. When in 1966 the Trustees proposed a special class in second year for students considered weak in Latin, there was general opposition from the teaching staff, led by the departments of Classics and Science. It was pointed out, not indeed for the first time, that it was becoming increasingly difficult to provide for the philosophy requirements of a seminarian together with a course for a BA or BSc, and that further overloading was quite impossible. The entry of lay students made the position of Latin more difficult. In 1967 it had to be accepted that it would be a compulsory subject at First Arts for seminarians only. In 1973, in common with other institutions, a course was offered in 'Greek and Roman Civilisation', for which no knowledge of Latin or Greek was required. Courses in the languages were still available, but they were very much a minority interest, having in some years no students. There is a certain irony in the fact that in that same year a proposed course in Biblical Languages and Literature was judged impracticable because of the expertise it would require in two admittedly difficult languages, Greek and Hebrew.

It has been seen that when the numbers of lay students grew so rapidly after they were first admitted in the autumn of 1968 the physical facilities that could be provided for them were inadequate. Badly needed additional teaching staff also came very slowly. In June 1968 the Trustees authorised temporary classroom accommodation; a library assistant; and temporary part-time lecturers in Modern History, French, English and Biology. A first-year course in Biology was offered in 1968/69. This was a major advance for the scientists, but amid indications that the 'centres of excellence' might be hard to achieve. For quite a while it was a question of making do with very inadequate resources. The Trustees, of course, could not hope to finance developments from the college's own funds, but for some years now there had been a government grant, and the opening had been decided in an atmosphere which made it reasonable to count on expanded state support, but everything had to be negotiated in a fluid situation, because as yet not merely were there no firm decisions but little even in the way of precedents. The grant in 1966/67 had been £27,500, quite inadequate to meet the new demands. It rose only slowly: £47,500 in 1968/69, £75,700 in 1969/70. In the early summer of 1970 a printed 'Submission to the Higher Education Authority' was presented, setting out in detail current needs and future projections. The annual grant for 1970/71 rose to £90,000, together with, as already noted, the first grant of £60,000 for capital needs. These grants marked the slow stabilisation of a situation in which the National University section of the college attracted government grants in parallel with other university institutions. Maynooth, however, had the disadvantages of the late starter. For some time additional posts were offered on one-year contracts, some of them part-time. If a priest were available he generally got preference, primarily because he came cheaper. But there was a fairly rapid decline in

SVD House of Studies 1969

Plate 80

Centenary of birth of Eoghan O'Growney 27 October 1963: centre front Donnchadh Ó Floinn and Sinéad Bean de Valera

Plate 81

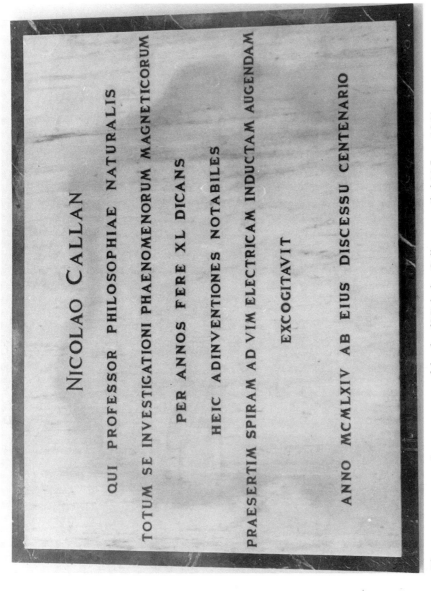

NICOLAO CALLAN

QUI PROFESSOR PHILOSOPHIAE NATURALIS

TOTUM SE INVESTIGATIONI PHAENOMENORUM MAGNETICORUM

PER ANNOS FERE XL DICANS

HEIC ADINVENTIONES NOTABILES

PRAESERTIM SPIRAM AD VIM ELECTRICAM INDUCTAM AUGENDAM

EXCOGITAVIT

ANNO MCMLXIV AB EIUS DISCESSU CENTENARIO

Plaque commemorating centenary of death of Nicholas Callan, unveiled 23 June 1964

Plate 82

The Park on a day of recollection *c.* 1960

Plate 83

St Joseph's Square *c.* 1970

Plate 84

The College Library early in the century before cataloguing

Plate 85

The College Library c. 1970

Plate 86

Archbishop Dermot Ryan cuts the first sod for the New Arts Building, 1 October 1974

Plate 87

Pope John Paul II with Irish youth by Imogen Stuart

Plate 88

EC grant for Biology 13 September 1989 with Mary O'Rourke, Minister for Education, Associate Professor Martin Downes and Monsignor Ledwith

Plate 89

The Taoiseach, Albert Reynolds, lays the foundation stone of the Callan Building, 24 June 1992

Plate 90

Student Restaurant and Sports Complex 1991

Student Centre 1993

Plate 91

Foyer of Callan Building 1993

Plate 92

Monsignor Ledwith with President Hillery on the occasion of his receiving an honorary doctorate, 27 January 1988

Plate 93

Professor Séamus Smyth, appointed Master of the Recognised College 22 June 1994, with Monsignor Ledwith, President 1985-94

Plate 94

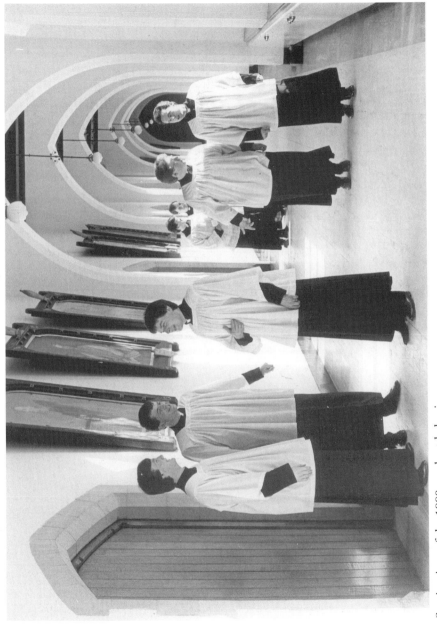

Seminarians of the 1990s on best behaviour

Plate 95

priest teachers on the National University staff. Some of them left the priesthood and in consequence left the college, and soon there were no new priests appointed. It might perhaps be regretted that so little effort was made to prepare credible priest-candidates for posts in the 'traditional' subjects, Classics, Irish, History, this last a latecomer as a Maynooth university department but long established in Ireland as an ecclesiastical interest.[8] Indeed, there was what in retrospect must be seen as inadequate planning even in philosophy and theology, and the days were gone when it could be assumed that with very little planning there would be a suitable candidate whenever a vacancy occurred.

Yet the priesthood continued to attract talent in a way that more might have been made of. The appointment of a priest led to the beginning of a German department in 1970/71. The same year the professor of Sociology, up to this a member of the Faculty of Theology, headed a department in Arts, with service teaching only in theology. But that year there were eleven new posts in the National University courses, with a head for the language laboratory, almost all filled by lay people. The situation was now fairly well irreversible, certainly after 1973, when the new departments were stabilised by appointing senior lecturers to head them—German, Biology (with a professor in 1978) and Geography (also with a professor that same year). In 1978 too there was provision for eight appointments to permanent posts as junior lecturers. The various departments were taking shape. The majority of the teaching staff was non-resident, nearly all lay. There were lay non-resident heads of departments. The process continued. When the priest-bursar, James Cosgrove, died in 1979 his successor was a layman, and in 1986 a layman, Séamus Smyth, professor of Geography, was appointed a third vice-president. The College Executive Council was struggling to resolve issues new to Maynooth, from absolutely basic matters like assessment boards and contracts of employment to lesser but important things such as the provision of offices, secretarial assistance, departmental budgets, telephones, right down to stationery and stamps. A little later, as permanent lay staff became established, the question of promotions and promotions procedures would arise, always a thorny issue, and calculated to be thorny above the average in Maynooth, where it was another of the problems being faced for the first time.

Resources were severely stretched, even overstretched, but this did not prevent large projects being mooted. Courses for an evening degree were first spoken of in 1971/72, courageous indeed but probably to the point of rashness. A report by a committee of the Academic Council in the spring of 1972 made clear how many difficulties there were. As well as the strain on resources, the limits imposed by the time available dictated a programme that must fall well short of the daytime courses. What continued for a while was a series of public lectures, dealing with many subjects, but heavily oriented towards theological issues. The department of Education mounted an annual lecture series each spring. The most enduring initiative, however, came from the Faculty of Celtic Studies, beginning in February 1971 and long continuing.

The lectures were published annually as *Léachtaí Cholm Cille*. The title recalls the student organisation, Cuallacht Cholm Cille, but the lecture series was a product of the Faculty, not of the students. It was highly professional, and became even more so. The Centre for Adult and Community Education was formally set up in 1975/76 under the aegis of the Department of Sociology, and a diploma was first awarded in 1976/77. A wide rage of extramural studies was begun at once. In the first year 430 were enrolled in courses in a number of centres. By 1983 there were 2,109 students, attending eighteen courses at various centres in seventeen counties. It was indeed a vast organisation run with very slender resources.

Anthropology also came in under the auspices of the Department of Sociology. A 'head of department' is first noted in the *Calendar* for 1985/86. There was no such department in University College, Dublin, nor indeed anywhere in the state. A Department of Economics within the Faculty of Arts had been a high priority for years before the appointment of a professor in 1984. As well as functioning as an Arts subject, from the year 1992/93 it offers the degree of BA (Finance). Science, as has been seen, carried on in conversions of old buildings and in prefabricated accommodation until the opening of the Callan Building in 1993. Experimental science subjects are by their nature costly in terms of staff and equipment, and it was a disadvantage that there was no applied science subject. Computer Science came in 1988/89. All departments were small, and sustaining them ranged from difficult to nearly impossible, particularly when it came to single-subject honours courses. In the Faculty of Arts the honours degree comprised two subjects, both taken at honours level. This was admittedly demanding, and in 1992/93 there was introduced, together with the BA (Finance), a 'special' degree, one subject taken at honours level and one at pass. By now too there was the development of career-oriented diplomas, because for quite some time teaching no longer offered an almost automatic career prospect to graduates in arts and science.

The funding of the National University college appeared generous indeed from the viewpoint of the Pontifical University, but it was on the meagre side compared with other institutions, inevitable perhaps in a college beginning from so small a base and seeking an identity. The harsh cutbacks in public funding generally in the late 1980s were a real anxiety. There was much misgiving when the Government's unit cost study began to operate in the college in February and March 1989. Yet it would appear that it brought benefits, that this quantitative comparision of institutions revealed Maynooth as understaffed. The riches of seventeen new academic posts were announced in the spring of 1990.

But the fact that individual departments and even the college itself were small was not without compensating advantages. The early days especially may have been passed in some confusion, but there was also much fellowship, as theologian, philosopher, humanist and scientist felt themselves part of a community where it was easy to share experiences. This was inevitably to some extent diluted as numbers grew, but at least within departments the element of personal relationship could still be strong. The frictions academic communities are prone to remained under control at this level even at times of real stress. There was much hard work in genuine co-operation, making Maynooth the kind of place to which many of its students come for no discernible reason except that they prefer it.

A few notable achievements might be mentioned, keeping them few if only because the more are mentioned the more feel omitted. Maynooth scholarship made the news in 1987, when the 'Giotto' mission to explore Halley's Comet carried an experiment devised in the Department of Experimental Physics, from which there developed the enterprise Space Technology Ireland Ltd. There has been distinguished work in the Department of Biology, attracting large research grants—in 1989 research into nematodes to secure pest control without the need for pesticides, with its obvious implications for the developing world in particular (Plate 89), and in 1992 studies of gene development in cancer growth and the factors affecting hereditary diseases. In 1991 the Department of Modern History became the first chosen to join the inner circle of the European Community course transfer system, and the first students appeared in 1992/93. The same department has introduced an evening postgraduate course leading to an MA degree in local history. The first graduates were in 1994.

With the Single European Act in 1990 large Community grants became available for fostering joint research projects, for co-operation between universities and industry, and for exchange of staff and students under what were known as 'Erasmus scholarships'. These developments opened Europe to Maynooth students, and they also brought Europe to Maynooth in numbers large enough to be a visible presence. Africa had been a visible presence from the earlier days, deriving mostly from the Irish missionary movement (Plate 79). So too had America. There had been 'occasional students' for a long time. In the mid-1970s St Mary's College, Notre Dame, made Maynooth one of the European centres for its 'junior year abroad', sending up to forty students a year; and in 1992 St John's University, New York, with a student body of about 26,000, chose Maynooth as the locale for its Irish programme.

EPILOGUE

Centenaries must surely be a time for communing with the ghosts of the past, bicentenaries even more so, and the place to commune with these ghosts must surely be the college cemetery. When Sir Francis Head visited it in 1852 he noted, in what was not a very well-kept place, 'four flat stones, each resting on four plain pedestals about four feet high . . . to the memory of great dons of the college.'[1] The visitor today, when facing the many memorials to great dons now resting there, will be conscious of a fairly clear distinction. To his right are monuments of the type described by Head, more of them there now indeed, but still recalling the afternoon and evening of the Catholic Enlightenment, the immediate heirs of the founding fathers of 1795. Most of the students' graves also date from this period, each marked with its simple cross, only the later ones having the luxury of a brief inscription. To the visitor's left, however, there arise the monuments to what may be called by the same extension 'the voice of 1895', a forest of Celtic crosses, the exceptions marked by plain slabs—Walter McDonald and Peter Coffey—being, it might be symbolically, those who were not comfortable within the system.

In 1995 it may be easier to feel more in tune with 1795. 1895 had too many certainties for our times. They are expressed in the opening of the 'Centenary Ode', and go on for all of its hundred and sixteen lines:

> Who is this ye crown with chaplets? Who is this ye bless today?
> Why the scene of jubilation? Why these guests from far away?
> Has the world's wild mirth and laughter all the buried years betrayed
> That this festal hour of triumph stirs the quiet cloistral shade?[2]

There cannot but be more sympathy with the less certain men of the founding generation, refugees from a revolution that had thrown their world into uncertainty and confusion, prefiguring the uncertainties and confusions two hundred years later, with so many landmarks swept away. It is somehow easier to be in sympathy with Francis Power, approaching the authorities in Dublin

Castle in 1799 to plead for the release of 'an inoffensive harmless young man' who had been arrested simply because he was called 'Power', and surely conscious that he himself had the same dangerous name. It is easy too to feel for Louis Delahogue, forced to leave an established academic career in Paris, but grateful for a new opportunity, and indeed for such basic things as a roof over his head, and fire and food, and learning not just to tolerate but to appreciate the young 'peasants' that he must have found trying when he had to live with them in crowded and noisy conditions.

Stability is not a word widely applicable in these times, but Maynooth is at least less unstable than in turbulent times in the recent past. It is not the same kind of place as it was a generation ago, but if there had been no change at all the cause for concern might be undiluted. Neither has it developed into quite the kind of place it was then expected it might become, though it would be hard to think of any human institution that has followed precisely its planned course through these turbulent years. In particular, theological studies have not had as great a role as had been hoped for. No doubt expectations were pitched too high at the time, not just in Maynooth but everywhere. Pope and Council were urging that religion speak to the world using the methods of research and literary forms of modern thought. It seems fair to say that nobody had quite realised how very difficult this was going to be, had not accepted that there might be elements in the culture of these time that are simply not receptive to revealed religion.

Ireland lay wide open to the changing world: its language was the 'world language', English. It changed rapidly, in some respects more rapidly than other places, if only because it had been a very conservative society. The country has indeed gone a long way towards the belief that the answer to any problem is to remove prohibitions and inhibitions. 'Thou shalt not' is no longer an acceptable beginning to a sentence. 'Discrimination', of almost any kind, seems to be the only thing that still passes for sin. Yet it may be that the Irish on their way down the ladder of permissiveness are beginning to notice some rather unexpected people trying to climb back up.

The fact is that society cannot hold together unless its citizens are prepared to make sacrifices. In Ireland, it is not easy to find motivation for such sacrifices except against a background of religion. As the world measures achievement we have no great past to keep for pride, and there is no evading the fact that religious commitment has been very central to the shaping of Ireland. It is doubtful if a purely secular and humanist culture could hold society together anywhere, and in this matter it is not unreasonable to fear that the Irish may be particularly vulnerable. Here surely is an aspect of the Irish heritage that Maynooth must be expected—even required—not to forget. The mind travels back once again to the college cemetery, and from the gravestones of the dead dons there to those who lie elsewhere. The plain slabs marking the graves of Walter McDonald and Peter Coffey catch the eye in the forest of Celtic crosses. It does seem true to say that at the core of Walter McDonald's striving was an attempt to engage theologically with the Ireland of his day. As for Peter Coffey, his students saw in him the dauntingly austere philosopher, knowing little or nothing of the enthusiast for the Irish language or the fiercely radical social thinker; they may perhaps have had some inkling of the quality of 'dreamer' that he saw in himself, but probably not very much. Donnchadh Ó Floinn rests elsewhere, with his dreams that 'the one thing about the old Irish world it is most needful to revive is its holiness.' So does 'Gerry' McGarry, who set out among the pastoral guidelines for his periodical, the *Furrow*, that it would be loyal to 'the traditions of the Irish church'.

Since they died Maynooth has developed into an institution they could scarcely have thought of. Nowadays memories are getting shorter, and the past may mean little even to people who do not know what 'deconstruction-ism' means. Yet were Maynooth to break with its past it is hard to see anything very distinctive in its present, or indeed in its future. Hopefully, the past will not be forgotten: *olim meminisse iuvabit*.

'Brief Lives'

As material for a general history of Maynooth College came together facts about individual lives inevitably began to accumulate, that obviously could not be worked into a history of the institution. At an early stage I opened a file on people, and as it grew it seemed more and more desirable not to let this material be lost, especially at a time when the past so easily gets forgotten. It began to appear also that a good photographic record could be put together, and in the end 'likenesses' of about four out of every five were located. The main sources were in the college, portraits and photographs in 'class pieces', but search has been made very widely. This work was done by Dr Dermot Farrell, who not only had copies made of what was known but tracked down material in likely—and indeed unlikely—places. He cannot have missed very much.

There had to be severe restrictions on the length of individual entries, even with the adoption of a reduced format, if the appendix was not to threaten to grow longer than the book. I began to envy the commission to John Aubrey to include all he knew when he composed his 'Brief Lives' over three hundred years ago. It will be obvious that my 'brief lives' make no claim to complete research: the only substantial addition to what chanced to come my way has been the *Irish Catholic Directory*, which in more spacious days often carried biographical notices of the dead.

I have tried as far as possible to list all the human and academic 'rites of passage'— birth, ordination, appointment, publications, and, inevitably, death. Even a list of these basic facts is not always possible, at least without minute research into such things as baptismal registers and tombstones. Curiously, the record of ordination is often lacking in the nineteenth century. Those selected as 'Dunboyne Scholars' were not ordained with their class, and no record was kept of individual ordinations. There are problems too about who should be included. To say that the qualifications are to have been a staff member and to be dead does not solve everything. For most of Maynooth's history every member of the teaching staff was a 'professor', but at the beginning there were some ambiguities, especially because of a certain overlap between the ecclesiastical and lay colleges. I have included all who taught in these early years, even if sometimes in an indeterminate capacity. The Dominican Order in particular has been very generous in providing staff from time to time. I have included those who were designated 'professor', though conscious that this involves a measure of discrimination. The deans are all here, but not the spiritual directors. I can only hope it will be accepted there is some reason in the dichotomy.

I have listed publications—for obvious reasons the principal publications only, and I am quite conscious I must have missed some. And the biographical notice concentrates on time spent in the college, which will explain the brevity of the account given to those whose careers were in a sense only opening up when they left, such as Archbishops John MacHale and William Walsh, or Bishop Michael Browne.

Biographical studies are sparse, even for major figures, but there are notices of some of the lesser ones in unexpected places, though not of many of them. Regretfully, I have had to omit all such references because of constrictions on space.

François Anglade

Michael Barrett

Patrick A. Beecher

Henry Bewerunge

Daniel A. Binchy

Peter Birch

Ahern, Maurice (1735-1801) Born Co. Kerry; educated in Paris; doctor of the Sorbonne, professor of philosophy at the Collège de Navarre; canon and vicar-general of Chartres; Fellow of the Royal Society of Navarre; in 1790 refused the Oath and left France; professor of Dogma in Maynooth 1795; reputed 'as great a defender as any Frenchman of the Gallican liberties'; died 7 Feb. 1801; buried in Laraghbryan; memorial tablet in western wall of church, inscription printed in *Cal. 1884/85.*

Anglade, François (1758-1834) Born Milheu, department of Aveyron, France; read philosophy in Rodez and theology in Paris; professor in Paris 1789; refused the Oath and left France at the end of 1792; reputed to have spent six years as gardener to a Protestant family in Wales; professor of Logic in Maynooth 1802, of Moral Theology 1810; on his appointment took charge of church music, in charge of liturgy after retirement; would seem mainly responsible for the gardens laid out at the western end of Dunboyne House; principal patron in the foundation of the Presentation Convent, Maynooth; resigned 1828; died 12 Apr. 1834; buried in college cemetery.
Published: *Institutiones Philosophicae* (3 vols., 1813–15).

Barrett, Michael (d. 1945) Ordained priest of the diocese of Cloyne in Maynooth 1892; professor of Philosophy 1893; resigned 1901; successively president, St Colman's College, Fermoy, and parish priest of Blarney and Macroom, where he died 26 Jul. 1945.

Beecher, Patrick A. (1870-1940) Born Tallow, Co. Waterford; ordained priest of the diocese of Waterford in Maynooth 1896; held teaching posts in USA and Canada 1896-1904; appointed to newly created chair of Sacred Eloquence and Pastoral Theology 1904; retired 1939; died in Cork 2 Jun. 1940.
Published: *The Holy Shroud: a Reply to the Rev. Herbert Thurston, S.J.* (1928); F.X. Schouppe, S.J., *The Pulpit Orator* (trans., 1914).

Behan, Joseph (1822-50) Priest of the diocese of Meath; professor of Philosophy 1845, before ordination to priesthood; died 5 Aug. 1850.

Bewerunge, Henry (1862-1923) Born Lethmathe in Westphalia; family moved to Dusseldorf in his early youth; ordained 1885, studied church music at Ratisbon; his tombstone described him as a priest of the diocese of Paderborn, but he ministered in Cologne, where he was chanter in the cathedral and secretary to the vicar-general; appointed to Maynooth 1888, at first to a contract post, later as first full-time professor of 'Church Chant and Organ'; brought a new professionalism to church music in the college and throughout the country, both in plainchant and polyphony; was on holiday in Germany when war broke out Aug. 1914; did not get permission to return until Jun. 1921; returned broken in health; died 2 Dec. 1923.

Binchy, Daniel A. (1899-1989) A distinguished and wide-ranging scholar, 'the last link with the "heroic age" of Celtic Studies', as one obituary described him; served as Irish minister to the Weimar Republic 1929-32; published *Church and State in Fascist Italy* (1941); professor in Canon Law Faculty, Maynooth 1943, resigned 1946; published *Corpus Iuris Hibernici* (6 vols., 1978).

Birch, Peter (d. 1981) Ordained priest of the diocese of Ossory in Maynooth 1937; taught St Kieran's College, Kilkenny 1938-53; prominent in adult education—social study classes 1940, university extension courses 1949; appointed professor of Education and Catechetics 1953; resigned on appointment as coadjutor bishop in Ossory 1962; died 7 Mar. 1981.
Published: *St Kieran's College, Kilkenny* (1951).

John Blowick

Andrew Boylan

Patrick A. Boylan

Martin Brenan

James Browne

Michael Browne

Patrick J. Browne

Blowick, John (d. 1972) Ordained priest of diocese of Tuam in Maynooth 1913; professor of Theology 1914; resigned 1917; played leading role in foundation of Society of St Columban ('the Maynooth Mission to China'); became first superior-general; died 19 Jun. 1972 at St Columban's, Navan.
Published: *Priestly Vocation* (1932).

Boylan, Andrew (1842-1910) Born Crosserlough, Co. Cavan; ordained priest of diocese of Kilmore in Maynooth 1867; taught in Kilmore Academy; appointed 'minister or second bursar' 1875, bursar 1883; Walter McDonald (*Reminiscences*, 83) described him acidly as 'good-humoured, honest, weak'; resigned 1887 to join Redemptorists; distinguished career as a missionary, first superior of newly constituted Irish province 1898; bishop of Kilmore 1907; died 25 Mar. 1910.

Boylan, Christopher (d. 1832) Born Dunshaughlin, Co. Meath; student in lay college 1803-06, afterwards in ecclesiastical college; ordained priest of diocese of Meath 1815; sent to study oriental languages with Dr Barrett, late vice-provost Trinity College, Dublin; professor of Oriental Languages in Maynooth 1816; of English Rhetoric 1818; of English and French 1820; rector Irish College, Rome, 1829-32; returned to Ireland June 1832 and died shortly afterwards.
Published: *The Ecclesiastical Conferences ... of Massillon Bishop of Clermont* (trans., 2 vols., 1825).

Boylan, Patrick A. (d. 1974) Born Athy, Co. Kildare; studied at Clonliffe and Maynooth; ordained priest of diocese of Dublin 1903; professor of Scripture 1905; studied Egyptology and Semitic Languages in Berlin; vice-president 1922; resigned 1934 on appointment as parish priest of Dún Laoghaire; died 22 Nov. 1974.
Published: *The Psalms* (2 vols., 1920); *Thoth the Hermes of Egypt* (1922); *The Epistle to the Hebrews* (1922); *St Paul's*

Epistle to the Romans (1934); *Lectionary of Epistles and Gospels for Sundays and Festivals* (1965).

Brenan, Martin (d. 1982) Born Castlecomer, Co. Kilkenny; ordained priest of the diocese of Kildare and Leighlin in Maynooth 1926; professor of Education and Catechetics 1931; resigned 1949 to become president of Carlow College and subsequently parish priest of Edenderry; died 4 Mar. 1982.
Published: *Schools of Kildare and Leighlin* (1935).

Browne, James (1786-1865) Born Mayglass, Co. Wexford; ordained priest of diocese of Ferns in Maynooth 1812; junior dean 1814; professor of Scripture 1817 and of Hebrew 1818; coadjutor bishop in Kilmore 1827; succeeded 1829; died 11 Apr. 1865.

Browne, Michael (d. 1980) Born Westport, Co. Mayo; ordained priest of the diocese of Tuam in Maynooth 1920; professor of Moral Theology and Canon Law 1921; DCL in Rome 1924; resigned 1937 on being appointed bishop of Galway; resigned bishopric 1976; died 23 Feb. 1980.

Browne, Patrick J. (1889-1960) Born Grangemockler, Co. Tipperary; studied Rockwell, Clonliffe (MA and travelling studentship Royal University 1908), Paris (DSc Sorbonne 1912); ordained priest of diocese of Dublin 1913; professor of Mathematics and Natural Philosophy in Maynooth 1913; studied Göttingen 1913-14; deeply involved in the politics of the War of Independence and the Civil War; a brilliant mathematician, but with deep literary interests; translated classic works from Greek, French and Italian into Irish; for many years chairman Dublin Institute for Advanced Studies; resigned 1945 to become President UCG; retired 1959; died Dublin 5 Jun. 1960.

443

Robert Browne

Patrick Byrne

Nicholas Callan

John Cantwell

Patrick J. Carew

Thomas Carr

John Clancy

Browne, Robert (1844-1935) Born Charleville, Co. Cork; ordained priest of diocese of Cloyne in Maynooth 1869; dean 1875, vice-president 1883, President 1885; his lasting legacy the fitting out of the College Chapel, where he produced much from limited resources, and the Aula Maxima, where the resources were very limited indeed; Dean Mulcahy, a student when he was President, while admitting he was pompous, wrote ('Reminiscences', 146): 'We found him always kindly, affable, deeply interest in our welfare, engrossed in the improvement of the college. St Joseph's Square was redeemed by him from the condition of a wilderness; Virginia creepers and passion-flowers decorated the walls of the New House'; resigned on appointment as bishop of Cloyne 1894; died 23 Mar. 1935.

Byrne, Patrick (d. 1834) Born Co. Tyrone; educated Irish College, Paris; doctor of the Sorbonne; president Irish College, Nantes; refused the Oath and left France; appointed parish priest of Donaghmore; president of Maynooth 1807; resigned 1810; appointed parish priest of Armagh, where he died in 1834.

Callan, Nicholas (1799-1864) Born Dromiskin, Co. Louth, of wealthy farming stock; ordained priest of diocese of Armagh in Maynooth 1823; DD from Sapienza, Rome; professor of Mathematics and Natural Philosophy 1826; described as quiet, childlike, ascetic, spending all day in class hall or laboratory; his studies in applied electricity produced the first effective induction coil and greatly improved batteries; 'reputed to be the best moral theologian in the college', particularly in the theology of St Alphonsus, many of whose theological and devotional works he translated and published; his charities were extensive; a great benefactor to the Presentation Convent; died 14 Jan. 1864.
Published: *An Abstract of a Course of Lectures on Electricity and Galvanism* (1832); *Darré's Elements of Geometry* (1844).

Cantwell, John (d. 1866) Ordained priest of the diocese of Meath in Maynooth 1815; appointed 'sub-dean' and later dean 1816; resigned 1820 on appointment as parish priest of Kilbeggan; appointed bishop of Meath 1830; died 11 Dec. 1866.

Carew, Patrick J. (d. 1855) Born Waterford; educated there and at Maynooth; ordained priest of diocese of Waterford; professor of Humanity 1825; of Theology 1828; consecrated coadjutor to vicar apostolic of Madras 1838; died in Calcutta 2 Nov. 1855.
Published: *An Ecclesiastical History of Ireland* (1835); Pierre Nicole, *The Perpetuity of the Faith of the Catholic Church in the Eucharist* (trans., with William Kelly, 1835).

Carr, Thomas (1839-1917) Born Moylough, Co. Galway; ordained priest of diocese of Tuam in Maynooth 1866; dean 1872, professor of Theology 1875, vice-president 1880; bishop of Galway 1883, archbishop of Melbourne 1886; Walter McDonald (*Reminiscences*, 54) characterises him as 'not brilliant, steady rather, and sensible ... a man of blameless life, a priest and a gentleman'; died 6 May 1917.

Clancy, John (1856-1912) Born Riverstown, Co. Sligo; educated Sligo, Athlone, Maynooth; ordained priest of diocese of Elphin 1882; professor of English 1887; bishop of Elphin 1895; died 19 Oct. 1912.

Clancy, Thomas, OFM (1748-1814) Born Co. Leitrim; became a Franciscan; ordained Rome 1772; lecturer in theology in Prague 1775; returned to Ireland in early 1790s; professor of Scripture in Maynooth 1795; resigned 1797; returned to Prague as tutor to son of Count Thunn; died Prague May 1814.
Published: *Theses ex Universa Theologia* (Prague, 1782).

Patrick Cleary

Peter Coffey

Daniel Coghlan (Cohalan)

Patrick Connolly

Peter Connolly

William Conway

Cleary, Patrick (d. 1970) Ordained priest of diocese of Killaloe in Maynooth 1911; professor of Theology 1914; resignation accepted 1918 (joined the Maynooth Mission to China); died 23 Oct. 1970.

Clinch, James B. Professor of Humanity 1795; of Rhetoric 1798; resigned 1802; became prominent in the politics of the veto question, and had a number of publications, including *Letters on Church Government* (1812).

Coen, Thomas (1763-1847) Born parish of Fohena, Co. Galway; the first student to sign the Maynooth matriculation roll, 30 Jun. 1795, aged 24 and presumably already ordained priest of diocese of Clonfert; finished studies 1800, appointed dean 1801; more or less forced resignation 1810, after difficult years in office; appointed administrator of parish of Loughrea; coadjutor to bishop of Clonfert 1815; succeeded 1831; died 25 Apr. 1847.

Coffey, Peter (1876-1943) Born near Enfield, Co. Meath; ordained priest of diocese of Meath in Maynooth 1900; studied in Louvain (DPh 1905); professor of Philosophy 1902; an outstanding philosopher, he was a man of high spiritual seriousness that found expression in his enthusiasm for the Irish language and for social reform; for some details of his campaigns and his publications see above, pp. 313–15; died in Maynooth 7 Jan. 1943.

Coghlan (Cohalan), Daniel (1858-1952) Born Kilmichael, Co. Cork; ordained priest of diocese of Cork in Maynooth; professor of Theology 1886; of conservative views, he clashed with Walter McDonald (see above, pp. 251–7); auxiliary bishop of Cork 1914, consecrated in Maynooth; succeeded 1916; died in Cork 24 Aug. 1952.
Published: *De Gratia* (1902); *De Deo Uno et Trino et de Deo Creatore* (1909); *De Incarnatione* (1910); *De Sanctissima Eucharistia* (1913).

Coleman, Patrick (1773-1838) Entered Maynooth 1795 to complete studies; ordained Liffey Street chapel 1797; appointed to lecture in Scripture in Maynooth 1799, and president of lay college 1800; resigned both posts 1802; ministered in various Dublin parishes; died 25 May 1838, aged 65.

Connolly, Patrick (d. 1945) Ordained priest of diocese of Clonfert in Maynooth 1911; assistant bursar 1917; resigned 1919 to join 'Maynooth Mission to China'; died Oct. 1945. Gratefully remembered for introducing table-cloths, an improvement to the midday lunch, and three-course dinners.

Connolly, Peter (1927-87) Born Drumconrath, Co. Meath; ordained priest of diocese of Meath in Maynooth 1951; studied Oxford 1951-4; in the words of a tutor 'one of the most intelligent students it has ever been my good fortune to teach'; professor of English 1954 and in his turn a brilliant teacher; regretfully his attempts to probe topics it was soon clear must be probed met a harsh response; in consequence his written work is much less than it might have been; retired 1985 after an incapacitating illness; remained in college; died 9 Feb. 1987.
James Murphy (ed.), *No Bland Facility: Selected Writings on Literature, Religion and Censorship: Peter Connolly* (1990).

Conway, William (1913-77) Born in the Falls Road area of Belfast; ordained priest of diocese of Down and Connor in Maynooth 1937; DD 1938; DCL (Rome) 1941; professor of Moral Theology 1942; vice-president 1957; auxiliary bishop in Armagh 1958, archbishop of Armagh 1963, cardinal 1965; died 17 Apr. 1977.
Published: *Problems in Canon Law* (1956).

James Cosgrove

George Crolly

William Crolly

Bartholomew Crotty

Terence Cunningham

Bernard Curran OP

Robert Cussen

Cosgrove, James (d. 1979) Ordained priest of diocese of Kilmore in Maynooth 1943; junior dean 1947; acting bursar 1955; bursar 1957; died 8 Dec. 1979.

Crean, Edward Ordained priest of diocese of Meath in Maynooth June 1886; dean 1888; resigned 1891.

Crolly, George (1813-78) Born in the parish of Downpatrick, Co. Down; entered Maynooth 1829, Dunboyne student 1835, ordained 1837 and recalled to diocese; professor of Theology 1844; for his conflict with Archbishop Cullen see above, pp. 149–54; died 24 Jan. 1878.
Published: *Disputationes Theologicae de Institia et Iure, ad norman iuris municipalis Britannici et Hibernici conformatae* (3 vols., 1870-77); *The Life and Death of Oliver Plunkett, Primate of Ireland* (1850); *Life of the Most Rev. Dr Crolly, Archbishop of Armagh and Primate of Ireland* (1851).

Crolly, William (1785-1849) Born in the parish of Downpatrick, Co. Down; entered Maynooth 1801; ordained and appointed lecturer in Philosophy 1806; professor of Philosophy 1810; resigned on appointment as parish priest of Belfast 1812; bishop of Down and Connor 1825; archbishop of Armagh 1835; died 6 Apr. 1849.

Crotty, Bartholomew (1769-1846) Born Clonakilty, Co. Cork; sent to Salamanca for studies by Bishop McKenna of Cloyne; persuaded to remain at Lisbon where he was successively professor (1791) and rector (1801); during French occupation (1806-08) resisted attempts to transfer him and his students to Paris; returned to Ireland 1811;

President of Maynooth 1813; provided much-needed stability by his sturdy courage; appointed bishop of Cloyne 1833; died 4 Oct. 1846.

Cummins, John A shadowy figure; probably the 'John Cummins' ordained priest of diocese of Dublin in Maynooth 1815; appointed 'procurator' 1816; resigned because of ill health at the end of 1827.

Cunningham, Terence (1922-86) Born in the parish of Lavey, Co. Cavan; ordained priest of the diocese of Kilmore in Maynooth 1948; DCL (Maynooth) 1951; taught in All Hallows College, Dublin 1951-6; professor of Canon Law in Maynooth 1956; deep interest in local history; many contributions, especially to diocesan historical journal *Breifne*, of which he became editor in 1980; died 22 Sep. 1986.
Published (with Daniel Gallogly): *St Patrick's College and Earlier Kilmore Academies* (1974).

Curran, Bernard, OP (1909-85) Born in Cork; became a Dominican 1927; ordained Rome 1933; taught philosophy in Tallaght; came to Maynooth in Jan. 1943 after the sudden death of Peter Coffey; remained until Sep. 1944; after this spent most of his life abroad; returned in poor health 1975; died in Cork 26 Aug. 1985.

Cussen, Robert (d. 1865) Appointed junior dean 1836, when he is described as curate of St Michan's, Limerick, formerly honorary canon and professor of theology at Meaux; resigned 1838 on appointment as parish priest of Bruff; died 1865.

John F. D'Alton

André Darré

Louis-Gilles Delahogue

Cornelius Denvir

John Derry

Joseph Dixon

450

D'Alton, John F. (1882-1963) Born Claremorris, Co. Mayo; studied in Clonliffe and Irish College, Rome; after ordination spent some time in Oxford and Cambridge; appointed lecturer in Classics Maynooth 1910, professor 1912; vice-president 1934, President 1936; coadjutor in Meath 1942, bishop of Meath 1943, archbishop of Armagh 1946, cardinal 1953; died 1 Feb. 1963.
Published: *Horace and his Age* (1917); *Roman Literary Theory and Criticism* (1931); *Selections from St John Chrysostom* (1940).

D'Arcy, Morgan (1761-1831) His family lived at Annagh, Co. Wexford; studied at Nantes and Bordeaux; ordained priest of the diocese of Dublin; served for a time in England, but was back in Dublin by 1793; president of lay college 1805; resigned 1807. Taught in a number of schools in Dublin; parish priest of St Audoen's 1813; died 16 Jul. 1831.

Darré, André Born Montau, department of Gers, France; ordained priest of diocese of Auch; professor of philosophy at Toulouse; appointed professor of philosophy in Maynooth 1795, arrived 1797; professor of Natural Philosophy 1801, in succession to Pierre-Justin Delort; sought leave of absence 1806, 1813; returned to his native diocese of Auch; his text-book of Geometry, as revised successively by Nicholas Callan and Francis Lennon, was in use in Maynooth for the whole of the nineteenth century; they considered its arrangement greatly superior to Euclid.
Published: *Elements of Geometry* (1813).

Delahogue, Louis-Gilles (1739-1827) Born Paris 1739; priest of diocese of Paris, canon of Saint-Honorat, professor of Moral Divinity and Fellow, Sorbonne; refused Oath and left France 1792; lived in England 1792-8; appointed professor of Moral Theology in Maynooth 1798 and of Dogma 1801; wrote textbooks covering much of the course; retained his horror of revolution and his admittedly moderate Gallicanism; invited to return to help to reorganise the Sorbonne in 1816, but did not go; retired 1820; died in Maynooth 9 May 1827.
Published: *Pensées chrétiennes* (Paris, n.d.); *Sanctus Cyprianus ad Martyres et Confessores* (1794); *S. Cyprien consolant les fidèles persécutés de l'Église de France* (1797); *De Religione* (1808, Paris printing 1815); *De Ecclesia Christi* (1809); *De Sacramentis in Genere et de Eucharistia* (1810); *De Incarnatione Verbi* (1811); *La journée du Chrétien* (1811); *De Mysterio SS. Trinitatis* (1812); *De Sacramento Paenitentiae* (1813).

Delort, Pierre-Justin Born Bordeaux, priest of diocese of Bordeaux; appointed professor of Natural Philosophy in Maynooth Jun. 1795; arrived October to find three students and little if any equipment; clearly did not settle down; sought leave of absence Feb. 1801, went to France and did not return.

Denvir, Cornelius (1791-1866) Born Lecale, Co. Down; ordained priest of diocese of Down and Connor in Maynooth 1814; lecturer in Natural Philosophy 1814, professor 1815; resigned 1825 on appointment as parish priest of Downpatrick; bishop of Down and Connor 1835; resigned 1865; died 10 Jul. 1866.

Derry, John (d. 1870) Entered Maynooth 1827; ordained priest of diocese of Clonfert; appointed 'second junior dean' 1833; resigned 1836 to take a parish in his diocese; bishop of Clonfert 1847; died 28 Jun. 1870.

Dixon, Joseph (1806-66) Born Coalisland, Co. Tyrone; entered Maynooth 1822; ordained priest of diocese of Armagh; appointed 'sub-dean' 1829, professor of Scripture 1834; resigned 1852 on appointment as archbishop of Armagh; consecrated in College Chapel; died 29 Apr. 1866.
Published: *A General Introduction to the Sacred Scripture* (1852).

James Donnellan

Philip Dowley

James Duff

Malachy Eaton

Thomas Esser OP

Donaghy, John Ordained priest of the diocese of Raphoe in Maynooth 1903; professor of 'Experimental Science and Mathematics' 1912; resigned 1921; subsequently taught in Marquette University, Milwaukee, and Incarnate Word College, San Antonio, Texas.

Donnellan, James (1856-1932) Born Ballinlough, Co. Roscommon; entered Maynooth 1871; ordained priest of the diocese of Tuam; dean 1884, bursar 1887; presided over the extensive modernisation around the turn of the century; prominent in foundation in 1902 of the Irish Catholic Church Property Insurance Co. (now Church and General Insurance plc); retired on pension 1923; died 4 Feb. 1932.

Donovan, Jeremiah (d. 1862) Born Macroom, Co. Cork, entered Maynooth 1811, ordained priest of diocese of Cloyne; professor of Rhetoric 1820; resigned because of poor health 1833, travelled extensively in Italy; died 11 Dec. 1862.
Published: *The Catechism of the Council of Trent ... Translated into English* (1829); *Rome Ancient and Modern and its Environs* (4 vols., 1822-4).

Dowley, Philip (1790-1865) Born Waterford. Ordained priest of diocese of Waterford and Lismore in Maynooth 1816; 'sub-dean' 1816, dean 1820; brought a badly needed stability to the office; vice-president 25 Jun. 1834, but left college next day to join a group of young priests he had encouraged to lead a common life, who were to develop into the Irish Vincentian Congregation; died 31 Jan. 1864.

Duff, James (d. 1959) Ordained priest of diocese of Down and Connor in Maynooth 1922; professor of 'Rhetoric' 1922; vice-president 1942; resigned 1950 on appointment as parish priest of Castlewellan, Co. Down; died 6 Feb. 1959.
Published: *The Letters of Saint Jerome* (1942); *St Augustine's Autobiography* (1946).

Dunne, Andrew (1746-1823) Educated at Bordeaux; priest of the diocese of Dublin; appointed secretary to the Maynooth Trustees 1795, 'librarian and treasurer' 1800, President 1803; resigned presidency 1807, re-appointed secretary to the Trustees and nominated parish priest of St Catherine's, Meath Street; resigned parish and returned to the college, taking on the duties of librarian; died 17 Jun. 1823.

Eaton, Malachy (1882-1929) Born Beakan, Ballyhaunis, Co. Mayo; ordained priest of the diocese of Tuam in Maynooth 1906; dean 1911; ill during summer of 1929, but resumed duties in Sep.; died suddenly 26 Nov. 1929.

Eloi, François Appointed professor of Sacred Scripture and Ecclesiastical History 1808; resigned 1809.

Esser, Thomas, OP (d. 1926) Appointed professor of 'Higher Philosophy' 1887; lectured in Latin because of imperfect command of English; recalled 1891 to take up an appointment in Fribourg (Suisse); died in Rome 13 Mar. 1926.

Eustace, John (d. 1815) Born Co. Kildare, educated Douai, priest of Kildare and Leighlin; appointed professor of Rhetoric in Maynooth 1795; resigned 1797; died Naples 1815.

Patrick Everard

Thomas Fahy

Michael Fallon

Thomas Farrelly

John Fennelly

Edward Ferris CM

Michael Fogarty

Everard, Patrick (1751-1821) Born of 'old gentry' stock in Fethard, Co. Tipperary; entered Salamanca 1778, ordained priest 1784; accepted rectorship of the Irish College, Bordeaux; barely escaped with his life when the mob broke in Oct. 1793; returned by way of Spain and England; opened a successful school in Ulverston in Lancashire; accepted presidency of Maynooth 1810, a commitment he clearly regarded as short-term; resigned 1812; appointed coadjutor in Cashel 1814, succeeded as archbishop 1820, died 31 Mar. 1821.

Fahy, Thomas (d. 1973) Ordained priest of diocese of Clonfert in Maynooth 1912; lecturer in Classics 1915; professor 1919; resigned 1927 to take up appointment in University College, Galway; died Galway 18 Jun. 1973.
Published: *New Testament Problems* (1963).

Fallon, Michael (d. 1965) Ordained priest of diocese of Galway in Maynooth 1919; DCL Maynooth 1921; junior dean Oct. 1929, professor of Canon Law 1933; resigned 1947 on appointment as parish priest; died Craughwell, Co. Galway, 16 Feb. 1965.

Farrelly, Thomas (1814-90) Born Ballintubber, Kells, Co. Meath; entered Maynooth 1837, ordained priest of the diocese of Meath; assistant bursar 1843, bursar 1845; retired on pension Jun. 1881, lived in the college; died 30 Dec. 1890.

Fennelly, John (d. 1868) Ordained priest of the diocese of Cashel in Maynooth 1833; bursar 1834; appointed vicar apostolic of Madras 1841 to succeed Patrick J. Carew, transferred to Calcutta; died Madras 23 Jan. 1868.

Ferris, Edward, CM (1738-1809) Born, he himself says, at Glencar, Co. Kerry; went to France 1754, joined Clare's regiment; left army and joined Vincentians 1758; held posts of vicar general and seminary rector at Toul and Amiens; appointed third assistant to the general 1778; badly beaten when the mob stormed Saint-Lazare on 13 Jul. 1790; became an *émigré* in 1793, going first to Rome, then to Switzerland when the French invaded Italy; dean in Maynooth 1898, professor of Moral Theology 1801; austere in his life and rigoristic in his teaching; died 26 Nov. 1809, buried in Laraghbryan; remains removed to Castleknock 19 Oct. 1875.

Fitzpatrick, William Priest of diocese of Dublin; curate in Mary's Lane chapel when appointed dean 1810; resigned and returned to Mary's Lane 1811; appointed vice-president 1813, resigned 1814; secretary to the Trustees 1823-5.

Flood, Peter (d. 1803) Born near Edgeworthstown, Co. Longford; entered Collège des Lombards, Paris, 1772, presumably already a priest, for after 1769 only priests were admitted there; superior of the college 1782; professor of Theology Collège de Navarre 1788; Collège des Lombards invaded by mob 1792 and students dispersed; refused oath, imprisoned in the Carmes; dramatically rescued at time of September massacres; given leave to return to Ireland, appointed parish priest of Edgeworthstown; refused Maynooth chair of Moral Theology 1795, but appointed President 1798; experienced much trouble in his office; died 26 Jan. 1803; buried in north aisle of College Chapel (St Joseph's).

Fogarty, Michael (d. 1955) Entered Maynooth 1878; ordained priest of the diocese of Killaloe; professor of Moral Theology 1889; vice-president 1903; appointed bishop of Killaloe 1904; died 25 Oct. 1955.

Michael Forker

Thomas Furlong

Denis Gargan

Richard Gibbons

Laurence Gillic

Thomas Gilmartin

Thomas P. Gilmartin

John Gunn

Forker, Michael (d. 1944) Born at Carrickfin, Co. Donegal; ordained priest of the diocese of Raphoe in Maynooth 1892; appointed 'to the vacant chair of Mental Philosophy' 1905; PhD Louvain; taught the Ethics courses; resigned 1929 on appointment as parish priest; died 5 Mar. 1944 in Glenties.

Furlong, Thomas (1802-75) Born Mayglass, Co. Wexford; ordained priest of the diocese of Ferns in Maynooth 1826; junior dean 1827; professor of Humanity 1829; of Rhetoric 1834; and of Theology 1845; appointed bishop of Ferns 1856; died 12 Nov. 1875; on hearing the news of his death Patrick Murray wrote in his diary: 'Of all the men, whose characters I have had opportunity of knowing well, he was the most faultless, the most perfect.'

Gaffney, Miles Priest of diocese of Dublin; not an alumnus of Maynooth; described as 'curate in Townsend Street' when appointed senior dean 1834 (the old penal-day chapel had been abandoned when St Andrew's, Westland Row, was blessed and opened on 2 Jan. 1834). Resigned on grounds of health 1855; was awarded a pension; a search through the likely sources has revealed nothing more of him.

Gargan, Denis (1819-1903) Born Cromwell's Bush, Duleek, Co. Meath; ordained priest of diocese of Meath in Maynooth 1843; in old age recalled he was present at the 'Monster Meeting' on Tara the following August; taught in the Irish College, Paris; appointed professor of Humanity in Maynooth 1845; of Ecclesiastical History 1859; for his acceptance of the parish of Duleek and subsequent return to the college in 1863 see above, p. 160; his lectures in Ecclesiastical History tended to be remembered for the amusing stories told of them but, as Dean Mulcahy summed up ('Reminiscences',

153): 'Humanity exuded from him, urbane, courteous, witty'; appointed vice-president 1885, President 1894, he devoted himself to building the spire; died 26 Aug. 1903.
Published: *The Ancient Church of Ireland: a Reply to Dr Todd's Life of St Patrick* (1864).

Gibbons, Richard Ordained priest of the diocese of Tuam in Maynooth 1813; lecturer in Humanity 1814, professor 1815; resigned 1824.

Gillic, Laurence (1820-54) Ordained priest of diocese of Meath in Maynooth 1849; professor of Scripture 1853; died 24 Jan. 1854.

Gilmartin, Thomas (1857-92) Born in parish of Achonry, Co. Sligo; ordained priest of diocese of Achonry in Maynooth 1881; professor of Ecclesiastical History 1886; died of consumption 8 May 1892; two volumes of *A Manual of Church History* published, a third projected; left copyright to establish a prize in ecclesiastical history; became a sizeable fund because the work proved a very successful textbook.

Gilmartin, Thomas P. (1861-1939) Born near Castlebar, Co. Mayo; entered Maynooth 1880; ordained priest of the diocese of Tuam; dean 1891; vice-president 1904; bishop of Clonfert 1909; archbishop of Tuam 1918; died 14 Oct. 1939.

Gunn, John Entered Maynooth (as 'John McGunn') 1829; ordained priest of diocese of Elphin 1837; appointed 'second junior dean' 1838; resigned 1852, ostensibly on grounds of ill health, but possibly more because he found the work uncongenial; awarded a pension, but served in a number of pastoral appointments. Wrote on Maynooth in *IER* in 1883 and 1884; disappears from *Irish Catholic Directory* after 1886; no obituary traced.

John Hackett

Richard Hackett

John Harty

Barbara Hayley

John Healy

William Higgins

Hackett, John (1913-70) Born Ballinonty, near Killenaule, Co. Tipperary; ordained priest of diocese of Cashel in Maynooth 1939; professor of Ancient Classics 1943, where he impressed his students by 'the razor sharpness of his intellect'; resigned on grounds of ill health 1958; served as curate in Tipperary and parish priest in Cappamore; did much work as translator for International Committee on English in the Liturgy; died suddenly 19 Jul. 1970.

Hackett, Richard (1823-87) Born Knockbridge, Co. Louth; ordained priest of the diocese of Armagh in Maynooth 1852; 'third or junior dean' 1853; professor of Philosophy 1862; Walter McDonald, who would have known him as pupil and colleague, describes him as an uninspired teacher, uninterested in his subject (*Reminiscences*, 43-5); Dean Mulcahy, who would have known him only by posthumous reputation, paints him as a conservative and martinet, insisting, for example, on addressing his colleagues as 'Mister' instead of the now popular 'Father' ('Reminiscences', 154), suggesting Canon Murray in Sheehan's *Luke Delmege*, who indeed may be to some extent modelled on him (Sheehan had been in his class in the year 1869/70); he died 9 Mar. 1887.

Hammond, Thomas (d. 1898) Ordained priest of diocese of Limerick in Maynooth 1857; 'junior dean' 1858; for the complaint of the Duke of Leinster's Scottish gamekeeper on his propensity to keep greyhounds and course hares see above, p. 186; candidate for vice-presidency 1883, but another dean, Robert Browne, his junior, appointed; resigned 1885, appointed parish priest of Newcastle West, where he died 5 Aug. 1898.

Hart, Andrew (1785-1815) Ordained priest of the diocese of Dublin in Maynooth 1808; parish priest of Lucan when appointed dean 1811; resigned 1812; parish priest of Rathcoole; died 19 Nov. 1815; an epitaph and panegyric composed by Delahogue have survived (Clogher DA, 1/3/2, 4).

Harty, John (1867–1946) Born Murroe, Co. Limerick; ordained priest of diocese of Cashel in Maynooth 1894; professor of Theology 1895; was given 'the new and most favourable privilege' of a year's study in Rome; resigned on appointment as archbishop of Cashel 1913; died 11 Sep. 1946.

Hayley, Barbara (1938-91) Educated at Alexandra College and Trinity College, Dublin; after a career in marketing turned again to academic life at Kent (PhD 1977) and Cambridge; professor of English Maynooth 1986; killed in a car accident May 1991.
Published: *Carleton's Traits and Stories and the 19th Century Irish Tradition* (1983); *A Bibliography of the Writings of William Carleton* (1985); *Three Hundred Years of Irish Periodicals* (1987, with Enda McKay); *Ireland and France: a Beautiful Friendship* (1992, ed. with Christopher Murray).

Healy, John (1841-1918) Born Ballinafad, Co. Sligo; entered Maynooth 1860, ordained priest of diocese of Elphin; professor of Theology 1879; Prefect of Dunboyne and editor *Irish Ecclesiastical Record* 1883; coadjutor bishop in Clonfert 1884; succeeded 1896; archbishop of Tuam 1903; died 16 Mar. 1918.
Published: *Ireland's Ancient Schools and Scholars* (1890); *Maynooth College: its Centenary History* (1895); *The Life and Writings of St Patrick* (1905); and several collections of addresses and essays.

Higgins, William (1793-1853) Went to Paris 1812, studied in a French seminary, ordained 1816; professor in the Irish College; went to Rome 1820, secured DD 1825; returned to Ireland 1826; professor of Theology in Maynooth 1826; bishop of Ardagh 1829; died 3 Jan. 1853.

John Hogan

Daniel Hourihane

James Hughes

Thomas Hussey

William Jennings

Thomas Judge

John Conleth Kearns OP

Matthew Kelly

Thomas Kelly

Hogan, John (1858-1918) Born Coolreagh, Co. Clare; studied in Paris (Saint-Sulpice) and Freiburg-im-Breisgau; ordained priest of diocese of Killaloe 1882; professor of Modern Languages in Maynooth 1886; editor *Irish Ecclesiastical Record* 1892; vice-president 1910; President 1912; resigned at Trustees' meeting Oct. 1918; died in a Dublin nursing-home 24 Nov. 1918.
Published: *Life and Works of Dante* (1897): *Irish Catholics and Trinity College* (1906); *Maynooth College and the Laity* (1910).

Hourihane, Daniel (1909-74) Ordained priest of diocese of Ross in Maynooth 1934; assistant bursar 1938; bursar 1944; as assistant bursar discharged heavy task of seeing college through 'emergency' of Second World War; serious car accident Aug. 1955 affected his health; resigned 1957; took up appointment in his diocese; parish priest of Timoleague 1970; died 23 Apr. 1974.

Hughes, James (1830-77) Born Clashganny, Co. Carlow; ordained priest of diocese of Kildare and Leighlin in Maynooth 1859; junior dean 1862; historical and antiquarian interests, wrote for *Kilkenny Archaeological Journal*, left three manuscript volumes of genealogical material to college library; died of a heart complaint 16 Nov. 1877.

Hussey, Thomas (1741-1803) For biographical details see above, pp. 26–7.

Jennings, William (1825-62) Born Tuam, Co. Galway; ordained priest of diocese of Tuam in Maynooth 1852; professor of Philosophy 1852; died 12 May 1862. Published: *Logicae seu Philosophiae Rationalis Elementa* (1861).

Judge, Thomas (d. 1907) Ordained priest of diocese of Achonry in Maynooth 1887; professor of Philosophy 1887; resigned 1893; went to Chicago and ministered there until his death 15 Dec. 1907.

Kearns, John Conleth, OP (d. 1985) Studied at the Biblical Institute, Rome and École Biblique, Jerusalem; appointed 'extraordinary professor' of Scripture in Maynooth for two years 1934; taught Scripture in OP House of Studies, Tallaght; died 10 Mar. 1985.

Kelly, Matthew (1814-58) Born Maudlin Street, Kilkenny; ordained priest of the diocese of Ossory in Maynooth 1838; taught theology in Irish College, Paris; professor of English and French at Maynooth 1841; mainly instrumental in founding the Celtic Society 1845 for the preservation and publication of early Irish manuscripts, later merged with the Archaeological Society (founded 1840) to become the Irish Archaeological and Celtic Society; accepted invitation to become vice-rector of the Catholic University c. 1 May 1857, then declined because of ill health; professor of Ecclesiastical History in Maynooth 1857; died 30 Oct. 1858.
Published: Editions of John Lynch, *Cambrensis Eversus* (3 vols., 1848-52); Stephen White, *Apologia pro Hibernia adversus Cambri calumnias* (1849); Philip O'Sullivan Beare, *Historiae Catholicae Hiberniae Compendium* (1850); *Calendar of Irish Saints: the Martyrology of Tallagh* (1857). He also published an Ecclesiastical Map of Ireland, and wrote extensively in periodicals. At his death he was preparing for publication Laurence Renehan's *Collections on Irish Church History* (finally published in 1864), and collecting material for a 'continuation of Lanigan', Irish ecclesiastical history from the twelfth century to the Reformation.

Kelly, Thomas (d. 1835) Native of Armagh; matriculated into Logic class 1814, obviously of mature years; ordained priest of diocese of Armagh 1820; dean 1820; professor of Theology 1825; bishop of Dromore 1826; coadjutor in Armagh 1828; archbishop of Armagh 1832; died 14 Jan. 1835.

Peter Kenney SJ

Neil Kevin

Jeremiah Kinane

Edward Kissane

John Lane

Michael Leahy

Walter Lee

Francis Lennon

Kelly, William (1804-42) Entered Maynooth 1823; ordained priest of the diocese of Ferns; professor of English and French 1830; went to Madras with Bishop Carew 1838; died in Calcutta 21 Mar. 1842.

Kenney, Peter, SJ (1779-1841) Born Straffan, Co. Kildare; ordained Jesuit priest at Palermo 1808; returned to Ireland 1811; at Archbishop Murray's request undertook vice-presidency of Maynooth for one year, 1812/13; founded Clongowes Wood College 1814; several times returned to Maynooth to preach retreats; died Rome 19 Nov. 1841; buried in the church of the Gesù.

Kevin, Neil (1903-53) Born Templemore, Co. Tipperary; ordained priest of diocese of Cashel in Maynooth 1929; professor of English 1932; died 16 Aug. 1953.
Published: *I Remember Maynooth* (1937); *I Remember Karrigeen* (1944); *No Applause in Church* (1947); *Out of Nazareth* (1953).

Kinane, Jeremiah (1884-1959) Born Upperchurch, Co. Tipperary; sent to Rome in 1909 to study for the DCL at the beginning of his fourth theology year; ordained Rome 1910; professor of Canon Law 1911; resigned 1933 on appointment as bishop of Waterford and Lismore; archbishop of Cashel 1946; died 18 Feb. 1959.

Kissane, Edward (1886-1959) Born Lisselton, Co. Kerry; ordained priest of the diocese of Kerry in Maynooth 1910; one of the first students of the Pontifical Biblical Institute (founded 1909); in Rome stayed at the Canadian College, 1910-13; went to Toronto to teach Scripture at the newly opened seminary there; professor of Scripture in Maynooth 1917; vice-president 1941; President 1942; an internationally renowned Old Testament scholar; brought Maynooth into the International Federation of Catholic Universities as one of the first members; died 21 Feb. 1959.

See also above, pp. 340, 345–6.
Published: *The Book of Job* (1939); *The Book of Isaiah* (2 vols., 1941. 1943); *The Book of Psalms* (2 vols., 1953).

Lane, John (d. 1968) Ordained priest of the diocese of Kerry in Maynooth 1927; dean 1928; resigned 1949 on appointment as parish priest of Cahirsiveen; later parish priest of Tralee, where he died unexpectedly 12 Dec. 1968.

Leahy, Michael (d. 1971) Born Knockanore, Co. Waterford; studied in Irish College, Rome; ordained priest of diocese of Waterford and Lismore 1935; studied at Pontifical Biblical Institute 1935-7; professor of Scripture in Maynooth 1942; resigned 1962 on appointment as parish priest of Dunmore East; later parish priest of Ballybricken; died 6 Dec. 1971.

Lee, Walter (1809-93) Born Cavendish Row, Dublin, grandnephew to Archbishops Carpenter and Troy; entered Maynooth 1826; ordained priest of diocese of Dublin; went to Rome for further study; 'second junior dean' 1837; resigned for reasons of health 1856 and appears to have been in poor health for some time; secretary to the Trustees 1856, retained office until his death; parish priest of Bray 1861; died 13 Dec. 1893.

Lennon, Francis (1838-1920) Born Tyholland, Co. Monaghan; entered Maynooth 1853, not yet fifteen years old; ordained priest of diocese of Clogher; professor of Natural Philosophy 1864; also given charge of the 'singing classes' but resigned this 1866; retired 1911 because of failing health, received pension of two-thirds of salary as entitled under Irish Church Act (1869); lived with his niece in Dalkey; died there 22 Dec. 1920.
Published: *Elements of Plane and Solid Geometry* (1872: revised edition of Darré, *Elements of Geometry*); *The Elements of Plane and Spherical Trigonometry* (1875).

Michael Logue   Edward Long

Cornelius Lucey

James MacCaffrey

Loftus, Martin Entered Maynooth 1816, ordained priest of the diocese of Tuam; professor of Irish 1820; resigned 1826, returned to Tuam; a later publication shows continuing interest in catechesis through Irish; appears to have died during the Great Famine.
Published: *An Teagasg Criostaighe do reir Comhairle Ard Easpoig Tuama agus Easpog na Cuige sin* (parallel text in Irish and English, Dublin, n.d. but c. 1839).

Logue, Michael (1840-1924) Born Carrigart, Co. Donegal; ordained priest of diocese of Raphoe in Maynooth 1866; taught in Irish College, Paris, and served in diocese; dean 1876, also to teach Irish; professor of Theology 1878; resigned 1879 on appointment as bishop of Raphoe; coadjutor in Armagh Apr. 1887, succeeded Nov.; cardinal 1893; died 19 Nov. 1924.

Long, Edward (d. 1975) Ordained priest of diocese of Raphoe in Maynooth 1926; obtained DCL; dean 1930; professor in Faculty of Canon Law 1943; resigned for reasons of health and returned to his diocese 1946; died as parish priest of Donegal 22 Dec. 1975.
Published: *The Church Prays for Her Dead* (1937).

Long, Paul (d. 1837) Studied in Paris at Irish College and Saint-Nicolas-du-Chardonnet; ordained priest of diocese of Dublin 1785; ministered in diocese of Laon; forced to flee by mob violence 1792; returned to Dublin; president of lay college, Maynooth, 1807-12; sent to Paris by Irish bishops 1814 to sort out problems of Irish College; returned to Dublin 1819; died parish priest of Meath Street, 1 Jul. 1837.

Lovelock, Charles (d. 1814) Native of Co. Galway; educated Paris; ordained priest of diocese of Tuam; parish priest of Monivea; professor of 'second class of Greek and Latin' 1795; arrived 1798, to be appointed to the 'first class'; professor of Rhetoric 1802; died 2 Mar. 1814; the last member of staff to be buried in Laraghbryan.

Lucey, Cornelius (1902-82) Ordained priest of diocese of Cork in Maynooth 1927; appointed lecturer in Philosophy 1927; studied in Innsbruck (DPh); professor of Philosophy 1933; lectured in Ethics, deeply interested in social issues; resigned on appointment as coadjutor in Cork 1950; succeeded 1952; resigned 1977 and went to work as a missionary in Africa; returned to Cork and died 24 Sep. 1982.

Luzio, Salvatore Appointed the first professor of Canon Law 1897; experienced very poor health in Ireland; resigned and returned to Italy 1909.

Macauley, Charles (1830-89) Entered Maynooth 1847; ordained priest of diocese of Down and Connor; professor of Rhetoric 1854; of Scripture 1878; died 2 Jun. 1889.

MacCaffrey, James (1875-1935) Born Alderwood, Clogher, Co. Tyrone; ordained priest of the diocese of Clogher in Maynooth 1899; professor of Ecclesiastical History 1901; studied École des Chartes and Institut Catholique in Paris; PhD from Freiburg-im-Breisgau; appointed editor of journal when Catholic Record Society of Ireland founded 1911; first number of *Archivium Hibernicum* published 1912; vice-president 1915; President 1918; died 1 Nov. 1935.
Published: *The Black Book of Limerick* (1907); *History of the Catholic Church in the Nineteenth Century* (2 vols., 1909); *History of the Catholic Church from the Renaissance to the French Revolution* (2 vols., 1915).

Daniel McCarthy

John McCarthy

Walter McDonald

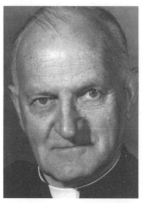

James Gerard McGarry

James McGinley

John MacHale

Patrick McKenna

Peter McKevitt

McCarthy, Daniel (1820-81) Born Tullagha, Co. Kerry; entered Maynooth 1837; ordained priest of the diocese of Kerry; professor of Scripture 1854; vice-president 1872; bishop of Kerry 1878; died 16 Jul. 1881.
Published: *The Life and Times of Florence MacCarthy Reagh* (1867); *The Epistles and Gospels of the Sundays throughout the Year* (2 vols., 1866, 1868); *The Gospel of St Matthew, with Notes Critical and Explanatory* (1877); *The Life of Saint Columba or Columbkille, translated from the Latin of St Adamnan* (n.d.). He also saw through the press uncompleted works of dead colleagues: Laurence Renehan's *Collections on Irish Church History* (2 vols., 1861, 1873) and *History of Music* (1861), and Matthew Kelly's *Dissertations on Irish Church History* (1864).

McCarthy, John (1909-83) Born Ahascragh, Co. Galway; ordained priest of the diocese of Elphin in Maynooth 1932; dean 1934; professor of Moral Theology 1938; resigned 1955 on appointment to the parish of St Peter's, Athlone; secretary to the Maynooth Trustees 1970; died 21 Mar. 1983.
Published: *Problems in Theology* (2 vols., 1956, 1959)

McCormick, Clotworthy Augustine (d. 1807) Born Co. Antrim; educated Paris; Augustinian Canon and 'abbot-general of Bangor'; military chaplain; appointed 'sacristan of the Roman Catholic College' 1798; died 7 May 1807 and buried in Laraghbryan.

McDonald, Walter (1854-1920) Born in parish of Mooncoin, Co. Kilkenny; entered Maynooth 1870; ordained priest of the diocese of Ossory; professor of Theology 1881; Prefect of Dunboyne 1888; died 1 May 1920. For details of his career and writings see above, pp. 251–7.

McGarry, James Gerard (d. 1977) Ordained priest of the diocese of Tuam in Maynooth 1930; professor of Pastoral Theology, Sacred Eloquence and Elocution 1939; founded the *Furrow* 1950; resigned 1969 on appointment to parish of Ballyhaunis; died 4 Aug. 1977.
Published: *The Word of Life: Essays on the Bible* (1959, ed.).

McGinley, James (d. 1960) Ordained priest of diocese of Raphoe in Maynooth 1891; dean 1892; resigned 1923 on appointment as parish priest of Ballyshannon; died 6 Jul. 1960.

MacHale, John (d. 1881) Born Tubbernavine, Co. Mayo; entered Maynooth 1807; ordained priest of diocese of Tuam 1814; assistant to Delahogue 1814; professor of Dogmatic Theology 1820; 'Letters of Hierophilos' begun 1820; coadjutor in Killala 1825, beginning his long career after leaving Maynooth; bishop of Killala May 1834, archbishop of Tuam Aug.; died 7 Nov. 1881.
Published: *Letters of Hierophilos* (1st edn., 1821); *Catholic Emancipation Proved to be Necessary for the Peace and Prosperity of Ireland* (1824); *The Evidence and Doctrines of the Catholic Church* (2 vols., 1828); many later publications, chiefly of an 'occasional' character.

McKenna, Patrick (1868-1942) Born in parish of Errigal Truagh, Co. Monaghan; ordained priest of diocese of Clogher in Maynooth 1894; professor of Theology 1904; bishop of Clogher 1909; died 7 Feb. 1942.

McKevitt, Peter (d. 1977) Ordained priest of diocese of Armagh in Maynooth 1925; professor of 'Catholic Sociology and Catholic Action' 1937; resigned 1953 on appointment as parish priest of Termonfeckin; died 3 Nov. 1977; see also above, pp. 315–16.
Published: *The Plan of Society* (1944).

Patrick McLaughlin

John McMackin

James J. McMahon

Charles McNally

Kevin McNamara

Joseph McRory

Patrick MacSweeney

Daniel Mageean

468

McLaughlin, Patrick (d. 1973) Ordained priest of diocese of Raphoe in Maynooth 1923; studied Paris for two years (DSc); professor of Experimental Physics 1928; curator of the museum 1943; vice-president 1951; resigned on becoming parish priest; died as parish priest of Lifford 16 Oct. 1973.
Published: *The Church and Modern Science* (1957); *Nicholas Callan* (1965).

McMackin, John (1904-88) Born in Glasgow; ordained priest of diocese of Raphoe in Maynooth 1929; professor of English and Elocution 1935; retired 1976, remained in college; died 22 Dec. 1988.

McMahon, James J. (d. 1981) Ordained priest of diocese of Clonfert in Maynooth 1950; studied in USA; lecturer in Mathematics and Experimental Physics 1954; professor of Mathematics 1960; resigned on leaving the priesthood 1974; died 28 Sep. 1981.

McNally, Charles (1787-1864) Born Clogher, Co. Tyrone; ordained priest of diocese of Clogher in Maynooth 1813; professor of Philosophy 1815; Prefect of the Dunboyne 1829; coadjutor bishop in Clogher 1843; succeeded 1844; died 21 Nov. 1864.

McNamara, Kevin (1926-87) Born Newmarket-on-Fergus, Co. Clare; ordained priest of diocese of Killaloe in Maynooth 1949; professor of Theology 1954; vice-president 1968; resigned on appointment as bishop of Kerry 1976; archbishop of Dublin 1984; died 8 Apr. 1987.
Published: *Christian Unity* (1961, ed.); *Truth and Life* (1968, ed.); *Vatican II: the Constitution on the Church* (1968); *Sacrament of Salvation* (1977).

McNicholas, Patrick (1781-1852) Born Co. Mayo; ordained priest of diocese of Achonry in Maynooth 1804; lecturer in Classics 1806; professor of Philosophy and librarian 1812; president, lay college, 1815; professor of Humanity 1817; bishop of Achonry 1818; died 11 Feb. 1852.

McRory, Joseph (1861-1945) Born Ballygawley, Co. Tyrone; entered Maynooth 1878; ordained priest of the diocese of Armagh; professor of Sacred Scripture 1889; vice-president 1912; resigned 1915 on being nominated bishop of Down and Connor; archbishop of Armagh 1928; cardinal 1929; died 13 Oct. 1945.
Published: *The Gospel of St John* (1900); *The Epistles of St Paul to the Corinthians* (1915).

MacSweeney, Patrick (1872-1935) Born in Dublin; studied Clonliffe College; ordained priest of diocese of Dublin; taught in Clonliffe College; MA of Royal University; professor of English in Maynooth 1912; editor, *Irish Ecclesiastical Record* 1913; deeply interested in Irish studies; died unexpectedly 7 Feb. 1935.
Publications: *The Martial Career of Conghal* (Irish Texts Society, 1904); *A Group of Nation-Builders* (1913).

Mageean, Daniel (1881-1962) Born Lisowen, Co. Down; ordained priest of diocese of Down and Connor in Maynooth 1906; dean 1919; resigned 1929 on appointment as bishop of Down and Connor; died 17 Jan. 1962.

Edward Maguire

John R. Maguire

Daniel Mannix

Thomas Gerard Meagher

Gerard Mitchell

Gerald Molloy

Magennis, Francis (d. 1847) Ordained priest of the diocese of Clogher in Maynooth 1829; professor of Theology 1830; resigned 1841 on appointment as parish priest of Clones, where he died May 1847.

Magennis, Peter, OP (1759-1818) Born Monknewtown, diocese of Meath; made Dominican profession at Drogheda; in Corpo Santo, Lisbon, 1782-99 as student, professor, rector; vice-president Maynooth 1810; professor of Scripture 1812; Prefect of Dunboyne 1815; left 1817 after differences with Delahogue and Anglade; died Drogheda 1818.

Maguire, Edward Entered Maynooth 1883; ordained priest of diocese of Clogher; professor of Rhetoric 1883; resigned 1886.

Maguire, John R. (1877-1948) Ordained priest of diocese of Clogher in Maynooth 1902; assistant bursar 1919, bursar 1923; resigned because of failing health 1944; died 10 Mar. 1948.

Malone, Daniel Ordained priest of the diocese of Armagh in Maynooth 1811; dean 1812; lecturer in Moral Theology and librarian 1814; resigned 1823.

Mannix, Daniel (1864-1963) Born Charleville, Co. Cork; ordained priest of diocese of Cloyne in Maynooth 1890; professor of Philosophy 1891; of Theology 1894; vice-president and President 1903; coadjutor archbishop of Melbourne 1912; succeeded 1917; died 6 Nov. 1963. See also above, pp. 283–99.

Meagher, Thomas Gerard (1932-82) Ordained priest of diocese of Cashel in Maynooth, 1958; student at Biblical Institute, Rome; professor of Scripture 1964; died 12 Feb. 1982.

Mitchell, Gerard (d. 1990) Ordained priest of diocese of Tuam in Maynooth 1929; called to the Master's degree (STM) after completion of his doctorate; this unfinished when appointed professor of Theology 1932; vice-president 1958; President 1959; resigned on appointment to parish of Ballinrobe 1967; died 17 May 1990.

Molloy, Gerald (1834-1906) Born Mount Tallant House, Terenure, Dublin; entered Maynooth 1849; ordained priest of the diocese of Dublin; professor of Theology 1857; resigned 1874 on appointment as vice-rector and professor of Natural Philosophy in Catholic University; rector 1883; in the view of Walter McDonald, a brilliant man who 'frittered away his life on trifles' (*Reminiscences*, 51-2); Senator of Royal University 1880, later vice-chancellor; remained a good friend to Maynooth, making notable gifts to the College Chapel; the final residue of his will founded the 'Molloy Prize' in Experimental Physics; secretary to the Trustees 1895; died suddenly while attending a congress in Aberdeen 1 Oct. 1906.
Published: *Geology and Revelation* (1869); *The Passion Play at Oberammergau* (1872); *Outline of a Course of Natural Philosophy* (1882); *Gleanings in Science* (1888); *The Irish Difficulty: Shall and Will* (1897).

471

Michael Montague

William Moran

Patrick Morrisroe

Cornelius Mulcahy

Daniel Murray

Patrick Murray

Henry Neville

Montague, Michael (1773-1845) Born Errigal Kieran, Co. Tyrone; entered Maynooth 1795, already a deacon; ordained priest of diocese of Armagh 1798, remained in college; bursar 1802; vice-president 1814; President 1834; became terminally ill 1844, resigned Jun. 1845, died 29 Oct. See also above, p. 57.

Moran, William (d. 1965) Ordained priest of the diocese of Meath in Maynooth 1910; his doctorate thesis caused contention between Walter McDonald and Daniel Coghlan (see above, p. 256); professor of Theology 1917; Prefect of Dunboyne and librarian on becoming senior professor 1932; resigned both offices 1939; very energetic as first curator of museum 1934; resigned 1943 on appointment as parish priest of Trim; died parish priest of Tullamore 1 Oct. 1965.
Published: *The Government of the Church in the First Century* (1913); *What is Christianity?* (1940).

Morrisroe, Patrick (1867-1946) Born Charlestown, Co. Mayo; entered Maynooth 1885; ordained priest of diocese of Achonry in Ballaghaderreen 2 Feb. 1893; dean 1896; bishop of Achonry 1911; died 27 May 1946.

Mulcahy, Cornelius (d. 1961) Ordained priest of the diocese of Limerick in Maynooth 1895; professor of English 1896; resigned 1932 on appointment as parish priest of Kilmallock; died 6 Jul. 1961.
Published: *The Hymns of the Roman Breviary and Missal* (1938); 'Reminiscences' in *IER*, lxvi, 145-73 (Sep. 1945).

Murphy, Thomas Priest of diocese of Waterford and Lismore; not an alumnus of Maynooth, dean 1814; died 1816.

Murray, Daniel (1768-1852) Born Sheepwalk, Arklow, Co. Wicklow; studied in Salamanca, but ordained in Dublin; coadjutor archbishop 1808, consecrated 30 Nov. in the penal-day Liffey Street chapel, 'one of the first which had taken place in Ireland for a long time'; succeeded on death of Archbishop Troy 1823; accepted presidency of Maynooth for one year at a time of crisis 1812; a good friend to the college until his death 26 Feb. 1852.

Murray, Patrick (1811-82) Born Clones, Co. Monaghan; ordained priest of diocese of Clogher in Maynooth 1837; served briefly in Francis Street, Dublin; professor of English 1838; of Theology 1841; Prefect of Dunboyne 1879; strongly ultramontane (author of 'A Song for the Pope') though ironically suspected of 'Gallican' leanings by Archbishop Cullen; strongly nationalist but grew more conservative because of fate of Papal States; impressed Carlyle when he met him in 1849: 'a big, burly mass of Catholic Irishism . . . head cropped like stubble, red-skinned face, hard grey Irish eyes; full of fiery Irish zeal too, and rage, man of considerable strength, not to be loved by any manner of means'—it catches some traits, but in true Carlyle fashion in the form of a caricature; most people had affectionate personal recollections of him; died 15 Nov. 1882.
Published: *The Irish Annual Miscellany: Essays Chiefly Theological* (4 vols., 1850-53): *De Ecclesia Christi* (3 vols., 1860-66); *Prose and Verse* (1867); *De Ecclesia Christi: Editio Compendiosa* (1874); *De Gratia* (1877).

Neville, Henry (1820-89) Ordained priest of diocese of Cork in Maynooth 1847; professor of Philosophy 1850; of Theology 1852; resigned on grounds of ill health 1867; parish priest of St Finbarr's, dean and vicar-general 1875; rector of Catholic University 1879 while retaining diocesan offices; resigned 1883; died 15 Dec. 1889.

Edward O'Brien (Dublin)

Paul O'Brien

Charles O'Callaghan

Thomas O'Dea

John F. O'Doherty

Thomas O'Doherty

Michael O'Donnell

O'Brien, Edward (1832-1908) Born Limavady, Co. Derry; entered Maynooth 1850; ordained priest of diocese of Derry; professor of Humanity 1859; of Rhetoric 1878; resigned on grounds of ill health 1879; as described by Walter McDonald (*Reminiscences*, 32), 'a man of genius', imaginative and poetic, who, however, 'did not press us'; president, St Colum's College; served in a number of parishes; parish priest of Limavady 1890, where he died 4 Sep. 1908.

O'Brien, Edward (d. 1974) Ordained priest of diocese of Dublin in Maynooth 1918; DCL (Maynooth) 1920; professor of Canon Law 1943; died 31 Oct. 1974.

O'Brien, Paul (1763-1820) Born Breaky, Moynalty, Co. Meath, 1763, grand-nephew to Turlough Carolan; developed an interest in the Irish language about the age of eighteen; entered Maynooth 1801; ordained priest of diocese of Armagh; immediately afterwards appointed professor of Irish, 20 Jul. 1804; active member of the Gaelic Society (a volume of 'Transactions' published 1808); died 13 Apr. 1820.
Published: *A Practical Grammar of the Irish Language* (1809).

O'Callaghan, Charles (d. 1982) Ordained priest of diocese of Raphoe in Maynooth 1929; professor of Church Chant and Organ 1951; resigned 1967 on appointment as parish priest of Dungloe; died 14 Jul. 1982.

O'Dea, Thomas (1858-1923) Born Carron, Co. Clare; ordained priest of diocese of Kilfenora in Maynooth 1882 (Galway, Kilmacduagh and Kilfenora united 1883); professor of Theology 1882; vice-president 1894; bishop of Clonfert 1903; of Galway, Kilmacduagh and Kilfenora 1909; died 9 Apr. 1923.
Published: *Maynooth and the University Question: Evidence before the Royal Commission* (1903).

O'Doherty, John F. (d. 1954) Ordained priest of the diocese of Derry in Maynooth 1926; lecturer in Ecclesiastical History 1928; professor 1931; studied Munich (PhD); resigned 1946; took up appointment in diocese; died 15 May 1954.
Published: *Laurentius von Dublin und das irische Normannentum* (1934); *A History of the Catholic Church for Schools* (1942); John Lynch, *De Praesulibus Hiberniae* (ed., 2 vols., 1944); Theobald Stapleton, *Catechismus seu Doctrina Christiana Latino-Hibernica* (ed., 1945).

O'Doherty, Thomas (1877-1936) Born Lisacul, near Loughglynn, Co. Roscommon; ordained priest of diocese of Elphin in Maynooth 1902; dean 1905; bishop of Clonfert 1919, of Galway, Kilmacduagh and Kilfenora 1923; died 15 Dec. 1936.

O'Donnell, James (1828-61) Born at Curragh Lane, Graiguenamanagh, Co. Kilkenny; entered Maynooth 1847; ordained priest of diocese of Kildare and Leighlin; dean 1856, professor of English Elocution and French 1858; died 23 Nov. 1861.

O'Donnell, Michael (d. 1944) Ordained priest of the diocese of Raphoe in Maynooth 1904; professor of Theology 1909; Prefect of Dunboyne 1920; resigned 1922; took up appointments in diocese; died 1944.
Published: *Penance in the Early Church* (1907).

Patrick O'Donnell

Tomás Ó Fiaich

Donnchadh Ó Floinn

John O'Flynn

Eoghan O'Growney

John O'Hanlon

Michael O'Hickey

James O'Kane

O'Donnell, Patrick (d. 1927) Ordained priest of diocese of Raphoe in Maynooth 1880; professor of Theology 1880; Prefect of Dunboyne 1884; according to Walter McDonald (*Reminiscences*, 83), 'handsome, well-bred, polite, but firm, as became a friend of John Dillon's'; bishop of Raphoe 1888; coadjutor in Armagh 1922; succeeded 1924; cardinal 1925; died 22 Oct. 1927.

Ó Fiaich, Tomás (1923-90) Born Cullyhanna, Co. Armagh; entered Maynooth but left because of health problems; ordained priest of diocese of Armagh in St Peter's College, Wexford, 1948; studied in UCD (MA) and Louvain (LicScHist); lecturer in Modern History 1953, professor 1959; vice-president 1970, President 1974; archbishop of Armagh 1977; cardinal 1979; died 8 May 1990.
Published: *Gaelscrínte i gCéin* (1960); *Irish Cultural Influence in Europe: VI-XII Century* (1971); *Columbanus in his own Words* (1974); *Oilibhéar Pluincéid* (1974); *Oliver Plunkett: Ireland's New Saint* (1975); *Imeacht na nIarlaí* (ed. with Pádraig de Barra 1972); *Art Mac Cumhaigh: Dánta* (ed. 1973).

Ó Floinn, Donnchadh (d. 1968) Born Kanturk, Co. Cork; ordained priest of diocese of Dublin in Maynooth 1927; taught philosophy in All Hallows College, Dublin 1929-39; many interests where spirituality and Irish language linked, especially An Réalt (Irish-speaking Legion of Mary); professor of Irish 1940; resigned because of ill health 1964, appointed parish priest Putland Road, Bray; died 2 Apr. 1968.
Published: *Seanchas Cléire* (1937); *Caoga agus Meanman* (1957).

O'Flynn, John (1909-74) Born Annaghadown, Co. Galway; ordained priest of diocese of Tuam in Maynooth 1933; studied Biblical Institute, Rome, 1934-6 (LSS); professor of Scripture 1936; died 23 Apr. 1974.

Published: Pierre Veuillot, *The Catholic Priesthood According to the Teaching of the Church* (1957, trans.); Gaston Courtois, *The States of Perfection According to the Teaching of the Church* (1961, trans.).

O'Growney, Eoghan (1863-97) Born Ballyfallon, Athboy, Co. Meath; ordained priest of the diocese of Meath in Maynooth 1889; professor of Irish Language, Literature and Antiquities 1891; editor of *Gaelic Journal*, organ of Gaelic League, of which he was vice-president; leave of absence because of 'threatened consumption' Oct. 1894; went to USA; resigned 1896; died Los Angeles 18 Oct. 1897; see also above, pp. 213, 287–8.
Published: *Simple Lessons in Irish: giving the pronunciation of each word* (1894).

O'Hanlon, John (1803-71) Entered Maynooth 1820; ordained priest of diocese of Ossory; professor of Theology 1828; Prefect of Dunboyne 1843; made good friends, e.g., Daniel McCarthy, who described him in his diary as 'always kind and considerate', but also attracted strong criticism, e.g., Laurence Renehan, Walter McDonald; died 12 Nov. 1871.

O'Hickey, Michael (1861-1916). Born Carrickbeg, Co. Waterford; ordained priest of diocese of Waterford and Lismore in St John's College, Waterford, 1884; professor of Irish Language, Maynooth, 1896; dismissed 1909; carried an appeal to the Holy See, which he lost; returned to Ireland 1916; died suddenly 19 Nov.; see also above, pp. 288–96.

O'Kane, James (1825-74) Born Newtownstewart, Co. Derry; entered Maynooth 1840; ordained priest of diocese of Derry; junior dean 1852, after three years as Dunboyne student; senior dean 1856; described as a model of all virtues, in everyone's confidence; resigned because of ill health 1871; died 16 Feb. 1874.
Published: *Notes on the Rubrics of the Roman Ritual* (1867).

Patrick O'Leary

Daniel O'Loan

John O'Neill

John G. O'Neill

Patrick O'Neill

Gerald O'Nolan

Edmund O'Reilly

Hugh O'Rourke

Séamus Ó Súilleabháin
CFC

O'Leary, Patrick (d. 1932) Entered Maynooth 1868; ordained priest of diocese of Kerry; dean 1878; resigned 1902; died parish priest of Millstreet 20 Jun. 1932.

O'Loan, Daniel Ordained priest of diocese of Down and Connor in Maynooth 1884; professor of Ecclesiastical History 1892; resigned 1901 and returned to his diocese.

O'Neill, John (1880-1947) Born in Tipperary town; ordained priest of diocese of Cashel in Maynooth 1903; taught in Carlow College 1903-08; professor of Philosophy in Maynooth 1908; studied Louvain (DPh); died 7 May 1947.
Published: *Cosmology* (1924).

O'Neill, John G. (d. 1965) Ordained priest of diocese of Cork in Maynooth 1924; studied Chicago (DPh); professor of Classics 1928; resigned 1941; died 10 Aug. 1965.
Published: *Ancient Corinth* (1930).

O'Neill, Patrick (1890-1958) Born Grange, Fedamore, Co. Limerick; ordained priest of diocese of Limerick in Maynooth 1915; professor of Theology 1918; studied Rome (DCL), vice-president 1936; health impaired after riding accident 1941; resigned 1942 on appointment as parish priest of Bruff; bishop of Limerick 1945; died 26 Mar. 1958.

O'Nolan, Gerald (1874-1942) Born Belfast; ordained priest of diocese of Down and Connor in Maynooth 1899; professor Irish Language, 1909; retired 1940; died 26 Mar. 1942.
Published: *New Era Grammar of Modern Irish* (5 parts, 1919-22).

O'Reilly, Edmund (1811-78) Born London, came to Limerick at age of six; entered Maynooth 1826; left after a few years, doubting his vocation; continued ecclesiastical studies in Rome; ordained priest of diocese of Limerick; professor of Theology in Maynooth 1838; resigned 1851 to join SJ; professor of Theology Catholic University 1854; founder and first rector of Jesuit House of Studies, Milltown Park, 1859; provincial 1863; died 10 Nov. 1878.
Published: *Theological Essays* (1892, ed. Matthew Russell).

O'Rourke, Hugh (1837-85) Born Maam, Co. Galway; entered Maynooth 1854; ordained priest of diocese of Tuam; professor of English and French 1862; health became poor late 1870s; died 9 Oct. 1885.

Ó Súilleabháin, Séamus, CFC (1921-86) Born New York; family returned to Ireland 1933, settled at Doonbeg, Co. Clare; joined Christian Brothers 1939; final profession 1946; teaching career in Belfast; head of Education in Marino Training College 1961; lecturer in Education, Maynooth, 1966, professor 1968 (see above, p. 428); died 7 Jun. 1986.

Richard Owens   William J. Philbin

Garrett Pierse

Laurence Renehan   Jean-Louis Rigal

Owens, Richard (1840-1909) Born Aghavea, Co. Fermanagh; ordained priest of diocese of Clogher in Maynooth 1866; dean 1878; professor of Theology 1884; resigned 1894 on appointment as bishop of Clogher; died 3 Mar. 1909.

Philbin, William J. (1907-91) Born Kiltimagh, Co. Mayo; ordained priest of diocese of Achonry in Maynooth 1931; professor of Theology 1936; resigned 1954 on appointment as bishop of Clonfert; bishop of Down and Connor 1962; resigned 1982; left his art collection to Maynooth, where it is displayed in the Renehan Hall; died 22 Aug. 1991.

Pierse, Garrett (1883-1932) Born Ballydonoghue, Ballybunion, Co. Kerry; ordained priest of diocese of Kerry in Maynooth 1906; taught in seminary of St Paul, Minnesota, 1909-14; professor of Theology in Maynooth 1914; prefect of Dunboyne 1923; died 31 Mar. 1932.
Published: *The Mass in the Infant Church* (1909); *Virtues and Vices* (1935).

Power, Francis (1737-1817) His epitaph describes him as 'civis Clonmel., alumnus Parisien., presbyter Cloynen.', which suggests Clonmel on Great Island, Co. Cork; family were, however, natives of Clonmel, Co. Tipperary (he describes himself in the parliamentary paper of 1808 as having been born in Co. Waterford); strong family links with France, specifically with Avignon; studied and ordained priest in Paris; became canon of Avignon; fled France; came to Maynooth 1796 as 'vice-president and procurator'; effectively president and dean until arrival of Peter Flood and Edward Ferris (1798); relieved of procuratorship on appointment of Michael Montague (1802), but asked to teach French; retired 1810; died 5 Jun. 1817; the first to be buried in the college cemetery.

Quinn, Richard Apparently not an alumnus; junior dean 1856; resigned 1876.

Renehan, Laurence (1798-1857) Born Gortnahoe, Longford Pass, Co. Tipperary; entered Maynooth 1819; dean 1825, still a Dunboyne student and not ordained; professor of Sacred Scripture 1826; vice-president 1834, bursar in addition 1841-5; President 1845; interested in music and Irish ecclesiastical history, friend of John O'Donovan and James Henthorn Todd; vice-president Celtic Society; spent vacations travelling in Europe copying manuscripts; in 1847 warned Henry Pepys, bishop of Worcester, against Denis Brasbie, ordained priest of diocese of Kerry 1834, became minister in Church of Ireland; Brasbie sued for 'gross and malicious libel', claiming £5,000 damages; jury awarded £25 with costs (over £300); died 25 Jul. 1857; his manuscripts are in the college library.
Published: *A Choir Manual of Sacred Music* (n.d); *A Requiem Office Book* (n.d.); *A History of Music* (ed. Daniel McCarthy, 1858); *Grammar of Gregorian and Modern Music* (ed. Richard Hackett, 1865); *Collections on Irish Church Church History* (2 vols., ed. McCarthy, 1861, 1873).

Reynolds, Laurence Born Kilkenny; educated Nantes; professor of Greek and Latin in lay college 1800; resigned 1802.
Published: *The Satires of Persius, translated into English verse* (1827).

Rigal, Jean-Louis (1875-1962) Born Alberot, department of Aveyron, France; ordained priest of the diocese of Rodez 1898; studied at Institut Catholique, Toulouse, and École des Chartes, Paris; lecturer in French in university of Breslau; professor of Modern Languages Maynooth 1914; arrived 1916; retired on pension 1938; returned to Rodez; diocesan archivist 1947; many substantial publications on local history; died 13 Mar. 1962.

Charles W. Russell

Arthur Ryan

Hubert Schild

Michael Sheehan

Michael Slattery

James Staunton

Russell, Charles W. (1812-80) Born Killough, Co. Down; entered Maynooth 1826, aged fourteen; ordained priest of diocese of Down and Connor 1835; professor of Humanity 1835; of Ecclesiastical History 1845; President 1857; 'one to be proud of' (Walter McDonald); best remembered for his role in the conversion of John Henry Newman; prolific writer on many topics; frequent contributor to the scholarly reviews, especially the *Dublin Review*, where he had also an editorial and management role; instrumental in opening of Vatican Archives to scholars; founding member of Historical Manuscripts Commission (1869); trustee of National Library (1877); injured in a fall from his horse 16 May 1877, never fully recovered; died at home of John O'Hagan in Dublin 26 Feb. 1880.
Published: *Tales Chiefly for the Young* (trans. from German with Matthew Kelly, 3 vols., 1845-6); *A System of Theology by Godfrey von Leibnitz* (trans., 1850); *The Life of Cardinal Mezzofanti* (1858); *The Carte Manuscripts in the Bodleian Library, Oxford* (with J. P. Prendergast, 1871); *Calendar of State Papers relating to Ireland, James I* (with J. P. Prendergast, 5 vols., 1872-80).

Ryan, Arthur (d. 1982) Studied in Rome; ordained a priest of diocese of Down and Connor; professor of Theology in Maynooth 1923; resigned 1925 to take up post in Queen's University, Belfast; died 16 Jun. 1982.

Scannell, Malachy (d. 1889) Entered Maynooth 1868; ordained priest of diocese of Kerry; professor of Rhetoric 1879; resigned 1883 to take up a diocesan appointment; died 7 Jan. 1889.

Schild, Hubert (1915–91) Born Lorraine; ordained priest of diocese of Toulouse; professor of Modern Languages in Maynooth 1950; resigned 1958, returned to France; died Paris Jul. 1991.

Sheehan, Michael (1870-1945) Born Newtown, Co. Waterford; entered Maynooth 1890; for health reasons finished his theology course and ordained in St John's College, Waterford 1895; professor of Rhetoric in Maynooth 1897; studied at Griefswald, Bonn and Oxford; founded Ring College, Co. Waterford 1906, president 1906-22; vice-president Maynooth 1919; coadjutor archbishop of Sydney 1922; returned in poor health 1937; lived in a Dublin nursing home with frequent visits to Ring; died Dublin 1 Mar. 1945 and buried in Ring.
Published: *Sean-chaint na nDéise* (1906); *Cnó Coilleadh Craobhaighe* (1907), *Cnuasacht Trágha* (1908); *Ladhar den Lus Mór* (1910); *Arthrach an Óir* (1910); *Gabha na Coille* (1910); *Gile na mBláth* (1912); *Apologetics and Catholic Doctrine* (pt 1, 1918, pt 2, 1923).

Slattery, Michael (1783-1857) Born Tipperary town; entered Trinity College, Dublin, to study law; studied for priesthood in Carlow College; ordained priest of diocese of Cashel there 1809; taught there for four years; returned to serve in diocese; President of Maynooth 1832; resigned 1834 on appointment as archbishop of Cashel; died 4 Feb. 1857.

Slevin, Nicholas (d. 1828) Entered Salamanca 1796; ordained priest of diocese of Clogher 1804; served in diocese for some years; in Rome 1815-21; taught in Salamanca 1821-2; Prefect of Dunboyne in Maynooth 1823; referred to as 'deceased' in minute of appointment of successor 13 Feb. 1829.

Staunton, James (d. 1963) Born Ballyouskill, Ballyragget, Co. Kilkenny; ordained priest of diocese of Ossory in Maynooth 1913; St Kieran's College, Kilkenny, 1913-18; DD Fribourg (Suisse); dean in Maynooth 1923; resigned on appointment as president of St Kieran's 1928; bishop of Ferns 1939; died 27 Jun. 1963.

Patrick Toner

Michael Tracy

James Tully

Paul Walsh

William Walsh

Toner, Patrick (d. 1941) Ordained priest of diocese of Armagh in Maynooth 1897; professor of Theology 1904; resigned 1912, returned to Armagh; died 12 Sep. 1941 as parish priest of Middletown, Co. Armagh.

Tracy, Michael (1892-1954) Ordained priest of diocese of Limerick in Maynooth 1916; acted as organist and choirmaster in absence of Bewerunge 1914-21; studied in Rome; professor of Church Chant and Organ 1927; retired on pension in poor health 1951; died 19 May 1954.

Tully, James (d. 1876) Born Mountbellew, Co. Galway; ordained priest of diocese of Tuam in Maynooth 1825; professor of Irish 1828; taught until his death, but without enthusiasm for either teaching or the Irish language; generous to the poor and a sought-after confessor; died 2 Oct. 1876.

Usher, Mark Born in Co. Meath; father, descended from Archbishop Ussher, became a Catholic and later a priest; educated Paris; professor of English Elocution Maynooth 1797; taught also in the lay college, and appears to have kept a school in Maynooth; retired because of 'old age and infirmity' 1811, but taught French 1818-20.
Published: *Synonymous Terms in the English Language Explained* (1816); *A Latin Grammar* (1823).

Walker, John (1732-1807) Born Colney Hatch, Middlesex; theatrical career, visited Dublin and Cork; converted to Catholicism Dublin 1768; quitted stage, lived as teacher of elocution; professor of English Eloquence Maynooth 1795; resigned and returned to London 1797; died 1807.

Walsh, Paul (1885-1941) Born Ballinea, Mullingar, Co. Westmeath; entered Maynooth 1903; interest in Irish studies aroused; remarkable role in the early years of Cuallacht Cholm Cille; involved in the troubles of 1909; ordained priest of diocese of Meath in All Hallows College; BA in Celtic Studies 1912, MA and travelling studentship 1914; studied Aberystwyth 1914-16; part-time lecturer in Welsh Maynooth 1916; professor of Ecclesiastical History 1919, continuing to lecture in Welsh; large classes and general courses uncongenial to a shy and scholarly man; resigned 1928. Died as parish priest of Multyfarnham 18 Jun. 1941. One of the many eulogies, from another great scholar, Francis Shaw SJ, in *Studies*, xxx, 447-50 (1941) said: 'It is probable that none since O'Donovan had such an all-round interest . . . a very great scholar, but he carried his learning lightly . . . he often published in a local weekly newspaper an article which would have graced a scientific periodical'. The list of his writings, compiled by John Brady, in *IHS*, iii, 193-208 (Sep. 1942) runs to sixteen pages of small print.

Walsh, Reginald, OP (1855-1932) Became a Dominican, ordained 1878, appointed Maynooth 1898 to the second chair of Scripture recently established, until a diocesan priest should be trained; resigned 1905 on appointment of Patrick A. Boylan; among other things deeply interested in promoting the cause of the Irish martyrs; died Tallaght 7 Apr. 1932.

Walsh, William (1841-1921) Born Dublin; student of Catholic University in rectorship of John Henry Newman; ordained priest of diocese of Dublin in Maynooth 1866; professor of Theology 1867; vice-president 1878; President 1880; archbishop of Dublin 1885, opening a life in public affairs, where he had already shown remarkable interest and capacity; died 9 Apr. 1921.
Published: *Harmony of the Gospel Narratives* (1879); *Tractatus de Actibus Humanis* (1880).

James Watters

Robert ffrench Whitehead

Cornelius Williams OP

William J. Williams

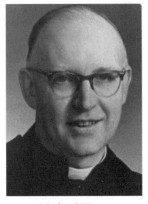

Michael Harty

Denis Meehan

Watters, James (d. 1854) Ordained priest of diocese of Down and Connor in Maynooth 1928; dean 1933; resigned 1934 and returned to diocese; died Belfast 8 Dec. 1954.

Whitehead, Robert ffrench (1807-79) Born Lower Dominick Street, Dublin; student of lay college; entered ecclesiastical college 1820, aged thirteen; professor of English and French 1828; of Philosophy 1829; ordained priest of diocese of Tuam 1830; vice-president 1845; left on vacation summer 1848, not heard of for more than twelve months; adventures included shipwreck off coast of Florida; resigned vice-presidency 1872; appointed librarian but resigned 1876; died 31 Dec. 1879.

Williams, Cornelius, OP (d. 1993) Studied philosophy at Tallaght, theology at Fribourg (Suisse); taught Tallaght, Rome (Angelicum) and Fribourg; appointed to the new chair of Moral Theology in Maynooth 1976; resigned 1977; died in Switzerland 17 May 1993.

Williams, William J. (d. 1952) Born in Co. Galway; secondary teacher, founder-member of ASTI 1909; lecturer in Education in Royal College of Science 1919; transferred with college to University College, Dublin, 1926; professor of Education Maynooth 1926; taught course until appointment of Martin Brenan in 1931, but from 1927 referred to as 'lecturer'; professor of Education UCD 1943; retired 1949; died in Dublin 19 Dec. 1952.

ADDENDA

Harty, Michael (1922–94) Born Toomevara, Co. Tipperary; ordained priest of diocese of Killaloe in Maynooth 1946; dean 1949; resigned on appointment as bishop of Killaloe; died 8 Aug. 1994.

Meehan, Denis (1914–94) Born Castlebar, Co. Mayo; ordained priest of diocese of Elphin in Maynooth 1940;

taught in Kiltegan 1941/42; professor of Ancient Classics in Maynooth 1943; librarian 1947; resigned because of ill health 1959; went to California; joined OSB at Valyermo Abbey 1963; died 6 Aug. 1994.
Published: *Window on Maynooth* (1949); *Adamnan's De Locis Sanctis* (ed., 1958); *Maynooth Again Remembered* (1982).

A Note on Sources

It would be laborious, and to a certain extent not very useful, to try to list everything relating to the two hundred years' history of Maynooth College. In any case, the work has been done, more or less completely, for the years from 1795 to 1869, the period when Maynooth was in the public eye as a 'political' issue to a degree it was not afterwards, at least until very recent times. It has been done in the kind of place where such work is normally best done, as a bibliography to a doctoral dissertation, *Englands Staats- und Kirchenpolitik in Irland 1795-1869 dargestellt an der Entwicklung des irischen Nationalseminars Maynooth College* by Karl Wöste (Bonn, 1976), pp. 322-51.

The key source for this study is material in the archives of Maynooth College (see pp. 399–400). And in the story of an institution the key record must be the minute-books of the administrative bodies. One such record is continuous from the very beginning, the minute-book or 'Journal' of the Trustees. As noted in the text, no formal record was kept of the activities of the Visitors until 1845, after which the newly constituted Visitors had to keep formal minutes and on the basis of them present an annual report to the Queen in Parliament. There is such a minute-book (MCA B1/1/1), but it has records of only some of the meetings which were held; records of all of them survive as Parliamentary Papers. When the episcopal Trustees got complete control of the college after the Irish Church Act (1869) they set up a committee of Visitors from among their number. Regrettably, the first minute-book of the episcopal Visitors has disappeared, but all the others are extant.

As already noted (pp. 68, 92–3), the position, indeed the very existence, of internal college councils was in the early years quite uncertain. The recommendations of the Commission of Inquiry in 1853 were not put into effect, but when he became President in 1857 Charles Russell had minutes kept of the meetings of the 'college council' (MCA B4/3/1); the last entry is in the year of his disabling accident, 1877. Before then, however, the episcopal Trustees had set up official councils and outlined their functions in the 1872 statutes. Originally there were two of them, the Administrative Council and the Scholastic Council or Council of Studies. In due course the two committees of the Administrative Council divided, with the 'seminary committee' retaining the original title, while the 'finance committee' became the Finance

Council. Minute-books are extant for both councils. As well, there are printed reports from the Finance Council. Printed reports on financial affairs in fact begin in 1865 with an annual 'Bursar's Financial Statement' which grew out of the dissatisfaction of the Trustees with Thomas Farrelly at this time. In 1877 this was superseded by an annual report from the Finance Committee, as the Trustees determined to subordinate Farrelly to it. Again as part of the changes of the early 1870s, the President was required to submit a printed report annually to the June meeting of the Trustees. The first was made in 1874. About ten in all are missing, but from this date on it is obviously a key document.

The Scholastic Council divided to meet university developments. On the one side was the Pontifical University, in practice more and more its Faculty of Theology. The National University courses led to the Faculties of Arts, Science, Philosophy and Celtic Studies, with the Academic Council to oversee and co-ordinate. In all cases there are minute-books, with an ever-growing supplementary documentation, most of which came to the President and into his archives. The latest development has been the minutes and documentation of the College Executive Council.

The dossier which the President has to compile for meetings of the Trustees has become so large that there is a temptation to feel that the history of the college can be written from it. This is to an extent true for the rather general summary which is all that can as yet be attempted for the last twenty-five years or so. From the 1870s the temptation is to write history from the minute-books. It is a temptation better resisted. The most promising supplement to official records is correspondence, even official correspondence, but most of all private correspondence. Here the Maynooth resources are disappointing. There is in fact no extant correspondence before the presidency of Laurence Renehan (1845-57) He was the first to live in what have since been the President's rooms, and his successor Charles Russell preserved his papers. From this time onwards there is a growing amount of administrative correspondence. The core of it is letters from bishops concerning their students in the college. Almost all is routine, with little historical significance. The same is true of the massive documentation connected with the 'Belgian burses'. But there are other collections that are richer in content. The most useful is concerned with wills and bequests, especially in that many of the bequests came from members of the staff and include personal details. The dossier on the building and fitting out of the College Chapel is well worth exploring, as is that on the land mortgages taken out after 1870, especially the disastrous Granard mortgage, though much of the detail is more relevant to the history of Irish land than to the history of Maynooth College. It was exciting to come across a substantial dossier on the case of Michael O'Hickey, sealed away in 1915. However, it consisted almost altogether of documentation prepared for the Roman court of the Rota. O'Hickey too would have had a copy of this, and it was presumably used by Leon Ó Broin in his study written in 1963.

The annual printed *Calendar* begins in the academic year 1863/64. It has precursors in two manuscript volumes, 'Ordinations and Prize Lists'. The title is descriptive, but the first volume also contains additional miscellaneous information, notably brief accounts of the early visitations and professorial staff—very welcome indeed for a time when information is so scanty. As far as individual students are concerned, the loss of the original matriculation register in the fire in New House in 1940 was grievous indeed. For each student there was his name with date of matriculation and class he matriculated into, with date and place of birth and names of parents. The 'official' information was printed in early numbers of the *Calendar*, but not the personal details. For all students, date and class of matriculation and date of ordination were put together some years ago by Monsignor Patrick J. Hamell (*Maynooth Students and Ordinations, Index 1795-1895* and *Maynooth Students and Ordinations 1895-1984*).

The early college statutes, dated 1800 and 1820, together with a student rule dated 1820, are bound together in a little volume in the library, with *Directorium* lettered on the spine. The documents dated 1820 are reproduced in the report of the Commission of Inquiry of 1853, together with the revisions introduced in the late 1840s. The later statutes—1872, 1918 and 1962—are available in copies as issued.

All this is indeed highly institutional, and the more personal note, the voice from below, is heard only from time to time. MCL has a treasure in the 'Conwell Letters', written by Eugene Conwell, a student of the diocese of Armagh in early and disturbed times. There are letters of William McMullan, a student expelled after the troubles of 1803, in the diocesan archives of Down and Connor. For the 1820s there are the letters written by Charles W. Russell as a student to his sister Margaret, which he obviously found among her papers when she died in 1877. But material like this is rare. The diaries of two professors have survived from the third quarter of the century. That of Daniel McCarthy runs from 1850 to 1878: it is heavily preoccupied with deaths among the staff and students. Patrick Murray's, now in MCL, covers the years from 1863 to 1882. His preoccupation is the labours of the academic life, but there is a vivid and detailed description of the great fire in St Mary's in 1878, and there is a loose sheet of paper with an account of the confrontation between the staff and Archbishops Cullen and Dixon in 1853, obviously written while the wound was still raw. There are surviving student diaries for a later date, but the few that have come my way are not very informative. Student publications are more useful, but they came relatively late, the most important being *Irisleabhar Muighe Nuadhat* at the beginning of the century and the *Silhouette* in the 1940s.

In theory, the Irish diocesan archives should complement those of Maynooth. The Dublin archives are quite important. Two great archbishops, Troy and Murray, watched over Maynooth with solicitous care from its foundation in 1795 to the death of Murray in 1852. The extensive material in their archives is all the more important because Maynooth sources for these years are so scanty. They were followed by Paul Cullen (1852-78), who also watched, with solicitude indeed, but with a suspicious eye as well. The next archbishop, William Walsh, had been staff member and President, but by now the documentation, though growing, is becoming more routine, with copies normally available in Maynooth as well as at the other end. By comparison with Dublin the archives of other Irish dioceses are disappointing for the crucial first seventy years or so, though material can turn up anywhere, and can be quite important for individual bishops, such as Laurence Gillooly in Elphin (1856-95) or Bartolomew Woodlock in Ardagh (1879-94).

In Rome, material is to be sought in the archives of the Congregation of Propaganda until the curial reform of Pope Pius X in 1908. As is to be expected, Maynooth surfaces there only from time to time. The documents from the time the college was founded are reasonably well known, as are those from the crisis years of the 1850s. Less well known, indeed it might be said unknown, is the documentation arising from the failed attempt to secure the right to confer degrees around 1820, and the investigation into studies in the college in 1884, with its consequence, the grant of university status, in 1895. In 1908 Maynooth affairs passed to the Roman Congregation for Seminaries and Universities, but by this date documentation will normally exist in both Maynooth and Rome. Finally, at least from its re-establishment in 1826 until the appointment of a Papal Nuncio in 1929, Irish Roman business normally passed through the hands of the rector of the Irish College, and left its traces in its archives, particularly during the rectorships of Paul Cullen (1832-49) and Tobias Kirby (1850-91).

From its establishment in 1795 to the Irish Church Act in 1869 Maynooth had very definite relations with Government and Parliament. This has left material in the Chief Secretary's Office, and with the Board of Works for its years of association with the college between 1845 and 1870 (both of these are now in the National Archives). The Gladstone Papers in the British Library are important for details of the shaping of the provisions for Maynooth in the Irish Church Act. Relations with Parliament produced more in the way of documentation, though it is of uneven quality. Until 1845 the vote for Maynooth was debated in Parliament every year. It is putting it kindly to say that these debates produced heat rather than light, diatribe rather than discussion. They contain little of interest to the historian. Of much greater interest is the information laid before Parliament and published as parliamentary papers (listed in Wöste, op. cit., 325-30). Many of these were routine and slender, presented in connection with the petition for the annual grant, but even these can be valuable in the early years when information is otherwise scarce. There is a copy of most of them in MCA. Three might be singled out as especially valuable. The first was presented in 1808, in connection with the petition for a building grant for New House. It is slender enough, but for that date the information it gives is considerable. Most important of all, however, are the reports of the two Commissions of Inquiry, in 1826 and 1853, large folio volumes packed with detail that would have gone quite unrecorded had it not been necessary to explain things to the Commissioners. The Act of 1845 had prescribed a routine visitation every year, with minutes to be kept and a report presented to Parliament. Only nine were held between 1846 and 1869, and minutes have survived for only some of them, but in each case there is a Parliamentary Paper.

Pamphlet literature is voluminous and in general disappointing. Like the debates in Parliament, it is normally abusive and seldom informative (the long list in Wöste, op. cit., 338-48 is not altogether complete). A particularly bad example is *Maynooth in 1834; by Eugene Francis O'Beirne, late student of Maynooth College* (Dublin, 1835). It is a wild diatribe, obviously 'ghosted', much of the information coming from a slanted reading of the report of the Commission of 1826, with personal contributions from O'Beirne, a student who had been expelled, to make it more plausible and convincing. Regrettably, it is typical rather than exceptional, reflecting the rise of bigotry in Ireland and 'no popery' in England in the early nineteenth century. Informative pamphlets are few indeed. One very valuable one gives the only surviving detail of the law case that proved decisive in the matter of Lord Dunboyne's will (*Some Particulars of the Case ... tried at the Trim Assizes, Aug. 24, 1802*). Two others, in each case a reply to an attack on the college, are Peter Flood, *A Letter from the Rev. Peter Flood, D.D. .... relative to a Pamphlet .... by Patrick Duigenan* (1800), and Bartholomew Crotty, *A Letter to the Rt Hon. Lord Bexley* (1829). Bits and pieces of information are to be picked up elsewhere but in general the pickings are thin indeed. One valuable exception might be noted. It is James Lord, *Maynooth College: or the Law Affecting the Grant to Maynooth, with the Nature of the Instruction there given, and the Parliamentary Debates thereon* (London, 1855). This is indeed a short cut to a great deal of information.

The first half of the nineteenth century was in many respects the heyday of the wealthy traveller, for cheap travel came only with the railways. Such a traveller usually had a good education and normally planned to write a book about his experiences. Many of those who came to Ireland came to Maynooth. They were mostly English, and in general approached the institution with English prejudices against Irish popery. Yet some of them can be quite informative. Among them the following deserve mention: J. N. Brewer, *The Beauties of Ireland, being Original Delineations, Topographical, Historical and Biographical for each County* (3 vols., London, 1826); Henry Inglis, *Ireland in 1834* (London, 1835); B. W. Noel, *Notes of a Short Tour through the Midland Counties* (London, 1837); and Mr and Mrs S. C. Hall, *Ireland: its Scenery, Character etc.* (2 vols., London, 1842). Two books with sharply contrasting approaches appeared in 1852. W. M. Thackeray's *Irish Sketchbook* is sourly critical, unjustly so it is reasonable to speculate, especially if judged against his contemporary, Sir Francis Bond Head, whose life as a colonial administrator had given him a capacity for detail of an almost photographic quality. The long chapter on Maynooth (*A Fortnight in Ireland*, pp. 66-99) is indeed a good substitute for a photographic album.

The French travellers who came to Ireland can be a valuable corrective to the English, in that whether they are personally believers or unbelievers they came from a tradition that was Catholic. But even the believers among them who came to Ireland were more interested in political theory than in seminaries. Montalembert paid a short visit to Maynooth in 1830. The relevant portion of his 'Journal de voyage en Irlande' has been printed in the *Dublin Magazine*, xvi, no. 2, 62-4 (Apr.-Jun. 1941).

Many books might be listed. At the head of the list there must surely be John Healy's monumental *Maynooth College, Its Centenary History* (Dublin, 1895). It bears the marks of hasty composition, but in the circumstances it was a remarkable feat. Nobody could call it very readable, but it did put down on paper a great deal of information, together with an impressive photographic record. Healy also produced the following year a detailed *Record of the Centenary Celebrations held in Maynooth College in June 1895*. Denis Meehan's book on the college buildings, *Window on Maynooth* (Dublin, 1949) must surely come next, followed by the study by Karl Wöste already noted. If these three figure slenderly in the annotation it is because detailed reference would be repetitious to the point of being wearisome.

Many of the Maynooth staff became public figures because they became bishops, but in Ireland there are comparatively few episcopal biographies. George Crolly's study of his uncle, *The Life of the Most Rev. Dr Crolly* (Dublin, 1851), is a dutiful tribute, but it does preserve some of the lore of the earliest days of the college. Archbishop Crolly spent only two years on the Maynooth staff, so even the full-length recent biography can find little to add (Ambrose Macaulay, *William Crolly* (1994)). William Meagher's *Notices of the Life and Character of His Grace Most Rev. Daniel Murray* (Dublin, 1853) is also dutiful, but as far as Maynooth goes quite uninformative. Bernard O'Reilly, *John MacHale, Archbishop of Tuam* (2 vols., New York, 1890) was a commissioned defence, and in any case MacHale's years in Maynooth were a comparatively short prelude to a long life. There is more information in Patrick J. Walsh, *William J. Walsh, Archbishop of Dublin* (Dublin, 1928) and in P. J. Joyce, *John Healy Archbishop of Tuam* (Dublin, 1931).

There are two very different books by staff members about life in the college. Walter McDonald's *Reminiscences of a Maynooth Professor* (London, 1926) chronicles fifty years' association from his coming as a student in 1870 to his death in 1920 with some bitterness but rather more tranquillity. Neil Kevin's *I Remember Maynooth* (London, 1937) caught the spirit of the inter-war tranquillity so brilliantly that for many of that generation the college as he described it became a kind of 'eternal Maynooth'. Of worthwhile books about members of the staff there are not many: Agnes O'Farrrelly (ed.), *Leabhar an Athair Eoghan* (Dublin, 1904); P. E. Mac Fhinn, *An tAthair Mícheál P. Ó hIceadha* (Dublin, 1974); and Ambrose Macaulay, *Dr Russell of Maynooth* (London, 1983).

Much incidental information comes from many places, especially in the earlier years, as is clear from the annotation to the opening chapters. As is only to be expected, very much of the material from the periodicals comes from the *Irish Ecclesiastical Record*. Attention might be called to the commemorative number issued in September 1945 as part of a very modest celebration of the sesquicentenary year of the college; and though it may seem invidious to single out one contribution few would quarrel with mention of the modestly titled 'Reminiscences' of Dean Cornelius Mulcahy of Limerick, ordained in the centenary year 1895, and for forty years a member of the staff.

Bibliographical Abbreviations

AAS	*Acta Apostolicae Sedis* (Rome, 1909 ff.)
APF	Archivio ... della Sacra Congregazione ... 'de Propaganda Fide'
SOCG	Scritture riferite nelle Congregazioni Generali
Archiv. Hib.	*Archivium Hibernicum* (journal of the Catholic Record Society of Ireland, Maynooth, 1912 ff.)
BL	British Library
Add. MS(S)	Additional Manuscript(s)
Cal. 1863/64 etc.	*Kalendarium Collegii Sti Patricii apud Maynooth A.D. MDCCCLXIII-IV* etc.
Castlereagh corr.	Marquis of Londonderry (ed.), *Memoirs and Correspondence of Viscount Castlereagh* (12 vols., London, 1848-53)
Cogan, *Meath*	Anthony Cogan, *The Ecclesiastical History of the Diocese of Meath, Ancient and Modern* (3 vols., Dublin, 1867-74)
Cornwallis corr.	Charles Ross (ed.), *The Correspondence of Charles 1st Marquis Cornwallis* (3 vols., London, 1859)
DA	Diocesan Archives
DDA	Dublin Diocesan Archives
FJ	*Freeman's Journal*
HEA	Higher Education Authority
HMC	Historical Manuscripts Commission

ICRA	Irish College Rome Archives
IER	*Irish Ecclesiastical Record*
IHS	*Irish Historical Studies*
McDonald, *Reminiscences*	Walter McDonald, *Reminiscences of a Maynooth Professor* (London, 1926)
MCA	Maynooth College Archives
MCL	Maynooth College Library
Mulcahy, 'Reminiscences'	Cornelius Mulcahy, 'Reminiscences', in *IER*, lxvi 146-73 (Sep. 1945)
NA	National Archives
NLI	National Library of Ireland
PRONI	Public Record Office of Northern Ireland
Rep. 1826	*Eighth Report of the Commissioners of Irish Education Inquiry. Dated London, 2nd June 1827. Roman Catholic College of Maynooth. Ordered, by the House of Commons, to be printed, 18 Jun. 1827* (H.C.1826-7 (509) xiii)
Rep. 1853	*Report of Her Majesty's Commissioners appointed to inquire into the Management and Government of the College of Maynooth. I: Report and Appendix; II: Minutes of Evidence, etc.* (HC 1854-5 [1896, 1896 I] xxii)
ME	*Minutes of Evidence*

NOTES

CHAPTER I (pp. 1–25)

1. HC 1808 (152) ix 371, reprinted in John Healy, *Maynooth College 1795–1895*, 696–7.
2. Eugene Conwell to Henry Conwell, 14 Apr. 1800 (MCL, Conwell Letters).
3. Peadar Mac Suibhne, 'The early history of Carlow College' in *IER*, lxii, 230–48 (Oct. 1943); Peter Birch, *St Kieran's College, Kilkenny* (Dublin, 1951). According to Thomas L. O'Beirne, Church of Ireland Bishop of Meath, students at Kilkenny attended 'only occasionally and at stated periods,' otherwise living at home, which he judged 'very pernicious' (O'Beirne to Castlereagh, 27 Apr. 1799, *Castlereagh corr.*, iii, 282–91).
4. The political background to the establishment of Maynooth College has been the subject of a number of studies over the past generation. Sources and previous studies are indicated in the most recent works: Hugh Fenning, *The Irish Dominican Province, 1698–1707* (Dublin, 1990), 573–6, and Dáire Keogh, *The French Disease* (Dublin, 1993), 68–88.
5. A. Paul Levack, 'Edmund Burke, his friends, and the dawn of Irish Catholic Emancipation' in *Catholic Historical Review*, xxxvii, 385–414 (Jan. 1952).
6. Denis Gwynn, 'Dr Hussey and Edmund Burke' in *Studies*, xvii, 529–46 (1928); Patrick Power, 'Dr Thomas Hussey' in *IER*, xlv, 460–72, 561–75 (May, Jun. 1935); Martin Murphy, 'Cloak and dagger: Dr Thomas Hussey, 1746–1803' in *Recusant History*, xix, 1, 80–94 (1988).
7. On 23 December Troy wrote to Archbishop Bray of Cashel saying he was convening all the bishops (Cashel DA, 1794/20).
8. Eamon O'Flaherty, 'Ecclesiastical politics and the dismantling of the Penal Laws in Ireland, 1774–82' in *IHS*, xxvi, 47–50 (May 1988).
9. Cashel DA, 1795/14.
10. *FJ*, 2 May 1795.
11. John Brady, 'The Oath of Allegiance at Maynooth' in *IER*, xciv, 129–35 (Sep. 1960).
12. Maurice R. O'Connell, 'The political background to the establishment of Maynooth College' in *IER*, lxxxvi, 9 (Jul. 1956).
13. Troy to the Duke of Leinster, 6 Jun. 1795 (DDA, 116/6/78); Troy to Bray, 28 Jul. 1795 (Cashel DA, 1795/26).

14. J. Warburton, J. Whitelaw, Robert Walsh, *History of the City of Dublin* (London, 1818), 1321–2.

15. These are a bound volume of hand-tinted maps of the Leinster estates, made in 1821 and now in Carton House. For the college lands see Plate 34.

16. *Castlereagh corr.*, iii, 77–8.

17. Troy to Pelham, 2 Dec. 1795 (DDA, 116/6/77); Pelham to Troy, 9 Dec. 1795 (ibid., 116/6/98); Troy to Bray, 8 Dec. 1795 (Cashel DA, 1795/32). In his letter to Bray Troy mentioned a sum of £40,000 for buildings.

18. Quoted in A. P. W. Malcomson, *John Foster* (Oxford, 1978), 414–15, from the original in the Kent Archives Office.

19. Camden to Pelham, undated but enclosing Marshall to Camden, 15 Jun. 1796 (PRONI, Calendar of the Pelham Papers, T 755/3, 19, 21).

20. Cashel DA, 1796/4.

21. For the lay college see below, pp. 40–42.

22. There is a full report in *Finn's Leinster Journal*, 30 Apr. 1796.

23. Printed in W. J. Fitzpatrick, *Ireland Before the Union* (Dublin, 1867), 44.

24. Printed in Hugh Fenning, *The Irish Dominican Province, 1698–1797* (Dublin, 1990), 576. See also Bishop Plunkett's 'Visitation Diary' for this date, printed in Cogan, *Meath*, iii, 277.

25. J. B. Clinch, *The following Odes were delivered before the Earl of Camden . . .* (Dublin, 1796).

26. Warburton, Whitelaw, Walsh, op. cit., at pp. 1316–17.

27. Troy to Bray, 24 Apr. 1798 (Cashel DA, 1798/9).

28. These details are given in a pamphlet published by the President, Peter Flood, *A Letter from the Rev. Peter Flood . . . Relative to the Pamphlet Entitled 'A Fair Representation of the Present Political State of Ireland' by Patrick Duigenan, LL.D. etc.* (Dublin, 1800). Duigenan's pamphlet was published in 1799.

29. *Rep. 1826*, 355–7.

30. Statement issued from the Trustees' meeting on 22 Apr. 1799 (*Castlereagh corr.*, iii, 78).

31. These three letters are in Cogan, *Meath*, iii, 226–8, 232.

32. Francis Power's statement, with a covering letter from Archbishop Troy dated 2 Oct., is in NA, State of the Country Papers, 3359, printed in *Archiv. Hib.*, xi, 10–11 (1944). For further information on Hearn and Power see ibid., 3353–6.

33. NA, Rebellion Papers, 620/18a/10/3, printed in *Archiv. Hib.*, xi, 11–13 (1944).

34. Clare to Cornwallis, 18 Apr. 1799, Cornwallis to Clare, 18 Apr. 1799 (*Cornwallis corr.*, iii, 277–9); Cornwallis to Portland, 18 Apr. 1799 (ibid., iii, 90–92); Memorandum of the Earl of Clare, 28 Dec. 1801 (ibid., iii, 372–3); Troy to Bray, 18 Apr. 1799 (Cashel DA, 1799/4).

35. *Castlereagh corr.*, iii, 79–80.

36. Cornwallis to Portland, 29 Apr. 1799 (NA, Miscellaneous Official Papers, 129/3, draft).

37. Troy to Bray, 30 Apr. 1799 (Cashel DA, 1799/6); Eugene Conwell to Henry Conwell, 5 May 1799 (MCL, Conwell Letters).
38. O'Beirne to Castlereagh, 27 Apr. 1799, May 1800 (*Castlereagh corr.*, iii, 282–91, 310–16); Luke Fox, later Chief Justice of the Common Pleas, to Castlereagh, 7 Oct. 1799 (ibid., ii, 413).
39. Cashel DA, 1800/6.

CHAPTER II (pp. 26–55)

1. Printed from the original in APF by Patrick Boyle, 'Documents relative to the appointment of a . . . coadjutor to the Bishop of Waterford in 1801' in *Archiv. Hib.*, vii, 17–18 (1918–21).
2. This letter is in private hands. A copy was given to me by Canon Matthew O'Donnell.
3. These developments appear clearly in two drawings now in MCL. See also letters from Maynooth to William McMullan, 19 Jun., 8 Dec. 1803 (Down and Connor DA, B/03/7, 9).
4. See below, pp. 42–4.
5. Michael Montague, the bursar, gave detailed and specific information on these matters to the Commission of 1826 (*Rep. 1826*, 112–13).
6. For the full details see Liam Swords, *The Green Cockade* (Dublin, 1989), 160–77.
7. *History of the City of Dublin*, 1322.
8. Young to Archbishop Bray, 3 Jul. 1804 (Cashel DA, 1804/5).
9. *Rep. 1826*, 43, 47–8.
10. Edward Power to James Burke, 3 Jul. 1803 (NLI, MS 1562).
11. Plunkett to Troy, 19 Dec. 1798 (DDA, 116/7/85).
12. *The Veto: a Commentary on the Grenville Manifesto* (London, 1810), 21–2.
13. *Rep. 1826*, 57–8, 96–7, 109, 150, 373.
14. See above, p. 16.
15. For a student view of the situation vis-à-vis Trinity College see Edmund Power to James Burke, 14 Jun. 1803 (NLI, MS 1562).
16. His evidence on this point is in *Rep. 1826*, 444–5.
17. *Cornwallis corr.*, 365–71; Colchester MSS, in *HMC Rep. 4*, 344–5.
18. See below, p. 269.
19. Their printed report is in DDA, 28/2/10.
20. John F. Hogan, 'The Lay College at Maynooth' in *IER*, xxvi, 225–39, 352–70 (Sep., Oct. 1909); John Brady, 'The Lay College, Maynooth', ibid., lxi, 385–8 (Jun. 1943), lxii, 94–7 (Aug. 1943), lxxiv, 201–6 (Sep. 1950).
21. *Dublin Evening Post*, 15 Sep. 1802.
22. DDA, 28/2/15; MCA, 5/9.
23. The student memorial, dated 3 Jan. 1803, is in DDA, 28/2/8; John Archbold to Eugene Conwell, Maynooth 14 Jan. 1803 (MCL, Conwell Letters).

24. Clogher DA, 1/1/2, 5.
25. Down and Connor DA, B/03/8.
26. Patrick Conway to Laurence Ward, Maynooth, 27 Jul. 1803 (NA, Official Papers, 153/55); Information of Daniel Collison of Maynooth, 26 Jul. 1803 (ibid., Registered Papers, 620/11/129/7); Philip Yorke, Earl of Hardwick, Lord Lieutenant, to Charles Yorke, Home Secretary, Dublin Castle, 29 Aug. 1803, printed in Michael McDonagh, *The Viceroy's Post-bag* (London, 1904), 385–6; Report of the Solicitor-General, summarised from the original in the Home Office Papers in Thomas Bartlett, *The Fall and Rise of the Irish Nation* (Dublin, 1992), 276; testimony of John Cousins, then a student, in *Rep. 1826*, 355–7.
27. Archbishop O'Reilly of Armagh to Bishop Plunkett of Meath, 23 Jan. 1807, printed in Cogan, *Meath*, iii, 364–5.
28. Ferris to McMullan, 19 Feb. 1807 (Down and Connor DA, B/07/1).
29. Ferris to McMullan, 27 Jan. 1808 (ibid., B/08/3).
30. Printed in Cogan, *Meath*, iii, 374–6.
31. Cashel DA, 1809/31.
32. So Bishop Plunkett noted in his diary (Cogan, *Meath*, iii, 382–3).
33. Letters of 17 Dec. 1809 (*Irish Magazine*, Jan. 1810); 28 Dec. 1809, 19 Jan. 1810 (ibid., Feb. 1810); undated (ibid., May 1810).
34. Cogan, *Meath*, iii, 387.
35. Everard to Rev. W. Strickland, Ulverston, 9 Jul. 1810 (DDA, 29/12/30); Daniel Murray to Archbishop Bray, 26 Jul. 1810 (ibid., 29/12/27). Both appear to be copies.
36. DDA, 34/8/2.
37. Armagh DA, A/9/1.
38. *Rep. 1826*, 142–3.
39. Ibid., 110, 358.
40. His evidence is in *Rep. 1826*, 349–53. In addition there might be noted *A Letter on the Reasons that led the Rev. Matthias Crowley . . .* by 'A clergyman', reputed to be one of the Maynooth staff (Dublin, 1811); *Irish Magazine*, Feb., Sep., Oct., Dec. 1814; W. J. Fitzpatrick, *Irish Wits and Worthies*, 90–93.
41. See below, pp. 153–4.
42. *History of the City of Dublin*, 1323.
43. *HMC Rep. Fortescue MSS*, viii, 120–21, 126, 193–4.
44. Printed in *Archiv. Hib.*, xliii, 22–3 (1988), from the original in Clogher DA, 1/2G/69.
45. Archbishop Troy's Affidavit in Chancery (DDA, 28/2/7); *Some Particulars of the Case, wherein the Lessee of Catherine O'Brien was Plaintiff and the Rev. A. Dunn, Secretary to the Roman Catholic College of Maynooth, Defendant: tried at Trim Assizes, Aug. 24, 1802. With a Circumstantial Account of the Testimony given by the Rev. William Gahan* (Dublin, 1802). See also John Kingston, 'Lord Dunboyne', in *Reportorium Novum*, iii, 62–82 (1962).

CHAPTER III (pp. 56–87)

1. Printed from the originals in Clogher DA in *Clogher Record*, vi, 482–5 (1968).
2. Montague to James Duffy, PP, Clontibret, 11 Feb. 1816 (Clogher DA, 1/46/43).
3. See Brendan MacEvoy, 'The parish of Errigal Kieran in the nineteenth century' in *Seanchas Ardmhacha*, i, 122 (1954).
4. *Rep. 1826*, 103–4.
5. There are brief biographical notices of the five in Donald H. Akenson, *The Irish Education Experiment* (London, 1970), 94–5. All except Blake are in *DNB*. For a more extended account of him see Donal A. Kerr, *Peel, Priests and Politics* (Oxford, 1982), 136–8.
6. *Eighth Report of the Commissioners of Education Inquiry . . . Roman Catholic College of Maynooth* (HC 1826–7 (509) xiii).
7. Correspondence on this point is referred to in Kerr, op. cit., 230.
8. *Thoughts upon the Catholic Question, by an Irish Roman Catholic* (Dublin, 1828).
9. Doyle to Jeremiah Donovan, professor in Maynooth, 4 Dec. 1828, printed in W. J. Fitzpatrick, *The Life, Times, and Correspondence of the Right Rev. Dr Doyle* (Dublin, 1880), ii, 98–9. The date can hardly be correct, for a reply, also dated 4 Dec., has survived in Kildare and Leighlin DA.
10. *A Letter to the Right Hon. Lord Bexley* (Dublin, 1829).
11. Crotty to Bishop Doyle, 26 May 1830 (Kildare and Leighlin DA); Richard Lalor Sheil to Archbishop Murray, 14 May 1831 (DDA, 31/3/44).
12. See especially John Gunn, 'The foundation of Maynooth College' in *IER*, iv, 316–26 (May 1883); 'Reminiscences of Maynooth', ibid., v, 160–69 (Mar. 1884); George Crolly, *The Life of the Most Rev. Doctor Crolly* (Dublin, 1851).
13. Fitzpatrick, op. cit., i, 328–51.
14. The process is described in detail by Crotty in *Rep. 1826*, 97ff.
15. APF, Acta 1826, 274r–275r.
16. Return made to Parliament 23 Jul. 1835 (HC 1835 (488) xxxviii, 569).
17. DDA, 34/8/6; MCA, 5/2/2.
18. *Dublin Review*, iii, 166 (Dec. 1836).
19. *Rep. 1826*, 50.
20. *Beauties of Ireland* (London, 1826), ii, 68.
21. *IER*, v, 163–4 (Mar. 1884).
22. Crotty's evidence, in *Rep. 1826*, 49.
23. Ibid., 65, 69.
24. *Irish Magazine*, Nov. 1813.
25. MCA, 14/35.
26. *Ireland in 1834*, 393–4.
27. *Rep. 1826*, 62–4, 199.

28. Ibid., 63–5, 127.
29. MCA, 5/2/4.
30. *Ireland in 1834*, 394.
31. *Rep. 1826*, 167, 447.
32. Ibid., 107, 111.
33. Ibid., 421–2.
34. Clogher DA, 1/1/41.
35. Printed copy in DDA, 28/2/36,
36. *Rep. 1826*, 136.
37. Ibid., 69.
38. Ibid., 378.
39. Clogher DA, 1/1/41.
40. *Rep. 1826*, 71.
41. Clogher DA, 1/1/41.
42. John Raymond Browne OP to the Master-General, Dublin, 17 Sep. 1819 (copy in APF, Congressi, Irlanda 22, 298r–300v).
43. *Rep. 1826*, 92–3, 150.
44. *IER*, v, 165 (Mar. 1884).
45. Pádraig Ó Súilleabháin, 'Brenan, Carew and their Ecclesiastical Histories' in *Archiv. Hib.*, xxvii, 104–6 (1964).
46. Evidence for the earliest period is considered above, pp. 29–31.
47. *Rep. 1826*, 141.
48. DDA 121/7/251.
49. APF, Lettere 299, 377v–378v, 556v–558r.
50. APF, Congressi, Irlanda 22, 298r–300v.
51. Ibid., 365r–366r.
52. Ibid., Irlanda 23, 207r–208r.
53. This letter is filed with the minutes of the General Congregation of Propaganda on 12 Feb. 1821 (APF, Acta 1821, ff. 109r–112v).
54. Christopher Boylan to John Ennis, 23 Jan. 1820 (Clogher DA, 1/1/44).
55. APF, Congressi, Irlanda 23, 115r–116r.
56. *Rep. 1826*, 135, 317.
57. APF, Acta 1821, 103r–116v; Lettere 302, 396rv.
58. APF, Lettere 302, 157rv; DDA, 121/7/287. This letter, as addressed to the Bishop of Ossory, has survived in the diocesan archives.
59. APF, Lettere 302, 164 rv; Congressi, Irlanda 23, 457r–458v.
60. APF, Congressi, Irlanda 23, 414r–418v, 426r–439r.
61. APF, Lettere 302, 396rv.
62. DDA, 121/7/292.
63. APF, Congressi, Irlanda 24, 462r–463r. See also 924r–926v.
64. Ibid., 471r–473r.
65. APF, Acta 1826, 274r–275r.
66. There is a very detailed minute in the Trustees' Journal for 27 Jun. 1823 and what is at least a final draft of the committee's report is in DDA, 28/2/29.

67. Pádraig Ó Súilleabháin, 'Nicholas Slevin, Maynooth Professor (1823–29) in the McCormack Papers 1815–16' in *IER*, civ, 80–85 (Aug.–Sep. 1965).
68. *Rep. 1826*, 54, 96, 185.
69. DDA, 34/8/8.
70. *Rep. 1826*, 183, 188.
71. *The Beauties of Ireland*, ii, 68.
72. *Ireland in 1834*, 392.
73. *Rep. 1826*, 61, 131–2.
74. John Brady, 'The Oath of Allegiance at Maynooth' in *IER*, xciv, 129–35 (Sep. 1960).
75. *Rep. 1826*, 62, 111, 372, 375; MCA 5/10.
76. The dispensation is entered in 'Ordinations and Prize-Lists', i, 370–71 (MCA, B4/2/1).
77. *A Fortnight in Ireland*, 79.

CHAPTER IV (pp. 88–126)

1. See below, pp. 142–6.
2. *Rep. 1853*, 27, 35.
3. Ibid., *ME*, 1–2, 39, 379–80.
4. ICRA, Additional Cullen Papers, 4/1/44.
5. Ordinations and Prize Lists, i, 381 (MCA, B4/2/1).
6. Renehan to Archbishop Murray, 19 Nov. 1845 (MCA, 6/11/13).
7. DDA, 58/2/1.
8. *Rep. 1853*, Appendix, 10–29, prints the 1848 statutes, with an English translation and indicating the changes introduced.
9. Ibid., *ME*, 379–80.
10. *Rep. 1853*, Appendix, 12–13; Cullen to Miley, 17 Nov. 1852 (DDA, 40/8/6).
11. 'Ordinations and Prize Lists', i, 401 (MCA, B4/2/1).
12. DDA, 38/4/63–76, 117–18.
13. Ibid., 40/8/6.
14. Anon., 'A Rural and Ecclesiastical Walk Through Ireland' in *The Catholic Luminary and Ecclesiastical Repertory*, 204 (10 Oct. 1841). The account of Maynooth is in the issues of 12, 26 Sep., 10, 24 Oct. They are reprinted in *IER*, lxi, 1–20 (Jul. 1940). Pádraig Ó Súilleabháin identified the author as W. J. Battersby in *IER*, ciii, 88 (Feb. 1965). The proposal that all should move to the new buildings was made by the Office of Public Works on 20 Sep. 1845 (MCA, 130/6/4).
15. *A Fortnight in Ireland* (London, 1852), 74–5, 94–5.
16. There is a contemporary account of Carew's consecration in 'Ordinations and Prize Lists', i, 400–401 (MCA, B4/2/1). See also T. Gavan Duffy, 'An Irish missionary effort: the brothers Fennelly' in *IER*, xvii, 464–84 (May 1921): Denis Meehan, 'Maynooth and the Missions', ibid., lxvi, 223–8 (Sep. 1945); T. P. Corbett, *Ireland Sends India a Noble Prelate* (Calcutta, 1955).

17. ICRA, Cullen Papers, 575.
18. Drafts of letters from Murray to the Lord Lieutenant are in DDA, dated Nov. 1841, 30 Nov. 1841, and 2 Dec. 1841 (34/8/51–3).
19. The political events of the next few years have received extensive coverage. See, for example, 'The Protestant Association and the anti-Maynooth agitation of 1845' in *Catholic Historical Review*, xliii, 273–308 (Oct. 1957); Edward R. Norman, 'The Maynooth Question 1845', in *IHS*, xv, 407–37 (Sep. 1967); Donal A. Kerr, *Peel, Priests and Politics* (Oxford, 1982), 242–89.
20. Renehan to Murray, 7 Nov. 1844 (copy in MCA, 6/11/2).
21. The petition to Peel is in BL Add. MS 40564, 186, 270. There is a draft in MCA (104/29/1). See also John O'Hanlon to Bishop McNally, 28 Apr. 1845 (Clogher DA, 1/10b/32).
22. For extensive correspondence on these points see MCA, 131/10.
23. For the Minute Book see MCA, B1/1/1, and for the Parliamentary Papers ibid., 131/3.
24. *Rep. 1853, ME*, 222–3.
25. Ibid., 160–61.
26. *Notes of a Short Tour through the Midland Counties*, 353.
27. *The Irish Sketch Book*, 306, 354 (Bohn edition).
28. *A Tour in Ireland*, 256.
29. *A Fortnight in Ireland*, 66–9.
30. Quoted in Kerr, op. cit., 250, from the Clarendon Papers in the Bodleian Library, Oxford.
31. Renehan to Murray, 19 Nov. 1845 (MCA, 6/11/33).
32. Communication of 19 Aug. 1845 (MCA, 130/6/1).
33. Op. cit., 204 (10 Oct. 1841).
34. *Rep. 1853*, 36–7.
35. Ibid., Appendix, 49–51.
36. MCA, 8/31/22.
37. Ibid., 8/31/29–31.
38. Gaffney to Archbishop Cullen, 17 Jan. 1850 (DDA, 325/8/106).
39. *Ireland in 1836*, 350–53.
40. *Irish Sketch Book*, 250.
41. MCA, 6/13/16.
42. Their correspondence is in MCA, 6/11/4–6 and DDA, 34/8/77, 98.
43. *Rep. 1853, ME*, 120.
44. *Rep. 1853*, 46.
45. Correspondence with the Board of Works on these matters is in MCA, 130/6/6, 11, 13, 14, 16.
46. *Rep. 1853, ME*, 401–03.
47. MCA, 6/6/30.
48. O'Reilly to Kirby, 23 Jul. 1839 (ICRA, Kirby Papers, 30).
49. O'Reilly to Cullen, 23 Jul. 1839 (ibid., Additional Cullen Papers, 4/4/30).
50. These essays were discovered in a locker in the Physics department in 1988 and presented to the college archive (MCA, 5/11/11).

51. See above, pp. 80–86.
52. MCA, 6/11/1, dated 16 Oct., DDA, 34/8/60, dated 29 Oct.
53. *A Fortnight in Ireland*, 79–80.
54. James Murphy to Renehan, 19 Jan. 1848; Renehan to James Murphy, 21 Jan. (MCA, 8/31/61–2).
55. McNally to Cullen, 21 Jan. 1840 (ICRA, Cullen Papers, 570).
56. Devereux to Cullen, 13 Sep. 1836 (ibid., 298).
57. Young to Cullen, 9 May 1850 (DDA, 39/2/26).
58. O'Reilly to Kirby, 23 Jul. 1839 (ICRA, Kirby Papers, 30).
59. *Rep. 1853, ME*, 91, 100.
60. Ibid., 21–7.
61. DDA, 34/8/94. There is an undated draft in MCA, 6/11/21.
62. Murray to Gavan Duffy, 12 Feb. 1855 (NLI, Duffy Papers, MS 8005).
63. *Rep. 1853, ME*, 16, 37, 57, 85–6, 295.
64. Murray, Crolly, Neville to Bishop Haly of Kildare, 15 Jun. 1852 (Kildare DA).
65. Clogher DA, 1/100b/12.
66. Murray to Renehan, 15 Jun. 1847 (MCA, 7/11/11); Browne (Kilmore) to Renehan, 18 Jun. 1847 (ibid., 18/6/47). See also Edmund O'Reilly to Cullen, 13 Jul. 1847 (ICRA, Cullen Papers, 1437).
67. Letters of Murray to Renehan, with drafts of replies, 18 Feb. to 4 Aug. 1849 (MCA, 7/11/11–22).
68. MCA, B4/2/4.
69. Murray to Renehan, 9 Aug. 1849 (MCA, 6/11/23).
70. Undated cutting from *The Times*, enclosed in a letter from Matthew Flanagan, secretary to the Trustees, to Renehan, 23 Oct. 1849 (MCA, 8/28/15).

Chapter V (pp. 127–48)

1. There are a number of accounts of the building programme, not always altogether in agreement. There is a forthcoming study by Frederick O'Dwyer, 'A. W. N. Pugin and St Patrick's College Maynooth' in *Irish Arts Review Yearbook*, xi (1995). The principal sources are: a set of 'contract drawings', numbered 1 to 14, signed 'A. W. Pugin 1846', of which there are tracings in NA (37325/57) and originals numbered 7 to 10 and 12 to 14 in MCL; miscellaneous drawings, mostly signed 'Richard Pierce', in both archives, including (in NA) a drawing of the proposed extension of the 'south pane'; the minute book of the Trustees; a letter-book of the Office of Public Works (NA, 2d/60/11); correspondence between the college and Office of Public Works (MCA, 130/6); annual reports of the Commissioners of Public Works and of the Board of Visitors established in 1845 (both published as Parliamentary Papers); a few items in the Registered Papers in the Chief Secretary's Office; evidence given to the

Royal Commission in 1853. The Report of this commission includes two perspective drawings of the college buildings (Plates 18, 19), one showing what was actually built, the other, described as 'reduced from a drawing by A. W. Pugin 1845', clearly indicating Pugin's first proposals as submitted in Sep. 1845; the original appears to have been in the custody of the Board of Works, but is now lost or mislaid.

2. 5 Jul. 1845 (Armagh DA, C/45/9).
3. Pugin to Board of Works, Ramsgate, 15 Jan. 1846 (NA, CSO, Registered Papers, 1846/1254w. Copy).
4. Staff to Archbishop Murray, 11 Mar. 1846 (DDA, 34/8/79).
5. HC 1847 (1098) xxiii 433, p. 6.
6. Matthew Flanagan, secretary to the Trustees, to Renehan, 18 Apr. 1846 (MCA, 8/28/3).
7. MCA, 8/31/19 (copy).
8. Ibid., 8/29/3.
9. ICRA, Cullen Papers, 1689, 1754.
10. *Rep. 1853*, Appendix, 91.
11. Ibid., 186.
12. *A Fortnight in Ireland*, 92.
13. MCA, 130/6/36.
14. HC 1851 (213) i 661; 1867–8 (301) liii 805; 1868–9 (102) xxiv 321.
15. *Rep. 1853*, 68.
16. Russell to Dixon, 3 Jan. 1858 (Armagh DA, MIC/451/E/32/13).
17. Bowyer to Cullen, 17 Jun. 1859 (DDA, 319/2/104).
18. This letter is printed in HC 1860 (422) liii 655.
19. DDA, 319/7/59.
20. More O'Ferrall to Cullen, 3 Jun. 1860 (DDA, 333/4/10).
21. Irish Office to Larcom, 12 Jun. 1860 (NLI, Larcom Papers, MS 7581).
22. This correspondence is published in HC 1860 (422) liii 655.
23. Details in John O'Ferrall to Cullen, 11 Aug. 1860 (DDA, 33/4/18).
24. *Evening Mail*, 9 Jul. 1860; *Evening Packet*, 31 Jul. 1860.
25. See student petitions of 1862 and 1868 (MCA, 13/45/10, 39).
26. HC 1868–9 (117) xxiv 319.
27. Copies of Russell's letters to the Treasury in MCA, 13/45/12; Treasury to Russell, 26 Oct., 7 Nov. 1863 in DDA, 340/8/302, 214/2/99.
28. Board of Works to Russell, 16 Jun. 1864 (NA, 2d/60/11).
29. Thomas Farrelly, bursar, to John O'Hagan, 12 Jul. 1864 (MCA, 13/45/15).
30. Board of Works to Sir Robert Peel, Chief Secretary, 23 Jan. 1865 (NA, 2d/60/11).
31. Russell to Cullen, 1 Dec. 1861 (DDA, 340/1/210).
32. Russell to Cullen, 20 Feb. 1865 (DDA, 327/2/3). A copy of the memorial is in DDA, 34/8/120.
33. Board of Works, 29 Aug. 1865; Instructions to Architect, 2 Oct. 1865 (NA, 2d/60/11).

34. Board of Works to Farrelly, 15 Feb. 1871 (ibid.).

35. What follows is drawn mainly from the Board of Works correspondence in NA 2d/60/11 and MCA, 130/7.

36. Russell to Cullen, 11 Nov. 1866 (DDA, 327/2/12).

37. Russell to Cullen, 27 Jul. 1864 (DDA, 214/2/5).

38. McCarthy to Russell, 14 Oct. 1858 (MCA, 130/7/2).

39. *A Fortnight in Ireland*, 92–3.

40. Daniel McCarthy to Cullen, 19 Oct. 1860 (DDA, 333/4/46).

41. Detailed in HC 1867–8 (301) liii 805.

42. Cullen to Kirby, 19 Oct. 1850 (ICRA, Additional Kirby Papers, 1/2/50).

43. O'Reilly to Cullen, 14 Feb., 26 Mar. 1851 (DDA, 39/3/2, 45/3/3).

44. Murray to Cullen, 29 Oct., 15, 22, 25 Nov. 1851 (ibid., 39/3/58, 71, 74, 79).

45. Ibid., 42/3/38.

46. Monsell to Cullen, 14 Mar. 1853 (ibid., 40/3/18).

47. Patrick Murray to Propaganda, 4 Nov. 1849 (APF, Congressi, Irlanda 30, 363r–364v).

48. *The Irish Annual Miscellany*, ii, 348.

49. Cullen to Kirby, 25 Dec. 1850 (APF, Congressi, Irlanda 30, 533r–534r).

50. Smith to Cullen, 10 Jan. 1851 (DDA, 42/3/2); Cullen to Kirby, 17 Jan. 1851 (Smith Papers, St Paul's); Cullen to Kirby, 20 Jan. 1851 (ICRA, Additional Kirby Papers, 1/2/68); Cullen to Smith, 25 Jan. 1851 (ibid., 1/2/74); Smith to Cullen, 20 Feb. 1851 (DDA, 39/3/24); Cullen to Propaganda, 28 Sept. 1851 (APF, Congressi, Irlanda 30, 713v).

51. DDA 39/3/24.

52. APF, Congressi, Irlanda 30, 653r–654r.

53. Ibid., 646r–652r.

54. Smith to Cullen, 10, 11 Jul. 1851 (DDA, 42/3/20, 21); Cullen to Smith, 15, 28 Sep., 7 Oct. 1851 (Smith Papers, St Paul's).

55. APF, Congressi, Irlanda 30, 712r–716v, 718r–719v.

56. Matthew Flanagan to Renehan, 7 Jul. 1847, 10 Sep. 1853 (MCA, 8/28/12, 22).

57. Flanagan to Renehan, 9 Apr. 1853 (DDA, 58/2/7).

58. Patrick J. Corish, 'Gallicanism at Maynooth: Archbishop Cullen and the Royal Commission of 1853' in Art Cosgrove and Donal McCartney (eds.), *Studies in Irish History Presented to R. Dudley Edwards* (Dublin, 1979), 176–89.

59. This point is developed in a lengthy notice of the Commission's *Report* in *Dublin Review* xxxviii, 461–506 (Jun. 1855). It was written by C. W. Russell.

60. HC 1854–5 [1896, 1896 I] xxii.

CHAPTER VI (pp. 149–72)

1. The complete documentation is in APF, Congregazioni Particolari 158, 36–155.

2. Cullen to Monsell, 10 Mar. 1855 (NLI, Monsell Papers, MS 8317).

3. Cullen to Kirby, 24 Feb. 1854 (ICRA, Additonal Kirby Papers, 2/1/9).

4. Moran to Cullen, 4 Sep. 1855 (DDA, 42/3/6).

5. Ibid., 449/7/80.

6. Dixon to Cullen, 28 Sep., 30 Oct. 1855 (DDA, 332/5/51, 55).

7. Murray to Gavan Duffy, 16 Mar. 1855 (NLI, Duffy Papers, MS 8005).

8. The document, dated 15 Oct., is in DDA, 58/2/18, and a covering letter from the signatories, Walter Lee and Matthew Kelly, ibid., 332/7/115.

9. DDA, 339/1/96.

10. Dixon to Kirby, 22 Oct. 1855 (ICRA, Kirby Papers, 1661); Dixon to Cullen, 6 Nov. 1855 (DDA, 332/5/77); MacHale to Dixon 1855 (Armagh DA, E/67/1); MacHale to Cullen, 8 Nov. 1855 (DDA, 332/5/80); Dixon to Cullen, 10 Nov. 1855 (332/5/82); MacHale to Propaganda, 11 Nov. 1855 (APF, Congressi, Irlanda 32, 573 rv).

11. Murray's memorandum is on a sheet of paper in his diary in MCL. See also Cullen to Miley, rector of the Irish College, Paris, 18 Nov. 1855 (DDA, 40/8/108); to Kirby, 29 Nov. 1855 (ICRA, Additional Kirby Papers, 2/1/86); to Propaganda, 2 Dec. 1855 (APF, Congressi, Irlanda 32, 585r–588r).

12. MacHale to Propaganda, 16 Nov. 1855 (APF, Congressi, Irlanda 32, 577r–578r).

13. The minutes of the meeting, including the two letters, are in DDA, 339/1/96. See also Cullen to Propaganda, 13 Jul. 1856 (APF, Acta 1857, 43r–44v).

14. APF, Acta 1857, 43r–50v; Propaganda to Cullen, 20 Feb. 1857 (DDA, 449/8/36).

15. Dixon to Cullen, 10 Mar. 1856 (DDA, 339/1/27); same to Kirby, 28 Mar. 1856 (ICRA, Kirby Papers, 1746).

16. Dixon to Propaganda, 20 May 1857 (APF, Congressi, Irlanda 33, 287r); Propaganda to Dixon, 8 Jun. 1857 (ibid., Lettere 348, 312v); Propaganda to Giuseppe Berardi, substitute Secretary of State, 12 Jun. 1857 (ibid., 323r–324r); Denvir to Propaganda, 15 Jun. 1857 (ibid., Congressi, Irlanda 33, 348r).

17. Propaganda to Cullen, 5 Apr. 1861 (DDA, 326/2/12); Cullen to Propaganda, 3 May 1861 (APF, Congressi, Irlanda 34, 85r).

18. Dorrian to Kirby, 21 Sep., 28 Dec. 1877 (ICRA, Kirby Papers 1877, 299, 395).

19. APF, Congregazioni Particolari 158, 149v–151v.

20. C. B. Lyons to Cullen, 2 Apr. 1855 (DDA, 332/5/16).

21. See above, pp. 122–3.

22. NLI, Monsell Papers, MS 8317.

23. Cullen to Propaganda, 26 May 1854 (APF, Acta 1854, 336rv).

24. John Derry, Bishop of Clonfert, to Cullen, 15 Oct. 1867 (DDA, 334/4/72).

25. NLI, Larcom Papers, MS 7681.

26. There is no record in the 'Liber Poenarum' (MCA, B4/2/4), which other-

wise appears to be written up in full for the presidencies of Renehan and Russell.

27. Cullen to Russell, 12 Nov. 1861 (MCA, 10/16/60); Russell to Cullen, 13 Nov. 1861 (DDA, 214/2/59).

28. Russell to Larcom, 27 May, Peel to Larcom, [early] Jun., Pigot to Larcom, 9 Jun. 1864 (NLI, Larcom Papers, MS 7586); Lee to Cullen, 28, 30 May, 21 Nov. 1864 (DDA, 320/5/56, 57, 126).

29. NA, Registered Papers 1869, 5515; Russell to Cullen, 11 Apr. 1869 (DDA, 321/1/48).

30. Details in Austin Gough, *Paris and Rome: the Gallican Church and the Ultramontane Campaign 1848–1853* (Oxford, 1986), 195–8, 214–15.

31. Propaganda to Cullen, 24 Nov. 1852 (DDA 449/6/45); Smith to Cullen, 23, 30 Nov., 12, 24 Dec. 1852 (ibid., 42/2/37, 38, 39, 41); Kirby to Cullen, 8 Dec. 1852 (ibid., 42/2/40).

32. Cullen to Kirby, 3 Jan. 1853 (ICRA, Additional Kirby Papers, 1/3/56); Kirby to Cullen, 10 Jan. 1853 (DDA, 42/2/1); Miley to Kirby, 28 Nov. 1852 (ICRA, Kirby Papers, 1082).

33. J. P. Cooke to Kirby, 15 Feb. 1853 (ICRA, Kirby Papers, 1140); Cullen to Propaganda, 21 Feb. 1853 (APF, Congressi, Irlanda 31, 395r).

34. APF, Congressi, Irlanda 31, 336v.

35. Smith to Cullen, 4 Feb. 1853 (DDA, 42/3/1); Propaganda to Cullen, 16 Feb. 1853 (ibid., 449/7/9).

36. Cullen to Propaganda, 30 Apr. 1853 (APF, Congressi, Irlanda 31, 439rv).

37. This extract from Blake's diary is printed in Peadar Mac Suibhne, *Paul Cullen and his Contemporaries*, ii (Naas, 1962), 343.

38. MCA, 13/45/10.

39. Edward Walsh, Bishop of Ossory, to Cullen, 17 Aug. 1857 (DDA, 339/5/106).

40. Cullen to Propaganda, 16 Feb. 1854 (APF, Acta 1854, 167rv).

41. Cullen to Propaganda, 17 Jan. 1860 (ibid., Acta 1860, 166v).

42. *Reminiscences*, 63.

43. Gargan to Cullen, 4 Apr. 1859 (DDA, 319/7/33).

44. Russell to Cullen, 18 Sep. 1863 (ibid., 340/8/196).

45. O'Hanlon to Cullen, 25 Sep. 1863 (ibid., 340/8/197); Russell to Cullen, 29 Sep. 1863 (ibid., 340/8/199).

46. Russell to Cullen, 8 Oct. 1863 (ibid., 340/8/201).

47. Lee to Russell, 3 Nov. 1857 (MCA, 13/45/1).

48. Murray to O'Hagan, 13 Oct. 1859 (NLI, O'Hagan Papers, MS 1874).

49. MCA, 13/45/10, 26.

50. Memorandum from Patrick Murray, 13 Oct. 1867 (DDA, 334/5/98); Gerald Molloy to Cullen, 17 Oct. 1867 (ibid., 334/5/103).

51. Cullen to Kirby, 12 Mar. 1854 (ICRA, Additional Kirby Papers, 2/1/11).

52. Woodlock to Bishop Moriarty, 16, 18 Apr. 1867 (NLI, Monsell Papers, MS 8319); same to Cullen, 26 Apr., 5 May, 20 Jun. 1867 (DDA, 45/5/3, 5, 18).

53. NLI, Mayo Papers, MS 11217.

54. Documentation in MCA, 13/45/17–22.

55. For the extant correspondence see DDA, 214/2/86, 87; MCA, 9/2/44, 45, 10/13/24.

56. Correspondence cited in Ambrose Macaulay, *Dr Russell of Maynooth* (London, 1983), 254–5.

57. MCA, 13/44/8, 9.

58. Furlong to Russell, 8 Nov. 1859 (MCA, 11/21/22).

59. Leahy to Russell, 11 Oct. 1861 (ibid., 9/4/41).

60. See above, p. 111.

61. MCA, 13/45/10.

62. Cullen to Kirby, 15 May 1856 (ICRA, Additional Kirby Papers, 2/1/21).

63. MCA, 13/4/35.

64. Russell to Cullen, 22 Apr. 1860 (DDA, 333/4/19).

65. MCA, 13/45/24.

66. *Nation*, 15 Feb. 1862.

67. A. M. Sullivan to Russell, 22 Feb. 1862 (MCA, 13/47/10).

68. Lawrence Gillooly, Bishop of Elphin, to Russell, 24 Apr. 1870 (MCA, 11/20/14).

69. Russell to Monsell, 29 May 1867 (NLI, Monsell Papers, MS 8319).

70. Newman gives the exact dates in his diary (C. S. Dessain and V. H. Blehl (eds.), *The Letters and Diaries of John Henry Newman*, xv (London, 1964), 91). See also Henry Tristram (ed.), *John Henry Newman: Autobiographical Writings* (London, 1955), 323.

71. *Cardinal Wiseman's Tour in Ireland* (Dublin, 1859), 226–40.

72. Details in Macaulay, op. cit., 216–18.

73. A copy of the printed ceremonial arrangements is in DDA, 44/1/13. No copy has survived in Maynooth, but they are reprinted in *Cal. 1866/67*, 127–32.

CHAPTER VII (pp. 173–205)

1. Cullen to Kirby, 10 May 1868, Delaney to Kirby, 2 Jun. 1868 (ICRA, Kirby Papers, 1868, 154, 185).

2. Russell's letters are in BL Add. MSS 44416-20 and Gladstone's replies in MCA, 13/47. See also E. R. Norman, *The Catholic Church and Ireland in the Age of Rebellion 1859–1873* (London, 1965), 282–409; Macaulay, op. cit., 267–86.

3. BL Add. MS 44798.

4. DDA, 321/2/57.

5. 14 Mar. 1860 (ibid., 121/4/104).

6. Ibid., 321/3/93 (incomplete and undated).

7. MCA, 13/46/31b.

8. Chief Secretary Hartington to Russell, 13 Mar. 1873 (ibid., 13/47/38).

9. Letters of resignation ibid., 13/45/41a.
10. Opinion of John T. Corballis, 14 Nov. 1859 (ibid., 131/12/13).
11. Ibid., 13/46/39.
12. O'Hagan to Gillooly, 19 Jan. 1875 (Elphin DA).
13. Text in MCA, 130/1/31.
14. George Conroy, Bishop of Ardagh, to Cullen, 25 Jun. 1875; Gillooly to Cullen, 1 Dec. 1875 (DDA, 342/7/23, 81).
15. Cullen to Gillooly, 13 Oct. 1870, 3 Jun. 1871 (Elphin DA); Gillooly to Cullen, 6 Mar., 2 Jun. 1871 (DDA, 328/3/24).
16. DDA, 335/1/33.
17. *Reminiscences*, 36.
18. Gillooly to Cullen, 9 May 1872 (DDA, 328/8/38); Gillooly to Russell, 9 May 1872 (MCA, 11/20/37); Russell to Gillooly, 10 May 1872 (DDA, 329/1, misplaced with letters of 1877).
19. A copy of the 1897 reprint is in MCA, 100/3/4.
20. Cullen to Gillooly, 22 Dec. 1875, 19 Jun. 1876 (Elphin DA); Gillooly to Cullen, 20 Jun. 1876 (DDA 322/3/69); Minutes of Administrative Council, 29 Jun. 1876 (MCA, B4/3/2); and a very frank and forceful letter from William Walsh to Cullen, 17 Jun. 1876 (DDA, 58/2/95).
21. Walsh to Edward McCabe, coadjutor archbishop of Dublin, 14 Jun. 1878 (DDA, 58/2/99).
22. Gillooly to McCabe, 14 Sep. 1879 (DDA, 337/4/57); Walsh to McCabe, 8 Jul. 1881 (ibid., 346/6).
23. Three reports by the bursar, Thomas Farrelly, dated 14 Aug. 1869, 6 Aug. 1870 and 1 Jun. 1871 (MCA, 13/47/33, 34, 35) give very detailed information.
24. MCA, 131/11.
25. Ibid., 13/46/32b.
26. See, for example, Archbishop McEvilly of Tuam to Browne, 20 Apr., 21 Nov. 1888 (MCA, 16/26/8, 9).
27. Ardagh DA.
28. As well as the Trustees' Journal and the annual reports of the President there is a file of correspondence in MCA, 15/29.
29. Andrew Murray, gamekeeper, to Cullen, 2 Mar. 1871 (DDA, 328/4/63); Russell to Cullen, 3 Apr. 1871 (ibid., 328/7/3).
30. The minutes of the Trustees and of the Administrative Council are full and informative. There is correspondence in MCA, 105/3/11-33, 4/1-25, and a long valuable letter from Walsh to Archbishop McCabe, 21 Dec. 1879 (DDA, 337/4/129). The subject is treated fully in Patrick J. Walsh, *William J. Walsh* (Dublin, 1928), 95–114.
31. Myles O'Reilly MP to Cullen, 4, 20 Feb. 1865 (DDA, 121/4/12,13).
32. Details in MCA, 113/2/5.
33. Archbishop Leahy (Cashel) to Russell, 10 Sep. 1868, 22 Jan. 1872 (MCA, 9/5/24, 63).

34. MCA, 113/4/23, reprinted in *Cal. 1868/69*.
35. Denis Kelly, Bishop of Ross, to Michael O'Riordan, rector of the Irish College, Rome, 19 May 1906 (ICRA, O'Riordan Papers, 1906/136).
36. What follows is drawn from the Trustees' Journal; the Bursar's Financial Statement (annual, from 1864); the reports of the Episcopal Finance Committee for 1879, 1881 and 1882 (a report for 1880 has not been traced); and the minutes and reports of the College Finance Committee.
37. *Reminiscences*, 83.
38. Ibid., 56.
39. William Hague, architect, to Walsh, 19 Jan. 1880 (MCA, 15/27/15); Walsh's Reports to the Trustees, Oct. 1879, Jun. 1881 (ibid., 132).
40. Ibid., 15/27/38.
41. Russell to Cullen, 6 Feb. 1875 (DDA, 335/7/1).
42. Russell to Cullen, 6 Feb., 22 Mar. 1875 (ibid., 335/7/1, 2).
43. Croke to Russell, 1 Dec. 1875 (MCA, 101/8/47); Croke to Cullen, 19 Jan. 1877 (DDA, 329/2/5); Gillooly to Cullen, enclosing a copy of Russell to Gillooly, both dated 1 Dec. 1875 (DDA, 342/7/81).
44. MCA, 102/18/1.
45. As agreed 15 Jul. 1876 (ibid., 101/9/10).
46. Ibid., 101/9/37.
47. Correspondence in MCA, 102/8.
48. McGivern to Browne, 26 Mar. 1888 (MCA, 16/11/3).
49. As early as 1884 Bishop Gillooly had commissioned a window from the firm of Lobin of Tours and it was erected in the position now occupied by Archbishop Croke's window. There is reason to surmise that the theme was the Immaculate Conception. This window was later removed, apparently to his diocese of Elphin, after a theme for the whole series had been agreed, together with a decision to reserve the four 'prime' places for the metropolitans.
50. The correspondence with Mayer is in MCA, 102/10.
51. There is a very extensive and interesting correspondence in MCA, 101/3, 4, 5.
52. These phrases are from two letters to Browne, 5 Jun. 1889, 30 Jan. 1890 (MCA 101/3/18, 23). In many places Buckley expounds his ideas of ecclesiastical art in a quite interesting way.
53. Hague to Browne, 22 Nov. 1887 (MCA, 101/8/5).
54. Westlake to Browne, 25 Jul. 1894 (ibid., 102/13/31).
55. Buckley to Browne, 21 Mar. 1891 (ibid., 101/5/28).
56. Mulcahy, 'Reminiscences', 146, repeated in Denis Meehan, *Window on Maynooth* (Dublin, 1949), 114.
57. *National Press*, 25 Jun. 1891, reprinted in *Cal. 1891/92*, 173.
58. Hague to Browne, 25 Sep. 1889 (MCA, 101/9/29).
59. Five letters between 6 Jan. and 15 Feb. 1892 (MCA, 102/15/62–6).
60. Mulcahy, 'Reminiscences', 147–8.

61. The documentation is in MCA, 102/14.
62. Ibid., 102/14/13, reported in *FJ*, 7 Aug. 1890.
63. Extensive documentation is printed in *Cal. 1891/92*, 168–89.
64. Buckley to Browne, 5 Oct. 1891 (MCA, 101/5/67).
65. Dated 12 Oct. 1891 (ibid., 18/50/2).
66. Hague to Browne, 14, 16 Dec. 1891 (ibid., 101/8/95, 18/51/2); Brownrigg to Browne, 19 Dec. 1891 (ibid., 16/23/10).
67. Hague to Browne, 29 Jan. 1892 (ibid., 18/51/5); Lalor to Browne, 16 Feb. 1892 (ibid., 18/50/4).
68. The extensive correspondence is in MCA, 18/50, 51.

Chapter VIII (pp. 206–39)

1. Moriarty to Cullen, 9 Jun. 1869 (DDA, 341/8/48).
2. Gillooly to Cullen, 2 Dec. 1877 (DDA, 329/1/66); Cullen to Gillooly, 8 Jun. 1878 (Elphin DA).
3. Gillooly to Walsh, 26, 30 Aug. 1878 (MCA, 15/12/4, 5).
4. Walsh to McCabe, 22 Jun. 1880 (DDA, 346/1/8).
5. Walsh to McCabe, 3, 7, 9, 17 Oct. 1883 (ibid., 358/8).
6. There is an interesting memorandum from Dr Patrick Murray, dated 13 Oct. 1867, on the problems of the theology courses even at that date. Two copies have survived in DDA (58/2/100, 334/5/98). There is also some information in the minute-book of the 'President's Council', kept by Russell between 1857 and 1877 (MCA, B4/3/1).
7. Walsh to Cullen, 1 May 1871, enclosing a memorandum from the professors of Theology (DDA, 58/2/74).
8. Walsh to Cullen, 11 Oct. 1874 (ibid., 58/2/89).
9. There is much detailed documentation between 1874 and 1881 in the minutes of the Trustees, the annual reports of the President, and the minutes of the Scholastic Council. See also in particular Walsh to Cullen, 11 Oct. 1875, 17 Jun. 1876 (DDA, 58/2/90, 95), and to McCabe, 22 Sep. 1879 (ibid., 337/4).
10. *Reminiscences*, 50–57.
11. It is unsigned and undated (ICRA, Kirby Papers, 1878/436).
12. Pius Devine CP to Walsh, 19 Nov. 1879 (DDA, 350/2).
13. *Reminiscences*, 177.
14. Ibid., 59–60.
15. Ibid., 39–49.
16. Ibid., 58–9.
17. A copy of the printed report, dated 6 Jun. 1876, is in DDA, 45/6/2.
18. Walsh to McCabe, 15 Jan. 1882 (DDA, 353/3); to Woodlock, 26 Jan. 1882 (Ardagh DA); to Gillooly, 16 May 1882 (Elphin DA); President's annual report, Jun. 1882.
19. Walsh to McCabe, 5 Jan. 1881 (DDA, 346/6); to Woodlock, 14 Sep. 1881, 16 May 1882 (Ardagh DA); to Gillooly, 16 May 1882 (Elphin DA).

20. Gillooly to Healy, 17 Dec. 1881, printed in P. J. Joyce, *John Healy Archbishop of Tuam* (Dublin, 1931), 64; Walsh to McCabe, 3 Dec. 1881 (DDA, 346/6).

21. Walsh to Woodlock, 30 Mar. 1882 (Ardagh DA).

22. See especially Walsh to Gillooly, 3, 12 Apr. 1882 (Elphin DA); Walsh to Woodlock, 5, 17 Apr. 1882 (Ardagh DA), and also Moran to Kirby, 19 Apr. 1882 (ICRA, Kirby Papers, 1882/56).

23. The story can be traced through the minute books of the various bodies. McCabe's intervention in Propaganda has left documentation there: McCabe to Bernard Smith OSB, undated copy; McCabe to Simeoni, 13, 17 Oct. 1882; report of the Episcopal Commission, 17 Jul. 1882 (all these in APF, Acta 1882, 605r–607r, SOCG, 1021, 116v–123r); Simeoni to McCabe, 6 Nov. 1882 (ibid., Lettere 378, 505v).

24. From APF, Congressi, Irlanda 41, 297r.

25. Ibid., SOCG, 1021, 107r–108v.

26. Ibid., Congressi, Irlanda 41, 295rv.

27. Ibid., Acta 1884, 561r–577r.

28. Ibid., Congressi, Irlanda 41, 547rv.

29. Ibid., Lettere 381, 133v.

30. Minutes of the meetings and final decisions ibid., SOCG, 1021, 282r–312r, 338r–339v. The decisions on Philosophy and Theology are printed in John Healy (ed.), *Maynooth Centenary Record* (Dublin, 1896), 239–41.

31. DDA, 360/4.

32. *Reminiscences*, 180, footnote. There are indications in the text that this part of it was being written in 1913.

33. A history of the *Irish Ecclesiastical Record* would be desirable. See Thomas Wall, 'The Irish Ecclesiastical Record and Maynooth' in *IER*, lxvi, 322–30 (Nov. 1945).

34. *Reminiscences*, 65–6.

35. 'Rare Books in Maynooth College Library' in *IER*, lii, 46–59 (Jul. 1938).

36. APF, Acta 1895, 234r–241v.

37. Printed in *IER*, 3rd series, xvii, 450–51 (May 1896).

38. Ibid., 4th series, vi, 564–7 (Dec. 1899); viii, 81 (Jul. 1900).

39. *Reminiscences*, 177.

40. Ibid., 38–9.

41. Gillooly to Russell, 29 Mar., 11 May 1871, 9 May 1872 (MCA, 11/20/26, 29, 37).

42. *Reminiscences*, 48–9, 66–7.

43. Ibid., 61–3.

44. There are some informative letters: Cullen to Gillooly, 22 Dec. 1875 (Elphin DA); Gillooly to Cullen, 28 Dec. 1875 (DDA, 342/7/93); George Conroy, Bishop of Ardagh, to Cullen, 21, 23 Dec. 1875 (ibid., 342/7/15, 16).

45. This letter seems to have fallen into Gillooly's hands. It ended up in DDA, 335/7.

46. Ardagh DA.

47. APF, Acta 1885, 576r–577v, SOCG, 1021, 288r–293v.

48. Obituary notice in *FJ*, 18 Oct. 1869.

49. McCabe to Simeoni, 18 Oct. 1884 (APF, Congressi, Irlanda 41, 403r–404v).

50. Undated memorandum, filed with the documents of 1884–5 (ibid., 686r–687v).

51. APF, SOCG 1021, 107r–108v.

52. Cullen to Conroy, 3, 6 Mar. 1870 (Ardagh DA).

53. APF, Congressi, Irlanda 41, 686r–687v.

54. Undated, filed with the documents of 1883 (ibid., Congressi, Irlanda 40, 626r–632v).

55. Printed in Agnes O'Farrelly (ed.), *Leabhar an Athair Eoghan* (Dublin, 1904), 228–30.

56. *Reminiscences*, 80–90.

57. McCarthy to Cullen, 5 Nov. 1877 (DDA, 329/4/58); H. C. G. Matthew (ed.), *The Gladstone Diaries*, ix (Oxford, 1986), 284; J. B. Hall, *Random Records of a Reporter* (London, n.d.), 224–5.

58. *FJ*, 3 Mar. 1879, 16 Feb. 1880, reprinted in *Cal. 1879/80*, 141–3, *1880/81*, 145–7.

59. John Healy, *Maynooth Centenary Record* (Dublin, 1896), 110–13.

60. *L'Irlande contemporaine* (Paris, 1907); English translation *Contemporary Ireland* (Dublin, 1908), 368, 461.

61. London, 1901, 23.

CHAPTER IX (pp. 240–66)

1. The 1900 statutes are printed in *Cal. 1901/02*, 180–99. Correspondence with the Congregation is printed here and in the calendars for 1909/10, 1918/19, 1919/20.

2. *Reminiscences*, 200–01.

3. Ibid., 195–202.

4. 'Reminiscences', 151; notebooks by courtesy of the Coffey family.

5. For an undated draft see MCA, 22/32/8.

6. Ibid., 22/30/7.

7. McDonald to Mannix, 7 Apr. 1906 (MCA, 20/3/11, copy in Mannix's hand).

8. Minutes of the first general meeting in *Archiv. Hib.*, ii, 347–50 (1913).

9. E. A. D'Alton to James McCaffrey, 16, 21 Jan. 1919 (MCA, 27/19/74a).

10. *Reminiscences*, 328–9.

11. J. F. O'Doherty, 'Maynooth 1895–1945' in *IER*, xvi, 210 (Sep. 1945).

12. ICRA, O'Hagan Papers.

13. Pp. 185–7.

14. 'Reminiscences', 162.
15. This is McDonald's account (*Reminiscences*, 111–14), supplemented by letters from Cardinal Logue to Archbishop Walsh, 21 Feb. 1898 (DDA) and Walsh to Logue, 4 Mar. 1898 (Armagh DA).
16. *Reminiscences*, 126.
17. Walsh to Logue, 4 Mar. 1898 (Armagh DA).
18. Hogan to Walsh, 13, 17 Feb. 1898 (DDA, 357/8); Logue to Walsh, 15, 21, 28 Feb., 5, 20 Mar. 1898 (DDA); Walsh to Logue, 14, 26 Feb., 4 Mar. 1898 (Armagh DA).
19. Healy to Hogan, 26 Mar. 1898; O'Doherty to Hogan, 25 Mar. 1898; McRedmond to Hogan, 13 Mar. 1898 (MCA, 21/6/5, 9/2, 19/11); O'Dwyer to Hogan, 13 Mar. 1898 (ibid., 22/21/3).
20. *Reminiscences*, 111–66, including extensive documentation.
21. McDonald to Walsh, 14 Feb. 1899 (DDA, 364/5).
22. McDonald to Walsh, 10, 13, 19 Nov. 1899 (ibid.).
23. Hogan to Walsh, 2 Dec. 1902 (DDA, 358/4); Logue to Walsh, 24 Oct. 1905 (DDA).
24. McDonald to Walsh, 30 May, 8, 27 June 1903 (DDA).
25. *Reminiscences*, 331–5, 403–6.
26. Reprinted in *Reminiscences*, 407–11.
27. MCA, 20/6/4.
28. Documentation ibid., 22/3/3.
29. The above is pieced together from the annual calendar and reports of the President, the minutes of the Trustees and Visitors, and of the academic bodies.
30. His evidence was published as a pamphlet, *Maynooth and the University Question: Evidence before the Royal Commission* (Dublin, 1903).
31. Mannix to Walsh, 7 Jul. 1906 (DDA, 374/7).
32. *Minutes of Senate*, ii, 455–9.
33. There is a detailed exposition in the President's report to the Trustees in June 1911.
34. *Minutes of Senate*, iii, 317, with 'Printed Paper 14-1' (27 Feb. 1914).
35. Birrell to Hogan, 14 Jan., 27 Nov. 1914 (MCA, 23/42/4, 23/43/12).

CHAPTER X (pp. 267–82)

1. The number of bodies keeping minutes and presenting reports increased steadily. This means there is much less need for detailed annotation in most matters. The above account is pieced together from the minutes of the Trustees and Visitors; the annual reports of the President (MCA, 132); the annual and 'special' reports of the Finance Council (ibid., B 3/10/3,4); and the minutes of the Finance Council (ibid., B3/11/1,2,3.
2. Material on the college farms is in MCA, 105, 106.

3. See above, pp. 185–6.
4. 'Reminiscences', 155–6.
5. There is no specific reference to this, and the lamp itself bears no inscription; but see Ashlin and Coleman to Hogan, 6 Mar. 1918 (MCA, 23/46/38).
6. There is a file on the decoration of the Lady Chapel in Hogan's papers (MCA 23/46).
7. Mulcahy, 'Reminiscences' , 169.
8. Ibid., 159.
9. *I Remember Maynooth*, 25–6.
10. 'Reminiscences', 170.
11. Ibid., 156–8.

CHAPTER XI (pp. 283–304)

1. Walsh to Logue, 8 Mar. 1903 (Armagh DA).
2. Donnchadh Ó Floinn, 'Magh Nuadhat agus an Athbheochaint' in *IER*, lxvi, 201–7 (Sep. 1945).
3. Printed in *Maynooth Centenary Record*, 232–4.
4. A full list of these papers, from 1903 to 1938, is printed in *Catholic Truth Society of Ireland: First Fifty Years 1899–1949* (Dublin, 1949), 45–51.
5. *Reminiscences*, 188–92.
6. The minute book of the Committee is in MCA, 20/12.
7. *Cal. 1903/04*, 187–91, reprints the account in *FJ*, 28, 29 Sep. 1903.
8. 'The Gaelic League and the chair of Irish at Maynooth' in *Studies*, lii, 348–62 (1963).
9. *Reminiscences*, 235–75.
10. MCA Box 100. The most important documents are:
    1. A typescript statement, 15 pp., large quarto, drawn up by Arthur O'Hagan and Sons, college solicitors, as instructions to the Trustees' lawyers in Rome. Title: 'Re Dr O'Hickey: Statement of the Trustees of Maynooth College, 30 June 1910'.
    2. *Summarium*, 1912, 180 pp., printed. The evidence presented to the Roman Rota on behalf of the Trustees.
    3. *Restrictus facti et iuris*, 1912, 38 pp., printed. The case for the Trustees as presented to the Rota by their lawyer.
    4. *Memoria*, 14 Feb. 1911, 18 pp., printed. Statement drawn up by Michael O'Hickey.
    5. *Memoria ulteriore*, 14 May 1912, 7 pp., printed. Further statement by Michael O'Hickey.
    6. *Memoriale nell' appello dal decreto del Turno . . . con sommario annesso*, 19 Jul., 27 pp., printed. O'Hickey's appeal to the Signatura.
    7. *Ricorso all Ecc.mo Collegio Rotale*, 10 May 1913, 13 pp., printed. O'Hickey's appeal from the Signatura to the full College of the Rota.
    8. A collection of the Irish newspapers relevant to the case.

11. Cited in Ó Broin, art. cit., 355, from the short-lived Catholic nationalist periodical *Irish Opinion* (1917).
12. See above, pp. 261–2.
13. O'Hickey to Walsh, 14, 17 Nov. 1904 (DDA, 365/8).
14. *Reminiscences*, 251.
15. Mannix to Walsh, 12 Jun., 12, 23 Jul. 1909 (DDA).
16. Logue to Walsh, 26 Oct., 2, 5 Nov. 1909 (DDA).
17. Luzio to O'Riordan, 26 Jun. 1913 (MCA, 100/5/55).
18. MCA, 100/4/19.
19. Judgement printed in *AAS*, v, 52 (1913).
20. *Reminiscences*, 368–70.
21. Art. cit., 360.
22. Argued in some detail in Colm Kiernan, *Daniel Mannix and Ireland* (Melbourne, 1984).
23. MCA, 20/3/5.
24. *Doomsland*, 187–8.
25. 'Reminiscences', 158.
26. DDA, 379/3. A further opinion, dated 28 May 1918, is in MCA, 35/19/82.
27. See above, pp. 219–20.
28. Hogan to Walsh, 16 May 1917 (DDA, 379/3).
29. MCA, 23/47/5, 5a.
30. Mulcahy, 'Reminiscences', 149.
31. John Blowick in *The Far East*, Jan. 1918, Jun. 1919; Denis Meehan, 'Maynooth and the Missions' in *IER*, lxvi, 229–34 (Sep. 1945); James Hogan, *The Irish Missionary Movement* (Dublin, 1990), 91–7; Bernard J. Smyth, *The Chinese Batch* (Dublin, 1994).
32. MCA, 26/1/20.
33. *Reminiscences*, 380–87.
34. M. T. Casey, 'Memories of 1916 in the Golden Jubilee Year' in *Vexilla Regis 1966*, 45–8.
35. Bishop Morrisroe of Achonry to Hogan, 11 May 1917 (MCA, 21/1/13).
36. Details in MacCaffrey to Logue, 2 Mar. 1923 (Armagh DA).

CHAPTER XII (pp. 305–28)

1. 'Maynooth 1895–1945' in *IER*, lxvi, 210 (Sep. 1945).
2. Mulcahy, 'Reminiscences', 172.
3. Walter McDonald to D'Alton, 23 Sep., 15 Oct. 1941 (MCA, 35/21/122).
4. For correspondence between 1945 and 1949 see MCA, 44/5/39.
5. *I Remember Maynooth*, 101–3.
6. Ibid., 90–91.
7. A list of those given between 1888 and 1898 was entered in a volume kept specially for the purpose (MCA, B4/2/5).
8. 31 Aug. 1933 (ibid., 27/17/62).

9. Ibid., 39/53/181.

10. There is an important file of correspondence in MCA, 27/21/77.

11. 'James Connolly's campaign in the light of Catholic teaching', pp. 212–29, 275–9, 346–59, 407–12, 489–92.

12. In addition to the minutes of the Trustees and Visitors there are letters from MacCaffrey to Logue in Armagh DA. See also MacCaffrey to the secretary to the Trustees, 7, 22 May 1923 (MCA, 27/15/28).

13. In addition to the minutes of the Visitors there is correspondence in MacCaffrey's papers (MCA, 27/18/73d).

14. He had earlier spelled his name 'Coghlan'. See above, p. 250.

15. MCA, 35/18/80.

16. See below, p. 322.

17. In addition to the relevant minute books there is extensive correspondence in MCA, 27/16, 17.

18. MCA, 27/17/62.

19. There are letters from two distinguished lawyers, Messrs Murnaghan and Ryan, both closely connected with the college, each dated 14 Jul. 1933, in MCA, 27/18/73a.

20. Extensive documentation in MCA, 35/19.

21. *Vexilla Regis 1959*, 65–9.

22. Corcoran to MacCaffrey, 21 Jun. 1926 (MCA, 27/23/87d).

23. The typescript 'Seán Corkery, librarian 1951–73. Edited transcript of an interview recorded on 12 June 1985' (Library Archives, no. 2) contains much valuable material on the history of the library.

24. Thomas Wall, 'Rare books in Maynooth College Library' in *IER*, lii, 46–59 (Jul. 1938).

25. William Moran, 'The projected Maynooth Museum: statement by the curator' in *IER*, xliv, 561–72 (Dec. 1934).

CHAPTER XIII (pp. 329–54)

1. His report is in MCA, 48/53/169.

2. Ibid., 43/14.

3. Memoranda ibid., 48/43/129.

4. Ibid., 53/59.

5. Ibid., 48/44/137.

6. Details of reconstructions and repairs are taken from the minutes of the Trustees and Visitors, the annual reports of the President, and the minutes and reports of the Finance Council.

7. See above, pp. 64–5.

8. A file giving details of this work in Humanity House (MCA, 48/46/144) shows only too clearly how inexorably costs could rise as work went on.

9. All this is very competently summarised in an unsigned but obviously supplied contribution in the *Standard*, 23 May 1958.

10. MCA, 43/15.

11. There is a copy of the High Court judgement in MCA, 48/48/149.

12. *I Remember Maynooth*, 23.

13. Documentation in MCA, 49/3.

14. Ibid., 49/1, 3.

15. *Hostage to Fortune* (Dublin, 1951), 105.

16. Documentation in MCA, 51/28,30, 53/61.

17. 'New directions for the Maynooth Union' in *Irish Theological Quarterly*, xxii, 282–92 (Oct. 1955).

18. MCA, 43/16.

19. President to Trustees, 9 Oct. 1959, 15 Jun. 1962 (MCA, 49/2).

20. MCA, 43/16.

21. Memorandum from Faculty of Science, 1 Jun. 1961 (MCA, 49/3).

22. There is extensive documentation in MCA, 49/1–3.

23. Correspondence with the French and German embassies is in MCA, 53/60.

24. MCA, 43/16.

25. MCA, 49/3.

CHAPTER XIV (pp. 355–69)

1. *Real Presences*, 44–5.

2. Ibid., 26.

3. *The Idea of the University: a Re-examination*, 40.

4. *The Closing of the American Mind*, 147.

5. What follows is based on material in the college archives. Such material inevitably gets more voluminous with the new developments. It has been put in order, but the documents have not yet been given definitive numeration, so that precise references are not possible.

6. *Commission on Higher Education: Report*, 423–5.

7. Ibid., 420–26.

8. Ibid., 652–5.

CHAPTER XV (pp. 370–91)

1. For further details see below, pp. 405–6.

2. For the text of both addresses see *The Pope in Ireland: Addresses and Homilies* (Dublin, 1979), 67–75.

CHAPTER XVI (pp. 392–413)

1. For the College Executive Council see below, pp. 402–5.

2. See above, pp. 387–8.

3. See above, p. 391.

4. See above pp. 389–90.
5. See above, p. 383.

CHAPTER XVII (pp. 414–35)

1. Bede McConville OSB to J. F. Hogan, MCA 23/42/5.
2. See above, p. 410
3. See above, pp. 378–81.
4. See above, pp. 319–20.
5. See above, pp. 381, 421.
6. See above, p. 419.
7. Correspondence in MCA, 53/54.
8. A diocesan priest was appointed to the department of Modern History in June 1994.

EPILOGUE (PP. 436–8)

1. *A Fortnight in Ireland*, 92–3.
2. *Maynooth Centenary Record*, 111–13.

Index

The section 'Brief Lives' (pp. 440–87) gives personal and professional details for all deceased members of staff. In the Index the principal entry in this section for each individual is marked by an asterisk.